10/23/75

*Radio and Television Broadcasting
in Eastern Europe*

The contribution of the McKnight Foundation to the general program of the University of Minnesota Press, of which the publication of this book is a part, is gratefully acknowledged

Radio and Television Broadcasting in Eastern Europe

by Burton Paulu

THE UNIVERSITY OF MINNESOTA
PRESS □ MINNEAPOLIS

Library of Congress Catalog Card Number: 74-79505

ISBN 0-8166-0721-4

To Frances

Preface and Acknowledgments

I first observed foreign broadcasting in 1944–1945, while working for the United States Office of War Information in the United Kingdom and Luxembourg. In the fall of 1958, as a member of an official exchange group, I took the first of six trips to the USSR. Impressed with the broadcasting of this vast country, and aware of the lack of published information about it, I studied the subject again in 1964–1965, while doing research in Geneva for a book on radio and television on the European continent, although work did not begin in earnest on the present volume until a quarter's leave from the University of Minnesota in 1970 made possible trips to eight Eastern European socialist countries.

All told, the present volume has drawn upon the findings of six trips to the Soviet Union; three each to East Germany, Poland, Czechoslovakia, Hungary, and Romania; two to Yugoslavia; and one to Bulgaria. These were made possible by grants from the Office of International Programs, the McMillan Fund, and the Graduate School at the University of Minnesota, as well as from the Ford Foundation. The Graduate School also provided funds for research assistants and some book and magazine acquisitions.

Many individuals and organizations assisted in the preparation of this manuscript. Very important was help from the broadcasting organizations of the several countries named above. During my visits I invariably was received courteously, was able to talk freely with a number of executives and programmers, and was provided with much printed and manuscript material. Also helpful were personnel in Radio Free Europe and Radio Liberty in Munich, the European Broadcasting Union and the International Telecommunication Union in Geneva, and the Voice of America in Washington, D.C. Some of these people also read and commented on portions of the manuscript. Needless to say, none of them bears any responsibility for what is said here.

Finally, there were those at home and in the office. To my wife, Frances, I dedicate this book. My three graduate assistants were Reuben Valdez, Robert Bjerke, and David Horgan, while typists included Jane Brown, Margaret Mattlin, and Barbara Tkach.

B. P.

Minneapolis
December 1973

Table of Contents

Radio and Television Broadcasting
in Eastern Europe

I

Introduction

The Western democracies should have much more information than they now possess about mass communications media in Eastern Europe.

Much that is said and done throughout the world is a consequence of the confrontation of Communist and democratic ideologies. Europe often functions as two units—the socialist countries of the East and the democratic countries of the West; and their underlying rivalry persists despite periodic rapprochements and détentes. Globally, many activities are polarized between the United States and the Western group on the one hand, and the Soviet Union, the People's Republic of China, and the other socialist countries on the other.*

The democracies should study the socialist states in order to learn as much as possible about their history, politics, economics, education, culture, industry—and mass communications media. Only by knowing can

---

* This study applies the term "socialist" rather than "Communist" to the Eastern European countries, in accordance with their own practice. In 1917 Lenin wrote: "From capitalism mankind can pass directly only to socialism, i.e., to the social ownership of the means of production and the distribution of products according to the amount of work performed by each individual. Our Party looks farther ahead: socialism must inevitably evolve gradually into communism, upon the banner of which is inscribed the motto, 'From each according to his ability, to each according to his needs.' " (V. I. Lenin, *Collected Works* 24:84–85.)

The latter phrase is commonly credited to Karl Marx (*Selected Works*, p. 325), although nearly identical expressions are to be found in the works of Morelly (c. 1774), Louis Blanc (c. 1840), and Mikhail Bakunin (1870). It—or expressions like it—appear in Article 12 of the Soviet Constitution, and in the constitutions of Poland (see p. 272), Czechoslovakia (p. 316), and Yugoslavia (p. 466).

we understand; and if the differences are so basic as to preclude agreement, then knowledge at least may facilitate coexistence.

Despite the importance of the subject, however, there has been no comprehensive study of broadcasting in the socialist states of Eastern Europe. There are good descriptions of the mass media generally, although they emphasize the printed press rather than broadcasting, and there are some excellent monographs on a few specialized aspects of the electronic media, but there has been no one place to which a reader could go for a reasonably complete description and appraisal of broadcasting in that part of the world.

The purpose of this book, therefore, is to describe and appraise the theory and practice of radio and television in the socialist countries of Eastern Europe, here defined as including Albania, Bulgaria, Czechoslovakia, East Germany, Hungary, Poland, Romania, the Soviet Union, and Yugoslavia. This is not easy to do. To begin with, there is a shortage of basic material. One reason for this is that these countries lack the motivation to do research like that conducted in the United States, the United Kingdom, and some Western European countries.

Until recently, the socialist states did not regard radio and television as proper subjects for university-level study. Certain types of research were hindered by the late development of fields like sociology—which provide some techniques for audience research—because they were considered in conflict with Communist theory. Research and writing also were discouraged by the close links between mass media and government, since socialist states do not necessarily feel obliged to inform either their citizens or the world about their activities. In addition, the engineering aspects of the electronic media often are related to national defense.

Of course there are some publications, such as the excellent *Yearbooks* in Yugoslavia—the least typical socialist state. Nevertheless, compared with the output of the United States, the United Kingdom, Italy, Switzerland, or West Germany, their number is very limited. Just because the task is made more difficult by a shortage of material is no reason for not collecting and interpreting those data available, so that those who wish to read may do so now and those who plan to write in the future will have a better foundation upon which to build.

There are good reasons for treating this group of countries as a unit. They are geographically contiguous; they are historically related; they are one-party states with close relationships between government and mass media; and they are closely involved with the Soviet Union.

This book rejects as incorrect the term "Iron Curtain" as a description of the barriers between these countries and the rest of the world, even though barriers do exist, and despite the convenient verbal shorthand provided by the famous phrase.* The expression is inaccurate because much communication does take place, and its amount is steadily increasing.

Also rejected is the popular dichotomy of the USSR on the one hand and a group of Eastern European "satellite" nations on the other. Obviously, the large and powerful Soviet Union is in a dominant position and from time to time has used its strength to influence the policies and to interfere in the affairs of various countries in the bloc. But if they are "satellites," it is not because most of them want to be. In any case, some of the main differences among them relate to their varying attitudes toward the USSR.

In dealing with these countries, it is important that we be aware of their separateness and their individuality, since they differ in size, nationality, history, culture, and political alignments. A glance at a map shows their geographical relationships. Poland and Romania share long borders with the Soviet Union, Czechoslovakia and Hungary very short ones, and East Germany, Yugoslavia, Albania, and Bulgaria none at all. They vary greatly in area. Arranged in order from small to large, and matched with American states of approximately equal size, they are as follows: Albania, 11,000 square miles (Maryland); Hungary, 35,919 square miles (Indiana); East Germany, 41,718 square miles (Ohio); Bulgaria, 42,729 square miles (Tennessee); Czechoslovakia, 46,467 square miles (New York); Romania, 91,699 square miles (Oregon); Yugoslavia, 98,740 square miles (Wyoming); and Poland, 120,359 square miles (New Mexico). The USSR is the largest country in the world, occupying over one-sixth of the global land area. Its total of 8.65 million square miles makes it almost three times the size of the United States.

* Winston Churchill was not the first person to use this expression. Bartlett's *Familiar Quotations* cites two uses of it during World War I, when the references were to Germany, not Russia. In 1945 both Joseph Goebbels, the Nazi propaganda chief, and Churchill applied it to the Soviet Union. Whether he borrowed or recoined the expression, however, Churchill's use of the term in his speech at Fulton, Missouri, in 1946 brought the phrase into general circulation.

Although about half the Soviet Union consists of Slavs, the USSR has over a hundred national groups, and there are minority nationalities in most of these countries. The Germans, Hungarians, and Romanians are as different from one another as from the Slavic groups constituting the major population blocs in Poland, Czechoslovakia, and the Soviet Union. There often are internal conflicts among these groups, as with the Czechs and Slovaks in Czechoslovakia, the Serbs and Croats in Yugoslavia, and various nationalities in the USSR.

The tongues of Albania, East Germany, Hungary, and Romania are entirely dissimilar and also stand apart from the Slavic languages of Poland, Czechoslovakia, the Soviet Union, and Yugoslavia. Hungarian and Romanian are mutually understandable with no other languages in the world—the latter, incidentally, being the only Romance language in the group. Although the Soviet Union uses Russian as its national tongue, the population speaks one hundred different languages and dialects, of which about sixty-seven are used in domestic radio and television broadcasting. Most Eastern European countries, in fact, use two or more languages in their domestic transmissions.

Relationships among these countries are complicated by centuries of changing political patterns, in which Germany and Russia often have played key roles. All or parts of Albania, Bulgaria, Hungary, Romania, and Yugoslavia belonged at one time or another to the Ottoman Empire before its dissolution following World War I, a process to which Imperial Russia contributed greatly. Portions of Czechoslovakia, Poland, Hungary, Romania, and Yugoslavia were in the Austro-Hungarian Empire. Poland, although a powerful and independent kingdom in medieval times, was partitioned among Prussia, Austria, and Russia toward the end of the eighteenth century and was not reconstituted until after World War I. Then, after twenty years of independence, it was divided in 1939 between Germany and the USSR, becoming independent again after World War II. The Balkan Wars (1912–1913), World War I (1914–1918), and World War II (1939–1945) found all these countries in a bewildering sequence of relationships.

Their political alignments since 1945 have been greatly affected by the World War II occupation of many of them by Germany and their subsequent "liberation" by the Soviet Army. The fact that Soviet troops freed them from Hitler's Germany provided the USSR with a major propaganda weapon in establishing and maintaining hegemony in that part of the world.

In recent years the Soviet Union has intervened militarily in East Germany, Hungary, and Czechoslovakia, and now maintains troops in East Germany, Czechoslovakia, Poland, and Hungary. Yet these countries maintain different degrees of independence from the USSR—not always with reference to the presence or absence of Soviet garrisons. Freest of all is Yugoslavia, with Romania and Hungary not far behind. Czechoslovakia, Poland, East Germany, and Bulgaria are less so, although this is not necessarily a reflection of their wishes. Obviously, the present Czechoslovak regime is the consequence of the Soviet occupation of 1968.

Generally speaking, the extent of mass media freedom in these countries is in inverse proportion to the amount of Soviet influence, an influence which also affects their foreign trade and economic independence. For this reason the history, foreign policy, and economic status of each state are briefly reviewed before its broadcasting is taken up.

It is important that we not explain too much about these countries on the basis of their being Communist. Unquestionably, political ideology determines some of their most distinctive features. But centuries of history, culture, and tradition were at work long before communism emerged. For example, we must not assume that limitations on freedom of speech in the Soviet Union are related only to Communist ideology. There never was a free press in Imperial Russia, and there always was enough censorship to prepare the Soviet Union for all the limitations on freedom of expression it has experienced since 1917. Therefore, while recognizing the importance of communism in shaping the policies and procedures of the socialist countries of Eastern Europe, we must recognize that it is only one of the factors making them what they are.

In the next chapter some of the basic features of broadcasting in Eastern Europe are reviewed in order to provide a frame of reference for the detailed descriptions that follow. Thereafter, each country is examined in turn. Treated first is the Soviet Union, the largest and most important of the group. Thereafter, the systems of the German Democratic Republic, Poland, Czechoslovakia, Hungary, Romania, Bulgaria, Yugoslavia, and Albania are reviewed. At the end a brief chapter offers some interpretations and judgments of socialist broadcasting.

II

Summary

The predominant feature of the mass media in Eastern Europe is their firm control by party and government and their consistent use to support Communist ideology and government policies. Because this approach is so different from that of the Western democracies, it will be documented in the actual words of party leaders and broadcasters.

A natural starting point is Lenin's seminal statement of 1901: "A newspaper is not only a collective propagandist and a collective agitator, it is also a collective organizer." His successors in all these countries have applied this policy not only to the mass media, but by extension to schools and all other aspects of organizational life. A combination of affirmative guidance and censorship assures the performance of the mass media in accordance with these principles.

Along with this has always gone the assumption that the opposition should be denied access to the media. Again to quote Lenin: "Why should a government which is doing what it believes to be right allow itself to be criticized? It would not allow opposition by lethal weapons, and ideas are much more fatal than guns." Accordingly, the Soviet Constitution guarantees freedom of speech only "in conformity with the interests of the working people, and in order to strengthen the socialist system," and the other socialist countries take the same position. Soviet jurist Vyshinsky made this definitive: "In our state, naturally, there is and can be no place for freedom of speech, press, and so on for the foes of socialism."

8

In contrast to Communist ideology, the democratic countries proceed on the assumptions that freedom of speech is good in itself; that the best way to arrive at the facts is for all points of view to be readily available; and that from a comparison of diverse opinions the best course eventually will be chosen.

But the democracies, too, place limitations on freedom of expression, and these were well expressed by Justice Oliver Wendell Holmes: "The question in every case is whether the words used are used in such circumstances and are of such a nature as to create a clear and present danger that they will bring about the substantive evils that Congress has a right to prevent. It is a question of proximity and degree."*

It would appear, however, that Holmes's dictum is accepted by both sides as a basis for operations, although there are differences in defining a "clear and present danger." The more secure Western democracies can allow greater questioning of basic concepts before approaching their danger points, whereas the younger and less established totalitarian regimes risk public debate only about details within the system. Nevertheless, actual practice everywhere seems to be predicated on the "clear and present danger" theory.

Yugoslavia, the freest of all the socialist countries, illustrates this very well. It prohibits criticism of the basic Communist system. It rules out attacks against Chief of State Tito. But Yugoslavia also proscribes two other things. Nothing can be published or broadcast that might exacerbate the troublesome animosities dividing the various Yugoslav nationalities. Furthermore, criticism of the USSR may be censorable, because Yugoslavia does not want to give the Soviet leaders an excuse to inter-

---

* In the United States there are more legal limitations on freedom of expression in broadcasting than for the printed press. The Federal Communications Commission (FCC) is instructed to license stations only if they operate in the "public interest, convenience, and necessity," and this involves some judgments of program promises and performance even though the law also bars the FCC from censoring programs. Sections of the criminal code prohibit the broadcasting of profanity and lottery information, while the Communications Act of 1934 requires the equal treatment of candidates for public office. All of these might be regarded as limitations on a station's freedom of expression. The Fairness Doctrine requires stations to afford a reasonable opportunity for the presentation of opposing viewpoints on controversial issues of public importance, and assures the right of reply in cases of personal attack. Although this is an FCC rather than a legislative requirement, it has the force of law, and its constitutionality was upheld by the United States Supreme Court in the famous Red Lion case.

vene, as they did in Czechoslovakia in 1968. However, there may be—and is—much criticism of government operations.

Party spokesmen in several countries have complained severely of insufficient *samokritika* or self-criticism in both the press and broadcasting. Presumably it is hoped that a reasonable amount of constructive—but restrained—criticism will assist in effecting needed improvements, at the same time that it releases some of the frustrations resulting from the generally severe controls. It is not clear how much criticism may be undertaken in the absence of prior approval. But however this may be, there is much self-criticism in all these countries, and at times the media are very outspoken indeed.

Although most Western observers disagree with Communist mass media concepts, they must concede that Lenin and his followers decided how they wanted to use radio long before the principal democratic countries determined their directions. One reason for this was that in 1917, when broadcasting was developing, the USSR had a very pressing problem which radio could help to solve. The leaders of the new state wanted to proselytize their people at home despite a breakdown in normal communications and to reach foreign publics over the heads of hostile governments. Another reason was that absolute control enabled policies to be set more quickly and firmly than in the democratic states. But for whatever reasons, the Soviet Union systematically utilized broadcasting from the outset and has continued to do so ever since.

The democratic countries, on the other hand, had difficulty setting their course. Even the commercial possibilities, which eventually played such a dominant role in the United States, were overlooked. In 1920 David Sarnoff, who later as head of NBC did so much to mold American broadcasting, saw the profits not in broadcast advertising, but in income from a program magazine and the sale of receivers. Herbert Hoover, when secretary of commerce in 1922, said it was "inconceivable that we should allow so great a possibility for service to be drowned in advertising chatter." Not until the passage of the Radio Act in 1927 was broadcasting legally structured as a mass medium, with stations required to serve the "public interest, convenience, and necessity."

But in spite of that law, the public service potential of broadcasting was so neglected that educational groups soon set up their own stations, fearing that they could not be adequately served by the American commercial system; and it was not until 1967 that the Public Broadcasting

Act pledged federal funds for nationwide educational programming. Although definitive concepts emerged in the United Kingdom earlier than in the United States, they still were not formulated as quickly as they were in the Soviet Union. When Lord Reith became managing director of the British Broadcasting Company in 1922, he recognized the public service potentials of radio and led the new British Broadcasting Corporation in that direction when it was founded in 1927.

Throughout the socialist bloc, broadcasting is a state-controlled monopoly. (This also is true of many other countries, although the fact that a system is government related does not mean that it must be closely controlled.) All Eastern Europe follows the Soviet pattern, with programming responsibility assigned to broadcasting committees of actual or near ministerial status and with financial support derived mainly from public funds. Most systems have some advertising, although except in Yugoslavia such revenue is not a significant part of the total budget. Transmitters and connecting links are run by ministries of communications. Also involved are the government agencies concerned with education, culture, propaganda, and censorship. Always important is the Communist party, although it is difficult to determine the exact relationship among government, party, and broadcasters.

There no longer is much direct censorship, although the possibility always remains. Seldom must a government official read and approve all material before it goes on the air, and rarely does anyone sit with his finger on a button to be pressed should unacceptable content come forth. This does not indicate relaxation of control, but rather acceptance of the reality that regulation is best achieved by appointing dependable people to key positions.

The broadcasting organizations themselves are subdivided according to such major functions as radio, television, external programming, and support activities. Most of them, incidentally, in Eastern as in Western Europe, are overstaffed. Moscow, for example, has 8,000 or 9,000 television employees—far more than are needed for its daily output of about twenty-four hours of programs.

The people who run Eastern European broadcasting—and they include both men and women—are able and dedicated. Although the executives usually belong to the Communist party, membership is not required of all key personnel. Needless to say, they must support communism—which is to say, oppose Western-style democracy—and be prepared to discharge both the letter and the spirit of their instructions. But then, how many American broadcasters oppose democracy and advocate communism?

I have talked to many of these people. Although appointments sometimes are difficult to arrange, once received, a foreign visitor usually is well treated. Some administrators are more political than professional in background, but this also is true of many American government officials. We might recall too that American broadcast executives often come not from the media but from business—which is the orientation for much of American broadcasting just as the party is in socialist countries.

The heads of such operating sections as news, education, and children's programs usually are well informed and experienced. Top executives are more willing to admit and discuss shortcomings than are their subordinates. Some old-line Communists, who began as street fighters and worked up to executive status, speak with a refreshing frankness and honesty which makes for rewarding exchanges. One need not accept their basic point of view to recognize their sincerity, admire their dedication, and appreciate their professional accomplishments.

In order to alleviate shortages of qualified personnel, many broadcasting organizations have their own training programs, and mass media instruction is beginning to develop in colleges and universities. This was one reason some people I talked to showed great interest in American mass media education. As might be expected, Eastern European curriculums emphasize Marxist-Leninist theory, but there are practical courses as well, and student laboratories are being set up.

Because these countries lagged behind the West in industrial and economic development, it was inevitable that their broadcasting should develop more slowly. The record of the Soviet Union in the 1930s was astonishingly poor. Thereafter, the widespread destruction of World War II wiped out most Eastern European installations, and the lower priorities placed on broadcast, as compared with other, reconstruction delayed replacement. But new buildings now are going up, although some have faulty construction owing to inadequate planning or poor materials. Undeveloped electronic manufacturing together with a shortage of foreign currency has delayed the acquisition of modern television equipment, while American strategic considerations slowed the acquisition of video tape recorders. Nevertheless, well-equipped studio centers are being built.

All these countries have two or more radio networks plus local services, which taken together cover almost their entire populations. There are both AM and FM transmitters, the latter usually with stereophonic capability. Except for Albania, all have at least one if not two regular television services. Several Soviet cities have three channels, and Moscow, with four, leads Eastern Europe. As rapidly as technology and funds permit, color is being introduced. There is an obvious relationship between political alignments and engineering standards. Except for the German Democratic Republic, all the socialist countries use Eastern European system "D" for black-and-white transmissions. (East Germany accords with West Germany and employs the West European CCIR standard.) Except for independent Romania and maverick Yugoslavia, all follow the Soviet example and transmit French SECAM rather than West German PAL color. (Here East Germany casts its lot with the socialist group.)

Eastern Europe leads the world in the distribution of radio programs by wire. In 1940 the USSR had over four times as many wired as wave sets; by 1970 the number of wave sets exceeded wire sets; but by 1972 the balance had swung back, and there were 50 million of each. In the other socialist countries, however, the proportion of wired sets has steadily decreased. The Soviet emphasis on wired receivers may follow from the belief that wired radio is controlled radio. Yet, it is not difficult to buy all-wave receivers in the USSR, many Western countries have some wired radio, and the United States is moving toward cable television.

The Soviet Union is pre-eminent in using satellites for the domestic distribution of television programs, the first Molniya satellite having been launched in 1965. This leadership undoubtedly was stimulated by the absence of an extensive ground-based microwave system as well as by the country's enormous size. Distribution, however, is not directly to home receivers, but rather to a set of Orbita ground stations which transmit the signals to conventional transmitters for general dissemination. To date, these countries have had no direct reception from Western satellites, although they have carried satellite relays received by Intervision from Eurovision.

Broadcasting services everywhere are planned to be complementary rather than competitive. Usually there is contrasting radio fare: one network features light entertainment, another more serious material, while a third may be a good music service. Other networks and stations provide regional and local programs. Twenty-four-hour radio schedules are beginning to appear, and several countries broadcast twenty hours a day. Radio and television are expected to cooperate rather than compete, each being programmed to its best advantage.

The role of the second television service, when there is one, varies from country to country. In some countries it is educational, whereas in others there is no difference between the two. In the Soviet Union second channels are regional and third channels educational. But in any case, the Eastern European television day is short. In the morning and afternoon there are mainly in-school programs, while adult offerings run from 4:30 or 5:00 until 11:00 P.M. or midnight. Shortages of both funds and material are the main reasons for the limited schedule, although the absence of competition is another factor, since the public has nowhere to turn when television is off the air except to radio services maintained by the same organization.

Languages complicate Eastern European broadcasting. In order to accommodate its many linguistic groups, the Soviet Union broadcasts in approximately sixty-seven languages. All these countries serve their substantial foreign-language populations. Yugoslavia, with its continuing nationality problems, broadcasts regularly in nine languages. Hungary's and Romania's unique languages complicate the exchange of programs with foreign countries and increase costs. Some of these countries, especially during holiday seasons, have short news, weather, and information programs in the languages of their principal foreign visitors.

News and public affairs are important program areas in all countries, but especially so in the socialist bloc since they provide opportunities for proselytizing. Such programs are of great interest to foreign observers, too, because they so clearly indicate broadcast objectives. The range of news sources is considerable, including national as well as foreign agencies, both Eastern and Western, which supply items on an exchange basis. Television also has closed-circuit feeds from Intervision and Eurovision. Less Eurovision material is broadcast during periods of East-West tension, although items still may be received and recorded for reference.

The radio services of each country usually offer hourly reports, ranging from short bulletins to thirty-minute features. Although many domestic and international items are covered, the emphasis is on socialist bloc, party, and government events, and there also are many stories about industrial achievements and national accomplishments. Everywhere it is standard policy to delay or omit items apt to embarrass the regime.

Public affairs broadcasts, discussion and information programs, and documentaries conform to the same pattern. Again and again the public is told of the benefits of life under communism and of the citizen's obligation toward his government and party. This is supplemented by much criticism of nonsocialist countries and institutions, and there often is severe treatment of West Germany and the United States. The purpose of all this, it is said, is to offset misleading "capitalist and imperialist" propaganda; but there also must be the hope of alleviating concern about shortcomings at home by reporting that things are "even worse" in the democratic societies. While many of these criticisms are drawn from authentic Western sources, the absence of balance material makes the total effect inaccurate.

Although most Eastern European broadcasts are "educational" in terms of Communist objectives, all these countries have programs which merit the word as used in the Western democracies, and these include some of the best productions turned out in that part of the world. Responding to many of the same problems encountered elsewhere, and planned in cooperation with educational authorities, these programs command a good share of the personnel and funds of their organizations.

The high national priorities placed on educating youth explain the emphasis on broadcasting for young people. In-school programs are mostly supplementary rather than direct instruction, although there is direct teaching in such specialist areas as language and music, because of a shortage of qualified personnel. Radio programs are available on tape, and many schools record programs off the air. Great pains are taken to encourage effective utilization, and there usually is some accompanying research.

Care and effort also are expended on instructional and entertainment programs for out-of-school reception. Some of this is a reaction to programs from Western sources, many of which have Communist youth as their target. Topics range from cultural subjects to traffic safety, and presentation devices include popular singers and orchestras, competitions, and prizes. Daily blocks of radio time may be assigned to "youth clubs." To discourage passive listening and viewing, some broadcasts invite direct participation in such varied fields as music and sports. In planning programs, socialist leaders indicate their awareness of the generation gap, which they often describe in exactly the terms applied to parent-child relationships in the United States.

On and off the air these countries excel in continuing education for adults. All have made conspicuous advances in public education during the last half century. Illiteracy, previously at a very high level, has been virtually eliminated, and there now are the more sophisticated problems of the "illiteracy" of industrial societies, second-chance universities for dropouts, and advanced training for college graduates. Many programs are scheduled during peak listening and viewing hours with the rationale that it is proper to use the mass media to train the few so that they may serve the many. Although most Western educators would disapprove of the political indoctrination built into these programs, they would accept many of their objectives and surely would applaud the consistent emphasis on education. I have reviewed with Soviet and other socialist educators our common problems in persuading academicians to broadcast effectively. There, as in the United States, teachers are apt to regard radio and television as better suited to entertainment than to instruction, in spite of the generally serious nature of Eastern European program schedules.

There also is strong emphasis on the spiritual life, and the media are expected to help develop the "man of the future," to use a phrase which turns up periodically in the literature. The purpose may be partly to indoctrinate a nonthinking automaton to serve the state without asking questions, but anyone could approve such objectives as good health habits, respect for law, and improved work standards. Except for a few broadcasts of church services in Hungary, there are no religious programs in Eastern Europe, although some series treat religions historically. Because organized religion is regarded as an enemy of Communist doctrine, the Voice of America and other foreign broadcasters have been strongly criticized for programs about Christianity and other faiths. But men still need something to believe in, and so the Eastern Europeans have replaced Christianity with communism and Christ with Lenin.

A broadcasting executive in Poland told me that a constant program objective is to bring culture to the masses, and this purpose is well realized in all the socialist countries. Literature receives much attention. For many years radio has had poetry readings, plus talks and discussions of literary subjects, and television now has such programs too. Most radio services have serial readings of novels, done in the United States only by educational stations. Drama also is well served, and despite a proselytizing emphasis, both radio and television present good performances of an excellent classical and modern repertoire. In earlier days many broadcasts originated in theaters. This is still somewhat true, it being argued that people without live theater like to have access to it through the media, but most presentations now are from studios.

The growth of television has not eliminated radio drama, which is regarded as an important art form and often is described as "the theater of the imagination." Original writing is encouraged for both media. In addition to serializing literary masterpieces, some of these countries have daytime radio serials which are the counterpart of those produced in America in pre-television days. Their enthusiastic followers—as in the United States—often regard the characters as real people. Although none of these broadcasting organizations has a permanent repertory company, broadcast drama nevertheless is a major income source for actors.

Music has been an important part of cultural life in this part of the world for centuries, and the broadcast media serve it very well. The repertoire is wide and international, but at the same time encouragement is provided to local composers. Like their counterparts elsewhere, television producers have encountered difficulties with serious music, and commentators have observed that "young television" has not succeeded in "capturing" music. Nevertheless, it continues to try and does particularly well with staged works.

Folk music, a staple of Eastern European broadcasting, is very effective when televised with native costumes. But there are problems in presenting contemporary popular music, particularly of Western origin, since many socialist programmers regard it as undesirable, either because it springs from an alien culture or because it is bad in itself. Nevertheless, much of it is broadcast in response to public demand and in order to keep young listeners from turning to foreign services.

Each radio network usually specializes in a different kind of music, ranging from light popular to extended classical works. The media everywhere encourage and commission new compositions. They maintain large organizations of instrumentalists and singers, and engage many free-lance artists. Their extensive libraries of records and tapes also contain spoken word materials of archival value. All things considered, music programming is one of the bright spots in Eastern European broadcasting, even though it is used to advance ideological objectives whenever possible.

Television needs a great deal of film. Although the close relationship between governments and motion picture production simplifies the telecasting of cinema films, there still is a shortage of material, partly because most of these countries have limited production capacities. Therefore, much old film, both domestic and imported, is put on the air, and the making of telefilms is encouraged. The latter are regularly exchanged among the socialist countries.

Films also come from Western sources, partly because of their audience attractiveness and partly because of low cost, basic investments already having been amortized by domestic use. This, of course, involves problems both of ideology and of foreign exchange. Yet, telefilms ranging from *Bonanza* to *The Forsyte Saga* have been broadcast, although in the Soviet Union it was deemed necessary to introduce the latter by explaining that it illustrated the decline of British upper-class society. Foreign films pose a language problem. Countries which can afford it dub them into their own languages or provide a running translation by a single voice, although some films are broadcast with their original soundtracks for language students. In other cases—as in Romania— subtitles are added.

Each country has its documentaries, which usually praise the current government while castigating pre-Communist regimes along with the Western countries, including especially the United States. There is frequent emphasis on World War II, especially in the German Democratic Republic and the Soviet Union. East-West détente may soften this, but is unlikely to remove it entirely, since so much Soviet propaganda depends on references to the joint victory over nazism.

Light entertainment is less good, and much of what passes for it on television is basically old-fashioned vaudeville. One reason for this deficiency is the consistently serious assignment given to the broadcasters, political and social objectives always having much higher priorities than entertainment. Another is the absence of competition: If two or more systems in a country competed for audiences, the popularity of entertainment would bring more of it to the air. Finally, there is the fact that a producer's assignment is complicated when he is told to work a "message" into his show. At the same time, some programs have been vetoed for fear that humor might conceal criticism. Throughout the centuries social and political critics have expressed themselves through literature, and the socialist programmers do not want that to happen on the air.

Nevertheless, much light entertainment is broadcast, although a great deal of it remains close to the stage forms from which it grew. There are guessing games, contests, and light music, but relatively little freewheeling entertainment of the type so prevalent on American television.

The Eastern European media do meet public demands for competitive sports, since much material is available, and its presentation does not raise ideological problems—even though occasional attempts are made to turn it to propagandistic objectives. Major domestic and international contests are broadcast, and scores are reported on newscasts, as in the United States. Interest in international competitions was one of the main reasons for the development of both Eurovision and Intervision, and many programs are exchanged, a good example being the 1972 Summer Olympics in Munich, which were carried on radio and television by most of these countries. As in the West, there are problems with sports promoters who fear that their audiences will be reduced by broadcasting. Valiant efforts are made to encourage amateur participation in sports, since it is not deemed sufficient merely to relay or report major contests.

All these countries have services for foreign audiences, the two most interesting examples being the Soviet Union, which leads the world in output hours, and Albania, whose heavy schedule results from its role as the European spokesman for the People's Republic of China. There are long-, medium-, and short-wave radio transmissions. Although ostensibly disseminating news, information, and culture, each country also expounds its own ideology. The United States is among the active participants, with its Voice of America, Radio Free Europe, Radio Liberty, and Rundfunk im Amerikanischen Sektor, Berlins (RIAS).

There is much casual viewing across international boundaries, such as between Czechoslovakia and Hungary on the one side, and West Germany and Austria on the other, and there are daytime repeats of television programs by each of the two Germanys for viewers in the other one. But the only true examples of international television broadcasting are the programs in their native languages beamed by the Soviet Union to viewers in Sweden and Finland.

The jamming of unwanted radio programs is an inevitable concomitant of domestic media censorship. Bulgaria has been most consistent in this, with the Soviet Union a close second. The frequency and regularity of jamming document the potential of international broadcasting, at the same time that they testify to the insecurity of the countries which do it. (Currently, only Hungary, Romania, and Yugoslavia do no jamming.) When satellite technology permits direct telecasts to home receivers, there may be a new kind of jamming, in view of the strong Soviet concerns in the fall of 1972 about the possibility of such transmissions.

Nevertheless, there is much cooperative production, involving not only the socialist but also the democratic countries. Almost all the Eastern systems maintain extensive contacts with their opposite numbers abroad, and there are live exchanges of quiz, discussion, and musical programs. Foreign crews frequently are admitted, working sometimes alone and sometimes with crews from their host countries. However, American correspondents, who must use Novosti personnel when filming, complain that this increases their costs and limits their freedom. Almost all the socialist countries give and sell radio and television programs for use abroad. Many of these are taken by American stations, the musical programs often being carried by educational outlets.

Audience research was late to emerge. Perhaps the socialist broadcasters did not consider it necessary to study their audiences: they knew what the public should get, so why take the time and trouble to find out what it wanted? (Actually, in view of their very systematic use of the media, it is important for them to study results and improve services.) The absence of competing stations and advertisers may be another reason for this delay. Other factors probably include slowness to develop mass media departments in universities, along with ideological hesitation to encourage disciplines such as sociology which provide certain research techniques. In discussing research, spokesmen sometimes sound embarrassed, perhaps because of their long association of audience studies with Western broadcasting. But now that they are involved, they claim that whereas in the West research is done to increase financial returns, in the East it is done to improve service.

For a long time research consisted largely of mail analysis, though scientific polling now is done everywhere. But the results are not widely published, even though they may be circulated internally. Those findings available show that audiences are much the same everywhere, with the highest ratings going to sports, entertainment, cinema films, and popular music, and the lowest ones to cultural programs and serious music. The effects of age, socioeconomic status, and education are similar in East and West.

Programs emphasizing propaganda and ideology receive low ratings except from the party faithful, and it may be that they demonstrate the "halo effect" in reporting enthusiasm for such offerings. Supplementing domestic data are the figures periodically reported by Radio Free Europe, which claim low credibility for many domestic newscasts, along with increased listening to Western transmissions at such times as the Hungarian revolution in 1956, the Czechoslovak occupation in 1968, and the Polish events of December 1970.

The strong appeal of the electronic media is shown by the extensive ownership of receivers. It began slowly, but penetration figures now compare favorably with those in many Western countries. Ownership clearly is related to economics, since the wealthier countries have better coverage, broadcast better programs, and own more receivers than do the poorer ones. Notable is the recent growth of television ownership, even though black-and-white sets may cost several months' salary. But figures on the extent of listening and viewing are hard to obtain, and in any case cannot be compared directly with those from Western countries, in view of the much shorter television day in Eastern Europe.

III

Union of Soviet Socialist Republics: Structure and Organization

The Union of Soviet Socialist Republics (USSR) is the largest, most powerful, and most important Eastern European socialist country. The mass media theories followed throughout the socialist bloc were first applied there on an extensive scale. Accordingly, certain concepts fundamental to this study will be introduced during this examination of Soviet radio and television.

Facts about the Soviet Union

Radio and television are integral parts of the countries they serve. Like all important national functions, they both grow out of and contribute to their environments. A study of any country's broadcasting, therefore, must take into account its geography, people, education, culture, history, economic standards, and international political status. Awareness of these factors is particularly important for Westerners observing radio and television in Eastern Europe because of the many differences between democratic and socialist concepts and procedures.

The USSR is the largest country in the world, making up more than half of Europe and nearly two-fifths of Asia. It is almost as big as all of North America, occupying one-sixth of the world's total land area. The Soviet Union covers 8,647,200 square miles: east to west it stretches 6,800 miles; north to south about 2,800 miles. (The total area of the continental United States is 3,022,260 square miles. It is 2,451 miles from New York to Los Angeles and approximately 1,800 miles from

the southernmost tip of Texas to the Canadian border.) There are
eleven time zones in the Soviet Union, so that when it is night in Moscow, it is morning of the next day in eastern Siberia. (There are four
time zones in the United States.) It is farther from the west to the east
border of the Soviet Union than from Kansas City across the United
States, Atlantic Ocean, and Europe to Moscow. The Soviet Union's size
has an obvious effect on its planning for broadcasting, requiring many
transmitters and extensive interconnections. It, therefore, was the first
country in the world to distribute domestic television programs by
satellite.

The USSR is the third most populous country in the world. The 1970
census put its total population at 241,720,000, an increase of 15.8
per cent over the 1959 figure of 208,826,000. The Soviet Union has
less than one-third of China's estimated 787,176,000 people and less
than one-half of India's 547,368,000, but it leads the United States,
which ranks fourth with 203,235,000.[1]

Like the United States, the USSR has undergone a population shift
in recent years.[2] In 1959 the majority of Soviet people lived in rural
areas, whereas in 1970 56 per cent (136 million) were urban and 44
per cent (105.7 million) rural. In 1959 only three cities had populations
over one million (Moscow, Leningrad, and Kiev), but in 1970 there
were nine: Moscow, 6,942,000; Leningrad, 3,513,000; Kiev, 1,632,000;
Tashkent, 1,385,000; Kharkov, 1,223,000; Gorki, 1,170,000; Novosibirsk, 1,161,000; Kuibyshev, 1,045,000; and Sverdlovsk, 1,025,000. (In
1970 New York had 7,895,000 people; Chicago, 3,367,000; and Los
Angeles, 2,816,000. Tokyo is the world's largest city with 8,841,000
inhabitants, and London is third with 7,379,000.)

The population of the Soviet Union is very unevenly distributed. In
1959 70 per cent lived in European Russia, which constitutes approximately one-fifth of the nation's total territory.[3] In 1970 the population
density of the various republics ranged from 277.5 people per square
mile in the Moldavian SSR, 221.3 in the Armenian SSR, and 203.7 in
the Ukrainian SSR, down to 11.8 people per square mile in the Turkmen SSR. Although the huge Russian Soviet Federated Socialist Republic (RSFSR) had an overall density of only 19.8, density in the eastern
RSFSR is even lower, since most of its people live in European Russia.
Most Soviet citizens can be reached by radio and television stations serving an area about the size of the continental United States, yet the

Soviet Union is almost three times as large as the United States. But it is necessary for the Soviet government to provide broadcasting services for the remaining 30 per cent of its citizens too, even though they are sparsely settled and widely separated.

The Soviet Union is composed of 100 different nationalities, speaking over 110 separate and distinct languages.[4] The Slavs, who can be divided into three principal subgroups, make up 75.6 per cent of the total Soviet population. Of the total population, the Russians constitute 53.4 per cent (although all Soviet people sometimes are inaccurately called Russians), Ukrainians 16.9 per cent, and Byelorussians (also called White Russians) 3.7 per cent. In the southern and eastern portions of the USSR there are many Moslems, who make up more than 10 per cent of the total population of the country. People of the same ethnic group and language tend to be concentrated in the same area, although there are many exceptions.[5]

In addition to the over 110 languages, numerous dialects are spoken by the scores of ethnic groups inhabiting the country. Some languages are spoken by millions, others by only a few hundred persons.[6] The most widely used language is Russian, the native tongue of at least 110,000,000 persons. Other languages spoken by 1,000,000 or more inhabitants include the following: Ukrainian, 35.0 million; Byelorussian, 8.2 million; Uzbek, 5 million; Kazakh, 3 million; Azerbaijani, 2.3 million; Georgian, 2.2 million; Moldavian, 2.0 million; Lithuanian, 2 million; Latvian, 1.6 million; Chuvash, 1.4 million; Moksha, 1.4 million; Erzya, 1.4 million; Tadzhik, 1.2 million; and Estonian, 1.2 million. At the other extreme are such languages as Tat with only 30,000 speakers; Vodian, 700 speakers; and Budukh, 200 speakers.

Even though Russian is the official national language, the government not only permits but encourages other indigenous tongues. Primary and secondary school instruction usually is available in local languages, although Russian is universally taught. In areas with a non-Russian majority, or where political and territorial divisions give recognition to non-Russian nationalities, there are many newspapers and magazines in local languages. The national radio and television networks use Russian, but local broadcasting is done in some sixty-seven other languages. (The international services use even more.)

Religion is systematically attacked in the Soviet Union, and atheism disseminated through the schools and other media. Although claiming to allow freedom of worship, and perserving some classical churches and mosques in excellent condition as monuments to the country's cultural history, in practice the government is consistently hostile to religion. There are no religious broadcasts, and religious indoctrination is outlawed.

Despite its many political and economic problems, and the tremendous devastation of both human and material resources it underwent during World War II, the Soviet Union is second only to the United States in the size of its economy, having made remarkable advances since the Bolshevik Revolution of 1917. But it should be noted that this required a great deal of foreign aid, much of it from the United States. The Soviet Union has extensive deposits of iron ore, oil, and natural gas. In coal production it now leads the United States, and while the USSR is second to the United States in electric power, it operates the world's largest hydroelectric station at Bratsk in south central Siberia. (The first great Soviet hydroelectric dam, located on the Dnieper River, was erected under the supervision of Colonel Hugh Cooper of the United States Corps of Engineers, using turbines built in the United States.)

In 1971 the Soviet Union realized a long ambition by becoming the world's largest steel-producing nation, maintaining that position during the following year.[7] In 1972 it overtook the United States in commercial sea power, ranking fifth to America's seventh, the Soviet fleet consisting of 16,734,000 gross tons to the United States figure of 15,024,000.[8] On the other hand, 1972 food crops were poor, although this could be attributed to bad weather. This forced Soviet leaders to import a great deal of grain, which, among other things, posed problems in news reporting (see below, p. 113).

In 1970, 65 per cent of the USSR's foreign trade was with other socialist countries, 15 per cent being with East Germany, 10 per cent with Poland, and 8 per cent with Bulgaria. Although in 1970 less than 1 per cent was with the United States, this trade increased so much during 1972 that the United States became the Soviet Union's fifth largest Western trading partner. In that year the German Federal Republic, as a consequence of improved political relations, became Moscow's principal trading partner, others in rank order including Japan, Finland, the United Kingdom, France, and the United States.[9]

Although its great expanses require an extensive transportation system, the Soviet Union lags seriously in this respect. It has only 83,800 miles of railroads, compared with 222,000 in the United States.[10] Its highway construction program also is very inadequate. By the end of 1969, the total length of its roads was 843,900 miles, of which only 300,000 miles were hard surfaced. In the same year the United States had 3 million miles of paved roads. In air transportation, 48.7 billion passenger miles were flown in the Soviet Union in 1970 compared with 130.6 billion passenger miles in the United States.[11]

A characteristic of totalitarian systems is their freedom to emphasize heavy industry, defense, or space exploration instead of the consumer goods that may be in public demand. Soviet space exploration is highly advanced, and Sputnik I, launched on October 4, 1957, was the world's first manmade satellite. Russian weaponry likewise is highly sophisticated. But despite tremendous improvements since 1917, the living standards of the Soviet population are much below those of Western Europe and the United States. Broadcasting is an example of this. In the manufacturing of radio and television equipment, and the distribution of receiving sets, the USSR has lagged far behind the Western countries. However, its extensive natural resources make it almost entirely self-sufficient, and since its people do not lack ability or dedication, sooner or later the Soviet Union's living standards will be second to none.

Advances have not been limited to the material realm. The government places a high priority on cultural and educational achievements, and Soviet literature, music, opera, and theater are thriving. Most Western observers criticize the consistent efforts to direct the creative arts to political objectives, but this has not caused any deterioration in volume of output. Medical services are universally available at no charge, and education is free from the primary grades through technical schools and universities. One of the most commendable achievements of the Communist regime has been the virtual elimination of illiteracy. In 1897 only 26 per cent of the total population between 9 and 39 years of age were literate; by 1926 this figure had climbed to 56.6 per cent; by 1939 to 89.1 per cent; by 1959 it had reached 98.5 per cent.[12]

Accompanying the growth of literacy has been a great increase in mass media circulation.[13] Thousands of newspapers are published in more than 50 languages, and 25 major newspapers are available throughout the country. *Pravda* (*Truth*), the publication of the Communist party, has a daily circulation of over 9 million, the largest in the world. *Izvestia* (*News*), the official newspaper of the Soviet government, is second with 8.5 million. Five thousand magazines are published regularly, plus 80,000 books and pamphlets every year, a world record. In 1970 the Soviet Union had 157,000 cinema theaters, with 30 studios producing films.

The USSR includes 15 constituent or union republics, each inhabited mainly by the nationality giving its name to the area. Within these are further subdivisions, bearing such names as autonomous republic, autonomous region, oblast (region), rayon or okrug (district), and dray (territory). The huge RSFSR includes 6 territories, 49 regions, 16 autonomous republics, 5 autonomous regions, and 11 national areas.[14] There, as elsewhere, administrative divisions often coincide with economic, ethnic, or linguistic areas. Broadcasting administration is directly related to these government units, since, in addition to the committee responsible for the entire country, there are committees for each republic, with still further decentralization in the larger republics.

The 15 republics vary greatly in size. The RSFSR's 6,591,100 square miles compose about 76.2 per cent of the nation's 8,647,200 square miles, and its 130,700,000 inhabitants are 54.1 per cent of the population of 241,748,000.[15] The RSFSR extends from the Gulf of Finland in the west to the Pacific Ocean on the east, including the huge area known as Siberia.

Second largest is the Kazakh SSR with slightly over 1 million square miles and 13.1 million residents, while the Ukrainian SSR is third with 233,000 square miles and 47.5 million inhabitants. (The American state of Texas covers 267,339 square miles.) At the other extreme, 8 of the 15 republics contain 55,000 or fewer square miles each, and Armenia, the smallest, has only 11,500 square miles and 2.5 million persons. Geographically as well as politically, therefore, the USSR is much dominated by the RSFSR as well as by the Slavs who constitute most of its population.

Both the Soviet government and the Communist party are structured like pyramids, with each unit theoretically electing the one above it. At the top of the national government is a two-chamber federal parliament, the Supreme Soviet of the USSR, which meets twice a year for a week or less, and whose members are elected to four-year terms. The Soviet of the Union, with 767 deputies, is elected on the basis of 1 deputy for every 300,000 people; the Soviet of Nationalities, with 750 deputies, has 32 deputies from each union republic, 11 from each autonomous republic, 5 from each autonomous region, and 1 from each national area.

Elections for the Supreme Soviet are by universal suffrage. Voting age is 18, although a candidate must be 23. But selection must be from the single slate of candidates approved by the party, voters having a choice only of voting for or striking out names. The Supreme Soviet elects a 37-member Presidium to serve between its sessions, and the president of the Presidium is the official head of state. The highest executive and administrative organ is the Council of Ministers, with some 90 members, titled minister or chairman, heading such departments as foreign affairs, defense, finance, health, agriculture, higher education, culture, electric power, conservation, foreign trade, and railroad communications. Of particular importance to this study are the minister of the radio industry, the minister of communications, and the chairman of the State Committee for Radio and Television.[16] Organization within union republics is similar to that of the All-Union government.

Paralleling the government at each level is the Communist party, the only legal party in the USSR, whose 14 million members and candidates for membership constitute about 9 per cent of the adult population, but whose leaders are the real rulers of the Soviet Union. In 1970, 55 per cent of its members were workers and peasants, and over 5 million were specialists with higher or secondary educations.[17] At the bottom of this pyramid are some 370,000 primary groups, in such places as factories, farms, government offices, and schools. Above them, and roughly paralleling the divisions of the federal government, are successively smaller cadres topped by the All-Union Party Congress of about 5,000 representatives, which is supposed to meet every four years. However, the most recent Congress, the twenty-fourth, met in 1971, five years after the previous one. The All-Union Congress elects the Central Committee, whose members, in theory, elect the Politburo and the Secretariat.

The Politburo (Political Bureau), the policy-making body of the Communist party, with fourteen regular and seven alternate members, is the center of national power. The Secretariat, with eleven members, some of whom also belong to the Politburo, manages the day-to-day affairs of the party. Heading both Secretariat and Politburo is the general secretary, the head of government and party. However, news stories also make frequent references to the chairman of the Council of Ministers and to the president of the Presidium of the Supreme Soviet, the latter being the titular president of the country.

Beginnings of Soviet Broadcasting

Although Westerners are told that the Italian Guglielmo Marconi (1874–1937) invented radio communication, the Russians claim the discoverer was Alexander Stepanovitch Popov (1859–1905). Actually, the two men, working independently and without knowledge of each other's experiments, achieved successful breakthroughs at approximately the same time. Regardless of who was first, though, both built upon scientific foundations laid by others. In 1873 James Clerk Maxwell, the great British theoretical physicist, published his basic *Treatise on Electricity and Magnetism*, advancing the concept of electromagnetic energy. In 1888 the German scientist Heinrich Hertz, in his *Electro-Magnetic Waves and Their Refraction*, reported experimental results based upon Maxwell's wave theory of electromagnetism.* On June 1, 1894, the British physicist Oliver Joseph Lodge (1851–1940) gave a lecture titled "The Work of Hertz and Some of His Successors," in which he described and demonstrated various methods of detecting electromagnetic waves.[18]

Marconi began experimenting with radio transmission during the fall of 1894 on his father's estate in Italy.[19] "After having worked for a month or more to perfect the instruments," wrote Marconi's principal biographer, "Guglielmo . . . demonstrated [to his family] that he was able to ring a bell on the ground floor by pressing a button on the third floor without any connecting wires." In *Wireless over Thirty Years* R. N. Vyvyan, who worked closely with Marconi for some years beginning in 1900, wrote that the first experiments were held in 1894 "across a distance of only a few yards in a room."[20] Although Vyvyan mentions a number of other pioneers besides Marconi, he makes no reference at all to Popov. W. Rupert Maclaurin, in *Invention and Innovation in the Radio Industry*, accepts Marconi as the discoverer without ever examining the case for Popov, whom he mentions only briefly in passing.[21]

---

* Radio waves were originally known as Hertzian waves, and now "kilohertz" and "megahertz" have replaced "kilocycle" and "megacycle" as the terms used to denote radio frequencies.

In a paper written in 1899, Marconi mentioned some "experiments in Italy in 1895."[22] During a 1904 court case he declared under oath that he conceived the idea of radio "during the fall of 1894 or early in 1895." However, he added: "I commenced my experiments on this subject in the early summer of 1895." In any case, Marconi went to Britain in mid-February 1896 and first published reports of his system on June 2 of that year, the day he applied for a patent.[23] When granted on July 2, 1897, it was the world's first patent for a radio transmitting and receiving instrument.

A. S. Popov, mathematician and physicist, graduated from St. Petersburg University in 1882, and later was director of the St. Petersburg Institute of Electrical Engineering, where he conducted research in physics and electronics. While visiting the World's Columbian Exposition in Chicago in 1893, he attended a meeting presided over by the German physicist Hermann von Helmholtz, during which there was a discussion of Hertzian waves. Thereafter Popov conducted experiments at Russia's Torpedo School. A Russian source states that on May 7, 1895, Popov, "at a meeting of the Russian Physico-Chemical Society, demonstrated an apparatus capable of receiving signals sent without wires—the first radio receiver in the history of mankind."[24]

Later the same year Popov established an experimental ship-to-shore wireless communication system over a distance of 750 feet, and the following year extended this to three miles. On March 24, 1896, he gave a public demonstration of the transmission by radio of the Morse Code symbols spelling the name of Heinrich Hertz.[25] The official minutes of the demonstration were very brief: "A. S. Popov shows instruments for the lecture demonstration of the experiments of Hertz. A description of their design is already in the Zh. R. F.-Kh. Obshchestva." Popov first read accounts of Marconi's demonstrations in September 1896. Although the Western world did not become generally aware of the Russian claims for Popov until 1945, when Soviet authorities formally declared him to be the inventor and accordingly designated May 7 as Radio Day, Russian assertions of priority were made during his lifetime.

The question is, Which man first used a radio device to both transmit and receive information? In October 1962 the *Proceedings of the Institute of Radio Engineers*, an American publication, carried a scholarly article by Charles Süsskind which reviewed the controversy. Süsskind pointed out that there were no contemporary accounts of either the

1894–1895 Marconi experiments or the 1896 Popov demonstrations. The Marconi claims depended upon testimony given in 1904 and later accounts, while the Popov claims depended upon reports made in 1908 and 1925. The term "lightning recorder" was applied to Popov's 1895 receiver by some writers, including Popov himself, and it probably was only a device for detecting electromagnetic impulses. However, Marconi probably transmitted and received radio signals in the fall of 1894, and most certainly by early summer of 1895. But Popov's supporters could argue that Marconi's 1894 and early 1895 experiments—that is, those conducted before May 7, 1895—were observed only by his family and friends, whereas Popov's May 7, 1895, demonstration was before a scientific gathering.

Süsskind concludes that Marconi definitely was first. Surely Marconi's patent application documented the fact that he had invented radio transmission sometime before his application of June 2, 1896. Süsskind admits there is indirect evidence that Popov had a successful demonstration on March 24, 1896, but contends that Marconi "demonstrated the transmission of intelligence at an even earlier date (though admittedly not before a scientific audience) . . . [and that Popov's] work was *at the most* contemporary with Marconi's and probably later."[26] But he also declares: "All credit should go to Popov for independently evolving the same practical receiver design from Lodge's first suggestion as Marconi did, and for carrying out further experiments in the face of substantial obstacles."[27]

Though neither physicist nor engineer, I feel that the data available do not establish either Marconi or Popov indisputably as the inventor of radio communication, although the case for Marconi is stronger. But, even so, the matter should not be regarded as closed until more information—unlikely at this late date—is discovered. In any case, we do know that both men—independently of each other—were working on radio transmission at about the same time and that the original discovery was made either in the fall of 1894 or in the spring or early summer of 1895.

Regardless of who invented radio, there is no doubt that it developed much more slowly in Russia than in the Western countries. To some extent this was due to the backwardness of the old regime: the Eastern countries frequently ascribe their pre-Communist shortcomings to the inadequacies of former governments. A Soviet source cites a related reason: "The development of radio engineering in Russia between the time A. S. Popov invented the radio and the October Revolution was hampered by the dependence of the Russian industry on foreign firms."[28] World War I challenged Imperial Russia's economy even more than it did the advanced industrial systems of the Western Allies, and after the Bolshevik Revolution in 1917, the struggles of the new government to sustain itself against domestic and foreign foes retarded plans to develop radio, despite Lenin's appreciation of the medium's propagandistic and educational value.

Radio broadcasting developed all over the world following World War I, just as television's growth followed World War II. In both cases, war delayed civilian applications of broadcasting technology, at the same time that it expedited the electronic developments that provided the basis for first radio's and later television's growth.

When the United States lifted wartime restrictions on nongovernment radio in 1919, experimenters became active, and many stations went on the air, with first code and then voice transmissions.[29] Several years of regulatory and administrative confusion followed. Because the authority of the government under the Radio Act of 1912 was inadequate to control radio's massive growth, there was chaos on the airwaves, and stations often interfered with one another's transmissions. But it was not until 1927 that the new Radio Act laid the foundations for the orderly development of American broadcasting.

Although large companies struggled to control the expanding—and lucrative—radio manufacturing industry, the commercial pattern that later characterized American broadcasting was not immediately foreseen. In 1920 David Sarnoff, later head of RCA, suggested that if people purchased "Radio Music Boxes" they might subscribe to the program magazine *Wireless Age*, which then could become profitable from its advertising revenue. Furthermore, there would be profits from the sale of receivers to the public.

From all this there emerged gradually the concept of broadcasting as a mass medium, regulated under the Radio Act of 1927 to serve the "public interest, convenience, and necessity." But with most stations privately owned and commercially supported, broadcasting became a business, though one with public service attributes. To this day, profits rather than service provide the continuous and underlying motivation in determining the program policies of American broadcasting.

In the United Kingdom there were experimental broadcasts by a Marconi transmitter in Chelmsford, near London, in 1920, one of the high points of which was a live broadcast on June 15, 1920, by Dame Nellie Melba, the great soprano.[30] Although the radio fans of the day responded enthusiastically, the Post Office, which in Britain discharges the technical regulatory functions assigned to the American Federal Communications Commission (FCC), disapproved of these early radio telephone broadcasts, lest they interfere with point-to-point message services. For that reason broadcasting for the general public developed initially against the wishes of the government departments concerned and in the complete absence of any wide appreciation of its social potentialities.

The British Broadcasting Company, which first broadcast November 14, 1922, was incorporated December 15, 1922, and licensed January 18, 1923. It was succeeded by the British Broadcasting Corporation, which began operations January 1, 1927. Before long John Reith, first director general of the company and the succeeding corporation, who recognized the public service potentials of radio, gave British broadcasting its permanent character; but in the first years after the war, British, like American, broadcasting lacked the firm guidance that Lenin provided from the very beginning in the Soviet Union.

Although the Soviet Union greatly lagged behind the United States and the United Kingdom in station construction and receiver distribution, its leaders immediately saw in radio, as in the printed media, a means to spread the message of communism domestically and internationally. The basic situation in the Soviet Union, of course, was conducive to innovation. In 1917 and following, Lenin and the Bolsheviks were hard pressed to maintain themselves in power at the same time that they were repelling foreign invaders. They needed to get their message to the population at home despite a breakdown in normal communications channels and to reach foreign publics over the heads of their governments. Therefore, they enthusiastically seized upon radio as a medium to achieve those objectives.

At two o'clock in the morning of November 7, 1917, the day the Russian Revolution began, the cruiser *Aurora* in St. Petersburg (later Leningrad) broadcast a message to "The Citizens of Russia" written by Lenin, and the next day the Second All-Russian Congress of the Soviet appealed to "All Railwaymen" to "undertake all measures necessary for the preservation of order on the railways."* On November 12 another broadcast announced that the Soviet government had been formed and that "decrees regarding land and peace have been adopted." On November 22 Lenin addressed "all soldiers of the revolutionary army and sailors of the revolutionary fleet," asking them not to "allow the counter-revolutionary generals to stand in the way of peace," but rather to "immediately select delegates to start formal negotiations with the enemy." Soviet leaders also began at this time to broadcast to governments and people abroad (see below, pp. 199–200).

To ensure the wider distribution of such messages, Lenin supported experiments in radio. In 1918 an engineer named M. A. Bonch-Bruyevich was appointed head of the radio laboratory in Nizhni Novgorod (now Gorki), about 270 miles east of Moscow.[31] A report from Lenin on December 2, 1918, described this laboratory as "the first stage in the organization of [a] State Radio Engineering Institute in Russia." In November 1919 experimental broadcasts from this station were heard by surprised amateurs in various cities, who wrote: "We heard human speech over the radio. Please explain." During January 1920 the Nizhni Novgorod laboratory conducted regular experiments in radiotelephony.

On March 17, 1920, Lenin signed a resolution ordering the installation of a radio telephone station in Moscow from which transmissions soon were received at such distant points as Tashkent, Irkutsk, and Berlin.[32] On January 26, 1921, he referred to the work of the new Nizhni Novgorod radio laboratory as "gigantically important," characterizing radio as a "newspaper without paper or wires, for through the microphone and the loudspeaker . . . it will be possible for all Russia to hear a newspaper being read in Moscow."[33] Accordingly, he requested

* S. V. Kaftanov et al., *Radio and Television in the USSR*, p. 217, hereafter cited as Kaftanov. On November 6, 1955, a plaque was placed in the radio room of the *Aurora*, which read: "The first radio station in the service of the proletarian revolution was the radio station of the Cruiser 'Aurora' " (Kaftanov, p. 239). The evidence is not clear whether this was a code or a voice broadcast. Kaftanov (p. 6), after stating that Lenin "valued radio very highly even during the very first days of the revolution," goes on to say that transmissions then were "by means of agreed telegraphic signals." But a more recent Soviet source (A. Y. Yurovskiy and R. A. Boretskiy, *Osnovy televizionnoy zhurnalistiki* (*The Fundamentals of Television Journalism*), p. 11) refers to the November 7 *Aurora* announcement as being "in the 'live' notes of the human voice." On later pages of the present study there are references to the apparent introduction of voice broadcasting at dates later than 1917, but the data are not complete. At any rate, there were voice broadcasts in both the United Kingdom and the United States before 1917.

that he be informed twice a month "about the progress of the work."

On May 19, 1922, Lenin wrote to Stalin about the great practical significance for propaganda, agitation, and the education of the masses of being able to "broadcast human speech over great distances by means of wireless radio communication."[34] He later wrote: "I ask the members of the Politbureau to take into consideration the exceptional importance of the Nizhegorodskaya radio laboratory, and the great services which it already performed, as well as the considerable assistance which it may extend to us in the near future both in a military sense and in the matter of propaganda."[35] A Russian source commented: "Having the continued support of Vladimir Il'yich, the laboratory personnel worked much and persistently over the development of a design for a radio-telephone transmitter, conducted experiments and attained good results, justifying V. I. Lenin's hopes."

In 1922 a twelve-kilowatt transmitter—claimed to be the most powerful broadcasting station in the world—was installed in Moscow. Its first speech broadcasts began August 21 of that year, and on September 17 it transmitted the first Soviet radio concert, "thus inaugurating Soviet broadcasting."* The September 17 broadcast was described by a Soviet newspaper as "the most visible and perceptible proof of the regeneration of our country and its emergence on the broad path of construction. . . . Let us hope that the idea of communion with multimillion masses through radio over the entire expanse of Soviet Russia will gradually turn into reality."[36] On October 8, 1922, the station went into regular operation. In December 1924 the country's second broadcasting station was activated in Gorki. In 1925 stations were built at Kharkov, Minsk, Rostov-on-Don, and other cities. That same year the central stations in Moscow and Leningrad were connected by line to a number of local theaters and concert halls, an arrangement which gradually evolved into nationwide network broadcasting.[37] In 1927 new stations went on the air in Tashkent, Kazan, and elsewhere.†

---

* *Radio Engineering and Electronics* 2:11 (1957), pp. 5, 9, hereafter cited as *REE*; Kaftanov, pp. 9–10, 222. The KDKA reports of the Harding-Cox election returns took place in 1920.

† Kaftanov, pp. 227–228. The total number of broadcasting stations authorized in the United States during this period was reported by the FCC as follows: 1922, 30; 1923, 556; 1924, 530; 1925, 571; 1926, 528 (*Broadcasting Yearbook 1972*, p. A-112). (This matter is further discussed in the section on technical facilities for Soviet broadcasting, pp. 67n, 68n.) Thereafter the number never dropped below 600

Broadcasting in the Soviet Union, more than anywhere else in the world, has involved the distribution directly to homes of programs by wire. As early as June 17, 1921, loudspeakers were installed in six Moscow squares to broadcast news daily from 9:00 to 11:00 P.M.[38] Concerts and lectures also were disseminated in that way. On November 7, 1922, a truck equipped with loudspeakers transmitted programs in Moscow to demonstrators celebrating the fifth anniversary of the October Revolution. These and similar steps were preliminary to the first experiments in wired broadcasting in Moscow in 1925, which led to the extensive radio diffusion networks which provide the Soviet Union with half its radio reception facilities (see below, pp. 70–71).

The first Russian proposals for the transmission of images by radio were made in 1880 by the Russian biologist P. N. Bakhmet'ev.[39] But a Russian source states that "the founder of contemporary electronic television" was B. L. Rozing, who demonstrated as early as 1907 that an electron ray tube could be used to transmit pictures at a distance.[40] On May 22, 1911, Rozing showed a picture "for the first time in the world," consisting of "intersecting dark lines on a light-colored background." On April 8, 1921, Lenin received a letter from a member of the Ministerial Committee of the People's Commissariat of Posts and Telegraphs reporting that the radio laboratory in Novgorod had discovered a "new photo element" which, when perfected, would transmit television pictures.

On April 29, 1931, test transmissions were begun with pictures using a mechanical scanning system and a Nipkow disc with 30 lines definition at 12½ frames per second.* In October 1931 experimental television broadcasts began in Moscow, and demonstrations were conducted in Leningrad.[41] These transmissions originally were only of still pictures, but beginning August 15, 1932, moving pictures were transmitted. On November 15, 1934, the first television transmission with sound was made in the Soviet Union.[42] All these experiments were very ele-

---

at any time. Although these figures were for the number of stations *authorized*—which was not necessarily the number on the air—there nevertheless was a pronounced difference between the number of stations in the Soviet Union and in the United States. Clearly, the Soviet Union lagged far behind the United States and most other Western countries.

* *REE*, p. 18; Kraftanov, p. 230; Yurovskiy and Boretskiy, p. 42. For an explanation of the division of television pictures into lines, see below, pp. 510–511.

mentary, using screens smaller than matchboxes. Nevertheless, public demand for television was so great that by 1939 amateurs had made themselves some 3,000 receivers. In 1932 motion pictures were telecast in Moscow, and in the same year an iconoscope tube was built experimentally.[43]

In 1938 the Moscow Television Center was fitted with American 343-line equipment, and the Leningrad Center with Soviet 240-line equipment.[44] The first transmission from the Moscow Center took place in March of that year, and by December several dozen tests had been completed. Regular transmissions began in March 1939.[45] One Russian account states that for this reason 1939 "was considered to mark the beginning of television in the Soviet Union." In February 1939 the first experimental programs were transmitted in Kiev.[46] Shortly before World War II it was decided to switch over to a 441-line standard, but during the wartime hiatus the 625-line standard was adopted.[47])

In 1945 the practice of observing May 7 as Radio Day—in honor of Popov's invention of radio on that date in 1895—was inaugurated, and to further mark the occasion, television broadcasting was resumed—"the first in Europe to renew its programs" after the war.* Programs were transmitted until September 17, 1948, when service was interrupted for the reconstruction of the Television Center, resuming June 16, 1949, on the new 625-line standard.[48]

As to other television developments: experiments with color television began November 5, 1954; daily black-and-white programs January 1955; a second Moscow station February 14, 1956; a third channel for educational programs opened in Leningrad September 1964; the first Molniya satellite for relaying television programs within the Soviet Union was launched April 23, 1965; and regular color telecasting began in November 1967. In 1967 the new Television Center was completed at Ostankino, a Moscow suburb, which began transmissions from its 1,750-foot tower in November of that year.[49]

Legal Structure

Printing was introduced into Russia in 1553, although no newspapers appeared until early in the eighteenth century.[50] From the very begin-

---

* Kaftanov, p. 236, Yurovskiy and Boretskiy, p. 47. BBC television, on a 405-line standard, was resumed on June 7, 1946 (*BBC Handbook 1973*, p. 249).

ning publishing was accompanied by some combination of licensing and censorship. Policies varied, but seldom if ever was there a truly free press in Imperial Russia. Censorship always was tightened following such events as the French Revolution, the revolutions of 1848 and 1849, the Polish uprisings of 1853, and the periodic regicide attempts. Nevertheless, great writers like Dostoyevsky, Pushkin, and Gogol flourished during the nineteenth century, and there even was an emerging revolutionary press preceding the October Revolution. But there always was enough censorship to prepare Communist Russia for all the limitations on freedom of expression it has experienced since 1917.

A few statements from the founders and leaders of the Soviet regime will provide a background for understanding certain basic aspects of its broadcasting.[51] Lenin, Stalin, Khrushchev, and other Communist spokesmen frequently have talked about the importance of a "free" press, meaning not freedom for dissenting voices to be heard, but rather the removal of barriers to the wide dissemination through all media of officially approved facts and opinions. As one Russian broadcaster told me: "Freedom of speech is freedom to tell the truth"; and although he did not say so, he meant the "truth" as defined by party and government. But let the Communist leaders speak for themselves.

In 1905 Lenin, in his article "Party Organization and Party Literature," wrote: "We want to create and we shall create a free press, free not only from the police, but also free from capital, from careerism. It will also be free from bourgeois-anarchistic individualism."[52] A few months before the Bolsheviks seized power in 1917, he wrote again: "The capitalists (followed, either from stupidity or from inertia, by many Socialist Revolutionaries and Mensheviks) call 'freedom of the press' a situation in which censorship has been abolished and all parties freely publish all kinds of newspapers. In reality, it is not freedom of the press, but freedom for the rich, for the bourgeoisie, to deceive the oppressed and exploited masses of the people."[53]

Immediately before the revolution Lenin stated: "Only a Soviet government could successfully combat such a flagrant injustice as the capitalists' seizure of the largest printing presses and most of the papers with the aid of millions squeezed out of the people. It is necessary to suppress the bourgeois counter-revolutionary papers . . . , to confiscate their printing presses, to declare private advertisements in the papers a state monopoly, to transfer them to the paper published by the

Soviets, the paper that tells the peasants the truth. Only in this way can and must the bourgeoisie be deprived of its powerful weapon of lying and slandering, deceiving the people with impunity, misleading the peasantry, and preparing a counter-revolution."[54]

These ideas were written into the clause on press freedom in the first Constitution in 1918: "To the end of assuring in behalf of the toilers actual freedom to express their opinions, the RFSFR annuls the dependence of the press upon capital and hands over to the worker class and poorer peasantry all the technical and material resources for publishing newspapers, pamphlets, books, and all sorts of other productions of the press, and guarantees that they may circulate freely throughout the land."[55] In the same year Lenin wrote: "We must convert—and we shall convert—the press from an organ for purveying sensations, from a mere apparatus for communicating political news, from an organ of struggle against bourgeois lying—into an instrument for the re-education of the masses, into an instrument for telling the masses how to organise work in a new way."[56]

In 1919 his stress still was on excluding opponents from control. " 'Freedom of the press' is another of the principal slogans of 'pure democracy.' . . . This freedom is a deception while the best printing-presses and the biggest stocks of paper are appropriated by the capitalists, and while capitalist rule over the press remains. . . . The capitalists have always used the term 'freedom' to mean freedom for the rich to get richer and for the workers to starve to death. In capitalist usage, freedom of the press means freedom of the rich to bribe the press, freedom to use their wealth to shape and fabricate so-called public opinion. . . . Genuine freedom and equality will be embodied in the system which the Communists are building, and in which there will be no opportunity for amassing wealth at the expense of others, no objective opportunities for putting the press under the direct or indirect power of money, and no impediments in the way of any working man (or groups of working men, in any numbers) for enjoying and practicing equal rights in the use of public printing-presses and public stocks of paper."[57]

Lenin never was willing to allow the opposition a hearing. In 1920 he declared: "Why should a government which is doing what it believes to be right allow itself to be criticized? It would not allow opposition by lethal weapons, and ideas are much more fatal than guns."[58] The next year, in a letter to a friend, he elaborated on this point: "All over the world, wherever there are capitalists, freedom of the press means freedom to *buy up* newspapers, to *buy* writers, to *bribe*, buy and fake 'public opinion' for the *benefit of the bourgeoisie*. . . . Freedom of the press . . . means freedom of *political organisation* for the bourgeoisie and its most loyal servants. . . . The bourgeoisie (all over the world) is still very much stronger than we are. To place in its hands yet *another* weapon like freedom of political organisation (freedom of the press, for the press is the core and foundation of political organisation) means facilitating the enemy's task, means helping the class enemy. We have no wish to commit suicide, and therefore, we will not do this."[59]

But it is not sufficient merely to exclude from control those who would misuse the press; the information media must assume a positive role. In 1901 Lenin wrote that communism needed "a political newspaper" without which "a political movement deserving that name is inconceivable in the Europe of today. Without such a newspaper we cannot possibly fulfill our task—that of concentrating all the elements of political discontent and protest, of vitalizing thereby the revolutionary movement of the proletariat."[60]

He continued with some words quoted by almost everyone who writes of Soviet mass media theory: "The role of the newspaper, however, is not limited solely to the dissemination of ideas, to political education, and to the enlistment of political allies. A newspaper is not only a collective propagandist and a collective agitator, it is also a collective organizer. In this respect it may be likened to the scaffolding round a building under construction which marks the contours of the structure and facilitates communication between the builders, enabling them to distribute the work and to view the common results achieved by their organised labour."* Later Stalin enlarged on this statement: "The press is a most powerful weapon by means of which the Party daily hourly speaks in its own language, the language it needs to use, to the working class. There are no other means of stretching spiritual threads be-

* This oft-quoted statement appeared originally in Lenin's article "Where to Begin?" first published in 1901 in the periodical *Iskra*. The following year he reviewed and discussed reactions to it in an extended essay, "What Is to Be Done?" (Lenin, *Collected Works*, Vol. 5, pp. 502–503.) For further comment, see Leo Gruliow, "How the Soviet Newspaper Operates," *Problems of Communism*, Vol. 5, No. 2 (March-April 1956), pp. 3–12.

tween the Party and the class, there is no other apparatus of equal responsibility."[61]

A Soviet authority on press theory stated: "The purpose of information is not that of commercializing news, but of educating the great mass of the workers, and organizing them under the exclusive direction of the Party according to clearly defined objectives. . . . Information is one of the instruments of the class war, not one of its reflections. As a result an objective concern with events prevents information from being used for its true purpose, mainly to organize the workers."[62]

Nikita Khrushchev declared in 1957: "Just as an army cannot fight without weapons, so the Party cannot carry out its ideological work successfully without the sharp and militant weapon of the press. We cannot put the press in unreliable hands. It must be in the hands of the most faithful, most trustworthy, most politically steadfast people devoted to our cause."[63]

The 1923 Constitution had no bill of rights, since it was assumed that the safeguards in the 1918 Constitution of the RFSFR would apply also to the Federal Constitution. However, the "Stalin Constitution," adopted December 5, 1936, contained a section titled "Fundamental Rights and Duties of Citizens," taken over with slight rephrasing from the constitutions of various constituent republics.[64] This assured Soviet citizens of the rights to work, rest and leisure, education, and medical care. Women were accorded equality, as were all races and religions.

"In conformity with the interests of the working people," citizens were guaranteed "the right to unite in [certain specified] mass organizations."[65] The article went on to state that "the most active and politically conscious citizens in the ranks of the working class, working peasants and working intelligentsia [would] voluntarily unite in the Communist Party of the Soviet Union, which is the vanguard of the working people in their struggle to build communist society and is the leading core of all organizations of the working people, both government and non-government."

Citizens of the USSR were guaranteed "inviolability of the person," and privacy of correspondence was "protected by law."[66] The right to asylum was guaranteed to "foreign citizens persecuted for defending the interests of the working people, or for scientific activities, or for struggling for national liberation." As to "duties," every citizen was to abide by the Constitution and laws of the country, was subject to military service, and was to defend the fatherland against all enemies.[67]

All these rights, however, were subject to certain qualifications, and Article 125, dealing with freedom of expression, was no exception: "In conformity with the interests of the working people, and in order to strengthen the socialist system, the citizens of the U.S.S.R. are guaranteed by law: (a) freedom of speech; (b) freedom of the press; (c) freedom of assembly, including the holding of mass meetings; (d) freedom of street processions and demonstrations. These civil rights are ensured by placing at the disposal of the working people and their organizations printing presses, stocks of paper, public buildings, the streets, communications facilities and other material requisites for the exercise of these rights."

Commentary on this clause was provided by a speech given by Stalin before the Eighth Session of the Supreme Soviet in November 1936: "What distinguishes the Draft of the new Constitution is the fact that it does not confine itself to stating the formal rights of citizens, but especially stresses the guarantees of these rights, the means by which these rights can be exercised. . . . It does not merely proclaim democratic liberties, but legislatively ensures them by providing definite material resources. It is clear, therefore, that the democratism of the Draft of the new Constitution is not the 'ordinary' and 'universally recognized' democratism in the abstract, but *socialist* democratism."[68]

These earlier writings on the uses of the mass media were effectively summarized by Andrei Vyshinsky, noted jurist as well as diplomat, who, in his 750-page *Law of the Soviet State* published in 1938, spelled out the official position on freedom of expression.* Initially, he stated the importance of these freedoms in terms most libertarians would accept: "Freedom of speech, of the press, of assembly, of meetings, of street parades and of demonstrations, being natural and indispensable conditions precedent to the manifestation of freedom of thought and freedom of opinion, are among the most important political freedoms. No society can be called democratic which does not afford its citizens all of them. Only in a state which actually guarantees these most important political

---

* Before entering the Ministry of Foreign Affairs, Vyshinsky was an eminent teacher and writer on Soviet law, had been prosecutor of the USSR, and played a leading role in the treason trials of the 1930s. In recent years Soviet jurists have emphasized civil rights more than Vyshinsky did, although the quotations from his writings given here still apply.

freedoms, and in behalf of all citizens without exception, is expanded and completely logical democracy to be found."[69]

Vyshinsky contended that the press in the United States and Great Britain was enslaved by capital, even though these countries, where censorship was long ago abolished, often were rated as places "where the press is absolutely and completely free. The *Times* of London is the organ of banks, connected through its directors with Lloyds bank, with the largest railroad companies, with insurance companies, and with a number of the biggest capitalist firms. . . ."[70] American newspapers also were indicted, particularly the Hearst Press, which carried on a "bloodthirsty agitation against the Communist Party, the revolutionary workers' movement and the USSR."

The Bolshevik victory in 1917, which transferred control of press resources to the working class, gave freedom of expression to people "for the first time in the world."[71] But once this was done, it was necessary to be on guard against the enemy, for which reason the government "explicitly excluded the nonlabor classes from enjoyment of this freedom," since it obviously would have been "folly to promise freedom of meetings to exploiters at a time . . . when the latter are resisting their overthrow and defending their privileges." After all, when the bourgeoisie were the revolutionaries in earlier centuries, they did not grant freedom of assembly to the ruling classes who had brought in foreign troops to put them down. "Having assured genuine freedom of the press to the toilers, the Soviet government did not extend this freedom to nonlaboring strata."[72]

Accordingly, one of "the first and most important measures" of the new government was the closing of "numerous organs of the counter-revolutionary press," so that the liberal screen of "free press" would not become simply a means for the "have" classes to poison the minds of the workers and to confuse their thinking. A new government decree said: "Everyone knows that the bourgeois press is one of the bourgeoisie's most mighty weapons. Particularly was it impossible at the critical moment when the new authority, the authority of the workers and peasants, was only in the process of being stabilized to leave this weapon—at such moments no less dangerous than bombs and machine guns—entirely in the hands of the foe."[73]

Fortunately, though, the October Revolution "destroyed each and every possibility of the rich bribing the press and capitalists being free to employ their wealth to fabricate social opinion. It created in the Soviet state, for the first time in the world, a truly free press, a means of expressing the opinions of the toilers with genuine freedom. Guided by the Bolshevik All-Russian Communist Party, the press in the USSR became a mighty instrument for the true education of the masses, for their self-organization, for fostering new discipline among them, for criticism and self-criticism, and for mobilizing the masses to eliminate all shortcomings in state and social building—for the building of socialism."[74]

Finally, to summarize the issue completely and neatly, the famed Soviet jurist wrote: "In our state, naturally, there is and can be no place for freedom of speech, press, and so on for the foes of socialism. Every sort of attempt on their part to utilize to the detriment of the state— that is to say, to the detriment of all the toilers—these freedoms granted to the toilers must be classified as a counter-revolutionary crime to which Article 58, Paragraph 10, or one of the corresponding articles of the Criminal Code is applicable."[75]

In other words, there is freedom of speech in the Soviet Union only for those who use it to support the established order and never for those who wish to question its basic principles. The mass media are not to present uncensored information from a wide range of sources; they are to play a "positive" role in developing the socialist system.

During my first visit to the Soviet Union in the fall of 1958, I wrote out a summary of what appeared to be the official view about the purposes of broadcasting: "Support of the basic ideologies of Communism, of the Communist Party, and of current government policies and practices, is the principal, underlying and continuing objective of all Soviet broadcasting." Several key broadcasting executives in Moscow, Leningrad, Tbilisi, and Kiev endorsed this statement without hesitation. One of my four American traveling companions, noting that almost all programs seemed to have a propaganda objective, remarked that Soviet broadcasting might be considered a commercial for the state 50 per cent of the time. Our hosts reacted vigorously: "If you want to put it that way," they said, "better to count it as 100 per cent!" Discussions during five subsequent trips brought renewed endorsements of this concept, although broadcasters in some of the other Eastern countries were reluctant to accept the statement without qualifications.

But this is not to say that the Soviet media do not carry material critical of the performance of party and government. Under the *samo-*

kritika (self-criticism) principle, they not only are permitted but are encouraged to deal with inadequacies of operation.[76] Stalin said that "without self-criticism there can be no proper education of the Party, the class, and the masses; and . . . without proper education . . . there can be no Bolshevism."[77] But this does not extend to the point of questioning the system itself or those party leaders currently in favor. Broadcasting is among the media which frequently have disseminated such criticisms, and various examples are given during discussions of programs in the chapters below.

Supplementing the constitutional provisions pertaining to freedom of expression are various parts of the Criminal Code and the Code of Criminal Procedure.[78] Included in chapter one, "Crimes against the State," and in the category of "Especially Dangerous Crimes against the State" is Article 70 of the RSFSR, entitled "Anti-Soviet Agitation and Propaganda":

Agitation or propaganda carried on for the purpose of subverting or weakening the Soviet regime or of committing particular, especially dangerous crimes against the state, or the circulation, for the same purpose of slanderous fabrications which defame the Soviet state and social system, or the circulation or preparation or keeping, for the same purpose, of literature of such content, shall be punished by deprivation of freedom for a term of six months to seven years, with or without additional exile for a term of two to five years, or by exile for a term of two to five years.

The same actions committed by a person previously convicted of especially dangerous crimes against the state or committed in wartime shall be punished by deprivation of freedom for a term of three to ten years, with or without additional exile for a term of two to five years.

Article 71 provides for the imprisonment or exile of those found guilty of the "propagandizing of war, in whatever form it is conducted." Article 74 prohibits "propaganda or agitation for the purpose of arousing hostility or dissension of races or nationalities. . . ."

Clearly, these provisions, particularly Article 70, which deals with "agitation or propaganda . . . for the purpose of subverting or weakening Soviet authority" and with the circulation of "slanderous fabrications which defame the Soviet state and social system," leave wide scope for the punishment of those making public statements deemed hostile to the regime. Article 125 of the Constitution, pertaining to freedom of speech, provides little defense, since it guarantees freedom of expression only in "conformity with the interests of the working people, and in order to strengthen the socialist system," qualifications which the party and the government may define as they wish.

Important to any study of Soviet mass communications is the Russian censorship agency, commonly known as Glavlit (from *Glavnoye uprav-lenie po delam literatury i izdatelstvo*), the Chief Administration for Literary and Publishing Affairs.[79] Three days after the November 7, 1917, coup d'état, Lenin issued a decree prohibiting the publication of opposition newspapers, but accompanied it with the assurance that the limitations would be only temporary: "As soon as the new order is consolidated, every administrative measure of restriction with regard to the press will be lifted; it will be granted a full freedom within the limits of its responsibility before the courts, in conformity with the broadest and most progressive press laws."[80] But the restrictions never were lifted, and there has been censorship ever since.

Glavlit is the only government agency to have functioned—and under the same name at that—since czarist days, having been a department of the old Imperial Ministry of Internal Affairs from 1865 to 1917. It was revived June 6, 1922, by a decree which, among other things, stated that one of its two deputy chiefs should represent the security police. Glavlit's authority was redefined and enlarged under a decree of June 6, 1931:

1. For the purpose of putting into effect all types of political, ideological, military, and economic control over items prepared for publication or distribution in the press, over manuscripts, pictures, drawing, etc., and also over radio announcements, lectures and exhibitions, there shall be organized under the People's Commissariat of Education of the RSFSR a Chief Administration for Matters of Literature and Publishing Houses (GLAVLIT).

2. In order to carry out the tasks placed upon it GLAVLIT shall be permitted to forbid printing, publication, and distribution of productions which (a) contain agitation or propaganda against Soviet authority and the dictatorship of the proletariat; (b) reveal state secrets; (c) stir up ethnic and religious fanaticism; [or] (d) have a pornographic character. . . .[81]

(In July 1941 when the German Army captured the Russian city of Smolensk, it acquired a large number of government and party records covering the period from 1917 to 1939.[82] Those files, after being shipped back to Germany, were captured by the Americans at the end of the war and now are housed in Alexandria, Virginia. Included in this so-called Smolensk Archive is much information about the operations of Glavlit up to the outbreak of World War II. Unfortunately, no comparable documents are available for the years since then.)

(The complete list of censorable items during the 1930s was comprehensive.[83] On February 26, 1934, for example, special criteria were established for the censorship of plays, films, ballets, broadcasts, and even circus acts. Among the reasons for which material could be banned were the following: "propaganda directed against the Soviet system and the dictatorship of the Proletariat," "divulging of state secrets," "arousing national and religious fanaticism," "pornography," "ideological weakness," "mysticism," and "anti-artistic character.' Other prohibited items included classified information on military developments, agriculture, and economics; epidemics (of both animals and people); crime figures; police activities; attacks on Soviet officials; ideological deviations and "misrepresentations of Soviet reality"; election disorders; and almost everything else that could conceivably affect security or the national image.[84] However, the Smolensk Archive contains many complaints by the censors that newspaper editors not only disobeyed but even ridiculed some Glavlit instructions.)

Glavlit is now in the Ministry of Information, although it operates more as an agency of the Security Police. Its work is supplemented by the censorship departments of the military, the secret police, and the atomic agency. In 1953 its name was changed to "Chief of Administration for the Protection of Military and State Secrets in the Press," and sometime before 1966 the word "military" was dropped.[85] In 1972 the Soviet government formally celebrated Glavlit's fiftieth anniversary, by which time its official name had become Main Administration for Safeguarding State Secrets in the Press.[86] The censors still operate under a complex set of guidelines and among other things have to approve all page proof before publication. (Related to their work is rigorous control of copying machines, which are guarded with great care to prevent the unauthorized copying and circulation of forbidden material.[87]) They also have representatives in radio and television stations, although few details are available about the ways in which broadcast materials are censored. Most Soviet observers now regard Glavlit as of limited importance. The affirmative aspects of information policy are organized so efficiently and the key staff members of the press and broadcasting organizations are so carefully chosen that censorship assumes secondary status.

When the Soviet governmment on February 27, 1973, formally notified UNESCO that it would adhere to the International Copyright Convention on May 27 of that year, there was extensive speculation about its motives.[88] Previously, the USSR had freely published works by foreign authors and composers without securing permission, although it did set aside royalties in its own currency which could be spent inside the Soviet Union. Many observers believed that the USSR did so in order to control the publication abroad of works by dissident authors.

In view of the generally strict controls maintained by the Soviet Union, it is surprising to note that from time to time there are unauthorized radio stations in the USSR, which, depending upon the mood of their operators, broadcast everything from light music to antigovernment propaganda. On April 7, 1970, the Presidium of the Supreme Soviet issued a decree stating that "the construction and use of radio transmission equipment without the required permission" would be punished by a fine of 500 rubles and the confiscation of the unlicensed apparatus.[89] It further provided that any evidence of the "illegal construction and use" of such equipment should be brought before a judge within seventy-two hours of its discovery, and it stipulated that there was to be no appeal from fines levied upon those convicted of such offenses.

Articles in Soviet periodicals in 1963 complained of "radio hooliganism" and "radio pirates," who had discovered ways to make low-power transmitters out of their radio receivers.[90] First they worked the short- and later the medium-wave bands, sometimes with sufficient power to cover a radius of thirty or forty miles. In the Kiev area alone authorities located some two hundred illegal transmitters. Although some of these "pirates" broadcast light music of merely nuisance value, others transmitted critical political polemics. Religious programs were presented on behalf of such varied groups as the Jehovah's Witnesses and the Russian Orthodox church, and there also were indecent songs and profanity.[91] One ingenious eighteen-year-old, imitating the voice of a well-known announcer, declared that American rockets with atomic warheads were on the way. In another case, a transmitter working on a television sound channel made indecent comments during a ballet performance.

"Radio Camomile," run by a young lady, specialized in "reactionary rumors and base tittle-tattle" for the industrial town of Kuibyshev.[92] "Station Cinderella" featured Latin-American cha-cha music, while "King" discussed the sex life of fellow broadcasters and arranged rendezvous. Still others transmitted jazz and popular music recorded off the air from the Voice of America. The pirate broadcasters even became so bold as to arrange a convention, which led to the arrest of all in attendance. Yet, such activities continue, since at the end of 1973 there were reports of illegal broadcasts in Moscow and some of the southern republics by "radio hooligans," who gave themselves such names as The Diamond, Dragon, Ninochka, Black Soul, Sea Devil, and Tempest.

Needless to say, the Soviet Union, like all countries, tries to eliminate unlicensed broadcasters. On one occasion, hoping to frighten illegal operators off the air, authorities circulated false rumors that signals from such stations interfered with airplane and ship direction finders, causing airplanes to crash and ships to run aground.[93] But this scare strategy was not effective, and it was dropped in favor of more conventional electronic detection and legal prosecution.

Although illegal broadcasting stations are eliminated as quickly as possible, there is encouragement for properly licensed amateur radio operators. In 1972 the Soviet news agency TASS boasted that the country's amateur operators had made 330,000 contacts with 220 countries and territories during a recent 105-day period, calling this "the greatest event in the history of radio hamming."[94] Although it might appear that such activities would breach the information barrier, the authorities feel that the advantages outweigh the disadvantages. Amateur operators are regarded as an important source of trained personnel; they have headed local campaigns to service radio receivers; and they have contributed to the tracking of artificial earth satellites. Finally, they are regarded as a reserve supply for military electronic technicians.

More important than censorship are the affirmative measures taken by the government to use all available media to achieve desired political and social objectives.[95] In 1920 the Central Committee set up Agitprop (Department of Propaganda and Agitation). From the very outset its heads usually were high-ranking members of the party. A list of the areas in which it works suggests the agency's comprehensive scope: party propaganda and agitation; culture; schools; science; fine arts; sports and gymnastics; and the mass media.[96] Decrees implementing its work were released in 1921 and 1924. In 1925, Agitprop indicated the proper ideological direction for radio news broadcasts, lectures, and concerts, the radio rules duplicating those previously issued for the press.[97]

Agitprop and related government agencies provide directions for all Soviet information media. However, Agitprop is a policy-making rather than an operational agency, and the execution of its instructions is entrusted to such organizations as the State Committee for Radio and Television. In addition, nonmetropolitan newspapers often take their leads from *Pravda* and the national news service TASS. The Smolensk Archive documents such instructions from the 1930s as these: unmask enemy elements on the collective farms; campaign for improved and increased agricultural output; criticize inadequacies in the work of local party and government organizations; and praise certain individuals scheduled for promotion.[98] In 1940 a 220-page volume was published summarizing all the principal press pronouncements to that date, and this was revised and extended to 675 pages in a postwar edition released in 1954.[99] It is difficult to describe the work of Agitprop, since its directives are secret and its activities rarely come to public view. However, it can be said that Agitprop instructions have tended to become less restrictive with the passing years, particularly since Stalin's death in 1953.

The administrative structure for Soviet radio and television has undergone a number of transformations since April 1, 1918, when the Council of People's Commissars decided to centralize radio telephony to provide an "evenly distributed service throughout Russia." Later the same month Lenin signed a decree delegating nationwide responsibility for station construction to the Commissariat of Posts and Telegraphs.[100] On July 21 another Lenin decree, "Centralization of Radio Engineering," authorized this commissariat to organize a radio council to plan for the construction and operation of the network of permanent stations.[101] On January 27, 1921, the Commissariat of Posts and Telegraphs was instructed to build stations in eleven cities and relay scientific lectures originated in Moscow.[102]

In July 1924 the Council of People's Commissars took an important step toward the permanent organization of broadcasting by creating in Moscow a joint stock company, "Radio for All," shortly renamed "Radio Transmissions," stock in which was held by trade unions and education authorities.[103] In June 1925 the Radio Commission with the

Central Committee of the Russian Communist party was created to manage the ideological and artistic aspects of "radio agitation," and in October the Central Radio Council was created under the Main Administration of Political Education to coordinate the work of the other organizations involved with broadcasting.[104] In July 1926 the Central Committee of the All-Union Communist party studied the problem of how best to organize talks on political and economic subjects, and six months later it adopted a resolution "of considerable significance," which, to quote an official source, "liquidated that certain spontaneity which heretofore existed in the organization of local radiobroadcasts, and assured a systematic party guidance of radiobroadcasting."

From 1928 until 1933, broadcasting was the responsibility of the Commissariat of Posts and Telegraphs. A directive issued July 13, 1928, liquidating the previous joint stock company and assigning broadcasting to Posts and Telegraphs, complained that the previous company did not sufficiently meet its responsibilities for "economic and cultural construction."[105] Later that year, a central radio council was created to assume direct management of broadcasting. As an official source put it: "Instead of the outdated programs that failed to justify themselves, new, livelier and more profitable programs were created. Interesting programs made their appearance, devoted to technical propaganda, on-the-spot reporting of various events, programs for kolkhoz members, for young people and so on. Musical and literary-dramatic programs were expanded. Many interesting programs in native languages were organized by radiobroadcasting editorial boards in the union republics." On September 10, 1931, the Committee on Radiobroadcasting with the People's Commissariat of Posts and Telegraphs USSR was created.[106]

The next important change came on January 31, 1933, with the appointment of the All-Union Committee for Radiofication* and Radiobroadcasting attached to the Council of People's Commissars.[107] The accompanying decree stated: "In view of the fact that radio is acquiring exceptional significance in the entire economic and political life of the country it is recognized as necessary to create the All-Union Radio

* The Russian word "radiofikatsiya," part of the name of this committee, is often translated as "radiofication," although English-language dictionaries contain no such term. A meaningful translation might be "radio development and expansion," meaning the construction and development of technical facilities as opposed to program activities.

Committee under the Council of People's Commissars USSR and to charge it with the development and execution of problems pertaining to: radiofication and radiobroadcasting, the . . . production of radio equipment, . . . and the organization and coordination of scientific research work in the field of radiofication and radiobroadcasting."[108]

The new committee was to be responsible for "the organization, planning, and operational direction of all radiobroadcasting in the USSR, including radio diffusion by lower radiobroadcasting exchanges in district centers, Machine Tractor Stations, and so forth."[109] An announcement of November 29, 1933, stated that transmitters and lines would be the responsibility of the Commissariat of Communications, with the All-Union Committee responsible only for programs.[110] To this day the USSR, like most other continental European countries, divides responsibilities for transmission and programming. This committee proved more enduring than any of its predecessors, since it continued to function until the middle of 1949.

The 1933 organization was the lineal forebear of the several committees that followed it.[111] The All-Union Radio Committee was headed by a chairman and two associate chairmen, appointed by the Soviet of People's Commissars. It was divided into three boards: radiofication; central broadcasting; and local broadcasting. The first, in charge of station and network construction and development, was involved principally with technical matters, including liaison with the Ministry of Communications, which supplied the transmitters and connecting lines. It also was responsible for developing the wired distribution network as well as the assignment of stations to wavelengths.

The Board for Central Broadcasting, which planned centrally originated broadcasts for national distribution, was divided into such functional departments as propaganda and education, news, literary-dramatic broadcasts, children's broadcasts, and musical programs. The Board for Local Broadcasting supervised and coordinated the work of the local radio committees. By 1935, two years after the All-Union Committee for Radiofication and Radiobroadcasting was created, there were 67 local committees in the various constituent republics. By 1950 this had grown to 168 broadcasting committees, plus 2,000 editorial boards in charge of local diffusion exchanges.

Among other things, the All-Union Committee collected the required receiver license fees from set owners (the charges were abolished in

1962); operated a department of publications; maintained laboratories for sound and television recording; and was in charge of broadcasts for audiences abroad. It also served as the broadcasting committee for the Russian Republic; as was pointed out above, other committees supervised broadcasting in the remaining fourteen republics.

On July 6, 1949, the All-Union Radio Committee gave way to the Committee on Radio Information attached to the Council of Ministers.[112] This was followed on March 30, 1953, by the Main Administration of Radio Information of the Ministry of Culture.[113] Another change was made May 15, 1957, when the State Committee on Radiobroadcasting and Television under the USSR Council of Ministers took over all responsibilities for broadcasting. A Soviet comment on this change referred to "the constantly growing significance of radio and television broadcasting, as powerful information media, means of mobilizing the workers for the solution of the tasks of communist construction, and of political and esthetic education of Soviet people."[114]

A decree of April 19, 1962, stated that the Soviet Presidium had decided "to convert the State Committee on Radio and Television under the U.S.S.R. Council of Ministers to the U.S.S.R. Council of Ministers' State Committee on Radio and Television"—the organization now responsible for Soviet broadcasting.[115] This change, however, made no important functional differences in the Committee's activities. The chairmen of the ten state committees listed on the roster of the Council of Ministers are regarded as members of the government, although they are below ministers in status.[116] Broadcasting, therefore, ranks with labor and wages, foreign economic relations, forestry, vocational technical training, price control, and the state bank. However, the council has a minister of radio industry and a minister of communications.

At present, the chief officers of the State Committee for Radio and Television (sometimes referred to as the Committee for Television and Radio) include a chairman, four deputy chairmen, and twelve members of a board of management. Each deputy chairman heads a main department: domestic radio; domestic television; broadcasts for foreign audiences; and technical and financial operations.[117] Under each deputy are several "chief editors," directly responsible for the work of their respective departments.

Domestic radio is divided into fourteen sections, all of which contribute programs to the country's several radio networks. Program responsibilities are divided as follows: (1) news and information (including, particularly, the nationwide information network Mayak, in addition to news and information programs on the other networks); (2) propaganda (subdivided into six sections: social and political, economics and industry, agricultural, international affairs, scientific and technological, physical culture and sports); (3) children; (4) youth; (5) literary and dramatic (subdivided into prose and poetry, foreign literature, drama, satire and humor, stage, and spectaculars); (6) music; (7) programs for the city of Moscow; (8) programs for the Moscow region; (9) planning and coordination for All-Union Radio; (10) planning and coordination for local transmissions; (11) centrally produced programs for local dissemination; (12) publications dealing with radio; (13) audience research; and (14) liaison and program exchanges with foreign countries.

Domestic television also has fourteen sections, although it is not organized exactly like radio: (1) social and political programs; (2) news and information; (3) films; (4) children and youth (both in and out of school); (5) programs for the Moscow region; (6) music; (7) literary and dramatic programs; (8) planning and coordination; (9) program exchange within the Soviet Union; (10) education; (11) operations; (12) design; (13) sound production; and (14) audience research.

The department dealing with broadcasts for foreign audiences, the Soviet equivalent of the Voice of America and the External Services of the BBC, is subdivided according to target areas: the other socialist countries; North America; Latin America; Western Europe; Near and Middle East; Southeast Asia; the Far East; and Africa. Other departments and sections of the State Committee are responsible for personnel selection and training; engineering; publications; the collection of information; financial planning; and labor and wages. The committee also maintains and operates the various buildings in Moscow used for broadcasting.

The State Committee for Television and Radio is responsible generally for television and radio throughout the Soviet Union and also serves as the broadcasting committee for the RSFSR. In addition, there are many republic, regional, oblast, and local committees, organized in much the same way as the All-Union Committee in Moscow. In 1965, for example, there were 14 broadcasting committees in the union republics, 20 in the autonomous republics, 112 in regions and oblasts, 7 in districts, and 153 in cities or subdivisions of cities. In addition, many public councils and editorial staffs were involved in planning and appraising broadcasting. Over the entire country there were more than 300 such groups, ranging from 14 in the Ukraine and 92 in Uzbekistan down to 5 in the small republic of Lithuania.

Although broadcasting is the formal responsibility of the State Committee for Television and Radio, which reports to the Council of Ministers, the Communist party always is involved, as it is in all important Soviet functions. The Council of Ministers is composed entirely of party leaders, while most if not all the members of the State Committee, as well as the key broadcasting officials, are tested party leaders. The censorship agency Glavlit and the complementary Agitrop, both of which have indirect if not direct influence over program content, are under party control. Education for broadcasting includes extensive indoctrination in party theory, and some broadcasting schools are run by the Communist party.

The party often issues detailed instructions to the State Committee. In February 1960, the Central Committee produced a 4,500-word document entitled "On Improving Soviet Radiobroadcasting and on Further Developing Television."[118] This extensive review of broadcasting must have had a considerable effect on the State Committee. A resolution of the Central Committee issued July 6, 1962, "On Measures for the Further Improvement of the Work of Radio Broadcasting and Television," again criticized and instructed.[119]

In April 1966, at its Twenty-third Congress, the party stated: "Fuller use must be made of the press, radio, television, and cinema in order to mold a Marxist-Leninist outlook and promote the political and cultural development of all the Soviet People."[120] Annually on Radio Day, May 7, there are statements about broadcasting by party leaders. Editorials and letters in such major newspapers as *Izvestia* and *Pravda,* and articles in the important ideological journals like *Kommunist,* constitute implied if not direct instructions.*

---

* For an interesting appraisal of press freedom, in which countries are rated on a scale of 1 (high) to 9 (low), see Raymond B. Nixon, "Freedom in the World's Press: A Fresh Appraisal with New Data," *Journalism Quarterly,* 42:1 (Winter 1965), 3–14, 118–119. In the European area, Professor Nixon gave 1 ratings to Belgium, Denmark, the Netherlands, Norway, Sweden, Switzerland, and the United Kingdom. Ranked 2 were Austria, Finland, France, the Federal Republic of Germany, Ireland, and Italy. Ratings of 7 were assigned to Hungary, Poland, Portugal, and Spain, and 8 to Bulgaria, Czechoslovakia, the German Democratic Republic,

Finances

Very little information is available about the financing of Soviet broadcasting. Neither the government nor the State Committee for Television and Radio reports the amount of money spent each year, and because of the many complexities involved, there is no point in guessing. Obviously, the sum must be very large, in view of the size and extent of the broadcasting establishment. One thing is certain, however: costs are met mainly from general public funds, since there are no receiver license fees, although there is a tax on new sets plus some income from broadcast advertising.

For many years each receiver owner had to purchase an annual license, but this requirement was eliminated on January 1, 1962, at which time an excise tax was levied on each set, the money being applied toward the support of the service.[121] The end of licensing was announced in *Izvestia* on August 27, 1961, in an article that described the decree as a "Gift to 10,000,000."

A month later the same newspaper published a letter from a listener-viewer complaining that he had paid far more in license fees over the years than the programs were worth, and that set owners thereby had been forced to give money to the state without getting value in return.[122] The heading of the original *Izvestia* editorial, said this writer, should have been "Gift from 10,000,000." This evoked over 450 letters arguing the pros and cons of license fees and broadcast quality.[123] Among other things, the letters documented the fact that the USSR, like many other countries, encountered a problem in getting set owners to buy licenses. Soviet citizens, like everyone else, do not like to pay taxes, and may try to evade them!

A few days after the Bolshevik party seized power in November 1917, the Revolutionary Committee made advertising a state monopoly in order to eliminate the possibility of financial support for opposition newspapers.[124] Radio advertisements were officially banned from 1935 to 1947.[125] For some years after the Revolution there was a great shortage of consumer goods, but when output began to equal demand, there was pressure from producing groups to bring their products to public

---

and the Soviet Union. The only European country with a 9 was Albania, although elsewhere Afghanistan, Mali, Yemen, mainland China, Mongolia, North Korea, North Vietnam, and Cuba received that rating.

attention.[126] Whenever miscalculation led to overproduction, there were calls for advertising, and the introduction of credit and installment buying created additional opportunities for sales. As the labor supply became more adequate and more highly specialized, both employers and employees wanted to advertise. Accordingly, advertising gradually reappeared, though more as a shopper's service than as a means of increasing the sale of goods.

Examples of this change of attitudes are provided by the references to advertising in two editions of the *Great Soviet Encyclopedia*.[127] The 1941 edition said that "hullabaloo, speculation, and a race . . . for profits have made advertising a means of swindling the people and of foisting upon them of goods frequently useless or of dubious quality." But a more recent edition described advertising in these words: "The popularization of goods with the aim of selling them, the creation of demand for these goods, the acquaintance of consumers with their quality, particular features, and the location of their sales, and explanation of the methods of their use." An *Izvestia* editorial in April 1969 pointed out that "advertising is art plus science, not a simple business."[128] But it was felt necessary to draw a distinction between American and Soviet practices, so *Izvestia* emphasized that "Americans, thirsting for profit, forgot common sense and flooded their media with ads." This the USSR would not do, "though we must admit that advertising is a prime element of commerce and of production efforts."

Broadcast advertising in the Soviet Union resembles that in a number of Western European countries. Direct "sponsorship"—the production of entire programs by advertisers—is not allowed, although spot announcements are broadcast. Radio advertisements are grouped into ten- or fifteen-minute blocks, and scheduled between 7:00 and 9:00 A.M. and 5:00 and 8:00 P.M. Television advertising, which first appeared in the 1960s, also is broadcast in clusters, between 6:00 and 11:00 P.M. Individual announcements vary in length from thirty seconds to two minutes.

Information rather than hard sell is the objective, with perhaps some encouragement to buy. There are advertisements for various kinds of consumer goods (food, clothing, and furniture), cinemas, lotteries, employment availabilities, and railroad and airline transportation. In 1970 I saw some food commercials on Kiev local television. The scene opened on a restaurant facade, after which the camera panned over an attractive food display as a woman's voice described the product. On the local Moscow channel in 1972 I saw a five-minute cluster of advertisements very similar to those aired in many Western European countries. An abstract symbol separated the commercials, which were for household articles and clothing. Narration was by a single voice, with music in the background. As with American television too, the production skill shown in the commercials sometimes exceeds that in the programs themselves. There are no data on the results achieved from broadcast advertising, although one Western journalist reported that the demand for a certain type of foreign cheese rose by 7 per cent after it had been advertised on Moscow television.*

The advertisements on Soviet radio and television, like those in all the Eastern European socialist countries except Yugoslavia, do not bring in enough revenue to be of financial importance. However, an Estonian television official suggested in 1967 that Estonian television could be improved if advertising were actively solicited and the organization made self-supporting. But nothing came of his proposal.[129]

International Radio and Television Organization (OIRT)

The Soviet Union and the other Eastern European socialist countries, except for Yugoslavia, belong to the International Radio and Television Organization, usually referred to by the initials of its French name— Organisation Internationale de Radiodiffusion et Télévision.[130] (The OIRT evolved in stages from the International Broadcasting Union (Union Internationale de Radiodiffusion), founded in Geneva in 1925, which had twenty-eight European members plus twelve associate members from outside the Continent.) Because of international political differences, the UIR was succeeded by the International Broadcasting Organization (Organisation Internationale de Radiodiffusion—OIR), created in Brussels in 1946. Tensions related to the cold war led the

---

* *London Times*, February 7, 1967, p. 15. Some foreign firms advertise in Soviet trade and technical publications to bring their products to the attention of prospective buyers in the Soviet Union. Soviet magazines circulated abroad by Novosti frequently advertise Intourist, Soviet airlines, Soviet railroads, automobiles, watches, souvenirs, and other things available for purchase by tourists. Some Soviet corporations which manufacture products to sell abroad buy souvenirs from foreign firms for distribution to their customers.

Western countries to withdraw and establish the European Broadcasting Union in 1949, with administrative headquarters in Geneva and technical offices in Brussels. Thereupon the OIR—which became the OIRT in 1959—moved to Prague.

Most OIRT members are socialist states. In 1973 these included Albania, Algeria, Bulgaria, China (which has not been actively participating in recent years), Cuba, Czechoslovakia, Finland, the German Democratic Republic, Hungary, Iraq, Mali, Mongolia, North Korea, Poland, Romania, the Sudan, North Vietnam, the United Arab Republic, and the USSR (with individual memberships for Byelorussia, Estonia, Latvia, Lithuania, Moldavia, and the Ukraine).

The OIRT is concerned with the administrative, legal, engineering, programming, and other problems common to all broadcasting organizations. Between the annual sessions of its General Assembly, the OIRT is governed by an administrative council. It has four standing committees. The Radio Program Commission deals with all matters related to radio programming and includes four specialized groups working on music, dramatic, children's, and science programs. The Television Program Commission is responsible for all aspects of television programming, including Intervision. The Technical Commission works with such matters as links between stations, studio equipment, recording, and transmitters. The Economic and Legal Commission is concerned with administrative, financial, and legal problems. OIRT activities are financed by membership dues.

OIRT publications include the *Review of the International Radio and Television Organization,* issued six times a year, with one edition in English and French, a second in Russian, and a third in German; the monthly *OIRT Information,* a news bulletin about programming in the member countries; and a catalog of programs suitable for exchange, issued twice yearly.

The OIRT takes part in international meetings when its interests are involved. It also participates in some sessions of the International Telecommunication Union in Geneva, to which most of its members belong, works with certain UNESCO groups, and has increasingly close contacts with the European Broadcasting Union.

An important OIRT activity is the exchange of radio and television programs among its members as well as with EBU stations. The OIRT Radio Program Commission arranges exchanges by network line and tape recording of concerts, athletic events, children's programs, and special broadcasts for such anniversaries as the October Revolution of 1917, the Lenin Centennial in 1970, and the Beethoven Bicentennial of the same year.[131] To promote radio dramaturgy, both scripts and directors are exchanged. OIRT countries may receive most EBU exchanges, although there are no data on the extent to which they are actually used.

It was inevitable that Europe should develop bilateral, regional, and Continent-wide television program exchanges as soon as technology permitted. Western Europe set up Eurovision in 1954, and Eastern Europe began Intervision in 1960, both networks being preceded by frequent ad hoc exchanges. Early in 1956 some stations in East Germany and Czechoslovakia broadcast part of the European coverage of the Olympic hockey matches relayed by Eurovision from Italy, and in 1957 connections were extended to Poland.[132] In January 1960 the OIRT Administrative Council created Intervision, its formal inauguration coming on September 1, 1960, with participation by Hungary, East Germany, Poland, and Czechoslovakia. The Soviet Union joined the following year and at the same time began to provide occasional programs for Western Europe. On October 19, 1961, the USSR fed to London, via Helsinki, pictures of the Moscow reception for Yuri Gagarin, the first Soviet cosmonaut, which the BBC relayed to various continental stations by way of Eurovision. Shortly thereafter, there was international distribution of the May Day Parade from Red Square, and in August of the same year a transmission from Moscow to Rome when the Italian premier Amintore Fanfani was visiting the Soviet Union.[133]

All European OIRT members except Albania, which has only experimental television, belong to Intervision: Bulgaria, Czechoslovakia, Finland, the German Democratic Republic, Hungary, Poland, Romania, and the USSR. Finland, the only member of both EBU and OIRT, receives programs from both, while Yugoslavia, a member of EBU but not of OIRT, receives Eurovision programs as an EBU member and some Intervision programs too. The television organizations of Austria, Sweden, and Yugoslavia participate as observers in some Intervision meetings.

Programs are exchanged by surface microwave only and not by satellite. More and more of them are in color—such as the Munich Olympic games in 1972—with transcoding from PAL into SECAM done by the user countries (for a description of Europe's two color television systems, see below, pp. 512–515). Intervision and Eurovision now are connected on the frontiers of the two Germanys as well as on the West German–Czechoslovak, Austrian-Czechoslovak, and Austrian-Hungarian borders. The daily news exchanges are carried out through the Schönbrunn studio of Austrian television.

These program activities are directed by the Intervision Council, with the chairman of the Television Program Commission as ex officio head. Program and technical coordination centers in Prague organize all relays and implement decisions taken by the council, which meets every three months to establish a quarterly plan. Fourteen specialized groups coordinate exchanges in such program fields as children and youth, sports, drama, music, entertainment, news, science, in-school, art, economics, and films.

The OIRT also organizes competitions and festivals, to which there are frequent references on the pages below. These include a children's radio play festival scheduled alternate years, an international television film festival in Prague, another film festival in Riga, and a popular song festival in Zopoty, Poland.

Between 1960 and 1965 more than 3,700 programs were exchanged by Intervision members. A Ukrainian television executive classified them as follows: sports, 43.5 per cent; topical, 30.5 per cent; cultural, 9.8 per cent; children's 9.4 per cent; and entertainment, 6.7 per cent.[134] Figures from Intervision headquarters indicate that the number of programs increased from 394 (572 hr. airtime) in 1960 to 2,246 (2,776 hr.) in 1968, with a drop to 1,854 programs (2,591 hr.) in 1969. From 1960 to 1970, 13,012 programs (15,447 hr.) were exchanged. These were categorized by Intervision headquarters as follows: sports, 40.0 per cent; news, 27.3 per cent; cultural, 12.2 per cent; children's, 8.7 per cent; and entertainment, 7.8 per cent. In 1969 almost a third were from the Soviet Union, other major contributors including the German Democratic Republic and Poland.

Exchanges between Intervision and Eurovision are becoming increasingly important to both groups. Negotiations began in February 1960, although there were few exchanges before 1965. Table 1, based on EBU reports, indicates the participation of all Intervision countries in Eurovision exchanges from 1961 to 1972. In 1961, for example, the Soviet Union originated 14 programs for Eurovision, with a duration of

Table 1. Participation of Socialist States in Eurovision (Eurovision Figures)

| Country | Programs Originated[a] | | Programs Received[a] | | News Exchanges | |
	No.	Dura-tion[b]	No.	Dura-tion[b]	No. of Items Originated	No. of Items Received
1960						
Czechoslovakia			73	68h		
Hungary			43	37h		
GDR			97	94h		
Poland			54	62h		
Yugoslavia			67	97h		
1961						
Czechoslovakia	11	23h	41	62h		
Hungary	3	6h	19	23h		
GDR	2	4h	73	92h		
Poland			26	38h		
Yugoslavia	20	22h	4	6h		
USSR	14	30h	3	2h		
1962						
Czechoslovakia	17	44h	21	42h		
Hungary	3	4h	24	47h		
GDR	7	16h	31	78h		24
Poland	13	13h	13	34h		
Yugoslavia	7	27h	49	68h		
USSR	9	21h	2	11h		
1963						
Bulgaria	1	2h	4	7h		16
Czechoslovakia	8	21h	51	90h		17
Hungary	9	20h	30	46h		17
GDR	8	11h	79	133h		16
Poland	3	3h	27	37h		16
Romania			5	9h		16
Yugoslavia	10	25h	118	168h	35	10
USSR	20	30h	20	32h		16
1964						
Bulgaria			19	26h		3
Czechoslovakia	11	15h	95	127h	1	10
Hungary	4	4h	69	85h		26
GDR	3	4h	158	205h	2	46
Poland	6	8h	76	74h		6
Romania			29	32h		
Yugoslavia	1	2h	144	216h	15	21
USSR	10	13h	65	99h		33
1965						
Bulgaria			14	34h45		
Czechoslovakia	10	15h45	56	94h15	11	23
Hungary	7	13h30	49	84h	6	162
GDR	15	25h30	113	160h15	17	198

Table 1—*Continued*

Country	Programs Originated[a] No.	Duration[b]	Programs Received[a] No.	Duration[b]	News Exchanges No. of Items Originated	No. of Items Received
Poland	6	11h30	35	53h15	10	5
Romania	1	4h15	14	27h45	1	1
Yugoslavia	9	16h45	88	154h45	28	14
USSR	20	40h	35	54h	40	3
1966						
Bulgaria			31	57h45	1	
Czechoslovakia	13	28h15	79	137h45	12	22
Hungary	14	37h	69	107h	11	457
GDR	7	17h	130	211h	24	403
Poland	4	6h30	52	84h45	22	1
Romania	4		45	84h45	5	
Yugoslavia	31	60h15	130	208h15	24	7
USSR	24	24h30	69	126h45	92	
1967						
Bulgaria	4	7h15	17	30h15		1
Czechoslovakia	13	28h	53	77h45	10	251
Hungary	9	16h15	44	65h30	7	529
GDR	4	7h	103	143h	10	483
Poland	7	6h	35	57h	19	16
Romania			46	77h45	4	1
Yugoslavia	8	8h30	144	213h30	19	520
USSR	10	21h15	56	86h	43	7
1968						
Bulgaria	1	2h	115	187h15		
Czechoslovakia	4	5h	151	222h30		
Hungary	4	7h	144	216h		
GDR			201	311h15		
Poland	1	1h45	170	230h45		
Romania	7	17h30	128	211h45		
Yugoslavia	4	5h45	172	277h30	46	1,517
USSR	3	4h15	176	265h15		
1969						
Bulgaria			27	55h15		
Czechoslovakia	29	47h	155	222h45	84	
Hungary	7	10h45	123	173h		
GDR	11	19h45	108	189h		
Poland	3	11h	110	134h		
Romania	14	28h45	108	148h30		
Yugoslavia	27	62h45	228	321h15	62	2,390
USSR	4	6h45	124	181h45		
1970						
Bulgaria			43	80h		
Czechoslovakia	21	24h45	89	157h30	37	

Table 1—*Continued*

Country	Programs Originated[a]		Programs Received[a]		News Exchanges	
	No.	Duration[b]	No.	Duration[b]	No. of Items Originated	No. of Items Received
Hungary	2	4h15	66	115h30		
GDR	8	18h45	114	220h45		
Poland	1	3h30	59	90h45		
Romania	20	32h30	65	101h15		
Yugoslavia	46	92h	158	277h	79	2,810
USSR	21	57h	100	179h		
1971						
Bulgaria	7	22h30	70	125h15		
Czechoslovakia	3	4h15	98	198h30		
Hungary	5	9h30	94	196h		
GDR	9	24h30	121	242h		
Poland			105	195h45		
Romania	6	11h45	107	183h30		
Yugoslavia	17	37h	191	325h45	72	2,803
USSR	10	23h15	117	225h30		
1972						
Bulgaria	2	2h15	121	224h30		
Czechoslovakia	36	83h30	142	277h15		
Hungary	4	6h	160	304h15		
GDR			180	354h15		
Poland			184	351h45		
Romania	12	30h15	171	321h45		
Yugoslavia	14	26h	266	472h15	50	2,675
USSR	4	5h45	183	351h		

SOURCES: *EBU Review* as follows: 67B (May 1961), p. 14; 73B (May 1962) p. 17; 79B (May 1963), p. 27; 85B (May 1964), p. 25; 91B (May 1965), p. 51; 98B (July 1966), p. 26; 104B (July 1967), p. 32; 109B (May 1968), p. 30; 115B (May 1969), p. 27; 121B (May 1970), p. 36; 127B (May 1971), p. 31; 23:3 (May 1972), pp. 37–38; 24:3 (May 1973), pp. 46–47.
a Excluding news.
b In hours (h) and minutes.

30 hours, and received 3, with a duration of 2 hours.* By 1966, 24 programs were originated (24 hr., 30 min.) and 69 programs received (126 hr., 45 min.). During 1969, 4 programs (6 hr., 45 min.) were originated by the USSR and 124 programs (181 hr., 45 min.) received.

* Figures for the reception of programs indicate only that those programs were *received* by one or another organization. They may not have been broadcast.

In 1971, 10 programs (23 hr., 15 min.) were originated and 117 programs (225 hr., 30 min.) received. The 1972 figures—4 programs (5 hr., 45 min.) originated and 183 programs (351 hr.) received—show fluctuation owing to the Olympic Games. News and cultural materials are exchanged without payment, although charges are made for some types of programs. Sporting events may involve payments to the organizers, as in the case of the Olympic Games. The rates depend on the number of sets in the receiving countries.

However, Intervision statistics often show more originations than do those from Eurovision. As is indicated in Table 2, during 1972 the USSR, for example, contributed 14 programs (20 hr. 51 min.) while receiving 62 (143 hr., 2 min.).

It is interesting to speculate about the long-range effects of these East-West exchanges, particularly in the field of news. On October 1, 1969, Intervision members began a regular exchange of video news items by way of closed circuit, and there also are daily news exchanges between

Table 2. Participation of Socialist States in Eurovision (Intervision Figures)

	Programs Originated[a]		Programs Received[a]		News Exchanges	
					No. of Items Origi-	No. of Items
Country	No.	Dura-tion[b]	No.	Dura-tion[b]	nated	Received
1971						
Bulgaria	8	18h38	56	107h35		
Czechoslovakia	10	25h29	69	140h38		
GDR	18	36h53	107	198h24		
Hungary	6	8h47	76	154h23		
Poland	4	4h5	85	171h41		
Romania	19	29h31	85	149h20		
USSR	17	29h13	108	203h7		
1972						
Bulgaria	7	8h59	33	74h31	9	31
Czechoslovakia	42	94h52	42	104h44	30	1,334
GDR	10	15h1	58	119h20	25	947
Hungary	9	14h34	43	84h44	15	1,587
Poland	6	6h52	55	112h26	37	1,917
Romania	23	48h42	68	151h26	10	1,532
USSR	14	20h51	62	143h2	94	1,270

SOURCE: Information provided by Intervision.
a Excluding news.   b In hours (h) and minutes.

Intervision and Eurovision (for details, see pp. 105–107). One only can hope that this will provide a window on the world for countries with limited information sources. Surely these exchanges permit sports fans to participate energetically, if vicariously, in the international contests of their teams. Furthermore, live transmissions and news clips of such major events as the November 7 and May Day parades in Moscow and the American moon walks may bring the people of the world closer together. But there is no evidence to support this hypothesis.

Technical Facilities

Soviet technical facilities are extensive, as befits the largest country in the world. The USSR has three radio networks and much local broadcasting, the world's largest wired diffusion service, a rapidly growing television service with a national network, many regional and local stations, and the world's first satellite system to distribute domestic television programs.

In spite of what Lenin and his colleagues said about its importance, however, broadcasting developed much more slowly in the Soviet Union than in the United States and most other Western countries. This was partly due to the general technological and industrial backwardness of the country. The political insecurity accompanying the Bolshevik Revolution of 1917, dislocation following World War I, and threats from outside also were factors. The internal turmoil of the 1930s must have played a role. The severe shortage of electricity, particularly in the 1920s and 1930s, delayed the distribution of off-the-air receivers. The emphasis on heavy industry and war matériel rather than consumer goods may have been a factor, although that might have been counterbalanced by the propagandistic potentials of broadcasting. The high illiteracy rate should have stimulated radio development in the 1920s and 1930s, but it clearly was more than offset by other considerations.

Then came the devastation of World War II, during which the number of radio transmitters and receivers greatly declined. Thereafter, food and shelter took precedence over mass communications. Finally, there was the lack of any competitive or commercial stimulus, which in the United States may have put more stations on the air than were needed, but in the Soviet Union probably delayed development. Whatever the reasons, the record is one of great gaps in broadcast coverage and service until recent years.*

There is no lack of documentation from the Soviet side on the slowness in recent years in installing facilities. On Radio Day, 1956, *Pravda* in a lead editorial criticized the ministries of communication and radiotechnical industries for their inadequacies.[135] The editorial complained that radio installations on collective farms were way behind schedule and that there was a lack of coordination among the various institutes and laboratories responsible for developing new equipment. "It is an obvious anomaly for these research institutions to take up problems . . . that have long since been tackled and solved by neighboring or foreign institutions."

In 1960 the Central Committee of the Communist party, in the course of a 4,500-word discourse on the needs of Soviet broadcasting, mentioned poor radio reception in outlying sections of the country and generally inadequate coverage for the second and third radio services.[136] Some provinces had no radio stations at all, and many local transmitters had poor coverage owing to insufficient power. Shortly thereafter, on Radio Day of the same year, the minister of communications accepted the Central Committee's complaints and said that efforts were being made "to eliminate the serious shortcomings, and also to develop FM broadcasting." In addition, he promised three-program wired broadcasting and reported on experimental color television programs in Moscow.[137] In recent years conspicuous improvements have been made in providing radio and television service to the Soviet Union. Almost the entire country now can receive radio singnals, while about 70 per cent is served by television.

For its domestic radio services, the Soviet Union operates a great

---

* In 1922 the USSR had 1 radio transmitter and the USA 30. Figures for other representative years follow: 1929, USSR 23, USA 618; 1940, USSR 90, USA 765; 1950, USSR 100, USA 2,819; 1966, USSR 600, USA 5,485. Soviet data are from Markham, p. 76, Hopkins, p. 246, and the Novosti publication, *Communications in the USSR*, by P. Rubina and F. Ramsin, pp. 6–7. Information also was supplied by Soviet broadcasting authorities. United States data are from *Broadcasting Yearbook 1972*, p. A112. Soviet figures may exclude some relay transmitters. American figures for 1922 and 1929 are for AM stations authorized; for 1940, AM stations licensed; thereafter for FM and AM stations on the air. Data for United States stations in 1973 are given in the note on p. 68 below.

many long-wave, short-wave, medium-wave, and FM transmitters.*
Some of these have accompanying studio installations, whereas others
serve only as relays. In addition to Moscow, there are production facilities in all republic capitals and other large cities, as well as modest
installations in many smaller towns.

It is difficult to obtain detailed information about the number and
location of these transmitters. There are periodic references to them in
the press, but when tabulated the figures contain many gaps and some
contradictions. However, one standard reference work lists 50 long-wave
AM transmitters, some with power up to 500 kilowatts.[138] (Although in
the United States domestic transmitters are limited to 50 kilowatts of
power, in the Soviet Union, as elsewhere in Europe, many have much
higher power.) Also listed are 127 medium-wave transmitters, with
from 5 to 300 kilowatts power, many being in the 100- to 150-kilowatt
range. In addition, there are 178 short-wave transmitters for the domestic
services. (Like Canada, Australia, and Brazil—also large and in many
areas sparsely settled countries—the USSR uses short-wave to reach
widely separated listeners.) But some of these figures may be much too
low, since they probably omit many low-power relays.†

FM broadcasting has been developing steadily in the Soviet Union
since it was introduced shortly after World War II, and 235 cities now
have one or more stations.[139] The new Ostankino television tower in
Moscow, completed in 1967, was designed to carry six FM as well as
at least five television antennas. The USSR began experimenting with
stereophonic FM in 1955, and in 1957 and 1958 Soviet engineers developed a "polar-modulation" system for stereo, of which tests were begun
in Leningrad in January 1960.[140] This was formally adopted at the end

---

* As used here, the term "transmitter" denotes the apparatus that sends out
radio or television signals by electromagnetic waves for off-the-air reception by
broadcast receivers. "Studio" or "studio installation" refers to the combination of
rooms and equipment used to originate radio or television programs, which are
recorded and/or distributed by line, microwave relay, and satellites to transmitters
for broadcasting. The term "station," which in the United States usually means a
transmitter and accompanying studio installation, is used less frequently in Europe,
where a number of transmitters often carry the output of one studio center.

† By way of comparison, as of August 31, 1973, the United States had 4,436
authorized medium-wave broadcasting stations, 2,581 commercial FM stations, and
693 educational FM stations (Broadcasting, September 17, 1973, p. 56). But since
many American cities have between 15 and 25 radio stations, the differences in
the extent of national coverage are nowhere near so great as might be concluded
from the differences in the total number of stations in each country.

of 1963, in preference to the pilot tone system of the United States used in most Eastern European countries. Several types of stereophonic receivers have been on sale since 1969.

The Soviet Union now operates three nationwide radio networks from its Moscow headquarters, disseminated by long-, medium-, short-wave, and FM transmitters to the entire USSR.[141] Two of these are subdivided. Program I has five sections, serving respectively: European USSR; Caucasus and Urals; Kazakhstan and Central Asian Republics; the Far East; Eastern Siberia; and Western Siberia. Program II—Mayak ("beacon" or "lighthouse")—is in seven subdivisions: European USSR; Caucasus, Urals, and North Kazakhstan; Kazakhstan and Central Asia; the Far East; Eastern Siberia; and Western Siberia. Program III covers the central European USSR, the South Urals, and the Volga River area, plus some regional centers by FM only. The wired relay centers all take Program I, while those with two or more channels often carry other central services along with local programs.

There also are many local and regional radio broadcasting services, whose boundaries approximate the various republics and their subdivisions. Their output too is on long-, medium-, short-wave, and FM, and is relayed by the exchanges. In addition to carrying programs from Moscow and their own capitals, these stations also have local originations.

Moscow has approximately ten long- and medium-wave transmitters plus six FM outlets. Among them, they broadcast national as well as Moscow regional and local material. There also are some twenty-five short-wave stations in Moscow transmitting domestic programs, although most of these are not receivable in the immediate area owing to short-wave propagation characteristics. They are intended to provide off-the-air national network service to distant regional and local stations and wire diffusion centers without line interconnections, and they offer direct reception to people inadequately served by other stations. Elsewhere in the USSR another 150 short-wave transmitters carry other domestic services.)

Listeners in Kiev, the capital of the Ukraine, have a choice of three radio services, the first two on long-, medium-, and short-wave, and the third on FM only. Ukrainian citizens also have access to national and other regional services on long- and short-wave. In addition, many smaller Ukrainian cities have their own services. This same general pattern is followed in the other republics.

The national radio headquarters, located in the State House of Radio Broadcasting and Sound Recording in Moscow, includes four large concert studios and fifty-six other studios, along with extensive remote facilities. Since these are shared with the international services, however, they are not always available for domestic productions. There also are large studio installations in the republic capitals.

Outside of the principal metropolitan areas there are five classes of radio production centers.* First class centers originate at least 10 hours of local programs per day and have staffs of 100 or more people. Each has 6 studios, ranging in size from a large concert studio, with floor space of from 3,230 to 3,765 square feet, down to speakers' studios of 160 to 215 square feet. There is accompanying production, engineering, and office space. Second-, third-, and fourth-class centers are progressively smaller and less elaborate. The smallest, or fifth-class installations, are responsible for not more than 1½ hours per day of local programming and are staffed by about 20 persons. These have only 2 studios, the total area of such centers averaging 4,300 square feet.

About half of the loudspeakers in the Soviet Union receive programs by wire from diffusion centers rather than from off-the-air receivers. (The Soviet terms are "wire sets" and "wave sets.") In 1940 there were 1,123,000 wave sets to 5,934,000 wired sets.† By 1950 there were 3,600,000 wave to 9,700,000 wired sets and in 1960, 27,800,000 wave to 30,800,000 wired sets. In 1970 the figures were 48,600,000 wave sets to 46,200,000 wired sets. In 1972 Soviet figures indicated about 50 million wired and the same number of wave sets, the former serving between 170 and 180 million people. Cities with wired services at that time contained over 95 per cent of the total population.[142] A forecast that by 1980 there would be from 60 to 70 million wired receivers, of which 4½ million would be in Moscow, might be taken as a statement of official policy to increase the proportion of wired receivers.

A typical diffusion exchange gets programs from central, regional,

---

* Kaftanov, pp. 197–198. These data are as of 1960.

† It is impossible to obtain definitive figures on the number of radio receivers in the Soviet Union. This study uses the data in Table 3 below, which have been assembled from both official and unofficial sources. Information about the development of wired services is given in Inkeles, pp. 239–245, and F. Gayle Durham, *Radio and Television in the Soviet Union*, pp. 1–5. Data on the number of diffusion exchanges between 1928 and 1958 are given in Kaftanov, p. 204. See also A. A. Zvorykin, *Cultural Policy in the Union of Soviet Socialist Republics*, p. 53.

and local studio centers either by telephone line or off the air. In some cases the exchanges also have modest origination facilities of their own. Programs are fed by lines to individual speakers in homes, apartments, offices, and hotel rooms. In some instances there are loudspeakers in assembly halls and public squares. Wired systems now serve all parts of the Soviet Union. The largest in Moscow feeds 3 million speakers, although those in smaller towns, collective farms, and elsewhere in rural areas may have relatively few subscribers.

For many years these diffusion systems provided only a single program, but in the early 1960s multichannel systems grew up.[143] Initially they were limited to urban areas (Moscow was the first city in which they were widely available), because technical considerations precluded their use with lines over six miles in length, but they now have appeared everywhere. As of 1964 cities with populations up to 50,000 had two-channel systems; cities with between 58,000 and 250,000 inhabitants two- or three-channel services; and metropolitan centers with 300,000 or more people three-channel diffusion networks.[144]

It is now planned to install three-channel services wherever possible. In 1972 between 15 and 20 per cent of all wired sets could receive three channels, although the costs of installing such systems were two and a half to three times those of single channel systems. Of the five Moscow hotels in which I have stayed at one time or another, four had one-channel systems, and only one—the new Intourist Hotel—a three-channel system. All my hotels in other Soviet cities had single-channel systems. Another sophistication is automation, first introduced in the early 1940s and more general since the early 1950s, making it possible to dispense with day-long personnel at rural distribution points.[145]

To put the Soviet situation in perspective, it should be noted that many countries distribute radio programs by wire to homes, offices, hotel rooms, and places of business, and that in the United States there now is a great mushrooming of community antenna systems which feed television programs to homes by cable. Wired radio services grew up in many European countries in the 1920s.[146] Switzerland now has a six-channel system, which provides subscribers with the three basic Swiss programs in French, German, and Italian; the second channel of their respective regions; and assorted programs from Austria, Germany, France, Italy, the United Kingdom, and the Swiss short-wave service. Italy offers *filodiffusione* on five channels in a number of major cities, providing the three national services, a wide range of light and serious music, and special stereophonic concerts. Although the United States has had little or no wired radio, except in some hotels and apartment buildings, it has had Muzak-like services for many years, and some cable television systems relay FM radio signals.

By 1960 a dozen continental countries had extensive distribution of radio programs by wire. The Soviet Union was first with 30,800,000 wired sets, and Poland second with 1,331,000.[147] In 1966 the leaders included the Soviet Union with 37,000,000 wired sets; Poland 1,073,-501; Bulgaria 675,152; Czechoslovakia 649,504; Switzerland 463,848; Sweden 399,175; and the Netherlands 383,500.[148] At the end of 1970 the figures were as follows: Soviet Union 46,200,000; Poland 960,010; Bulgaria 723,024; Czechoslovakia 687,290; Switzerland 434,033; the Netherlands 222,497; and Italy 175,176.[149] As indicated above, in 1972 the USSR had approximately 50 million wired receivers. In 1969 all of Western Europe had 148,000,000 off-the-air receivers to 1,556,000 wired sets, while the socialist countries had 73,000,000 wave sets to 44,297,000 wired sets.[150]

It is easy to conclude that the USSR and the other socialist countries favored wired sets in order to make it more difficult to hear programs from abroad. One might say: "Wired radio is controlled radio." The fact that the system is being expanded would support that conclusion. But that cannot have been the only—if indeed it was even the main—factor in view of the extensive wire distribution in other countries too. Soviet authorities cite various reasons for the widespread use of wired sets. In the 1920s there were not enough radio transmitters to cover the country; there was a shortage of receivers; and in many areas there was a shortage of electricity. Some diffusion centers even had to use windmill-powered generators to obtain sufficient current to feed programs to loudspeakers. (The speakers themselves usually operate, as does a telephone, on centrally supplied power.)

Wired sets are very simple in design and hence easier to manufacture. They also are more economical to operate and maintain than wave sets. It is claimed that a wired system provides better quality reproduction with less interference. (There may be less interference, but tone will depend on the system's quality. The speakers in the Soviet hotels where I have listened to wired programs were very poor.) Wired systems may carry programs of strictly local interest originated at the neighborhood diffusion exchanges. (This also is given as one of the advantages of CATV in the United States, and most plans for its development include provisions for local programming.)

Finally, so long as they are intact, wired systems can deliver programs during hostilities without enemy interference. During World War II, when Leningrad was under siege and broadcast programs were subject to interference from the Germans, many Leningraders kept their speakers turned on twenty-four hours a day.[151] When no program was on the line, the ticking of a metronome indicated that the system was operating. If an emergency statement was to be made, the metronome rate was increased, thus alerting the public to the forthcoming announcement.

The Soviet Union, like the rest of Eastern Europe, except the German Democratic Republic and Yugoslavia, uses a different black-and-white television system (system D) than does Western Europe. Furthermore, all the Eastern countries, except Romania and Yugoslavia, use French SECAM color, whereas the Western countries, excepting France, use the West German Phase Alternating Line (PAL).* Despite attempts by the International Radio Consultative Committee (CCIR) of the International Telecommunication Union to establish uniform standards, Europe now has four basically different and incompatible† black-and-white systems, plus two color systems. These usually are identified by the number of horizontal lines in their pictures: 405, 525, 625, or 819. Actually, besides the number of lines, many other variables also must be determined in establishing a television system.

Fortunately, this multiplicity of standards does not prevent the exchange of programs, since methods of transcoding have been developed. But because of these differences in standards, the sets used in the socialist countries (excepting East Germany and Yugoslavia) will not easily receive programs from their Western neighbors. In practice, however, some kind of signal usually can be picked up, though with poor quality, thus enabling residents in border areas to receive Western programs. However, the limited more-or-less horizon coverage of television

---

* For an explanation of these and other technical expressions, see the appendix.

† The expression "incompatible" means that a camera, recorder, transmitter, receiver, or other instrument designed for one system will not work on another one. A color and a black-and-white system are said to be "compatible" when signals from the color system can be reported in monochrome by the black-and-white system.

excludes such reception in the Soviet Union, except of Finnish stations in the northwest part of the country.

In earlier years, Russian television experimented with several line standards. In May 1931 there were tests using a mechanical scanning system with 30-lines definition at 12½ frames per second.[152] In 1938 there were experiments in Leningrad with Soviet 240-line equipment and in Moscow with American 343-line equipment. Shortly before World War II it was decided to change to a 441-line system.* After a wartime hiatus, broadcasting was resumed using this standard on the first Radio Day, May 7, 1945. Operations were suspended in September 1948 for the reconstruction of the Moscow Television Center, to be again resumed in June 1949 on the 625-line standard now universal in Eastern Europe.

The Soviet Union now has one nationwide television network serving about 70 per cent or some 170,000,000 of its 241,748,000 population.[153] Supplementing the Moscow installations are 131 studio centers in republic capitals and other large cities. In 1974 there were over 1,700 television transmitters, and forty-five cities—including most of the republic capitals and other larger metropolitan areas—had two channels or more.[154] Both Leningrad and Moscow have third educational channels, and Moscow has a fourth channel. However, with television as with radio, it is difficult to determine the exact scope of Soviet installations. Published data mention high-powered centers and low-powered relays along with retranslation facilities.

Soviet transmitter power is low by Western European and American standards. Of the 150 principal installations listed in one standard reference work, only three had vision transmitters with as much as 50 kilowatts ERP and 10 kilowatts sound (50/10); one was rated at 25/5; one at 20/8; two at 20/4; and all the rest at 15/4 or less.[155] Western Europe has many installations with vision transmitter ERP from 100 to 500 KW, and some up to 1,000 KW. In the United States most stations on channels 2–6 utilize the authorized 100 KW ERP and on channels 7–13, 316 KW ERP. American UHF stations may go up to 5,000 ERP, although few if any do so.

Color television is devloping slowly but surely in the Soviet Union.[156] Experimental transmissions began in Moscow on November 5, 1954,

* Kaftanov, p. 237. See above, pp. 36–37, for more details about these early experiments.

and regular broadcasts, using the SECAM system, were inaugurated in October 1967. Color programs are relayed from Moscow to seventy other cities and towns, although only Leningrad, Moscow, Kiev (capital of the Ukraine), Tbilisi (capital of Georgia), and Baku (capital of Azerbaijan) have origination facilities. There are about twenty-five hours of color network programs each week.

As a multilingual country, the Soviet Union faces a problem because many television viewers do not know the Russian language used on centrally originated programs. Therefore, a method was developed to transmit a bilingual sound track. First tried in Tashkent in 1961, by 1965 such systems were operating in ten USSR capitals with plans for further extension.[157]

The new All-Union Television Center in Moscow includes twenty-one studios with a total floor area of 107,640 square feet, supplemented by relay facilities in the Palace of Congresses, the Bolshoi Theater, the Lenin Stadium, and various theaters in the center of the city. In recognition of the propaganda potentialities of an anniversary, the center has been named the 50th Anniversary of the October Revolution Television Center.[158] It includes a fine new studio complex completed in 1967, an adjacent office building, and a 1,750-foot tower. The new facility is in the Moscow suburb of Ostankino, adjacent to the All-Union Agricultural and Industrial Exhibition. Construction was begun in 1964, the foundation for the main building being laid on April 22 of that year, on Lenin's birthday.

There are twenty-one studios: two of 10,764 square feet each; seven of 6,458 square feet; five of 1,614 square feet; and seven of 645 square feet. The total floor area of these studios is approximately 80,730 square feet. The large- and medium-sized studios are equipped with six television cameras each, and the smaller ones with from two to four cameras. Each studio has two 35-millimeter and two 16-millimeter film projectors and two video tape recorders. Equipment elsewhere in the building can record from the Eastern European 625-line 50 field standard to the American 525-line 60 field standard, and vice versa. There are elaborate lighting facilities plus all the other ancillary equipment found in major television installations.[159] In addition to individual studio video and sound control rooms, there are a central control room, a video recording unit, several studios for film sound recording, editing rooms, laboratories for film processing, makeup and dressing rooms for 1,500 people, workshops for props and costumes, extensive storage space, rehearsal rooms, and a television museum. The building also contains an auditorium with seats for 800 people.

Most equipment is Soviet made, although there are some Japanese video tape recorders.* The first experimental video tape recorders in the Soviet Union were tested in 1961, but now the USSR produces recorders that will record and reproduce color as well as black-and-white signals.[160]

Adjacent to the studio complex is a twelve-story building with offices for administrative, editorial, and program staff. It has a dining room with seats for 500, a snack bar seating 125, three cafés each seating 70, and medical facilities. The old studio center is still used for certain educational programs, and there also is a building with 107,640 square feet of floor space which houses mobile units and related equipment.

The most visible feature of the new Ostankino Center is its 1,750-foot tower. Although the Soviets say it is the highest structure in the world, it actually is exceeded in height by eight television towers in the United States. However, since the American towers are all supported by guy wires, it may be that the Moscow tower is the tallest self-supporting structure in the world.† Transmitters and other technical services are housed in the tower base. There are public viewing platforms at 482,869 feet

---

* Only recently have the Eastern European countries had anything like an adequate number of video tape recorders. For a long time the United States refused to sell VTRs, as they are called, to Eastern European countries, because they are used for radar—as well as television—recordings and hence are of strategic importance. The United States also persuaded Japan to withhold equipment. Consequently, the Eastern countries had relatively few recorders even as late as 1967, and not all of these were of compatible design.

† The American stations are as follows: KTHI-TV, Fargo, North Dakota, 2,003 feet; KCAU-TV, Sioux City, Iowa, 2,000 feet; a tower near Des Moines, Iowa, serving WHO-TV, WOI-TV, and KDIN-TV, 2,000 feet; KELO-TV and KSOO-TV, Sioux Falls, South Dakota, 1,985 feet; WREO-TV, Columbus, Georgia, 1,749 feet, WBIR-TV, Knoxville, Tennessee, 1,749 feet (*Television Factbook 1969–1970*; *Variety*, June 16, 1971, p. 35). But the Ostankino Tower is higher than any American office building. The Sears Roebuck Building in Chicago reaches 1,454 feet, and the World Trade Center in New York 1,353 feet. The Empire State Building in New York City, 1,250 feet tall, the highest building in the world for almost forty years, may be extended up to 1,494 feet, which would put it above both the Sears Roebuck Building and the World Trade Center, although it still would be shorter than the Ostankino Tower. Construction now is under way of a 1,800-foot self-supporting television tower in Toronto, Canada, which would top the Ostankino Tower by 50 feet. In May 1974 Poland announced construction of a 2,120-foot radio and television tower in the city of Plock. If the report is correct, that tower would be the world's tallest structure, although information is not available as to whether it is self-supporting.

and 1,105 feet. In anticipation of a wind of hurricane strength once every twenty years, the tower was designed to permit maximum deflection of 26 feet in the upper steel portion and 3.28 feet in the lower concrete section.

Like many television towers, this one has a restaurant at 1,076 feet, which rotates once each hour, with accommodations for 288 people. A public contest to name it brought 400 suggestions, of which the one most often proposed and chosen was "The Seventh Heaven." In October 1972 I had a meal in the restaurant and found the view better than the food. But all things considered, the All-Union Studio Center is very impressive, both outside and inside. In addition to visiting studios and control rooms, I have had meetings in some of the offices, that of the program director in particular being up to the best American executive suite standards.

There are good reasons why the USSR was the first nation in the world to use satellites to connect domestic television stations. Its size is an obvious one. Another was the absence of extensive cable and microwave networks like those in Western European countries and the United States.[161] The first Molniya satellite (the word means "lightning" in Russian) was launched April 23, 1965. Approximately fifteen or twenty have been put up since then, because their batteries burn out in approximately six months.* On November 24, 1971, the first Molniya 2 was launched, containing certain technical advances over the original series.[162] Among other features, the new series can be tuned to the frequencies used by the Western Intelsat satellites, thus becoming a potential component of a worldwide system. Solar batteries supply the Molniya transmitters with sufficient power to relay signals to earth stations, but not enough for pick-ups by home receiving sets.

The Soviet satellites are nonsynchronous, meaning that they do not maintain a constant position relative to the earth's surface, and hence can be used to relay signals only when within sight of both transmitting and receiving points. They have an elliptical orbit, reaching a height of 24,593 miles over Siberia and 292 miles over North America. Extreme northern latitudes do not have good reception from synchronous equatorial satellites, which is the reason the USSR uses non-synchronous satellites with elliptical orbits. Their period of orbit is a little less than twelve

* Telstar was launched by the United States July 10, 1962; Syncom III, August 19, 1964; Early Bird, April 6, 1965; and the fourth in a series of Intelsat 4 satellites, June 13, 1972. The latter are capable of handling 6,000 simultaneous telephone calls or 12 color television programs.

hours, which gives them about eight hours of useful coverage of the Soviet Union and four hours to swoop down for a swift passage over the Southern Hemisphere. Three satellites are sufficient to cover all USSR territory with its eleven time zones.

Separate agreements cover the satellite activities of the Western and the Eastern countries.[163] On August 20, 1971, fifty-four nations signed the permanent charter of the International Telecommunications Satellite Organization (INTELSAT), although the Soviet Union and the other bloc countries were not among them. But only the socialist states signed the Intersputnik agreement in Moscow on November 15 of the same year. (The Intersputnik group, although limited now to nonsynchronous satellites, has plans for a stationary satellite located over the equator.)

Molniya satellites provide television signals to some thirty-seven ground stations in all parts of the Soviet Union (the ground reception system is called "Orbita"); long-distance telephone, telegraph, and other electronic services; and relay communications with manned spacecraft. However, they have yet to be used for exchanges between two or more socialist countries or for the beaming of programs to Western countries, except for one experimental color television exchange with Paris. But the USSR does have frequent radio and television exchanges with the rest of Europe through land lines and microwave relays.

Thus far, the Western world has made very limited use of satellites for domestic program distribution. There are proposals for a satellite to provide educational television in the sparsely populated Rocky Mountain region of the United States, servicing cable television systems and local broadcasting stations. After a year's test, the satellite then would be repositioned for use in India.[164] Other plans involve Brazil and Australia. On November 9, 1972, a communications satellite, Anik I, to provide radio, television, and telephone relays for Canada was launched at Cape Kennedy, and on April 20, 1973, it was joined by Anik II. The latter has twelve color television channels and also can relay over 5,000 telephone conversations at a time. Although one of the major purposes is service to the far north and the Arctic islands, these also will serve the entire country through thirty-seven ground stations.[165] Some of these channels are rented to American users, although most are utilized by Canada. In January 1973 the FCC authorized the Western Union Corporation to launch a domestic satellite for telegraph and related services in the United States. Undoubtedly other countries also will use satellites for domestic as well as international program distribution, but up to now the Soviets clearly are in the lead.

Anticipating the time when developing technology will make it possible for the United States, the United Kingdom, and other countries to beam television programs by satellite directly into Soviet homes, Foreign Minister Andrei Gromyko in August 1972 suggested an international agreement severely limiting the use of artificial satellites for direct broadcasting.[166] A convention, he said, was "necessary to protect the sovereignty of states against any outside interference and prevent the turning of direct television broadcasting into a source of international conflicts and aggravations of relations between states."

The Soviet proposal would prohibit the transmission of "materials propagandizing ideas of war, militarism, Nazism, national and racial hatred and enmity between peoples, and equally, material of immoral or provocative nature otherwise aimed at interference in internal affairs of other states or their foreign policy."* Mr. Gromyko advocated prohibiting programs "containing propaganda or violence," horror, pornography, and the use of narcotics, as well as programs "undermining the principles of local civilization, culture, everyday life, tradition and language." If the agreement were violated, the countries concerned might use any available means to eliminate the broadcasts, presumably including jamming their signals or shooting down the satellites. The Soviet position, of course, was entirely consistent with its long history of excluding foreign publications and jamming unwanted radio signals.

The United States opposed the Soviet proposal as a limitation on freedom of expression, but when the matter came up for its first vote at a UNESCO meeting in Paris in October 1972, the United States was defeated 47 to 9. Voting against the American position were the socialist states, plus many African, Asian, and Latin-American countries, apparently concerned that the international distribution of programs by satellite would be principally from major to minor powers, thus creating a need to erect barriers to protect local cultures, attitudes, and customs.

Soviet radio and television receivers look and perform like those elsewhere in the world. But their owners have encountered the same problems of quantity, quality, and service that have plagued Soviet consumer

---

* For references to Soviet legislation prohibiting the dissemination of such materials by domestic sources, see p. 45 above.

goods for years. In 1961 a technical magazine reported getting many letters about the poor quality of receivers and tape recorders as well as about difficulties in obtaining repairs.[167] In reply the publication explained that there were too many designers and too few producers of such items and that there was a lack of standardized components. Furthermore, prices were too high. The article concluded: "It is hardly necessary to offer proof that the situation in the production and sale of radio parts to the population is extremely unsatisfactory. . . . We would like to know the opinions of the officials of the U.S.S.R. State Planning Committee and the State Committee on Radioelectronics concerning these matters."

At the November 1962 meeting of the Communist Party Central Committee, Party Chief Nikita Khrushchev, according to *Pravda*, "subjected the production of television sets to sharp criticism. The designers must take the comments made into consideration and must reorganize their work."[168] When the chairman of the State Radioelectronics Committee reviewed the state of Soviet electronics on Radio Day, May 7, 1963, he agreed there had been "just criticism" of the production of receivers. The demand for television sets, he said, greatly exceeded the supply, and "quality, reliability and durability" had fallen below the desired standards. He promised everything possible would be done to improve the situation.[169]

But on Radio Day 1966 it still was necessary to offer explanations, since the same minister of the radio industry wrote in *Izvestia*: "The standardization of radio apparatus is an enormous reserve for reducing labor consumption in manufacturing, for heightening output quality and simplifying repairs. This makes it possible to adopt standard technological processes and to specialize production."[170] Whereas in 1965 there had been thirty-three models of television sets on fifteen types of chassis, in 1970 there were forty-five models on only nine chassis.

I have visited a number of stores selling radio and television receivers, and have operated Soviet sets in hotel rooms and lobbies.[171] Basically, controls and performance are similar to those of American sets, which is not surprising since they perform the same functions. Table and floor model radio sets usually have long-, medium-, and short-wave bands, as well as FM. It is unusual to find a large set without short-wave, since some Soviet domestic programs are broadcast on that band. Stereo sets have begun to appear, although to date there has not been much stereo broadcasting. Depending upon size of set and speaker, tone quality is comparable to that of radio receivers elsewhere, although for economic reasons Soviet hi-fi and stereo development is far behind that of the United States. Stores also show monaural and stereophonic phonographs and tape recorders, in addition to combination sets. Component parts from which radio receivers may be assembled also are on sale.

Older radios and phonographs are rather bulky, with ornate cabinets, in this respect being similar to Soviet furniture of the same period. Recent models are smaller, lighter, and frequently in plastic cases, with bright chrome trim. There is an increasing number of transistor sets, both large and small, and it is not unusual to see Soviet teen-agers listening to transistor radios as they walk along the street, like their American counterparts. There are relatively few Soviet automobiles, so even if a large percentage of them had radios—which is not the case—there still would not be the "drive-time" audience for which American stations compete.

Similar generalizations can be made about Soviet television receivers. The older ones have small screens and somewhat garish cabinets. The new ones come with screens ranging from twelve to twenty-three inches in diameter and with plainer, often plastic cabinets. Most sets can receive twelve VHF channels, although few areas of the country use more than two channels. There also are some projection-type receivers for group viewing. In 1970 the set in one of my hotel rooms had no power switch and therefore could be turned on or off only by plugging in or pulling out the power cord. But this is unusual, since my other sets had all the normal controls: off and on switch; volume and tone controls; station selecter; brightness control; contrast control; vertical and horizontal holds; and picture height and width adjustment. Some television receivers cover the FM radio band too, and color sets are beginning to appear. With the OIRT 625-line standard, pictures are of high quality. The receiver in my room in the Intourist Hotel in 1972 in Moscow worked very well, being fully comparable with the best American sets.

It is difficult to get meaningful price information, although real costs are high. In 1972 I found small portable transistors, many imported from Japan, priced at the ruble equivalent of $40 to $100, with larger radios ranging from $85 to $125.* Radio-phonograph combinations sold for

* Throughout this book, dollar currency equivalents are given as of 1972, unless otherwise indicated. In the case of the Soviet Union, therefore, the rate is $1.20 per ruble.

$180, and elaborate all-wave sets, including tape-recording and reproducing facilities, for $310. A ten-inch black-and-white television receiver could be had for $172.50, and twelve-inch sets ranged from $260 to $325. One twenty-one inch black-and-white receiver was priced at $420, while others of the same size recently had been reduced to $462.50. Color receivers ran from $420 to $780. These prices were less than they had been six months previously, when reductions of 25 per cent were announced.

But it is not very meaningful to translate rubles—or other Eastern European currency—into dollars in search of real prices. Soviet workers, of course, receive much less than their opposite numbers in the United States; but many of their expenses are lower too. Education and medical care, for example, are free, and taxes—by our standards—ridiculously low. It would take an economist to devise a price translation formula. It should be noted, however, that the average pay for Soviet workers is about 130 rubles per month. In many cases there are two or more wage earners in a family unit. Television receivers, like other household items, may be purchased on the installment plan with low interest rates. Nevertheless, these receivers cost their Soviet purchasers far more in real wages than an American would pay for similar sets. Under these conditions, therefore, the fact that television ownership in the Soviet Unon is growing at the rate of 5 million a year surely indicates the wide appeal of the medium.

The special stores that sell only for hard currency, mainly to tourists, stock some attractive transistor radios which are recommended by American residents in the USSR. Their ruble cost in other stores would probably be twice their hard currency prices, since special rates are quoted to stimulate foreign currency sales. I also found television receivers at about half the regular price. Since it obviously would be uneconomical to transport these to Western countries and adapt them for use there, I asked why they were offered for sale at all. The answer came: "You can buy them as gifts for friends or relatives." Refrigerators and automobiles also are on sale to foreigners.*

* In 1970 a Soviet citizen had to pay over $6,000 for a four-cylinder Volga four-door sedan, and wait two or three years for delivery, whereas a foreigner could have one immediately for about $1,500 (*New York Times*, August 18, 1970, p. 14C).

Networks and Programs

The Soviet broadcasting organization is large and complex, as befits a country three times as large as the United States and with eleven time zones to its four. In 1973 the USSR operated three basic radio services and one television network out of Moscow in addition to a great many regional and local services.* Radio Program I, whose five sections serve different geographical areas, is a general service with information, literary and dramatic programs, and programs for young people. It is available virtually around the clock. Program II, Mayak, also nationwide and with seven geographic subdivisions, is on the air twenty-four hours a day. Because it is the equivalent of an American news and music network, foreign correspondents frequently monitor it to keep informed of the latest Soviet developments. Program III, for the Central European USSR, broadcasts from 6:00 A.M. to 10:00 P.M. and is essentially a literary and musical service, with a strong educational emphasis. For Moscow there are six FM stations, which serve not only the capital city itself but also the entire Moscow district. Among them these transmitters carry the three national networks, a fourth program intended for the Moscow area alone, a stereo service consisting basically of music, and a Moscow city network. During a typical day, Moscow puts out over 100 hours of programs, while the total of all the local broadcasting centers is about 850 hours.†

UNESCO reported that in 1964 domestic USSR programs totaled 540

---

* *WRTH 1974*, pp. 106–107. Information about the technical and coverage aspects of the several programs is given above on p. 69.

In Europe the term "program" may be applied to a network or to an individual broadcast. When used at all, the word "station" usually means a transmitter rather than a studio-transmitter combination as in the United States. Seldom is a single transmitter programmed independently; normally two or more are joined together to provide coverage of an area or region. "Channel" may refer to a single local television transmitter, just as Americans say "Channel 2" or "Channel 10" in identifying a specific local station, or to a national network—"the First Channel," for example.

† A. A. Zvorykin, *Cultural Policy in the Union of Soviet Socialist Republics*, p. 42. Most European radio networks play short themes during station breaks to identify themselves. These are compositions by native composers, national folk songs, or themes written especially for the purpose. Both Eurovision and Intervision have broad, sweeping themes with which to begin their transmissions. The first Soviet radio network and the foreign service of Radio Moscow use the same Russian folk song as a theme, while Network II (Mayak) uses the popular song "Moscow Nights." The radio section of all editions of the *World Radio-TV Handbook* lists many of these themes.

hours a week, with the following divisions of program types: music 55.3 per cent; news 16 per cent; sociopolitical 10.6 per cent; literature and drama 9 per cent; programs for children and young people 6.6 per cent; and miscellaneous 2.5 per cent.[172] In 1965 official figures indicated 69.9 per cent of all radio network material to be sociopolitical. Programs concerning the arts (presumably including music) were second with 29.8 per cent, while advertising made up 3 per cent.

To further illustrate network fare, the schedule for one of the Moscow network stations for the day of February 4, 1970, is reproduced below. On the air from 5:00 A.M. until 1:00 A.M., it had eleven news-oriented programs, scheduled on the hour, plus a sports journal (23.10) (figures refer to program times by the twenty-four-hour clock). Since nationwide Network II (Mayak) scheduled news and information on the hour and half hour, Soviet listeners therefore had wide access to news. There were programs for rural listeners (05.30, 06.30, 17.00); literary programs (09.15); and calisthenics (05.15, 06.15, 11:00). Material for children and youth included exercises (07.10), "The Dawn of the Pioneers" (07.40), "A Dramatization of R. Kipling" (10.05), a feature for schoolchildren (16.15), a French lesson (16.50), something for "village youth" (17.00), and two "Radio Youth" late evening broadcasts (22.30, 23.30). Music included a morning concert (05.30), "Songs by Soviet Composers" (08.25), "The Songs of A. Dvoskin" (11.30), Romanian Melodies (12.15), a "Concert-Essay on Composer A. Melikov" (13.00), "The Music around Us" (19.30), "Her Songs Live in the People" (21.15), and "After Midnight" (00.03).

Schedule of Moscow I (Radio) for February 4, 1970

0500	Kremlin bells. News
0515	Calisthenics
0530	"Rural Radio"—morning concert
0600	Kremlin bells. News
0615	Calisthenics
0630	"Rural Radio"—radio-journal "Land and People"
0700	Review of Pravda
0710	Exercises for children
0720	Commentary
0735	Billboard
0740	"The Dawn of the Pioneers"

0800	News
0815	Billboard
0825	Songs by Soviet composers
0845	For adults about children. "Together with Marat"
0900	Review of the Central Press
0915	"Library of New Works of Soviet Literature"—A. Chakovsky's *Blockade*, a chapter from volume II
0945	Instrumental music
1000	News
1005	Children's program. 1. A dramatization of R. Kipling. 2. A talk on the Russian balalaika and Ukrainian bandura.
1100	Calisthenics for workers
1110	"Party Comrades"—about the director of Kiev's "Tochelektropribor" plant P. A. Shilo
1130	The songs of A. Dvoskin
1200	News
1210	Billboard
1215	Romanian melodies
1230	"Workers' Newspaper of the Air"
1300	Concert-essay on composer A. Melikov. Radio Azerbaijan production
1345	Program preview for February 5 and 6
1400	"Festival of Soviet Republics." "A Worker's Word to Ilyich," a production of the Udmurt ASSR radio
1430	"Voices of Our Friends"—programs from socialist countries
1500	News
1515	In socialist countries
1530	"Festival of Soviet Republics"—"Russia Is One," a literary musical production of the Udmurt ASSR radio
1600	"On the 25th Anniversary of Victory"—V. I. Lenin on the character and mission of the Soviet Armed Forces, a lecture
1615	For schoolchildren, from the notebook of radio journalist L. Magrachev
1650	For schoolchildren learning French
1700	"Rural Radio" and "Radio Youth"—village youth
1800	Amateur performers on the stage of the House of Labor Unions

1830	The rostrum of the party worker: interview with the secretary of the Kabardino-Balkar Party obkom M. Kh. Shekikhachev
1840	"The Lenin University of the Millions"—a talk on the significance of Lenin's teachings on the revolutionary party of the working class
1900	News
1918	Billboard
1920	Commentary
1930	"The Music around Us"—radio almanac
2030	Ministries and bureaus reply
2045	International diary
2100	For adults about children. "The Father of Volodya Ulyanov"
2115	"Her Songs Live in the People" (Oksana Petrusenko), direct broadcast from Kiev
2200	News
2230	Evening program of "Radio Youth"; *Don Juan*, a musical interpretation
2310	Sports journal
2330	Continuation of "Radio Youth" evening program
2350	News
0003	After Midnight—musical program
0100	End of broadcasting day

With obvious political objectives were the programs about a plant director (11.10); a lecture reviewing Lenin's ideas "on the character and mission of the Soviet Armed Forces" (16.00); an interview with a Communist Party secretary (18.30); and the "Lenin University of Millions" presentation about "the significance of Lenin's teachings on the revolutionary party of the working class" (18.40). Originating outside Moscow were a concert from Radio Azerbaijan (13.00); the "Festival of Soviet Republics" by Udmurt Radio (14.00, 15.30), and a concert from Kiev (21.15). There were programs from or about other socialist countries (14.30, 15.15). Largely absent was light entertainment, although there was a half hour of "Amateur Performers on the Stage of the House of Labor Unions" (18.00).

Regional and local services throughout the country are on the air from early morning until late night, exact schedules varying from place to place. In 1971 there were three Radio Kiev services.[173] The first program was on the air 17 hours per day or about 120 hours per week. About half of this consisted of relays of Radio Moscow, which therefore were in the Russian language. The remainder of Program I, and the second and third services, were in Ukrainian or other local languages. Radio Kiev II, the local equivalent of the national Mayak program, was broadcast from early morning until late at night. Program III, on FM, was on the air daily from 4:00 to 9:00 P.M., with stereo concerts from 4:00 to 5:00 P.M.

As previously noted, there are over 110 languages and dialects in the Soviet Union, the number of people speaking each ranging from 110,000,000 for Russian and 35,000,000 for Ukrainian down to 200 for Budukh. The number of languages used nationwide in domestic radio broadcasting varies from time to time. Since 1960, it seldom has been less than 60, and in 1972, 67 were used.* All the autonomous republics, oblasts, and okrugs broadcast in at least one native language plus Russian. But in Armenia in 1972 four languages were used (Armenian, Azerbaijan, Kurdish, and Russian); in Azerbaijan three (Azerbaijan, Armenian, and Russian); and in Uzbekistan four (Kazakh, Tatar, Russian, and Uygur).[174]

The Soviet Union's only national television network is on the air weekdays from 7:00 to 10:00 A.M. and from 2:00 to 10:00 P.M. The Saturday and Sunday schedule is from 6:00 A.M. to about 10:00 P.M. Day-long programming is unusual in Europe, so that the Soviet procedure conforms to that of the Continent generally.

Program II, for the Moscow region, is on the air Monday through Friday from 3:00 to 10:00 P.M., and Saturdays and Sundays from 2:00 until 10:00 or 11:00 P.M., or from seven to eight hours a day. Program III, an educational service, offering in-school programs, adult education,

---

* The annual issues of the *Europa Year Book* list the number of languages used in both domestic and external broadcasting, and in most recent years more languages are used at home than for listeners abroad. An official Russian source, listing the 64 languages used for domestic broadcasting in 1960, included, among others: Russian, Ukrainian, Byelorussian, Armenian, Georgian, Kazakh, Turkmen, Uzbek, Latvian, Luthuanian, Polish, Hungarian, Bulgarian, German, and Finnish. The entire list as of that date is given in Kaftanov, p. 118.

Although there is nowhere as much foreign-language broadcasting in the United States as in the Soviet Union, there is more than most Americans realize. A total of 253 stations use Spanish, 92 Polish, 67 French, 66 Italian, 51 German, and one each Armenian, Estonian, Lebanese, and Tagalog (*Broadcasting Yearbook 1973*, pp. D39–D54).

and evening courses, operates an average of four hours daily. Program IV, whose schedule consists mainly of repeats from the other services, operates three hours on weekdays.

Because of the country's many time zones, the national network, fed out of Moscow, has elaborate provisions for repeating programs for different parts of the country. In the office of the All-Union program director, I saw a number of sets, each with a different picture, indicating the various feeds in progress at the moment. Most programs are prerecorded to make possible transmission by satellite and ground relays to other time zones during prime viewing hours.

The staff is large. There are from 8,000 to 9,000 employees in Moscow alone, including program and production personnel and studio engineers, but excluding transmitter engineers. Here, as in so many other respects, the Soviet Union's boasted absence of unemployment is achieved by overemployment!

The forty-five second channels in the republic capitals and other large cities, which concentrate on regional and local material, usually broadcast from 5:00 or 6:00 to 10:00 or 11:00 P.M., with additional periods on Saturdays and Sundays. As long ago as 1961, these channels were using a total of twenty-five languages, and at present Uzbekistan alone, to take just one example, telecasts in five languages.[175] These stations emphasize programs of regional and local interest, including news, education, competitive sports, and broadcasts about local industries and collective farms. Since there are 131 originating centers outside Moscow—20 in the Ukrainian Republic alone—there must be considerable diversity in local programming.

With television as with radio, there are incomplete data about program categories. However, the program director of All-Union Television provided the following analysis of the national network's output: music (both serious and light), 15.9 per cent; cinema films, 13.2 per cent; information (including news), 9.5 per cent; educational programs, 9.4 per cent; dramatic programs, 9.2 per cent; children's programs, 8.9 per cent; sports, 8.5 per cent; documentary films, 6.6 per cent; political material and economics, 6.3 per cent; cultural programs, 4.3 per cent; youth programs, 3.8 per cent; folk music, 2.3 per cent; miscellaneous (including advertisements), 2.1 per cent.[176] Another Russian source, citing older data provided the following figures for local television; programs of artistic nature, 48.7 per cent; sociopolitical, 30.6 per cent; children's, 12.6 per cent; advertising, local want ads, and test patterns, 8.1 per cent.[177]

An American viewing Soviet television is immediately aware of the short program day: Not even in 1973 was the national network on the air continuously from early morning until late at night, and schedules for the other services were very irregular. As the above figures indicate, the emphasis is on serious material, despite a good share of music, films, and sports. The percentage of information, documentaries, and children's programs is high, certainly much higher than in the United States. Entertainment is apt to consist of cinema films or drama, although there is considerable emphasis on sports, and the starting time of the main evening newscast—surely an important item for Soviet planners—is frequently delayed so that an outstanding athletic event can be aired live. Finally, there is much propaganda, evidenced by such program titles as "The Building of Communism" and "The Marxist Story of History."

From time to time there has been severe criticism from the public about the seriousness of the programs and the lack of contrast among channels, although this is less a problem today than it was in the past. In February 1960 the Central Committee of the Communist party remarked that channels serving the same region should not duplicate programs "to the dissatisfaction of the public."[178] In 1965 a Soviet journalist voiced the same criticism: on changing stations the viewer frequently saw the same thing, with obvious similarity between first- and second-channel programs.[179] In 1967 a journalist masquerading as a television serviceman visited a number of homes to check surreptitiously on audience reactions.[180] One respondent remarked that "there are some shrewd people in television. If one channel's got a lecture, without fail the other one has a round-table discussion."

After a month of television viewing in the Soviet Union in October 1970, I felt that these criticisms were largely justified. Sometimes two sports events, a drama and an opera, or two discussions would be broadcast simultaneously by the two channels in a city. On other occasions, one channel might sign off early in the evening, while the other carried a program of limited interest. But after viewing Moscow television during a week in October 1972, I noticed a pronounced improvement. Other cities may still lack contrast, but the four Moscow channels then provided good range of material, although there still were occasions when two or more channels might have very similar programs.

Training for Broadcasting

The Soviet Union recognizes its need for more and better trained broadcasting personnel. In 1960 the Party Central Committee adopted a resolution criticizing the "extremely limited complement of skilled workers" and "authoritative commentators," and went on to say: "The main cause of shortcomings in radio broadcasting is the unsatisfactory selection, training and indoctrination of cadres of radio workers. Those sent to work in broadcasting are often persons who failed in journalism or in some other sector of ideological work."[181] Accordingly, the Radio and Television Committee was told to "take steps to improve the selection and placement of cadres for broadcasting, to improve radically the training of broadcasting personnel and to raise their political level and professional skills in every way possible."

The following year regular courses were provided in the Ukraine for producers, editors, and others, the curriculum including production, design, staging, film editing, and related subjects.[182] There also were responses in Moscow in 1962 from the film and television sections of the Union of Soviet Journalists, which laid plans for joint meetings of film and television workers to improve both the ideological and the production aspects of television.[183]

In 1965 Alexander Yakovlev, in the party's ideological journal *Kommunist*, complained because the United States was so far ahead of the USSR in training broadcasting personnel.[184] He pointed out that over 400 American schools had departments training specialists in broadcasting, and that colleges and universities often had their own television stations. Furthermore, he said these institutions did research and gave degrees in broadcasting, while many agencies, corporations, and firms conducted audience surveys. Regretting that much Soviet writing about television was concerned with details rather than fundamental concepts, he declared: "There is a need for serious works analyzing the specific features of TV art and exploring its genres and forms, the characteristics of TV playwriting and reporting, TV's civic functions, the relationship with the audience and principles of preparing programs." He suggested that training and research be concentrated in a single central institute.

In 1969 *Pravda* editorialized that although the creation of significant television programs "depended entirely on the ideological level and professional qualities" of staff members, many television employees did not meet the demands placed upon them. Accordingly, there was a great need "for the professional training of all those who have been entrusted with the creation of TV productions."[185] A member of the Faculty of Journalism at Moscow State University wrote in the same year that the training of television journalists at universities and party schools was "not yet fully up to the level of those specific requirements to which the profession of television journalism should conform."[186]

Such training now is available at universities in Moscow, Leningrad, and Tbilisi, at theater and cinematography institutes throughout the country (half of whose graduates go into radio and television), as well as in some Communist party schools. In-service training is offered by broadcasting organizations in many cities, as well as by the journalist and cinematography unions.

University-level instruction in broadcasting is very new, as indeed are schools of journalism. The Moscow Faculty of Journalism, founded in 1952, is the largest and most influential school of its type. It has approximately 900 full-time and 1,000 correspondence students. Approximately 400 students graduate each year. There is a teaching staff of about 70. During the five years of course work (it takes six years for correspondence students to finish), students take both general and specialized subjects. Major sequences include newspaper and magazine journalism, editing, publishing, and broadcasting. There is laboratory and fieldwork for all students.

The Department of Radio and Television in the Moscow Faculty of Journalism was organized jointly by the university and the State Broadcasting Committee in 1961. Originally, it dealt only with domestic broadcasting, although courses on international and foreign broadcasting were added later. Students are chosen competitively, most having had previous experience in the media. In 1970, thirty full-time television and forty full-time radio students were registered for each year of the five-year course. Theoretical material is presented by members of the university faculty, and practical courses are taught by people from the State Committee for Television and Radio and Moscow Radio and Television.

At the outset, all Faculty of Journalism students take certain basic courses: a history of the national press since the nineteenth century; the theory and practice of the party and Soviet press; and a review of the contemporary foreign press. Later, students in television journalism take such courses as "Theory and Practice of Television Broadcasting"; "The Role of Television in Social Life"; "The Organization of Television in the USSR"; "The Relationship between Television, Radio, Cinema, and Theater"; "Media of Expression of Television"; "Script Writing"; "Documentary Television"; "Artistic Television"; "Television for Children and Youth"; "The Principles of Planning and Preparing Programs"; and "Television Abroad."[187]

Laboratory and fieldwork are emphasized, and there also are radio and television laboratories for student exercises. At the time of my visit to the Soviet Union in October 1970 only the University of Moscow and the University of Tbilisi had such facilities, and I was able to examine and photograph the Moscow installation freely. Although it certainly was adequate to provide students with some training, almost any American university, and many small colleges, have much better equipment than did the University of Moscow. There undoubtedly will be expansion and improvement in the future, but in 1970 facilities were very modest indeed.

Telecommunications engineers are trained at institutes in cities throughout the USSR, including Moscow, Leningrad, Kuibyshev, Novosibirsk, Odessa, and Tashkent.[188] The radio and television curriculum includes network and local radio programming, satellite communications, and program distribution.

Although the Soviet Union is making progress in training broadcasters, much remains to be done. Discussions with radio and television authorities during several visits to the USSR indicated their interest in this area, since they asked many questions about American curriculums, teaching methods, and bibliographies. But in view of the great need for staff enlargement and upgrading, the number of schools now available cannot serve adequately an organization which already has some 50,000 employees.

Universities, of course, can provide the personnel for executive and administrative positions. But many of the production shortcomings of Soviet broadcasting could be solved at a much lower level. Any American university with production courses could organize workshops in the Soviet Union which would affect significant improvements in just a few months. Although it would be naive to suggest that the USSR would get its teachers from the United States, American experience surely could provide a model if not a source of instructors. Basic programming concepts are another thing, of course, since the differences between Western and Communist ideologies would make an exchange in personnel here difficult if not impossible.

IV

Union of Soviet Socialist Republics:
Programs

Programs are the product of broadcasting. Organization and structure exist solely to create them, and audience reactions are the measure of their results. In the pages that follow, Soviet radio and television programs are described and appraised in terms of their objectives. These are so different from those of the democratic West that we first should review the instructions provided to the broadcasters. These directives implement the basic information theories laid down by Lenin and other leaders who wrote about the Soviet press (see pp. 38–41).

Program Objectives

Lenin and the other leaders of the Soviet state often spoke and wrote about the important role of the mass media in organizing support for party and government, and the Central Committee of the Communist party has frequently reiterated the broadcasters' assignment. On February 26, 1925, the committee adopted a resolution pointing out the importance of radio, and on July 27 of the same year it published a letter referring to "the significant role which must be performed by radio as a powerful means of agitation and propaganda."[1] On August 8, 1932, *Pravda* carried an article titled "About Soviet Radiobroadcasting," which stated that radio should "become a true meeting place for the millions," and on March 24, 1940, a *Pravda* editorial advised: "Some of the best and most experienced propagandists should be drawn into radio work."[2]

In 1935 a Soviet-produced article for an American periodical ex-

94

plained: "The basic characteristics of radio broadcasting in the Soviet Union are its mass character and the fact that it is produced and directed for the purpose of serving the cultural needs of the toilers and establishing for them a pleasant, sensible recreation."[3]

In 1945, to commemorate the fiftieth anniversary of Popov's invention, the Council of People's Commissars resolved: "Taking into consideration the very important role performed by radio in the cultural and political life of the population and in the defense of the country, and in order to popularize the achievements made by our science and technology in the field of radio as well as to encourage radio amateur activities among wide-spread segments of the population, the 7th of May will be designated as a Day of Radio every year."[4]

In the summer of 1954, "to attain successfully the objectives of television," reads a Soviet history, various program committees were set up in Central Television with some journalist members.[5] "These new people brought into television the traditions and experience of the Party and Soviet press and radio broadcasting; it was only as a result of this factor that the objective of turning television into a means of Party propaganda could be attained." On November 12, 1959, in a message to the All-Union Conference of Soviet Journalists, the Central Committee "underscored the great significance of radio and television, which along with the press, performed an important role in the historical matter of building a communist society, in the education of the new man and in the struggle for peace throughout the world."[6]

In February 1960 another Central Committee statement stressed that "radio plays a greater and greater role in the Party's ideological work, in the political and cultural education of the masses and in the implementation of the program of communist construction."[7] Some accompanying criticisms further documented the committee's intentions. The State Radio and Television Committee did not "check on the work of the radio stations." Furthermore, "there is no well-thought-out system or consistency in radio propagandizing of the historic decisions of the 20th and 21st Party Congresses, the subsequent plenary sessions of the Party Central Committee, the domestic and foreign policies of the Soviet state, the achievements and tasks of communist construction, or the advantages of socialism over capitalism."

The committee also declared: "The main task of Soviet radio broadcasting and television is the mobilization of our country's working people for the comprehensive construction of communism in the U.S.S.R., for raising labor productivity and stepping up technical progress in all branches of the national economy, for discovering new reserves and applying advanced experience, for economy in the use of state, collective farm and public funds and property, and for the struggle to eliminate shortcomings. Radio and television must inculcate in all Soviet people a communist attitude toward labor and the need for the participation of every Soviet person in socially useful work."

Several chairmen of the State Committee for Radio and Television have written in similar vein. In his introduction to a Russian-language description of *Radio and Television in the USSR* published in 1960, S. V. Kaftanov stated: "The Central Committee CPSU stresses that radio-broadcasting performs a constantly expanding role in the Party's ideological work, in the political and cultural education of the masses, in the mobilization of the creative energy of the people for the realization of the program of communist construction."[8]

On May 7 the head of the Broadcasting Committee often makes a pronouncement. In 1963 Chairman M. Kharlamov wrote: "Soviet radio has become a mighty ideological weapon in the struggle to build communist society. It would be no exaggeration to say that radio and television constitute one of the Party's right-hand helpers in ideological work. The ability of radio and television to penetrate everywhere make it possible to carry the Party's work to millions of listeners, to carry the great ideas of communism to their minds and hearts."[9] In 1972 S. G. Lapin, then chairman, was reported by *Pravda* as saying in a speech dedicated to Radio Day that through broadcasts related to major national events "the Party uses television and radio as a rostrum from which to make a direct appeal to the entire Soviet people."[10]

The head of the Political Programs Department of Central Television wrote in 1962: "Our chief task is to ensure that TV programmes contribute to the successful realization of the Party programme: the creation of the material technical basis of communism, the formation of communist social relations, education of the people of the communist society."[11] Soviet sources frequently emphasize the importance of using radio and television "to explain Marxist-Leninist ideas to the workers constantly, profoundly, and multilaterally. . . ."[12] It also is necessary "to constantly wage an aggressive struggle against bourgeois ideology which is alien to Marxism-Leninism, against imperialistic propaganda and revisionism on a basis of vivid lifelike examples, by revealing the advantages of the socialist order and of the Marxist-Leninist ideology which provides remarkable samples of the communist life and work."

One of the assignments of the Radio Propaganda Editorial Office is to eradicate "capitalist residues in people's minds."[13] This is essential because "present day bourgeois ideologists and their followers—revisionists, are stubbornly attempting to hide the defects of the capitalist order." Therefore, Soviet broadcasts should "expose the unsubstantiated nature of such fabrications, their incompatibility with reality and give a scientific, Marxist-Leninist analysis of it. These broadcasts widely utilize facts from the lives of the capitalist countries, materials yielded by investigations conducted by conscientious scientists of the bourgeois world, and official statistical data from capitalist governments."

Broadcasts are to point out to Soviet citizens the nation's desire for peace and, at the same time, to develop a feeling of community with other socialist countries. In 1960, Chairman of the Broadcasting Committee S. V. Kaftanov wrote, "By daily explaining the peaceloving foreign policy of the Soviet Union on a basis of concrete facts of the struggle for a realization of Leninist principles of peaceful co-existence, our radio and television must educate the Soviet citizenry in a spirit of pride for their great Homeland, which is proceeding in the vanguard of the forces for peace and progress, to bring about a whole-hearted aspiration in every man to strengthen the power of the USSR and of the entire socialist camp through his unselfish labor, and to help in every possible way in the consolidation of peace throughout the world."[14]

Premier Nikita Khrushchev in a broadcast on June 15, 1961, emphasized the continuing task of uniting all the socialist countries into one friendly family.[15] A Soviet treatise published at about the same time urged the presentation of information to the Soviet people "about successes obtained in socialist construction in countries of the people's democracies [as well as] about the national liberation struggle of the peoples against colonial and imperialist oppression."[16]

Broadcasting also is to present a wide range of general information about the nation and the world. A senior lecturer in radio and television at Moscow University wrote: "It is obvious that the informative possibilities of other kinds of journalism cannot be compared with the possibilities of television. It was not by chance that the Central Committee of the Communist Party of the Soviet Union called television 'one of the main methods of informing the population about events occurring in our country and abroad as well as about the achievements of industry, agriculture, science, technology, art, literature, and sports.' "[17]

A people's artist of the USSR emphasized the importance of radio not only as "the most powerful means for propagandizing ideas of communism [but also as] a means for political and cultural education of the people."[18] The head of the Radio and Television Committee in the Byelorussian Republic wrote that its programs pay "considerable attention to moral and ethical themes."[19] The Central Committee of the All-Union Communist party complained in a resolution adopted July 6, 1962, that "radio and television contribute insufficiently to the spreading of good aesthetic tastes."[20] The Central Committee's Bureau for the Russian Republic on Improvements in the Work of Television emphasized in 1965 that television has an important role "in popularizing the achievements of Soviet literature and art, in the development of people's creativity and in organizing the cultural leisure time of the working people."[21]

Good work habits are another continuing objective. The Central Committee wrote in 1960: "Radio and television must demonstrate the people's condemnation of loafers and good-for-nothings who try to live at the expense of others and must describe in concrete terms how labor becomes a need of Soviet people."[22] Another Soviet source put it this way: "A high cultural level of everyday life consists not only of a well-organized public service, but an observance of the rules of socialist communal life as well. The radio newspaper is struggling with phenomena alien to those rules—drunkenness, hooliganism and rudeness."[23]

Broadcasters are to discharge these responsibilities not only in propaganda programs, talks, documentaries, and news, but at all times. A former chairman of the State Committee pointed out: "Explanation of the policies of the Communist Party is not limited to operational commentaries; it is heard on many programs devoted to the activities of the Party, to its theoretical, political and organizational principles."[24] The head of the Broadcasting Committee in Byelorussia wrote: "We consider it our sacred duty to help the State and Party in educating new, politically broad-minded people with communist traits and widely developed aesthetic tastes. This noble aim is pursued by each of our programmes—no matter whether it be a classical music concert, a theatrical play, a commentary, or an on-the-spot report."[25]

In an article, "Music on Television," a Russian broadcaster declared:

"Meeting the viewers' requirements for a pleasant rest and entertainment at their television screens, we must not forget our basic task, which results from the great mission of television to educate the social consciousness to be of help in the cultural education of the viewers and to form their aesthetical taste. Television must propagate the progressive ideas of our times among the masses of the population and must be a medium of their spiritual enrichment. Musical telecasts, disposing with the great force of emotional influence, have a noteworthy place here."[26] The author continued that "the most important task of the musical department is to propagate, by means of music, those contemporary ideas which dominate the Soviet people and which determine the basis of our life. These are ideas of struggle for constructing a Communist Society, the struggle for peace and friendship between peoples; the idea of Soviet patriotism and spiritual development of the Soviet people."

All Eastern European broadcasters have these assignments. Reading such instructions, and discussing them with both officials and audiences, I frequently have felt that their recitation is comparable with the praising of products by American advertising, for which audiences—consciously or unconsciously—make allowances. Nevertheless, whatever its immediate topic, Soviet broadcasting always has the continuing objective of supporting party and government. Frequent examples are given below, and news, one of the most sensitive program areas, is the best place to begin.

News

One of Lenin's best-known comments about the mass media was his statement of 1901 that "a newspaper is not only a collective propagandist and collective agitator, it is also a collective organizer."* Soviet as well as Western writers frequently quote this phrase. Thus, Alexander N. Yakovlev, who later became deputy chairman of the party's propaganda and agitation section, wrote in the party's ideological journal in 1965: "Giving the news is certainly not the whole of television's task. The blue screen, like the newspaper, should be not only an effective propagandist and agitator but also a collective organizer of the masses. It should not

* Lenin, *Collected Works*, vol. 5, p. 22. For additional information about this statement, see above, pp. 40–41. Other references to the mass media in Soviet ideology are given above (pp. 38–44).

only explain the Party's decisions to the audience but work from day to day for their implementation and check on their fulfillment."*

In 1960 the Communist Party Central Committee emphasized the need for broadcast news to support the decisions of the party congresses and the Central Committee, and stressed the importance of concentrating the attention of the radio audience "on the chief problems of communist construction."[27] In 1963 the State Committee on Radio and Television published a guidebook that left no doubt about how news should be reported.[28] What was wanted was "not the impartial photographing of that which occurs on our enterprises and construction sites, on our collective and state farms, in scientific institutions and higher educational institutions." Rather, "it is a question of the purposeful, directed selection of those facts and events, which represent the broadest social interest, which graphically, covincingly propagandize the policy of our Party, mobilize the people for the successful construction of the Communist society. In other words, information by radio should bear a militant aggressive character."

The head of the Information Section of Soviet Radio reviewed his department's work in 1967 upon the thirty-fifth anniversary of its assuming responsibility for news broadcasting:[29]

The 'latest news' releases which describe our achievements are of great importance in the purposeful formation of social opinion. By information media and through daily facts the 'latest news' propagate the foremost experience and everything new that takes place every day and every hour in factories and mines, on building sites as well as kolkhoz and scientific laboratories.

Every day the broadcasts show the advantages of socialism over capitalism and reflect its international significance and revolutionary influence on the peaceful development of the USSR and the achievements attained in the building-up of communism. It also exposes the inventions of bourgeois propaganda and comments on the most important international events. . . .

Similarly as during the first years after the war the 'latest news' department plays not only the role of propagator, but also of organizer of many great deeds accomplished by our people. It supports everything new and progressive in all fields of the national economy, science and culture.

* A. Yakovlev, "Television: Problems and Prospects," *Kommunist*, No. 13 (September 1965), translated in CDSP, 17:39 (October 20, 1965), p. 15. In the Soviet Union "blue screen" is a popular term for television, corresponding somewhat to the American "tube."

As broadcasting developed, the Soviets became increasingly aware of the differences between printed and broadcast news. Although Lenin realized the importance of all communications, he necessarily was concerned mainly with the printed media since radio then was only beginning. But he did recognize radio's potential, and he encouraged its development. Nevertheless, the Soviets were slow to adapt to broadcasting. During my first visit to the Soviet Union in the fall of 1958, a broadcaster told me there was little need for television news, since the public could get news from radio anyway; and there is reason to believe that somewhat the same attitude prevailed earlier about radio's relationship to the press. Furthermore, all the news media, including the local press as well as radio, for a long time were expected to wait on *Pravda* for policy guidance, and to some extent still do. Nevertheless, the authorities were driven inexorably by the force of events to utilize first radio and then television as effectively as possible.

In response to the frequent complaint that radio was too slow with the news, the Party's Central Committee in 1960 stated: "Because radio should give the population the important news before the newspapers do, TASS has been instructed to transmit news immediately to central and local radio stations. . . ."[30] Three years later a handbook for radio journalists instructed: "Radio should communicate to the population all important news earlier than do the newspapers."[31]

In turn, television was scored for not going beyond radio techniques. Beginning in 1956, it merely repeated radio news programs, not developing its own newscasts with visual material until 1960.[32] But even in August 1965 an editorial in *Pravda*, after observing that the public got news of domestic and international affairs from newspapers, magazines, and radio, argued: "From television they expect additional information, lively and clear commentaries, expanding their horizons and helping them to understand better the meaning of the events taking place. One cannot, for example, agree with those commentators on international news who merely repeat the content of the newspapers they have read in the morning without giving a profound evaluation of the phenomena of world-political life. Television, as distinguished from radio, has a full opportunity with its visual means (film clips, photos) to disclose more convincingly and sensibly to the viewer the meaning of any particular fact and to show it to him visually. Unfortunately, the studio workers by no means always make use of the very rich possibilities of films and television technology."[33]

Another publication complained: "Many times television cannot find really vivid visual material, and news items are simply read aloud. In such cases television is still at a disadvantage in competition with press and radio."[34] An article in the journal of the Union of Soviet Journalists, whose title read in part "What Television Lacks," referred to "television without television, when we tell viewers about important events but do not show them."[35]

But the Soviets definitely want the mass media to be used cooperatively rather than competitively. During visits to the USSR and to other Eastern European countries, I have been lectured about the wasteful manner in which American radio and television compete. In 1962 at a Moscow meeting of the film and television section of the Union of Soviet Journalists, speakers stressed the importance of "uniting film and TV journalists in one section, corresponding to the close kinship between these two media of spreading information."[36] A member of the party's propaganda and agitation section said that the "blue screen and the press can and should complement each other," and commended a television program on which the commentator advised his viewers to obtain further details from the newspapers, while the latter recommended certain television programs to their readers.[37] "Thus, through combined efforts, a single theme gets utmost development, visual and analytical." Likewise, the chairman of the State Committee for Radio and Television Broadcasting, addressing the All-Union Creative Conference of Publicists in July 1964, called on press and broadcasters to improve their output through cooperation.

Related to insistence upon more comprehensive utilization of the broadcast media˙has been the growing realization that Soviet citizens frequently check the completeness and accuracy of domestic accounts against outside sources. The jamming of foreign broadcasts had almost ceased in 1963, but it was stepped up during the August 1968 occupation of Czechoslovakia and continued until September 1973, when, for reasons not entirely clear, it was stopped, except for Radio Liberty, Israel and China.*

* Jamming consists of broadcasting noise, or putting another station on or near the frequency of the transmitter whose programs it is desired to exclude. For more on this, see below, p. 215n.

I heard jamming in the Kiev area in October 1970, and a great deal in Moscow two years later. But despite this periodic jamming, programs do get through, and in any case, the English-language broadcasts seldom are interfered with. The BBC, the Voice of America, and Radio Liberty continue to beam programs into the USSR, Radio Liberty in languages of the Societ Union only, the BBC and the Voice in English too. Increases in the number of wave sets have made these programs available to more people; and since the Soviet Union does some domestic broadcasting on the short-wave band, many sets equipped to receive domestic short-wave programs also can tune in those from abroad.

Although Soviet broadcasters are reluctant to admit that foreign transmissions have any significant effect on their programming, they are quite aware of them and—as I learned in conversations—frequently listen to them. Periodic and often savage criticisms in Soviet media document their concerns about the Voice of America, the BBC, and—particularly—Radio Liberty. For example, an article in *Komsomolskaya Pravda* in 1966, entitled "An Alliance of Dirty Hands," criticized American attempts "to undermine the socialist camp from within, sow lack of faith in the existing system, compromise leaders and calumniate the political parties that are in power." It went on to complain about the Crusade for Freedom, Radio Free Europe, and the United States Information Agency.[38] Recently, the number and intensity of these attacks have increased.

F. Gayle Durham concluded that certain changes in news schedules in October 1952 were "brought in by the then new chief of the broadcasting committee, M. A. Kharlamov. His policy was to decrease the jamming and increase the news and commentary from the Soviet operated stations."[39] The official report of the All-Union Creative Conference of Publicists in July 1964 urged workers in all media to "respond promptly to various, perhaps unfavorable phenomena and incidents that occur in our life. Or else it turns out that, while we keep silent, the people learn about them from foreign radio broadcasts, and, furthermore, learn about them in incorrect and distorted interpretations. We still consider ourselves to have a monopoly in the field of information. But this isn't so. After all, by lagging in information, we sometimes involuntarily orient people to foreign radio, and once any false version begins to circulate it is difficult to stamp it out."[40]

If Soviet news output differs in emphasis or substance from that of the Western countries, it is not due to a shortage of material. Basic, of course, are the worldwide resources of the central news gathering organization TASS (Telegrafoi Agentstvo Sovetskovo Soyuza). In the mid-1960s, in the RSFSR alone, TASS had 6 branch offices, 120 staff correspondents, 140 part-time correspondents, 65 staff photographers, and 200 part-time photographers.[41] TASS has exchange agreements with the agencies of the 14 other USSR republics, which have some 360 correspondents of their own. Currently, it maintains 103 bureaus in 97 countries in all parts of the world, and exchanges news with 69 agencies outside the Soviet Union, including Reuters, AP, and UPI. TASS lists 6,600 subscribers for its general services and 7,200 for its photo services, of which 75 are in foreign countries. Each day TASS transmits 1 million words in Russian, 80,000 in English, 60,000 in French, 25,000 in Spanish, 12,000 in Arabic, and 10,000 in German.*

Since February 1961 the USSR also has had Novosti (Agentstvo Pechati Novosti—APN), which provides feature stories, commentaries, and photographs. Novosti has its own foreign correspondents, as well as exchange agreements with AP, UPI, AFP (Agence France Presse), Reuters, and others. Soviet radio and television obtain a great deal of news from government and party sources, as well as from their own correspondents.[42] In 1968, for example, central radio in Moscow received an average of 100 reports daily from domestic correspondents, plus dispatches and much tape-recorded material from outlying radio stations. All this is supplemented by an elaborate informal network of part-time correspondents. Regional and local centers follow similar procedures.

The news sources for television are even more extensive. To assemble and edit the daily half-hour "Vremya" telecasts, there are 145 people in Moscow, plus 15 or more special correspondents elsewhere in the Soviet Union.[43] Over 131 regional studios provide supplementary material on both film and tape. Television also has permanent correspondents in Western Europe, Japan, and the United States. In addition to wire copy from TASS and the various foreign agencies serving radio, "Vremya"

---

* One well-informed Western observer told me that TASS has three classes of output: one for "trusted persons," which provides fairly complete coverage; a second for a somewhat larger group; and a third, which may be broadcast. This situation parallels that in Czechoslovakia, described below on p. 319. It is commonly believed in the West that TASS functions as an intelligence as well as a news agency. For a development of this view, see Theodore E. Kruglak, *The Two Faces of TASS.*

secures material by closed circuit feeds from Intervision as well as from Eurovision.

Intervision, the international network organized by the OIRT, began weekly news exchanges in May 1964 and now regularly serves seven OIRT members—Bulgaria, Czechoslovakia, the German Democratic Republic, Hungary, Poland, Romania, and the USSR—plus Yugoslavia.* By April 1965 there were biweekly exchanges involving Czechoslovakia, the German Democratic Republic, Hungary and Poland. As line facilities became available, other countries joined. In January 1966, when Soviet and Bulgarian television came in, there were four news exchanges per week. Romanian television joined in December 1967, and in January 1968 Yugoslav television also participated. Starting in May 1970 there were daily exchanges.

Intervision headquarters in Prague coordinates this activity. By 10.15 hours (Central European Time) participants must indicate what program material they have to offer. This information is relayed by telex to all members by 11.00 (incidentally, in the Russian language), and they must respond within forty-five minutes. Following telephone conference calls between 15.30 and 16.00, items are transmitted on a closed-circuit basis at 16.25 for recording. Since most major news programs are at 18.00 hours or later, material is received in time for the main evening broadcasts. These line feeds are supplemented by air exchanges of films and video tapes of non-timely material.

There has been a steady increase in both the number and the duration of news items exchanged. In 1966, 1,440 items were transmitted and 3,205 received. By 1969 this had almost doubled, with 2,432 items transmitted and 6,512 received. An analysis of exchanges in June 1970 showed that the Intervision members participating offered 224 items and received 699, so that most items were taken by 3 or more organizations. The average duration of items was 1 minute and 13 seconds, and the breakdown of the 224 by themes was as follows: sociopolitical, 109; science, technology, and economics, 61; cultural life, 46; sports, 8. Most exchanges are of silent film without sound, in which respect Intervision is behind Eurovision, although Intervision is steadily increasing its use of sound film. In 1972 Intervision exchanges were mainly black and white,

* Waclaw Wygledowski, "IVN—Daily News Exchange on the Intervision Network," *OIRT Review* 1971/1, pp. 3–10. For a description of Intervision see pp. 60–61.

although most Intervision members were doing some color telecasting.

A guide to the subject matter of these programs is provided by the telex copy sent to participating Intervision members on November 3, 1970.[44] The original text, which was in English, is as follows:

USSR: session of the presidium of the supreme soviet to ratify a new soviet-finnish treaty; preparations in moscow for the military parade. Film shows arrival of tamans division; arrival to moscow of italian parliamentary delegation, visit of the president of the interparliamentary union of the supreme soviet; meeting of a soviet soldier and a czechoslovak teacher, who got acquainted 25 years ago, at the end of the war (sound); international geological exhibit in Moscow. Czechoslovakia: festive meeting and performance in a prague theatre, marking the anniversary of the october revolution and opening of the 'month of czechoslovak-soviet friendship'; session of the czechoslovak-soviet friendship union; unveiling of Lenin's memorial in the area of ancient charles university. East Germany: decorations and promotions of new officers and generals attended by walter ulbricht; return from hungary of the ministry council's vice-chairman wolfgang rauchfuss, interview at the arrival (sound). Poland: arrival to warsaw of west german foreign minister walter scheel, film shows welcome at airport; statement of polish foreign ministry representative on the coming polish–west german talks; walter scheel paying visit to his polish counterpart minister jedrychowski; start of official polish–west german talks attended by walter scheel, his deputies egon franke and ferdinand duckwitz as well as a group of experts. Poland is represented by foreign minister stefan jedrychowski, his deputy josef winiewicz and a group of experts.

Intervision and Eurovision began regular news exchanges in September 1965, and news experts from the two groups have met periodically since 1969. The Prague and Geneva headquarters exchange daily telex messages preliminary to working out exchanges for the day. The technical link-up for news is through Austrian television in Vienna, which receives and forwards items in both directions. Eurovision offerings include not only the material collected by the participating organizations, but also the output of UPI and Visnews, so that Eurovision offers a very considerable service to Intervision.

Data on Eurovision-Intervision news exchanges are published annually by the European Broadcasting Union (see Tables 1 and 2 above). During 1965 Soviet television supplied 40 items to Eurovision while receiving only 3 in return. The next year it supplied 92 items but took none. There are no EBU data on the extent of news exchanges between the

Soviet Union alone and Eurovision after 1967, but Intervision figures indicate that in 1972 the USSR took 1,270 items from Eurovision and originated 94.

The Soviet Union uses its Molniya satellites not only to distribute programs to domestic transmitters, but also to feed news items to Moscow from distant parts of the country like Vladivostok. Between October 6 and 13, 1970, color relays of the visit of President Pompidou to the Soviet Union were sent to Paris.[45] Thus far, the USSR has had no direct reception from any Western satellites, although through Intervision it has received American satellite feeds from Eurovision.

There are many news programs on Soviet radio. At the outbreak of the Revolution in November 1917, the limited broadcast facilities available were used to report the progress of the revolt, although there were few sets to receive the programs.[46] The same procedure was followed for the invasions that took place during the early months of the Communist regime. Thus, on November 11, 1920: "Flash. To everyone, to everyone. . . . The valorous troops of the 51st Moscow Division broke through the last white line of resistance and have a firm hold in the Crimea. The enemy is fleeing in panic. . . ." November 23, 1924, was the date for the "first issue of a radio newspaper," a project continued through 1932. In September 1933 the "radio newspaper editorial office" was replaced by the more radio-oriented "editorial office for central political information," which inaugurated "The Latest News" programs, a title applied ever since to Soviet radio newscasts.

In 1959 All-Union Radio broadcast eighteen news programs each day, and in 1967 Moscow radio transmitted Russian-language news on its several network and local services an average of four times each hour, the 100 daily programs filling 17½ hours of air time.[47] A good share of this now is provided by Program II, the nationwide Mayak, although all the radio services have newscasts. Introduced in the summer of 1964, Mayak offers news and information on the hour and half-hour twenty-four hours a day. Few Soviet citizens are ever more than twenty-five minutes away from radio news from a Moscow source. These national services are complemented by regional and local newscasts in area languages over local stations and wired exchanges.

Radio newscasts are of several types. There are straight summaries of five or ten minutes duration, surveys of the domestic and world press, interviews, and commentaries. For the most part, staff announcers read copy, but there also are short actuality inserts.[48] The voices of correspondents from Tashkent, Vladivostok, Paris, and Washington are heard. Basically, the same techniques are used in the Soviet Union as elsewhere.

But the substantive emphasis is often quite different. A publication of the State Committee on Radio and Television opened with the following sentence: "Political information occupies a place of importance in Soviet radio broadcasting; its organization and broadcasting concern the editorial office of 'The Latest News.'"[49] Therefore, materials about the Seven-Year Plan for the Development of the National Economy "occupy a place of importance," along with "information on themes dealing with political, party, Komsomol and trade union life."

Much emphasis is given to friendly relations with other socialist countries. As the head of radio news put it: "Our correspondents talk daily about the successes and experiences of brotherly countries in the building-up of socialism. . . . In their materials correspondents acquaint Soviet people with numerous achievements attained through the joint efforts of socialist countries. The 'Friendship' international pipeline, the industrial power plant in the Mongolian town of Darkhan, the 'Ost' metallurgical complex in the German Democratic Republic and the 'Iron Gate' power plant in Rumania as well as many others have become symbols of the friendship and proletarian internationalism of the peoples of brotherly countries."[50]

News of the West, especially of the United States, often is selected and interpreted to indict these countries and their leaders as imperialist warmongers. Much also is made of government problems, economic weakness, racism, and poverty, partly to brighten the Soviet picture through contrast.[51]

An example of the reporting of American developments is provided by a radio newscast presented early in 1971. On January 9 the Moscow domestic service carried the following Russian-language item from its Washington correspondent.[52]

The American public reacted with profound indignation to the report on the latest act of banditry perpetrated by the ultrareactionary Zionist organization calling itself Jewish Defense League. Militant thugs of this league, on the sly and under the cover of night, organized an explosion near the building which houses the information and trade departments of the Soviet Embassy in Washington. . . .

Many Americans with whom I had occasion to speak condemned this provocation. Judging by reports from various towns, a considerable part of the Jewish population of America reacts with similar condemnation to the escapade of the Zionists and the notorious league. As far as the league itself is concerned, it is only a mob of fascist thugs, little different from storm troopers.

Nevertheless, this so-called Jewish Defense League is acting at large under the protection of American laws and under cover of millionaire patrons. . . . One must say that the American public always reacted to these outrages with condemnation. Not infrequently at concerts of Soviet artists, the indignant public threw the hooligan thugs out of the hall.

The behavior of the American authorities causes surprise. It is quite obvious that neither Zionist extremists nor any other militant anti-Soviet elements could behave with such a lack of restraint if the American authorities took resolute measures to cut short the acts of banditry.

It is interesting to notice the distinction drawn between the American people, reported as condemning such conduct, and the American government, which if it did not actually encourage, at least condoned these activities.

The radio domestic service—like most throughout the world—covered the blocking of traffic by demonstrators in Washington in May 1971.[53] The affair of the Pentagon Papers also was reported. *Pravda*'s line on this, probably taken by the broadcasters too, was that the publication of this material was not the consequence of America's free press, but rather the result of a clash between two power groups. Because the economy was beginning to suffer on account of the war, certain business interests decided to use the Pentagon Papers to embarrass the government and those who had "ruled undividedly in Washington until now."[54] However, much news is covered as in broadcasts anywhere else. The visit of Premier Khrushchev to the United States in August 1961 was treated as broadcasting in the United States would treat a trip by its president. Rocket launchings and moon landings are heralded. Inevitably, there are weather forecasts.

The national television network offers one or more five-minute newscasts during its late morning and early afternoon periods; has short newscasts at 5:00 and 6:00 P.M., as well as preceding sign-off; and presents its main thirty-minute newscast "Vremya" ("Time") at 8:30 P.M. All second channels throughout the country have newscasts in local languages; third channels, when available, and Moscow's fourth channel have occasional short summaries.

Content and procedure can be illustrated by reference to "Vremya," broadcast nationally by Soviet television since January 1968. Normally this is aired from 8:30 to 9:00 P.M., although the hour is changed if extended dramas, cinema films, or sports require rescheduling. I asked the editor how they chose items. For one thing, he said, they try to show the main events in the "hot places." He also mentioned political values: they cover the class struggle in capitalist countries, and he referred to the UAW General Motors strike then (October 1970) in progress. Their programs reflect the socialist point of view, while encouraging feelings of solidarity between Moscow and Detroit workers. I reminded him that in the United States we then were televising President Nixon's news conferences and suggested they do the same thing. But he proved equal to my quip: "You'd better ask Mr. Kosygin about that."*

During October 1970 and again in October 1972, I had opportunities to watch many national and local newscasts. On a typical evening, the "Vremya" camera opens on a man and a woman announcer team. The set is plain, and neither then nor later is there much rear screen projection. At that time no American national program had an anchor woman, although the Soviets had several television news programs on which women played key roles. However, the two participants do not engage in any of the small talk which often accompanies American television news, at least on the local level. Although they are pleasant, both announcers are on the serious side, and they get right down to business.

First there is a rundown of the main items—without slides, films, or other teasers—although if a big story involves a top official, the program may open directly with a film report of it. Almost every program, whether five, fifteen, or thirty minutes long, has at least one film feature reporting industrial, economic, agricultural, or scientific achievements. We see tractors and combines in fields; we visit factories; we are addressed by workers as they turn aside from their lathes; we see fishermen pulling fish from a lake; we see a film report of the Komsomol youth's fiftieth anniversary and are told about their achievements over the years.

I asked several Soviet broadcasters why they give so much time to such features, a characteristic, incidentally, of news in all Communist

* When Kosygin visited Canada in October 1971, he held a thirty-minute live televised press conference. *Winnipeg Free Press*, October 21, 1971, pp. 1, 8; *Windsor Star*, October 21, 1971, pp. 1, 2.

countries. They replied that this is important: the people want to know these things. Furthermore, television should be used to ennoble labor and encourage the improvement of work standards.* However, during my 1972 trip, several high-ranking Soviet broadcasters agreed with me that there were too many such reports. It is my view that these countries use the mass media to report rising standards of living partly because of the many shortages the public is required to accept. People must wait for apartments; their housing has shortcomings and limitations; and there may be years of delay before they get that new car—which in any case will cost much more than would a bigger and better car in the United States. But be patient: progress is being made. And indeed it is—impressive new apartment buildings are going up everywhere, even though there still is a great housing shortage.

Government and party leaders constantly appear on television, sometimes to make long announcements or statements. They also are seen taking part in various ceremonial events, many of which are intrinsically unimportant. Planes land or take off; passenger loading ramps are moved in or out of position; celebrities with their staffs, and perhaps wives, get on and off; hands are shaken; and flowers are presented by attractively dressed little girls. Visitors invariably place wreaths on Lenin's tomb and on the tomb of the Unknown Soldier. And, of course, important party meetings are reported in great detail. Most short and all longer newscasts include weather information, with maps, charts, and some pictures, often done quite ingeniously.

During my visits to the Soviet Union in the falls of 1970 and 1972, I listened regularly to the short-wave programs of the Voice of America and the BBC and found that many of their international items turned up also on Soviet television. In addition, "Vremya" carried additional news from the other socialist countries, reporting coal mining advancements in Czechoslovakia, the completion of new buildings in Cuba, and the dedication of a subway and art exhibit in Budapest.

Many American items are covered in short factual bulletins read by the announcers. Picture presentations tend to take an editorial approach. For example, during the UAW strike in Detroit in October 1970, meetings were organized in several Moscow automobile plants to mobilize

* After living in Soviet hotels during six trips to the USSR, I understand the problem!

support for the American workers, and collections were taken up in their behalf. Moscow television showed Detroit scenes, with workers carrying signs bearing such legends as "UAW on Strike." Then we would see meetings in Soviet factories with speakers citing the American strike as just one more example of the way capitalist employers oppress their workers. No one, of course, explained that the striking Americans were living much better than the Soviets who were being asked to contribute toward their support.

On April 16, 1972, the Apollo moon launch was featured equally with news from Vietnam, although this has not always been the case with American launchings.[55] On the other hand, the trial of Angela Davis was reported as an example of racial discrimination and injustice in American society, the charges against her being described as "fabricated." Her subsequent acquittal was hailed as "a victory for the progressive American and world community."[56]

The Soviet media did not provide much build-up for President Nixon's visit to Moscow in May 1972, although once he arrived television carried his twenty-minute speech to the Soviet people. In accordance with usual practice, a Russian translation was superimposed over the English version, which was faded down, though left high enough to be intelligible.[57] But the president's speech did not have a monopoly of airtime, since one Moscow local channel carried a program for youth and another had a classical concert. The Soviet media ignored the early stages of the Nixon-McGovern campaign, but as voting day approached indicated preference for Nixon on the grounds that his re-election would assure continuity of the negotiations then in progress looking toward a Soviet-American rapprochement.[58]

To a great extent, coverage of any United States events varies with the international climate, although interpretation is apt to be critical in any case.[59] During President Nixon's visit to Moscow the policy was one of restraint, and the mining of the Haiphong Harbor was not mentioned for twenty-one days. But shortly thereafter criticism was renewed, sometimes even surpassing pre-summit levels. Angela Davis, who had become a virtual folk heroine during her months of incarceration and trial, dropped out of sight while Mr. Nixon was in Moscow, but thereafter returned to the news.

Early in 1973 the Soviet press responded to requests for easier East-West exchanges by saying that the USSR would never tolerate the free

entry of people and ideas unacceptable to party ideologists. But as
Leonid Brezhnev prepared for his visits to Bonn and Washington, Soviet
newspapers began printing stories favorable to the United States, while
barely mentioning the Watergate affair, then beginning to emerge. In fact,
a 500-word article in a weekly Soviet newspaper on May 17, 1973, was
the first extended treatment of Watergate in the Soviet Union. Nevertheless, only a few weeks preceding Brezhnev's visit to America, a long
Pravda article warned that only "naive people could expect . . . the
basic conflict . . . between capitalism and socialism . . . to lose its
significance in the international arena."[60] Furthermore, the week preceding Brezhnev's flight to America the Soviet police began to tighten
controls over the leisure-time activities of Americans in Moscow.

Nevertheless, some television programs were changed because of the
Brezhnev trip.* Several American documentary films were shown, along
with shorts of Soviet and American soldiers meeting on the Elbe at the
end of World War II. There also was a documentary treatment of a successful Soviet tour by American pianist Van Cliburn. Yet, at the very
same time, some Soviet bookstores began selling a 1,280-page book
entitled *Accents*, reported to have gotten its name because it accented
"the most important and typical events and problems" in the world today.
An American correspondent in Moscow who examined the book—
available in an edition of 100,000—said that it contained "some of the
crudest anti-American propaganda seen here in some time. It has club-
swinging policemen, poverty, racism, American Nazis, and a picture of
the Pentagon 'where 300,000 employees are plotting aggressive plans
against peace.' " The correspondent also noted that the latest volume of
Soviet foreign trade statistics for 1972 had been edited to conceal the
heavy purchase of American grain during the previous year.

The Soviet media covered Brezhnev's visit thoroughly. Its affirmative
aspects were emphasized, and the hope was posed of its leading to a new

---

* *New York Times*, June 25, 1973, p. 18M. At about the same time, a Moscow
program in an Indian dialect (Quechua) beamed to Bolivia, Ecuador, and Peru
said: "We ask, how many Watergate-type scandals have occurred in previous US
elections? Imperialism's information media have always criticized and attacked
corruption in other countries. However, they have never been able to criticize
their own country. This leads us to believe that political corruption within
Yankee imperialism has existed, still exists, and will continue to exist. This
scandal . . . casts shame on US democracy" (FBIS *Daily Report*, June 12, 1973,
p. G1).

era of harmony and expanded trade. Broadcast coverage was by a news team which used the facilities of the National Broadcasting Company to beam several hours of transmissions per day to the Soviet Union by satellite. Some of these events were offered to other Eastern European countries by Intervision. Brezhnev's broadcast to the American people on June 24, 1973, also was relayed by the Soviet media. These broadcasts, incidentally, gave the Soviets their first chance to see Brezhnev in an ebullient mood in contrast with the more formal stance he normally maintains at home.

Although Soviet coverage of American events usually reflects government policy at the moment, there is continuity in the omission or delay of certain types of items. There are no speculations about government plans and no references to differences among party leaders. Although American broadcasts may raise doubts about the veracity of government news releases, or call for the publication of secret documents, such an approach is completely taboo for Soviet loudspeakers and screens.

At any time, unduly critical items may be kept off the air. For example, during interviews with Radio Moscow and TASS on August 30, 1962, U Thant, then acting secretary general of the United Nations, criticized USSR policy in the Congo and complained that the Soviet public was not hearing both sides of the Congo story.[61] However, Radio Moscow used only a brief portion of the interview, omitting the critical sections, while the only Soviet newspaper mentioning it, *Pravda*, omitted U Thant's complaint that the Soviet people were not getting the full Congo story.

Although the Soviet media cover the exploits of their cosmonauts, they do not always do so with the immediacy or the detail to which the American public has become accustomed. On the day of Yuri Gagarin's pioneering flight in the spaceship *Vostok,* April 12, 1961, radio news reports were broadcast every fifteen minutes.[62] On April 23, 1971, Soviet television broadcast recordings made during the launching of the spacecraft *Soyuz 10* the previous day, although it did not cover the actual launching live.[63] However, while the flight was in progress, there were live broadcasts from the orbital station. During an hour-long program on May 9, the three cosmonauts answered questions about their mission and then watched a variety show and some acrobatic acts performed in their honor.[64] The following month, television carried pictures of the three other *Salyut* cosmonauts working in a compartment of their orbital station and showed how the Earth appeared from that height.[65] But when all three were killed during re-entry at 1:35 A.M. (Moscow time) on June 30, 1971, the news was withheld until 8:15 A.M., and details were not forthcoming until the following day.[66]

Also delayed were reports of the death of Nikita Khrushchev, which occurred at noon on September 11, 1971.[67] This information was relayed to Western newsmen by family friends almost immediately, but it was not until the morning of September 13 that *Pravda* published a brief obituary which subsequently was read over the radio.* For almost two days, therefore, Soviet citizens were able to learn about the death of the man who had led them for a decade only by listening to Radio Liberty and other foreign stations which broadcast frequent bulletins about Khrushchev's death as soon as they received the information.

There is no reporting of fires or disasters unless they are very dramatic, nothing at all about the personal lives of the Soviet great, and few human interest stories. These are not regarded as sufficiently important; in any case, since the ultimate purpose of broadcasting is to build the Communist society, too much reporting of that kind might provide bad examples at the same time that it took space and time from items of more basic and lasting importance. In 1970 a man who shot four cosmonauts in Moscow, perhaps trying to kill party leader Leonid Brezhnev, who was in another car in the same motorcade, was tried and sentenced to a mental hospital, but the press made no reference to the incident until the trial was completed.[68]

Airplane crashes usually are not reported unless there are foreigners aboard, although if too many rumors are circulating, there may be a small item referring to the crash and to the fact that there were casualties, but not indicating how many. No reports of the dramatic crash of the Tupolov-144 supersonic transport at the Paris airshow on June 3, 1973, were broadcast on the day it occurred, although late evening telecasts mentioned the closing of the airshow.[69] TASS distributed a three-sentence story about the disaster, but this was not broadcast until the following day. Early in 1971, when American diplomats' cars were being vandalized in Moscow in apparent retaliation for the harassment of Soviet personnel in the United States by militant Jewish organizations, the

---

* *New York Times*, September 13, 1971, p. 1M; *London Times*, September 14, 1971, p. 6. Hundreds of Soviet police and troops were present in the cemetery area, holding down attendance to twenty or thirty people.

Soviet media gave no publicity whatsoever to these acts of reprisal, probably in order to avoid building a mass anti-American campaign.[70]

Although Communist broadcasters do not criticize the form of government, the party itself, or basic political concepts, they do participate in the national pastime of self-criticism (*samokritika*).[71] In fact, they are expected to work with the other media in exposing faults and inefficiencies at the operating level. People write to newspapers raising embarrassing questions. Television newscasts show uncompleted buildings, leaky roofs, or falling tiles, while the announcer indicts the agency or individuals allegedly responsible for the failure.

In 1962, Leningrad *Pravda* published a 1,200-word statement from the City Party Committee noting that there had been "profound critical statements in the pages of the press and in radio and television broadcasts exposing shortcomings in the work of individual enterprises and institutions."[72] The newspaper went on to observe that many of these had "gone unanswered, which lowers the organizational role of the press substantially and confuses public opinion." Such criticisms are "warning signals" and should lead to action which subsequently should be reported.

One example of such a project was the series in which two radio reporters, to point up the poor quality of consumer goods, went into stores pretending they were clerks and praising the items on sale, then surreptitiously recording the criticisms of the buyers.[73] Writers in *Sovetskaya pechat* in 1965, under the title "Radio and Television: What Television Lacks," urged the widespread use of television to "criticize and root out shortcomings." An example was given of the chief engineer of a Moscow factory who had criticized another factory for delaying the delivery of gasoline engines necessary for some new construction, to which the director of the second factory had a chance to reply. "The editor succeeded in carrying the case about engines to the end and discussed this with television viewers."[74]

In 1967 several *Zhurnalist* authors complained that television was not willing to be as controversial as the newspapers.[75] They referred to an interview about a factory in which a new system of incentives had been introduced. This they faulted because the program had not mentioned that the incentive system was highly controversial. It was not sufficient, they said, to treat important events only through the dispatches of TASS. Such a procedure might be safer, but it was not satisfactory.

In the city of Kuibyshev a television program showed cluttered store windows, with the result that they were arranged more attractively.[76] In the same city, when it appeared likely in 1968 that construction for a public building might be unduly delayed, three television journalists produced several programs to show how slowly the work was proceeding and thereby expedited the construction.

In 1972 there were reports from the city of Omsk that 15,000 apartments were built each year without any coatracks. This led to a nine-month comic opera sequence of bureaucratic confusion which produced much laughter—but still no coatracks.[77] At about the same time, in another part of the country, labels were mixed on shipments of fertilizer and coffee beans.[78] In February 1972 the minister of consumer services was quizzed on Moscow television by three newspaper reporters who asked about such services as tailoring and coin-operated laundries.[79]

How much freedom do the broadcasters have in making such criticisms, and to what extent is everything planned in advance? It is reasonable to assume that if party or government approval are not specifically received in advance, they at least are expected; and it may be that criticisms are coordinated by the government and sometimes planned as a prelude to future political changes. In any case, samokritika is limited to operational rather than policy problems.

The few audience data available indicate considerable dissatisfaction with news output. In 1967 a survey was made of the television viewing of 1,916 individuals in Leningrad.* Asked among other things to indicate their satisfaction or dissatisfaction with news and current events programs, 38 per cent indicated they were satisfied; 27 per cent said they did not like such programs; 20 per cent took a neutral position; and 18 per cent had no opinions at all. On a question about spot news coverage, approval was expressed by 36.2 per cent, a neutral position was taken by 24.5 per cent, and disapproval was registered by only 6.7 per cent. In the "hard-to-judge" and "rarely watched" category were 32.6 per cent of the respondents.

However, when requested to rank thirty-one types of programs in order of popularity, the respondents put Central Television newscasts 17th, while two other news programs were rated 19th and 20th respectively. Among broadcasts of low popularity was the local Leningrad news

* Boris Firsov, There Is No 'Average' Viewer, a Soviet TV Survey, pp. 18, 20, 22. For more details on this and other research, see below, 186–189.

program, which was in 24th place. Interest in news and current affairs tended to increase with the age of respondents, as was to be expected. But it was low among the better educated too, although the lowest rating of all was by the group with a fourth-grade education or less. This did not necessarily indicate a lack of interest in news and current events per se, but perhaps a distrust of the regime-controlled media, with the result that these respondents were seeking other news sources, one of which could have been foreign broadcasts.

In 1968 the State Committee for Radio and Television conducted a nationwide poll of 5,232 persons in 30 different locations, both urban and rural, all over the country.[80] Newspapers were the favored source for foreign news, followed in descending order by radio, television, and lectures by Communist party propagandists. Except for collective farmers, 60.2 per cent of whom were "fully satisfied" with the amount of international news, 70 per cent or more felt that radio and television did not provide enough foreign items. Although 46.6 per cent of the collective farmers, and 36.2 per cent of Communist party members and government workers, were "fully satisfied" with interpretation and comment on international affairs, 70 per cent or more of the remainder were less than satisfied. These and other data led the author of the study to conclude "that among all audience groups there are serious complaints with radio and television concerning the volume and information on foreign affairs and the credibility of commentary."

Official Soviet spokesmen too have criticized broadcast news. In July 1964 the All-Union Creative Conference of Publicists heard from the editor in chief of All-Union Radio news. After pointing out that the information broadcast by Moscow each twenty-four hours would fill twenty-six issues of *Pravda*, and noting that many outstanding journalists were taking an active role in the work of the radio center, he went on to regret that "not many journalists have yet mastered the art of speaking into a microphone. Yet journalists of the capitalist West are at the microphone day and night, they use radio to the utmost, particularly in broadcasts to the Soviet Union."[81]

In 1965 a *Pravda* editorial complained: "Broadcasts of television news on domestic matters must be brought to a higher level. Of course, it is difficult to give a complete picture in brief reports of a particular event or phenomenon. But why not invite to the studio prominent scholars, or specialists, who, with their knowledge could comment upon today's news from scientific laboratories, factory shops, construction sites and fields?"[82] A writer in *Kommunist* stated that despite progress and some successes, "it would be wrong to consider TV news programs satisfactory. Frequently they do not respond to events quickly enough. Much of the presentation is hackneyed and inexpressive, especially on economic themes. There are few professionally trained reporters, commentators and announcers."[83] A professor in the Faculty of Journalism at Moscow State University wrote in December 1969 about the inadequacies of television news.[84] In many cases, he said, owing to a shortage of journalists who could convincingly read newscopy, their roles were taken by announcers who "do a rather good job of concealing the fact that they are mouthing other peoples' words." The writer condemned this practice: it is necessary to train journalists to be newscasters; and although this now is being done by universities and party schools, there still is a long way to go.

During several weeks of viewing television news programs in four Soviet cities in October 1970, I noticed that production quality varied from day to day, sometimes being quite good and at other times rather poor. On the whole, though, it was below American standards. I was surprised to see much poor film, in view of the excellence of Soviet cinema film. Furthermore, most of the film was silent. Television camera shots often were held much too long, and camera movement was limited, giving programs a static effect. Several times I saw newscasts in which an important person or perhaps the announcer read an official statement while one camera held the same shot for as long as five or six minutes, with only some in-and-out movement. Apparently one does not tell a Soviet party leader: "When I give you the signal, turn your head and look at the camera with the red light." But with news as with other types of programs, I noticed great improvement in 1972 over 1970. The newscasters were better, had more personality, and read their copy more smoothly. There was more and better film, and overall production had become much more professional. There even were a few light items to relieve the monotony of the propaganda message!

How can one judge content, in view of the great differences between socialist and democratic theories on dispensing information? Only, it appears, on their own terms. From the Soviet point of view, content selection is good: They report those items they want their audience to know about and emphasize "acceptable" attitudes. Nevertheless, credibility would be increased with more objectivity in selection and presentation—although official doctrine clearly would oppose such a change. One of the studies cited above reported a low level of credibility, and my own impressions, after talking to a good many Soviet citizens, bear out the reports of other foreign observers that the Soviet people are more critical of the mass media than their leaders believe them to be.

Public Events and Documentaries

Like all countries, the Soviet Union uses radio and television to bring its major public events before the nation and the world. Moscow's Red Square—the national center for observances of the two major patriotic holidays, the anniversaries of the Revolution and May Day—provides an excellent setting for television coverage.* The sides of the square, 1,320 feet long and 420 feet wide, are bordered by the Kremlin wall, St. Basil's Cathedral, the GUM Department Store, and the Historical Museum. On such occasions these buildings are decorated with huge posters, large plaques, and much bunting.

Ranking members of the political hierarchy stand on the Lenin Mausoleum, while several thousand fortunate spectators, both Soviet and foreign, occupy the viewing stands on the two long sides of the square. The gigantic parades, usually including much military hardware and many marching delegations, enter at one end, sweep past the watching thousands, and exit at the other end. The high buildings provide excellent sites for television and film cameras, and special stands are erected for additional camera angles.

These parades are very impressive. I was among the spectators in Red Square on November 7, 1958, and a dozen years later watched portions of the 1970 parade on television.† Events like these are broadcast to the entire Soviet Union and are sent to other socialist countries by Intervision. Eurovision members and the rest of the world can get all or portions of the pickups by direct feed or through videotapes and films. Coverage techniques are similar to those used in the United States for

---

* The uprising that overthrew the provisional government in 1917 took place on October 25 by the Old Style calendar, but the Soviets now refer to it by the New Style date of November 7. Nevertheless it is known as the October Revolution or sometimes as The Glorious October Revolution.

† The first Red Square event to be televised was the May Day parade in 1956 (Yurovskiy and Boretskiy, p. 65).

presidential inaugurations and in the United Kingdom for ceremonial state occasions. The many cameras, located strategically at various points in Red Square and the surrounding area, and equipped with a wide range of lenses, show the parade itself, the presidium atop the tomb, the crowds, and the marchers. For variety there are interviews with participants and spectators.

Inevitably in 1970, the Soviet Union and all the other socialist countries had a year-long observance of the birth centenary of Vladimir Ilyich Lenin. Spending October of that year in the Soviet Union, I constantly saw pictures, posters, and displays extolling Lenin's role in building the country. It seemed that the Soviet Union had replaced the Russian Orthodox church with communism and Jesus Christ with Lenin. All the information media were mobilized for this project. Writing in 1969 the deputy chief editor of USSR Central Television stated: "The most experienced and talented scriptwriters and editors, producers and tele-operators, political reviewers and artists are enthusiastically preparing television programmes devoted to the Lenin Jubilee. They are endeavouring to show systematically on the television screen and from all aspects the preparations for the hundredth anniversary of Lenin's birthday in our country as well as abroad, to reveal in a clear and penetrating way the image of Vladimir Ilich, his life and revolutionary activity, the riches of his theoretical heritage, to inform viewers of the fight of the Soviet people for the practical application of Marx-Leninist ideas, of the most penetrating influence of Lenin's ideas on the general development of the world."[85]

The Soviet leaders were motivated not only by the intrinsic merits of the Lenin story, but also by the opening it provided to propagandize for the basic Communist articles of faith. They also saw this as an opportunity to tell the younger generation about Lenin, since half the country's population in 1970 was made up of people thirty years of age or younger, several generations removed from the Lenin era.

Subjects and titles indicate the nature of the programs. There was a television cycle "devoted to the heroic working class of the Soviet Union [and] to glorious revolutionary and labour traditions." There were three series intended particularly for youth: "The Relay of Generations"; "We Are Reporting to Ilich"; and "Leninist Trials." More instructional in concept was "The Lenin University of Millions," in both radio and television versions, dealing with the history of the Communist party,

Marxist-Leninist philosophy, and socialist-political economy. I saw one of these when it was repeated in October 1970. It consisted largely of readings from Lenin, plus accompanying pictures and commentary comparing the Soviet Union and the United States to the great disadvantage of the latter. We saw slides of New York and Chicago; heard about Standard Oil of New Jersey; were told that the cost of living in the United States was rising; and saw pictures of slums. There also were strike scenes from France, Italy, Japan, and West Germany, plus a reference to the General Motors strike then in progress. Other Lenin University programs were straight lectures, some of which committed all the sins of low-budget American educational television in its least inspired moments.

Lenin also received much praise during the fiftieth anniversary of the Revolution in 1967, when all the media were used to propagate the ideals of the Revolution at home and abroad.[86] There was one cycle of programs about Lenin, plus another entitled "The Party of the Revolution," dealing with the role of the party during the Revolution and afterward. "Science and Culture of the Soviet Union" showed how the Revolution had awakened the creative forces of the nation. "The Atlas of the Peoples of the USSR," produced by television centers all over the country, described the contributions of the various national groups of the Soviet Union. Over 100 telecasts were based on literary works by Soviet writers and dramatists, and many broadcasts for both adults and children developed musical and artistic themes.

The highpoint was a series of fifty documentaries, "Chronicle of a Half Century," which presented a year-by-year panorama of Soviet history from 1917 to 1967. Developed with great care, this project was assigned to twelve filming teams. Originally telecast during the anniversary year with the last program on November 6, the eve of the anniversary, the series has been repeated several times.

I saw some of the documentaries in the series. On the whole they were well produced, with effective film selection and editing. But one thing that emerged clearly was the difference in concept between Soviet and American "documentaries." Whereas in the United States many documentaries present a range of facts and opinions, in the USSR—and other socialist countries too—they almost always propagandize for a single point of view. A case in point was the program in this series dealing with 1958. This telecast, devoted mainly to events taking place within the USSR, showed tractors and combines in fields; ships and submarines being launched; smiling workers harvesting grain; a children's chess tournament; a horsemanship demonstration; girl gymnasts; new power stations; advances in coal mining; and other Soviet events of productive and peaceful nature.

Then it showed Van Cliburn playing in Moscow, since 1958 was the year he was launched on his successful career by winning the Tchaikovsky Piano Competition. Clearly, the Russians were boasting of discovering this talented young American. There followed several pictures of American events: Ku Klux Klan members in full regalia abusing blacks; slum conditions in big city ghettos; and the U.S. military in Vietnam. The obvious propaganda objective was to demonstrate how the peace-loving Soviet Union had advanced the career of the talented young pianist Van Cliburn, while his countrymen at home were doing reprehensible things.

In 1961 Ukrainian radio produced "The Way to Space," which dealt with Yuri Gagarin, the first Soviet spaceman.[87] In the same year Moscow told the story of the courageous Arctic scientist and explorer Otto Yuyevich Schmitt, while Azerbaijan radio and television devoted an entire day to programs about workers on some oil rocks in the Caspian Sea.[88] Estonian television planned a five-year series of 300 or 350 broadcasts entitled "25 Years Ago Today," each of thirty-five or forty minutes' duration, about World War II.[89]

The propaganda lesson is constantly repeated. In Leningrad, on October 8, 1970, I saw a documentary, illustrated by pictures and slides, arguing that capitalism breeds strikes and violence. On October 31, 1970, in Kiev, several days before the November 3 election in the United States, I watched "America Faces the Election." It began with some filmed Washington scenes, after which the studio commentator spoke against a rear screen projection of buildings in Washington and the Statue of Liberty in New York. We saw Governor Rockefeller riding a bicycle, Arthur Goldberg shaking hands, and several other typical American campaign scenes. A chart with English captions showed comparative party strength in the House of Representatives, and there were pictures of demonstrators carrying signs which read "Long live Vietnam." *U.S. News and World Report* was the source of graphs detailing the increase in unemployment, the high crime rate, and growing national defense expenditures. There also were pictures of police making arrests. This was one of the best produced programs I saw during four weeks in the Soviet Union in the fall of 1970. Yet its obvious purpose was to demonstrate that things were falling apart in the United States and that no matter who won the election, disaster was inevitable. It is interesting that a program with that message was chosen for superior production.

Severe treatment also was provided mainland China in a one-hour documentary broadcast January 31, 1972, which depicted that country as a thoroughly regimented state determined to stamp out the individuality of its citizens.[90] Based on films by Italian, French, Danish, British, and Chinese cameramen, the programs ridiculed Chinese mass indoctrination and regimentation in much the same way Western observers formerly described the Soviet Union. At one point the commentator observed that in China "to think is harmful. Any emotional feeling is rotten bourgeois individualism."

A year later the USSR took an equally severe line during a three-episode treatment of the United States—at the very time the Soviet government was negotiating an agreement for technical cooperation with the General Electric Company. Built around the life and work of a Soviet newsman stationed in Washington during the 1960s, "Washington Correspondent" impressed an American newsman in Moscow as "dedicated to the theme that the United States is a land of violence which kills its public leaders.* To the accompaniment of discordant rock music, the program dealt with the assassinations of President Kennedy, his brother Robert Kennedy, and Martin Luther King; the fighting in Vietnam; and games in which young people in automobiles tried to run down one another. There were quick cuts from pictures of GIs watching an exotic dancer at a Christmas show to people burned by napalm in Vietnam. Yet, at about the same time, in connection with a visit of President Pompidou of France to the Soviet Union, Moscow television carried two films highly complimentary of the French cities of Paris and

---

* *New York Times*, January 15, 1973, p. 8. Very similar was the program telecast nine months earlier, describing the United States as a highly militaristic country, which also emphasized racial strife, unemployment, slums, and pornography (*Los Angeles Times*, March 5, 1972, p. 6A). In 1972 Moscow television released a full-length film titled "On the Struggle of the Laos People against American Imperialism" (*OIRT Information* 1972/4–5, p. 10). An official description stated that it "bears witness to the heroism and indomitable national liberation struggle of the Laos people that can be broken neither by napalm nor by American bombs of which already more have been thrown on the liberated territory of Laos than on the territory of Hitlerite Germany during the Second World War."

Marseilles.* Only time will tell whether the summit meetings between Brezhnev and Nixon will soften or eliminate such treatments of the United States. But past experiences indicate that the basic approach will remain much the same, even though the emphasis may vary with the current international climate.

Political Education

Political education is a constant objective of all the Soviet media. During my first trip to the USSR in the fall of 1958 with four other American mass media specialists, one of my traveling companions, noticing that every program seemed to have a propaganda purpose, remarked that Soviet broadcasting might be considered a commercial for the state 50 per cent of the time. To this our hosts, several Soviet broadcasting officials, reacted vigorously: "If you want to put it that way," they said, "better count it as 100 per cent!"

In the same vein, the chairman of the State Committee on Radio and Television wrote on Radio Day in 1963: "Soviet Radio has become a mighty ideological weapon in the struggle to build communist society. It would be no exaggeration to say that radio and television constitute one of the Party's right-hand helpers in ideological work. The ability of radio and television to penetrate everywhere make it possible to carry the Party's word to millions of listeners, to carry the great ideas of communism to their minds and hearts."[91]

Addressing itself to the improvement of Soviet broadcasting, the Communist Party Central Committee in Februrary 1960 made several references to the importance of political education.[92] "In spite of the very large number of political broadcasts from Moscow and from republic and province centers, the attention of the radio audience is not concentrated on the chief problems of communist construction. Unimportant, isolated scraps of material are often broadcast. Valuable initiative in production and in serving the population, striking examples of Soviet

---

* Since 1967 Byelorussian Television in Minsk has transmitted the cycle "Streets and Squares Narrate," drawing upon the recollections of eye witnesses and participants in World War II to "remind viewers of the history of that struggle and the fates of heroes once living and fighting in these places. In the reportages the glorious history . . . is shown together with the present life of the Byelorussian people who have built up new cities, housing estates and villages on the war ruins" (Niniel Kasianova, "Reportage à suivre," *OIRT Review* 1972/1, pp. 3–5).

patriotism, the friendship of people's high ideals and the communist attitude toward labor are propagandized feebly."

Therefore, the committee instructed: "There must be regular, consistent and profound radio propaganda of the decisions of Party Congresses and plenary sessions of the Party Central Committee, explanations of the domestic and foreign policies of the Soviet Union and elucidations of the people's struggle to complete the seven-year plan ahead of schedule and to create an abundance of material and spiritual values and of the growth of the forces of communism."

Five years later the Central Committee's Bureau for Improvements in Television reported that, despite much improvement, television still was "insufficiently utilized in the mobilization of the working people for the fulfillment of political and economic tasks, in the communist upbringing of Soviet people, in popularizing the achievements of Soviet literature and art, in the development of people's creativity and in organizing the cultural leisure time of the working people."[93]

The head of Political Programs for USSR Central Television described the responsibility of his department as the production of "a new man."[94] Writing in 1961 he declared: "A new man is being formed in the process of active participation in the building-up of communism, development of communist principles and economic cultural life, under the influence of the whole system of the educational work of the Party, the State, and social organizations in which the press, radio and television play an important role."

The following year he detailed this pronouncement: "The main contents of our political broadcasts is wide and systematic propagation of the decisions of the 22nd Congress of the Communist Party of the Soviet Union, explanation of the new programme of the Party, of the programme of the building-up of communism in the USSR, and of the political and working upsurge among the working people, aroused by the Party Congress. Our chief task is to ensure that TV programmes contribute to the successful realization of the Party programme. . . ."[95] Every political broadcast, he said, must meet two requirements: "Its theme should not be casual, but connected with basic problems of contemporary life and thus interconnected with other broadcasts. . . ." Secondly, it must be given responsible handling, and if possible well-known and prominent people should participate.

Party congresses are a continuing subject. In 1959, according to the

State Committee for Radio and Television, it was necessary to expound the "grandiose program" for the building of communism laid down by the Twenty-first Congress of the CPSU which met that year in Moscow.[96] There were broadcasts by old Bolsheviks who had worked with Lenin; talks by economists on the transition from socialism to communism; and reports of successes of the Soviet economy. Automation was discussed in order to demonstrate how, under a socialist economy, technology improved working conditions, whereas under capitalism the very opposite might be true. There were talks on such topics as "The Concern of the Communist Party for the Welfare of the People" and "To Everyone According to His Needs—The Communist Principle of Distribution." Comparable programs on television intermingled political education with economics.[97]

In 1962, following the Twenty-second Party Congress of the previous year, Ukraine radio had a series of talks on such topics as "The Building of Communism" and "The Historical Significance of the 22nd Congress."[98] The national television network developed programs to explain and propagate the decisions of the congress.[99] A decade later there were television programs to prepare for the Twenty-fourth Congress of the Communist party, and the following year both radio and television broadcasts marked the fiftieth anniversary of the V. I. Lenin All-Union Pioneer Organization.[100]

National television broadcast an interview with the leader of the American Communist party Gus Hall on October 8, 1970, to commemorate his birthday. Recorded in the United States, both questions and answers were in English. During the telecast the original soundtrack was faded to the background, and a Russian translation read by a single voice. Mr. Hall's statement was mainly an explanation of why he had devoted his life to communism.

Two Russians writing about Soviet television as it was in the mid-1950s complained that the screen "was filled with an endless stream of speeches, interviews, lectures, and talk. The commentator talked constantly on and off the screen. It was during this period, between 1955 and 1957, that tables of all sizes, podiums, and so on, began to appear on television screens. The noble desire to tell television viewers about all the events of the public and cultural life of the country led the professionals of Central Television astray onto the easy but wrong road of blindly imitating radio broadcasting.[101]

These faults, unfortunately, are still prevalent. In Kiev on October 31, 1970, I saw a program called "International Life," intended to prepare the audience for the All-Union Party Congress scheduled the next year. The specific subject was the effects of political changes in China on world communism. The three participants—all men of considerable status—sat stiffly in a straight row and talked, with no assisting visuals and hardly any camera movement. Although this program dealt with a topic of great importance to the USSR, it suffered from the most obvious production shortcomings.

Some programs involving a measure of confrontation now are emerging on Soviet radio and television, although the USSR is by no means ready to accept the free marketplace of thought conceptualized by Justice Oliver Wendell Holmes. The official report of a publicists' conference held in 1964 had one section headed, "The Truth Is Born in Argument," which stated that great progress had been made since "the years of the Stalin personality cult."[102] During those years, unfortunately, the Soviet Union had "lost the habit of good, fruitful discussion . . . [of] businesslike argument from which the truth emerges." But, fortunately, "the situation has changed."

At any rate, there are some programs on which officials answer questions over the air. The magazine *Zhurnalist* reported in 1967 a monthly program in Estonia in which government ministers answered questions from viewers.[103] The first secretary of the Communist party in the city of Kuibyshev wrote in 1969 that the local station had been carrying for several years a program called "Television Meeting of the City Executive Committee" on which a journalist asked committee members questions from the public.[104] The questions must have been probing since the author commented: "Appearances of city, district, and enterprise leaders on television simply are essential, although I myself know that to find oneself before the television camera is not pleasant." Reference already has been made to the February 1972 broadcast during which the minister of consumer services was questioned by three newspaper reporters about inadequacies in his department.[105]

With political education as with planning for the Lenin centenary, it is essential to eliminate from people's minds any remaining "bourgeois ideology and . . . vestiges of capitalism." It also is necessary to combat those "revisionists" who try to conceal the defects of capitalism by claiming that it has been reborn and made democratic by presenting programs exposing the "unsubstantiated nature of such fabrications." A part of this is the elimination of religious belief, identified as among the "capitalist residues in people's minds."* Accordingly, talks and discussions on antireligious themes are developed with such titles as "Religion—A Harmful Residue of the Past," "How Religion Treats the Woman," and "Religion Is Incompatible with Communism." Attempts are made to undermine belief in such superstitions as the "self-rejuvenation" of icons and the "spontaneous ignition" of candles. Dramas with antireligious themes are broadcast, but religious services and programs involving acts of faith are never aired in the USSR.

Article 124 of the Soviet Constitution deals with freedom of religion: "In order to ensure to citizens freedom of conscience, the church in the USSR is separated from the state, and the school from the church. Freedom of religious worship and freedom of anti-religious propaganda is recognised for all citizens." In spite of this guarantee, political and professional advancement are virtually impossible for a dedicated church member, while the schools and all other information media constantly preach atheism. Although most cities have some churches, often well kept up, in which services are conducted regularly, in addition to many cathedrals and churches maintained in excellent condition as museums, worshippers tend to be elderly people. If this continues to be true, it is hard to see how any religion except communism can endure for long. Leningrad has a former cathedral made into an atheist museum, containing displays illustrating such shortcomings of the prerevolutionary church as fake icons. Nevertheless, attending Moscow churches in 1972, I noticed more—and also more young—people in attendance than on earlier visits and was told by both Soviets and Americans that religion was becoming a fad with some young intellectuals.† A Western correspondent reported in 1973 that in a town of 250,000 located 125 miles east of Moscow, three or four thousand people struggled against police lines in an attempt to take part in an Easter Eve mass.

* Kaftanov, pp. 52–53. The report of the All-Union Creative Conference of Publicists in 1964 complained that "many newspaper editors pay insufficient attention to atheist propaganda. The materials carried by some newspapers are often aimed not at believers but at people who are already atheists" ("The Publicism of High Ideas," *Sovetskaya pechat*, No. 7 (July 1964), p. 17; translated in CDSP 16:42 (November 11, 1964), p. 13).

† *New York Times*, April 30, 1973, p. 7C. See p. 214 below for official complaints of religious broadcasts beamed into the USSR by foreign short-wave services.

On the positive side, there is emphasis on molding "a new man with communist features, habits and morality."[106] Less sympathetically, one might say that the objective is to develop a new Soviet man corresponding to the Christian of the Middle Ages, who questions nothing, while developing his personal and professional potentialities to better serve the state. The cycle "Good People—Together with You" dealt with "generosity, moral integrity, honesty, selflessness, and the devotion of the Soviet people to the ideas of communism and internationalism."[107] A premium is placed on good moral standards, dedication to family, and the elimination of indolence and drunkenness. Alcoholism is the subject of a continuing campaign. On at least one occasion this problem was handled very crudely. The senior editor at Kharkov television wrote in the journal of the Union of Journalists toward the end of 1963 about a program entitled "Under the Lens": "A dozen photographs: close-up large-scale pictures of the raddled features of alcoholics. The broadcaster, trying to get as much anger as possible into his voice, reads out names and addresses, and asks naively: 'It would be interesting to know where he gets the money he spends on drink, since he had done no work for several months.' The end of this strange transmission is something on the lines of: 'Comrades, let us see to it that there are no idlers or drunkards among us.' "[108]

Workers and Farmers

It is an easy transition from programs to develop the "new Soviet man" to those which glorify the country's workers and stimulate them to become more productive. The Constitution declares the USSR to be a "socialist state of workers and peasants," so it is not surprising that the heads of political programming for central television wrote that "it is necessary to reflect and propagate all the best and most progressive experiences in the fight for development in the productive use of the country, to propagate the examples of the communist work and make them accessible to millions of people."[109]

In 1960 an article in *Izvestia* mentioned approvingly, in the course of some highly critical references to Soviet radio, a series entitled "News about Agriculture."[110] In addition to commending the programs as "conversational," the writer said that they contained repartee with an imaginary character "who in talking with correspondents, tells his opinions or ridicules negligent officials."

Broadcasts for workers and farmers often are developed cooperatively with representatives of the target audiences. Programs in the series "Replies to Questions of the Working People" were organized at clubs and houses of culture where working people gather. In cities as well as in rural areas, factory employees, farmers, teachers, physicians, engineers, and others banded together to organize programs for their fellow workers.[111] In the district of Voronezh (approximately 300 miles south of Moscow), there were in 1961 some 300 program planning groups involving over 2,000 persons. In the Ukraine, with over 1,000 such units, training courses were organized for members. Moscow then had a council of television viewers that took an active part in program planning.[112]

In Kiev in 1962 workers from the Ministry of Agriculture and the Academy of Agricultural Science discussed "topical questions of agriculture as seen in the light of the decisions of the 22nd Congress of the Communist Party" on the radio series "Attention, Important!"[113] In 1969 Lithuanian television invited proposals on improving farm life and agricultural processes.[114] The winning team received a prize plus a trip to East Germany. In 1972 Lithuania televised a series in which teams from cities and industrial plants competed in solving problems related to increased output.[115]

"The School of Agricultural Knowledge" was a series of television programs broadcast in 1968 to present practical information on such subjects as how to eliminate weeds and when to cultivate before sowing.[116] While the programs were in progress, peas and maize were grown on a small test plot, and the experimental results were reported on the telecasts. On one broadcast a poultry expert told of waterless duck raising. Turkmen radio conducted a campaign to enlist young women to drive cotton harvesting machines.[117] One woman made a commitment to harvest at least a hundred tons of cotton as well as to each three relatives to drive harvesters. Thereafter, many girls volunteered to run harvesting machines "and to mark the 22nd Congress of the Communist Party of the Soviet Union by increasing efforts in cotton harvesting." One Saturday afternoon at the end of September 1972, national television carried a short documentary showing rows of harvesters in a large field, women checking grain, and trucks taking it to elevators.

The Party's ideological journal *Kommunist* offered some very frank criticisms of a program telecast on August 1, 1965, in connection with All-Union Railroad Workers' Day.[118] In fact, its comments could be applied as well to a good many educational television programs in the United States which have introductions that promise more than the programs deliver. "Semaphore lights flashed across the screen, and you were invited to take a trip along the country's chief railroads. Accompanied by a guide, a future railroad engineer, the audience was all ready to set out. But stop! First there was an interview, giving statistics on freight shipments and load capacity and information about new railroad mileage. All this is very important, but one wonders whether it was really necessary for the screen to repeat what had already appeared in central newspapers. The semaphore lights invited us to start out again; but it was not a real trip, it was make-believe; there was a map on the wall, a model on a stand, and a lecturer with a pointer, waiting for the signal to start lengthy technical explanations . . ."

On October 8, 1970, on the local Leningrad station, I saw a telecast of a ceremony from the assembly hall of a collective farm, during which speeches were made, medals awarded, and prizes given to members of a farm group. There also was some light entertainment, including the merriment resulting when a live pig was carried into the room. Although this program may have been a morale builder for members of the farm unit involved, the television handling was very poor, there being almost no attempt to adapt the ceremony to the medium. This was neither a sophisticated nor an effective use of television.

Although most programs for agricultural workers are vocationally oriented, one of the objectives of the Peoples' Television University is the general educational and cultural upgrading of agricultural and industrial workers.[119] Such programs are designed for both individual and group viewing, and in rural areas they frequently are watched in palaces of culture on sets purchased by collective farms. Sometimes discussions follow the telecasts.[120]

Broadcasts on industrial subjects often use the self-criticism formula. In one radio program the spokesman for a metallurgical plant criticized another factory for slowness in supplying the machinery necessary to automate the controls of an open hearth furnace. Subsequently, representatives of that plant went on the air, accepted the complaint, and explained what was being done to remedy the situation.[121] On a series in Gorki, factory rejects were shown to television viewers, and the workers responsible were asked to offer explanations.[122] Appropriately the program was called "Attention, Reject!" This was described as "a vivid and effective form of the fight against careless workers." Workers in seasonal sugar beet factories were invited to make suggestions about servicing equipment. Scores of them replied, and the preparation of the factories for the next season was expedited.

Some programs are designed to stimulate competition among various factories.[123] Production innovators, high-output workers, and special labor brigades, representing metallurgical workers, machine builders, textile workers, and lumbermen, have exchanged experiences and complaints by radio and have criticized their respective organizations. Thereafter, management spokesmen appeared to explain what they were doing about the shortcomings. The series "Under Equal Conditions" was a competition among organizations achieving different levels of output while working under similar conditions. In 1959 and 1960, radio, television, and the press combined to facilitate the introduction of new automated machinery in Stalino, in the Donbass region.[124] A decade later the television cycle "Seven Days of the 'Dynamo' Works" presented a daily fifteen-minute report on the work of various agricultural collectives and industrial plants.[125]

In addition to factual presentations about industry and agriculture, the broadcast media present glamorizing documentaries with such titles as "Heroes of Our Day." Subjects may be workers in cement factories, tractor brigade foremen, metal workers, electric engine drivers, railroad engineers, dairymaids, or poultry maids. A helicopter was used to gather material for a series about the "victories" of village workers.[126] Ukrainian radio had features about the "master of high sugar beet crops"; a "heroine of socialist labor"; and a woman who twice received recognition for high maize yields.[127] "The Master of Fire River" described the life of the foundry worker who led his comrades in smelting so much steel above the target level as to make possible "several thousand more cars in the streets of our towns." Another person was honored for finding a way to reclaim marshlands which subsequently grew abundant cereal crops.

Finally we should notice the "Workers' Radio Gazette," a thrice weekly radio series originated in Moscow for national distribution, which attained its 200th broadcast in mid-1970.[128] *Pravda*, after describing with approval the way in which the series instilled young workers with regard for their occupations, and referring to "the romance of heroic work," went to to comment: "It would be well for the Radio Gazette to deal more consistently and in greater depth with the important problems of the work of industry and propagandize more widely the achievements of competing collectives. . . . It would be very useful regularly to familiarize listeners with the life and work of the working class in the socialist countries. And one can still learn only a little about the life and struggle of the proletariat in the capitalist countries from the programs."

Children and Youth

If there is one country that plans for the future, it is the USSR, so it is not surprising that the Soviet Union pays much attention to its younger generation. In May 1970, Leonid I. Brezhnev, head of the Communist party, told the opening session of a Young Communist League Congress in Moscow that the "stormy upsurge" of youth in the Western countries was evidence of the "deepening social crisis of capitalism." Western youth, he said, was no longer willing "to put up with a system of exploitation and with the bloody adventures of imperialism." Meanwhile, Soviet youth was "growing up morally healthy, energetic and ambitious . . . full of energy and enthusiasm for the fight for the Party, for the cause of Communism."[129]

In view of all this, it is inevitable that Soviet radio and television should have many carefully designed programs for children and youth. There are broadcasts for use in school and for reception at home. Between 5 and 10 per cent of the radio and from 10 to 12 per cent of the television output is for young people.

These programs are originated by both national and local services, and all the larger broadcasting units have departments devoted to children's features. In Leningrad and Moscow, most—though not all—educational television programs are carried by the third channels and, as more third stations are added elsewhere, they will carry the major share of educational material for their areas. But the national network also has such programs, as do the second channels now on the air.

With these programs as with all others, service to state and dedication to party are fundamental objectives. In January 1957 a department to prepare radio broadcasts for young people was established "to educate the Soviet youth in the spirit of high communist awareness, a profound sense of devotion to the party, the Homeland, and to the matter of communism."[130] Several years later the Central Committee maintained there should be at least an hour a day of children's television programs in which "special attention must be given to the development of children's labor habits, initiative, self reliance and desire for knowledge and to enlisting children in various socially useful tasks in collectives of young technicians, naturalists, and athletes. Propaganda on healthy living, physical culture and sports, programs of mass gymnastic exercises, various sports competitions and calisthenics lessons must take an important place in television programs."[131]

In 1965 the party's Bureau for the Russian Republic on Improvements in Work of Television reiterated this position:[132] "Programs for children and young people must be imbued with revolutionary romanticism and the heroics of daily labor; they should raise burning questions in the life and upbringing of the young generation and portray the work of Young Communist League and Young Pioneer organizations and sports societies on a broad scale. These broadcasts must attract young viewers with vividness of form and diversity of subject matter."

The chief editor of broadcasts for children and youth, writing in the same year, pointed out the importance of using radio to bridge the gap between today's youth and the days when Soviet citizens were undergoing severe hardships to assure the triumph of the Revolution, as well as to "show listeners the wonderful character of Vladimir Ilyich, the greatest leader and teacher of the working people of the whole world."[133]

Other comments from Soviet sources further document the objectives of youth programs. In 1965 Pravda praised the Leningrad youth series "Horizon": "No matter the subject, the chief thought, the leading idea of each program is the inculcation of civic activeness in young people." But there were shortcomings too: the series lacked "lively, vivid programs on problems of Marxist-Leninist theory and questions of international politics that are disturbing young people."[134] At the same time a prominent party theorist, writing under the title "Television: Problems and Prospects," complained of a lack of purpose in youth programs.[135] When serious problems are raised, it is done "briefly and hastily," whereas the audience "seeks a direct, frank and pointed discussion."

In 1967 the associate editor in chief for radio broadcasts for youth used the Twenty-third Congress of the Communist party, held the previous year, as a reference point in writing about the "Education of Young Citizens."[136] High moral principles were among the concepts to be transmitted, with Lenin as the example. The purpose was to develop the man of the future; but since the future grows from the present and the foundations of the present rest on the past, it was necessary to use stories about older generations to transmit revolutionary traditions to youth.

These references to communism may cloud the fact that in many respects the objectives and problems of broadcasts for youth are the same everywhere. One writer contended: "In radio broadcasts for school children we talk about people marked by high moral standards whose love for their homeland, discipline, audacity and faithfulness to friendship and many other noble traits represent an example to be followed by young people."[137] What the same author said about Soviet youth and the generation gap could apply almost anywhere: "It is well known that adolescents are often skeptical to [of] the opinions of adults, have their own ideas of life, the surrounding world, and painfully receive every discrepancy between the words and deeds of adults. Their opinions are often one-sided. Lacking vital experience they may confuse individual facts with vital truths while considering some vital truths to be exceptions. Adolescents would like to re-build life in accordance with their ideals, but have not enough experience of public work and, after meeting their first obstacles, tend to be depressed and convinced of the futility of their efforts."

In recent years the Soviet Union has had radio and television programs for use in schools, as well as supplementary programs for reception at home. But these developed much later and are less elaborate than comparable programs in West Germany, the United Kingdom, and the United States. The USSR's eleven time zones and many languages may partly explain its slowness in developing national services, although that would be no reason for the delayed emergence of such programs in the individual republics. Perhaps there were equipment shortages or inadequate funds. In any case, increases in the number of tape recorders now make it possible for schools to record national presentations for use at convenient times.

Soviet in-school programs supplement rather than duplicate school lessons and seldom if ever do direct teaching. Soviet theory in this respect has shown remarkable consistency through the years. An article written for American readers in 1935 explained that programs for children were not intended to instruct or substitute for schools "but to assist the school to instill into the children certain knowledge and habits. . . ."[138] Exactly thirty years later, the chief editor for radio broadcasts for children and youth said the same thing: "In spite of the ever-increasing use of radio and TV sets in schools and their application in the educational process, in our country broadcasting is primarily intended to help teachers and parents in the education of children out of school."[139]

Radio programs, serving all ages and dealing with many subjects, are developed by staff specialists working cooperatively with academic authorities and educational administrators.[140] For young children there are programs about nature and the world in which they live; for primary and intermediate classes, Russian, English, French, and German lessons, as well as broadcasts about literature and music; and for senior students, programs about literature and social sciences. Although ten years ago there was a trend toward long programs, ranging from thirty to forty-five minutes in length, they now run from ten to twenty minutes. Much ingenuity is shown in their development. One technique is taking children on imaginary trips, something well suited to radio, since it is not tied to definite visual images. Geography was taught that way. In a series for older children called "What the Clock Narrated," clocks drew upon their memories to retell facts and events.

Some literature programs use a narrator who talks about famous Soviet writers, while others are in dramatic form.[141] Broadcasts about history often emphasize recent findings not yet reported in textbooks. Space exploration brought programs about spaceships and the cosmos. Programs on physics describe technological developments like electricity and radio, and other broadcasts explain how chemistry is involved in industry, agriculture, and construction. Contests are a frequent interest-generating device. A biology series was moved to a farm so that senior students could receive practical training in livestock handling.

Soviet sources have provided an interesting description of a program about the circulation of water in nature called "The Story of the Rain."[142] An older and younger person often walked together in the woods and fields. Preparing to go out one day to pick mushrooms, they were kept inside by the rain.

Thousands of small drum players banged their instruments on the roof, windows and leaves, the drops began to dance and play leapfrog with the bubbles in the puddles.

It rained the whole day, the next, the third. . . . On the fourth day it seemed that it had stopped, but then it changed its mind and started again.

Our travellers sat round the table, a cricket scraped behind the oven, the clock ticked and the rain hummed.

"You could tell us something, uncle," said Dimka yawning, "you are silent all the time."

"I am not only silent, I am listening," said the big man.

"What are you listening to?"

"The rain."

"What is there to listen to in the rain?" said Dimka with surprise. "It bores one to death."

"It narrates a story."

"The rain? A story?"

Dimka also started to listen. He turned this way, and that, but could not understand anything.

"It seems you do not understand the rain," said the forester. "I will help you because we are good friends."

He filled his pipe, lighted it with a small piece of coal from the oven and started to narrate.

The children listened to the fascinating fairy-tale with great interest and it was obvious that a boring fairy-tale could not have been tolerated.

Music is a natural for radio. The USSR has had in-school music programs since 1925, and beginning in 1963 offered, as a counterpart to the former NBC Music Appreciation Hour with Walter Damrosch, the series "About Music for Children," presented by the noted Russian composer D. B. Kabalevsky.* Kabalevsky's series was set in a simulated Pioneer camp and in a Moscow school. Of universal application was the talk in which he differentiated between the verbs "to listen" and "to hear."

It sometimes happens that a radio set is switched on from the morning till the evening. And the remarkable musical art then turns into one of the noises accompanying our life similarly as the noise coming from the street. A lorry passes by, water drops from the tap, the radio plays. . . . All noises. It is not possible to listen in this way. From a great advantage radio becomes a great misery. We develop a neglectful attitude towards music. We stop being interested in it, loving it and understanding it.

* A. Menjshikova, *OIRT Review* 1965/1, pp. 15–16; see also Menjshikova, *OIRT Review* 1965/5, p. 21. Dmitri Kabalevsky was born in 1904. In addition to fame as a pianist, particularly for playing his own music on concert tours throughout Europe, he has many compositions to his credit, including piano works, string quartets, symphonies, concertos, and operas. He is best known in the United States for the opera *Colas Breugnon*, first produced in Leningrad in 1938, as well as the orchestral suite *The Comedians*.

Everywhere you hear music—on the radio, at concerts, at school—try to listen to it attentively, similarly as you read a book. And then music, similarly as books, will become your dear and faithful friend.

There also were two musical quiz programs, "In What Republic?" dealing with music in the various Soviet republics, and "In What Country?" about other lands. On both of these an area studies approach was used, since material on literature and geography was included too. In addition, there were the radio lessons called "We Learn to Sing."

An official analysis stated that in 1970 central television in Moscow originated 2,145 educational transmissions, including 304 in-school programs for secondary school students and 377 foreign language lessons for young children.[143] There also were 201 programs for home viewing by secondary school students, plus 144 to prepare students entering higher educational institutions.

In-school television began in 1965, and by 1972 programs were being originated in twenty studio centers. In the latter year a thousand Moscow schools were receiving programs in chemistry, biology, geography, music, literature, foreign languages, social science, and zoology.[144] These (including repeats) are on the educational channel between 9:30 A.M. and 2:00 P.M., as well as in the late afternoon for home viewing. Programs for the entire country are carried by the national network between 4:00 and 5:00 P.M. In-school programs begin ten minutes after classes start and conclude five or ten minutes before they finish, enabling teachers to discuss programs without interrupting them. In-school broadcasts run from fifteen to twenty-five minutes, those for home reception being a little longer.

Programs are scheduled for all ages. There are broadcasts to teach young children to speak English and French, it being intended that children will watch at school with their teachers or at home with their parents. These are supplemented by special transmissions for teachers and parents, previewing the programs and suggesting how best to use them. There also are printed outlines for teachers.

In the Ukraine an instructional project was organized in 1964, becoming a separate unit on July 1, 1967, with the name Ukrainian Educational Television.[145] In addition to programs for extramural students, Ukrainian Educational Television produces "The School Screen" for secondary schools, of which fifty-three hours were aired in 1968, on Tuesday, Wednesday, and Friday mornings from 11:35 to 12:05. Since the school period extended from 11:30 to 12:15, teachers had a few minutes with the class before and after each telecast. Subjects included history, social studies, physics, Russian literature, biology, and zoology.

Other programs are intended for home reception, and many teachers make home listening and viewing assignments. In 1960 Ukrainian radio launched a series called "School Hour" for high school pupils.[146] Broadcast once every two weeks, these programs were intended to arouse interest in such subjects as physics, chemistry, mathematics, literature, music, and agriculture. For young people finishing high school, there were programs to provide transitions to the next stages of their personal and professional careers. One radio series, "On Student Affairs," provided advice to young people enrolled in correspondence, technical, and night school courses.[147]

Less didactic broadcasts for home reception serve all ages. Radio programs for preschool listeners, intended for both parents and children, introduce children to the world in which they live.[148] This project calls to mind the BBC radio series "Listen with Mother," begun in 1950 and continued for many years, and its television successor, "Watch with Mother"—both of which aimed to provide a common experience for parents and children, instead of setting up radio and television barriers between them.[149] "How Do They Live?" heard once a month on Ukrainian radio, set out to explain to younger listeners such natural phenomena as plants, animals, insects, and birds.[150] "Let Us Sing, Let Us Play!" was designed to teach preschool youngsters to enjoy and understand music.[151] A musical program on Ukranian radio, "The Snowball Pipe," had two girl characters responding to listeners' requests, which were played by the magic "snowball pipe."[152]

On April 19, 1925, a young people's "Newsreel" was inaugurated on Soviet radio, and it has continued ever since.[153] Although designed as a counterpart of the morning newscasts for adults, it is not limited to news, since it includes other types of information along with some propaganda. At one time children were invited to become correspondents, and from 700 applicants 100 were chosen for participation. The Ukrainians developed a similar program on a weekly basis in 1952, and comparable broadcasts have been introduced elsewhere.[154]

Out-of-school as well as in-school programs take listeners on fictitious journeys. The radio series "Traveling to the Sun" involved a trip through the Soviet Union.[155] The "Pioneer Arrow" was a ship which followed a route suggested by the audience. Other programs help children to organize their leisure time. Some emphasize fellowship with young people abroad, particularly in the socialist countries, while world youth festivals, both West and East, get special radio and television treatment.[156] In 1963 Ukrainian radio scheduled broadcasts giving advice to young poets and actors, programs for school literary groups, talks on new books, and discussions with contemporary authors.[157]

In June 1969 Moscow radio broadcast a series of children's plays using scripts from most of the socialist countries as well as by French, Norwegian, and Swedish authors.[158] During the festival, eighteen radio plays from ten countries were performed. The play by Helmut Schulz entitled *One Day of a Great Life*, dealing with Marxist doctrine, was accompanied by music adapted from works of the contemporary British composer Benjamin Britten. In 1971 Byelorussian radio was devoting three hours a day to programs for young children. Much of this time was given to radio plays, of which the motto was "to learn to know while playing."[159]

One of the most charming of all Soviet programs is "Good Night Children!" broadcast by the national television network evenings at 8:15. On this daily series, several whimsical and amusing puppets—children, adults, and animals—enact stories with skill sufficient to capture both the under-five and the over-fifty audience. After seeing a number of these during several visits to the USSR, I would rank them among the best Soviet television productions. Many programs utilize puppets, a natural and commendable development in view of the Soviet Union's great skill in puppetry. There also have been local projects, such as Kiev television's "Good Night Children!" introduced in 1962, on which Grandfather Taras told fairy tales.[160] Ukrainian radio had an "Evening Tale" to help "education in children, goodheartedness, respect for other people, love for work and nature."[161] There also was a series on Georgian radio called "Before Falling Asleep," which related the adventures of various Soviet heroes.[162]

Inevitably there are programs for and about Communist youth.* For

* Young people of ages nine through fourteen are eligible to become Pioneers, whose distinctive three-cornered red ties signify the three generations of Communist workers: Pioneers, Komsomols, and party members. Pioneers take part in organized activities such as athletics, dramatics, music, ballet, art, crafts, cooking, photography, and drama, always with a strong admixture of Communist ideology. I visited an old Pioneer center in Tashkent and a splendid new one in Kiev, which

the very young there was the radio series "Uncle Fekya's Stories about the Seven Year Plan," built around Uncle Fekya, a locksmith born at the turn of the century, and his Pioneer grandson.[163] The grandfather told how hard life was for workers and peasants under czarist rule and how much communism had done for the country. Programs for older children deal with such things as the revolutionary traditions of the working class and the heroes of the civil war and World War II. There are special programs about Communist work brigades to encourage young people to contribute time to public enterprises.[164] But the appeal is not only for physical activity. In Kiev on October 29, 1970, I saw a program, originated jointly by the television studios in Kiev and Lvov, presenting poetry and music in observance of the anniversary of the founding of the Komsomol organization.

Youth programs, like the entire broadcasting schedule, emphasize work rather than play and serious more than lighthearted material, but there is entertainment too. Cartoon films are broadcast on Saturday mornings much as in the United States; and although Mickey Mouse has not yet included the USSR on his itinerary, some Soviet presentations recall the famous Walt Disney character. In the middle 1960s Ukrainian radio had an afternoon series, "The Club of Sunday Meetings."[165] In a simulated club setting, this aimed "at helping young people to spend their leisure time in an entertaining, sensible, and interesting way." The program included information (about animals and interplanetary flights, for example); music (folk songs, dance music, quizzes); a sports commentator; discussions of films; and advice for hobbyists (fishing, radio, and photography.) Television programs following the same format have have been developed in Minsk, Ashkhabad, Kuybyshev, Odessa, and elsewhere.[166]

There also are programs by children. In 1961 Lithuania had had for five years a radio and television children's choir, which sang at school

---

would qualify as a well-equipped youth center in any American city. Pioneer Palace staff members, incidentally, are paid more than schoolteachers, with the rationale that since attendance is optional, the programs must be presented by the best possible personnel. The Pioneers have their own publications, the best known being *Pionerskaya Pravda* (Pioneers' Truth). Qualified young people between fifteen and twenty-five years of age may join the Communist Union of Youth or Komsomol, modeled after the party itself. Komsomol groups also have well-developed activities. Their principal publication is *Komsomolskaya Pravda*. Eventually, some Komsomol members go on to become members of the Communist party.

affairs and on broadcasts.[167] In October 1970 in Kiev, I saw two television programs in which young people participated. A national production from Moscow consisted principally of ballet exercises done by young girls in a studio equipped with standard exercise bars and mirrors. (At the same hour, 6:00 P.M., the local channel was carrying a program of sports for schoolchildren.) Several days later I saw the Saturday morning "Pioneer Theater" presentation, with amateur actors. These programs may have been of some interest to their intended audiences, but neither achieved the level of excellence one would expect from national or republic capital organizations. In 1972 a Soviet spokesman told an Intervision meeting about programs by and for young people.[168] Some of these programs, he said, had been on the air for over ten years, including "Hello We Are Looking for Talent," a young people's amateur hour. That particular series illustrates how socialist television can stress long-term youth development over entertainment values, since some of the programs impressed me as providing an undeserved amount of exposure to performers of little talent.*

Adult Education

In the USSR the distinctions between propaganda and education are not always clear. In fact, many newscasts, documentaries, and public affairs features, as well as programs for workers in industry and agriculture, serve both functions. The State Television and Radio Committee wrote in 1970 that "most of the radio and television programmes for home listeners can in one way or another be considered educational."[169]

---

* Although several socialist countries are using America's tremendously successful *Sesame Street*, the Soviet Union has taken a strong stand against the program. Using a technique often employed to editorialize, the Soviet newspaper *Sovietskaya kultura* in August 1973 reprinted an attack on the program from the Mexican magazine *Siempre* denouncing the series as cultural imperialism. The Soviet publication said that the Mexican article exposed the "politics of America's so-called educational television, one of whose programs titled 'Sesame Street' serves as a clear example of veiled neocolonialism in cultures." The article went on: "We don't know whether the authors of the program gave it that title intentionally. The word 'sesame' came from the Orient and means 'open up.' One thing is certain: With that type of program, imperialism is seeking to penetrate into other people's homes, even if door and windows are tightly locked. The passkey is to be global television" (*New York Times*, August 17, 1973, p. 6C). Further quotations are given in *CDSP*, 25:32 (September 5, 1973), pp. 5–6). It is interesting to note that this attack came at the same time that the United States was providing more and more capital and technical aid for the Soviet economy. The reference to "global television" undoubtedly was to the possibility of program distribution directly to home receivers by satellite (see p. 79).

But however defined, there surely are many such programs. During the school year 1970–1971, Moscow television presented 2,145 educational transmissions, which included the following for adult viewers: 457 broadcasts for external students; 195 foreign language lessons; 172 programs for medical doctors; 144 broadcasts for students entering higher educational institutions; 69 programs for teachers; 64 programs in the People's Television University; 38 broadcasts on science and technology; 36 programs for engineers; 34 agricultural programs; and 18 Parents' University programs.

In the 1920s, the assignment of educational broadcasting was to eliminate illiteracy and offer basic general education. Necessarily, the medium was radio, but now the "main mass teaching medium in the USSR is television." Adult education broadcasts always are important in a country like the Soviet Union, with its great distances and its delays in developing rapid transportation and communication.[170] Television particularly has brought educational and cultural opportunities to people living in remote areas and small towns, such as explorers, farmers, shepherds, cotton growers, and hunters, who otherwise would be cut off from the world.

In 1935 a Soviet writer declared: "We state without exaggeration that in the Soviet Union everyone is studying."[171] One aspect of this, she said, was radio broadcasting developed by the unit named "In Aid of Self-Education." Subjects included natural science, psychology, philosophy, the history of art and literature, geography, religion and atheism, and mathematics. These were developed both as individual programs and in cycles, at different levels of difficulty. Bibliographies were prepared for many of the topics treated.

In 1960 there were adult education offerings on international affairs, particularly involving relations with other socialist countries; industrial problems; the development of the chemical industry; the uses of atomic energy; artificial satellites and rockets; the International Geophysical Year; scientific developments in general; natural phenomena; and medical information for doctors and laymen.[172] In 1971 Estonian Radio had three blocks of information programs daily, ranging from short announcements to long presentations. These included fifteen to eighteen five-minute programs each day in addition to some extended units.[173]

By the late 1950s the term "university" began to be applied inexactly to some series. In October 1959 a "People's Television University" was inaugurated, with lectures by scientists, journalists, writers, composers, producers, actors, and teachers.[174] Among the subjects taught was English. The next year there was a "Radio University of Literature and Art," although this was "only a symbolic title, since it does not in the least offer a 'University' education."[175] But the programs did attempt to "incite listeners' interest in books, the theatre, music, and fine arts." The "Radio Cultural University" of the Ukraine, begun on September 1, 1960, tried "to acquaint listeners with the achievements of Soviet and world literature, music, and art."[176] There were cycles on Ukrainian and Russian literature (including broadcasts on the fight for peace in Soviet literature, with reference to Tolstoy, Ehrenburg, and Sholokov, among others), as well as programs on Ukrainian and Russian music.

At about the same time Moscow television developed a "People's University" with three divisions: science and technology, arts, and English.[177] Its broadcasts, varying from thirty to forty-five minutes in length, were presented on Wednesdays and Sundays. Subjects included "Technical Reading," "Lessons on Geography," "literary-musical evenings," health, and English. Currently the People's Television University, originated in Moscow for the national network, offers programs for industrial and agricultural workers with intermediate school education, living in towns and villages.[178] A spokesman for the broadcasting committee said that these aim "at familiarizing viewers with scientific, technical and cultural achievements at home and abroad. Leading Soviet experts and artists help to prepare and also take part in the television university programme, which lasts for two academic years."

Chess lessons may or may not be "educational," but Soviet broadcasters have legitimized the game by coverage on both radio and television. Perhaps the fact that chess is so widely played in the USSR and that the country has won so many international chess tournaments may be determinative. At any rate, during October 1970 I watched several well-produced chess programs. In midevening on October 8, the Leningrad educational channel had a lesson using a large chessboard placed upright on a wall with magnetized chessmen. A "professor" of charming manner and a good sense of humor explained the moves in a way that should be emulated by some of his more academic colleagues. There also have been radio broadcasts about chess.[179] Muscles as well as brains are toned by television, since there are calisthenics for young and old. I found interesting and amusing a Saturday morning program during which three men of different ages did exercises to piano accompaniment while an off-screen voice gave instructions in Ukrainian.

The most sophisticated educational uses of the electronic media take place in Kiev, Leningrad, and Moscow—and for many of the same reasons similar projects have developed in other countries.[180] There are not enough school places to accommodate all applicants. Since only half of all higher school students graduate, some way must be found to salvage the talents of the dropouts. Accordingly, programs are planned to supplement correspondence study and to improve the professional skills of employed workers. Broadcasts give correspondence students an opportunity to equalize their chances with full-time students and with students in night classes. Television may raise the general level of teaching by giving wide exposure to outstanding teachers.

In Kiev the "Extramural Student's Screen" was developed jointly by educators and broadcasters to supplement correspondence and evening classes. Subjects include social studies, history, mathematics, chemistry, physics, English, geography, and the technology of materials; and students have requested an increase in the number of mathematics, physics, and theoretical mechanics programs. Lecturers are chosen "from among the most eminent specialists," according to the director of the project, with regard to "both appearance and erudition."[181] The telecasts usually employ visual aids; and museums, theaters, and assembly halls are brought onto the screen by film. These programs are broadcast evenings between 6:00 and 7:40, each presentation consisting of three half-hour lessons separated by five-minute breaks. They are carried by the local channel in Kiev and by stations in five other Ukrainian cities.

Writing about one set of courses in the project, the director stated that the "Extramural Students' Screen" set out to collect and train gifted young mathematicians. After a severe selection process, 150 pupils were chosen to view 22 telecasts. The 20 most gifted of these were offered advanced training. The director concluded: "It is our conviction that, even if only a few members of the group will become eminent mathematicians in the future, the existence of such televised forms of teaching as that conducted by Ukrainian Television is fully justified."

Viewing is done at home, although there are consultation centers in several local participating universities. Courses are appraised through meetings of teachers, conferences between students and teachers, and letters from viewers. Meetings also are arranged among educational authorities, television personnel, and teachers. Although the report of the director of the project implies success, he does not cite the firm evidence of achievement given in some of the other experiments described below.

The outstanding uses of instructional television in the Soviet Union are provided by Moscow and Leningrad. Direct teaching by television was first introduced into the USSR on September 8, 1965, in Leningrad, and since then has developed rapidly in both cities.[182] During 1964–1965 Leningrad broadcast approximately 180 lectures to supplement high school and college work, though these did not carry credit by themselves. By 1968–1969 the number had grown to 350 early evening broadcasts on mathematics, geometry, physics, and chemistry. Much of the time of the third Leningrad channel is devoted to such material, and about a fifth of the channel's time is used for languages, including English, French, and German.

Instructional television in Moscow emphasizes service to correspondence and evening class students as well as to employed specialists. During each academic year since 1965, there have been approximately 400 hours of such programs, and 480 hours were scheduled for 1968–1969. Current courses cover the history of the Communist party in the Soviet Union, scientific communism, political economy, chemistry, physics, mathematics, geometry, theoretical mechanics, and the resistance of materials. For general adult viewing, "Foreign Languages for You" offers instruction in English, German, and French.

Scheduled during late afternoon and early evening hours, with frequent repeats, these broadcasts are designed to supplement courses taken in technical institutes by full-time students, and hence are not complete in themselves. The number of telecasts per course varies from seventeen to eighty-four, most programs being thirty-five minutes long, although lectures in four series were fifty minutes each. The number of programs varies from series to series: the physics course consisted of eighty-four, the higher mathematics course of eighty-two, and the foreign language courses of thirty-four.[183]

As in the United States and the United Kingdom, special telecasts are presented for professional groups, and for much the same reason: because of the knowledge explosion, the skills of doctors, engineers, and teachers soon become outdated, so that ten years after leaving college, an engineer, for example, is operating at only 50 per cent of his potential.[184] In Moscow in 1970–1971, to improve their working skills and to provide further training for various specialist categories, there were 172 programs for doctors, 69 programs for teachers, and 36 for engineers.[185] The medical programs were organized in cooperation with the Central Institute for the Improvement of Doctors and were widely promoted in medical circles. Physicians enrolled in the courses were relieved of professional obligations during the hours the programs were telecast. Some 1,500 doctors took part in each of the three cycles: cardiovascular diseases; organization of health services; and micropediatry. Almost all the doctors registered successfully completed their courses. Each "Doctors' Corner" program is repeated. I saw a well-done program of this type in Moscow in October 1972. There were filmed scenes from operating theaters, and several physicians used charts and diagrams as they explained the procedures being demonstrated. One of the engineer's courses is a weekly daytime program, "The School for the Engineer," dealing with topics like inventions, labor organization and industrial esthetics.

The director of the Moscow educational channel believes there are three ways to use television. The first is as a supplementary teaching aid, an example being Central Television's foreign language lessons.[186] In the second method, the assignment is divided between television and an educational institution. Thus, "Doctors' Corner" combines theoretical presentations on television with laboratory work in a Moscow clinic. The third approach is total television teaching, with the educational institution providing only books, counseling services, laboratories, and examinations. Moscow experience favors the last of these choices.

The Soviets have given much attention to good teaching on television. The director of educational programs in the Moscow area, Vladimir Klyuchansky, echoes many American educational broadcasters: "But let us not conceal the fact that we still have some programs whose authors merely reproduce ordinary classroom lessons on the screen. The result is monotonous and dull. At the other extreme, in the chase after 'entertainment value' authors sometimes forget that the main purpose is to instruct the students. . . ."[187]

The director of the Leningrad Television Center wrote in much the same vein: "It is a well-known fact that a television lecturer should make the invisible viewer his participant and partner. . . . (A TV lecturer does not deal with scores of students at a time, as it is . . . in colleges of higher studies, but with each viewer individually.) That is the reason why there is a general agreement that a TV lecture requires an element

of dramatization. . . . [The] television screen emphasizes and under-
lines the shortcomings of the lecturer which are not visible in a normal
lecture hall."[188]

But it is not always easy to get the professors to adapt to the medium.
During a meeting in September 1968 in Moscow, Mr. Klyuchansky and
I exchanged anecdotes about the difficulty of persuading professors not
to repeat conventional lectures before the camera. It was clear that problems in Moscow approximate those in Minneapolis. He also observed
that teachers are apt to belittle television as being good mainly for entertainment, despite the fact that Soviet television on the whole is much
more serious than ours.

Soviet writers emphasize the importance of instructional television
being developed cooperatively by educational and television experts.
Although "autonomy of the teachers" is emphasized, there still must be
cooperation.[189] Sometimes owing to basic conservatism, teachers use traditional teaching methods on television, with poor results. But it is
equally bad when television tries to decide matters of pedagogy. In Leningrad, television teachers are chosen competitively by a panel of directors, writers, and subject matter experts.[190] Plans then are made for each
telecourse, with visual materials, models, captions, drawings, films, animation, diagrams, and designs introduced as required. The director of the
Moscow project stressed the importance of providing students with written outlines. Students, he believes, should not take notes, since that
divides their attention between note taking and viewing.

Although there is both individual and group viewing in Leningrad,
only 15 per cent of the extramural students watch at home, partly because other members of their families want to see entertainment broadcasts, a problem encountered by television students in the United States
too.[191] This is one reason viewing rooms have been set up in more than
100 Leningrad factories and business places, and some programs have
been scheduled immediately after closing time. One Soviet telecaster
remarked that these viewing rooms "must become genuine study centers."[192] Usually a knowledgeable discussion leader is present to answer
questions after the programs are finished. Moscow too reports a trend
from individual to group viewing, principally because a consultant then
can be present to answer questions and to lead discussion. Moscow had
about 20 such groups, totaling some 1,500 students.[193]

Consistent efforts are made to appraise these programs. In Leningrad each broadcast is evaluated immediately after transmission by producers and subject matter experts, and all programs are subject to weekly analysis by the editorial staff.[194] Since the introduction of television, the number of students passing from the first to the second year of studies rose from 58 to 80 per cent. In Moscow, when experimental and control groups were compared in 1967–1968, it was found that technical students supplementing day school attendance with evening viewing got slightly higher test scores than did non-viewing students.[195] In Leningrad it was learned that because the target audiences often were young people who had been at school or work all day, only a limited amount of material should be presented, because the students were too tired to follow long concentrated presentations.[196]

Leningrad reported that the instruction of a full-time student by conventional methods costs between 6,000 and 7,000 rubles. (The official exchange rate of the ruble in 1972 was $1.20.) The cost of training an employed evening class student, formerly 4,700 rubles, was lowered to 3,000 rubles with the introduction of television. There are, of course, no tuition charges to students, since all education is supported by the state in the Soviet Union.

The total numbers of viewers are not available. In Leningrad it was found that school programs were among the least popular television broadcasts, being watched by only 3 per cent of the public.[197] However, since extramural students composed less than 3 per cent of all inhabitants anyway, the television producers thought they were doing well. In 1967–1968 Moscow had 6,000 student viewers at home, plus uncounted casual viewers among the general public. Authorities were pleased to report that within a day or two of the announcement of a new series, 10,000 or more copies of the accompanying printed materials might be sold. Furthermore, it was assumed that many students who viewed regularly did not have the materials at all. Enquiries showed that from 30 to 60 per cent of the audience were not extramural students, but engineers, teachers, technicians, and full-time workers, who viewed to supplement other studies or professional activities.

I viewed Soviet educational television in 1968, 1970, and 1972, and noted great improvements over those years. In the summer of 1968 I saw a straightforward geometry lesson for adults, with few gimmicks. After the lecturer was briefly identified on the screen, he disappeared from view and talked for five minutes while the camera showed the blackboard or other visuals. When he returned, though, his manner was pleasant and his personality attractive. Although the general approach was that of an American college closed-circuit lecture, less effort was made to attract and hold viewers than would be normal in the United States.

In 1972 I saw two more mathematics lectures. One was quite conventional, presented by a man who proceeded in typical classroom fashion, alternately writing symbols on a blackboard and talking from behind a desk. The other one showed more production skill, being accompanied by symbols projected directly on the screen as well as written on the blackboard.

The greatest improvement of all was in the area of language lessons. In the summer of 1968 I saw an English lesson for adults built around a scene in which a young man came to dinner with his girl friend's family. Things proceeded quite well, although the acting was stiff. On a Saturday afternoon in Kiev, October 31, 1970, I saw a thirty-minute English lesson during which two middle-aged women presented a formal lesson which combined reading from *Moscow News*, a Soviet English-language newspaper with heavy Communist overtones, and some grammar. There was effective visual presentation of the phrases and sentences discussed. But neither teacher had an attractive television personality, and both spoke heavily accented, though understandable English. This contrasted unfavorably with various foreign lessons from the BBC and East Germany.

But in October 1972 the Moscow educational channel had a well-done "English for You" program. It was opened by a young woman who spoke briefly in Russian and thereafter in English. Most of the program was a simulated tryout for roles in an English-language play. One young lady read a nursery rhyme in both English and Russian, and a group of aspiring "actors" sang American folk songs in both languages. There was some formal drill at the conclusion. All the participants spoke good English, which, though Russian rather than British or American in accent, nevertheless was entirely acceptable.

In Leningrad, on the evening of December 7, 1970, I saw a program prepared by East German television. Following a well-done discussion of the repertoire of several East Berlin theaters, we saw a play which had been prepared in order to teach German. The actors' lines were superimposed at the bottom of the screen, and there was repetition of various phrases. In addition to effective teaching, this program also presented some information about a country friendly to the USSR. Less admirable was a German lesson aired in October 1972, also from East Germany, during which propaganda got in the way of instruction. Film inserts emphasized the achievements of the German Democratic Republic following World War II. But Moscow television did have a well-done French lesson, illustrated with film footage from France. A number of Eastern European countries use teaching material from French television as well as Soviet-prepared inserts for their Russian lessons.

Although Soviet television has its dull and lifeless lecturers, with visuals held so long that one almost forgets the teacher, there is no question that USSR educational productions have improved tremendously during the last several years. This reflects the feeling of Russian educators that educational television has a promising future. In September 1968 the director of Leningrad educational television ended his report to a European meeting of experts on television in continuing education by stating that the medium had great potentialities because of its quality and efficiency as a teaching device, convenience of reception, and low cost.[198] The Moscow report to the same meeting concluded that four things remain to be done: (1) research must be developed, and an experimental approach maintained; (2) reception and utilization should be improved; (3) there must be continuing scientific inquiries into all aspects of television teaching; and (4) the audience must be increased, largely by expanding viewing facilities in schools.

Music

No country has a better record in music than the Soviet Union and its imperial predecessor. In the days of the czars, such Russian composers as Tchaikovsky, Glinka, Rimski-Korsakov, and Musorgski were praised throughout the world. Rachmaninoff and Stravinsky began their careers under the old regime and after World War I moved to the West, finally settling in the United States. Despite recurring differences between artists and political leaders, the USSR has had composers like Khachaturian, Prokofiev, and Shostakovich; pianists on the order of Richter and Gilels; violinists such as the Oistrakhs and Kogan; and cellists like Rostropovich. Russian ballet and opera have won worldwide recognition. The folk music of this country of many nationalities has survived in its original form at the same time that it has inspired many composers of concert works. There also is a light music repertoire, although it has not achieved the world acceptance of that produced in the United Kingdom and the United States.

Why this high premium on the arts and willingness to support them lavishly, despite relatively low living standards and shortages of consumer goods? Partly tradition: czars and rulers under whatever name, together with their courts and the upper classes, placed a high value on the arts, and this practice has been continued, with the important change that what was limited to the few now is available at low cost to the many.

It is significant to recall that Lenin, in the early months of the Revolution, ordered that museums, art collections, and the like be preserved. These were wise instructions, since the illiterate peasants and workers upon whom fell the brunt of the fighting probably did not appreciate such things and associated them with the state, the church, the landowners, and the other groups and institutions which had joined forces to oppress them.

Then there is the great appreciation of things of the mind and spirit. Christianity and Christ have been replaced by party and Lenin, but dedication to an ideal and to a spiritual leader remains—even though application may not always match theory. The benefits of education have been extended enormously, along with insistence that the rewards of modern technology be available to all. If the objective is the best of everything for everybody, then the performing arts are part of the national heritage to be shared. Westerners criticize the economic theories and political practices of the socialist countries, and disapprove of their ideological uses of the arts. Furthermore, concert and opera repertoires are on the conservative side, one reason being government dictation of composition styles. But nevertheless, concerts, operas, and ballets are well done and widely enjoyed. It comes as no surprise, therefore, to find extensive coverage of music by radio and television.

An article published in 1960 summarized what probably still are the principal objectives for music broadcasts in the Soviet Union.[199] Political assignments are foremost: "We find that the most important task of the musical department is to propagate, by means of music, those contemporary ideas which dominate the Soviet people and which determine the basis of our life. These are the ideas of struggle for constructing a Communist Society; the struggle for peace and friendship between peoples; the ideas of Soviet patriotism and the spiritual development of the Soviet people."

Although few Western writers would endorse the use of music for political ends, most of the other objectives listed by the author would be accepted almost anywhere. The basic task "results from the great mission of television to educate the social consciousness, to be of help in the cultural education of the viewers and to form their aesthetical taste." Television should bring its audiences the musical heritage of the past. "The popularization of the classical heritage of Russian and world musical culture is the most important task of musical programmes."*

Similar viewpoints were expressed by the director of music broadcasts in 1963: "The tasks faced by the workers of our department are complex and responsible: to seek new forms of musical broadcasts in order to make the music of the peoples of the USSR more accessible, to propagate Russian classical music and Soviet music among all the peoples of the USSR, to deal regularly with the whole musical culture of our country, to strengthen contact with life, to establish close contact with artistic organizations and listeners, to fully satisfy the ever increasing demands of the builders of the communist society."[200]

With music as with education, the media are expected to bring the advantages of metropolitan centers to outlying rural areas. Commentator A. Yakovlev wrote in 1965: "Until recently only residents of big cities could watch opera. The remainder of the population knew opera music only from the radio and could not watch opera. This year the Central TV studio organized a series entitled 'Getting Acquainted with Opera.' Productions of opera classics by the best theatres appeared on the blue screen. The studio, newspapers and magazines received many letters of gratitude, many of them from villages and small towns. It is noteworthy that there was an increase, not a drop, in opera attendance in the cities from which the productions were broadcast."[201] In 1970, Novosti published the story of a woman living in a small village far north of the Arctic Circle who had never been to a large city nor had seen a professional opera company, and yet had developed a love of opera from listening to the radio.[202]

Although complete figures are not available, there is much music on both radio and television. In 1959 the main ingredient of All-Union

---

* This statement is remarkably similar to one published fifteen years earlier by a Soviet writer who referred to the "task of familiarizing the radio listener with contemporary music of the Union as well as the classical music and the music of foreign composers" (Ziglin, p. 66).

Radio was music, and each month Moscow broadcast up to 2,000 concert programs.[203] An analysis of the three radio services then on the air listed their respective music percentages as 47.7, 70.1, and 87.9, the third program being mainly a classical music service.[204] In the early 1960s there were more than forty hours a day of music on All-Union Radio; by 1965 this had grown to sixty-seven hours and thirty-four minutes; and in 1970 it reached sixty-eight hours.[205] About 65 per cent of all radio programs now are music, and of these 40 per cent are of serious and 60 per cent of light music. Some 18 per cent of the Central Television output is music, including light music, musical films, full-length concerts, and operas.

Music is distributed among all the radio services, national and local. The Soviet Union does not have the equivalent of the France Musique network, the individual "good music" stations in many American cities, or day-long music programs in lighter vein, except for the Mayak network. On Mayak, approximately forty-five minutes of each hour consists mainly of middle-of-the-road music plus a rather strange combination of jazz and concert music, together with news and information on the hour and half hour. Typical program titles might include "State Music by Soviet Composers," "Foreign Movie Music," "Morning Melodies," "Instrumental Music," "Light Music," and "Dances."[206]

Both the radio and television sides of Central Broadcasting have music departments.[207] In 1965 the Chief Editorial Board of Musical Broadcasting for Radio was subdivided into sections for concert, symphonic, and chamber music; theater and operetta music; popular music; music of the people; amateur productions; music abroad; and music education. There also were divisions for the record library, music library, and music production. Television is divided in much the same way.

Broadcasting resources include the Bolshoi Symphony Orchestra, which also plays for the Bolshoi Opera and Ballet; the Opera Symphony Orchestra; the Theatre Orchestra; the Orchestra of Native Songs; vocal soloists; and many free-lance instrumental soloists and accompanists. These groups contribute to both radio and television, and also present concerts in Moscow and elsewhere. In addition, there are broadcasts on both radio and television, live and by recordings, of public concerts by all sorts of musical organizations and soloists. The country's best artists and entertainers are heard and seen regularly.

An article in *Izvestia* in 1962 complained about the inadequate phonograph record library.[208] Although there were 80,000 titles, library growth and replacement were inadequate. There then were no Beethoven symphonies conducted by Toscanini; not enough recordings of Wagner's *Ring of the Nibelung*; few performances by Egon Petri, Alfred Cortot, Fritz Kreisler, and Jascha Heifetz; and only a few recordings by Dietrich Fischer-Dieskau, Boris Christoff, Maria Callas, and Renata Tebaldi. The record library of All-Union Radio, said *Izvestia*, should be in the same category as the Lenin Library (the Soviet equivalent of the Library of Congress). It should be stocked with all the records made in the country as well as the best from abroad. The editor of the Department of Musical Broadcasts wrote in 1963 that there were difficulties "in connection with the very slow renewal of the supply of musical recordings." Local recordings frequently were unsatisfactory, and there were poor contacts with record companies.[209]

Like all broadcasters, those in the Soviet Union face the problem of audiences with different tastes.[210] It was found "that people of various ages, professions and cultural levels have various and often conflicting claims and wishes with regard to musical programmes." Some want television to entertain them, while others seek intellectual stimulation and education. However this may be, the musical fare on Soviet radio and television runs the gamut from great masterpieces to current popular selections.

During a typical week, there are radio broadcasts of music by composers of all nationalities.[211] In 1959 Central Radio had 600 concerts of "classical music," and that output level probably still is maintained.[212] One point of emphasis is the performance of little-known compositions by great composers. For example, some unpublished compositions by Tchaikovsky were heard for the first time on Soviet radio in 1958. But there also are many standard works, such as those presented on "A Panorama of 20th Century Operas," which included compositions by Rimski-Korsakov, Puccini, Richard Strauss, Bartók, Kodály, Ravel, de Falla, Schönberg, Janaček, Berg, Martinů, and Szymanowski.[213] In addition to music by such outstanding twentieth-century Eastern European composers as Prokofiev, Miaskovsky, Glière, Shostakovich, Khachaturian, Penderecki, and Kabalevsky, there also are works by Vladigherov, Stolanov, Pipkov, Koutev, Goleminov, Marinov, Raitchev, Eisler, Meier, Kokhan, Dessau, Schwein, Gerster, Zechlin, Wieber, Szabó, Mihály, Dimitresco, Profeta, Popovitch, Lutaslawski, and Berté.

A favorite program device is the commemoration of anniversaries. In 1961 there were special programs in the Ukraine to observe the 160th anniversary of the birth of Franz Liszt.[214] The cycle "underlined the fact that . . . the great Hungarian musician visited the Ukraine several times and liked to listen to Ukrainian music." The following year the 120th anniversary of the birth and 50th anniversary of the Ukrainian composer Nikolai Lysenko were observed in special programs.*

There also is a large amount of concert music on television. Operas arranged for studio production have included works by Arensky, Bizet, Borodin, Glazunov, Gounod, Offenbach, Rimski-Korsakov, Tchaikovsky, and Verdi.[215] There are direct relays from opera houses and concert halls.

It is not surprising to find emphasis on patriotic subjects. One survey of musical broadcasts mentions some "unjustly forgotten works written by Soviet authors," including the Fourth Symphony by Kniper, about a Komsomol fighter.[216] Ukrainian radio broadcast the cantata by Danjkevich called "The Star of Communism Is above Us," as well as "National Holiday" by Borisov.[217] There was a song by an unnamed composer dedicated to Yuri Gagarin, the first Soviet cosmonaut. A tractor driver on a collective farm was the author of a composition for accordion entitled "The Virgin Soil."[218] Some of these compositions were the consequence of "a surge of creative activity among Ukrainian composers" inspired by the upcoming Twenty-third Congress of the Communist party. The Music Department makes its plans on a year-long basis with special reference to anniversaries and public events.[219] Special music was scheduled for the 50th anniversary of the Revolution, the 50th anniversary of the founding of the Young Communist League, and the Lenin centenary.

The world's first demonstration of electronic music, according to Soviet sources, was given in Moscow in 1921 by L. S. Termen.[220] Later Termen played his Etherophone (or Termenovox) in Berlin, London, and New York. In 1958 an electronic instrument invented by A. A. Volodin won a gold medal at the Brussels exhibition.[221] This "Ekvodin Model V-11," with a range of seven octaves, had 600 possible tone combinations. Up to 1963, fourteen types of electronic instruments had been

---

* OIRT Information 1962/9, pp. 7–10; OIRT Information 1963/4, p. 14. Nikolai V. Lysenko lived from 1842 to 1912. After being justice of the peace in the Kiev district (1864–1866), he studied music in Leipzig and later worked with Rimski-Korsakov in St. Petersburg. An ardent nationalist, he utilized Ukrainian melodies in some of his compositions.

produced in the Soviet Union. These were used to provide background music for plays and films, and in other situations where special music and sound effects were required.

Both radio and television have music appreciation programs.[222] "How to Understand Music" presented information about melody, harmony, and counterpoint, with both classical and contemporary illustrations. There were dramatized treatments of the lives of the great composers, including two programs about Beethoven, each lasting an hour and a quarter; two for Grieg; and single programs dealing with Paganini, Haydn, Miaskovsky, Sibelius, Schubert, and Rossini.

With music as with other educational presentations, Soviet broadcasters like to challenge and test the audience. The series "An Hour of Music for Young People" ended with a description of a composition which listeners were asked to name. Selections are played without introductory announcements, and the audience is asked to identify them. Folk music is performed on native instruments, with listeners challenged to identify music, instruments, and performers. One such program elicited more than 12,000 letters.

Prominent composers discuss the music of their countries in programs running from forty-five minutes to an hour, including musical examples.[223] One series presented spokesmen from East Germany, Czechoslovakia, Finland, Japan, the United Kingdom, France, Switzerland, and the United States. Americans taking part included Samuel Barber, Alan Lomax, and Aaron Copland.

Television too has music appreciation. "Introduction to Musical Instruments" took up the sections of the symphony orchestra in turn.[224] There also are programs about such national instruments as the accordion and balalaika. "Musical Dictionary" dealt with terms like "concerto," "serenade," and "tarantella." Television has musical quizzes along with programs on such topics as "V. I. Lenin's Favorite Music" and the history of revolutionary songs.

Public symphonic, operetta, and ballet performances often are broadcast on radio and television, either live or from recordings.[225] In June 1965 I attended the premiere of a new choreography of Stravinsky's *Rite of Spring* in the Bolshoi Theater in Moscow and observed cameras recording the performance, which I saw on television several evenings later, together with a discussion of the ballet and an interview with the prima ballerina.*

Complementing broadcasts of concerts are public presentations by the radio and television musical organizations. In the early 1960s the Ukrainian Radio Symphony Orchestra and Song Ensemble were giving up to twenty-three concerts a year in factories and palaces of culture.[226] As an example of the repertoires, at a concert for workers in a carriage repair factory, the orchestra played the overture from Lysenko's opera *Taras Bulba*, selections from Tchaikovsky's *Swan Lake*, and Enesco's First Romanian Rhapsody. The State Choir of Lithuanian Radio and Television gives performances throughout the country.[227] One was presented on the 100th anniversary of the birth of Lenin.

With music as with other program areas, there are production faults. In 1960 a Moscow producer pointed out that since it is not possible to show effectively a whole orchestra on a television screen, it is essential to put on camera the center of musical interest.[228] "The best way is when the mounting of pictures coincides precisely with the movements of the conductor's baton and switches over to this or that group of instruments at the moment before they start performing. Such a presentation of the orchestra requires a perfect knowledge of the score according to which the pictures are then made. . . . It is extremely important that the main producer of the telecast be a musician, who knows the score, the beginning and the end of a musical thought, and the character of the transition from one piece to another."†

But after viewing many Soviet telecasts, I concluded that music production standards are quite uneven, even though sound pickups are good. In Leningrad on October 1, 1970, I saw a concert on the national television network which included Franz Schubert's "The Shepherd on the Rock" for soprano, clarinet, and piano, followed by some piano solos and

* Although the Bolshoi Theater, completed in 1824, must assign television cameras to boxes at the sides or back of the auditorium, buildings like the Palace of Congresses, completed in 1961, have permanent camera positions.

† After producing some telecasts by the Minneapolis Symphony Orchestra in Minneapolis in 1953, I wrote in much the same vein: "Throughout this series the musical content of the selections being telecast, rather than the pictorial possibilities of the instruments playing, determined the production techniques used. Television served musical objectives, and technique never became an end in itself. Thus, there were no harp-violin supers or other pretty trick shots without musical justification" (Paulu, "Televising the Minneapolis Symphony Orchestra," *Quarterly of Film, Radio and Television* 8:2 (Winter 1953), p. 160).

a selection for a small orchestra. Neither performance nor production was up to the standards one would expect on either the national television service of the Soviet Union or a local channel in its second city. In Moscow on October 17, 1970, there was a live telecast of a concert by a male choir and the All-Union Radio and Television Orchestra, during which the camera work was stiff and often unrelated to musical substance.

On the other hand, in Kiev on October 25, 1970, on "Pages from Beethoven's Life," a woman read material about Beethoven against a background of recordings from the *Eroica* Symphony and other compositions. At times a split screen showed a juxtaposition of the woman reading and photographs of Beethoven. Then came a performance of a Beethoven piano sonata. On this program considerable thought and effort achieved a good combination of pictures and sound to produce an effective telecast. On the Moscow local channel on October 4, 1972, an attractive woman announcer introduced some Beethoven and Schubert selections played by a male pianist formally dressed in white tie and tails. Performance was good and camera work acceptable, although quiet and routine. Several days before, however, I saw a program which ran well over sixty minutes, during which a man—apparently a famous singer now past his prime—appeared as both singer and interviewee. Fifteen or twenty minutes of this might have been worthwhile, but as a program on the national channel, it was much too long and would have benefited from cutting and editing.

At noon in Kiev on Saturday, October 31, 1970, I saw a telecast of Puccini's *Madame Butterfly* that had been recorded in the Kiev opera house before an audience. The performance was good. Several evenings before I had seen Bizet's *Carmen* well done in the same theater. However, absolutely no concessions were made to television, and so the results were only fair. During an early evening hour on the same day, there was a program by a choir from Lvov. Although the choir wore attractive Ukrainian costumes, the effect was static, since the camera panned over the choristers as they stood in rows. At one point a male soloist, though clearly heard, was not seen on the screen.*

---

* There was reference above, in the section on documentaries (pp. 122–123) to the telecast which showed Van Cliburn winning the Tchaikovsky prize. In that program there was such poor synchronization between pictures and sound as to suggest that the editors had tried to match a silent film recording of the performance with an entirely different sound track.

Much local and folk music is broadcast in all parts of the country.[229] In Tashkent I heard Uzbek music with a pronounced oriental sound, quite different from what one hears in either Moscow or Minneapolis. With its many nationalities and languages, of course, the USSR has a tremendous range of native music. In 1963 Central Radio scheduled five hours of "Music of the Peoples of the USSR" each day and on the first national network featured the music of the various republics in turn on Saturdays and Sundays, with special reference to anniversaries and local events.[230]

Kiev organized a "National Philharmony," with 2,000 amateurs who gave concerts in factories and farms as well as on radio and television.[231] At one time Kiev radio regularly transmitted concerts by fifty amateur Ukrainian symphony orchestras.[232] Lithuanian radio and television report with pride that they have popularized folklore by broadcasting it for over twenty years and that they have brought it to audiences abroad through Intervision.[233] In Moscow I have seen both network and local programs based on national folk dances and music.

In 1960 the State Committee for Radio and Television reported that each month All-Union Radio presented some 500 programs "consisting of works from the mass entertainment media (stage, operetta, song)."[234] Then as now, Soviet radio and television had many programs of light music. As was pointed out above, of the 65 per cent of all radio programs that are music, 60 per cent consist of light music.[235] There are such programs on the national networks, local radio, and television. The City Department for Culture in Vilnius cooperated with the Lithuanian Radio and Television Committee to organize "The Towers of Vilnius" competition to discover the best young interpreters of "variety songs," the winners later appearing in Moscow.[236] In 1970 more than 8,000 and in 1971 some 12,000 listeners and viewers took part in the poll that chose the winners.

Staff members responsible for popular music broadcasts are subject to special party and government instructions, although the current broadcast repertoire includes much music that would not have been approved by the spokesmen of ten years ago. In 1962 the Communist Party Central Committee, writing under the title "On Measures for the Further Improvement of the Work of Radio and Television Broadcasting," stated: "Weaknesses in the ideological-political and artistic treatment of materials and production have penetrated into the programs; in fact, there has been enthusiasm for modernistic, jazz music, intended for Philistine tastes. Radio and television contributes insufficiently to the spreading of good aesthetic tastes."[237]

It is not surprising, therefore, that the chief editor of musical broadcasts for Central Television remarked that it was difficult to devise programs of popular music "because we must protect our youth against evil influences, banality, decadent moods, naturalism, vulgarity, and erotic lyricism."[238] Dance telecasts, he said, must avoid "exaggerated twisting of the hips, an unnatural stance with the legs astride, and . . . erotic movements," and he quoted with approval—this was in 1964—a statement by Nikita Khrushchev: "We are for melodious music which moves human souls . . . music without melody cannot arouse anything but irritation." The editor also condemned the banality of popular song texts, a subject of complaint in all parts of the world: "Composers and poets writing songs full of the spirit of decadency, inconsolable langour, endless repetition of the theme of unrequited love, and cheap lyricism have been sharply criticized."

Although jazz and contemporary music fans in the USSR buy records when they can and listen to foreign radio programs, Soviet popular music differs from that in West Germany, the United Kingdom, and the United States. Soviet musicians often tape record short-wave broadcasts—the Voice of America Russian service has a daily fifteen-minute program called "Music for Recording," which is one reason that their performances are beginning to sound more like those in the West.

Whereas the music in Soviet hotels and other entertainment spots used to consist mainly of the show tunes of two or three decades ago, I noticed in 1970 and especially in 1972 changes toward the Western pattern. Among other things, amplifiers made the music loud—or too loud, depending on one's preferences. Nevertheless, it is still true that a tourist, tuning across the radio dial in his Moscow hotel room and finding a program of popular music such as he is used to hearing at home, is more apt to be listening to Warsaw, Budapest, Bucharest, or the Voice of America than to a domestic Soviet station. What does turn up is sometimes amusing. One evening in Moscow I heard "Hello Dolly!" sung in English by a deep-voiced Russian with a heavy accent.

There are many exchanges with foreign countries, both East and West.[239] Soviet radio uses tapes from the standard music festivals in Czechoslovakia, Norway, Finland, Yugoslavia, and elsewhere. Exchanges are conducted more systematically, however, with the socialist countries. The director of musical broadcasts for Central Television referred to Intervision exchanges as something "whose significance can hardly be exaggerated."[240] Such programs are of importance not only for their artistic contributions but also for "their support of the cause of communist education of the people."

In 1963 Ukrainian radio had a whole week of music from the German Democratic Republic, with emphasis on contemporary composers, including Kurt Schwaen, Hanns Eisler, Günter Heitman, Gerd Schlotter, Hans-Georg Görner, and Ottmar Gerster.[241] The exchange had its ideological aspects too, since this "week of the Musical Art of the German Democratic Republic" described "the successes of German workers and farmers in building-up their economy and culture." The following year Ukrainian radio had cycles of music from Poland ("Szymanowski in Russia"); Bulgaria ("Bulgarian Songs on Russia," described as "a musical poem on the unbreakable friendship between the two brotherly Slavonic peoples"); Hungary ("The Song of Peace," performed by a children's choir); Czechoslovakia; and Romania ("The Danube Carries Blue Waves, the Danube Carries Songs").[242]

None of the Intervision programs I saw, however, were propaganda. In the summer of 1966, Intervision relayed a Eurovision feed from La Scala in Milan. The singing was in Italian, although there were intermission explanations in Russian. In October 1970 I watched a well-produced symphony concert from Berlin, as well as another German presentation featuring Beethoven's Second Symphony, during which a three-man panel discussed the music, with illustrations from recordings plus an occasional piano theme. The German-language commentary, held at a low level in the background, was accompanied by a simultaneous translation.

Some American music is broadcast. There was reference above to appearances by Samuel Barber, Alan Lomax, and Aaron Copland on a series dealing with the music of foreign countries. In 1963 Ukrainian radio broadcast performances by Pete Seeger, "who sang 'The Way of Freedom,' the song of the unemployed 'All That I Want,' the folk songs 'Keith Jones' and 'Deep Sea,' negro songs 'Joshua' and 'Lullaby,' the Russian song 'The Moon Is Shining' and many others."[243]

In November 1958, as a member of an American exchange delegation, I took part in a 4½-hour meeting in Kiev with the president of the Ukrainian Radio and Television Committee. In the course of our discussion, which ranged over many aspects of broadcasting in the Soviet Union and the United States, he read with considerable pride a carefully prepared list of Ukrainian broadcasts of American music. He mentioned recordings by the New York Philharmonic and Philadelphia orchestras, Mario Lanza and Leonard Warren, plus selections by Gershwin and other American composers. All told, it was a convincing list of American music, composers, and performers. Since the implication of his statement was that they did much better by us than we did by them, I reviewed at some length the way American stations—particularly educational stations, since in 1958 there were few commercial good music stations—treated Russian composers and artists. But our host was not pleased with my one-upmanship!*

The data available, although interesting, do not provide comprehensive information about audience reactions. During 1958 the All-Union Radio music office received more than 200,000 letters from listeners in all parts of the country.[244] Most pertained to the thirty-five request programs presented each month, although letters are not a scientifically valid method of audience measurement. A 1961 publication told of a letter from "a group of listeners . . . against broadcasting serious music."[245] In response the broadcasting authorities scheduled a cycle of broadcasts, "An Hour of Music for Young People," featuring discussions of serious and light music, in which several composers participated.

In connection with Radio Day 1961, a 1,700-word article dealing with various aspects of Soviet broadcasting criticized musical programs.[246] "It is impossible not to notice how many trivial, primitive and sometimes simply vulgar things make their way into artistic programs. Good concerts composed with great taste are rarely heard on the first program in the evening hours. Music over the radio is often 'served up' in the form of brief introductions, 'musical interludes' and background music for spoken programs. There is no well conceived and well worked-out system for artistic education of the people over the radio through the propaganda of the best works of music, literature, and theater."

The next year *Izvestia* complained that in tuning across the dial a listener might go from a "magnificent Arturo Toscanini recording" to a

---

* He played us recordings of a Mozart symphony by a Ukrainian orchestra and of a Khachaturian ballet suite by an amateur group to demonstrate the excellence of Ukrainian musical organizations. It should be noted that many of the footnote references above are to Ukrainian examples.

"mediocre fantasia from bad operettas." Or, from a Beethoven sonata or beautiful Russian song to "the most boring potpourri for an orchestra of folk instruments."* The article stated that although the first radio network presented about eight hours of music every day, it was broken up into brief fragments as fillers between other broadcasts, the periods being too short to present complete major works. The author sounded like some critics of American commercial broadcasting in the pre-FM days: "There are days when a music lover . . . must wait until half past twelve at night; only then can he hear really wonderful compositions excellently performed in their entirety." Therefore, he concluded, the whole schedule should be reorganized so that music can be presented at better times and in larger blocks.

In 1965 there were criticisms of the new Mayak network. The magazine *Sovetska a muzyka* published a letter complaining that Mayak and some other stations broadcast too many excerpts from operettas and "unaspiring hit tunes of five years' vintage."[247] To this *Izvestia* replied that listeners need light as well as serious music and that in any case the two types of music are not mutually exclusive.[248]

In 1968 a 3,300-word article in *Ogonoyok* complained that those in charge of music broadcasts "do not always show a sufficient sense of responsibility, as witness the preponderance of light music in radio and television broadcasts. Mayak, our most popular radio station for music, offers mostly variety and dance music."[249] Not that the author was opposed to light music, but when it "practically displaces classical music it becomes detrimental to the development of good musical taste." Too much loud and dissonant music, he continued, can become a form of torture: "The press has already carried reports of the use of music for such purposes by the C.I.A. and the F.B.I." He also complained about jazz arrangements of popular classics.

Several months later the same magazine published twelve letters in reply, ten favoring and two opposing the critic's point of view.[250] One letter said: "The article was, if anything, too mild." Referring to the Sochi song festival on television, another writer stated that "it was embarrassing

---

* I. Nestyev, "Culture: Music on the Radio," *Izvestia*, August 5, 1962, p. 2, translated in CDSP 14:32 (September 5, 1962), p. 30. Ten years later, in 1972, I was surprised by the wide range of music on Mayak and by the abrupt transitions from one style of composition to another. During a single day I heard Rachmaninoff's Rhapsody on a Theme of Paganini for piano and orchestra, recent popular music, folk music, and much middle-of-the-road music.

to . . . watch singers in short skirts wiggle their hips." Another writer complained about a singer who sang Bach "in a cacophonic jazz arrangement." But one correspondent declared: "The article criticizes the young people in our country and all over the world. What is music supposed to give people? Everyone is sick and tired of all the symphony music, folk music and 17th and 18th century chamber music that fills the air."

Literature, Drama, and Entertainment

There are relatively few entertainment programs on Soviet radio and television, except for films, light music, and sports. An official analysis in 1959 assigned 9.6 per cent of network radio time to "literary-dramatic" programs, but nothing to light entertainment or sports, unless they were included in the 53.3 per cent ascribed to music or the 2.4 per cent not accounted for.[251] A 1964 UNESCO report, based on Soviet data, described 9 per cent of the radio output as "literature and drama," but contained no light entertainment category, and 1965 figures from the State Committee for Radio and Television did not list entertainment at all.[252] The UNESCO report also stated that Moscow Central Television devoted 22 per cent of its time to films, 19 per cent to literature and drama, and 18 per cent to music. The State Committee reported in 1965 that from 30 to 35 per cent of television time was occupied by fiction, art, spectacles, entertainment, opera, ballet, and drama, and 20 per cent by films.

One American observer, analyzing the programs on the two Moscow channels from January through June 1960, found that their combined output included 20.0 per cent film, 11.4 per cent plays, 10.8 per cent sports, and 10.5 per cent miscellaneous.[253] In 1965 a Soviet writer, after some intensive television viewing, calculated the proportion of television entertainment programs to be from 6 to 7 per cent, which he regarded as too low to achieve the "synthetic relaxation of which modern television claims a monopoly."[254] Currently, cinema films compose 13.2 per cent of national television, dramatic programs 9.2 per cent, and documentary films 6.6 per cent. Sports make up 8.5 per cent and music about 18 per cent of the output, of which a good share probably is entertainment material.[255] However, my impression after hearing and viewing radio and television during six trips to the USSR is that the Soviet situation is the reverse of ours: whereas we have too much light entertainment—probably more than the public wants, and certainly more than it needs—they do not have enough.

One basic reason for minimizing entertainment is the consistent policy of emphasizing ideological content, even within light entertainment formats. A Soviet article in 1935 pointed out that broadcasts for collective farms gave consideration "to contemporary literature which deals with agriculture," at the same time that they "acquaint the radio audience with the life of the Russian in the past."[256] Twenty-five years later the State Committee wrote about radio broadcasts of the best from "the multinational literature of the USSR," along with "works by progressive writers from capitalist countries."[257] At that time literary programs dealt with such subjects as "Writers on Communist Labor," "At the Building Projects of the Seven Year Plan," "Heroes of Our Time," "The Plowed Virgin Land," and "They Fought for the Homeland."

There were broadcasts of works by contemporary authors from Albania, Bulgaria, Czechoslovakia, East Germany, North Korea, Romania, Mongolia, and North Vietnam.[258] These were supplemented by programs about "present-day progressive writers from capitalist countries," including "A Song in Chains," dealing with "the struggle of the people in Portuguese colonies against their oppressors"; "The Poets of Black Africa," which was "saturated with anger and hate towards colonists"; as well as "Freedom for the Homeland!" described as "a bold statement made to the French colonizers by the literary workers of fighting Algeria." A radio piece based on the poetry of black writers in the United States was entitled "The Black and White Worlds Will Become One World."

By 1959 the Radio University of Literature and Art was presenting two-year lecture cycles on Russian literature and art from the fourteenth to the twentieth century, plus programs on literature and art abroad.[259] These broadcasts included talks about and readings of domestic literature from many parts of the USSR: Armenia, Byelorussia, Dagestan, Estonia, Georgia, Karelia, Kalmykin, Kazakhstan, Komi, Latvia, Lithuania, Tadzhikistan, and the Ukraine. Here, as with music and other subjects, there were discussions with authors and quizzes for audiences of all ages. In 1971 the USSR broadcast eleven types of radio programs dealing with literature, including dramatized excerpts from stories and novels by Soviet authors; broadcasts about new books; serial readings from Soviet classics; broadcasts about the revolutionary theater; readings from poets in socialist countries; and talks in which foreign socialist writers gave their impressions of the Soviet Union.[260]

Television proceeds in much the same way, with thirty- and sixty-minute programs bearing such titles as "Literary Panorama," "Talks about Literature," and "Poetry."[261] There also are book reviews, literary news, and other presentations dealing with Russian literature, actors, and theater. On a Saturday afternoon in September 1972, I was much impressed by "What's On at the Theater." After an opening montage of theater marquees and lobbies, there followed scenes from plays and interviews with actors and theater audiences. The program was well tied together by the anchor woman, who also conducted some of the interviews.

There always are poetry programs. One report stated: "Large literary presentations are devoted to the creativity of poets," including Aseyv, Bagritskiy, Bednyy, Blok, Brusov, Kazin, Lugovskiy, Mayakovski, Tikhonov, Yesenin, and others.[262] Byelorussian radio began its poetry programs in 1936 and since December 1964 has had a regular series called "Poetry," of which the director said: "Poetry is a radio natural."[263] In March 1961 there were programs nationally and in his native province of the Ukraine to observe the centennial of the death of Taras Shevchenko. His poetry was read, his dramas aired, and musical settings of his poetry, including some by the Ukrainian composer Nikolai Lysenko, were broadcast. (For the Lysenko anniversaries, see above, page 157.) In accordance with the usual ideological emphasis, it was pointed out that Shevchenko's poetry exposed "the landlordship and serfdom of czarist Russia, rousing the people to fight against oppressors."[264] On October 4, 1972, on national television, I saw a program of readings from poetry by Mayakovski. This effectively produced film first showed a book resting on a table. A hand opened the book, after which the camera pulled back for a shot of the actor who commented on and read from Mayakovski's works. This program was allocated forty-five minutes on national television one evening at 9:30.

In the Soviet Union as in other countries—the United Kingdom, for example—early radio dramas often were live pickups from theaters. But since these programs sometimes ran from 3½ to 4 hours, they soon were presented in condensed versions, "suitable under the conditions of radio broadcasting."[265] Then came studio presentations of dramatic works, dramatizations of novels and other literature, and finally plays written especially for radio. Through the years, a wide range of literature has been transmitted, extending from works by world-famous authors to productions by writers known only in the USSR. As elsewhere in Europe, radio drama has continued into the television era, and there still are many dramatic presentations, some originated in Moscow for nationwide distribution, and others produced in outlying areas in local languages.

The Lithuanian SSR has devoted much attention to radio drama. Some of its programs have emphasized patriotic themes.[266] One play told the story of a man "who spent 20 years in the prisons of bourgeois Lithuania," and another spoke of the feelings shared by the Lithuanian proletariat and Russian, Polish, and German revolutionaries. In 1971 Lithuania organized a festival of radio plays drawing upon all parts of the Soviet Union.[267] Scripts also are exchanged with other socialist countries.

Television drama too had its proscenium arch period. Originally there were relays from theaters or studios with little or no adaptation. Then came television versions of theatrical works and finally plays written especially for television, although there still are direct pickups from theaters. The first television drama was *Pavel Grekov,* performed by actors of the Theater of the Revolution in Moscow.[268] A history of USSR television remarked that during the early 1950s "the opinion was that television was exclusively a means of broadcasting productions created by other art forms. . . . It should, however, be pointed out that after television developed, this view began to correspond less and less to reality. Long years of practical experience were needed in order finally to refute the acceptance of the so-called transport function of television which is true only during the state of its initial development." The first remote telecast in the Soviet Union—a Moscow soccer game on June 29, 1949—led to live transmissions from the Bolshoi and other theaters in Central Moscow. At the end of 1951 the play "Truth Is Good but Happiness Is Better" was recorded on film in the Maly Theater in Moscow, and thereafter various public presentations were recorded for television.

Until 1958 most television drama consisted of adaptations of theater plays, but then theaters began to regard television as a competitor and objected to their plays being telecast, despite a ruling that television should have free access to their material.[269] All this encouraged the writing of plays for television and incidentally led to improved production standards. But in 1969 the director of television drama in Byelorussia concluded that in Intervision countries generally there were too few television plays and that those available often were of poor quality. He further regretted that the best plays often were adaptations of theatrical pieces or dramatizations of novels.[270] He concluded that "tomorrow belongs to works written especially for television." He also told about dramatizing a novel describing the building of socialism in a village. A prize-winning play dealt with "the distribution of land in the Byelorussian village in the post-revolutionary period of the twenties and the irreconcilable fight against the kulaks." Several years earlier a *Pravda* review of a television drama about crimes committed by the czars' ministers said: "On the eve of the 50th anniversary of the Great October Revolution millions of viewers saw a television play helping them to understand better some of the reasons resulting in the inevitable fall of czarism."

In addition to seeing some drama on the air, I have watched rehearsals in the Moscow television studios. While it obviously is impossible for anyone to judge the fine points of a production in an unfamiliar language, my overall impressions were good. Studios, control rooms, lighting boards, and all the rest were elaborate; settings were attractive; the actors appeared to be highly competent—I was told they were among the nations' best; and the whole procedure appeared very professional. In view of the excellent record of USSR drama and film, and the increasing availability of fine studio facilities (see pp. 75–76), Soviet television drama soon should rank with the best.[271]

The first cinema film broadcast in the Soviet Union was "A Great Synonym," transmitted on March 25, 1938.[272] By 1964, 30 or 40 per cent of Moscow television consisted of cinema or television films. These included historical series with such titles as "History of the World Film Art," "Film and the Spectator," and "The Film Panorama." Currently Central Television airs about 700 hours of films each year, and motion picture appreciation programs are standard features. As indicated above, about 20 per cent of national network programs are films. Cinema films cannot be telecast for periods varying from a month to a year after their theater release, depending upon the republic originating the program. There is little or no delay for documentaries, however. Television is not charged for the use of cinema films.

At present Central Television receives films from its own studios; from television studios elsewhere in the country; from motion picture studios; by exchange and joint production with other socialist countries; and through purchases from Western countries. The first film made originally for television in the Soviet Union was "The Riddle of NFI," produced by Andronikov in 1958.[273] The next year "The Witch," based on a story by Chekhov, received a prize at an international television festival. In 1962, twenty-five television films were produced, including "The Cuban Novel," "Mozart and Salieri," "Aesop," and "The Taming of the Shrew." In 1963 Soviet telefilms received international awards at Monte Carlo and Cannes. Reflecting the growth of amateur film making, USSR television also shows many films by amateurs.

On the whole, however, the production of films for television has lagged badly. Clearly, it began late. The first Soviet television serial, "We Called Down Fire upon Ourselves," describing guerrilla activities in the rear of the German army during World War II, was produced in 1965.[274] A Soviet critic pointed out then that only a few dozen television films were produced in the USSR each year, although 70 to 80 per cent of all USA film studios made television films. Things improved toward the end of the decade, however, since many documentaries were turned out in connection with the fiftieth anniversary of the October Revolution in 1967 and the Lenin Centennial in 1970.

One television series, a production of Lithuanian television, has been on the air since 1966.[275] It deals with the Petraitis family, consisting of a man, his wife, daughter, son-in-law, relatives, friends, neighbors, and colleagues. For it the producer and editor received the Prize of the Union of Journalists of the USSR, and there have been references to the series in both Lithuanian and East German newspapers. Lithuanian television also has produced films about old folk customs, its national musicians, and a Lithuanian shipbuilding works.[276]

In 1967 the State Committee created the Foreign Exchange Studio for Television Production (FES).[277] At the third Intervision Film Forum in Moscow in 1969, with attendance from both Intervision and Eurovision countries, more than 200 films on science, music, children's subjects, and other topics were shown. At that time FES sold $100,000 worth of features to West Germany, Italy, and Japan. When *Romeo and Juliet* and *Blind Rain* won awards at the Monte Carlo Film Festival, performance rights to both were bought by the Columbia Broadcasting System, the first such USA-USSR transaction. CBS paid $42,500 for the two pictures, selling $36,000 of its own productions to the USSR in return.

In 1970 CBS enterprises sold Soviet television its Peabody Award-winning program "The Secret of Michelangelo: Every Man's Dream," "Vladimir Horowitz: A Television Concert at Carnegie Hall," "Gauguin in Tahiti," and "Casals at 88."[278] In 1972 it was announced that Soviet film makers had turned the 6½–hour cinema version of Tolstoy's *War and Peace* into a thirteen-part television series, hoping to interest American networks and other foreign services.[279] Clearly, *War and Peace* is regarded as a salable item, since the BBC spent $650,000 on a twenty-part television serialization of the novel, again with American television as a prospective purchaser.*

Frequently there are joint productions.[280] Soviet and Italian crews worked on the series "Life in the USSR," while Finnish teams cooperated in the production of "Siberia Today." A documentary developed with Hungarian television dealt with research in the Antarctic. Soviet and Bulgarian crews produced Prokofiev's opera *The Love for Three Oranges.* "The Battle of Moscow," produced with the French broadcasting system, won a Monte Carlo Award.[281] Cooperation with West Germany led to "Moscow in Music," which one West German critic described as "the greatest musical art film on Moscow ever."

In 1970 Soviet television used film from Bulgaria, Czechoslovakia, and Hungary, and in 1971—with enthusiastic audience response—broadcast the twenty-six episodes of the British production *The Forsyte Saga.*[282] Purchased by the USSR in December 1968, its presentation was delayed for ideological reasons. Although not the first Western telefilm to be broadcast in the Soviet Union, it was the first Western serial to be shown. The Moscow correspondent of the *New York Times* reported that, preceding the first broadcast on July 8, 1971, a Soviet commentator explained that *The Forsyte Saga* was considered acceptable because it showed the decline of "the highest echelons of the ruling British bourgeois class." In presenting *The Forsyte Saga*, the USSR followed its usual

---

* A Soviet critic wrote that the British production "threw away the essence of the novel, its social and political nerve, its social meaning and message." The review added: "The shameful execution of the Tolstoy novel is one of a series of other anti-Soviet doings of British television. It has shown through its channels a sufficient number of hastily assembled films about Russian spies where Russia in general and its people appear as dirty, angry, dangerous and poor in spirit" (*Variety*, February 7, 1973, p. 29).

practice of fading down the original sound track while an announcer read a Russian translation.*

The first and only American television series (as opposed to single programs) ever shown in the Soviet Union was *Daktari*, a wild animal series laid in the African bush.[283] Although first broadcast in the United States in 1965–1966, the USSR did not telecast its fifty-six episodes until 1970. These have been repeated several times, one occasion being the summer of 1973 at the time of Leonid Brezhnev's visit to the United States. The USSR was the fourth foreign country to carry *Daktari*, and the presentation in Russian marked its seventh language. In the spring of 1971, NBC International sold two programs to the Soviet Union, *American Profile: Home Country USA* and *Vanishing 400,* the latter an examination of high society in America. This was NBC International's first sale to the USSR, although previously it had sold *Bonanza* to Poland, Romania, and Yugoslavia. One Saturday afternoon in 1972 I saw on the national network the American telefilm *The World of Animals*, about various sea animals. The original English narrative was held in the background while a Russian translation was read.

Almost every evening Soviet television shows two or more cinema films along with some telefilms. Some of these illustrate the jokes about old films on American television. Musicals of the Jeanette MacDonald, Grace Moore, and Nelson Eddy era are a staple, and in Tashkent I saw a musical film in the Georgian language, again reminiscent of the late 1930s. But during my 1972 visit I saw a number of recent films. A char-

---

* The BBC sold *The Forsyte Saga* to about fifty countries, including Romania and Czechoslovakia. American viewers first saw it on the National Educational Television Network in 1969. A writer for *Komsomolskaya pravda* who devoted 1,500 words to "The 'Saga' and TV" had this comment on the serial: "Soames Forsyte, the 'man of property,' destroyed the lives of the people around him and finally wounded himself. The television producers saw the 'Saga' as primarily a family chronicle, and the social content of the work as merely the background. Their production lost epic scale by this treatment, but gained television impact and thereby an audience of many millions. But the inevitable discussion of the series in the homes of television viewers has become a social phenomenon in itself. The appearance of 'A Man of Property' in 1906 was preceded by the suffragette movement. Now activists of the movement for women's equality deny the institution of marriage altogether; the disintegration of the bourgeois family is being hastened through the protest of the young against their parents' egotistical, money-loving mode of life" (A. Yefremov, "The 'Saga' and TV," *Komsomolskaya pravda*, August 18, 1971, p. 3. Quotation is from abstract of translation of original in CDSP 23:40 (November 2, 1971), p. 20).

acteristic of these, incidentally, was their preoccupation with World War II, something the Soviets regularly exploit.*

In 1960 a Soviet telecaster wrote that entertainment broadcasts were "one of the most difficult sectors of work in television."[284] Viewers, he said, "want to be entertained, to laugh, to be amused in front of their television sets and even to join in dance. Everything that evokes a healthy laugh, stimulates, amuses and entertains listeners is desirable and necessary for television." He continued: "Unfortunately, the influence of bourgeois music, banality, cheap erotism and low artistic tastes often penetrate into this variety genre. We must cope seriously with these phenomena, because for a certain section of the youth this is infectious and even influences student artistic amateur activities in a negative way." The author went on to say that they had experimented with "an original form of variety television concerts and satiric reviews," as well as with musical comedies and circus broadcasts.

Perhaps one reason for the difficulty in developing entertainment programs is the continuing assignment to combine entertainment with ideology. In the spring of 1957 an attempt was made to develop a television quiz series in connection with an upcoming World Youth Festival.[285] This led to "VVV-Gay Question and Answer Sessions," incorpo-

* Soviet movie makers, like television producers, are urged to turn out films glorifying communism, particularly since young people constitute 75 per cent of the Soviet film public (*New York Times*, May 12, 1971, p. 6C). The cinema is one of the Soviet state's major sources of internal revenue. Yet, the producers face the unpleasant fact that the films with the highest box office returns usually are not those that emphasize the party line (Edmond Stevens, "Russian Cinemagoers and Their Secret Passion," *Times*, December 9, 1968, p. 6).

In 1969, 185 feature films were shown in Soviet motion picture theaters (*Variety*, April 1, 1970, p. 33). Of these, approximately 50 per cent were domestic productions, 25 per cent were from other socialist countries, and approximately 20 per cent from the rest of the world. The most highly praised Soviet films were *The Brothers Karamazov, Dead Season,* and *Don't Sorrow!* Fifty films from socialist countries were mainly from Poland and the German Democratic Republic, although there also were some from Romania, Czechoslovakia, and Bulgaria. Forty other foreign pictures were from a number of countries. United States productions included *The Comedians, Born Free, Flipper, Sister Carrie,* and *The Best Years of Our Lives.*

When polled, a group of Soviet college students indicated that their favorite American cinema film was *Judgment at Nuremberg.* But on the whole, the student respondents preferred Continental—especially Italian and French—to American productions, said their favorite performer was Sophia Loren, and liked best certain Italian and French actors, although approving of Steve McQueen, Gregory Peck, and Sidney Poitier.

rating information about the festival. However, to quote a history of Soviet television, the program creators began to copy blindly the worst examples of American television, asking such silly questions as, "How does a cat climb down a tree, with its tail up or down?" Criticized for "lack of ideological content and spiritual emptiness," the series was dropped. Later, however, the format was revised for a new series, "Club for Gay and Resourceful People," accepted precisely because it was "full of factual and ideological content," and it presented a proper image of Soviet youth as "clever, educated, talented, and gay."

The year 1958 saw the beginning of the radio series "The Happy Companion," which deliberately set out to combine amusement and message, while engaging in some of the self-criticism on which the Soviet media pride themselves.[286] This series told "about the Seven Year Plan for the National Economy of the USSR in a lively and entertaining manner; it also speaks about the achievements made by science, agriculture and culture. At the same time it appears with criticisms of the different inadequacies evident at enterprises or institutions, it ridicules inept directors of factories, plants or kolkhozes, conservatives who hinder technical progress, drunks, loafers, sluggards, and violators of labor discipline." There also was a sixty-minute monthly radio review called "On Saturday Night," with satire and humor from the magazines of the USSR and other socialist countries. This and the preceding project, incidentally, were the responsibility of the Editorial Office on Satire and Humor. Initiated in 1962 and terminated in 1970 was the Saturday evening Central Television series "Blue Fire," usually broadcast from Moscow, but sometimes originated in Leningrad, Kiev, and other cities. The program had a simulated nightclub setting, viewers being invited to "join" the studio audience.*

With this background, it is informative to examine an article published several years ago by a Soviet writer entitled "Television: 7% Fun."[287] After a hard day in the office, he wrote, a worker returns home looking forward to six or eight hours of enjoyable television viewing. He anticipates laughing "like a child"; he expects to "pass the time pleasantly"; he is going "to have a glorious time." But these things he cannot do

---

* Vladimir Murkulov, "Blue Fire, "*OIRT Review 1963/5*, pp. 6–7. "Obviously the custom of visiting friends exists in every country. We say in this case 'to go to the fire' and as the TV screen is considered to be blue we have painted our invitation with this colour, too."

because only 6 or 7 per cent of all television broadcasts have any entertainment value. To make matters worse, "elements of serious broadcasts seep into cheerful entertainment programs. Hence, every evening the television screen offers us a thoroughly mixed, monochrome cocktail of the instructive and entertaining."

Although a few programs parody such well-known aspects of Soviet life as consumer goods shortages, nothing approaching America's *Laugh-In* is going to stay on the Soviet air for very long. In 1972 an attempt was made to develop a series based on eighteenth-century fables, but the project fell through when the editor responsible rejected one after another of the proposed stories, fearing possible hidden meanings.[288]

However, one program, "The Pub of 13 Chairs," has lasted for a good five years, despite its obvious criticism of bureaucracy. It was in fact recommended to me by the program director of All-Union Television as a good example of light entertainment.[289] Adapted from a format originally devised by Polish television—and scheduled irregularly—the series is produced and filmed in the Soviet Union, although the program is set in Poland. Each program includes a dozen or so skits with interspersed songs, built around stock-comedy characters: a muddled professor, an office sex siren, a dumb athlete, a henpecked husband, and a hard-driving plant manager.

A bartender may ask the plant director, "How's it going?" When the answer comes, "Not so good; we are behind on fulfilling the plan," the bartender may reply, "Keep up the good work." Another skit might deal with shoddy construction and paper-thin walls between apartments. When a man says that a woman "is a nice girl" but that the key to any automobile will fit her heart, the Soviet viewer takes this as a reference to the difficulties of buying an automobile. If the wife of a Soviet businessman gives her husband, just before he leaves on a trip to the West, a list of the clothes she wants him to buy, the audience regards this as a comment on the shortage of good clothing in Soviet stores.

My viewing of light entertainment telecasts has been disappointing. On October 1, 1965, I saw a Saturday evening variety show from a ship tied up in a harbor, during which the master of ceremonies introduced acts reminiscent of poor vaudeville in the 1920s. In Leningrad on October 7, 1970, I saw a filmed program from East Germany featuring several big bands, with singing in both German and English, and a nightclub act in German, all very well done. But on October 17 in Moscow, the "All-

Union Competition of Variety Artists," picked up from a theater, brought us acrobats, a singer accompanied by two accordionists, and similar acts. This was fairly good vaudeville, although the stage pickup left much to be desired. There also was "Hello, We Are Looking for Talent," during which an MC interviewed young people, who thereafter did performances.

On October 17, 1970, the Moscow regional channel carried, live from an auditorium, the finals of an amateur talent contest. The quality of entertainment varied: there was a clever act with dumbbells; a magician; a singer who offered "Mack the Knife"; and a young woman doing a difficult hula-hoop act while the orchestra played "Hello Dolly!" But the presentation made few concessions to television. In fact, the program periodically was interrupted as the curtains were closed and the stage rearranged for the next act. I have seen other light entertainment programs done in equally clumsy fashion, causing me to wonder why a country with a reservoir of talent like the Soviet Union would allocate long periods of time to so many poorly produced programs with mediocre talent.

Nevertheless, lighthearted musical programs are beginning to emerge on Soviet television, and in 1972 I saw several that were well done. One program, originated in Leningrad on a Saturday from 5:30 to 6:00 P.M., presented a group of singers and instrumentalists, including four young men, a woman, and a Dixieland group. They performed a rhythmic version of the "Song of the Volga Boatmen," some Russian music of folk song nature, and other light selections. The best entertainment I saw on Moscow television in 1972, however, was a recording from East Berlin which featured a lively group of young singers and dancers who performed (apparently) in Alexanderplatz, the center of the new East Berlin, although the excellence of the acoustics indicated that the sound had been prerecorded. This was better than anything of that type I saw on USSR television.

In many cases, the Soviets have not advanced beyond the original media to make use of television's unique potentials. For example, there was the very sedate dance program broadcast by the national network late one Saturday evening. In an ornate ballroom, ten couples—the women in party dresses and the men in business suits—did Viennese waltzes and polkas. Music came from a small live ensemble and, in the case of some of the waltzes, from phonograph records. Frequently broadcast are films of folk dances. One from Georgia running over an hour was aired shortly after a similar Estonian program the same evening. Also telecast that evening was a folklore festival film, with dancers, singers, and folk instruments, running for one and a half hours.*

The Soviet Union is second to no country in its enthusiasm for sports. Moscow's Lenin Stadium, built in 1955–1956, contains 72 tiers of seats with accommodations for 100,000 spectators.[290] In 1957 the USSR had 1,666 sports stadiums, 27,279 football (soccer) stadiums, 32,215 basketball arenas, and 167,990 volleyball courts. I saw a South American soccer team, staying in my hotel, besieged by fans seeking autographs. One Sunday afternoon in a restaurant, I noticed many people listening to a major athletic contest on transistor radios. Finally, I should note that my career as a student and writer about foreign broadcasting was nearly ended in the fall of 1958, when at a soccer match between two Soviet teams, I was swept down the stadium ramp by a crowd of enthusiastic Muscovites rushing to their seats just as the game began.

For many years the treatment of sports has approximated that in the United States. News programs usually include some sports news, and in the case of television scores often are flashed on the screen. In 1958 there were over 250 sports news programs on national radio, with an equal number of pickups direct from stadiums.[291] Soviet sportscasters have gone abroad to cover important contests in such places as Australia, China, Latin America, Poland, Scandinavia, the United Kingdom, and the United States.

The first Soviet telecast to originate outside a studio was a football match in the Dynamo Stadium in Moscow on June 29, 1949.[292] In 1963 a swimming meet between the two Ukrainian cities of Kiev and Lvov was conducted entirely by television. Forty-eight contestants, including two European champions, took part, and television cameras in both cities

---

* Apart from television, there is some excellent light entertainment in the USSR. When I was visiting there, Kiev had sellout performances for an ingeniously contrived entertainment ranging from duets in the style of Nelson Eddy and Jeanette MacDonald to presentations by long-haired young men with electronic instruments. I was unable to share the side-splitting laughter of the audience when the comedians came out; but one did not have to know Ukrainian to realize that everyone, from charwomen to party leaders, was having a hearty good time.

Circuses also thrive in the Soviet Union, and most cities of any size have a permanent circus building, with shows running many months of the year. Performances are of a high order, ranging from birds to bears and from dogs to elephants, along with an assortment of jugglers, trapeze artists, and clowns.

enabled viewers to see their teams in action. The nature of other television sports programs is indicated by such titles as "Sporting Panorama," "TV Stadium," and "Masters of Soviet Sports."

International sports coverage was a major factor in the development of Intervision, as it also had been of Eurovision. Of the more than 3,700 programs transmitted over the Intervision network between 1960 and 1965, the largest category—43.5 per cent—consisted of sports broadcasts.[293] Sports are a major ingredient of bilateral hookups, and there is international distribution of contests with wider interest.

The USSR took Eurovision and Intervision feeds of almost all the 1972 summer Olympics, although it broadcast only those in which Soviet athletes did well. In September 1972 I arrived in Moscow the day after the conclusion of a USSR-Canada hockey series, of which the first four games were played in Canada and the last four in Moscow. The project brought some 3,000 Canadians on a ten-day tour to the Soviet Union, during which time they virtually took over Moscow's Intourist facilities. The games were of enormous interest throughout the country, particularly the play-off, which Canada won 6 to 5 in the last minute of play. All the matches were televised.

Several days later the Soviet national network carried an Intervision feed from Czechoslovakia of a game between that country and Canada which ended in a 3–3 tie. During this transmission, surprisingly, the cameras periodically focused on a digital clock indicating game timing, which contained the name of the manufacturer, Longines. A day or so later the national network carried another hockey game at the same time the local Moscow channel took a football match. Between Intervision and its home resources, therefore, Soviet television covers major sporting events very thoroughly.*

It is difficult to judge production quality when unfamiliar languages are used to describe partly unfamiliar sports. But the voices of the Soviet radio announcers reflect the same quality of intense excitement and disappointment one hears at home. I have watched telecasts of soccer, water polo, ice hocky, and gymnastics, and found the coverage similar to that in the United States. There may be fewer cameras with zoom lenses,

---

* During the break in the Canadian-Czechoslovakian match, rather than providing commentary or analysis as would be done in the United States, Soviet television transmitted two animal cartoons.

fewer close-up shots, and slightly slower camera work, but the overall effect is about the same. As to audiences, on several occasions I have joined (largely male) viewing groups when major events were being telecast and could just as well have been watching an American contest in a bar or club at home. Soviet interest in the USSR-Canadian hockey matches mentioned above was very high indeed.

V

Union of Soviet Socialist Republics:
Other Services

Although the emphasis throughout this study is on broadcasting itself, all the socialist countries do some audience research, and certain ones of them place great emphasis on external broadcasting. The former activity is important as a measure of results and the latter for its relationship to international politics.

Audience Research

Audience research developed very slowly in the Soviet Union. One scholar reported that the first full-fledged study of the domestic audience was an inquiry in the spring of 1963 into the effects of television on radio listening.[1] Extensive research of this type, of course, has been conducted in many countries for years.

Why was the USSR so slow to initiate scientific audience studies? Since the Soviet government uses the communications media so purposefully, one would expect it to have a great interest in measuring the results. Perhaps the party maintains that since it knows what the public should get, there is no need to find out what it wants.

In any case, there were delays in developing research instruments. The noncommercial, monopoly status of Soviet broadcasting provided less motivation for research than did the American system, where competitive networks, stations, sponsors, and advertising agencies all urgently need such data. In the United Kingdom too there was delay in initiating research during the BBC-only days, although a fine organization eventu-

181

ally was developed; but the whole process was greatly accelerated by the advent of competitive commercial television in the 1950s.

The slowness of Soviet institutions of higher learning to train communications media personnel—especially for radio and television—may

Table 3. Radio and Television Receivers in the USSR

Year	Radio Wave Sets (Off the Air)	Radio Wired Sets	Television Sets
1925		200	
1928	70,000	22,000	
1932	97,000	1,361,000	
1937	321,000	2,946,000	
1940	1,123,000	5,934,000	400
1945	500,000	5,600,000	200
1946		5,700,000	
1947		6,500,000	
1948		7,300,000	
1950	3,600,000	9,700,000	15,000
1951	4,800,000	10,600,000	56,000
1952	5,800,000	11,700,000	114,000
1953	7,300,000	13,800,000	225,000
1954	10,000,000	16,400,000	450,000
1955	13,000,000	19,500,000	823,000
1956	16,300,000	22,200,000	1,300,000
1957	19,000,000	24,800,000	1,800,000
1958	21,700,000	27,100,000	2,500,000
1959	24,700,000	29,200,000	3,600,000
1960	27,800,000	30,800,000	4,800,000
1961	30,500,000	32,100,000	6,500,000
1962	32,800,000	33,100,000	8,300,000
1963	35,200,000	34,600,000	10,400,000
1964	36,700,000	34,600,000	12,800,000
1965	38,200,000	35,600,000	15,700,000
1966	39,800,000	37,000,000	19,000,000
1967	41,800,000	38,900,000	22,700,000
1968	44,400,000	41,000,000	26,800,000
1969	46,700,000	43,400,000	30,800,000
1970	48,600,000	46,200,000	34,800,000
1971	50,800,000	49,100,000	39,300,000
1972	50,000,000	50,000,000	45,000,000

SOURCES: This table is compiled from the following publications of the Central Statistical Board of the USSR: *Narodnoye khozyaystvo SSSR v 1958 g.*, pp. 602–603; 1962, p. 422; 1965, p. 514; 1968, p. 506; and 1970, p. 466; *Narodnoye khozyaystvo SSSR 1922–1972 gg.*, p. 314; *Soviet Union 50 Years*, p. 192; *The U.S.S.R. Economy*, p. 184. Also the following: *The Europa Year Book 1965*, p. 1001; Rubina and Ramsin, pp. 15–16; *Yezhegodnik bol'shoy sovyetskoy entsiklopediy 1964*, p. 77; Zvorykin, p. 53; and for 1972, quotations from Soviet newspapers supplied by Radio Liberty.

have been another factor. Undoubtedly significant was the delay in developing such fields as sociology, long regarded as ideologically hostile to Communist doctrine, whose techniques pertain to mass media research. But for whatever reasons, the scientific study of Soviet audiences was late to develop.

Table 3 provides information about the number of radio and television receivers in the USSR from 1925 to 1972, documenting the slow growth of both wave sets (off-the-air receivers) and wired sets (loudspeakers connected to diffusion systems) (for more information about both types of receivers, see p. 70). In 1928 the entire country had only 70,000 wave sets and 22,000 wired sets, a negligible number for a population (then) of approximately 147,000,000. In 1940 the number of wired receivers (5,934,000) was over five times that of wave sets (1,123,000). In 1963 the number of wave sets (35,200,000) exceeded the number of wired sets for the first time since 1928, but thereafter the number of wired sets gradually increased, until in 1972 there were an equal number of each (50,000,000). Radio Liberty estimates that about two-thirds of all off-the-air sets can receive short-wave programs. This means that in 1972 there were between 30 and 32 million such receivers. During 1970, the last year for which there are comparative data, the USSR had 39.0 radios (including both wave and wired sets) per hundred of population. This was more receivers per hundred than in any other Eastern European country or in the United Kingdom, Sweden, or West Germany. However, the United States had 141.2 radio receivers per hundred—all off-the-air—or 41.2 per cent more radios than people.[2]

Television also had a slow start, and even by 1950 there were only 15,000 sets in the entire country. Since then, the number has grown steadily: by 1968 there were 26,800,000, and by 1972 an estimated 45,000,000 television receivers. About 5,000,000 sets are added each year. In 1970 the USSR had 14.3 television receivers per hundred of population, which was proportionately more sets than in Yugoslavia, Bulgaria, or Poland, but fewer than in the other Eastern European countries, the United Kingdom, Sweden, or West Germany. In that year the United States had 41.2 television receivers per hundred, the highest rate in the world.* There is no cable distribution in the Soviet Union com-

* *United Nations Statistical Yearbook 1971.* For radio and television license statistics in most of the Eastern and some Western European countries, see Table 10 below. In 1972 a Soviet source reported that in the USSR, there are "about 90

parable with that country's radio diffusion system, although there is a trend toward central antennas for multiple-dwelling units. New apartments have only a few aerials on their roofs, whereas older ones are surmounted by forests of television masts.[3]

For some years, audience research consisted entirely of the analysis of letters, of which most pertained to request and quiz programs, or to broadcasts for children and youth.[4] The number of letters received between 1949 and 1964 is shown in the tabulation below.[5] The letters were

1949	. . . 246,210	1956	. . . 339,762
1950	. . . 202,796	1957	. . . 350,973
1951	. . . 194,063	1958	. . . 403,000
1952	. . . 222,057	1961	. . . 266,000
1953	. . . 256,625	1962	. . . 346,000
1954	. . . 303,000	1963	. . . 498,000
1955	. . . 390,720	1964	. . . 427,227

read, analyzed, and often answered. In 1958, 43,000 letters were answered by mail, and in the first half of 1959 over 40,000 were answered. In addition, some programs were organized around them, sometimes in reply and sometimes to develop ideas they presented.* People were invited to report stimulating experiences and to describe friends and surroundings, and the more "interesting and disturbing letters . . . [were] read on the air." At the outset, television also made a point of the number of letters received, but this was de-emphasized as research developed.

However, letters still are an important source of information. In March 1972 a member of the radio music section reported on their use to a meeting of OIRT music experts in Moscow.[6] In 1971, 219,468 letters were received about musical programs. A single series might bring 1,000 letters per broadcast—the ages of the writers ranging from 4 to 103! Letters are used to gauge general audience reactions as well as to plan pro-

---

television sets for every 100 families living in areas where television programs can be picked up," making it possible for 140 or 150 million viewers to watch "the most significant . . . programs at the same time" ("Creative Forces for the Fulfilment of the Party's Decisions," *Pravda*, May 7, 1972, p. 2, translated in CDSP 24:18 (May 31, 1972), p. 21).

* A long-time feature of Radio Moscow's North American Service has been "Moscow Mailbag," consisting of answers to questions from the United States. See below, pp. 209–210.

grams. But, scientific research aside, any network department receiving almost 220,000 letters in the course of a year would regard them as indicating something about the audience.

Apart from letter analysis, it appears that the first Soviet survey of the radio audience was conducted when Radio Moscow sent postcards to North American listeners inviting their reactions to various programs.[7] The first domestic research took place in the spring of 1963, when the State Committee for Radio and Television and the School of Journalism of Moscow University joined forces to study the impact of television on radio listening.[8] It was found that television already was beginning to affect the radio audience, although in 1963 only a small percentage of Russian homes had television receivers. Up to 1967, at least, cinema attendance had not been decreased by television. In that year the average Soviet citizen went to the cinema an average of eleven times.[9] In the same year, a University of Leningrad psychologist advocated more intensive audience research, including studies of such things as reaction differences between viewers in family groups and in classrooms.[10] He also suggested reviewing the work of such American scholars as Hadley Cantril, Bernard Berelson, and Gordon Allport, even though he stated that the purpose of Western research was to manipulate audiences in the interest of the ruling minorities, whereas the goal of Soviet research would be to make the individual a "conscious creator of new, communist social relations."

In 1966 two American researchers reported the amount of television viewing in the United States and eleven other countries: the USSR, East Germany, Poland, Czechoslovakia, Hungary, Bulgaria, Yugoslavia, West Germany, France, Belgium, and Peru. Although the data were collected in 1965 and 1966, they do provide some comparative information.* The figures must be used with care, however, since, in addition to being out of date, they report viewing in countries whose television output was then—and still is—much lower than that of the United States. The data were obtained from diaries of leisure time activities. Viewing was divided

---

* In 1967 the average American with access to a receiver watched television a little less than 19 hours a week (Roper Organization, *An Extended View of Public Attitudes toward Television and Other Mass Media 1959–1971*, p. 5). Although this indicates more viewing than in Eastern Europe, it must be remembered in 1967 American viewers usually had from 18 to 24 hours a day of program service, whereas USSR stations were on the air 8 to 10 hours or less. Exact comparisons are therefore impossible.

Table 4. Amount of Daily Television Viewing in Selected Countries (in Minutes)

Country	Primary Viewing	Secondary Viewing	Total
Bulgaria	17	17	34
Yugoslavia	39	48	87
Hungary	42	45	87
USSR	42	45	87
West Germany	62	72	134
Czechoslovakia	65	71	136
Poland	71	82	153
East Germany (GDR)	80	100	180
United States	90	127	217

SOURCE: J. P. Robinson, "Television and Leisure Time: Yesterday, Today, and (Maybe) Tomorrow," *Public Opinion Quarterly*, 38:2 (Summer 1969), pp. 216–217.

into primary viewing (done as a major activity) and secondary viewing (background activity). The results are indicated in Table 4.

A survey conducted in Leningrad in April 1967 demonstrated clearly that while official Soviet spokesmen may regard television primarily as a means of education and propaganda, most viewers considered it a medium for entertainment and escape.[11] Of the study's 1,916 respondents, 85.9 per cent had television sets. Of this group, 38.7 per cent were pleased with television programming, 39.2 per cent reported "some disillusionment," and 22.1 per cent found it "hard to say" what they thought. Asked how often they viewed, 27.7 per cent said "most days," 33.8 per cent three or four days a week, 24.6 per cent one or two days, 2.3 per cent less than once a week, and 2.3 per cent hardly at all. The time spent watching television averaged between thirteen and fourteen hours a week.

In accordance with findings in all countries, people of higher social, educational, and economic status tended to be light viewers, while those at the other end of the scale were heavy viewers. The 316 "very extensive" viewers included 56.6 per cent of the sample with a ninth-grade education or less, but only 8.6 per cent of those with higher education. The survey definitely established that most Leningraders watched television primarily for entertainment, although a large number still rated its information appeal high. When asked, "What does television mean to you personally?" 70.5 per cent said it was a way to relax; 60.2 per cent reported it to be a source of information about events at home and abroad; and 45.8 per cent found it a way of expanding knowledge and cultural outlook. (Since respondents were permitted more than one answer, percentages total more than 100.)

There were criticisms of how well television provided information. Asked, "What is it in television information broadcasts that you find most inadequate?" 19.0 per cent listed "on-the-spot reporting of events"; 17.4 per cent questioned the "candor" of programs; 15.4 per cent put down "diversity of facts"; 11.6 per cent said "day-to-day interpretation of events"; and 5.7 per cent said "ability to speak simply, understandably." However, 32.0 per cent said they had no complaints about television information broadcasts, and 25.3 per cent said that they watched such broadcasts so infrequently that they could not judge them. As to entertainment programs, 48.3 per cent said the quality should be improved; 41.4 per cent said there should be more; and only 8.4 per cent thought there were enough of them.

Of particular interest were the "like," "neutral," or "do not like" reactions to the twelve categories of programs listed in Table 5. Preference clearly went to entertainment—sports, quizzes, variety shows, and films—while the lowest-ranking categories were broadcasts on political themes, educational broadcasts, serious music, and opera. Most of these findings do not differ significantly from those reported elsewhere in the world, except for the high percentage (27.0) of negative votes for newscasts. Could this indicate dissatisfaction with basic news policies?

Table 5. Satisfaction with Television Broadcasts in USSR (in Percentages)

Category	Like	Neutral	Do Not Like	Rarely Watch; Hard to Say
Sports coverage	84.0	5.3	1.2	9.5
"Club of Cheer and Wit," and similar panel quiz shows	81.2	8.6	2.4	7.8
Variety shows	70.9	19.5	1.8	7.8
Films	66.5	22.5	4.3	6.7
Television plays	61.1	17.5	1.9	19.5
Programs for youth	58.1	18.0	3.9	19.8
Theater and literature broadcasts	45.0	24.0	4.0	27.0
News and current events	38.0	20.0	27.0	18.0
On-the-spot news coverage	36.2	24.5	6.7	32.6
Broadcasts on political themes	16.4	21.0	8.6	54.0
Educational broadcasts	16.0	16.0	7.0	61.0
Serious music and opera	15.0	14.0	25.0	47.0

SOURCE: Boris Firsov, *There Is No "Average" Viewer: A Soviet TV Survey*, p. 18, translated from *Zhurnalist*, No. 12 (December 1967).

The Leningrad study also rated thirty-one types of programs from most to least popular, as shown in the accompanying list. (The figures in the right-hand column indicate the number of the 1,916 respondents who reported regularly viewing each program category.)

Popularity of Program Types

A. Extremely Popular Broadcasts (Programs watched regularly by 50–74 per cent of the viewers; occasionally by 25–30 per cent; not at all by 10–12 per cent.)
1. Films 1,730
2. "Club of Cheer and Wit" 1,665
3. Serial films 1,600
4. "The Blue Fire" (light entertainment; see p. 75) 1,565
5. Variety shows 1,540

B. Highly Popular Broadcasts (Watched regularly by 35–50 per cent of the viewers; sometimes by up to 50 per cent; not watched by 10–20 per cent.)
6. Television plays 1,415
7. Concerts by top performers 1,365
8. Theatrical presentations 1,360
9. Documentary films 1,300
10. Popular science films 1,285

C. Broadcasts of Average Popularity (Watched regularly by 15–35 per cent of the viewers; sometimes by up to 70 per cent; not watched by 15–35 per cent.)
11. Satirical shows 1,275
12. "Tales of Heroism" 1,235
13. Theatrical interviews 1,210
14. Broadcasts about masters of literature and art 1,160
15. Amateur concerts 1,135
16. Informational Broadcasts 1,105
17. Central Television newscasts 1,100
18. Educational broadcasts 1,080
19. News bulletins 1,075
20. "The World Today" 1,065
21. Broadcasts on political themes 982
22. Broadcasts on themes of social duty, morals, and family ... 962
23. "Talks about the Theater" 926

D. Broadcasts of Low Popularity (Watched regularly by 2–15 per cent of the viewers; sometimes by up to 60 per cent; not watched by 30–70 per cent.)
24. News from the Leningrad television studio 920

25. Literary theater 883
26. "Interview 67" 857
27. "Neva Torch" 775
28. Broadcasts about the history of the government 720
29. "Pages of Poetry" 700
30. Broadcasts on economic topics 394
31. School programs 162

Educational programs were most popular among viewers fifty years of age and older, as well as those with four years of education or less, and least popular among viewers with fifth- to sixth-grade educations. Serious music was given its lowest rating by viewers under eighteen and its highest by those over fifty. Interest in news and current events increased with age and education, the lowest rating coming from the group with a fourth-grade education or less. Broadcasts on historical subjects were most popular among viewers between fifty and fifty-nine years of age; surprisingly, though, the rating dropped with increased education. Light music and variety shows ranked highest among respondents under eighteen, preference dropping with increased age and education. Broadcasts on political themes received low ratings from those under eighteen. The study concluded: the most critical attitude toward television is among viewers with a higher than secondary education.*

The world over, television viewing tends to displace such older pastimes as cinema attendance.[12] A 1973 study of leisure time in an industrial center with a population of 250,000 showed that over 46 per cent of the blue-collar workers and 42 per cent of the office employees had not been to a theater in over a year, although about half said they watched television. Similar studies in Moscow, Leningrad, and one other city indi-

---

* A study of the United States audience by the Harris organization in 1971 reported that although the average American then was watching television seventeen hours a week, people with eighth-grade educations were viewing twenty hours whereas those who had gone to college watched only fourteen hours. Respondents with incomes below $5,000 a year watched twenty-two hours, while those earning $15,000 or more watched thirteen hours. Four groups were identified, ranging from those who were "satisfied and watching more" to those "watching less and considered programs worse." The latter category was found to consist of the age group from fifty to sixty-four, of white-collar and skilled workers, and of those whose family incomes were between $5,000 and $10,000. The conclusion was: "Discontent is rising faster here than elsewhere, with increasing criticism of entertainment being offered and a tendency to stop tuning in 'just to see what happens to be on'" (Louis Harris, "But Do We Like What We Watch?" *Life* (September 10, 1971), pp. 43–44).

cated that 80 per cent of married women with families spent their free time either watching television or doing nothing. When asked what they did during their most recent free day, only one in five said she had been to the movies or a theater, had visited someone, or had taken a walk.

A "survey" of quite another sort was conducted in Moscow during the same year by a journalist masquerading as a television serviceman. Though hardly scientific, the results were interesting and on the whole critical of television programming.[13] A personnel director, who also was a Communist party worker, reported that when his set was new the family watched everything, later becoming more selective. Now they prefer sports: "At least, you never make a mistake; it's always interesting." He liked programs about cosmonauts and suggested that a booklovers' club be organized. A young lady preferred radio to television news, because she then could wash the dishes and listen at the same time.

A woman insurance agent pointed out that she spent eight hours a day at work, an hour and a half waiting in lines at stores, and the rest of her time in the kitchen. Accordingly, she thought television sets should be enameled to match refrigerators and kept in the kitchen. "Because of this, the husbands would also start sitting in the kitchen, and while they're there they might even give us some help." As to programs, she said, "There are some shrewd people in television. If one channel's got a lecture, without fail the other one has a round-table discussion."

Although there are incomplete Soviet data on the extent of television viewing, there clearly are addicts there as everywhere else. In 1971 a teacher of broadcasting courses at the University of Moscow quoted from a letter from a woman viewer that could have been written in the United States. "My attitude toward television might not have changed if the picture tube of our new set hadn't gone out of order. Silence has reigned in the house for almost a month. I used to think I couldn't live without television. Its absence proved a boon. We visited friends, went to the movies, and I found time to read several books during the month, even though I am busy with work, children, household cares and study. Now I believe that television consumes our leisure with little benefit. I think it even keeps us from using our minds. Some people may say that this unthinking state is a form of recreation. I disagree. The noise tires one more than a day's work. You can't pry your husband or children away from the set that blasts away from seven in the evening to midnight. We ought to be able to be selective as to programs, but how? The printed program listings provide no clues for choosing the good from the bad."[14]

The author of the article then speculated about what activities television had displaced. "If we turned off the TV sets in some homes, the ex-viewers would simply play dominoes, reach for a guitar, or even start drinking. Is television worse? In one village a salesclerk told me there was a direct relationship between television and the amount of liquor sold: When good programs were on the air, vodka sales fell off."

In 1968, in the first nationwide study of audience reaction to foreign news coverage, conducted jointly by the State Committee for Radio and Television and the Moscow Economics-Statistical Institute, 5,332 questionnaires were mailed to residents in 30 different cities and towns, divided proportionately between urban and rural areas.[15] Foreign news source preferences were, in declining order, newspapers, radio, television, and lectures (Table 6). Respondents higher on the socioeconomic and

Table 6. Sources of Foreign Affairs Information in USSR (in Percentages)

Group	Newspapers	Radio	Television	Lectures[a]
Collective farmers	63.7	52.0	38.0	30.6
Workers	64.9	56.2	44.1	14.8
Engineers and technicians	78.7	50.0	35.7	14.7
Students	70.4	34.7	30.2	14.0
Communist party members and government workers	82.5	50.0	45.0	31.3

SOURCE: Pavel Gurevich, *Soviet TV and Radio: Foreign News and Audience Reaction, Zhurnalist*, No. 7 (July 1968), pp. 47–48, translated in *The Soviet Press in Translation*, 7:1 (Fall 1968), p. 13.

[a] Lectures were considered as monthly rather than daily sources of information.

political scale were more apt to prefer newspapers over the electronic media. But collective farmers, party members, and government workers gave much higher ranking to lectures as a source of information than did workers or students.*

* Periodic Roper reports have shown that in the United States most people get their news from television, with newspapers ranking second, and radio a poor third. In fact, annual surveys since December 1959 have indicated an increasing preference for television. In December 1959 the rankings were television 51 per cent, newspapers 57 per cent, and radio 34 per cent. By November 1972 this had changed to television 64 per cent, newspapers 50 per cent, and radio 21 per cent (Roper Organization, *What People Think of Television and Other Mass Media 1959–1972*, p. 2).

Asked what themes should receive greater coverage, the respondents gave answers that were too "correct" to be credible, since those listed were as follows: "the worker movement and the class struggle in capitalist countries"; "the struggle against the rebirth of fascism"; "social-political and economic situations in countries freed from colonial dependence"; "the situation in Western Germany"; and "the military blocs of the West."

Table 7. Interests of Radio and Television Audiences in USSR
in Three Types of Broadcasts (in Percentages)

Group	Hard News	Interpretation and Commentary	Major Foreign Affairs, Issues
Collective farmers	40.0	27.5	49.3
Workers	49.0	28.9	56.6
Engineers and technicians	62.9	40.2	72.4
Students	53.8	38.7	74.9
Communist party members and government workers	61.3	55.0	81.2

SOURCE: Pavel Gurevich, *Soviet TV and Radio: Foreign News and Audience Reaction, Zhurnalist*, No. 7 (July 1968), pp. 47–48, translated in *The Soviet Press in Translation*, 7:1 (Fall 1968), p. 15.

The study also reported (Table 7) that respondents at the bottom of the professional scale had less interest in international issues than those at the top. Furthermore, they had relatively less interest in interpretation and commentary, but more interest in hard news. On the other hand, Communist party members and government workers, in addition to higher overall interest in broadcasts about foreign affairs, had much greater interest in programs of interpretation. The report concluded: "The lower the educational level of listeners, the more they need explanation and interpretation of events. But it appears that it is fruitless to provide it."

Table 8 reports more interest than satisfaction with news programs about international topics, except that collective farmers (who had less education) were quite pleased with what was available. In the case of programs on interpretation and commentary, all the groups polled (again, except for collective farmers) indicated more interest than satisfaction.

There is no evidence that the State Committee itself makes ongoing

Table 8. Interest in and Satisfaction Received from Radio and Television
Broadcasts on International Topics in USSR (in Percentages)

Group	Factual Dispatches (Not Necessarily Timely)		Hard (Timely) News		Interpretation and Commentary	
	Interest	Satisfaction	Interest	Satisfaction	Interest	Satisfaction
Collective farmers	49.9	52.7	40.0	60.2	27.5	46.6
Workers	56.6	25.2	49.0	29.1	28.9	28.1
Engineers and technicians ...	72.4	23.4	62.9	18.0	40.2	18.0
Students	74.9	27.8	53.8	21.6	38.7	22.1
Communist party members and government workers	81.2	40.0	61.3	28.7	55.0	36.2

audience studies such as are conducted in almost all Western European countries and the United States. If it does, then neither the fact nor the results have been publicized. However, an article in *Variety* in 1970 reported that the computer system that checks water consumption indicates a drastic drop whenever major sports events or other happenings of wide appeal are on television.*

It is impossible to determine if the research that has been conducted is used in determining program policies. However, the head of radio news wrote in 1968 that in order to increase the effectiveness of the service they used "data resulting from sociological investigations, thus ascertaining who listened to our broadcasts and when."[16] He went on to say that in response to audience interest, and in order to provide listeners with more information, they "revised the schedule of a broadcasting day. Today it can be said that our informative programme is ever more acquiring a union-wide character in the full meaning of the word." Whereas in

* *Variety*, April 8, 1970, p. 94. In May 1953 readers of America's *Business Week* magazine were amused by a story linking water consumption to television program popularity: Consumption was down during interesting telecasts, but when less attractive programs or commercials came on, there was a great increase, indicating fewer people before their sets ("Why Water Charts Zigzag at Night," *Business Week* (May 2, 1953), pp. 44–46). The late Lord Reith, the first BBC director general, in his autobiography, wrote that he told the Prince of Wales—later Edward VIII—"that water engineers could provide a pretty clear indication of the popularity of broadcast items. When there was anything specially interesting, water consumption fell; immediately afterward there was a sudden, sometimes alarming, peak load" (J. C. W. Reith, *Into the Wind*, p. 244).

the past, stories usually were designed for listeners in the European area, they now are written for the parts of the country that will hear them and with reference to the times of broadcast. He also mentioned that his department was guided by ideas from listeners' letters.

Combining the data from those surveys, reports from correspondents and other foreigners in the USSR, and conversations with Soviet citizens, my conclusion is that the general public does not hear or watch with enthusiasm, or accept uncritically, the heavy propaganda output of the Soviet media. As one Soviet citizen put it to me, after a hard day's work the public wants escape and relaxation, and these the electronic media do not provide. As for the commentaries, people regard them as long and boring, and tune them out mentally if not in fact.

There are surprising parallels between the reports in the few published surveys and some comments in the official press. Since the latter may be assumed to reflect government and party views, the need for improvement must be deeply felt. Some of these criticisms have been cited during the descriptions of program areas above; however, the total impact is greater when they are examined consecutively.

In February 1960, a USSR People's Artist, in a 1,200-word article in *Izvestia*, complained that many radio programs were monotonous and dull.[17] Complex subjects were treated in long sentences, and with too many technical terms. There was much "empty talk." Scheduling was repetitious: sometimes "the same song can be heard several times a day over different stations." A program for onion raisers "is hardly of much interest for a salesgirl in a haberdashery." On the same day the editor of the magazine *Kursk Truth* wrote that sometimes "we hear almost the same thing over and over," along with agricultural information "written in stiff language." There are too many "long, dull articles."[18]

In February 1960 the party's Central Committee released a 4,500-word statement about the need to improve Soviet radio and television.[19] After lamenting the ideological shortcomings of many programs, the committee offered some specific criticisms. Programs were not related to life; they were badly produced and thus aroused little interest; they were overloaded with figures; and there were not enough skilled writers. Owing to inadequate technical facilities, reception in certain outlying areas was poor. Radio and television workers were inadequately trained, and the State Committee did not keep close enough check on program output. There should be a greater range of programs and improved news coverage. Two stations covering the same area should not duplicate programs "to the dissatisfaction of the public." Furthermore, "radio broadcasts were everywhere dry and official sounding."

Two years later the committee offered more criticisms, many of which were repeated in a 14,000-word document issued in July 1964, following a conference of publicists.[20] The tenor of these reports was that although things had gotten better, there still was plenty of room for improvement. Many broadcasts were "put together monotonously" and had about them a "smell of boredom and indifference." Therefore, they did not attract attention or response. One reason for this was that broadcasters often "transfer to radio and television genres and methods peculiar to the press, movies, and theater."

In September 1965 an article with the title "Problems of Television: When There Are Many Channels" pointed out that public reaction to television then was known as a result of research in Leningrad and that this information should be heeded by those responsible for program policies.[21] Furthermore, there was too much similarity among the several Moscow channels. Each should develop its own distinctive character, and programmers should avoid scheduling similar material on two or more stations at the same time. (When this was written, Moscow had three channels. Now there are four.)

A writer in a Soviet youth journal in 1967 mentioned the monotony of television programming.[22] Unlike most critics, however, this author complained that television was too much a medium of light entertainment, that programs were superficial, and that they did not involve their viewers in the problems of the day. He agreed with other observers, though, that too many programs were based upon formats devised for other media, such as motion pictures, rather than being uniquely designed for television.

In 1970 *Pravda* ran a 1,000-word editorial about local radio, complaining that programs in outlying regions did not "adequately reflect the urgent problems of concern to radio listeners."[23] Although concerned mainly with ideological failures, the editorial also lamented equipment shortages at local stations, and charged local committees to turn out programs that were "timely, rich in content, varied in form." Three months later, in a follow-up, *Pravda* reported that the Bashkir Province Party Committee had discussed these criticisms and found them justified, whereupon the local broadcasters were ordered to improve their output "and to strengthen ties with listeners."[24]

From these survey data and official statements several conclusions emerge. Official statements are apt to emphasize the ideological role of broadcasting while audience surveys report, as boldly as they dare, that the public is bored by such material and prefers entertainment. However, both sources agree that programming often is ineffective; that there is monotonous scheduling, with inadequate contrasts among the stations serving a given area; and that production should be improved. Finally, there is the frequent complaint that radio and television, especially the latter, have not yet grown away from the older media of print, stage, and film. My own listening and viewing during several trips to the Soviet Union support these generalizations. Yet, as was pointed out above during discussions of radio and television programming, there have been tremendous improvements during the last several years, particularly between 1970 and 1972, so that Soviet broadcast executives must have concluded that changes were necessary. It is important to notice that most of the criticisms reported above were made before 1970.

External Broadcasting*

The USSR is deeply involved in foreign propaganda. To achieve its goals it utilizes all available methods and means, including both the printed and electronic media.

One of its weapons is TASS, the official news agency established in 1925, which provides news to both domestic and foreign clients.[25] Since April 3, 1961, the Soviet Union also has had Press Agency Novosti, which supplies the Soviet media with information about foreign developments and publishes newspapers and magazines for distribution abroad. In 1963 Novosti published 85 brochures for foreign circulation with a total press run of 12 million copies.[26]

A Novosti spokesman told me that TASS is run by the government, whereas Novosti is a "public agency like the BBC." However this may be, there is a parallel between Novosti and the Soviet Radio Station "Peace and Progress," which although housed in the same building as Radio Moscow and using some of the same transmitters, is claimed to be

---

* The British term "external broadcasting" is used in this study to denote radio and television services originated by one country for reception or use in another.

a private organization, supported by nongovernment groups, and hence not subject to government control (see below, p. 207).

In 1964, while maintaining ties with 102 countries, the Novosti output included 27 magazines and 5 newspapers. In 1965 it supplied information to 3,500 foreign newspapers and magazines, 70 information agencies, and 8 publishing houses.[27] Novosti magazines for foreign distribution include *Soviet Union*, available in Russian, Korean, English, Chinese, German, French, and Spanish; *Soviet Literature*, in Russian, English, French, German, Spanish, and Polish; *New Times*, in English, Chinese, German, French, Spanish, and Russian; and *Culture and Life*, *International Affairs*, *Soviet Film*, and *Social Sciences*.[28]

Among Novosti publications distributed in the United States are *Soviet Life* and *Sputnik*. Under a reciprocal agreement between the two countries, the picture magazine *Soviet Life* which tells the story of the Soviet Union for American readers using a format somewhat resembling the former *Life* magazine, is available by subscription at $3.95 a year or on newsstands at 50 cents a copy, while the United States Information Agency Russian-language publication *Amerika* is sold in the Soviet Union. (*Soviet Life* is printed in Rockville, Maryland, in the same plant that produces *Amerika* for distribution in the USSR.) *Sputnik*, with English, French, German, and Russian editions, a digest of Russian magazine articles, is comparable with the *Reader's Digest* in size and appearance. Printed in Helsinki, Finland, it sells at $5.00 a year by mail or 50 cents a copy on newsstands. Both of these magazines are carefully edited, and *Soviet Life* is very well printed, with excellent color reproductions.

Although an American radio correspondent in the Soviet Union may telephone his dispatches directly to the United States, Novosti must provide all film and television equipment and crews used on programs recorded in the USSR for broadcasting abroad. American correspondents regard this as an attempt to control their output, since "cooperation" may be forthcoming only when the Soviet government likes the program being produced. (Pickups for the coverage of President Nixon's visit to Moscow in May 1972 were provided by Soviet radio and television, but these were live rather than recorded programs.)

One fundamental fact underlies the development of international broadcasting: it is possible for radio waves to travel from transmitter to receiver over territory controlled by neither broadcaster nor listener. Because no intervening facilities are required, the broadcaster may be certain of reaching the listener with exactly the message he wishes him to receive, subject only to such factors as atmospheric disturbances or deliberate jamming. The transmission of written (letter, newspaper, magazine, book) or wired (telephone, telegraph, cable) messages in some way involves intermediaries. Under the best conditions this may be difficult or expensive; at the worst it may involve censorship. The dissemination of messages through press, film, radio, or television controlled by someone else encounters similar problems. But radio and television broadcasting is almost a certain way of bringing the broadcaster into direct, uncensored contact with listeners and viewers.

Therefore, the development of international broadcasting has been governed mainly by situations in which the government of one country has wished to reach listeners in another without using facilities or media controlled by either the listener's or any other government. In some cases the listener's government merely has not been consulted—as when the United Kingdom broadcasts to the United States. But in the most dramatic uses of international broadcasting, the sending government deliberately attempts to circumvent the wishes of the receiver's government. This situation has given rise to the frequent use of radio as a political instrument. "By broadcasting alone can the voice of one country be carried to another, regardless of the latter's government. Not even the most terroristic methods of control avail against the will of people to tune in what they want to hear. . . . Broadcasting [therefore] is our only assured channel of international communication."[29]

At present, radio is a much better medium for international broadcasting than television, because land-based television transmitters have little more than line-of-sight coverage, whereas radio, especially short-wave radio, may reach out thousands of miles. However, there are many examples of "spillover audiences" for television programs. In Western Europe, people who live in border areas frequently watch programs from neighboring countries, and where incompatible systems are involved, sets usually are equipped to receive signals from both countries.

Of much greater importance politically is cross viewing along the boundaries between the democratic and socialist states, such as West Germany and Czechoslovakia, Austria and Czechoslovakia, and Austria and Hungary. Prime examples, of course, are the two Germanys. Since these countries speak the same language and use the same television system, residents on either side can readily receive signals from the other.

Little programming is done exclusively for audiences across the line, but there nevertheless is much cross viewing. The only country maintaining television services primarily for foreign audiences is the Soviet Union, which beams some programs in their native languages to viewers in Finland and Sweden.

Future satellite developments may provide foreign programs directly to home receivers, but this is not yet possible. However, when that time comes, the Soviet Union will be among the contenders. Commentator Yakovlev, writing in the ideological publication *Kommunist* in 1965, after observing that communication satellites will bring "world-vision," went on to say: "This will signify an open clash between two ideologies in the air. Only one possibility can be considered here—victory!"[30] In 1969 a Soviet historian, Yuri Sheinin, writing in the Moscow *Literary Gazette*, warned that worldwide television might present a threat to communism: "It is enough to imagine what the malicious use of the latest channels of information for reactionary purposes might lead to. To a certain degree it could impede social progress."[31] In 1972 Soviet Foreign Minister Andrei Gromyko proposed a convention severely limiting international satellite television (see above, p. 79).

International broadcasting was first used to advance political objectives in 1915, when Germany developed a regular radio news service used by a number of neutral countries.[32] Messages in code to German espionage agents—a forerunner of devices used by both sides in World War II—were incorporated into some of these transmissions. Since Germany's cable contacts had been cut, it had more reason than the Allies to use radio.

The political isolation of the USSR after the 1917 Revolution motivated it to undertake international broadcasting. On February 4, 1918, Lenin addressed a radio report "to everyone," in which, according to a Soviet source, he "refuted the false information disseminated by foreign newspapers and gave information about the conditions in the Soviet country, and about the decrees adopted by the Soviet government."[33] The USSR frequently used radio during invasions of its territory by its former allies in 1918 and 1919. While the peace treaty with the Central Powers signed at Brest-Litovsk on March 3, 1918, was under discussion, the Soviet Union broadcast a daily account of the negotiations in order to present its case to the world while the conference was in progress.

During the Communist-inspired Bela Kun revolution in Hungary in

1919, the Soviet Union aimed some broadcasts at Hungarian listeners. On March 22 Lenin told the Hungarians that "constant radio communication between Budapest and Moscow is undoubtedly necessary." On April 18 the Ministry of Foreign Affairs appealed to working people abroad: "The workers and peasants of Russia now freed from all oppressors and exploiters, first to have shed the capitalist yoke, ask you to be alert and not to slacken your pressure on your leaders who aspire to choke the people's revolution in Russia. . . ." On July 17, 1919, a broadcast to Great Britain, France, and Italy invited workers to demonstrate against intervention in Soviet Russia, and on November 18, 1920, an address to the workers and peasants of the Entente countries said that "world reactionary forces" were working against the interests of the working people of Russia, and appealed for "fraternal assistance from the working masses of the Entente countries, whose powerful voice could once again paralyze the reactionary intrigues. . . ."

Most of the programs described above were in Russian, since a Soviet source indicates that the first external broadcast in a foreign language was in German during the autumn of 1920.[34] In November 1927 delegations visiting the Soviet Union for the tenth anniversary of the Revolution were given foreign broadcasting facilities to report on their experiences. The foreign-language broadcasting department was organized in October 1929, the year in which regular broadcasts in German, French, and English were inaugurated. Daily programs in those languages began the following year.

In 1933 there were regular programs in eight languages—Czech, English, French, German, Hungarian, Italian, Spanish, and Swedish—plus occasional broadcasts in Turkish and Portuguese. With the start of World War II, languages were added in response to Soviet political and military involvement. Finnish broadcasts began in 1939 (the year of the Russian-Finnish War); Serbo-Croatian in April 1941 (the Germans occupied Yugoslavia in that month); and Bulgarian the following month (Bulgaria was occupied by the Germans in March 1941). Then came Danish, Dutch, Greek, Iranian, Norwegian, Polish, Slovakian, Turkish, and Hebrew.

The Western nations, with less incentive to broadcast to their neighbors, developed international services more gradually. In 1929 the Netherlands began short-wave broadcasts for its citizens abroad.[35] The British experimented in 1923 and started regular transmissions in 1932.

It was not until January 1938, however, that the BBC broadcast in a foreign language—in Arabic, for listeners in the Middle East—and it was only on September 27, 1938, at the height of the Munich crisis, that it broadcast to Europe in German, Italian, and French.[36]

The United States was the last great power to develop international broadcasting on an extensive scale, because it lacked the incentives which encouraged such broadcasting by other countries.[37] It was not politically isolated, as was the Soviet Union after World War I. It had no designs on its neighbors, as did Italy and Germany. It had no empire to bind together, as did the Netherlands and the United Kingdom. Furthermore, American traditions were against "government in business"; there was a strong dislike of government propaganda operations of any sort; the radio industry was strongly opposed to such broadcasts; and international broadcasting could not be made commercially self-supporting. When the United States finally did enter the field, it did so for the same reasons that caused the United Kingdom to initiate foreign-language broadcasts to Europe: it was concerned generally about international politics, and it felt the need to reply to the Axis propaganda campaign. After a slow start by private short-wave stations in the 1930s, the United States government began to exercise some supervision in 1939, although it did not take over the short-wave transmitters until November 4, 1942, almost a year after entering World War II.)

The USSR, the United States, the United Kingdom, and all the other countries engaged in international information activities dispense "propaganda," a variously defined term, which does not need to have a bad connotation. According to Funk and Wagnall's *New Standard Dictionary,* propaganda is "any institution or systematic scheme for propagating a doctrine or system." Webster's *New International Dictionary* defines it as "a group or movement organized for spreading a particular doctrine or system of principles." L. John Martin, in his *International Propaganda,* reviewed twenty-six different definitions and found they all agreed that "propaganda is the art of influencing, manipulating, controlling, promoting, changing, inducing, or securing the acceptance of opinions, actions, or behavior."[38] He then offered his own definition: "propaganda is a systematic attempt through mass communications to influence the thinking and thereby the behavior of people in the interest of some in-groups."

It is interesting to compare United States and Soviet statements about the purposes of external broadcasting. In 1948 the legislation establishing a permanent international information agency for the United States provided a declaration of objectives: "The Congress declares that the objectives of this Act are to enable the Government of the United States to promote a better understanding of the United States in other countries, and to increase mutual understanding between the people of the United States and the people of other countries. Among the means to be used in achieving these objectives are (1) an information service to disseminate abroad information about the United States, its people, and policies promulgated by the Congress, the President, the Secretary of State and other responsible officials of Government having to do with matters affecting foreign affairs . . ."[39]

Referring specifically to the Voice of America, the United States Information Agency stated in 1970:

The long-range interests of the United States are served by communicating directly with the peoples of the world by radio. To be effective, the Voice of America must win the attention and respect of listeners. These principles will govern VOA broadcasts:
1. VOA will be a consistently reliable and authoritative source of news. VOA news will be accurate, objective and comprehensive.
2. VOA will represent America, not any single segment of American society. It will therefore present a balanced and comprehensive projection of significant American thought and institutions.
3. As an official radio, VOA will present the policies of the United States clearly and effectively. VOA will also present responsible discussion and opinion on these policies.[40]

The USSR State Committee on Radio and Television declared in 1960 that its foreign-language broadcasts offered an "explanation of the peace-loving foreign policy of the Soviet government, the efforts directed by the government of the Soviet Union towards lessening international tension and bringing an end to the 'cold war,' and towards achieving peaceful coexistence among states with different social structures."[41] In addition, these broadcasts were to "expose the aggressive policy of the imperialist powers and their intrigues . . . [and describe] the struggle by peoples of Asia, Africa, and Latin America for . . . independence and freedom. . . . "

The Central Committee of the CPSU in a resolution adopted July 2, 1962, entitled "On Measures for the Further Improvement of the Work of Radio Broadcasting and Television," dealt at considerable length with broadcasts for foreign audiences, clearly indicating that such programs were of great importance to the Soviet Union.[42] After declaring that "serious shortcomings exist in radio broadcasting to foreign countries, especially in propaganda on the Soviet way of life and the successes in the building of communism," the committee instructed the broadcasting authorities to "skillfully take into account . . . the peculiarities of individual countries and groups within the population, to elucidate widely the life, the internal and external policy of the Soviet Union; to propagandize the achievements of world socialism, to tell in detail the international significance of the success of communist construction in the USSR; to unmask the anti-peoples policy of the imperialist states; [and] to show that in the Soviet Union friendly and brotherly mutual aid between the peoples has secured remarkable successes in the political, economic and cultural development of the populations of all the republics, autonomous oblasts, and national okrugs."

The Central Committee then directed that, effective September 1, 1962, the Radio and Television Committee was to introduce around-the-clock short-wave Russian-language services for reception both in the Soviet Union and abroad. Furthermore, it was to differentiate among programs for Asia, Africa, and Latin America; restructure those to Western Europe, America, and Japan with reference to the development of television in those countries; and organize broadcasts to foreign countries "from the Soviet trade unions, the Union of Soviet Societies of Friendship and Cultural Contacts with Foreign Countries, Soviet Committee for the Defense of Peace, Committee for Youth Organizations and other public organizations, and also radio broadcasts about individual Soviet republics." In addition, it also was to increase the availability of Soviet-produced programs for use on foreign radio and television stations.*

As is shown in Table 9, the USSR and the United States lead the world in amount of external broadcasting: Since 1965, first one and then the other has been ahead. In 1972 the Soviet Union broadcast 1,884 pro-

---

* In 1965 the magazine *Sovetskaya pechat* referred to Moscow's foreign output as "the source of truth about the Leninist policies of our party and government, about the affairs and work of the first socialist country in the world" (A. Yakovlev, I. Chuprynin, and Y. Orlov, "Mighty Means of Propaganda," *Sovetskaya pechat*, No. 6, 1965, translated in *The Soviet Press* 5:1 (Spring 1966), p. 20).

gram hours per week, compared with the United States total of 2,001. (The USSR total includes Radio Moscow, the various republic external programs, and Radio Station "Peace and Progress." The United States figure is for the Voice of America, 929 hr.; Radio Free Europe, 574 hr.; and Radio Liberty, 498 hr.) All the other European Communist countries combined (Albania, Bulgaria, Czechoslovakia, German Democratic Republic, Hungary, Poland, Romania, and Yugoslavia) broadcast 1,901 hours per week.*

The figures summarizing yearly output do not tell the whole story, however, since there may be important variations from month to month in reaction to international political developments.[43] In August and September 1968, after the invasion of Czechoslovakia on August 21 of that year, Soviet broadcasts in Czech and Slovak rose from 17½ to 168 hours a week, and then declined to 84 hours a week. At that time, Poland resumed broadcasting in Czech and Slovak after an 18-year interval, and by early September 1968 was broadcasting 140 hours a week in those languages. But its output was reduced to 17½ hours by the end of the year. At the time of the crisis, a clandestine service using East German transmitters began broadcasting in Czechoslovakia 24 hours a day. When it discontinued programming in February 1969, East Germany started 120 hours a week of Czech and Slovak programs on the same transmitters, reducing its output to 40 hours a week in June 1969.

In the latter 1960s the USSR and China had what the BBC described as "probably the most hostile and extensive radio confrontation of its kind in the history of international broadcasting." During the period 1967–1968 Peking broadcast 300 hours a week in Russian, increasing this at the beginning of 1969 to 417 hours. At that time the USSR was using 12 medium-wave channels simultaneously to beam an average of 168 hours a week of Chinese-language broadcasts to the Chinese People's Republic.

There are no official data on the number, location, or power of the transmitters carrying the USSR's international services. Long-, medium-,

---

* Since this review of Soviet external broadcasting, and the corresponding portions of subsequent chapters, deals with broadcasts intended to achieve political objectives, no references are made to Radio Luxembourg, Europe Number I, Radio Monaco, or other commercial stations. Although these stations do have large foreign audiences, their orientation is commercial rather than political, even though their news programs are widely heard abroad and undoubtedly influence their listeners.

Table 9. Estimated Total Program Hours per Week of Selected External Broadcasting Organizations[a]

Country	1950	1955	1960	1965	1966	1967	1968	1969	1970	1971	1972
USSR	533	656	1,015	1,417	1,527	1,707	1,906	1,928	1,908	1,915	1,884
Albania	26	47	63	154	200	382	452	476	487	487	490
Poland	131	359	232	280	281	306	312	305	334	336	340
East Germany (GDR)		9	185	308	298	296	295	335	274	273	284
Czechoslovakia	119	147	196	189	182	193	191	201	202	211	225
Romania	30	109	159	163	167	176	184	185	185	188	190
Bulgaria	30	60	117	154	156	154	162	164	164	175	175
Hungary	76	99	120	121	121	114	128	102	105	104	111
Yugoslavia	80	46	70	78	81	76	76	74	76	86	86
United States	497	1,274	1,495	1,832	1,865	1,842	2,006	1,908	1,907	1,829	2,001
Voice of America	497	843	640	831	845	831	951	877	863	785	929
Radio Free Europe		431	444	523	536	537	540	541	547	547	574
Radio Liberty			411	478	484	474	515	490	497	497	498
Chinese People's Republic	66	159	687	1,027	1,103	1,203	1,180	1,290	1,267	1,309	1,292
German Federal Republic		105	315	671	700	719	721	706	779	792	806
United Kingdom (BBC)	643	558	589	667	667	719	725	718	723	720	746
Egypt		100	301	505	589	580	599	586	540	545	601

[a] Data supplied by the BBC, published in part in some BBC handbooks. There are, however, certain discrepancies between the BBC figures and those supplied by the individual countries. A Soviet source reported that in 1966 USSR external broadcasts totaled 143 hours per day, or 1,001 hours per week (Zvorykin, p. 42). The BBC put USSR broadcasting for 1966 at 1,527 hours a week. However, it may be that the Soviet source indicated the number of hours of different programs, whereas the BBC reported total output hours, which in external broadcasting usually includes many repeats. On June 30, 1970, the United States Information Agency reported an average VOA weekly output of 830 hours, which is not much different from the BBC figure of 863 (United States Information Agency, *34th Semiannual Report to the Congress, January-June 1970*, p. 17). At the end of 1972 the Voice of America reported broadcasting 931 hours (data from VOA), whereas the BBC figure was 929 hours.

and short-wave bands are used, depending upon whether the target audience is an adjacent country, a more distant place on the European continent, or an overseas area. One unofficial source indicated that in 1971, 233 short-wave transmitters, located in all parts of the Soviet Union, were used for external broadcasting.[44] These varied in power from 50 to 240 kilowatts. The list included 44 stations with 50 kilowatts, 19 with 120, 101 with 100, 5 with 200, 63 with 240 kilowatts, and 1 with 150 kilowatts. These stations carried the foreign services of Radio Moscow; the foreign services of the various republics; the relays of some home services for listeners abroad; programs of the Soviet Union Committee for Cultural Relations; the Merchant Marine and Fishermen's Services; and the programs of Radio Station "Peace and Progress."

The Soviet Union leads the world in the number of languages used in external broadcasting. The exact number varies from time to time, although the general trend definitely is upward. In 1933 there were 8; by December 1941, 21) and by 1960, 38 languages.[45] According to a Soviet source, in 1966 external broadcasting used 56 foreign plus 10 USSR languages, for a total of 66 languages. In 1972 the BBC reported the total to be more than 80, although the Soviets themselves claimed only 70,[46] But whatever the number, since it is so large, it must be expected to vary as needs change.

By way of comparison, in 1972 the BBC's external services used 40 languages, while the Voice of America used only 35.[47] But the United States figure comparable with the Soviet 70 (or 80) would be 49, adding to the 35 VOA languages the 8 of Radio Liberty and the 6 of RFE not used by the VOA.

An idea of the range of USSR languages is indicated by a list provided by the Soviet broadcasting authorities in 1965, at which time they named the non-Soviet languages as follows: Albanian, Amharic, Arabic, Bambara, Bengali, Burmese, Bulgarian, Catalan, Chinese, Czech, Danish, Dutch, English, Finnish, French, German, Greek, Hausa, Hindi, Hungarian, Indi, Indonesian, Italian, Japanese, Khmer, Korean, Lappish, Linagala, Macedonian, Malay, Maltese, Mongolian, Nepalese, Norwegian, Pashto, Persian, Polish, Portuguese, Quechua, Romanian, Serbo-Croatian, Slovak, Slovian, Somali, Spanish, Swedish, Swahili, Tama, Tamil, Turkish, Urdu, Vietnamese, and Zulu. The Soviet languages used included Azerbaijanian (from Baku), Armenian (from Erevan), Byelorussian (from Minsk), Kurdish (from Yerevan), Latvian (from Riga),

Lithuanian (from Vilnius), Russian (from Moscow), Tadzhik (from Dushanbe), Ukrainian (from Kiev), and Uzbek (from Tashkent.)

Although most USSR external broadcasts originate in Moscow, there are other production centers too. A number of the republics transmit programs in their native languages for listeners in adjacent countries, as well as by short-wave for Soviet emigrants living abroad. Programs of this type now come from Alma-Ata, Dushanbe, Kiev, Baku, Minsk, Riga, Tallinn, Tashkent, Vilnius, and Yerevan.[48] Radio Tashkent in the Uzbek SSR has been broadcasting to foreign listeners for nearly twenty-five years. In 1967 Tashkent originated six and one half hours a day in English, Urdu, Indi, Persian, and Uzbek for audiences in India, Pakistan, Afghanistan, Iran, Ceylon, Japan, Australia, Canada, Sweden, Britain, New Zealand, and the United States. Radio Kiev for some years has broadcast in Ukrainian, English, and German, mainly for Ukrainian emigrants in Canada. There also are the special services in Russian, one maintained by the Soviet Committee for Cultural Relations with Fellow Countrymen Abroad, with a mailing address in Moscow and a branch in East Berlin, and the other by the Merchant Marine and Fishermen's Services, in the city of Riga.[49] In East Germany the Soviet Union operates Radio Volga, comparable with the United States Armed Forces Network, for its military forces.

Roughly comparable with Radio Liberty and Radio Free Europe is Radio Station "Peace and Progress," located in the same building used by the other external services, which is on the air fifteen hours a day.[50] A Soviet advertisement in the *World Radio-TV Handbook* described this station as "The Voice of Soviet Public Opinion," while the description provided by the WRTH, which probably was based on Soviet information, said that "it belongs to Soviet public organizations." In any case, it broadcasts to Europe in German; to Asia in Mongolian, English, French, and several dialects of Chinese; to Africa in English, French, and Portuguese; to the Near and Middle East in Yiddish and Hebrew; and to Latin America in English. In 1967, when the Indian government requested the Soviet Union to discontinue some Radio Station "Peace and Progress" broadcasts on the grounds that they were unduly critical of the Indian government, the USSR said it could not do so because the station was privately controlled and expressed the views of the individuals operating it rather than of the government.[51]

The Soviet Union's external services are headed by the first of the four vice-presidents of the State Committee on Radio and Television.[52] As with most countries, there are subdivisions by target audiences, with separate editorial boards, as they are called, for the Communist countries, North America, Latin America, Western Europe, the Near and Middle East, Southeast Asia, the Far East, and Africa. There also is a department that coordinates the external broadcasts originated by the various Soviet republics, as well as one concerned with audience mail.

The North American Service may be used as an example.[53] Although its exact schedule depends upon the season, this service is on the air daily from approximately 4:00 to 11:00 P.M., Eastern Standard Time. A similar Pacific Coast Service is delayed by several hours for West Coast listeners. There are three or four hours of original programming each day, although the output, with repeats, totals some twelve hours. The North American Service uses nine or ten frequencies, the Pacific Coast Service employs four frequencies. For some years the staff worked from 7:00 P.M. to 2:00 A.M., Moscow time, but now they prerecord most programs and put in a more normal working day.

The director of the North American Service, the translators, and of course the announcers speak English, although the administrators are not as fluent as the announcers. Key administrators often have backgrounds as residents, correspondents, or scholars in the United States. Basic program materials originally are written in Russian—just as most Voice of America materials are first written in English—and so must be translated into English before they are broadcast. But North American programs are both cast and spoken in American English, just as programs for the United Kingdom utilize British English. Most North American Service announcers are natives of the United States and therefore speak fluent colloquial American English. They read American magazines (unlike most Moscow residents, they receive prompt delivery of current United States publications of their choice), listen to the Voice of America, and talk with American tourists in order to keep informed on current language trends. I have visited with them on several occasions and found their knowledge of American developments and their use of the language so good as to make me forget I was in Moscow.

Production procedures resemble those of any American station. Programs originate in talk-size studios, with the usual array of microphones, turntables, tape recorders, and loudspeakers. There is portable equipment for remote recordings as required. North American staff members are conscientious workers, and re-record and edit until they get satis-factory results. All programs are broadcast from recordings, which is one reason the latest news developments are not covered. Staff turnover is surprisingly low, and I encountered some of the same people when visiting in Moscow in 1970 as in 1958.[54]

Radio Moscow productions follow a fairly predictable pattern. Two or more voices, male or female, alternate during North American Serv-ice presentations, which usually begin with five or ten minutes of news on the hour, although news sometimes is given in shortened form on the half hour as well. After the main items are listed, the news is given in about the same detail as on an American program of the same duration, although the contents, of course, are different. As with domestic news programs, there is considerable emphasis on economic achievements and output norms. There is not, however, the "self-criticism" feature so often found on programs for home audiences. Current USA-USSR relations are covered, but there is no effort to achieve objectivity, nor are stories detrimental to the Soviet Union included either for their news value or to increase the credibility of the remaining items. Radio Moscow is slow to cover late news breaks: whereas the Americans and British try to be as timely with international as with domestic news programs, Radio Moscow apparently waits for the official line before putting anything on the air.

News usually is followed by commentary, sometimes from one of the domestic services or a Soviet publication and at other times written espe-cially for the broadcast. Although the author often is identified, reading usually is by one of the regular announcers. If the source is a broadcast in some language other than English, the feature may be introduced with a few moments of the original, after which it is faded out and a transla-tion read by the announcer. (The same procedure is followed for news program actualities.) The commentary often reports opinion on highly controversial issues and may be severe in its treatment of American policies and personnel.

A long-time feature in lighter vein is "Moscow Mailbag," on which two or three staff members answer questions from listeners. Skillfully done to suggest informality, "Moscow Mailbag" questions and answers are carefully organized to reflect maximum credit on the Soviet Union. There also may be talks on such subjects as "Life in the Soviet Union," "Science and Engineering," "Women in the USSR," "Medicine in Moscow," and "Youth Parade." There are interviews with visiting Americans and descriptions of major events like the annual November 7 parade. Most programs contain music too—concert music, folk songs, or light popular music. Musical features, however, often are unsatisfactory on short-wave, because of fading.

Although the North American Service does a creditable job, it does not compare in production or polish with either the BBC or the Voice of America. Surely it is much less professional than the magazine *Soviet Life*, which is printed in the United States in order to match the quality of reproduction to which Americans are accustomed. When asked to comment on the principal short-wave services, Europeans usually put the BBC first, the Voice of America second, and Radio Moscow a poor third. The British programs are favored because of their World War II record for accuracy and objectivity, and because of the skillful way in which their content and presentation imply—if not achieve—impartiality, even though they are part of the United Kingdom's propaganda apparatus. The Voice of America comes second, partly because it so often appears to be doing a "selling job" for its sponsors. Except among dyed-in-the-wool Communist sympathizers, Radio Moscow is ranked third. This is due to its obviously tendentious nature, because its news usually is limited to items of direct progaganda value, and because it so regularly disposes of the Soviet Union's opponents in severe and sarcastic terms, while reporting USSR activities in a consistently favorable manner.

The exchange of programs with foreign countries is the responsibility of the Chief Editorial Board for Program Exchange.[55] The board's three departments are responsible respectively for radio exchange, television exchange, and liaison with foreign organizations. This agency represents the USSR in its contacts with such international groups as the OIRT and arranges Soviet participation in international contests and exhibitions. Relations are maintained with eighty-six countries, many of which receive and use material provided by the Soviet Union. A number of American stations broadcast programs supplied by Radio Moscow. Most of these are musical programs, though some language materials are included too.* On May 31, 1973, the chairman of the State Committee on

* The broadcasting organizations of the United Kingdom, France, West Germany, Italy, and some Eastern countries provide tapes of musical and other programs to American stations. Educational stations, particularly, are frequent users of such materials.

Radio and Television and the president of the National Broadcasting Company signed an agreement for the exchange of programs and personnel.[56] Under its terms, incidentally, Soviet programs used in the United States may be sponsored. There also were provisions for the exchange of production, technical, and management personnel; manuscripts; program information; and catalogs.

The OIRT publishes several times each year the *Catalogue of Transmissions Suitable for Exchange*, listing programs from its members available for use in other countries. Prominent among Soviet offerings are musical programs. Thus, one issue listed tape recordings of little-known works by Martinů, Prokofiev, Dohnanyi, Schubert, Szymanowski, Paganini, and Saint-Saëns; better-known compositions by Stravinski, Scriabin, and Tartini; various popular songs by Soviet composers; and a great deal of Russian folk music.[57]

The output of Radio Moscow becomes more meaningful if reference is made to foreign broadcasts whose target is the Soviet Union. In all parts of the USSR it is possible to tune in programs from the Voice of America (VOA), Radio Liberty, the BBC, Radio Vatican, Radio Israel, West Germany, the Chinese People's Republic, and some other countries. The VOA and the BBC broadcast in English and some Soviet languages, while Radio Liberty broadcasts only in USSR languages.*

The Voice of America, an outgrowth of the international broadcasting begun by the United States during World War II, first broadcast in Russian to the Soviet Union on February 17, 1947. In 1972 VOA beamed 98 hours a week in Russian to the USSR, along with 28 hours in Ukrainian, and 7 hours each in Armenian, Estonian, Georgian, Latvian, Lithuanian, Ukrainian, and Uzbek. English-language services also are available 24 hours a day to Soviet listeners. These programs originate in Washington, D.C., and are beamed to the USSR by transmitters in the United States, with relays in Europe and Asia. Also generally available in the Soviet Union are the programs of the BBC's Eastern European service, which in June 1972 broadcast 31 hours each week in Russian, along with many English-language programs in the BBC World Service.[58]

---

* Paralleling Radio Liberty is Radio Free Europe, which broadcasts in their languages to Poland, Czechoslovakia, Hungary, Romania, and Bulgaria. A description of various clandestine radio stations which beam programs to the Soviet Union and other Eastern European socialist countries is provided in William A. Matthews, "Clandestines—The Political Voice of Radio," *How to Listen to the World 1971*, 6th ed., pp. 135–140.

The Voice of America is supplemented by Radio Liberty, now openly admitted to be of United States origin, which broadcasts to the USSR in 20 Soviet languages.[59] Radio Liberty, established in 1953 as Radio Liberation, and later renamed Radio Liberty, has administrative headquarters in New York and studios in Munich, Germany. Staffed by Americans and former Soviet citizens, it uses 17 transmitters, operating on 33 frequencies, located in Germany, Spain, and Taiwan. During a normal week Radio Liberty broadcasts 36 hours in Russian and 45 hours in other USSR languages, for a total of 81 hours of original programming. Through repeats its daily transmitter hours add up to over 2,000 per week.*

For a long time Radio Liberty—along with Radio Free Europe, founded in 1950, which broadcasts to the other socialist countries of Eastern Europe excepting Yugoslavia—claimed to be privately supported by foundations, corporations, and the public. But the truth began to emerge. A *New York Times* series on the Central Intelligence Agency published in 1966 referred to the CIA affiliations of Radio Liberty and Radio Free Europe.[60] On January 23, 1971, Clifford P. Case, United States senator from New Jersey, offered documentation to support his assertions that the CIA had spent several hundred million dollars during the previous twenty years supporting the two operations and announced that he would introduce legislation bringing them under the direct authorization and appropriations control of Congress.[61] The senator claimed that during the previous fiscal year their combined operating costs approximated $34 million. "Covert CIA funding of the two stations has been an open secret for two years," said the newspaper story. Under CIA operating procedures, their activities were approved by the National Security Council, with disclosure to Congress limited to a handful of senior legislators.

On June 25, 1971, the United States Senate passed a resolution appropriating funds for both organizations, this being the first time any part of the United States government had officially admitted the CIA relationship.[62] In October 1973 permanent enabling legislation was passed.

---

* Radio Liberty broadcasts in three Slavic languages (Byelorussian, Russian, and Ukrainian) and seventeen non-Slavic languages (Armenian, Azerbaijanian, Georgian, Adhige, Avar, Chechen, Karachai, Ossetian, Tatar, Bashkir, Karakalpak, Kazakh, Kirghiz, Tadzhik, Turkmen, Uigur, and Uzbek).

The USSR has claimed CIA involvement in Radio Liberty for a long time. Soviet broadcasting executives brought this up during my first visit to the USSR in 1958, and occasional articles have appeared in the Soviet press insisting there was government support of Radio Liberty.[63] Soviet spokesmen have complained about foreign broadcasting services generally, because they breach the information wall, but Radio Liberty has been particularly subject to criticism. In April 1966—the month of the *New York Times* series mentioned above—an article in *Izvestia* by "Observer" stated the case very firmly: "Born at the height of the 'cold war' as a medium of the notorious 'American Committee for Liberation from Bolshevism,' which united in its ranks all kinds of scum and traitors to the Soviet motherland, Radio 'Liberty' has become a tool of reactionary U.S. circles in their struggle against the soviet Union. The 'Committee for Liberation,' which was renamed the Radio 'Liberty' Committee at the beginning of 1964, now includes the Institute 'for Study' of the USSR and other organizations, in addition to Radio 'Liberty.' To support the reorganized committee the U.S.A. spends the round sum of $25,000,000 annually."

Examples of the types of broadcasts to which the Soviet government objected were cited in the article: "It was Radio 'Liberty' that for several months publicized with great fanfare the filthy anti-Soviet writings of the scum Sinyavsky and Daniel, who have been justly sentenced by a Soviet court. It repeatedly aired, in particular, Sinyavsky-Tertz's short stories 'The Trial Begins' and 'Lyubimov' and Daniel-Arzhak's short story 'Moscow Calling,' which contain not only outright slander of the socialist system, the building of communism in our country and the Soviet people, but frank appeals to terrorism and to the elimination of socialism by force and violence."*

One reason the USSR objects to Western programs, and especially to Radio Liberty, is that they bring the people of the USSR messages from Soviet dissidents that never would be published by the government-controlled domestic media.[64] A Soviet citizen who decides dramatically to oppose his government may write to several important officials, supplying copies of his letter to foreign correspondents. The correspondents

---

* Some of the Communist countries threatened to boycott the 1972 Olympic Games in Munich if West Germany renewed the licenses of Radio Liberty and Radio Free Europe when they expired in June 1971. However, the licenses were renewed (*Variety*, June 24, 1971, p. 36).

send this material abroad, after which it receives considerable circulation when broadcast back to the Soviet public by VOA, BBC, or Radio Liberty. In May 1968 Reuters was warned against sending dispatches abroad based on unauthorized contacts with private citizens, and in July of the same year Soviet leaders became very critical of VOA and BBC newscasts that spread information about the trial of four youths who had challenged the regime's restrictions on free speech.[65] In 1971 foreign stations were reporting the death of Nikita Khrushchev for two days before any of the domestic media referred to it at all (see above, p. 115).

On various occasions I have asked Soviet broadcasting officials to discuss and compare the Voice of America, the BBC, and Radio Liberty. Invariably, they reply that from their point of view the BBC is best (or least bad), the VOA a poor second, and Radio Liberty least acceptable. Radio Liberty, according to them, is irresponsible and dishonest, encourages unrest, and incites opposition to the regime. Although Radio Liberty claims to be as factually accurate as the VOA, it usually is more outspoken, this being one of the arguments for its establishment in the first place.

But there are Soviet objections to other foreign services too. In January 1973 the trade union newspaper *Trud* complained about broadcasts with religious themes from the VOA, the BBC, Radio Liberty, West Germany's Deutsche Welle, Vatican Radio, Radio Monte Carlo, and the Voice of the Orient. "The voices of religious radio advocates cease neither day nor night," said *Trud*. "They try to export to our country ideals alien to the Soviet people. They try to change their convictions and way of thinking . . . vain attempts."[66]

A new Soviet publication called *Questions of Theory and Practice of Mass Media* attested to the effectiveness of foreign radio broadcasts, at the same time specifying objections to them.[67] An article complained that foreign broadcasts aroused dissatisfaction among various nationality groups; that broadcasts to Central Asia tried to build up feelings of "national exclusiveness in that area"; and that the primary targets were Soviet youth and intelligentsia. As to youth programs, the publication said that the broadcasts try "to weaken the revolutionary enthusiasm of youth; to inculcate an apolitical attitude, apathy toward the historic fate of socialism, and individualism; to dull class consciousness; to stir up among Soviet youth feelings of admiration for the Western way of life, bourgeoisie norms and morals; and on this basis, to provoke dissatisfaction with Soviet reality." Interestingly, the article admitted that the VOA has a regular youth audience in the USSR and cited research from the Komsomol Committee as proving that "a certain part of the youth more or less regularly listens to broadcasts by American radio."

What is the Soviet Union to do when confronted by unwanted foreign broadcasts? To a country that believes in controlling and censoring news, such broadcasts are a breach of the information barrier. One reaction is to counteract them through its own media. There was reference above to the apparent effect of foreign broadcasts on the restructuring of domestic news programs. A study published in 1953 reported approximately 1,000 references in the Soviet media to Voice of America broadcasts between April 1, 1947, and March 31, 1951, the first under the title "A False Voice,"[68] The Voice of America was the subject of a generalized and, for the most part, unsystematic attack, whose nature and extent were more related to the state of the cold war than to specific VOA programs. USSR communications media, concluded the study, were trying to counteract the Voice "by posing a negative counter image of the United States, rather than by seeking to refute the negative image of the Soviet system disseminated by the VOA." During 1971 the Soviet Union made 416 separate attacks on Radio Liberty, 82 of them in publications distributed outside the USSR, and 334 in domestic media.[69] During the first half of 1972, the same source reported 255 attacks on Radio Liberty.

It was inevitable that sooner or later the USSR would try to prevent its citizens from listening to foreign broadcasts by jamming them.* This, of course, is not a new practice. It was begun in 1934 when the Dollfuss government in Austria jammed radio attacks from Nazi Germany.[70] The

---

* Jamming consists of broadcasting noise or another program on or near the frequency of the station whose programs it is desired to exclude. This can be done to long-, medium-, or short-wave transmissions. Powerful sky-wave signals can be radiated into the ionosphere and reflected back to earth at distant points. In this way it is possible to jam over large areas, even in foreign countries, as the USSR has done in Poland and some other countries from time to time. Alternatively, several low-power transmitters can be used to disrupt local reception by using ground-wave signals originated in the immediate vicinity. This procedure often is used in large cities. Through a combination of sky- and ground-wave propagation, a government may attempt to blot out reception in an entire country. (Information paraphrased and quoted from Voice of America statement, "Background on Radio 'Jamming.'") There are discussions of the legal aspects of jamming in Martin, pp. 85–87, and of both its legal and technical aspects in Delbert D. Smith, *International Telecommunication Control*, pp. 5–17.

next year Germany began jamming Moscow, and from then until the fall of Hitler there hardly was a time when jamming did not occur somewhere in the world. After 1945 jamming ceased for about twelve months, but a jamming war then broke out between Moscow and Madrid, after which there was much interference, particularly by the USSR and its neighbors, with programs from the BBC, the Voice of America, Radio Liberty, Radio Free Europe, and Vatican Radio.

The concentration has been on programs in Eastern European languages, English-language transmissions usually going unchallenged. Soviet spokesmen say that the English-language programs are more objective and accurate than those in USSR languages. Russian-language broadcasts are "distorted in an unfriendly way," one official told me. Actually, the basic factual content of VOA and BBC programs in English and USSR languages is about the same. But not many Soviet citizens understand English well enough to follow the programs, and those who do often are sophisticated intellectuals who might not be affected too much by what they heard. Furthermore, there may not be enough equipment to jam all the transmissions, and it provides better returns to concentrate on those in local languages. Finally, it may be that some of the Soviet leaders themselves, many of whom understand English, want to hear outside news sources. Most of the broadcasting officials I have talked to were familiar with VOA and English-language programs, and often heard them.

Soviet jamming of the Voice of America began in 1948, and during the next several years most other European socialist countries followed their example, as did mainland China in 1956.[71] When it came on the air in 1953, Radio Liberty was given the same treatment. United States protests against jamming went unheeded until June 19, 1963, when suddenly the USSR stopped jamming broadcasts in Armenian, Georgian, Estonian, Latvian, Lithuanian, Polish, Russian, and Ukrainian. Romania stopped jamming on July 29, 1963; Hungary on February 1, 1964; and Czechoslovakia on April 1, 1964. Bulgaria, however, continued to jam and still does.

The Soviet Union resumed jamming VOA and Radio Liberty programs in Russian, Ukrainian, Georgian, and Armenian in August 1968, when it invaded Czechoslovakia, presumably to prevent its own citizens from learning the full facts about the invasion and hearing about adverse world reactions. Since then Czechoslovakia, East Germany, and Poland have resumed jamming VOA and RFE, while the Soviet Union from its own territory often jams RFE programs for those countries. Romania, however, has done no jamming since 1963 and Hungary since 1964.[72] As an example of the measures taken to overcome jamming, in November 1969 the United States began using as many as twenty-seven short-wave frequencies, plus a million-watt long-wave transmitter in Germany, for one hour of evening broadcasts in Russian to the Soviet Union.

The United States government has tried periodically through diplomatic channels to persuade the Soviet Union to cease jamming.[73] While visiting the Soviet Union in 1970 I could find no Soviet broadcaster willing to admit that jamming was taking place, although I heard jamming on my radio. Subsequently, an account by a British correspondent, datelined Moscow, November 23, 1970, reported intensified jamming of VOA broadcasts in Russian.[74] In Moscow in October 1972 I heard jamming signals very clearly. On June 24, 1972, the Soviet Union began jamming Russian- and Hebrew-language broadcasts from Radio Israel, probably because they relayed accounts by Western correspondents of the arrest, trial, and persecution of Jewish citizens in the USSR. But on September 9, 1973, the jamming of transmissions from the Voice of America, BBC, and Deutsche Welle was stopped, although continuing for programs from Radio Liberty, Israel, and China. This might have been to provide the USSR with a propaganda advantage at the time of the reconvening of the European Security Conference in Geneva on September 18 of that year, at which the free exchange of ideas was expected to be a major agenda topic, although there is no documentation to support this hypothesis. In view of the vacillating policy of the USSR one can only conclude that jamming will start and stop depending upon current international and domestic pressures.

It must be realized that jamming is never entirely successful and that it requires a much larger installation to jam effectively than to transmit programs in the first place. For example, in April 1949, even though the Soviet Union was using more than 1,000 transmitters to jam the American and British services to the USSR and other Eastern countries, many programs still got through, particularly in areas away from the big cities where the jammers were concentrated.[75] An American writing from Moscow in September 1973 reported that there were 3,000 jamming stations, and that the Kremlin had spent between $200 million and $300 million building and installing this equipment plus another $100 million a year to operate it.

Jamming is illegal under international law, and the Western powers periodically have protested against it. Ever since 1906 international radio conventions have forbidden interference with other country's radio services. On December 14, 1950, by a vote of 49 to 5, the United Nation's General Assembly reminded members that Article 44 of the 1947 International Telecommunication Convention signed at Atlantic City required that all stations "be established and operated in such a manner as not to result in harmful interference to the radio service or communication of other members."[76] Since jamming constituted "a violation of the accepted principles of freedom of information," the Assembly therefore requested "the governments of all Member States to refrain from such interference with the right of their peoples to freedom of information."

On the other hand, at least one international telecommunications convention gives its members the right to stop transmissions "which may appear dangerous to the security of the State or contrary to their laws. . . ."[77] In the 1920s and 1930s the signatories of various international agreements pledged not to broadcast programs that might cause political difficulties for their neighbors. In September 1936 a League of Nations conference in Geneva, attended by delegates from thirty-seven countries, drew up an International Convention Concerning the Use of Broadcasting in the Cause of Peace, which among other things required the contracting states to prohibit broadcasts calculated "to incite the population of any territory to acts incompatible with international order or . . . security"; to ensure that their domestic transmissions did "not constitute incitement either to war . . . or acts likely to lead thereto"; and not knowingly to broadcast incorrect information which might lead to international misunderstanding.[78] Signatories included the USSR but not the United States. Following World War II this convention was revived in 1954 by action of the General Assembly of the United Nations, although with an amendment condemning jamming.

Eastern countries have justified jamming as a defense against incitement to disorder and revolution, contending that a country has the same right to exclude subversive propaganda as illegal drugs or pornographic literature. The representative of the Soviet Union at the United Nations session cited above asserted that the anti-jamming resolution had been introduced by countries wishing to "take advantage of the United Nations and its proclaimed principles of freedom of information in order to conduct unlimited 'psychological warfare.' " Such warfare, he said, had been undertaken by the ruling circles of the United States and the United Kingdom against a number of states, including the USSR, the People's Democracies, and the Chinese People's Republic.

"It was only to be expected," he continued, "that the countries against which such 'psychological warfare' was conducted should take measures to counteract it in order to paralyze the aggressor, to defend their peoples from the consequences of that type of attack, and to nullify and render ineffective a weapon of aggression which was formerly used only in the time of war. The States against which psychological warfare has been directed have, in fact, taken measures to counteract that type of aggression. There can be no doubt regarding the legality and justice of those counter-measures against aggression by radio."

The spokesman from Czechoslovakia supported the USSR, stating that his country also voted against the resolution because "the intention of its sponsors was primarily to divert the attention of the Assembly from an organized campaign of radio propaganda which constitutes a direct threat to peace, is based on this interpretation, misinformation and distortion of facts, and is beamed daily for ten full hours to my country."

A country which really believes in freedom of information, and does not fear the consequences of a free press, will seldom if ever jam foreign broadcasts, even if it dislikes them. On the other hand, countries which feel the need for a controlled press will—and do—jam programs that they consider objectionable. It is reasonable to assume, therefore, that despite the anti-jamming resolutions of the United Nations, the International Telecommunication Union, and other international bodies, whenever a country with a controlled press becomes concerned about the effects of foreign broadcasts on its domestic affairs, it may resort to jamming.

There are no studies of the results obtained from international broadcasting comparable with those available in many countries about their domestic programming. Nor are the data about foreign listening to Radio Moscow as comprehensive as the reports from the BBC and VOA about their audiences, inadequate as they are. However, since the audiences for external programs are likely to be in inverse ratio to the attractiveness of the receiving country's domestic communications media, the amount of Soviet listening to such programs should not be judged on the basis of short-wave listening in the United States, since Americans have few incentives to hear foreign programs.

To indicate the results received from its external broadcasts, Radio Moscow cites letters from listeners, of which 158,000 were received in 1958 and 248,000 in 1962.[79] The Central Committee of the CPSU said in 1962 that up to 170,000 letters were received each year from listeners in over 100 countries, thus testifying "to the interest of millions of foreigners in Soviet radio broadcasts."[80] By way of comparison, the BBC reported that during 1970 it received over a quarter of a million letters from foreign listeners.[81]

In 1962 and 1963 an American sociology professor studied a group of Americans who listened under test conditions to recordings of Radio Moscow's North American Service.[82] Sixty-one volunteer respondents—college groups and townspeople—were divided into experimental and control groups, the experimental group hearing an average of two hours of recorded Radio Moscow programs each week for three months, for a total of fifty hours of listening. The findings were favorable to Radio Moscow. The test group reported an increased belief in the Soviet government's sincerity; heightened feelings of identification with the Russian people; greater acceptance of the logic of Soviet viewpoints; and increased questioning of the objectivity of American news sources. But one reason for this was that the respondents had expected the programs to contain so much propaganda, to have so many distortions, and to be so illogical that they were pleased with what they heard. In other words, it was "*less* distorted, *less* biased, and *less* one-sided than they expected it to be." In any case, since most of the test group would not have listened to Radio Moscow under normal conditions, the programs would have had no effect on them without the experiment.

The impact of Radio Moscow on North America probably is very slight. Clearly, there is very little listening. Even though a good all-wave receiver in many places can pull in Radio Moscow one evening out of three, reception difficulties often discourage regular tuning. More important is the fact that most Americans are sufficiently satisfied with the news and information from their own printed and broadcast media to feel no need for short-wave programs from outside. Those who do listen are apt to be distressed by Radio Moscow's highly tendentious and hortatory style. In fact, Radio Moscow might increase its audience by providing more objective news treatment and presenting a less consistently roseate view of the USSR. But if it did so, Soviet citizens tuning in by chance might be distressed at the discrepancies between their domestic services and what their government sent abroad.

Why, then, does the USSR maintain such an extensive external broadcasting establishment? In many parts of the world, particularly Europe, the Middle East, and Asia, Soviet long-, medium-, and short-wave programs come in as well as domestic transmissions. Soviet broadcasters have pointed out to me that even if the percentage of listeners is very small, a fraction of 1 per cent of the public in any large country could constitute 50,000 to 100,000 people or more, a group well worth reaching. Furthermore, those who do listen may spread reports of what they hear among friends and associates. In many cases, listening is done by people disposed to accept the party line, who use the service as a propaganda guide. For all anyone knows, Radio Moscow—and indeed, those broadcasting in the other direction too—may transmit hidden messages, as was the case during World Wars I and II. Finally—and probably this is most important—the world's monitoring services pass along to the news agencies many statements made by Radio Moscow, which then give very wide coverage to at least some of its output.*

* A writer for the Canada News Agency reported in March 1971 that English-language broadcasts from Radio Moscow were the sole source of news for some 5,000 Canadians living in the northern part of the country. Scattered in tiny settlements in the Arctic Islands, and without good signals from the Canadian Broadcasting Corporation, they had good reception only from Radio Moscow (*Minneapolis Tribune*, March 7, 1971, p. 13A). However, Canada's new satellite may have the effect of hastening the installation of improved ground-based radio and television transmitters.

VI

German Democratic Republic

Broadcasting in the German Democratic Republic (the GDR or East Germany) is unique in the socialist world because of the special relationship between the two Germanys. The constant availability of broadcasts from the German Federal Republic provides continuing motivation for the improvement of the East German output, even though GDR broadcasting is complicated by government requirements for strong ideological emphasis. Nevertheless, many observers believe that East German broadcasting is the best in socialist Europe.

Facts about the German Democratic Republic

In 1945, at the end of World War II, the Potsdam Agreement assigned 14 per cent of the population and 24 per cent of the area of the former Reich to Poland and the Soviet Union. The remainder of Germany then was divided into four occupation zones, governed respectively by the USSR, the United States, the United Kingdom, and France. The eastern or Soviet zone evolved into the present German Democratic Republic.

East Germany, with an area of 41,718 square miles, is about the size of Ohio (41,222 square miles). Its population in 1970 was 17,057,000 people, and its capital city of East Berlin had 1,085,000 inhabitants.[1] The German Federal Republic (West Germany) with 95,860 square miles is nearly the size of Oregon (96,981 square miles). Its population in 1969 was 61,195,000; that of West Berlin was 2,134,000. The GDR's neighbor to the west and southwest is West Germany (half of East Germany's land frontiers border on West Germany); to the south Czecho-slovakia; and to the east Poland. The Baltic Sea is on the north. West Berlin is a political enclave 110 miles inside the GDR.

Much of the short history of the German Democratic Republic has been a result of its close association with the Soviet Union and its competitive relationship with West Germany. Recognizing the economic and political strength of the USSR, and aware of the many Soviet troops on its territory, the GDR must plan and act with reference to the USSR.* At the same time, it is responsive to the economic, political, and ideological magnetism of West Germany.

The GDR was proclaimed on October 7, 1949, a few months after the establishment of the Federal Republic on May 23 of the same year.[In 1953 popular discontent led to uprisings in several East German cities, which were severely suppressed by Soviet troops. In 1955 East Germany signed a peace treaty with the Soviet Union, and in 1964 a twenty-year treaty of friendship.

The erection of the Berlin Wall in August 1961 was a master stroke for economic self-sufficiency or a major public relations blunder, depending upon one's point of view. My hosts in East Berlin justified it on economic grounds. Although conceding it has caused much suffering to some individuals and families, they asserted that the Wall ended the brain drain (before it went up, 2,000 East Germans a day—almost 100 per hour—including some of the most productive citizens in the country, were deserting to the West), reduced smuggling, curtailed illegal currency transactions, and reduced West German espionage. However this may be, there is no doubt that the country's economic status has improved since the Wall was constructed.[3] But despite the détente between East Germany and the Soviet Union on the one hand and West Germany on the other, all reports indicate that the Wall will remain and that emigration will continue to be strictly controlled.

Until recently most of the GDR's foreign contacts were with socialist countries, although valiant efforts to establish Western ties eventually brought results. Diplomatic relations now have been established with the German Federal Republic, France, the United States, the United

---

* It was reported in 1970 that the USSR had stationed 260,000 soldiers, 1,000 heavy tanks, and 6,000 armored vehicles in East Germany, and a 1973 news story stated that 2,000 more tanks had been dispatched to strengthen a Russian garrison of 20 divisions (*New York Times*, February 19, 1973, p. 5C).

Kingdom, and some other Western states, and East Germany belongs to both the UN and UNESCO. All this has been accompanied by a progressively more relaxed attitude toward Western countries and visitors, apparent during my several visits to East Berlin. Nevertheless, at the same time that East Germany seeks more and closer contacts with Western countries, its Central Committee has called for "closer vigilance" in order to exclude unwanted Western influences, and has stated that the leading West German political party is offering "nothing more than another evil form of imperialism."[4] The GDR is prepared to benefit from close contacts with the democracies, but it surely will continue to maintain and protect its basic ideologies and procedures in every way possible.

Although the German Democratic Republic now is the second industrial power in Eastern Europe, and the seventh nation in the world in terms of production output, its early years were very difficult. It was stifled economically by the devastation of World War II; the USSR took all its German reparations from this sector of the country, at the same time requiring the GDR to contribute to the support of occupying Soviet forces; and it did not benefit from any counterpart of the Marshall Plan aid given West Germany by the United States.

In 1950 the GDR became a member of the Moscow-oriented Council for Mutual Economic Assistance (COMECON), and its foreign trade is mainly with Eastern socialist countries, although it now is establishing trade missions in a number of Western capitals. Nevertheless, in 1970, 41 per cent of the value of its foreign trade was with the USSR.[5] In second place, surprisingly, was the German Federal Republic with 14 per cent. Czechoslovakia was third with 10 per cent, Poland fourth with 8 per cent, and Hungary fifth with 5 per cent. Less than half of 1 per cent of the GDR's trade was with the United States. But in the same year 72 per cent of all tourists came from nonsocialist countries, the majority probably from West Germany. However, the easing of border formalities with Poland and Czechoslovakia early in 1972 undoubtedly will increase tremendously the number of tourists from socialist countries.*

---

* In the first six months of 1972, after visas were eliminated and currency and custom restrictions lifted for short visits between East Germany and Poland, it was estimated that over 6 million East Germans and Poles crossed their common frontier, though often for visits of less than a day (*New York Times*, January 4, 1972, p. 36M; *New York Times*, July 5, 1972, p. 8C). But at the end of the year, by which time some 16 million Poles and Germans had crossed the border, the experiment was curtailed, mainly because World War II enmities were surfacing

A visit to the East German capital provides dramatic evidence of the reconstruction taking place. With an eye to propaganda effect, East Berlin is rebuilding Alexanderplatz into a showplace to match West Berlin's Kurfürstendamm, with wide streets, efficient subways, new buildings, comfortable hotels, and well-stocked shops. The adjacent new television tower, 1,185 feet high, has a revolving restaurant at 690 feet providing a panoramic view of both Berlins. A popular Sunday pastime is to stroll down Unter den Linden, the most elegant street of the prewar city, which has been attractively rebuilt, and to be photographed with the Brandenburg Gate and the Wall in the background. Although there still is a great difference between the living standards of the two Germanys, any open-minded visitor must recognize that the German Democratic Republic is making remarkable progress. I stayed for several days in 1968, 1970, and 1972 in East Berlin hotels and was much impressed.

Legal Structure

The organization of broadcasting in the two Germanys parallels their government structures. Recalling how the Nazi party used centralized broadcasting for propaganda, the Western powers reconstituted their zones as a federal republic with eleven separate states or Länder, each with its own radio and television services. But the USSR organized its zone according to a highly centralized pattern.

The present constitution of the German Democratic Republic came into effect April 9, 1968, replacing the original constitution of 1949.[6] The Preamble, consistent with so many East German statements about the United States and West Germany, declared that the people of East Germany gave themselves this "socialist Constitution" partly because "the government of the United States of America, in agreement with circles of West German monopoly capital, [had] split Germany in order to build up West Germany as a base of imperialism and of struggle against socialism, which is contradictory to the vital interest of the nation."

The German Democratic Republic is described as "a socialist state of the German nation. It is the political organization of the working

---

again as a result of the Germans filling Polish camping sites and hotel rooms while the Poles cleared East German shelves of scarce consumer goods (*New York Times*, December 10, 1972, p. 17).

people in town and countryside who are jointly implementing socialism under the leadership of the working class and its Marxist-Leninist Party."[7] No article of the Constitution deals expressly with the mass media, although Article 12 declares that "post and telecommunications installations," like most other basic enterprises, "are nationally-owned property" and are not to be privately controlled.

The portion of the 1968 Constitution dealing with freedom of expression clearly was based on Article 9 of the original 1949 Constitution, which read: "All citizens have the right, within the limits of universally applicable laws, to express their opinion freely and publicly and to hold unarmed and peaceful assemblies for that purpose. This freedom shall not be restricted by any service or employment status, and no one may be discriminated against for exercising this right."[8]

Article 23 of the 1968 Constitution repeated some of this phraseology: "(1) Every citizen of the German Democratic Republic has the right to express publicly and freely his opinion in accordance with the spirit and aims of this Constitution. This right is not limited by any service or employment relationship. Nobody may be placed in a disadvantage for having made use of this right. (2) The freedom of the press, radio and television are guaranteed."

Although the limitations on these freedoms are not as positively stated as they are in the Soviet Union, there nevertheless is the qualification that freedom of expression is guaranteed "in accordance with the spirit and aims of this Constitution," implying that statements contrary to its "spirit and aims" are not protected (see above, pp. 42–44).

Although the GDR claims to have half a dozen parties, all are basically Communist. Political life is dominated by the Socialist Unity party (Sozialistische Einheitspartei Deutschlands), and many of the same people serve as top officials for both party and government.[9] The Council of Ministers consists of a presidium and some other members, one of whom is minister of postal services and telecommunications.

Broadcast administration and programming are controlled by two committees, on the basis of legislation passed in 1969: the State Committee for Radio (Staatliches Komitee für Rundfunk beim Ministerrat) and the State Committee for Television (Staatliches Komitee für Fernsehen).[10] Both have chairmen and several deputy chairmen, appointed and removed by the Council of Ministers. As in many European countries, however, transmitters and connecting links are the responsibility of the Ministry of Postal Services and Telecommunications. Although there is appreciable income from advertising, basic financial support is from license fees. The yearly charge for radio is 24 marks (about $6.96 in 1972). The charge for a television set capable of receiving only the first channel is 60 marks (about $17.40) and for a set that picks up both channels, 84 marks ($24.36).

The GDR, like the Soviet Union, has very strict information controls. This was particularly true during the Walter Ulbricht years (1953–1971), although things relaxed following the accession of Erich Honecker in May 1972.[11] Since then, some previously suppressed books have been published, and political cabarets even have been allowed to satirize government officials. However, during my last trip to East Berlin, in September 1972, no Western newspapers were on sale, either in news kiosks or in my hotel, East Germany's newest and best, although they were available at tourist hotels in all the other socialist countries except Czechoslovakia. It is reasonable to assume that, despite its improved international status and slightly more liberal domestic administration, the GDR will continue tight controls.

I had an opportunity to discuss these matters with a young East German television staff member in 1970. When I cited the Holmes phrase about the free marketplace of ideas, he replied that, although familiar with the concept, he firmly rejected it. "Information," he said, "is not neutral." It should be selected, and interpretations determined so as to support long-range political goals. Objectivity is no guideline, since the public should not be given the full range of facts and then be expected to decide.

Does East Germany's political and geographical status explain these strict controls of information? He accepted my suggestion that insecurity might be a factor: the countries farther east could risk selling Western newspapers to tourists—and therefore occasionally to their own citizens too—because they were more secure than the German Democratic Republic with its long exposed borders. Perhaps this also explains the security regulations for admittance to broadcasting studios, which are tighter than those in the other socialist countries. After having been vouched for by someone in authority, and having showed my passport to the guards at the door, I received an entrance pass. It was all polite— but very firm. The controls over entering and leaving East Berlin's broadcasting studios, in fact, are stricter than those enforced at the national borders of West Germany, Switzerland, and France.

A brief history of GDR Radio provided by the State Broadcasting Committee on its twentieth anniversary illustrates the approach taken frequently by East German spokesmen.[12] In spite of experiments in 1920, the introduction of broadcasting in Germany was delayed for three years becasue the ruling circles feared an "approaching revolutionary crisis." But after the "reactionary forces" had triumphed in October 1923, the first programs were transmitted. Thereafter, revolutionary workers, leaders, and artists were excluded from broadcasting until the establishment of German Democratic Radio on May 13, 1945. In West Germany, following World War II, all transmitters were put under the control of the military, but in the eastern zone the Soviet administrator assigned them to "the rule of the German administration of people's education."

Some understanding of the leadership of East German broadcasting may be provided by the record of Gerhart Eisler (1887–1968), former chairman of the State Broadcasting Committee. Eisler was born in Leipzig, became a journalist and then an active Communist following World War I. He lived and worked in Shanghai, Spain, France (where he was interned in 1940), Mexico, and the United States (of which he was a resident from 1941 to 1949). In 1949 the Un-American Activities Committee dubbed him "America's Number One Communist." Sentenced to four years' imprisonment for contempt of Congress and for falsifying his record, he stowed away on the Polish liner *Batory* in New York harbor in 1949. In Southampton, British police took him into custody at the request of the United States Embassy, but he subsequently was released and went to East Germany, where he became a member of the Central Committee as well as its propaganda chief, serving as chairman of the Radio and Television Committee from 1949 to 1953.[13]

The similarities of GDR and USSR mass media objectives were documented in an article published in 1960 by the deputy chairman of the State Broadcasting Committee. After referring to Lenin's famous statement describing a newspaper as "not only a collective propagandist and . . . agitator . . . [but] also a collective organizer of socialist transformation," he wrote: "There is no doubt that at present radio is one of the most important mass media of propaganda, since it can at any time and in any place address itself to the population of any region. In addition, socialist radio aims not only at providing various strata of listeners with entertainment, information and education, but also at attracting and mobilizing them to take an active part in the socialist transformation."[14] The chairman of the State Radio Committee wrote in similar vein: "By means of ideological and educational broadcasts from the main centres of the Republic radio and television aid the building-up and victory of socialism."[15]

When the second television network was launched in 1969, it was described as having "the same social task as the first programme. Its aim is to educate highly cultured personalities with all-round interests and a firm class standpoint. . . . It will help to satisfy better the growing intellectual-cultural demands of the working people."[16] Television also is to emphasize "the importance of friendly cooperation among the German Democratic Republic and socialist countries in the solution of long-term tasks set by the Party and the Government and, in particular, to elucidate the international role and importance of the Soviet Union."

Stations and Networks

German Democratic Radio, which began in 1945 with a single medium-wave transmitter on the air 156 hours a week, by 1973 was putting out over 700 program hours in the long-, medium-, and short-wave and FM bands for listeners in the GDR, West Germany, other parts of Europe, and countries overseas. The Deutscher Fernsehfunk was operating two television services with over 110 hours of programs each week.

The two nationwide radio networks are identified as Radio DDR I and Radio DDR II. Radio I, on medium-wave and FM 24 hours a day, is carried by 12 medium-wave transmitters (including 1 of 100 kilowatts, 1 of 120 kilowatts, 2 of 220 kilowatts, and 1 of 250 kilowatts), a number of low-powered repeaters, and 9 FM stations.[17] Radio II, on the air daily from 9:00 A.M. to 11:00 P.M., has 13 FM outlets, with power ranging from 1 to 10 kilowatts. East German FM transmitters operate on the portion of the band used in the Western countries (87.5 to 100 MHz) rather than on the lower frequencies (66 to 73 MHz) assigned to FM in the other socialist countries (see below, p. 510). Stereophonic broadcasting, introduced on September 15, 1964, of which there are about 45 hours each week, uses the Western pilot tone system.[18]

Program I, the basic service, offers a combination of information and entertainment. (The two networks together transmit approximately 65 per cent music and 35 per cent verbal material.[19]) An official description of Radio I stated that it broadcasts "an informative and entertaining programme consisting of news items, commentaries and dance music." There are news programs on the hour throughout the day; music, ranging from popular to concert; weather information; and evening dramatic and entertainment features. From midnight to 5:00 A.M. daily there are "Melodies in the Night." Radio coverage of sports and other special events is most apt to be on Program I.

Program II follows the pattern of the BBC Third Programme. One East German source, comparing it with the first service, said it would "probe deeper" and would be "an independent organizer of musical and literary contributions as well as political broadcasts."[20] A member of the program department wrote that it "should reflect not only all social, economic, scientific, and cultural-educational problems, but must represent a direct contribution to the intellectual discussion of our times." Program II carries broadcasts for schools, classical music, and serious drama.

Supplementing the two network services, which take programs from other parts of the country as well as from the Berlin headquarters, are FM regional services in Cottbus, Dresden, Frankfurt/Oder, Karl-Marx-Stadt, Leipzig, Potsdam, Rostock, Schwerin/Neubrandenburg, and Weimar. (There also are studios—though not transmitters—in Gera, Halle, Magdeburg, and Suhl.) The service in Dresden, begun in July 1964, was, in the words of its director, designed as "a politically effective and flexible programme."[21] Most regional services are on the air daily from 5:00 to 10:00 A.M., with area news, announcements of regional events, weather forecasts, police reports, suggestions for entertainment, and other locally based features. The Dresden studios contribute one evening a month of educational programs to the nationwide second network. An interesting variation in local broadcasting is provided by a station in Rostock, a city on the Baltic coast, which since 1966 has devoted fifteen hours of transmission time daily from May through September to programs for vacationers, including news, weather, and other information features of special interest to vacationers.* The domestic services also include Berliner Rundfunk, which uses five medium-wave AM and eleven FM trans-

---

* Ingrid Kuhfeld, "The GDR Radio Holiday Wave of the Rostock Transmitter," *OIRT Review* 1972/5, pp. 18–20. For references to similar services in Romania and Bulgaria, see below, pp. 408 and 437.

mitters to provide a twenty-four-hour service primarily for the Greater (East) Berlin area, but with coverage in other major population centers too.[22]

There are two services for residents in other political areas which cover East German territory too, and are listed in the nationally distributed program guide.* From the standpoint of people in East Germany, the most important of these is Stimme der DDR, formerly known as Deutschlandsender. Although Stimme der DDR reaches domestic as well as foreign listeners with its one long-wave, three medium-wave, two short-wave, and ten FM transmitters, its twenty-four-hour service is designed especially for West Germany.

Radio Berlin International uses a number of short-wave transmitters, plus a 150-kilowatt medium-wave transmitter (receivable in most of East Germany) to reach worldwide audiences with programs in twelve languages. Radio Volga, operated by the Soviet army, uses a 200-kilowatt long-wave transmitter in the Berlin area and shares some East German transmitters in other parts of the country to serve Soviet military personnel in East Germany with programs originated locally and in Moscow.[23]

In the GDR as elsewhere, radio had to change its pattern in response to television.[24] It adjusted not only by transmitting more music (up to two-thirds of its time), but also by serving as an adviser to parents, and emphasizing weather information, participation sports (swimming, sailing, skiing, and flying), and bulletins on road conditions. But a spokesman for the Broadcasting Committee noted in 1971 that even though television was widespread, there nevertheless were more radio sets than ever, and many homes had two or more radio receivers.

The foundation for the German Democratic Republic's television headquarters at Adlershof in Berlin was laid in 1951, and regular programs from the new Deutscher Fernsehfunk began the next year.[25] There now are two networks, the first covering the entire country, and the second about half the population. The first network is carried by a dozen high-powered (mainly VHF) transmitters, with vision power from 1 to 100 kilowatts, plus a large number of low-powered repeater stations (mostly, but not entirely, VHF). The second network, launched on

---

* *Internationales Handbuch 1971/72*, pp. C143–C146. The external services of the GDR, along with foreign broadcasts available to East German citizens, are described below on pp. 264–267.

November 3, 1969, the twentieth anniversary of the founding of the DDR, has nine UHF stations in large population centers plus some low-powered repeaters. There are color programs several evenings each week, usually—but not always—on the second network. In Berlin programs are transmitted from the television tower, which has facilities for radiating two television programs (on VHF Channel 5 and UHF Channel 27, respectively) and four FM radio services (in the band used in Western Europe and the United States.) Studio headquarters are in Berlin, with supplementary studios in Rostock, Halle, Leipzig, Dresden, and some other cities. The Deutscher Fernsehfunk has connections with Eurovision through West Germany; with Intervision through Poland and Czechoslovakia; and with the Scandinavian network Nordvision.

The GDR is the only socialist country using Western European television system B, since all the others use Eastern European OIRT system D. One might speculate that this was done so that viewers in West Germany could watch East German programs without set alterations. But the reverse also is true: East Germans can readily see programs from the West. However, for color, Deutscher Fernsehfunk adopted the French SECAM III system, used by all the socialist countries except Yugoslavia. Consequently, when West Germans tune in East German color telecasts, they see them in black and white.*

Program I is on the air weekdays from approximately 7:30 or 8:00 A.M. to 12:30 or 1:00 P.M., and from 3:30 to 11:00 or 12:00 P.M., with Saturday and Sunday schedules continuous from about 8:00 A.M. until 11:00 P.M. or midnight. Network II broadcasts daily from about 5:00 to 11:00 P.M. Both are general rather than specialized services, presenting news, public events, entertainment, sports, films and educational programs. It is planned that when a third program is added, it will be educational, following the pattern of the third channels in Leningrad, Moscow, and West Germany, and of Public Television in the United States.

---

* East Germany first reported video tape recorder developments in 1964, and by 1967 had five recorders of its own manufacture. It would appear that East Germany has secured top line VTR's, possibly of American design if not manufacture, through either Egypt or Czechoslovakia. In any case, after watching their programs I was convinced that they had good machines and were using them effectively. Although the GDR has no community television antenna systems, it is developing master antennas for the roofs of apartment buildings to improve reception and appearance.

During morning transmissions, the first network has telecasts to schools, educational programs for adults, and repeats of programs from the previous day for viewers unable to watch the original presentations. In fact, newscasts sometimes are repeated without any change at all. In the afternoon there are more school telecasts, educational programs for adults, news, women's features, and films. In the evenings there are newscasts, films, dramas, light entertainment, and sports. At 6:40 P.M. there is a five-minute cluster of commercials, and from 6:50 to 7:00 the program for small children called "Our Little Sandman."

In 1970 the program output of the two television networks was classified as follows: cinema and documentary films, 23.4 per cent; news and news-oriented programs, 20.0 per cent; sports, 12.1 per cent; music, dancing, and entertainment programs, 10.7 per cent; economic, scientific, and educational programs, 8 per cent; dramatic and cultural programs, 7.3 per cent; children's programs, 6.4 per cent; programs for youth, 2.1 per cent; advertisements, 1.7 per cent; agricultural programs, 1.1 per cent; program announcements and miscellaneous, 7.2 per cent.[26]

The second channel transmits black-and-white programs four days each week, and color programs for about four or five hours each week on Fridays, Saturdays, and Sundays.[27] Its schedule resembles that of the first channel during the evening hours. It also repeats some material from the first network, making it available to viewers who did not see the original presentations.

As the second most industrialized country of the socialist bloc, the German Democratic Republic manufactures a wide range of radio and television receivers. I inspected some of them in the Alexanderplatz area of East Berlin and found them well constructed. There are some attractive portable radios covering the AM and FM bands, cabinet radios covering the full broadcast band (long-, medium-, and short-wave, plus FM), and television receivers with screens of various sizes. The small AM-FM transistor radios were priced at around 245 marks ($71.05 in 1972); the larger all-wave table models between 360 and 455 marks ($104.40–$131.85); and the high-quality stereo sets between 500 and 925 marks ($145.00–$268.25.) Black-and-white television receivers, with screens from eighteen to twenty-one inches wide, ranged in price from 600 to 2,000 marks ($174.00–$580.00).

News and Public Affairs

Programs of news and political information are important in themselves, and also as indices of basic objectives. In September 1970 I asked an East German broadcaster what I should write about radio in the German Democratic Republic. The most important thing to report, he said, was that on May 13, 1945, East Germany created an anti-Fascist broadcasting service which consistently opposes nazism. In reviewing the history of German Democratic Radio, a spokesman for the Broadcasting Committee wrote: "Every day our radio journalists . . . help to change society by means of radio journalism . . . to the benefit of all."[28] In the same vein a lecturer in radio journalism at Karl Marx University in Leipzig declared that "the growing interest in journalism has arisen from the direct needs of the class struggle, by the wish and necessity to make journalism a more effective weapon in the service of this or that class."[29]

In one of its publications German Democratic Radio stated that the leading story in a newscast should emphasize the confrontation of socialism and imperialism and that the struggle of the working class against capitalism always should be reported.[30] Although such things as the "aggression of Israel" in June 1967 and natural catastrophes have high news value, the ultimate objective is to report the class struggle.

East Germans have access to many newscasts. In addition to the national and local services, there is news on Berliner Rundfunk, designed primarily for East Berlin but available by relay in other parts of the country too, and on Stimme der DDR, intended for West Germany but also available throughout East Germany. The German Democratic Republic also can pick up radio and television newscasts from the German Federal Republic and other Western European sources, plus the Voice of America and the BBC. An East German television executive told me in August 1965 that all their broadcasts were planned on the assumption that the public heard and viewed both sides, so they must compete for audience and enhance their reputation for accuracy— although it is my impression that the GDR's propaganda-laden newscasts defeat this objective.

In 1970 the domestic radio services transmitted 87 newscasts each day with a total duration of 540 minutes, which an East German source said equaled 6,480 typed lines, 216 typed pages, or more than 8 newspaper pages the size of *Pravda*.[31] The previous year a member of the radio staff reported that on a typical weekday, GDR's first network transmitted 21 newscasts ranging in length from 3½ to 10 minutes, plus one 12-minute program.[32] The 6:00 and 7:00 A.M. summaries dealt with "socially important events of the previous day that are still continuing," plus things that took place during the night. The 10:00 A.M. program reported further developments, while the 1:00 P.M. newscast reviewed events occurring during the morning and summarized "important articles in the socialist daily press." The 12-minute program at 7:00 P.M., the principal newscast on Network I, was scheduled for that hour because in most homes (this was 1968) television sets had not yet been turned on. The 10:00 P.M. newscast was similar to that at 7:00 P.M.

German Democratic Radio news is planned with its audience in mind. A two-part article published in 1969 discussed at some length the theories underlying the selection and placement of news. Determining factors included the repetition of important items; the emphasis of late news; the placement of late items, if important, in lead spots; and the systematic change of opening stories.[33]

On the first television network there are thirty-minute newscasts at 9:30 A.M. (a recorded repeat of the previous evening's program) and at 7:30 P.M. (the principal newscast of the day, also carried by Network II), plus bulletins at noon and at the end of the day's transmissions. There also are thirty-minute commentaries (Der schwarze Kanal—The Black Channel) several evenings each week. The Sunday pattern is similar, although because of the longer broadcasting day there are additional short bulletins.

The basic source of material is the national news agency Allgemeiner deutscher Nachrichtendienst. ADN draws upon 1,070 staff members (350 editorial) to put out each day 7,750 words in English, 6,500 in Spanish, 5,000 each in French and Arabic, 2,000 each in Russian and Greek, and 75,000 in German.[34] ADN has branches in all the major cities of the GDR, as well as in the principal world capitals, including Bonn, Geneva, London, Paris, and New York. It also has exchange agreements with TASS, some other socialist news agencies, Agence France Presse, Reuters, AP, and UPI. In addition, the broadcasting organization maintains permanent correspondents in Baghdad, Budapest, Cairo, Geneva, London, Moscow, Peking, Prague, Stockholm, and Warsaw, among other cities.

As an Intervision member, Deutscher Fernsehfunk has access to daily feeds from both Eurovision and Intervision. Statistics published by the European Broadcasting Union indicate that in 1962, the year the German Democratic Republic first exchanged news with Eurovision, it received 24 items and provided none (for details, see Table 1). The rate gradually increased until 1967, when it supplied 10 and received 483 items. But since 1967 EBU statistics have provided no individual data on news exchanges between East Germany and Eurovision. Intervision headquarters reports that in 1972 the GDR took 947 news items from Eurovision and contributed 25.

East German news programs are heavily burdened with propaganda and become increasingly so during times of international tension. In September 1966 I had an opportunity to compare West and East Berlin newscasts on the day Ludwig Erhard, chancellor of West Germany, was visiting in Washington, and Walter Ulbricht, chairman of the State Council of East Germany, was in Belgrade. Each service led with film reports about its own chief executive, but both also included some material about the travels of the other one. The subject matter during the remaining portions of the two programs was largely duplicative.

But subsequent viewing of GDR newscasts left a different impression. This may be partly because one of these occasions was in September 1968, shortly after the arrival of Soviet troops in Czechoslovakia. Television news then appeared to be mainly propaganda, two out of three items being stories, speeches, or editorials praising East Germany and its Warsaw Pact colleagues, or criticizing the West, particularly West Germany and the United States. The annual Leipzig Fair, then in progress, was extensively reported. Items relative to Walter Ulbricht received a disproportionate amount of time, even exceeding the emphasis given party leaders in other Eastern countries.

By 1972 the emphasis had shifted back somewhat from propaganda to information. I was in East Berlin during the week in September 1972 when Gustav Husak, the Communist party chief in Czechoslovakia, was visiting the GDR, and saw many items pertaining to his visit. Film coverage on newscasts was supplemented by live pickups of his arrival and departure. Production on these and other newscasts was good, presentation being smooth but not exciting, with the directors doing their best to realize the propaganda objectives of the programs.

A mainstay of East German television since March 21, 1960, has been the commentaries of Karl Eduard von Schnitzler, The Black Channel. An East German source said of von Schnitzler in 1966: "Recognized by friends as well as adversaries, his topical and fighting polemics against the practices of West German TV propaganda have appeared on TV screens weekly for six years."[35] On the air at least one evening each week, von Schnitzler warns and editorializes about alleged or real imperialistic, capitalistic, racist, and Nazi developments in West Germany, NATO, and the United States. His telecasts often include video taped excerpts from West German programs. He also turns up as the author of an occasional documentary.*

When I first saw von Schnitzler in 1968, he showed great energy in justifying the Soviet invasion of Czechoslovakia, which had just taken place. When I last viewed his commentary in September 1972, his presentation was basically as before—news analysis with interspersed recorded excerpts from West German television—but he had mellowed a bit. At the end of 1971 the *New York Times* reported that, as a consequence of the loosening of controls, even though von Schnitzler previously had been one of Walter Ulbricht's favorite commentators, one East Berlin cabaret had dared to satirize him as "a stuffed shirt capable of uttering only worn-out clichés even about the weather."[36]

On August 13, 1972, von Schnitzler discussed the Berlin Wall.[37] The reason for the GDR's progress during recent years, he said, was the construction of the Wall in 1961, which enabled East Germany "to enjoy all the advantages of socialism freely and without obstruction by anyone. We like our work better, we are living better, we have better houses, we can plan more . . . and implement more." The Wall, he said, made

* Both East and West Germany record each other's programs off the air and use them in propaganda programs. Although von Schnitzler apparently was out of favor for a time, he returned to the air and now broadcasts regularly. In 1964 *Variety* reported that he had been dropped by the East German Propaganda Ministry for making too many blunders (*Variety*, October 21, 1964, p. 39). "Schnitzler has never been a popular figure in either West or East Germany not only for his political views, but also for his arrogant attitude. Yet many agree that he's an outstanding commentator with some dubious qualities. He's a political conferencier and cynic par excellence, a slick and clever propagandist, undoubtedly a highly gifted journalist and also a brilliant speaker.

"Although having a genuine hatred for the Western regimes, he liked the Western way of living. He liked Western-style clothes, drove a West German car and frequently came over to West Berlin to enjoy the local nightlife until the West Berlin Senate put him on the list of 'undesired persons.' His predilection for the Western life apparently made him enemies in the East German party camp. Reports from the 'other side' say that he's fallen ill."

peace in Europe more secure and placed the GDR's boundaries "under protection and control." The Wall was bitterly opposed by the "eternal reactionaries," but nevertheless "humanity was rendered a great service" in that "peace on our continent" was "protected and strengthened."

The German Democratic Republic has both radio and television programs on which officials answer questions from the public. In 1964 the Department of Contemporary Events of East German Radio had a series, "Journalists Put Questions," during which ministers, scientists, and government officials were asked "outstanding and often burning topical questions," thus realizing "the civil right of the people . . . to receive an answer to every question."[38] The series "Frankly" was begun the same year to discuss "frankly and directly with our listeners all questions occupying their attention and concerning mainly political and economic life." People in regional studios outside the capital telephoned questions to a team of three experts and a moderator in Berlin. Each half-hour program dealt with eight to ten questions, ranging from "the relation of the German Democratic Republic towards West Germany and the friendship pact between the German Democratic Republic and the Soviet Union to the problems of reform of industrial prices, the technical revolution, distribution and trade." In one instance a Dresden listener complained of red tape in the local travel agency. A member of Parliament on the panel looked into the matter and on the following program explained when and how the problem would be solved. In 1972 "Frankly" was still on the air, dealing with topics like the relative importance of man and his bank account, and addressing itself to such questions as "Why does the working class constitute the only factor able to plan, realize and protect the further development of society?"[39]

"Your Burgomaster at the Microphone," on Berlin Radio for some years in the middle 1960s, brought together the Burgomasters of the eight Berlin districts and some citizens every five or six weeks to discuss the problems of the day, with the public invited to send in questions.[40] Other series have had as guests the chairman of the State Broadcasting Committee, the minister of national defense, the deputy minister of foreign and inter-German trade, and other high officials. During election periods the media are used to present information about issues and candidates, to urge support for the party, and to report election returns.

Education

In a broad sense almost all GDR radio and television is "educational," since it is expected to impart selected information and concepts to its audience. But in addition to meeting such assignments, East German broadcasting offers programs for children both in and out of school, along with adult education features ranging from a television academy to informal programs for the general public.

Education in the German Democratic Republic covers all ages from childhood through university and beyond.[41] There are crèches for the infants of working mothers, and nursery schools for younsters aged four through six. Beginning in 1959 elementary and secondary schools were replaced by polytechnics, which all children beginning at age six must attend for at least ten years. Thereafter are high school, vocational training, and university. Radio and television are used at all levels.

Although programs for in- and out-of-school use are organized and administered separately, their basic objectives—with indoctrination a constant feature—are similar. In 1960 the head of children's television wrote that all programs for children had the theme "the socialist education of the young generation," and should educate children "in the socialist way of life."[42]

Radio is to introduce children to their surroundings; establish a "positive attitude towards learning, correct behaviour, and the development of valuable character traits"; instill respect for workers and older people; provide mathematical skills "to develop logical thinking"; develop elementary accomplishments in painting, drawing, modeling, and making minor household repairs; introduce good literature; and offer spiritual inspiration.[43] In 1967 the head of Berlin Radio's programs for youth quoted Prime Minister Otto Grotewohl's statement to the delegates to the First Parliament of Free German Youth stressing the importance of cooperation between old and young: ". . . we do not want any division between adults and young people. . . . The building-up of this destroyed country can be effected only through the observation of a common approach from all sides, by both young and older generations."[44] In achieving these objectives, the unique features of the broadcast media are to be exploited. Television should be used to "stir people to activity" and to introduce new concepts and procedures.[45]

When I asked one East German broadcaster if in-school broadcasts had social and political objectives, the answer was yes: all programs must build better socialist citizens. There are no nonpolitical schools, since the GDR is a socialist state. Programs are developed cooperatively with teachers and educational administrators. Education is highly centralized, and all schools use the same curricula, textbooks, and examinations, although teachers may vary their presentations. Such procedures, of course, facilitate the use of broadcasts, and about 80 per cent of the schools use radio. Programs are available on tape as well as from Radio II, and many schools make their own off-the-air recordings. There are published materials for teachers and pupils.

In-school radio programs, scheduled daily for twenty- or thirty-minute periods in midmorning and midafternoon, are intended to enrich, but not directly to instruct. There are programs on foreign languages (French, English, German), chemistry, history, and literature. In 1967 there was a seven-part series on the plastic arts in the Soviet Union to observe the fiftieth anniversary of the October Revolution.[46] "From Learning to Studying," for students planning to attend college, offered advice on the selection of subjects and the development of good study habits. Individual program titles included "To Study Is More Than to Learn," "Technology and the Hygiene of Mental Activity," and "Studies in the Development of Personality."[47] A music series for primary and secondary school pupils took up part singing, folk songs, and musical form.

A series on psychological problems discussed managing an allowance, selecting a vocation, and nicotine and alcohol abuse. The final program, "What Will Future Parents Look Like?" was introduced with a statement first published in 1927: "Will future parents also annoy their children with superfluous things, with unreasonable teaching by rote, with severe verdicts and with a thrice damned pig-headed attitude ordering just for the sake of ordering, forbidding just in order to forbid, putting on airs, in short: the perverse game of parents?" Obviously, the problems of parent-child relationships in Germany in 1927 and 1969 approximate those encountered elsewhere in the world.[48] "Radiovision," on the air since 1968, provides slides for projection in classrooms as a series of thirty-minute broadcasts on history is heard.[49]

Out-of-school programs serve all ages. In the mid-sixties radio had a daily program for preschool listeners each morning from 8:40 to 9:00.[50] On Mondays a "fairy uncle" told fairy tales. On Tuesdays a "farmer" told about animals in a village. On Wednesdays "Marianne" conveyed birthday greetings, sang songs, and read poems. On Thursdays a child "talked" to the wind, the rain, and the plants, and there was dramatized "dialogue" among animals. On Friday mornings nursery school children sang and played, while on Saturdays an old sea captain recounted his adventures. In this series, as in others, there were programs about Christmas, a holiday observed in East Germany in accordance with long tradition.

Regular television transmissions for young people began January 6, 1955, with the series "Young Builders of Socialism."[51] A 1960 review of German Democratic Television said that preschool children should be introduced to the world outside their homes through fairy tales and films of trips to places like seaports and farms. Dolls and puppets are used on such telecasts. Very charming, and comparable to the Soviet Union's "Good Night Children," is "The Little Sandman," initiated November 2, 1959, which took over from a similar series first telecast on October 8 of the previous year.[52] Each time I have visited East Berlin I have seen several of these programs, and found them charming, well done, and enjoyable. It is reported that many West German parents prefer them to the comparable offerings of their own television service.

Programs for viewers between six and fourteen years of age are designed not as an extension of schoolwork, but "to help children spend their leisure hours in a sensible and suitable way." In 1960 telecasts for girls were to "stimulate interest in fashion, in good housekeeping, reception of guests and helping mother at home."[53] By 1969 television for children and youth dealt with a different theme each day of the week.[54] In spite of the great emphasis on political orientation, it should be noted that many of these programs would be acceptable under any ideology. In 1963 a series on traffic safety was initiated, in order to lower the accident rate.[55] Berlin Radio's Kiddietown had a Pretzel Street, a Waffle Street, a Noise Square, and a Cobble Street. Children were encouraged to make traffic signs and to practice riding their scooters and bicycles in closed-off streets. There were thousands of entries in a contest about traffic regulations, in which prizes included sixteen holiday excursions, thirty trips to a traffic museum, and fifteen airplane flights over Berlin.[56]

There are plays for children on both radio and television, one theme being the "history of the German and international children's movement, working youth and workers, the struggle of the working people in Europe against fascism, [and] the struggle of progressive elements in Federal

Germany against the seeds of German fascism and militarism."[57] An official analysis of 100 plays telecast between 1954 and 1963 found that 49 dealt with the problems of children in their environments, 34 dramatized fairy tales from various nations, 13 treated historical events, and 4 were musical plays.[58] There are radio plays throughout the year and also during special weeks when as many as 26 plays for children and youth may be transmitted.

Young people also are given a chance to broadcast, as with the youth clubs in Berlin, Leipzig, and Magdeburg.[59] Each weekday the Berlin Youth Club (DT 64) presents contests, literary competitions, and call-in programs, the latter having attracted as many as 1,000 calls per broadcast. During three months in 1967, 17,501 cards and letters were received. Some years more than 50,000 letters are received, including many from West Berlin, West Germany, and abroad.[60] DT 64 is now on the air five afternoons each week from 4:00 to 7:00 P.M. with lively music and other features for and by young people. The Magdeburg Youth Club, which began in 1964, holds weekly meetings to exchange ideas, write scripts, and select participants for its programs, which are broadcast monthly on Sundays from 9:00 to 10:00 A.M. East Germany being a musical country, there also are broadcasts by children's and young people's choirs.

The German Democratic Republic has applied the term "Television Academy" to certain adult education offerings since 1961.[61] The director of the Television Academy wrote that its primary intent was "to raise the general standard of education in adults." It was declared part of the state educational system in September 1962, although it is not intended to prepare students for matriculation in universities or to assist in university instruction. Rather, its broad range of courses is planned to assist employed adults increase their professional knowledge and skills. In November 1964 the academy was expanded to include several programs for high school students.

The Television Academy divides its offerings into five categories.[62] The first of these, "Socialist Management in the Economy," a forty-five–minute series broadcast once every two weeks (with two repeats) since January 1967, presents concepts of socialistic economy to Communist party officials, union leaders, members of production committees, educators, students, and workers. The academy pointed out: "Without qualified scientific management activity, without deep enquiries into the process of management, without application of new instruments of modern management, in the age of scientific technical revolution there could be no advance in the economy of the German Democratic Republic." In 1967 reprints of twelve broadcasts were distributed to more than 1,400 viewing groups.

Courses in the second category, which dealt with computer programming and were developed jointly by computer programmers, film producers, and publishers, consisted of sixty broadcasts of forty-five minutes each. These programs were broadcast alternate weeks and were repeated over a three-year period.[63] The third category, "Mathematics for Practical Use," begun in 1961–1962 in cooperation with various trade unions, included ninety-five weekly programs, each repeated once. Advanced courses were added later. After viewing these programs, students can take state examinations and receive credits in the national high schools. Over 150,000 viewers have written in connection with these broadcasts on mathematics. In September 1968 I saw some algebra courses marked by effective presentation and good visuals. Material about these and other Television Academy programs often is published in weekly radio and television program guides available throughout the country.

The fourth category, the "Winter Academy of Socialist Agriculture," was inaugurated in 1962. These in-depth treatments of agricultural subjects are planned cooperatively by scientists, farmers, journalists, and government officials involved in agriculture. The programs are broadcast at noon on Sunday and are repeated Wednesday evenings. Study material is published in newspapers with wide circulation in rural areas, and on alternate weeks seminars are held at some 16,000 local centers. The programs deal with such problems as the operation of an automatic tire adjustment device, the management and organization of food production, and the improvement of agricultural output.[64]

The fifth Television Academy category consists of lessons in Russian, English, and German.[65] (Russian now is the second and English the third language of East Germany, and both are required in secondary schools.) There have been several series on Russian: the basic course "Russian for You," first presented in 1964, consisting of sixty-two broadcasts, each of twenty-five minutes' duration; a continuation course began in 1965, made up of twenty-one thirty-minute programs (for which a handbook was prepared); the advanced "Russian Club—Druzhba," monthly thirty-minute programs initiated in January 1968; and "We Talk Russian," begun in 1971, consisting of thirty-five programs each lasting twenty-five minutes.

The excellent "English for You," launched in 1965, consists of thirty-minute programs broadcast at various early morning and late afternoon hours, described by a Television Academy spokesman as "an integrated constant part of school instruction in the extended secondary schools. Besides, it creates possibilities of further education for adults who study in evening schools or in national high schools." I have seen a number of these programs. In 1970 an attractive woman teacher presented information about grammar and pronunciation, while a small cast imported from London, speaking excellent—though not BBC or "southern"—English, took part in short skits designed both to sustain audience interest and to illustrate points about the language. The 1972 programs showed improvement and included episodes recorded both in London and in Berlin. I also saw several well-done Russian language programs recorded on location in the Soviet Union.

Excellent results are reported from these Television Academy programs. By April 1963, after some two years on the air, the academy had received half a million letters, and had awarded diplomas and badges to over 6,000 participants.[66] Between March and December 1965, the series "Russian for You" brought in 750,000 answers to questions plus 20 files of letters.

Both radio and television also present information for adults in less structured form. "The Board of Professors Meets," a monthly series initiated by Berlin radio in 1963, was intended "to establish direct contact with listeners who do not mind switching off their TV sets for a while when radio has something interesting to offer."[67] During the initial program, which lasted ninety minutes, one hundred calls from the audience were received for the nine professors—all with high academic as well as party qualifications—who answered questions on such subjects as whether people will ever free themselves from shortcomings like "hatred, envy and falsehood"; if it is unhealthful to smoke; and why mankind needs "to know how captive pelicans sit on eggs." Beginning in 1964 the programs were relayed by Deutschlandsender to West German listeners, and television also picked them up.[68] Somewhat similar was a series begun in 1966 on which the rectors of various universities discussed "problems of teaching research and learning."

German Democratic Radio has the Department of Economic Broadcasts which is concerned with labor and production output.[69] In 1966 the department initiated a three-hour evening series to stimulate listeners to think about the relationships between leaders and citizens, along with "questions of socialist morals." During the first program almost 4,500 listeners phoned in their comments. There was a series on the second radio network "devoted to the problems of scientific socialism and the marxist philosophy."

Broadcasting also has been used in attempts to raise production levels and develop correct work attitudes. Radio programs have been devised to improve food production, and the School and Life Department of television had a series, "How to Foster the Correct Attitude toward Work."[70] It was necessary, said a news release, to counteract the age-old association of work with slavery and compulsion, and to foster "the correct attitude towards work and socialist discipline in our children. Very often education in factories is limited to giving formal knowledge, this often being a consequence of the lack of a system of fostering a responsible attitude towards work."

Under the name "The Thieving Magpie," there was a three-day campaign for the return of "unused or insufficiently employed machines," which brought more than 1,180 telephone calls and led to the return of 5,000 machines and parts.[71] A twenty-five–minute television program asked people to save electric power and gas, with such good results that by the time the broadcast ended the consumption of power had been greatly reduced. One way to save electric power—which probably was not stressed—would have been to ask people to turn off their television sets!

A television cycle named after the doctor's waiting-room phrase "Next, Please" brought thirty-minute monthly broadcasts on such medical subjects as smoking, nutrition, and rheumatic fever. These programs utilized devices like a visit to a doctor's office, a physical examination on television, and a relay from a health spa.[72] Another medical program reported that the German Democratic Republic had developed artificial blood vessels superior to those developed in the United States, and there were several broadcasts for women entitled "Do You Feel Worn Out?"

Supplementing the programs for in-school use mentioned above are broadcasts for parents and teachers. A Saturday morning television series, "Pedagogical Adviser," invited parents to ask questions of experts.[73] On the Saturday morning radio series "Teachers' Consultation

Hour," broadcast regularly since 1964, teachers put questions to educators and psychologists about socialist education and the "concepts arising in the course of the educational process at the school and the family." During the first 300 of these programs 3,000 questions were discussed, out of the 8,000–10,000 received. The weekly program guide lists the name of the discussion leader along with a telephone number.

There are programs about citizens and the law. The television series "The Public Prosecuter Has the Floor," featuring the chief public prosecuter, reviewed the factors which induce people to crime, it being hoped that viewers would "draw conclusions governing their own behaviour and cooperate in the elimination of the causes and conditions of offenses and crimes."[74] Other legal programs dealt with arbitration, agricultural law, and "interesting and topical questions of the criminal, civil, labour and family laws." In 1966 radio observed the twentieth anniversary of the series "Juridical Quarter of an Hour," in which a legal expert answered "questions of citizens from all parts of the republic and many places in West Germany." By mid-1967 the first radio network had transmitted 150 programs in the series "Not Only Documents," dealing with such subjects as family conflicts, matrimonial property rights, and the causes of crime among young people.

German Democratic Radio and Television have their own training courses, in addition to which there is the School for Film and Television in Berlin as well as advanced training in the journalism section of the University of Leipzig.[75] During a visit to East Berlin in September 1970, I talked at some length with the directors of several of these programs. The School for Film and Television, then in operation for sixteen years, originally trained only film producers but now works in television too. Entrance requirements include twelve years of elementary and secondary education plus some field experience. The staff of between thirty and forty members, some part and some full time, includes many practical broadcasters, and there are from 300 to 400 students each year. The curriculum combines basic academic subjects with production training, for which there is laboratory work in the school and in the broadcasting studios. The theoretical portions of the curriculum emphasize Marxist-Leninist ideology: for example, producers are told that their assignment is to use television to interpret the cultural revolution.

The library of the Hochschule is fairly well equipped with books from both East and West, although the problems of obtaining material from

Western countries were such that the staff reacted most enthusiastically to my offer to supply some mass media publications from the United States. Instruction for radio journalists was begun by the faculty of journalism in the Karl Marx University in Leipzig in 1964. The curriculum includes general background subjects, foreign languages, typing and shorthand (commonly taught in European journalism schools), and some laboratory courses.[76]

Drama

East Germany broadcasts a great deal of drama. Each year radio transmits from seventy to ninety plays for adults, twenty-five for young people, and seventy for children.[77] In 1968 television produced and transmitted eighty-four plays and films.

The ideological potentials of broadcast drama are fully exploited. The deputy chief dramaturgist of German Democratic Radio referred to radio drama before the Nazis as "the first golden age of the radio play."[78] Only "modest" results were achieved following 1933, however, because some "fascist bards" tried to put the radio play to the service of the "blood and soil myth." During the 1950s original radio plays were still "on the decline," but now a new generation of playwrights has emerged. Accordingly, he noted with pride, "the radio play in the German Democratic Republic has attained a reputation in the last few years and in spite of many people pointing to the spectacular development of television, it has strengthened its position."

In 1970 the director of radio drama production wrote that the greatest successes were achieved with plays "dealing with important social and national themes and requiring the listeners' activity, (i.e., thinking, adopting an attitude and acting)."[79] Radio drama has two basic objectives: to inform the public about life and problems in the GDR, and to "influence the development of our society." At a symposium on "The Future of Radio Dramaturgy in the German Democratic Radio," the head of the State Broadcasting Committee praised radio drama for providing "an essential contribution towards the socialist way of thinking and behaviour of citizens in the German Democratic Republic."[80]

Television plays, too, are a propaganda weapon.[81] The television drama department was established to produce "humanistic and socialist works of world literature" in order to develop an "educated nation."

However, a play "wins real success [only] if it is based on a clear political conception." The same purpose prevailed in 1969, when a news release stated that "efforts will be concentrated on productions promoting the role of German Television in the formation of socialist state consciousness and in the creation of our socialist national culture." Therefore, "films and plays with socialist characters will also be transmitted which—as a paragon for millions of viewers—will provide impulses for the consolidation of the socialist community."*

Radio has annual play weeks during which scripts from East Germany and other countries are broadcast. The foreign countries represented tend to be in the socialist bloc, but there also are plays from Austria, Denmark, Finland, France, Great Britain, Iceland, Italy, Japan, New Zealand, Sweden, Switzerland, and sometimes West Germany.[82]

The head of radio feature drama has theorized at some length about the purposes of such programs.[83] He illustrated by referring to a weekly family broadcast entitled "Neumann—Please Ring Twice," transmitted on Program I Saturdays at 8:00 P.M. (still broadcast in 1972), which he described as "dealing in an entertaining and possibly gay manner with the everyday life of a family." Although he recognized that the idea for such a series was not new, he thought it was new to use the technique to "show, convey and render effective the socialist way of feeling which is finding expression in the socialist way of living." Accordingly, the radio family was planned as a counterpart of many listeners' families: the father, a forty-one-year-old foreman in a manufacturing plant; the mother, a schoolteacher; a seventeen-year-old daughter; a thirteen-year-old son; and a grandmother, a pensioner who still worked. The story line posed the range of problems such a family might normally encounter, with an emphasis on approved points of view. (Both radio and television in the United States and the United Kingdom have achieved success with "family" programs.) To observe the one-hundredth birthday anniversary of German writer Heinrich Mann (1871–1950), there was a six-part serial broadcast of his novel *The Youth of King Henry IV*. An official

---

* *OIRT Information* 1969/9, p. 8. An analysis by a Western writer of thirty short television plays broadcast between April 1 and July 31, 1962, classified them as follows: historical plays, 18 per cent; plays on the "building-up of socialism" in the GDR, 26 per cent; plays against "militaristic-clerical-fascist powers" in the GFR, 29 per cent; plays characterizing the "American way of life," 18 per cent; and plays on the theme of "flight from the Republic," 9 per cent (Jörg Lingenberg, "Das Fernsehspiel in der DDR," *Rundfunk und Fernsehen*, 1966, No. 3, p. 310).

description said that the treatment, which concentrated "on ideological problems," clearly indicated that its author's ideas "are preserved in socialist humanism and can be implemented solely in our society."[84]

In 1968 television produced and transmitted eighty-four plays and telefilms.[85] These included classical works by Lessing and Schiller as well as several plays dealing with "individual cases of the class justice of the period of the Kaiser and the Weimar Republic." Television, like radio drama has its "message": to mark the twentieth anniversary of the end of World War II, there were programs about fascism, the contributions of the Soviet Union to the GDR, the Polish army, and the tenth anniversary of the Warsaw Pact.[86] In 1963 a television play co-authored by Karl Eduard von Schnitzler—better known for his Black Channel series—and Lutz Köhlert told the story of a young black who went to West Germany and found it a racist country.[87] In 1970 programs observed the hundredth anniversary of Lenin's birth as well as the twentieth anniversary of "the liberation from Hitlerite fascism," the series being entitled "Peace."[88] The programs had the objective of expressing "in an artistic way the importance of the liberation of European nations and how the Soviet Army's fight inspired the political struggle in many countries."

The United States often is treated severely. Along with straightforward presentations of plays like that based on Mark Twain's "The Man Who Corrupted Hadleyburg," televised in 1961, there was the comedy which used Columbus's discovery of America as the basis for a satire in which some West Germans went to America vainly seeking a better world.[89] A play by a German author dealt very severely with the Sacco and Vanzetti case. At the time of the trial, said an East German commentary, "the ideas of the Great Socialist October Revolution were penetrating from Europe to America." East German writer Maximilian Scheer wrote "The Road to San Rafael—A Radio Play for Angela Davis," which "traces the background and connections of the murderous complot against the courageous fighter for civil rights and communist [sic]."[90] (A year after this broadcast, by which time Miss Davis had been acquitted of the charges against her and was touring the European socialist countries, I saw her on television news programs, observed pictures of her in store windows, and noticed that the hostesses in the East Berlin television tower had named themselves "The Angela Davis Hostess Collective.")

Both East and West Germany frequently broadcast plays by Bertolt Brecht (1898–1956), who during his later years lived and worked in East Berlin. There were special programs in 1973 to mark the seventy-fifth anniversary of his birth. In 1947, as a refugee in the United States, Brecht was examined by the House Committee for Un-American Activities during its inquiry into alleged Communist infiltration into the motion picture industry.* Brecht said he had written revolutionary literature in prewar Germany because of his anti-Hitler connections, but denied he had ever been a Communist, although admitting he had collaborated with Hans Eisler—brother of Gerhart Eisler, later chairman of the GDR State Broadcasting Committee—who wrote music for his play *In Praise of Learning.* J. Parnell Thomas, the New Jersey Republican who was chairman of the committee, accepted Mr. Brecht's assertion that his Communist links were mainly of an artistic nature, and in dismissing him said: "Thank you. You are a good example to other witnesses. . . ."†

Music

Germany's long musical tradition is maintained by both the Federal Republic and the Democratic Republic. Among East Germany's musical rallying points is Leipzig, where Johann Sebastian Bach was organist and choirmaster at the St. Thomas Church, and in whose conservatory were trained some of the greatest musicians of recent centuries. Berlin's State Opera House, located in the East Berlin area, only a shell after World War II, has been beautifully rebuilt in accordance with the original designs of 1743.‡

The Broadcasting Committee draws upon its own extensive musical resources as well as upon instrumental and operatic groups throughout the country. Radio maintains 20 performing groups, including a 112-

---

* *OIRT Information* 1973/2, pp. 2–3; *New York Times,* October 31, 1947, p. 3. In East Berlin the Theater am Schiffbauerdamm houses the Berliner Ensemble, founded by Bertolt Brecht in 1949 and directed by his wife after his death, which specializes in productions of his works.

† In September 1970 I saw several studios that had been constructed especially for radio drama. They were carefully designed, with variable acoustics, good control rooms, and a wide range of manual and electronic sound effects. GD Radio now is experimenting with drama in stereo (*OIRT Information* 1971/4–5, p. 11).

‡ A performance there of Puccini's *La Boheme,* sung in Italian by an excellent East German cast, was one of the finest I attended during a fourteen-week trip to Eastern Europe in the fall of 1970, and in the fall of 1972 I enjoyed a lively presentation of Smetana's *The Bartered Bride.*

piece symphony orchestra in Berlin and a 105-piece one in Leipzig; 2 other concert orchestras of 70 and 57 musicians, respectively; dance and light music ensembles of 34, 31, 30, and 17 members each; small groups of instrumental soloists; and 8 choral groups, including both children and adult members, varying in size from 35 to 100 members.[91] In addition to taking part in broadcasts, these organizations give public concerts. Symphony orchestras and opera companies in Berlin, Leipzig, Dresden, and other cities, as well as noted conductors and soloists, both East German and foreign, contribute regularly to German Democratic Radio and Television. Most guest artists are from the Eastern countries, but there also are appearances by many Westeners, including West German composers and conductors Robert Häger, Gustav König, Hans Werner Henze, and Wolfgang Sawallisch.[92]

The music played ranges from medieval to contemporary compositions, the latter by both socialist and other composers. Reflecting long tradition, there is no embarrassment about relaying, particularly during the Christmas and Easter holidays, Bach cantatas, oratorios, and passions. One East German source commented: "Nowadays, Bach's Passions have become an inseparable part of the socialist musical culture."[93]

Beethoven's Ninth Symphony is broadcast annually on May Day.[94] In 1970, in honor of the 200th birthday of Beethoven, who was born in Bonn, the capital of West Germany, German Democratic broadcasting had special programs, some of which were offered to Intervision and Eurovision. That year the State Broadcasting Committee transmitted 100 concerts, 440 other broadcasts of Beethoven's music, and a 12-part series entitled "Ludwig van Beethoven—A New Biographical Report Based on Letters and Conversation Books," which utilized "hitherto unknown materials from the German State Library in Berlin." In addition to being broadcast at home, these were widely circulated, being used by 70 broadcasting organizations in all parts of the world.[95] Also commemorative was a 10-part series on the German State Opera with which GDR radio celebrated the 225th birthday of that great institution in 1967.

Music appreciation programs include quizzes on operatic and concert music. One such series, presented monthly since 1962, which reached its 100th program in 1970, brings in an average of 950 cards and letters per program.[96] There has been a studio for experimentation with electronic music since 1962, the first concert results being aired on March 9, 1965. It also produces background music for films and dramas.[97] In 1966 the Berlin Radio Symphony Orchestra performed a four-movement com-position by Joachim Thurm, "Moments Musicaux 1965 for Electronic Sounds and Instruments," which combined electronic sounds with strings, brass, and percussion instruments.

There are many broadcasts of light and popular music, and any week's program guide lists such titles as "Melodies in the Night," "Light Music Review," "Rhythmical Dessert," and "Jazz." One American reporter wrote from Berlin in the mid-sixties that the question of accepting the Beatles (along with an "anarchistic individualist" poet-singer named Wolf Biermann) constituted a "cultural dispute" which was "creating the greatest internal turmoil in East Germany since the Berlin Wall was erected."[98] The story quoted a Communist official as saying that the Beatles would be accepted "because they are more like folk singers," but the Rolling Stones would be ruled out as "too animalistic." However, in order to meet competition from Western transmitters, East Germany now broadcasts almost all types of contemporary popular music.

But the reaction to unwanted musical styles is affirmative as well as negative, and there are consistent efforts to develop light music of an approved type. The head of radio dance music said that of 932 compo-sitions submitted in 1964, only 40 per cent could be broadcast.[99] Fur-thermore, people seeking employment as pop singers lacked good voices, training, or both. In 1965 a "variety music working group" was set up to develop "entertaining music." In response to the complaint that the current quality of light music did not match the level of education of the German Democratic Republic, working groups were charged to "achieve a new expression congruent with our time" and "to coordinate political, cultural-political and economic tasks and needs."[100] During the following year, fifty composers and song writers took part in seminars in the Berlin Radio Building for the authors of dance music.

Taste and ideology aside, much entertainment music is broadcast by GDR Radio. The Leipzig Radio Dance Orchestra aired several compo-sitions by the Cambodian chief of state Prince Norodom Sihanouk, a tape of the performance being sent to the prince as a gift.[101] Music for social dances was treated historically, as programs dealt in turn with the charleston, foxtrot, twist, and other dances. There also is folk music, par-ticularly from Eastern Europe, plus programs of currently popular music based both on commercial records and on tapes made at concerts. Of surprisingly commercial orientation have been song competitions developed by radio, television, and the state phonograph record monopoly. On Soviet television in 1972 I saw a well-produced light music program from East Germany, on which popular singers, against East Berlin background scenes, did a very professional job with some current hits.

Some—though not extensive—use is made of music and recordings from the United States. In addition to live performances of compositions by American composers and broadcasts of music recorded in the United States, there was a 1965 American folk song series presenting Pete Seeger, "a singer who plays an important role in American musical life"; Woody Guthrie; and Huddie Ledbetter, "the great Negro guitar player, who had to be freed from Southern prison to show his capabilities." The program was introduced "by American journalist Victor Grossman."[102]

Film, Documentary, Entertainment, and Sports

In the German Democratic Republic, as elsewhere, films are an important component of television. An official analysis in 1967, when there was only one network, indicated that 17.6 per cent of the output consisted of "feature films and foreign television films, television plays (our own productions), [and] serial films."[103] It is reasonable to assume that well over half of this was on film. The same publication indicated that 64 per cent of such materials from foreign sources were from socialist countries and 35 per cent from other countries. A cursory review of evening programming since the inauguration of the second network in October 1969 shows various kinds of film programs almost every evening on both services, varying in length from thirty minutes to two hours.

Deutscher Fernsehfunk produces much of its own material, but also gets television and cinema films from the East German film agency DEFA. In 1968 DEFA produced for television 30 feature films and 200 short films.[104] Programs from abroad in foreign languages are dubbed into German, often by DEFA, which, for example, dubbed the Robin Hood series from England.[105] Some are purchased from West Germany already dubbed, although in 1961 there were plans to dub in East Germany 250 feature films from other socialist countries. DEFA films normally cannot be telecast for 12 months after their cinema release, although there are exceptions, as when DEFA and Deutscher Fernsehfunk have joint productions.

The repertoire is extensive, including light entertainment, musicals, and other escape material. An announcement in 1969 of color programs for the new channel referred to various Soviet films, including Tolstoy's *Anna Karenina*, along with productions from French television featuring Josephine Baker, Marcel Marceau, and other entertainers.[106] In November 1972, commemorating fifty years of film making in the USSR, television combined forces with a number of cinema theaters to present some recent Soviet cinema and television films. In the words of the weekly program guide, which devoted a good deal of space and several accompanying photographs to the project: "GDR television has always seen one of its most important duties, continually and in ever more inclusive fashion, to be the opening up to its public of the cultural riches of the people of the USSR, thus to contribute to the deepening of the friendship and to the solution of our common problems in the interest of strengthening socialism."[107] A retrospective series of twenty Soviet films was telecast in 1973.

In any case, the overall emphasis is on propaganda. There is frequent reference to documentaries by Walter Heynowski, who in 1961 produced "Action J," which dealt with an official of the Adenauer cabinet who was "the intellectual instigator of the criminal Nazi laws concerning race, citizenship and matrimony."[108] In addition to being telecast and shown in cinema theaters in East Germany, this was carried by other socialist bloc stations, shown in a London theater, and given first prize in a contest in Leipzig.

A five-section documentary, "Seizure of Power by the Hanged," revealed "sensational facts from the fascist past and its links with the West German present."[109] "The Smiling Man," produced with sound tracks in five languages by Heynowski and Gerhard Scheumann, which exposed "the dirty work of the ill-famed Congo-Müller and the brutality of German militarism in the sensational way," was broadcast as well as shown at various international meetings.[110] In 1968 GDR Television broadcast the first installment of a series about Axel Springer, the West German publisher, which emphasized "the fundamental reactionary trends of development in West Germany since 1945." The next year there was a three-part treatment of the "unscrupulous speculations and intrigues" accompanying the West German art market.[111]

Highly touted was another documentary by Heynowski and Scheumann, "President in Exile," jointly produced in 1969 by East German and Czechoslovakian television. The program was based on an interview with the West German Walther Becher, described as a leader of revanchism. With sound tracks in several languages, it was broadcast by various Eastern European countries and was the subject of a special paperback book in German, Russian, French, and English, which quoted highly laudatory press reviews, mainly from Eastern European sources.[112] Over 100 million viewers saw the telecast during its first year.

The United States too has been treated in some of these documentaries. In 1962 a three-part film, "Stalin's Temple," showed "the senseless feverish building-up of the US Air Force," as well as the "unscrupulous methods of the press and television."[113] Five years later Heynowski and Scheumann went to North Vietnam to interview some American aviator prisoners for the cycle "Pilots in Pajamas."[114] In 1969 there was a film report of an "expert commission" appointed by President Kennedy in 1962, which "arrived at the conclusion that lasting peace was not desirable for the USA."[115]

During the week of the American presidential election in November 1972, the second network presented a two-installment Soviet version of Robert Penn Warren's *All the King's Men*, described in the program guide as a picture of American election procedures that had changed since the publication of the novel in 1946 only in becoming more expensive. During the same week "The Black Clan" ("an organization of the most reactionary circles in the US, whose essence is fascism") was telecast as the fourth in a series entitled "USA—Danger from the Right."[116]

Despite all the ideology, however, there still is much entertainment. The East Germans themselves have produced serializations of Dickens's *Nicholas Nickleby*, Shakespeare's *King Lear*, and Shaw's *Androcles and the Lion*, plus a 3½-hour dramatization of Dostoevsky's *The Brothers Karamazov*. On the lighter side, they carried the BBC productions of "Maigret," "Airline Detective," and "Sherlock Holmes." In November 1972 I saw a light entertainment feature recorded in a large theater during which music, dancing, and singing were effectively handled, along with relief shots of the audience, which obviously was enjoying itself. But it was not as well done as a program of similar nature from West Berlin which I picked up—with some difficulty, owing to the intentional maladjustment of my set—which equaled American network entertainment of this type.

Radio and television regularly broadcast news reports and play-by-play accounts of sports in which there is national and local interest, including ice hockey, soccer, gymnastics, boxing, skiing, and racing (bicycle, automobile, and motorcycle). There is much international cooperation in the coverage of these events, not only among countries of the Eastern bloc, but also between East and West. As occasion requires, there are bilateral arrangements with Austria, Czechoslovakia, Finland, Norway, Sweden, the USSR, West Germany, Yugoslavia, and other countries, along with elaborate hookups for Intervision and/or Eurovision.

For the world motorcycling championship in Sachsenring, GDR Television used eleven cameras, and in 1962 it broadcast the Baltic Sea Regatta from a tugboat three miles offshore.[117] A bicycle race was covered from a helicopter flying above the track, and there were twenty-second film portraits of all the racers ready to insert into the programs to supplement live reportage.

In 1964, to cover "the largest amateur cycling race in the world, the Peace Race," a relay van with sportscasters from East Germany, Poland, and Czechoslovakia transmitted reports to an airplane which, by a complicated series of relays, fed them to the GDR, Polish, and Czechoslovak radio networks.[118] The head of the television sports department, who supplemented experience in coproduction with Polish and Czechoslovak television by viewing broadcasts from Austria, England, France, Italy, Sweden, Switzerland, the United States, and West Germany, reported that it was not unusual to use a dozen cameras to cover competitive sports.

In 1972 both radio and television provided extensive coverage of the Munich Olympics, with pictures from West German television and their own commentary, supplemented by interviews with East German athletes. American observers report that this followed a highly nationalistic line. There is emphasis on participation as well as on spectator sports. Depending upon the season, radio broadcasts news for vacationers and tourists about spas, camping places, and other vacation activities.[119] Television has its morning setting-up exercises, along with information about health and physical training.

In 1962 candidates between the ages of twenty and thirty were invited to apply for positions as television sports announcers. Qualifications included a good knowledge of sports; at least a secondary education; and "correct diction, quick perception, prompt reproduction of observations, [and] correct pronunciation without dialectical traces."[120] But sports, like other program areas, have their political aspects. In 1963 television scheduled documentaries entitled "Boots and Trackshoes," which were to deal with "the militarization of West German sports."[121]

Audience Research

Although German Democratic broadcasters report extensive research plans, few findings have been published. The Council of Ministers resolved in April 1965 "to build an information and documentation system in the field of social sciences," and one staff member wrote: "Radio research work must serve as a . . . guide in this field. . . . If this is not the case, radio lags behind the requirements of society."[122]

Although letters receive less emphasis from German Democratic broadcasters than from Soviet broadcasters, they nevertheless remain an important source of information, and one department has responsibility for evaluating the 600,000 communications received each year from the home audience.[123] In addition, the public is invited to submit proposals for television programs; advisory councils have been set up to provide advice and audience feedback; and polls are taken of listeners and viewers to obtain information about program preferences. Audience research is conducted separately for radio and television.

The television research department was established first, in 1964, although between then and 1967 only seven surveys were carried out.[124] But beginning in 1968 there were surveys every two weeks, involving first 500 and then 1,000 respondents, chosen randomly from among television license holders. These surveys are conducted by 15 members of the research department aided by 200 part-time interviewers, with the data processed by computer.

The main purpose of this research is to "keep the executives of the GDR Television informed about the measure to which the intended effect of programmes has been realized." In addition to determining the number of viewers, studies have been made of the relationship between the two television networks; the effects of living conditions on program tastes; "heroes" in television drama; and the factors that make an entertainment program attractive. Results are reported for internal use, but are not generally circulated.

Regular radio research began in 1966.[125] The radio research staff employs 1,500 interviewers and 80 fieldworkers, and the data collected are processed electronically. Subjects studied include the quality of radio news; public reactions to morning programs; and young people's taste in music. Like television, radio does little publishing, except when staff members write for specialized journals.

As is shown in Table 10, based on data supplied by the European Broadcasting Union, the penetration of radio in the GDR remained about constant in 1966, 1967, and 1968, although the television ratio per 100 increased from 20.84 in 1966 to 24.42 in 1969. In the latter year West German radio figures were slightly below those for East Germany (31.63 compared with 34.71), and for television slightly higher (25.98 compared with 24.42.) In 1972 East Germany had 5,984,000 radio and 4,499,200 television licenses.*

The Robinson study of television viewing in the United States and eleven other countries reported in 1965 an average of 85 minutes of viewing in East Germany as a primary activity and another 85 minutes as a secondary activity, for a total of 170 minutes or about 3 hours a day of viewing. These were somewhat above the figures for West Germany, which averaged out to 140 minutes a day.†

In 1965 an inquiry was conducted to determine the effect of television on radio in a medium-sized city regarded as a microcosm of the entire country's population. It was found that with the coming of television, morning listening became more important, with television favored in the evening. Many listeners preferred radio to television drama, however, "because a radio play leaves place for the development of an individual's phantasy."[126] On the basis of listeners' polls, it was decided that between 5:00 and 8:00 A.M. announcers must be able to impart "a personal character" to their work.[127] A television inquiry in 1966 found that when working people returned home in the late afternoon, they wanted short and entertaining programs, so such productions were scheduled from 5:30 to 7:30 P.M.[128]

In 1965 a poll in Leipzig, with 600,000 inhabitants, and two other cities in the same area with 40,000 and 8,000 inhabitants, respectively, again showed that audiences react the same the world over.[129] During late afternoon and evening hours, 68 per cent of men without television

---

* The EBU does not provide any GDR data for 1970 or later. These 1972 figures are from the *Europa Year Book 1972*, Vol. I, p. 791.

† John P. Robinson, "Television and Leisure Time: Yesterday, Today and (Maybe) Tomorrow," *Public Opinion Quarterly* 33:2, (Summer 1969), pp. 216–217. For further details, see above, pp. 185–186.

listened to the radio, compared with 20 per cent of those with television, the corresponding figures for women being 61 and 17 per cent.

Unfortunately, few data have been published on the effects of programs on their audiences, although figures have been cited above showing considerable interest in and response to some educational broadcasts. A survey conducted in 1966 found that certain television literary programs caused increased demands in libraries for the books concerned, but this was hardly a startling discovery.[130]

Information received during conversations with East German broadcasters does not differ greatly from reports obtained in other countries. Young people like dance music and jazz, while older people prefer "middle-of-the-road" or concert music. Generally speaking, program preferences in East Germany, the United States, and elsewhere seem to be affected in the same way by such factors as socioeconomic status, education, and age.

External Broadcasting

It is inevitable that the German Democratic Republic should be active in external broadcasting. Because of the country's geographical position, and particularly because of the political enclave of West Berlin, almost every East German citizen is exposed to Western radio and television programs, at the same time that the GDR is well situated to propagandize its neighbors in return.

The chairman of the State Broadcasting Committee wrote in 1960: "The ideological struggle against the opinions disseminated by numerous transmitters hostile to our country plays an important role in our broadcasts."[131] He then sounded a motif frequently stressed by East German leaders: "One of our most important tasks consists in the struggle against German militarism, which is a great danger to peace and humanity in general." It is necessary to counteract broadcasts from Western Europe "directed against the German Democratic Republic." Unfortunately, "two thirds of the territory of our Republic are located within the radius of activity of West German television transmitters, while our television can cover only two fifths of television license holders in the other part of our Western border."

Another East German writer argued that because West German television "strives to prevent people from West Germany from forming even

Table 10. Radio and Television License Statistics, 1966–1972

Country	Total Radio Licenses	Total Television Licenses	Combined Licenses[a]	Population	Radio Licenses per Hundred	TV Licenses per Hundred
1966						
Bulgaria	1,468,930	287,880		8,285,000	25.88	3.47
Wire	675,152					
Czechoslovakia	3,179,143	2,375,105		14,300,000	26.78	16.61
Wire	649,504					
France	8,390,219		7,471,192	49,700,700	31.91	15.03
West Germany	5,512,534		12,719,599	60,000,000	30.39	21.20
East Germany (GDR)	5,811,731	3,559,240		17,079,500	34.03	20.84
Hungary	2,497,000	1,000,000		10,167,000	24.56	9.84
Poland	4,519,250	2,540,064		31,800,000	17.59	7.99
Wire	1,073,501					
Sweden	2,948,203	2,160,435		7,784,000	37.88	27.75
Wire, in total	399,175					
United Kingdom	2,512,993		13,919,191	54,435,700	30.19	25.57
Wire, in total	65,240					
Yugoslavia	3,003,321	777,595		19,900,000	15.09	3.91
1967						
Bulgaria	1,528,300	420,228		8,334,000	26.61	5.04
Wire	689,385					
Czechoslovakia	3,185,071	2,599,766		14,300,000	26.88	18.18
Wire	659,327					
France	6,939,591		8,316,325	50,083,000	30.46	16.61
West Germany	4,781,276		13,805,653	59,970,000	30.99	23.02
East Germany (GDR)	5,873,955	3,902,689		17,091,000	34.37	22.83
Hungary	2,439,475	1,168,781		10,236,000	24.22	11.42
Wire	39,343					
Poland	4,504,498	2,934,063		31,943,900	17.34	9.19
Wire	1,034,839					

Table 10—*Continued*

Country	Total Radio Licenses	Total Television Licenses	Combined Licenses[a]	Population	Radio Licenses per Hundred	TV Licenses per Hundred
Sweden	2,929,487	2,267,700		7,910,000	37.04	28.67
United Kingdom	2,582,949		14,910,346	54,500,000	32.09	27.36
Yugoslavia	3,053,767	1,001,929		20,000,000	15.27	5.01
1968						
Bulgaria	1,544,713	621,205		8,364,000	26.49	7.42
Wire	696,176					
Czechoslovakia	3,286,696	2,864,067		14,389,000	25.57	19.90
Wire	680,072					
France	6,306,207		9,251,555	49,778,540	31.25	18.59
West Germany	4,029,671		14,958,148	60,440,400	31.42	24.75
East Germany (GDR)	5,932,949	4,173,050		17,091,168	34.71	24.42
Hungary	2,500,000	1,350,000		10,274,000	24.33	13.14
Poland	4,587,814	3,389,142		32,374,000	17.29	10.47
Wire	1,009,745					
Sweden	2,529,664	2,343,007		7,910,000	37.03	29.62
Wire	399,211					
United Kingdom	2,501,580		15,531,471	54,744,000	32.94	28.37
Wire	224,921					
Yugoslavia	3,170,764	1,298,113		20,131,000	15.75	6.45
1969						
Bulgaria	1,564,237	833,201		8,472,000	27.00	9.83
Wire	723,024					
Czechoslovakia	3,224,265	2,996,798		14,439,000	27.09	20.75
Wire	687,923					
France	5,792,937		10,153,180	49,778,540	32.03	20.75
West Germany	3,459,114		15,909,146	61,232,300	31.63	25.98
East Germany (GDR)	5,932,949	4,173,400		17,091,168	34.71	24.42

Table 10—*Continued*

Country	Total Radio Licenses	Total Television Licenses	Combined Licenses[a]	Population	Radio Licenses per Hundred	TV Licenses per Hundred
Hungary	2,531,400	1,595,600		10,313,000	24.80	15.47
Wire	26,000					
Poland	4,661,610	3,827,000		32,691,400	17.28	11.71
Wire	987,805					
Sweden	417,000		2,404,000	8,012,000	35.21	30.00
Wire	400,000					
United Kingdom	2,375,224		15,632,978	55,283,000	32.93	28.63
Wire	183,534					
Yugoslavia	3,310,832	1,542,662		20,456,000	16.19	7.54
1970						
Bulgaria	1,564,237	1,027,000		8,472,000	27.00	10.27
Wire	723,024					
Czechoslovakia	3,173,653	3,091,243		14,439,000	26.74	21.41
Wire	687,290					
France	5,152,320		11,007,630	52,139,000	31.00	21.11
West Germany	2,947,701		16,674,742	61,926,000	31.69	26.93
Hungary	2,530,262	1,768,561		10,313,000	24.53	17.15
Poland	4,697,315	4,214,779		32,879,000	17.21	12.82
Wire	960,010					
Sweden	334,338		2,512,734	8,096,000	35.16	31.04
United Kingdom	2,120,788		15,818,388	55,283,000	33.34	29.50
Yugoslavia	3,379,853	1,798,462		20,613,000	16.40	8.72
1971						
Czechoslovakia	3,173,653	3,091,243		14,439,000	26.74	21.41
Wire	687,290					
France	4,495,780		11,311,865	51,487,000	31.46	23.31
Color			690,627			
West Germany	2,472,483		17,429,730	61,926,000	32.14	28.15

Table 10—Continued

Country	Total Radio Licenses	Total Television Licenses	Combined Licenses[a]	Population	Radio Licenses per Hundred	TV Licenses per Hundred
Hungary	2,507,701	1,942,677		10,315,597	24.62	18.83
Poland	5,800,000	5,000,000		32,604,000		
Romania	2,250,940	1,484,832		20,400,000	15.12	7.28
Wire	833,732					
Sweden	305,501		2,359,253	8,129,000	35.98	32.22
United Kingdom	39,000,000	15,264,000		55,347,000	70.47	29.94
Color		1,304,561				
Yugoslavia	3,481,361	2,057,238		20,656,000	16.85	9.96
1972						
Bulgaria	1,520,510	1,285,848		8,472,000	26.34	15.18
Wire	710,944					
France	3,954,551		13,198,675	51,914,600	33.04	25.42
Color, in total			1,199,454			
West Germany	2,225,679		18,063,892	60,650,599	33.45	29.78
Hungary	2,542,213	2,100,000		10,315,597	24.64	20.35
Romania	2,304,482	1,944,182		20,800,000	14.96	9.35
Wire	807,833					
Sweden	283,448		2,701,493	8,131,000	36.71	33.22
Color, in total			502,478			
United Kingdom	39,000,000	17,191,436		55,347,000	70.47	31.06
Color, in total		2,815,701				
Yugoslavia	3,627,106	2,359,357		20,877,000	17.37	11.30

SOURCE: This table is based on the compilations of radio and television license statistics published in the following issues of the *EBU Review*: 102B (March 1967), p. 36; 108B (March 1968), p. 32; 114B (March 1969), p. 38; 120B (March 1970), p. 39; 126B (March 1971), p. 34; 23:2 (March 1972), p. 37; and 24:2 (March 1973), p. 33. The actual number of receivers in use probably exceeds these figures in all cases, since—despite laws and regulations—licenses are not purchased for all sets.
[a] Licenses for both radio and television.

a vague idea of the scientific successes achieved in the German Democratic Republic and the socialist countries," one purpose of a projected series of programs about the natural sciences "was to inform that important part of the community of TV viewers of the successful efforts exerted in this field by the camp of socialism as well as to encourage their sound judgement."[132] A 1968 publication stated that because GDR's television could be received by millions of people in West Germany, West Berlin, Denmark, and southern Sweden, one of its functions was to present "truthful accounts of the peaceful economic and cultural socialist construction of our republic, the growing international authority of the GDR and the proposals of the Council of State and the government on European security and on all vital questions of the people."[133] Although the progressive détente between the Germanys may bring some relaxation of the propaganda war, it is unlikely that the basic thrust of East Germany's output will soon be changed.

No other Eastern European country is the target of as much foreign broadcasting as is the German Democratic Republic. East Germans can hear West German radio, and those living along the west border and in the Berlin area can watch West German television too. In West Berlin, 110 miles inside East Germany, there are, in addition to the West Berlin stations, relays of other West German services, plus the high-powered transmitters of RIAS (Rundfunk im amerikanischen Sektor von Berlin), operated by the United States Information Agency.* Transmitters in Hof and Munich bring RIAS programs to other parts of East Germany. East Berlin also receives service via West Berlin relays from American, British, Canadian, and French military radio, some of whose programs are available to other parts of the country too, as well as from the BBC. (Neither Radio Liberty nor Radio Free Europe broadcasts to East Germany, this being an assignment of RIAS.) West Germany's Deutschlandfunk, in German and other Central European languages, covers all of East Germany.

Although it is difficult to determine the sources, there is much jamming of Western radio signals in East Germany. The European Broadcasting

* *WRTH 1973,* pp. 57, 60–61. Although the East German authorities do not permit West German installations on their territory, it is possible for the stations of West Berlin to tie into the West German system by a single microwave relay between Berlin and the West German border (*EBU Review* 87A (October 1964), p. 224). However, RIAS has land line connections over East Germany as a result of treaty commitments made by the USSR following World War II.

Union's technical center reported that as of May 1, 1972, there were jamming transmissions on 583, 737, 854, and 989 kilohertz, all channels used by RIAS transmitters.[134] In East Berlin I picked up a good deal of jamming. Although it is not illegal to hear or watch foreign broadcasts in the GDR, the authorities clearly do what they can to discourage it.

The television sets sold to the public receive programs from both sides. However, in the Berolina Hotel in 1968, I found that, although the set in my room picked up the (then) one East German channel very well, it did not receive West Berlin stations at all. In 1972, in the new and elaborate Inter Hotel Stadt Berlin, my room had a built-in all-wave radio set that received programs from all sources, but again the television set had been altered so that only with great difficulty could I get any West Berlin stations.

For its part, the GDR maintains two services primarily for foreign listeners: Stimme der DDR (formerly Deutschlandsender) broadcasts mainly to West Germany, while Radio Berlin International uses short-wave transmitters to reach international audiences. Stimme der DDR also is available to East Germany, and its programs are listed in published program guides. Furthermore, East German domestic services are available to all of West Berlin and portions of West Germany. East German broadcasts intended primarily for foreign listeners averaged 284 hours a week, which placed the GDR fourth among Eastern European countries, after the USSR with 1,884 hours, Albania with 490 hours, and Poland with 340 hours. The German Democratic Republic, however, offers only slightly more than half the German Federal Republic's 724-hour output (see above, p. 205).

For its round-the-clock schedule, Stimme der DDR offers virtually a complete service, including news, political features, programs for young people, and a wide range of music.[135] Generalizations about its programs would apply to all the services maintained by the GDR for its Western neighbors. "The growing needs and interests of West German listeners in getting objective and all-round information about the German Democratic Republic is given expression in [these broadcasts]. . . . In arranging its programs . . . [Stimme der DDR] takes into account social developments in the two German states and the special political entity of West Berlin and gives special consideration to the living habits in West Germany."[136]

In 1965 there were plays by West German writers dealing with such topics as Russian war prisoners, the Hiroshima bomb, and the rise to favor and status in West Germany of former Fascist leaders.[137] Several West German poets read excerpts from their works in the series "Poetry Today," designed to provide "information about the standpoints and tendencies in West German literature." Programs for young people dealt with such subjects as "What Is the Difference between Military and Militarism," "Is Music a Distracting Element When Doing Homework," and "Can a Girl Become a Sailor?"

Commenting generally on talk and information programs for West Germany, an East German release stated in 1965: "The chief task of the 'Scientific World Opinion' series is to acquaint West German listeners . . . with fundamental problems of the marxist world outlook. . . ."[138] In 1966 a new series discussed "the relation of working people to work and questions of shared responsibility," which would meet "the growing need of West German listeners for substantial information about the German Democratic Republic."[139]

Instruction is "given in an entertaining manner" about history, geography, natural sciences, literature, music, theater, arts, and sports.[140] The midnight news bulletins summarize the most important events of the using "an informal personal approach" and provide "background information." With obvious propaganda intent was the 1969 series "Late Crop," dealing with "the late crop of sour grapes of the Bonn Vineyard," which had the purpose of exposing West German political life and revealing leaders like Kissinger, Brandt, and Strauss as wearers of "brown shirts."

Stimme der DDR musical groups make frequent contributions, sometimes playing from art galleries and airports (where there also are interviews with travelers and air crews).[141] It periodically relays Bach performances from the St. Thomas Church in Leipzig. Stimme der DDR also maintains a large dance orchestra, which both plays at home and travels abroad (for example, to the Soviet Union).

Radio Berlin International, in addition to broadcasting to Europe in Danish, English, French, Italian, and Swedish, uses Arabic, English, French, German, Hindi, Portuguese, Spanish, and Swahili in programs for the Near East, Africa, South Asia, and North America.[142] In 1955 it began regular newscasts to Africa, these becoming daily in 1960. About these, a spokesman wrote: "This decision was dictated by the necessity of spreading the truth about the first anti-imperialist German state on the African continent with the aid of the voice of radio. It was necessary to eradicate the false ideas about Germany invented by the propaganda of fascist regimes and further enhanced in the service of the neo-colonialist policy and to replace the distorted pictures drawn by the cold war by the presentation of German reality."[143] Since 1966 there has been a program guide for Radio Berlin International listeners, now issued in eight languages (English, French, Swedish, German, Italian, Spanish, Arab, and Swahili) and distributed in 102 countries.[144]

The television propaganda war between the two Germanys is unique.[145] (Some programs from the Soviet Union are beamed to Finland and Sweden, but this is a very small operation.) There are, of course, many instances of people in the border areas of friendly countries watching programs from their neighbors, some of which undoubtedly are developed with an awareness of foreign audiences, but nowhere is there a television propaganda contest like that between the German Federal Republic and the German Democratic Republic. Although few if any telecasts are developed especially for viewers across the boundaries, portions of the regular broadcasting schedule are repeated for those in the "other Germany," and each country videotapes off the air programs from the other which might be useful for reference or for broadcast.

One reason the GDR always cultivated close relationships with other broadcasting organizations was its long-time isolated international status. There are regular program exchanges with over 100 radio organizations in all parts of the world and with many television groups.[146] A great point is made of cooperative agreements, particularly with other socialist countries. In fact, almost every OIRT information brochure reports one or more such protocols. Although for many years the nonsocialist countries most frequently involved were in the Middle East, there are more and more references to cooperative projects with other countries.[147]

There is close cooperation with the Soviet Union. Gerhart Eisler, when head of the State Broadcasting Committee, wrote at the time of its twentieth anniversary that German Democratic Radio had "developed from modest beginnings to its present-day form with the great support of our Soviet friends."[148] In 1961 East German Radio broadcast a program produced in Siberia about the people of Yakutia, which told how the USSR had brought art and science to that Arctic region, the most backward part of the czarist empire.[149] German Democratic Radio also broadcast Othello's monologue in the Yakut language. In 1969, in preparation for the Lenin centennial, Deutschlandsender prepared special programs about Ulyanovsk, Lenin's birthplace.[150]

Reversing directions, in 1969 several Soviet regional networks had a "Day of the German Democratic Radio," and once each week Soviet radio now broadcasts "Berlin Speaking," recorded in Russian in Berlin for the USSR.[151] These programs acquaint Soviet listeners "with social life in our republic and—among other things—also with the musical production in the DDR." Examples of the latter have ranged from a thirty-minute program in the spring of 1971 entitled "Music as Presented by Renowned Organs" to programs of workers' songs.

Like most European countries, East Germany exchanges production teams and crews with both socialist and nonsocialist states. In 1967 a Dutch-Finnish team visited the GDR to record material for Reformation Day broadcasts.[152] Belgium, Cambodia, Czechoslovakia, Japan, New Zealand, Norway, Sweden, North Vietnam, the United Kingdom, the USSR, Yugoslavia, and other countries have either sent production teams or joined in other cooperative projects.[153] In 1972 East German and Italian television joined forces to produce Verdi's *Rigoletto* in East Berlin, with an Italian conductor and soloists plus the Dresden State Orchestra. It was planned to use the program on German, Italian, and French television.[154]

Services to foreign broadcasting organizations include program exchanges, in which music is a natural, since no language problems are involved. Performances available on tape from German Democratic Radio include symphonic, operatic, and choral music; light concert music; popular melodies; and novelty selections by East German composers.[155] Among users have been various American broadcasting organizations, including the Pacifica stations as well as some served by the Broadcasting Foundation of America.[156] German Democratic Radio took part in the EBU series "Panorama of Great Orchestras," providing programs by the Leipzig Gewandhaus and Dresden State orchestras.[157]

On the input side, German Democratic Radio has used the Sibelius Festival from Helsinki, the Zagreb Biennial from Yugoslavia, recordings made at the Salzburg Festival in Austria, and materials from Czechoslovakia, Poland, and the Netherlands.[158] There is a regular exchange of television films, particularly with the bloc countries, where East German telefilms have been used by both television and cinema.

Television participates regularly in Eurovision exchanges. According to EBU data, in 1960, although originating no programs, the GDR received 97 programs of 94 hours duration (see Tables 1 and 2). Its first contribution was of 2 programs the following year (4 hr.), when it received 73 programs (92 hr.). In 1971, according to the EBU, the GDR contributed 9 programs (24 hr., 30 min.) and received 121 programs (242 hr.). Intervision reported that in 1971 East Germany received 107 programs from Eurovision (198 hr., 24 min.) and contributed 18 programs (36 hr., 53 min.). The 1972 Eurovision figures—no originations but 180 programs (354 hr., 15 min.) received—reflect Olympic Games coverage, whereas the Intervision figures—10 originations (15 hr.) and 58 programs (119 hr., 20 min.) received—do not.

VII

Polish People's Republic

Poland's geography sets it apart from the other non-Soviet countries covered in this study. If Yugoslavia is regarded as somewhat Western oriented, then Poland is the only one of the group whose land frontiers are shared entirely with Eastern-oriented countries. Furthermore, it is located directly on the invasion road between Germany and the Soviet Union—a fact which has affected its history over the centuries. Yet, as international and domestic crises developed since World War II, Poland solved its problems without the Soviet intervention which occurred in East Germany, Hungary, and Czechoslovakia.

Facts about Poland

The Polish People's Republic is the largest nation in the Soviet orbit, with an area of 120,359 square miles (New Mexico has 121,666 square miles) and in 1970 a population of 32,604,000. Warsaw, the largest city and capital, has over 1.3 million inhabitants. Before World War II one-third of the population was Ukrainian, Byelorussian, German, or Jewish, but boundary and population shifts during the war and since 1945 reduced these minorities to less than 2 per cent of the total, and most of the population now is ethnically Polish. Poland's land frontiers are entirely shared with other socialist states: the German Democratic Republic to the west, Czechoslovakia to the south, and the Soviet Union to the east. The Baltic Sea is on the north.

For two centuries the history of Poland has been marked by partitions

270

of its territory. In 1772, 1793, and again in 1795, it was divided among Prussia, Russia, and Austria. After being reconstituted as an independent political entity from 1919 to 1939, it was divided between Germany and the USSR during the first month of World War II. Postwar arrangements gave portions of eastern Poland to the Soviet Union and portions of eastern Germany to Poland.

During World War II, Poland was the scene of heavy fighting, during which it suffered enormous property damage. From six to seven million people died, including over three million Jews killed by the Nazis. Since 1945 there has been extensive reconstruction, and the major cities have been largely rebuilt. In the course of three visits to Warsaw in 1965, 1970, and 1972, I have been much impressed by the progress made in this reconstruction. However, a relatively low standard of living and shortages of consumer goods have caused much unrest, contributing to several political crises.

Although most of Poland's recent history has involved domination or occupation by foreign countries—currently, the USSR—Poland has succeeded in maintaining some degree of freedom from Soviet control. In 1956, when revolt led to direct Soviet intervention in Hungary, unrest in Poland caused only a change in leadership, bringing to power Wladyslaw Gomulka in October of that year. When Gomulka was replaced in 1971 by Edward Gierek, realignment again occurred without Soviet military action. However, Poland is among the countries with USSR garrisons, there being some 50,000 Soviet troops stationed there.

Although Poland is far from being "free" in the Western sense, its mass media enjoy more independence than do those of its neighbors, the German Democratic Republic and Czechoslovakia. The Roman Catholic Church, although subject to varying degrees of government restrictions, has continued to function, and the 95 per cent of the population who are members frequently attend services. In fact, the Western tourist will notice in Poland the good condition in which churches are maintained, as well as the number and wide age range of worshippers. But Poland has no religious broadcasts, although it does mention religious events on news programs.

Poland belongs to the Warsaw Pact, COMECON, the United Nations, and UNESCO. (There is a description below of an elaborate adult education project partly financed by UNESCO.) Of Polish trade, 65 per cent is with the East and 35 per cent with the West; but while the Soviet Union far and away is Poland's most important trading partner, Poland has received considerable financial assistance from the United States. In 1970, 42 per cent of Poland's foreign trade was with the USSR, 13 per cent with East Germany, 10 per cent with Czechoslovakia, 6 per cent with West Germany, 6 per cent with the United Kingdom, and 5 per cent with Hungary. Trade with the United States came to a little less than 3 per cent.[1]

Legal Structure

The current Polish constitution, which resembles that of the USSR, was adopted July 22, 1952.[2] Article 1 declares that "the Polish People's Republic is a State of People's Democracy" in which "the power belongs to the working people of town and country." Article 8 states that "the national wealth"—including mineral deposits, forests, transportation, and "means of communication"—"is the subject of special care and protection by the State and by all citizens." Article 14, Paragraph 3, states: "The Polish People's Republic gives increasing practical effect to the principle: 'From each according to his ability, to each according to his work.' "* Unlike many of the socialist constitutions, that of Poland does not contain any provision qualifying freedom of expression, unless this might be inferred from the third part of Article 72: "The setting up of, and participation in, associations, the aims or activities of which are directed against the political or social system or against the legal order of the Polish People's Republic are forbidden."

The government is headed by the Council of State and the Council of Ministers, the latter including the minister of communications. The unicameral national assembly, the Seym, is elected every four years by all citizens eighteen years of age and over. De facto power is in the hands of the Political Bureau (Politburo) of the Polish United Workers' party, which is the dominant political group, although in 1969, 45 per cent of the 460 parliamentary seats were divided among three other Communist-controlled parties. In Poland, as elsewhere in the Eastern European bloc, party and government activities are closely integrated.

Decrees and laws relative to broadcasting were passed in 1944, 1949, 1951, and 1960.[3] Broadcasting is administered by the Committee for

---

* For the derivation of this phrase, see footnote on p. 3. For references to it in the Czechoslovakian and Yugoslav constitutions, see below, pp. 316 and 466.

Radio and Television, under the terms of a bill adopted by the Seym on December 2, 1960. Members of the committee are appointed—and may be dismissed—by the Council of Ministers. In addition, Parliament must approve all program and budget plans. The chairman of the Radio and Television Committee is not a member of the council, although he takes part in discussions when broadcasting is on the agenda. The party also is involved in broadcasting.

The committee is responsible for all aspects of domestic and external broadcasting, although—in accordance with the usual European pattern—transmitters and lines are the responsibility of the Ministry of Communications. Broadcasting is subdivided functionally into such areas as radio, television, external services, engineering, personnel, and research, with each major department headed by a vice-chairman. Although regional stations are administered locally, they too are eventually responsible to the committee.

Polish broadcasting is supported mainly by license fees, although there is some income from advertising. The annual charge per household for a radio license is 180 zlotys ($46.00) for a tube or transistor set and 72 zlotys ($18.50) for a wired receiver. The rate for a television receiver (which also covers all radio receivers in the household) is 480 zlotys ($122.65).*

There is careful supervision of both the printed and broadcast media in Poland. Under the law, the mass media may not criticize the system of government, disclose state secrets, damage the international relations of the country, induce violations of law and order, or publish inaccurate information.[4] Conformity with regulations is assured through the appointment of dependable people to the Radio and Television Committee and to important positions in the broadcasting organization. However, there is no censorship as such, nor is it necessary, since the broadcasting staff can be expected to conform to policy and to carry out directives. But Poland, like the other countries in the socialist bloc, engages in a certain amount of self-criticism. There may be complaints about housing, or debate whether children of party members have better

---

* In Poland, even more than in most European countries, it is difficult to provide dollar equivalents for local currency, since several exchange rates are quoted. In early 1973 the official rate was 3.68 zlotys to the dollar, the tourist rate 22.88, and the rate for transferring foreign currency 66.00. Diplomats had still another rate.

chances in higher education than do those from working-class families—but basic ideological tenets are not questioned (see the case of "The Bricked-Up Window," pp. 281–282 below).

On December 5, 1971, a report on party activities published in the Warsaw newspaper *Trybuna ludu* defined the role of the mass media: "The press, radio, and television represent an important link of the ideological front. The mass information media were partly responsible for the fact that the hopes of the forces which saw during the December crisis an opportunity for undermining the party's leading role in our country were not realized. . . . The mass information and propaganda media battled against passivity and routine in political, economic, and cultural life and emphasized the need to consolidate social discipline and the awareness that every citizen is responsible for the country and its development."[5]

This position was reiterated the following day by Edward Gierek, the new first secretary of the Central Committee, who told the Politburo: "We must speed up the development of Marxist-Leninist social sciences and undertake broader, more complex research in Poland's contemporary problems, into the socialist work and the international class struggle, and popularize the results of these works through training and propaganda, education and the mass media."[6]

All this had been anticipated by a statement from Polish Radio the previous year: "The Polish radio is at present playing an important part in forming the public opinion of the Polish people and its socialist economic and cultural policy. It also plays a vital role in interpreting public opinion, bearing in mind the importance of public opinion in the effort to eliminate faults and errors and helping to improve and make more productive the work of the whole of society."[7]

Yet Poland is freer than many socialist countries. In 1957 a Polish magazine ran excerpts from George Orwell's *1984*, and there have been reviews of such works as Arthur Koestler's *Darkness at Noon*, whose subject is Communist terrorism.[8] The very extensive repertoire of radio and television drama includes many Western plays, both classic and contemporary. A former Czech journalist now living in the West, writing in 1964 about the press in all the Eastern European countries, concluded that the coverage of events in Poland was "more complete and objective than in other communist countries," with the exception of Yugoslavia.[9]

In the spring of 1972, the Warsaw student State Theater Academy presented performances in Washington, DC, of excerpts from the play *Tango* by Polish writer Slawomir Mrozek, which had been widely performed in Western Europe but banned from the Polish stage. This fact, together with an announcement that Mrozek's complete works shortly would be published in Poland, was taken as evidence that the new Gierek regime favored a thaw in Poland's cultural life.[10] In mid-1973 it was announced that direct censorship would be ended for two major Warsaw newspapers, although since both were Communist organs staffed by party stalwarts, it would appear that no great risk was being run. Yet at the same time, heavier doses of Marxist philosophy were prescribed for Polish university students. My own impressions, after discussions with a number of Polish citizens, are that the Polish people exert constant pressure for freedom of expression and avail themselves of it at every opportunity. The government is at least moderately sympathetic to such pressure, even while continuing publicly to subscribe to the standard Communist line—perhaps partly, if not entirely, for Soviet consumption.

Stations and Networks

After some experiments dating from 1924 the Polskie Radio Company began regular programming on April 18, 1926.[11] During World War II all radio facilities and electronic manufacturing plants were destroyed, so when broadcasting was resumed on August 11, 1944, it was with a transmitter supplied by the Soviet Union, located in a renovated railroad car. The Poles are justly proud of having rebuilt broadcasting mainly with their own equipment. Currently, they have three radio and two television networks, plus regional and external services.

Radio Program I uses one high-powered long-wave station (500 kilowatts on 227 kilohertz), reinforced during certain hours of the day by several FM stations, to cover almost the entire country.[12] This general program, on the air twenty-four hours a day, is intended mainly for audiences in small towns and villages, and accordingly includes agricultural features, educational programs for in- and out-of-school use, light music, drama, and entertainment.

Program II, covering over half the country's territory and 70 per cent of its population, is carried by a 300-kilowatt medium-wave station in Warsaw, about 25 medium-wave stations in other cities, and some 14 FM stations. On the air twenty-one hours a day, from 3:00 A.M. to midnight, it is directed to provincial capitals and large industrial centers. It offers more challenging intellectual and cultural fare than does Program I, emphasizing literary material, serious music, and news.

Program III, on the air from 4:00 A.M. until 11:00 P.M. weekdays, and from 5:00 A.M. until 11:00 P.M. Sundays, is carried by 20 FM stations.[13] It reaches about 60 per cent of the country's territory and 70 per cent of its population. This is basically an entertainment service: 60 per cent of its time is given to light music, the remainder consisting of dramatic programs and some discussions. Consideration is being given to establishing a fourth network that would divide its programming equally between serious music and educational material, with strong emphasis on organized instruction.[14]

A UNESCO report made in 1964 categorized the content of the three national programs as follows: music, 52.7 per cent; news and information, 24.5 per cent; literary and theatrical presentations, 9.9 per cent; broadcasts for children and schools, 5.7 per cent; general educational programs, 2.0 per cent; and advertising, 3.7 per cent.[15] An analysis in 1966 classified centrally originated programs in this way: music, 52.0 per cent; literature and plays, 11.2 per cent; news and information, 7.3 per cent; commentaries and current affairs, 6.9 per cent; children and schools, 4.5 per cent; advertising, 3.5 per cent; sports, 2.4 per cent; educational programs, 2.3 per cent; agricultural programs, 2.1 per cent; special events, 1.7 per cent; variety shows 1.4 per cent; youth programs, 1.2 per cent; and, miscellaneous, 3.5 per cent.[16] An official source categorized programs in 1970 as follows:[17] The spoken word constituted 52.3 per cent of Network I, 48.5 per cent of Network II, and 33.4 per cent of Network III, the overall average being 46.8 per cent. Music made up 45.1 per cent of Network I, 48.7 per cent of Network II, and 64 per cent of Network III, for an average of 50.5 per cent. The remaining miscellaneous material averaged out at 2.7 per cent.

Regional stations located in sixteen cities relay some programs from Network II, present between two and five hours of local programs each day, and originate some material for the national networks.[18] Warsaw has three hours a day of local services, including news, weather, road information, Warsaw-oriented entertainment, and announcements of events in the area. At present, the national radio headquarters are in a building which formerly housed the secret police, although new construction is in progress adjacent to the television studios opened in 1969.

Polish FM broadcasting uses the spectrum space between 63 and 73 megacycles, as do the other Eastern European countries.[19] The first stereo experiments were launched in 1963, and programs have been presented regularly since October 1967. In the belief that FM represents the future of radio broadcasting, approximately eighty transmitters were in service in 1973, with more to come.

The Poles have some pragmatic theories about the relationships between radio and television. The general director of radio and television wrote in 1962 that although some people regarded television as radio's "irreconcilable enemy," television instead would cause radio to make its programs more attractive.[20] Nine years later the radio program director observed that radio finally was emerging from the shadow of television and said he looked forward to the three radio networks becoming more sharply differentiated so as to give their audience a greater range of choice.[21] Program I would become "an information program with light and folk music dominating," Program II "an artistic program with a predominance of literary forms and serious music," while Program III would "concentrate on entertainment and bring a large number of short magazine-type items." Radio, he said, is the best medium for information, as had been demonstrated by Soviet, Western European, and American stations. Nothing else can report the news as quickly, and the man who carries a transistor is always in touch with the world.

There were experiments with television in Poland in 1938, although these were cut off by the war.[22] Experimental programming was resumed in 1952, the regular broadcasting began on July 23, 1954, in Warsaw. By 1960 all the major regions of the country had their own stations.

Network I now is carried by 17 VHF transmitters in all parts of Poland, with ERP video power ranging from 1 to 265 kilowatts, reinforced by over 70 low-powered satellites.* These transmitters cover 68 per cent of the country's territory and 80 per cent of its population. A general service, it is on the air from 8:00 to 10:00 A.M. and 4:00 to 10:00 P.M. In the morning it carries in-school broadcasts and during the evening programs of general information, political broadcasts, entertainment, drama, sports, films, and Intervision relays.

The second network, inaugurated October 1, 1970, is carried by 6

---

* *WRTH 1973*, p. 279. The Eastern European D system is used. See above, p. 76n, on a radio and television tower at Plock, completed in 1974.

VHF transmitters to 2 per cent of the territory and 17 per cent of the population.* Regular color transmissions were begun December 5, 1971, with a broadcast of the Sixth Congress of the Polish United Workers' party. On the air 22 evening hours each week, between 12 and 14 hours of its output is in color, although it is hoped that by 1975, 70 per cent of the total output of both networks will be in color, with originations in the regional as well as the Warsaw studios. In contrast with the German Democratic Republic, where both services are general in nature, the second Polish channel is educational, emphasizing science, technology, fine arts, experimental theater, and foreign languages. In 1971 its program categories were approximately as follows: scientific-educational, 22 per cent; artistic, 22 per cent; films, 21 per cent; information and public affairs, 15 per cent; and sports, 6 per cent.[23]

On July 18, 1959, a new broadcasting center was opened in Warsaw for radio and television, with a number of studios, control rooms, offices, and related space.[24] When completed, this will be the largest construction project ever undertaken in the country. The building appears to be hastily built, although this is understandable in view of the tremendous reconstruction problems faced by Poland after World War II.

Poland manufactures all types of transmitting and receiving equipment, meeting most of its own demand and doing some exporting.[25] Although the production of video tape recorders began in the late 1960s, and it is reported that enough are produced to meet domestic needs, I saw several American Ampex machines in the television center, suggesting that the local product does not meet all demands. One Western observer reported that in May 1971 the television program guide contained an article apologizing for certain program inadequacies, which also said that "our equipment is far from satisfactory. Current investments can at best only smooth over the consequence of neglect for many years."[26]

Supplementing the national headquarters in Warsaw are television centers in seven other cities, which provide from thirty to sixty minutes of local programs each week, in addition to contributing to the national services. In Gdansk, on the Baltic coast, a studio center with film equipment and a remote pickup van was constructed in 1969.[27] Gdansk's chil-

* OIRT Information 1971/2, pp. 13–14. SECAM color is used with the Eastern European D system. OIRT Information 1969/12, pp. 4–5.

dren's program, "The Flying Dutchman," is fed to the entire country. Szczecin, in northwest Poland, produces for the national network about thirty hours annually of information, news, drama, entertainment, and popular science programs.

Although Poland has no cable television, an amplifier has been manufactured which allows up to 30 sets to use a single antenna for both radio and television signals, eliminating the need for a forest of antennas on apartment rooftops.[28] Television receivers have been manufactured since 1957, and the current production rate of over 700,000 sets a year allows some exports. A new black-and-white receiver costs between 5,200 and 10,000 zlotys, with 7,400 a good average. Color sets sell for 19,500, but when they get into production, prices may come down. (The country's average monthly wage is around 2,750, although some industrial workers earn as much as 4,200 zlotys.)

News

Residents of the Polish People's Republic have a choice of at least thirty domestic radio news programs every twenty-four hours plus two major television newscasts.[29] Since most people can hear Radio Free Europe and other foreign services, and residents in border areas often see foreign—albeit socialist—television, one could adopt an American promotional phrase to say that most of Poland is never more than an hour away from news.

Although the Poles have not said as much about the propaganda objectives of news as have some of the other socialist countries, they clearly recognize the ideological significance of information programs. In 1960 the radio program director wrote: "Polish radio is an organ of propaganda. . . . [Therefore], it explains many problems, comments on events, mobilizes public opinion, discusses incorrect tendencies, [and] struggles against hostile propaganda. . . ."[30] A former Polish journalist, Georges H. Mond, generalizing about mass media policy declarations in Poland between 1967 and 1969, identified two prevailing themes: written, spoken, and televised news should be improved to meet competition, presumably from abroad; and all the mass media should be strengthened for psychological warfare against "the ideological distraction of imperialism."[31]

The Polish news agency Polska Agencja Presowa (PAP), which

is legally a government department, has bureaus in seventeen cities throughout the country and correspondents abroad in such centers as London, Peking, Cairo, Paris, New Delhi, Bonn, Mexico City, Stockholm, Rome, and Washington, and in the socialist capitals.[32] PAP has exchange agreements with the Eastern European countries as well as with British Reuters and Agence France Presse. It publishes daily 60,000 words in Polish, 1,200 words in Russian, 1,000 words in English, and 300 words each in French and Spanish.

Eighty per cent of Polish broadcast news comes from PAP and TASS, although broadcasting has its own correspondents in Moscow, London, Paris, Rome, Belgrade, Prague, New York, East Berlin, Budapest, Bonn, and Mexico City, among other cities. Television also gets material from UPI, IPN, Intervision, and Eurovision, while both radio and television draw upon the news departments of their regional stations (see Tables 1 and 2). According to the EBU, the first year Poland got any news from Eurovision was 1963, when it received 16 items. In 1965 Poland contributed 10 items and received 5; in 1966 it contributed 22 while receiving only 1; and in 1967 it contributed 19 while receiving 16. There are no data from the EBU on Polish contributions to or reception of Eurovision news since then. However, figures from Intervision in Prague indicate that during 1972 Poland received 1,917 Eurovision news items and originated 37.

Polish network radio now transmits some thirty newscasts a day, most of them on Programs I and II. As described by a Polish source in 1967— and basic procedures remain about the same—these included nineteen programs ranging from five to ten minutes in length, plus several fifteen- and thirty-minute programs. All newscasts provide coverage of both domestic and international items. Typical thirty-minute evening programs include news, commentary, interviews, sports, and weather. A typical broadcast begins with a weather forecast, followed by late news from Poland and abroad, sports, and more weather. The final ten or twelve minutes, "Problems of the Day," present additional information plus several commentaries. The longer programs often include reviews of the domestic and foreign press, along with information about theatrical performances, films, books, exhibitions, and concerts.

Radio newscasters, who are very much aware of the competition from television at home and from foreign radio, try to make their presentations interesting and compelling. Many programs are built around journalists who read well rather than professional announcers, in order to stress authenticity, and emphasis is placed on good radio writing. In 1971 the editor in chief of radio news said that eight different styles were used, ranging from straight news to programs with background and supplementary material.[33] Inquiries by the research department showed that news was third in listener preference, top rank going to entertainment and second to music.

News is the most popular television item, for which reason additional equipment, studio space, and personnel have been assigned to it.[34] On a typical day the first television channel has a ten-minute newscast at 4:30 P.M., plus twenty- or thirty-minute programs at 7:30 P.M. (also carried by the second network) and 10:30 P.M.

In September and October 1970 I saw several newscasts. Gamal Abdel Nasser, president of the United Arab Republic, had just died, and therefore the programs reviewed his career and reported his funeral. One thirty-minute program, in fact, devoted over half its time to Nasser, an editorial judgment probably guided more by political than audience factors. In any case, there was a good deal of film, probably from Eurovision, about the Nasser story.

I also saw a report from New York by the Polish United Nations correspondent; film coverage of the Southeast Asian war; stories about visitors to Moscow; pictures of a fire in Los Angeles; material about the visit President Nixon paid Tito in Yugoslavia; a Polish exhibition in East Berlin; and such domestic items as building construction, the installation of a new university chancellor, and the opening of the academic year. Most of the film was silent, although sound film would have been more effective, especially on domestic stories with Polish speakers. The news readers tended to lack personality and were rather stiff, the overall effect tending toward dullness. On most programs a young woman, with map, pointer, and arrows, gave a rather colorless weather forecast. Additional viewing in 1972 confirmed previous impressions about news content, but indicated progress in presentation: news readers were definitely better and production improved.

Despite the requirement that comments be kept within ideological bounds, Polish broadcasting does engage in self-criticism, an example being the case of "The Bricked-Up Window."[35] An influential person living in a village near Warsaw had built a villa immediately adjacent to a farmer's house, thereby sealing up his neighbor's only window. Television documented the story on an hour-long program before an informal three-member tribunal, and the public was invited to react. This led to some 800 letters, many of which were published in a newspaper under the title "A Thousand Angry People." During a thirty-minute follow-up, some of the letters were read, and the conflict resolved right on the air. An article describing the project commented that such procedures constituted an important escape valve, and remarked that the letter writers were "angry people in revolt . . . against passivity and eternal discontent, people who attempt to improve all shortcomings, who wish the best for their homeland." In mid-1973 at the same time censorship was lifted from some Warsaw newspapers, self-criticism was intensified: grievances were sought out and publicized, and a campaign initiated to curb rudeness and poor work habits among civil servants, who in Poland, as in so many European countries, often have constituted an independent enclave in the nation's affairs.[36]

Major party meetings are covered at length by both media. In December 1971 radio broadcast a speech by the first secretary of the Central Committee, Edward Gierek, the written transcript of which took almost thirty-seven single-spaced typed pages, while a talk by Premier Piotr Jaroszewicz on the following day covered fifteen pages.[37] In September 1972 I noticed that the regularly scheduled programs on both television channels were delayed several hours one evening so that another party meeting could receive extensive coverage. But it also should be noted that Poland and Romania were the only two socialist countries with extensive live coverage of America's first moon landing in 1969.[38]

Programs also provide a forum for public exchanges with government officials.[39] In 1971 a short-lived ninety-minute series, "Citizens Forum," gave viewers a chance to quiz government and party leaders. To supplement questions received in advance, sixteen telephone lines were installed, one for each province of the country, and three remote television units set up to transmit questions live. The series was developed at the suggestion of party leaders to close the communications gap with the public, and it is reported that many searching questions were received. But it is no longer on the air.

Children and Youth

Poland does some outstanding educational broadcasting for audiences of all ages. These include youth programs for both in- and out-of-school use, all thoughtfully justified in terms of the national broadcasting objectives outlined above.

In 1965 the deputy chief editor of Polish Radio pointed out that there were several reasons for the "unwillingness of schools to accept new media," the chief one being "the obsolete technique of school work."[40] Traditional organization, she wrote, led to mechanical and rigid teaching, which discouraged creativity. Such problems still face media specialists in Poland as elsewhere. In 1971 the Program Council of Polish Radio and Television was seeking ways "to decrease discrepancies existing between the enormous effort developed by radio and television in order to promote educational broadcasts and the relatively low number of schools utilizing these broadcasts and programmes."[41]

The objectives of in-school broadcasting were determined at the outset. In 1961 it was decided that "school telecasts are no substitute for the teacher in the fulfillment of the tasks laid down for them in the compulsory school curriculum."[42] Nine years later another article stated: "The broadcasts are neither a repetition nor an extension of the school program. Taking advantage of the possibilities . . . [of] radio . . . they give a varied picture of the world which stimulates the child's imagination and adds new elements to the knowledge it acquires from textbooks."[43]

Broadcasting can compensate for shortages of up-to-date textbooks, assist nonexpert teachers in fields like music, bring performances (of literary works, drama, and music) into the classroom, enrich the curriculum, and motivate students. It can bring factory, foundry, museum, and laboratory to the school.[44] The media also can help introduce new curricula and teaching methods. Finally there is the political objective. The deputy chief of the Department of Popular Scientific Broadcasts wrote in 1965 that one task of school television was "to aid the development of the scientific, materialistic world outlook. The plan of school programmes has been prepared accordingly."[45]

In-school radio broadcasts deal with such standard subjects as languages, history, civics, geography, physics, biology, and chemistry.[46] Music is among the subjects stressed, and there are programs of children's songs, talks on composers, and series with names like "Works That Became Famous" and "The Lives of Instruments." In-school programs are aired at 9:00 A.M., 11:00 A.M., and 1:00 P.M., to coincide with class periods. Other programs, to extend the school curriculum, are heard at 7:45 A.M. and 1:00, 2:45, and 3:05 P.M. Programs range from twenty to thirty minutes in length, depending upon subject matter and grade level.

Programs are planned cooperatively a year in advance by teachers, broadcasters, and representatives of the Ministry of Education, and each series is supervised by a subject matter expert. The broadcasts are combinations of talks, discussions, interviews, and dramatizations, and there are pupil and teacher handbooks for both radio and television.[47] Emphasis is placed on teacher preparation, and broadcast times are set so as to leave a few minutes for class preparation and follow-up discussions.

In 1969 one out of every four teachers made some use of school radio. Sixty per cent of schools tuned in broadcasts, and 43 per cent used recordings of the programs. In 1972 it was reported that 20 per cent of the 27,000 elementary schools in the country used in-school radio programs "systematically," this figure reaching 50 per cent among village schools.[48] Many schools own tape recorders and have built extensive libraries of their own. Radio and television programs are planned to supplement—rather than compete with—each other. For example, television gave up music instruction to radio, replacing it with art programs. However, broadcasts for very young pupils are on radio only.

School television began in the spring of 1961 with 35 experimental programs of thirty minutes' duration received in some 300 schools.[49] In 1970–1971 there were 340 programs, including tape-recorded repeats from earlier years. Telecasts last about twenty minutes for younger and thirty minutes for older children. Since class periods run forty-five minutes, this leaves time for class discussion before and after broadcasts. In 1969–1970 there were programs for all grades, on such subjects as history, geography, physics, civics, chemistry, zoology, poetry, drama, and biology. The average series consisted of from 7 to 10 programs. In 1972 there were 1,200 hours of in-school television.

Studies of use and effectiveness accompany the broadcasts.[50] In 1967, 80 per cent of all secondary schools had at least one television receiver, and 70 per cent of the teacher's colleges were equipped. A recent investigation showed that 80 per cent of all schools used television regularly, the main limiting factor being scheduling convenience. It is hoped, however, that this problem will be met through the repetition of programs on the second channel. Of the teachers, 90 per cent rated the programs "good," while 33 per cent said they were "very good." Teachers put television ahead of films as teaching aids. Ever since 1963–1964 there have been programs to facilitate the adjustment of teachers to new curricula and textbooks, and in 1969 "there were weekly lessons to prepare them for in-school broadcasts dealing with new mathematical concepts."[51] Many programs are required viewing for teachers.

Like all socialist countries, Poland takes its out-of-school programs for children and youth very seriously. In 1964 a member of the radio staff observed that because young people born between 1940 and 1948 had "no criteria of comparison based on their own experience under capitalism," it was necessary for youth programs to clarify the differences between socialism and capitalism.[52] For example, the series "My Place in Life" was to fight "against egoism, antisocial attitudes, indifference, and uncritical admiration of the western way of life."

There are broadcasts for all ages.[53] A department to develop programs for preschool children was set up in 1948–1949, when there was a shortage of qualified teachers for the kindergartens then being opened. The best time for such broadcasts was found to be 9:40 A.M. on Tuesdays and Fridays. Subjects included attitudes toward animals, children of foreign lands, fairy tales, and stories from Polish history. Follow-up activities were strongly encouraged.

Polish broadcasters like block programming for children. In 1965 a daily twenty-five minute series was presented from 4:35 to 5:00 P.M., subjects including technology, economics, social problems, science, sports, and recreation. Beginning in 1966 "Meeting with Youth" was transmitted each weekday afternoon for two hours, and after February 1, 1969, there was a sixty-minute block of children's programs from 3:05 to 4:05 P.M.[54] In 1970 radio and popular science programs for listeners aged twelve to fifteen, dealing with laboratory experiments, astronomy, polar exploration, and geology.[55] In 1969 French lessons were broadcast during summer holiday periods as an extension of the services offered during the regular school year.

In 1960, when still in its development stage, television began to plan out-of-school programs for children, and by 1969, following the radio pattern, moved its young people's programs into one block on Tuesdays between 5:00 and 7:20 P.M.[56] Offerings included "TV for the Young Set," intended to inform young viewers about current events, help them solve their problems, and suggest ways to spend their leisure time. To make the programs as attractive as possible, there were popular singers, beat groups, song competitions, plays, student cabarets, contributions by drama students, and films. Polish, like Soviet and East German television, has its "Good Night" puppet series, whose two principal characters, Jacek and Agatka, are so popular that some children have been named after them.[57] Finally, in the spring of 1972, *Sesame Street* appeared experimentally on Polish screens.[58]

Adult Education

When I asked the director of foreign relations what I should stress about Polish broadcasting, he said I should report that it is trying to bring culture to the masses.

For many years Polish broadcasting has had educational programs for adults, although the Television Technical College, with credit arrangements, was not inaugurated until 1965. The Radio University set up in 1959 did not "include lessons dealing systematically with all problems of a given branch of science," but rather was "a school of independent thinking," which was to "enrich the stock of listener's knowledge."[59] These and other programs, often presented sequentially in weekly installments, dealt with the Polish language, world history and culture, science, medical information, and even "The Great Religions of the World."

The growth of television has not curtailed the enthusiasm of the Polish radio staff to develop educational programs for adults.[60] A series of training programs for the Society for the Popularization of Knowledge and for the Conference of Workers' Self-Governments occupies eighty minutes of time every day. In 1970 it covered six basic areas, including the Lenin anniversary, industrial subjects, theories on the development of the universe, and important anniversaries (the 20th anniversary of the defeat of Nazi Germany, the 150th birthday of Engels). "One Hundred Years of Europe" traced the Continent's history beginning with the Paris Commune of 1871. "The Radio Encyclopedia of Culture" included 200 programs, once a week for twenty-five minutes, reviewing Polish history and culture from the earliest times to date. Instruction in Russian, French, and English continued, and German lessons were begun.

Polish broadcasters have demonstrated a more international viewpoint than have those in many other socialist countries. In 1957 radio began a series from the International Radio University, coordinated by the French broadcasting system, and in 1971 was still carrying those programs along with similar ones from the OIRT in Prague.[61] Both series consist of talks on academic subjects by various world authorities which are read on Polish radio after being translated. Despite the names, however, neither was a "university" project with formal courses or credit.

This emphasis on education is encouraged by audience research findings. A research center reported that early in 1971 72.4 per cent of all listeners followed "popularized scientific" programs, which then occupied 3 per cent of all radio time.[62] It also was found that 6.5 per cent of the audience followed language lessons, of which 62 per cent heard those in English, 50 per cent in Russian, and 21 per cent in French.

The term "Television University" emerged as early as 1963.[63] "Horizon," a popular science magazine broadcast three times a week, tried to present "the most difficult scientific matters in an accessible way."[64] Several programs a week were devoted to economics—"broadcasts about workers, industrial questions, economy, and management"—with contributors ranging from workers to government ministers.[65] In 1970 radio, hoping to bring the facts of economics to the working man, offered "Five Minutes about the Economics" and "Under the Factory Roof."[66] For those of literary inclination there were telecourses in French, which also included information about French history and culture.[67]

In view of the importance of agriculture to its economy, it is not surprising that Poland has developed some excellent agricultural broadcasts. More than half the population lives in rural areas, and there are many agricultural workers. Despite government pressure to develop collective farming, however, about 85 per cent of the farms are privately owned. Because agricultural output has not kept pace with demand, large imports of wheat have been necessary to feed the growing industrial population, and Poland has had to supplement assistance from the Soviet Union with surplus agricultural commodities from the United States. The riots of December 1970 followed increases in food prices which had the objective of reducing the consumption of food to leave more of it for export.

The radio series "Scientific Workers to Farmers," begun in 1960 and involving 100 specialists from agricultural colleges all over the country, was received not only in homes but also by groups of listeners.[68] Between 60 and 80 per cent of the country's farmers heard these programs, and it was claimed that an increase of agricultural production occurred in those areas where the broadcasts were followed regularly. In 1965 sixty tape recorders were distributed in rural areas so the programs could be recorded and replayed; supplementary filmed materials were prepared; and in some localities agronomists led discussion groups after the programs had been heard.

Television programs for agriculturalists began in 1962, and by 1969 700,000 persons regularly watched twelve hours of programs each month.[69] Programs with "the character of an agricultural university" were begun in 1962, when there were thirty-nine broadcasts lasting from forty-five to fifty minutes, each combining formal presentations and answers to viewers' questions. The series dealt with new plants, cattle breeding, fodder stock, veterinary problems, vegetable growing, mechanization, gardens, beekeeping, and agricultural buildings.

I saw several first-rate farm programs. One provided instructions about the care of newborn lambs. Filmed on a farm, the program had shots of the delivery, followed by demonstrations of how to care for the lambs. A program about herbicides showed a tractor spraying as the announcer explained how this would improve crop output. There also was material on the life cycles of insects, illustrating why spraying is effective. A third program dealt with fire prevention on farms. Viewers saw the ashes of a barn that had burned after being struck by lightning and heard an interview with a farmer seeking money to install fire safeguards. This too was done on location, giving the impression of a program by farmers for farmers.

In Warsaw in September 1972 I viewed an interesting adult education program after having discussed it with the woman who both organized it and appeared as principal interviewer. The title was "Fear," and the purpose was to report both normal and psychopathic manifestations of fear through interviews with people recounting their own experiences. A surgeon, wearing his medical paraphernalia, discussed his doubts and concerns during two recent operations, after which we heard from the patients themselves in their hospital beds. A test pilot interviewed in the cockpit of his plane told of the role of fear in his occupation, while a mentally ill person dramatically related his constant concerns. From time to time two psychiatrists in the studio commented upon these episodes. This program was well planned and ably presented by a woman who was a highly effective broadcaster. It could be recommended as an intelligent treatment of an important subject to program planners in any country.

Poland's most significant broadcast education project was the Televi-

sion Technical College (sometimes referred to as the Television Poly-
technic), developed by the country's educational authorities and television staff in cooperation with the UNESCO Department of Mass Communication. It was in fact one of the major projects of its type anywhere
in the world. Its purpose was to provide advanced training for working
people who could not attend day schools or evening classes.[70]

In recent years there has been a tremendous increase in the number
of college students in Poland. Whereas in 1945 there were around 500,-
000, by 1970 the number had risen to 2,100,000. The growth was particularly rapid in the higher technical schools, where the number went
from 125,000 to 1,250,000.[71] In an effort to meet these demands, most
universities offer evening and correspondence courses. But evening
classes are available only to people living in large cities with institutions
and colleges, and such schools have limited capacity. Students in evening
classes receive generous allowances of time off to register, attend classes,
and take examinations. Correspondence is the only real choice in small
towns and rural areas. Nevertheless, the results often were disappointing.
Without a regular classroom teacher, many students became discouraged
and dropped out after a few months of independent study.

It therefore was decided to use television, and the most promising field
for experimentation appeared to be technical studies, both because of
their importance to the national economy and because of the many interested students. Accordingly, at the beginning of 1965 the Ministry of
Higher Education, at the request of Polish television, began systematic
planning, and on November 30, 1965, an agreement was signed between
the Polish government and UNESCO, which provided $120,000 to assist
in the project.

It was hoped that television would bring well-organized instruction to
isolated areas and make the best teachers available to all university and
technical schools. The publicity attending such a course should induce
the reappraisal and improvement of existing curricula and textbooks.
Broadcasting's fixed schedule might impose systematic discipline on correspondence students who otherwise lacked stimulation to maintain a
steady learning pace. In addition to bringing formal education to students
living too far from colleges to attend classes regularly, it was hoped the
project would attract as casual viewers daytime technical students, secondary school pupils, and persons interested merely in increasing their
knowledge. However, the objective was not to create a new institution,

as in the case of Britain's Open University, but rather to supplement the work of existing schools.

UNESCO was anxious to cooperate not only because the project was important in itself, but also because it would be of great interest to other UNESCO members with similar educational problems, especially to emerging countries. Therefore, it was agreed to develop a five-year project, with UNESCO contributing funds for additional television equipment and Poland organizing the broadcasts, arranging utilization, and conducting research.

Preliminary planning was shared by the Ministry of Education and Higher Instruction and Polish Radio and Television. A twelve-man advisory council was set up by the ministry to develop curricula, determine the number of programs in each subject, and nominate lecturers. A special research unit of sociologists, psychologists, economists, and educators was created to provide evaluation.

Preceding the main project, however, were some preliminary broadcasts—the Small Pilot—in 1966. This twenty-week preparatory series was intended to test the skill of the lecturers, try out different production techniques, determine the best ways of preparing and distributing study guides, and establish the procedures to be used in the fifteen consultation centers set up to assist students through face-to-face contacts with advisers. These centers were selected from forty already located at colleges and factories all over Poland in connection with existing adult education projects.

Public announcement of the Small Pilot early in 1966 brought 56,000 requests for study guides and even induced some prospective students to buy television receivers. At the time it was estimated that 30,000 of the people buying the guide were qualified to register for university courses, although the preliminary experiment had places for only 9,000 students. The experimental telecasts, broadcast from February to June 1966, consisted of introductory lectures in mathematics and physics. They were broadcast on Tuesdays and Wednesdays from 4:25 to 5:55 P.M. with repeats on the same days at times after 10:00 P.M. The experiment provided much curriculum and utilization information, as well as data about the social composition, geographical distribution, and study objectives of the students enrolled.

When a UNESCO representative visited one of the discussion centers set up throughout the country—in Olsztyn, a town in northern Poland—

he found that after the telecast by a university professor there was a discussion during which a counselor answered questions.[72] "There is a regular audience of about 40 people, aged 25 to 35," he wrote, "most of them mechanics, technicians or workers from nearby building concerns. Many of them left secondary or technical schools five to ten years ago, abandoning all ideas of further study. The fact that they have now decided to continue studying leads to the conclusion that they are stimulated and encouraged by this new medium—television."

This preliminary experiment was evaluated as it took place.[73] Of the 57,864 persons who ordered the guide, over two-thirds met the requirements for participation in a course of technical studies at a Polish university. Most of them were working in industrial enterprises, thus constituting the intended audience. An overwhelming number found the courses helpful, although it was not possible to determine any direct relationship between participation in television courses and success in final examinations. However, the total findings were sufficiently favorable to justify continuation.

Following the completion of the Small Pilot, the Television Technical College scheduled a series of experiments during the five academic years between 1966–1967 and 1970–1971.[74] Presentations augmented the curriculum for the first two years of higher technical studies for adult workers, supplementing both the independent study of correspondence and the regular class meetings of evening class students. The universities and technical colleges graded students and granted credit. Radio programs were developed to parallel some of the television series. Initially the Television Technical College faced a problem in presenting specialized material on the country's single network, since the average Polish viewer, like his counterparts everywhere else, does not want mathematics lectures during prime viewing hours. But when Polish television inaugurated a second network in October 1970, some programs were switched to it, although at first it served only a few major population centers.

During the first semester of 1966–1967 there were half-hour lectures for first-year students, fifty-five on mathematics, sixteen on descriptive geometry, and sixteen on chemistry. These were telecast Tuesdays from 4:00 to 5:00 P.M. and Sundays from 8:30 to 9:30 and 10:00 to 10:30 A.M. The following year the first-year courses were repeated for new pupils, while second-year students were offered continuation lectures on mathematics, physics, mechanics of materials, and electrotechnics. These were broadcast Tuesdays from 4:00 to 5:00 P.M. and Mondays and Fridays from 3:45 to 4:15 and 4:25 to 4:55 P.M.

During 1968–1969 entrance-level courses in mathematics and physics were added. The first-year lectures again were repeated, although those for the second year were dropped. During 1969–1970 all the preceding year's programs were repeated, and forty lectures on mathematics for secondary schoolteachers introduced. During the final year, 1970–1971, most of the 1969–1970 programs were repeated, and twenty lectures on physics added for secondary school students.

Upon the completion of the five-year experiment, a summary of all the research was published.[75] The audience was found to be many times larger than the number of people formally registered: about 3.5 per cent of all viewers in the country, or some 270,000 people, watched the telecasts. Their ages ranged from fourteen to seventy, and they had widely varied educational, social, and professional backgrounds. The typical registered student was a married male graduate of a secondary or vocational school, who held a middle job in industry and faced the problem of keeping up with his profession while continuing family activities. But viewers also included secondary school pupils and teachers who watched for general information.

Of one sample registered in technical colleges 20 per cent did not view the telecasts at all, 60 per cent did so sporadically, and less than 10 per cent systematically. One reason for not viewing was inconvenient viewing times: for many students the afternoon program came too early or the evening program too late. Viewing usually was done individually rather than in groups, and most viewers disregarded the advice to prepare for the lectures by reading the assigned textbooks. Although students were advised not to take notes in order to concentrate better on the telecasts, many did so nevertheless. Not surprisingly, Polish students like those elsewhere complained that television eliminated or reduced direct contacts with teachers.

It was not clear whether the telecasts actually increased viewers' learning, although a good majority of the students said they learned things from the telecasts which helped them in their examinations. During the first year, regular evening class and correspondence viewers received better scores on the mathematics tests than did nonviewing students.[76] But when the project had been completed and all results tabulated, it was found that viewers were seldom more successful than nonviewers in examinations, and that viewers who took examinations for admission to extramural studies seemed to benefit hardly at all, since only 80 out of 576 were admitted. But the researchers discounted these data, saying that the lectures were viewed mainly by older students with poor academic backgrounds and less time to study. Therefore, it was assumed students did benefit from the telecasts even though it was difficult to document the exact amount or nature of their learning.

After the experiment was over, it was decided that television can make important contributions to higher education provided it is used "to create new educational concepts, practices and institutions based upon the existing network of higher schools. It is not useful to duplicate classes organized in higher schools with TV lectures."[77] Television lectures were most effective when they used appropriate visual aids, and viewers should prepare for them by reading the textbooks. Although the consultation centers were not fully utilized, research indicated that future projects should have them nevertheless.

The final judgment favored television, which was described as "perhaps the medium which could be most effectively used in the effort to provide full access to education for all in the service of economic and social development."[78] Therefore, it was concluded, "education in the future will be largely based on the means of mass communication and above all, on television in all its technical forms."

The sincere interest of the Polish authorities in television teaching was further demonstrated by the meeting they arranged at the University of Warsaw in September 1968 to deal with the "Further Education of the Employed Particularly at the University Level." Invitations went to outstanding authorities in all of Europe, and acceptances were received from Bulgaria, Denmark, the German Democratic Republic, Finland, France, Great Britain, Hungary, Italy, Romania, the Soviet Union, Sweden, and Yugoslavia, with observers expected from Canada, the European Broadcasting Union, Japan, and UNESCO. But because the Soviet Union's occupation of Czechoslovakia on August 21 occurred shortly before the meeting was scheduled to open, a number of the Western participants cancelled plans to attend.

Drama and Entertainment

Reflecting nationwide interest in the theater, Polish radio and television have many outstanding dramatic programs. One author stated that the "permanent and successful development of radio dramaturgy representing a special branch of literary production governed by its own laws constitutes one of the special features of Polish cultural life."[79] He went on: "The primary concern of the authors of contemporary Polish radio plays is to follow the effects of the great historical transformation experienced by the whole nation in the course of the past twenty-five years upon the life of the common people of the various strata of population, upon their psychology, world outlook, morality and attitudes."

Polish writers often refer to radio drama as the Theater of Imagination, accepting the concept that radio is the medium permitting freest play of the imagination.[80] Polish radio theater dates from the early 1920s. During the eleven years preceding World War II, not counting programs for children, it produced more than 300 original radio plays; in 1969, 610; and, in 1970, 578, including adaptations of literary classics, full-length radio dramas, and several serials.[81] The radio drama department has eight staff members and over fifty free-lance producers. Despite its extensive output, however, it depends entirely upon free-lance actors, and during a year may employ almost a thousand of them.

All of Poland's stages together do not present as many premieres in a year as does the Polish Radio Theater. Some people specialize in writing for the broadcast media, and there are script competitions for both professional and amateur writers.[82] The public is invited to select the best "Premiere of the Year," and some years nearly 15,000 votes are received. There was experimentation with stereophonic production beginning in 1970, although the person then heading the Polish Radio Theater opposed stereo on the grounds that it hampered listeners' imagination. "It is excellent in music," he said, "but on the air, providing a right and left side . . . hinders the possibility of proper receiving." Nevertheless, the 1971 Prix Italia entry, *Arthur's Departure* by Polish playwright Andrezej Markarewicz, was done in stereo.[83]

There are frequent festivals, such as the Festival of Friendship, which began in 1963, during which a number of socialist countries present performances in translation of each other's scripts.[84] The Festival of Contemporary Radio Plays, which included forty plays from the previous twenty years' output, ran for three months in 1965. In 1969 a special festival, "Poland on the Fronts of the Second World War," commemorated the thirtieth anniversary of the German attack. Regional stations as well as Warsaw originate these productions.

Fixtures of Polish radio have been several long-running serials comparable with the daytime dramas formerly on American radio and now on television.[85] The oldest, "The Matysiak Family," on the air since December 15, 1956, and now broadcast from 8:30 to 9:00 P.M. on Sundays, deals with an urban family; the "Jeziorany" cycle, begun in 1960 and broadcast Sundays from 2:30 to 3:30 P.M., is about a country family. The Jeziorany story receives additional circulation by being printed in a magazine. A number of Clubs of the Friends of Jeziorany also have been established. For a time there was a third series, "The Rebels," with young Polish intellectuals as characters, but this was dropped.

A Polish writer observed that these programs "even lack a comprehensive plot; the individual problems developing from case to case are solved by means of insignificant conversations and chats using simple colloquial language and thus giving the impression that a hidden microphone is eavesdropping on the everyday events of an average family's life."[86] Another article pointed out that the events of the "Matysiak" serial take place on "the day of the transmission," the programs being "a contemporary topical chronicle of social, political and cultural events which influence the action of the heroes of the broadcasts."[87]

Many listeners to these programs—like those to American radio serials in the 1930s and 1940s—believe the characters to be real, send them gifts, and write them letters. On January 17, 1966, the twenty-first anniversary of the liberation of Warsaw, the Polish Radio and Television Committee opened the doors of the "Matysiak House" for old-age pensioners, constructed with contributions stimulated by the broadcast series.[88] By 1970 over 2 million letters had been received about the series, and once, when two of its characters were considering marriage, 2,736 letters of protest were received within a few days, causing the proposed story line to be changed.[89] Upon the fifteenth anniversary of the series on December 15, 1971, there were plans to publish a four-volume story of the "Matysiak Family" from its very beginning up to 1971.

The Children's Radio Theater, a responsibility of the Department of Programs for Children and Youth, produces original plays and adaptations. In 1961 the results of a competition for scripts by authors between the ages of seven and seventeen documented the problems facing some young Poles: the winning play dealt with alcoholic parents, while another treated the problems of school adjustment.[90] In 1966, when the department invited young listeners to write their reactions, 9,000 responses were received on productions ranging from Mark Twain's *The Prince and the Pauper* to modern works, the latter being preferred by a good majority.[91] Observing the twenty-fifth anniversary of the "Victory over Fascism," a series of thirteen plays with patriotic overtones was presented.[92]

A Polish writer observed that from the very beginning, Polish television was influenced more by drama than by variety shows, music, news, or public events. One reason was the generally high level of the theater in Poland, and another that actors and directors were the first source of television talent "and made it what it was in its first years."[93] First productions were derivative, leaning on theatrical conventions, but in the later 1950s and early 1960s scripts and productions emphasized the unique features of the medium. In the early days television receivers were owned by a small "sophisticated literate audience," which permitted the producers to emphasize plays by Sartre, Giraudoux, and Joyce as well as short stories and novels by de Maupassant, Zola, Balzac, Mark Twain, Howard Fast, and Dumas, among others. But the subsequent wider distribution of sets required television drama to become "socially committed, educational, diversified and popular."

In the course of a year Polish television has approximately 140 dramatic productions, of which about 40 per cent are classical and 60 per cent contemporary.[94] When the second channel is fully operative, the number may be raised to 200 a year. "Monday Theater," originated in Warsaw, presents Polish and foreign literary masterpieces along with original television plays of outstanding merit.[95] Authors include Sophocles, Racine, Schiller, August Strindberg, Arthur Miller, Tennessee Williams, and Eugene O'Neill. "Friday Theater," produced at regional television centers, features works by regional authors along with foreign plays currently being presented in local theaters.

"The Small Screen," which alternates on Wednesdays with "Contemporary Studio," features plays by contemporary Polish and foreign authors. "Studio 63," named for the year of its foundation, "is an experimental centre both in the field of presentation and repertory." It is intended for more sophisticated viewers.[96] "Sunday Theater" is light entertainment, while "TV Theater in the World" brings prize-winning and noteworthy productions from other countries. The "Cobra Theater" on Thursdays presents mystery and detective plays by authors like Arthur Conan Doyle, Agatha Christie, G. B. Shaw, Oscar Wilde, and J. B. Priestley. Beginning in 1963, provincial dramatic groups offered their best productions to national television audiences each summer.[97] In 1969 eight theaters in seven cities produced works by Gogol, Shakespeare, and some Polish writers. By 1971, when the "TV Festival of Theater Plays" had become "an integral part of the summer programme" of Polish Television, seven regional theaters contributed ten plays, including one classical and three contemporary Polish productions, one "antique drama," one Soviet play, two other foreign plays, and, "according to the festival tradition—two plays by Shakespeare."[98]

Major productions run from sixty to ninety minutes and are rehearsed as many as twenty or thirty times during one month. For years most plays were broadcast live, and one prominent Polish television producer believed that production was enhanced and viewer reaction sharpened if actors and viewers knew they were "participating in the actual event as it is taking place."[99] But now, most broadcasts are from videotape.

Except for light music, some entertainment drama, and certain film programs, Polish broadcasting offers relatively little light entertainment. The program analyses cited above (pp. 276, 278) leave no doubt about the low percentage of programs in this category, despite their audience popularity. One reason for this, Polish broadcasting authorities contend, is a shortage of good material. Another is the problem of costs, which are high for such programs. However, in 1970 radio presented for the fourteenth consecutive year the series "The Microphone Quiz," recorded in a Warsaw café, which used popular singers and actors before a studio audience.[100] Beginning in 1969 television had a similar program, "We Invite You to the Café," originated in turn in different Polish cities. There was one program from the Polish ocean liner *Stephan Batory*, with a number of entertainers as "guests."

In 1972 the head of radio entertainment described the four most popular programs on the air.[101] "Tea at the Microphone," in its fourteenth season, consisted of songs, readings, and parodies. The programs were recorded in a café with some 500 spectators, and before being broadcast the 2½-hour original was edited down to 90 minutes for presentation during an evening hour, with a subsequent afternoon repeat. "Program with a Carpet," recorded at factories or before professional groups, had the dual objective of publicizing the enterprise concerned and of entertaining by satirizing its faults and problems. It too was edited down for broadcasting from 2½ or 3 hours to about an hour. "The Merry Bus" took its cast around by bus to villages. The other "most popular" program, "Guess, Guess," also produced before an audience, used a contest format.

Television quizzes also elicit enthusiastic response. In one of them contestants select areas of knowledge in which to compete before a jury of experts in the field, with money prizes doubling after each set of correct answers, as with America's $64,000-question series—though with much smaller rewards. Another series, with students as performers, gives television receivers as prizes. Comedy shows are another favorite television genre, with humor ranging from simple to sophisticated. I have not watched any of these shows, although in September 1972 I did see a light entertainment film made in Italy in which popular singers and an orchestra presented a lively program on an elaborate Hollywood-style set. This was broadcast in the original Italian, suggesting that the supply of Polish light entertainment material must be limited.

Film and Documentary

Between 1960 and 1963, when nearly 30 per cent of Polish television consisted of films, about 260 feature films and 4,000 short films were transmitted annually.[102] Nevertheless, film production was regarded as "a weak point of the work of the Polish television," since the department spent most of its time preparing news inserts and other short items. But an agreement between television and film makers soon led to the production of 45 films annually, and in 1969 the television film studios provided 782 hours of broadcasting time.[103] In 1971, 24 feature and 70 half-hour telefilms were produced, plus 162 documentary films and newsreels, 41 scientific films, and 91 animated films.[104] Among these was a television serial about a little bear named Calargol, also broadcast with great success in France. Most of these productions were in color.

Film output includes both entertainment and propaganda material. In 1971 the Polish studios produced a thirteen-part color series based on the novel *The Peasants*, by Nobel Prize winner W. S. Reymont, along with treatments of literary classics by Mérimée, Robert Louis Stevenson, Balzac, and others.[105] During the previous year the cinema film *Mr. Wolodysjowske*, based on a novel by Nobel Peace winner Henryk Sienkiewicz, led to a series of thirteen television films. Television programs have been shown in cinemas, and the series *Four Panzermen and a Dog*, a humorous account of the adventures of a World War II tank crew and their dog, broke attendance records, attracting some 5,680,000 cinema viewers.[106] This series has been carried by other socialist countries too, including East Germany and the Soviet Union. In East Germany it was turned into a book for young readers, with 400 pages and many illustrations. But an American observer in Hungary told me it failed there because its consistent representation of American soldiers as stupid stereotypes proved unbelievable. Also popular was a series about the experiences of a resistance hero, "Captain Kloss," who week after week worked his way out of traps set by his German army adversaries. This cycle too was widely distributed in the socialist bloc. Despite a late start, Polish television has received awards in the Monte Carlo, Montreux, and Prix Italia exhibitions for its films as well as its plays.[107]

Most Polish television films publicized in English-language publications have political and propaganda overtones. In 1963 the four-piece cycle "The Flight" told the story of a young Yugoslav concert pianist who visited Zurich, Berlin, Moscow, London, Prague, Rome, Budapest, and Paris. The description of the series said it reviewed "the history of the friendly relations connecting today's people beyond the borders of their country."[108] The following year "A Stake Higher Than Life" told serially the story of a Polish citizen who cooperated with the underground while masquerading as a German officer during World War II.

Both radio and television develop documentary programs to commemorate patriotic events. Television news regularly presents "A Quarter Century," dealing with "the achievements of our country in the fields of economy, science and culture during the past 25 years of people's rule." In 1969 a program during an election campaign "let the viewers see how the election platform adopted by the present authorities has been implemented during their four years in office."[109] "Landscape 69" delineated the "extensive economic transformation which this country has undergone since the last war"; "Life Story" dealt with the social progress of the working classes; and other programs described the "dynamic expansion" of the shipbuilding and other industries.

In 1970 "The Nuremberg Epilogue," a "dramatized report on the trial of Hitlerite criminals in Nuremberg," was seen first on television and then adapted for the cinema.[110] In the same year, "Columbuses, Year of Birth 1920," based on a novel by Roman Bratny, related in five one-hour episodes the experiences of some resistance groups between 1940 and

1944. The release of this series was timed to coincide with the anniversary of the outbreak of the Warsaw uprising in 1955.

In July 1970 Polish television presented a seven-section serial dealing with postwar life which reported "Polish achievements in reconstruction."* To mark the twenty-fifth anniversary of the victory over nazism, eleven documentaries based on Polish and Soviet film sources reviewed the joint military operations of the two armies, the last episode being telecast on the armistice anniversary, May 8, 1970. This series was especially "for young people who do not remember the war."

The success of several foreign serials, including the Dr. Kildare series and one entitled "Cecily, the Village Doctor," led to the production of a Polish serial with nine forty-five–minute episodes which told the story of a young woman doctor who, after completing her internship, decided to leave the large city to work in a village where she became involved in local life. "The idea of the director was to present a hero entangled in the complicated problems of our times."[111]

There are regular broadcasts of American telefilms, dubbed into Polish. *Dr. Kildare* and *Perry Mason* have been seen, while Poland has the biggest of all fan clubs for the long-running *Bonanza*.[112] In the first months of 1971, NBC, the producer of *Bonanza*, supplied over 5,000 photographs of the Cartwright brothers to their Polish fans (and during the same period, only 2,000 to their followers in the United States). Both television and cinema films from France, Italy, and the United Kingdom are seen on Polish television. From the BBC came *The Forsyte Saga*, each episode broadcast twice, first with Polish narration over the English sound track, and the second time in the original version.

Poland is among the countries using the BBC's "English by Radio" and "English by Television." In 1972, 280 stations in 75 countries were carrying the radio series, and the television series was used by 60 countries, including most of Western Europe, Hungary, Poland, Romania, and Yugoslavia. The courses consist of instruction incorporated into dramatized situations. For a long time the dramatic bits in English

---

* *Polish Bulletin* 1970/7-8, p. 12; *Polish Bulletin* 1970/4–5, p. 18. Tourists on the standard bus tour of Warsaw are taken to a small theater to view a brief documentary about the outrages perpetrated by Nazi Germany upon Poland and the eventual liberation of the country by Soviet troops. The film has several sound tracks, the one used depending upon the language spoken by the majority of the tour group.

involved two attractive young Britishers, Walter and Connie, but beginning in 1972 they were replaced by the color series "The Bellcrest Story," which in thirteen episodes teaches the specialized English of modern business.[113]

Music

A member of the radio music department speaking at an OIRT meeting in Budapest in 1968 differentiated between music broadcasts in capitalist and in socialist countries.[114] Whereas in the former, he said, little attempt was made to raise the level of musical understanding because commercial attitudes prevail, in the socialist countries the objective is "not only to meet the need for entertainment, but also to raise the cultural and artistic levels of the population. Education and propaganda constitute one of the most important tasks of the entire socialist state. . . . The musical direction of all socialist broadcasting pursues the objective of meeting the cultural needs of the listeners, of elevating their culture, of presenting the most interesting events of musical life and of contributing largely to entertainment. It is at the same time a matter of attracting the largest possible number of listeners."

The amount of time devoted to music by the radio networks has remained stable through the years. In 1964, when there were only two networks, music constituted 55 per cent of the schedule, which came to 18 hours a day or 127 hours a week. Of this, "entertaining music occupied 75 per cent of the time."[115] In 1970 music took 55 per cent of the time, or 25 hours a day. There were 17 hours of popular and dance music, 6 hours of classical music, and 2 hours of folk music. But there is a difference among the three networks: in 1969 the first network devoted 80 per cent of its schedule to light music; the second 50 per cent to serious music; and the third 70 per cent to popular and light music.[116]

The Radio and Television Committee maintains a number of musical organizations of its own and also broadcasts performances by other groups. The Polish Radio and Television Symphony Orchestra in Katowice, founded in 1948, gives concerts at home, travels abroad, and does much broadcasting. Its 106 members also provide personnel for several chamber ensembles.[117] In 1963 the orchestra visited the Soviet Union, the Mongolian People's Republic, the Chinese People's Republic, Hong Kong, Japan, Australia, and New Zealand, giving 56 concerts with repertoire ranging from Chopin, Brahms, Tchaikovsky, and Strauss to Lutoslawski and Penderecki. There also are broadcasting symphony orchestras in Warsaw, Cracow, and Wroclaw, along with light music combinations, dance orchestras, and choral groups in all major studio centers. In 1972 the fifteenth anniversary was observed of an experimental electronic studio in which technicians, composers, and dramatists experiment with music and drama.[118] Through the years this team has produced music and sound effects for dramatic programs as well as entire compositions and stereophonic dramas.

The classical music repertoire is impressive. Between 1954 and 1960 Polish radio broadcast 183 complete and 20 abridged operas; 40 cantatas by Bach; 46 Haydn symphonies; 32 symphonies and 45 concertos by Mozart; and cycles of the major symphonies and concertos of Beethoven, Schubert, and Brahms. Modern composers received comparable treatment.[119] During 1968 there were over 200 broadcasts of 2 hours or longer (20 per cent being direct transmissions) of symphonic, chamber, and other serious compositions. There are regular live broadcasts by the National Philharmonic Orchestra and other organizations. Polish radio encourages the composition of music for broadcasting, and one of its radio operas received a Prix Italia first prize.

From the very beginning television also has presented much music, and by the end of 1956 a Mozart opera, two musical comedies, and ten programs of light music had been broadcast. In 1958 there were monthly presentations of operas, musical comedies, symphony concerts, recitals, and folk music.[120] Television producers have tried hard to disprove the statement by the eminent Polish composer Witold Lutoslawski that "music is of its very nature a non-telegenic art."[121] A member of the staff involved with entertainment and music wrote that the producers of such programs have three choices: first, they may make maximum use of the medium; second, they may present almost entirely static programs; or third, they may treat musicals or operas as television stage plays. Noting that Channel I is for the mass audience and that Channel II is to emphasize serious material, he said that the latter would introduce instructional music programs with such themes as the language of the dance, stories from opera, and world music development. It also would present concerts by outstanding performers, from classical to jazz.

At the end of 1971 a new department was established to be responsible for all aspects of television music.[122] At the same time it was announced that there would be an alternate week series on which four renowned Polish music critics discussed trends in music; a monthly premiere of a musical film; monthly concerts by radio and television orchestras; and weekly solo recitals by outstanding artists. But until it could organize its own musical theater, Polish television planned to broadcast foreign operatic films.

On October 7, 1970, in Leningrad I saw a symphony concert relayed by Intervision from Warsaw. Although the performance was good, television production was poor. After the opening overture there was a ten-minute pause while a piano was moved into place for the concerto. During this entire process the cameras showed us in turn the musicians, the audience, and the piano movers. The intermission contained material quite unrelated to the music, and the camera pickup of the concert itself was not distinguished.

Polish broadcasting offers much light music, although typically among socialist countries there is some opposition to current popular music.[123] In 1960 a Polish article stated that "the Department of Music is always under fire from listeners, who write many letters asking for light music, by which they mean only jazz and jazz songs."[124] Folk music—of which Poland has a great wealth—is both broadcast and recorded for the archives. The director of radio music referred to "a wide campaign for the presentation and popularization of Polish folk music which, although it is not fashionable at present, will in any case remain [an] invaluable treasury of our national culture."[125] Folk music, he said, is followed "with pleasure by those city and village inhabitants for whom more progressive forms of art are too difficult and contemporary youth music too irritating."[126] Even youth, he said, taken up with big-beat music, have shown an "unexpected inclination . . . to folk themes."

Various devices are employed to present information about music and to encourage listening. In the early days radio had "The Musical Alphabet," "The Composer of the Week," and "From the World of Opera." Quizzes challenge listeners to guess titles and composers, and on some programs members of the radio music department answer questions from the public.[127] In 1968 television developed "Listening and Watching," produced in Katowice for the entire network. The program was described as "both a concert and a show, in principle for young people, but it is an excellent concert for everybody, an entertainment by serious music."[128] The series was so successful that the principal participant was among the winners in an annual poll to select the most popular personalities on Polish television.

Music appreciation programs—by whatever name—are offered for all age groups from children to adults.[129] Special efforts are made to reach youth with "entertaining" as well as serious music. For the more sophisticated there are programs of new works by Polish composers and performances by young artists. The director of radio music concluded a discussion of the subject by saying: "A constant search for interesting themes and authors fully satisfying the requirements of musical propagation on the radio, constitutes a permanent task of the musical management of Polish Radio."

There are some interesting request programs. Lovers of serious music can select and dedicate compositions to friends. It was observed, however, that perhaps the chief point of the program for many participants was to get on the air their names and the names of the persons to whom they were making dedications.[130] A series of programs on which people who paid a nominal fee could dedicate light music to friends had so heavy a patronage that requests had to be made several months before broadcast time.

With music as with plays there are festivals, such as the Chopin International Pianists' Competition, and special anniversary concerts marking political events like the millennium of the Polish state and the end of World War II.[131] There also is an international festival of contemporary music, called Warsaw Autumn, which emphasizes contemporary composers from standard to avant-garde. Soloists and groups from Poland and abroad participate, and many of the concerts are broadcast.

Festivals staged especially for broadcasting include the National Festival of Polish Songs held one week each year in the city of Opole, which has become so popular that in 1971 over 200,000 persons applied for the 5,200 season tickets available.[132] Participants come from all parts of the country, and the winners compete in the International Song Festival in Sopoty with contestants from other Eastern European countries, Western Europe, Canada, and the United States. In the Sopoty Festival, which is relayed by radio, Intervision, and Eurovision to listeners and viewers in many parts of Europe, all entrants must present one selection by a Polish composer, although it may be sung in their native language. This festival is the counterpart of the annual Eurovision Song Contest sponsored by the European Broadcasting Union since 1956, the finals of which are heard and seen in both Eastern and Western countries. I saw the 1972 festival on Hungarian television in Budapest, presented from a recording with the original Polish announcements replaced by some in Hungarian. (Both the original and replacement announcers were women.) It was a well-done show, lavishly produced on a big stage before a large and enthusiastic crowd.

Audience Research

Poland has the most highly developed broadcast research organization of all the Eastern European countries. What is now known as the Center for Public Opinion and Broadcasting Research was established in 1965 as the Center for Research on Public Opinion and Program Studies, following the merger of the former radio research division and the Research Center on Public Opinion.[133] According to its director, it was created so that broadcasting policies could be based on a real knowledge of audience interests and needs.

In 1965 a Polish writer compared the motivations for audience studies in socialist and capitalist countries. Where there is private ownership of broadcasting facilities, he argued, research is conducted to increase profits or to preserve the capitalist system, while in the socialist countries its purpose is to "contribute to the formation of a new, socialist community."[134]

The Center for Public Opinion and Broadcasting Research analyzes mail, conducts inquiries into audience reactions, examines the impact of the media on society, and abstracts information from foreign publications for the broadcasting staff.[135] Headed by three administrators, it employs forty-two full-time people including sixteen sociologists, eight university-trained researchers, and fifteen other professionals.

Four thousand part-time workers conduct interviews to obtain audience data. Although not paid, they receive awards for good work. Audience samples—consisting typically of between 1,500 and 3,500 people—are selected by a quota system. Over the years more than 200 studies have been conducted, the yearly average being about 20. The center turns out a bulletin, a biweekly report, a quarterly set of studies, and miscellaneous other publications. Among them these brochures contain a wide range of information about many aspects of broadcasting.[136]

The number of radio licenses remained almost stationary between

1966 and 1970, the 1970 figure being 4,697,315, which is 17.21 sets per hundred of population. Poland is second only to the Soviet Union among countries with highly developed wired diffusion systems. In 1964 approximately 4,000 relay centers transmitted programs to 1,281,800 loudspeakers on farms, cooperatives, factories, hospitals, clubs, and schools.* By 1966 the number of wired sets had dropped to 1,073,501 and by 1970 to 960,010. The official Polish News Agency reported in 1972 that there were at least 5.7 million wave sets and perhaps as many as 7.5 million, since the published figures did not include transistors.[137] The number of television licenses increased from 2,540,064 in 1966 (7.99 per hundred) to 4,214,779 (12.82 per hundred) in 1970. A 1972 report put their number at 4,250,922.[138]

Through the years the findings of Polish researchers have not differed substantially from those reported by other countries. In 1963 it was found that films, dramatic productions, and news were among the most popular television programs, and serious music least popular.[139] Men preferred films, sports, and programs about science; women liked theatrical productions. Viewers between twenty and twenty-nine years of age wanted entertainment programs and quizzes; those between thirty and thirty-nine showed high interest in films and sports; while among viewers over forty interest in news and dramatic programs increased and in films lessened. Serious music had most of its followers among older groups. Interest in news and educational programs increased with educational level, while respondents with less education were more apt to prefer films, light entertainment, and sports. In Warsaw in 1964 and 1965, as the number of television sets increased by some 6 per cent, attendance at theaters and concerts dropped by 5.2 per cent, and cinema attendance dropped by 13.6 per cent.[140]

The director of the Research Center reported that in 1969 over 90 per cent of the population had access to radio and that 75 per cent listened regularly, the average person tuning in three hours a day.[141] Program preferences were expressed by the following percentages: entertain-

---

* UNESCO, *World Communications: Press Radio Television Film*, p. 316. See Table 10 above for comparative figures on both wired and wave sets in a number of European countries. One factor inevitably related to set ownership is electrification: as late as 1966, 20 per cent of all Polish villages still lacked electricity. In pre-transistor days, this could have been one reason for the many wired receivers, which can be powered from a central source (Miroslaw Dabrowski, "The Role of the Polish Radio in the Musical Life of Poland," *OIRT Review* 1966/4, p. 3).

ment, 77 per cent; plays and theater, 51 per cent; light music, 42 per cent; sports, 26 per cent; rural programs, 21 per cent; and scientific and socioeconomic programs, 18 per cent.

In 1969 the center surveyed musical preferences, using a sample of 2,000 people over the age of sixteen.[142] Light music lovers constituted 85 per cent of the audience; folk music, 82 per cent; and classical music, 20 per cent. The influence of age and education was as one would predict: older respondents preferred folk and classical to light music, while the better educated chose light and classical over folk music. Rural listeners liked folk bands and amateur folk ensembles. As to folk music from foreign sources, Russian music was preferred by 56 per cent of the folk music lovers, with Hungarian a poor second, receiving 10 per cent of the votes. Big-beat music was enjoyed most of all by young people aged sixteen and seventeen with the eighteen to twenty-four age group including only half as many big-beat fans. Among classical music lovers, opera was the favorite of 54 per cent; solo and vocal music, 27 per cent; choral music, 21 per cent; symphonic music, 18 per cent; and chamber music, 17 per cent.

A Polish report published in February 1972 contained some other interesting audience information. Of the group polled, 67 per cent listened to radio newscasts in the morning, 42 per cent to various light music broadcasts, 26 per cent to sportscasts, and 18 per cent to programs on politics and public affairs.[143] When asked, "Has your knowledge increased in the course of the last year as a result of your listening to the radio / watching television / reading newspapers?" the yes answers were as follows: radio, 36 per cent; television, 40 per cent; and newspapers, 44 per cent.* We should note the comment: "All surveys show that the number of those who purposefully select specific radio programs is extremely small. For the decisive majority radio seems to provide an accompaniment to various activities performed in the home."

In 1969 the average Pole watched television 2½ hours on weekdays, 3½ hours on Saturdays, and 5 hours on Sundays and holidays.† Television preference ratings were as follows: films, 75 per cent; news, 65 per

* In the United States there has been a constant trend toward television as the preferred news medium. See above, p. 191n.

† Robinson (pp. 185–186 above) reported that in 1966 average respondents in Poland viewed television 70 minutes a day as a primary and 82 minutes as a secondary activity, the total of 2 hours and 32 minutes being almost exactly that reported by Polish sources.

cent; entertainment programs, 54 per cent; theatrical programs, 45 per cent; popular scientific programs, 35 per cent; and serious public affairs programs, 27 per cent.

Broadcast drama ranked fourth in popularity on both radio and television, with radio theater preferred to television theater by the older and better-educated respondents. Audience preference figures for several radio plays put Victor Hugo's *The Hunchback of Notre Dame* at 32 per cent; Oscar Wilde's *The Ideal Husband* at 25 per cent; two Polish productions at 17 and 13 per cent respectively; and Arthur Miller's *The Grass Still Grows* and Sophocles's *Oedipus at Colonus* at 26 per cent. Translating these percentages into people, 6 million listened to Hugo and 350,000 to Miller. However, even radio plays with relatively small audiences reached many more people than did the most popular stage theater presentations.

For the most part television drama outdraws radio drama. A study made in 1968 showed that 68 per cent of viewers watched television drama "often" and 32 per cent "rarely."[144] Most popular was the "Theater of Sensation," with standard dramas second. Certain experimental dramatic and poetry programs were much less popular. White-collar workers composed the majority of the stage theater audience, although they made up only a small percentage of the total population. The audience for television drama consisted of 52 per cent white-collar workers, 35 per cent blue-collar workers, 7 per cent farmers, and 6 per cent other occupations.

These Polish data may be supplemented by reports from Radio Free Europe, even though it is difficult to accept uncritically RFE reports based on interviews with Polish nationals traveling abroad. RFE-sponsored interviews with 1,316 Poles visiting in the West between May and December 1970 showed that 99 per cent of the respondents listened to Polish radio programs, 55 per cent tuning in nearly every day and 34 per cent several times a week.[145] Favorite listening times were between 6:00 and 9:00 A.M., 12 noon and 1:00 P.M., and 4:00 and 10:00 P.M. Listening held up surprisingly well during midevening hours, with 28 per cent tuning in domestic radio between 8:00 and 9:00 P.M. As to television, 91 per cent of the respondents did at least some television viewing, 26 per cent viewed every day, and 34 per cent several times a week. Top viewing hours were between 7:00 and 10:00 P.M. From 8:00 to 9:00 P.M. 78 per cent often watched television.

Between May 1970 and March 1971 Radio Free Europe commissioned public opinion research institutes in six Western European countries to interview over 1,500 Polish nationals visiting in the West about their foreign radio listening.[146] Of the respondents 85 per cent stated that a major radio source of information on world events was Radio Warsaw; 40 per cent listed Radio Free Europe; 13 per cent the BBC; and 6 per cent the Voice of America. (It should be noted that with nineteen hours a day of programs in Polish, the extent of RFE's services to Poland is much greater than those of the other stations listed.)

As sources of information on Polish problems before the Baltic port incidents led to the replacement of Gomulka by Gierek in December 1970, the choices were Radio Warsaw 69 per cent, RFE 58 per cent, BBC 11 per cent, and VOA 7 per cent. But after Gomulka's fall, RFE rose to 76 per cent, Warsaw ranked at 70 per cent, VOA 11 per cent, and BBC 9 per cent. One reason given for the RFE increase was that it —like VOA and BBC—reported certain items before they appeared on Polish domestic programs.[147] Only 2 per cent indicated much confidence in the news from Radio Warsaw.

Interviews between June 1971 and February 1972 with 1,243 Polish nationals visiting the West revealed a continued high rate of listening to RFE programs.[148] The preferred Western station was RFE by 60 per cent, others being BBC with 25 per cent, VOA with 24 per cent, and Radio Luxembourg with 22 per cent. RFE listening trends from 1962 through 1971 began with 50 per cent of the public in the former year, rising to a peak of 67 per cent in 1968, dropping thereafter to 60 per cent, but rising to 83 per cent in early 1971, as a consequence of the "December Events."[149]

External Broadcasting

In 1972 Poland maintained an average weekly output of 340 hours of external broadcasts, which placed it third among the Eastern European group, after the USSR and Albania, and somewhat ahead of East Germany, Czechoslovakia, Romania, Bulgaria, Hungary, and Yugoslavia.* Supplementing its short-wave facilities, the external department shares several medium-wave transmitters with the domestic services. Poland broadcasts to Europe in Danish, English, Esperanto, Finnish, French,

* See table 9 above and *WRTH 1973*, p. 84.

German, Italian, Polish, Spanish, and Swedish; to Africa in English and French; to the Arab countries in Arabic; and to North America in English and Polish. A good share of its output is in Polish for Poles living abroad or at sea. The external services inform foreign listeners about life in Poland and maintain economic, social, and cultural ties between Poland and other countries. The programs in Polish have succeeded in persuading "an ever increasing number of Poles abroad" to acknowledge "the correctness of the present politics of their motherland."[150]

Hardly any part of Poland is beyond reach of foreign broadcasts. Programs from the Voice of America, the BBC, West Germany, and Radio Free Europe are readily available, as are services from the Soviet Union and other Eastern European countries. The radio program director, arguing for better coverage of the domestic services, said it was "incredible" that it was possible to get one or more foreign stations anywhere in Poland, while there still were "blank spots" not reached by any of the domestic services.[151] Television sets in border areas can easily pick up programs from East Germany, Czechoslovakia, and the Soviet Union, although East German television standards are not compatible with those used by the other bloc countries.

In Poland, as elsewhere in Eastern Europe, Radio Free Europe is the most resented foreign service, although one Polish broadcaster told me that the extent of listening to it is less now than formerly because of the country's improved domestic services. In 1970 I was told: "We have not jammed since 1956, I can assure you of that," although some foreign jamming of Western broadcasts to Poland, originating in the Soviet Union and other socialist countries, continued. But in March 1971 Poland resumed jamming Radio Free Europe—despite claims that Edward Gierek was allowing more freedom in cultural and intellectual life than had Gomulka (see above, pp. 274–275). I heard jamming in Warsaw in September 1972. It is not illegal to listen to foreign programs in Poland, but under a law which provides penalties for disseminating information detrimental to the state, a person may be punished for discussing with others what he has heard on foreign broadcasts. There is no question that jamming does discourage listening. In 1970 and 1971, when 2,821 Eastern Europeans visiting the West were asked why they did not listen to Radio Free Europe, 19 per cent of the non-listening Poles said that jamming was a major factor.[152]

The director of foreign relations for Polish broadcasting attaches great importance to international program exchanges.[153] There is increasing demand, he wrote, for the exchange of "political, social, cultural, entertainment and sports material." Exchanges with the Soviet Union receive special emphasis. On January 14, 1964, Radio Moscow broadcast the 1,000th edition of a biweekly broadcast in Russian prepared by Polish radio entitled "Warsaw Speaking," which informed Soviet listeners about political, economic and cultural events in Poland.[154]

June 1955 marked the twenty-fifth year of programs from the USSR to Poland, the first having gone on the air June 22, 1941, the day Hitler attacked the Soviet Union. These are relayed by Polish radio six days a week.[155] In 1967 Warsaw and Moscow organized the Constitution of Friendship for young listeners, with questions covering the history, geography and life of both countries. Winners received prizes and visits to each others' countries.[156] On the adult level were the "Warsaw-Moscow" television programs broadcast on July 25 and 27, 1968, in which actors and entertainers from both countries participated.[157]

The "Week of Hungarian Culture" and the "Week of Swiss Culture" involved radio exchanges between Poland and those two countries, and there was a similar project with Austria.[158] Polish radio also has done broadcasts with UNESCO (see above, pp. 289–293). On October 21, 1970, a radio discussion, "The Germans—As Seen by the Poles," was transmitted by Polish Radio and by stations in West Berlin, Munich, Cologne, and Hamburg.[159] A Polish description of the program stated that it included "viewpoints which are absolutely inacceptable in Poland" and went on to say: "In this transmission, which lasted almost two hours, the fundamental condition of a frank discussion was observed: both parties had the possibility to express their opinions which were accepted with full understanding by the Polish listeners and by the majority of West German listeners."

The director of foreign relations for Polish broadcasting regrets the limited international exchange of television drama; disputes "the prevailing opinion that foreign television art is different, strange, and couldn't possibly be smoothly absorbed"; and suggests that other countries follow Poland's example and exchange television directors and designers.[160] "Polish plays," he said, "performed by foreign actors and directed by Polish TV directors are a form of modern cooperation which improves the professional skill of the people involved and is a long range investment in the approach of cultures and ideas. We, of course, welcome foreign directors . . . and . . . authors of TV programs to our studios."

But Poland's participation in Eurovision has been limited (see Tables 1 and 2). Eurovision figures show that from 1965 to 1970 Poland contributed and received fewer programs than did any other socialist countries except Bulgaria and Romania. According to Intervision statistics, during 1971 Poland accepted 85 Eurovision programs (172 hr.) while providing 4 programs (4 hr.), which constituted only about 5 per cent of Intervision's contributions to Eurovision. During 1972 Poland received 55 Eurovision programs (112½ hr.) and contributed 6 programs (7 hr.). Of these, about 60 per cent were sporting events; 13 per cent, cultural programs; 10 per cent, entertainment; and 15 per cent, news.

Polish radio and television make recordings of many of their programs available for international exchange, these being listed in publications of the OIRT and in the Polish Radio and Television Bulletins. The Broadcasting Foundation of America distributes some musical programs to the stations it services in the United States.

VIII

Czechoslovak Socialist Republic

Broadcasting in Czechoslovakia is of particular interest because of the occupation of the country by the USSR in August 1968. During the preceding months all the media had taken a decidedly liberal and often an anti-Soviet position. While the occupation was in progress, the Czechoslovaks showed remarkable courage and great ingenuity in maintaining their broadcasting services despite the presence of foreign troops. Thereafter, conservative forces regained the ascendancy, and broadcasting, along with other aspects of national life, again was rigidly controlled.

Facts about Czechoslovakia

The Czechoslovak Socialist Republic (49,367 square miles) is about the size of New York State (49,576 square miles). With Poland to the north, East Germany to the northwest, West Germany to the southwest, Austria and Hungary to the south, and the Soviet Union to the east, Czechoslovakia borders on both Western and Eastern European countries.

Czechoslovakia has a population of 14,407,000, and its capital city, Prague, contains 1,082,000 inhabitants. Bratislava, the third largest city and the capital of Slovakia, contains 288,000 people.[1] From west to east the three major sections of the country are Bohemia, Moravia, and Slovakia, the first two inhabited by Czech- and the third by Slovak-speaking people. Czechs and Moravians compose about 65 per cent and Slovaks 30 per cent of the total population, the remaining 5 per cent being Hungarians, Germans, Ruthenians, and Poles. Before 1939 there were many more minority inhabitants than now, but postwar territorial arrangements placed most of them under other sovereignties. Rivalries between Czechs and Slovaks are a continuing problem, affecting broadcasting along with many other things. The two languages, both official, are mutually understandable, and there are broadcasts in both of them as well as in some minority tongues.

Industry accounts for two-thirds of Czechoslovakia's national income. Trade is oriented toward Eastern Europe since 70 per cent is with the socialist countries.[2] In 1970, 38 per cent of the value of all foreign trade was with the USSR, 14 per cent with the German Democratic Republic, 9 per cent with Poland, 6.5 per cent with West Germany, 6 per cent with Hungary, 5 per cent with Romania, and 4 per cent with Yugoslavia. Less than 1 per cent was with the United States. Recent decisions of the Soviet and Polish governments to increase their supplies of consumer goods helped the Czechoslovak economy, since it is a major producer of such items.[3]

After three centuries as provinces of the Habsburg Empire, the territories of Bohemia, Moravia, and Slovakia merged to become the independent republic of Czechoslovakia following the collapse of Austria-Hungary in 1918. During the next twenty years Czechoslovakia developed industrially, enjoyed a high standard of living, and showed a genuine talent for democratic self-government. But it could not escape further partitions. As a consequence of the Munich Agreement of September 1938, it was progressively dismembered by Germany, Poland, and Hungary. A government-in-exile returned with the Russian army in 1945. The Communists emerged triumphant in the ensuing elections, and in February 1948 assumed complete control, putting the country firmly into the Soviet orbit.

From 1948 until 1963 domestic policies followed a rigid Stalinist pattern, after which a gradual freeing of controls culminated in the appointment of Alexander Dubček as first secretary of the Czechoslovak Communist party on Janaury 5, 1968.[4] Dubček transformed Czechoslovakia into the most liberal of the Communist bloc countries, and during the first eight months of 1968, commonly referred to as the "Prague Spring," radio and television and the other mass media enjoyed a high degree of freedom. But evidence of Soviet concern about these trends became increasingly apparent, and at an Eastern European summit meeting in Dresden in March 1968 Dubček was questioned about his policies.

In July there were well-publicized Soviet troop movements along the Hungarian border, and long columns of tanks and armored vehicles maneuvered in East Germany. By the end of the month some twenty-eight divisions from the USSR and other Warsaw Pact countries completely surrounded Czechoslovakia.

Meanwhile, the Czechoslovaks continued to manifest their independence. There was a public investigation of the death in 1948 of Foreign Minister Jan Masaryk, with the press implicating the Soviet Union. International alignments were indicated by the visits of Presidents Tito of Yugoslavia and Nicolae Ceauşescu of Romania a few weeks before the invasion. Although Romania was and Yugoslavia was not a member of the Warsaw Pact, neither country took part in the invasion, and both publicly criticized the action, despite concern for their own safety.

At 11:00 P.M. on August 20, 1968, Czechoslovakia was occupied by Soviet, Bulgarian, Hungarian, Polish, and East German forces, of which about three-quarters were from the Soviet Union. The USSR announced that the invasion had been requested by the "party and Government leaders of the Czechoslovak Socialist Republic" as a consequence of the threat which had arisen to the socialist system from "counter-revolutionary forces" which had entered into "a collusion with foreign forces hostile to socialism."[5] Subsequently, Soviet party leader Leonid I. Brezhnev referred to the duty of socialist states to intervene in order to root out "revisionism." This concept, which came to be known as the Brezhnev Doctrine, was incorporated into the preamble of the Treaty of Friendship signed by the two countries May 6, 1970: "The defense of socialist achievements that were gained by the heroic efforts of the people of each country is the common duty of socialist countries."[6]

On October 16, 1968, following a series of conferences between Czechoslovak and Soviet leaders, a treaty was signed providing for the stationing of Soviet troops on Czechoslovak territory as "a step toward strengthening the defense of the Czechoslovak Socialist Republic and of all countries of the socialist community in the face of growing revanchist efforts of the West German militarist forces." Inevitably, this led to increasingly close supervision.[7] In April 1969 Dubček was replaced by Gustáv Husák as party secretary, and there has been a gradual tightening of controls ever since. In May 1971, at the Fourteenth Congress of the Czechoslovak Communist party, Dr. Husák thanked Brezhnev for sending troops in 1968, saying that he thereby averted a bloody civil war threatened by the policies of the Prague Spring.[8] By the summer of 1973, although Soviet forces were not frequently seen, it was estimated that there still were some 70,000 troops in Bohemia.

One aftermath of the occupation was the trials of former officials indicted for their roles in 1968 and thereafter. During ten days in July 1972, twenty-eight persons were sentenced and others placed on probation for alleged subversive activities.[9] In announcing one of these verdicts, the government press agency said that the accused formed "an illegal group" whose objective "was to overthrow the socialist state system." The Czechoslovak news media did not report all the sentences resulting from these trials.

Early in 1973 Prague announced its willingness to provide amnesty for some citizens who had fled in 1968, excepting those accused of subversion, betraying state secrets, or damaging the country's reputation abroad.[10] However, broadcasters and writers may not be among those covered, since their activities might be held damaging to the country's image. Yet, there is détente in Czechoslovakia as elsewhere: diplomatic relations with West Germany have been resumed for the first time since World War II, and a consular treaty signed with the United States.

Legal Structure

The Czechoslovak Constitution is preceded by a declaration which among other things says that the country is "already practicing" the socialist principle "From each according to his ability, to each according to his work."[11] It goes on to say that efforts are being made to create the conditions essential "for the transition of our society to communism," at which time it is hoped to realize "the highest principle of distribution—the principle of communism: 'From each according to his ability, to each according to his needs.'"

The Constitution proper begins: "The Czechoslovak Socialist Republic is a socialist state founded on the firm alliance of the workers, the farmers, and the intelligentsia, with the working class at its head." Recognizing the rivalry of the Czech and Slovak populations, it refers to the country as "a unitary State of two fraternal nations possessing equal rights, the Czechs and the Slovaks." Supplementing this concept, Article 25 reads: "The State shall ensure citizens of Hungarian, Ukrainian, and Polish nationality every opportunity and all means for education in their mother tongue and for their cultural development." This was further reinforced by the Constitutional Law on Federalization, effective January 1, 1969, under which Czechoslovakia became a federal state of two nations with equal rights, the Czech Socialist Republic and the Slovak Socialist Republic, each with its own government.[12]

Article 2 of the Constitution declares that all power "shall belong to the working people" and be exercised through "representative bodies which are elected by them, controlled by them, and accountable to them." Article 4 states that "the guiding force in society and in the State is the vanguard of the working class, the Communist Party of Czechoslovakia, a voluntary militant alliance of the most active and most politically conscious citizens from the ranks of the workers, farmers and intelligentsia."* The party underwent extensive changes in 1970 as an aftermath of the upheavals of 1968, and many members were expelled, had their memberships canceled, or chose to resign. In 1971 the party had some 1.2 million members.[13] Article 7 says that the economic foundation of the country "shall be the socialist economic system, which excludes every form of exploitation of man by man," while Article 8 (2) includes "broadcasting, television and motion picture enterprises" in the category of "national property."

Chapter II, "Rights and Duties of Citizens," guarantees equal rights without regard to nationality, race, or sex, plus the rights to work, to leisure after work, to social security, and to education.[14] Provisions relative to freedom of expression parallel those in other socialist constitutions, with limitations like those in the Soviet Constitution and some others. "Freedom of expression in all fields of public life, in particular freedom of speech and of the press, *consistent with the interests of the working people*, shall be guaranteed to all citizens. . . . These freedoms shall be secured by making publishing houses and printing presses, public buildings, halls, assembly grounds, as well as broadcasting, television and other facilities available to the working people and their organizations."†

---

* As in all socialist countries, the basic source of government power is the Communist party. *Europa Year Book 1972*, Vol. I, p. 616.

† Emphasis added. See above, pp. 42–44.

Although the Constitution of 1920 setting up the Czechoslovak Republic following World War I laid the basis for a highly democratic regime, it nevertheless contained provisions authorizing much more censorship than normally is found in a democratic country. Paragraph 113 stated: "Freedom of the press as well as the right to assemble peaceably and without arms and to form associations is guaran-

In the years following World War II Czechoslovak broadcasting was successively under the Ministry of Information, the Ministry of Culture, and the Committee for Radio and Television. Subsequently, the director general reported directly to the Council of Ministers.[15] Radio and television now operate under laws enacted in 1964. Their respective directors, responsible to the government, are assisted by boards of management made up of the senior officials heading the working sections of the organization, including the domestic, regional, and external services. The structure provides considerable autonomy for Slovakia.

Since 1959 radio and television have been administratively separated. Transmitters and connecting links, as usual in Europe, are the responsibility of the Ministry of Posts and Telecommunications. The annual fee for a radio license is 120 crowns ($18.22) per household and for a television license 300 crowns ($45.57) per household, each television license including also a radio license.[16]

The evolution of Czechoslovak broadcasting from close regulation in the early 1960s to freedom in 1968 and back again to firm control not only is interesting in itself, but also illustrates Communist procedures. A former employee of the Czechoslovak news agency, who also served as correspondent in London, has written about these information controls. When censorship was introduced in 1953 after the Soviet model, the official Czechoslovak journalists' publication—following Lenin's theories of earlier decades—explained that it was necessary during the transitional period to protect the public against bourgeois ideas: "Only very naive people can believe that the communists who did not hesitate to ban the bourgeois newspapers would perhaps hesitate to ban all expressions of counterrevolutionary bourgeois ideology in the pages of the legal press or even in the socialist press. We communists are not supporters of so-called free competition in the field of ideology!"

---

teed. It is therefore in principle inadmissable to place the press under preliminary censorship" (Czechoslovak Government Information Office, *The Constitution of the Czechoslovak Republic*. In the Austro-Hungarian Empire there had been strict censorship). But paragraph 117 declared: "Every person may *within the limits of the law* express either his or her opinion by word, in writing, in print, by picture, etc." (emphasis added). Paragraph 118 reads: "Scientific research and the publication of its results, as well as art is free so far as it does not violate the penal codes." Likewise, Paragraph 112 guaranteed all inhabitants "the right to profess and exercise publicly and privately any creed, religion or faith whatsoever, *so far as the exercise of the same is not in conflict with public law and order or with morality.*"

An example was provided by a railway accident in 1960, about which, although 110 people were killed and 106 injured, there were no radio reports until the following day and no newspaper stories until two days later. "Independent reporting or probing by the press of the wider circumstances of the disaster was forbidden since it would have brought into the open the real causes, namely the low standards of railroad equipment and safety measures, and the overworking of both train crews. . . ."[17]

A former Czech journalist and news broadcaster has described how censorship was enforced.[18] Mass media were never operated privately, but always by government-related organizations. Journalists and broadcasters had to have party approval, and specific clearance was required for appointment to important positions. Mistakes could lead to dismissal without appeal.

News copy was delivered on paper of different colors. Stories on white paper could be freely broadcast; those on blue paper were for staff information; and items on pink paper were for chief editors only. A final category went just to party headquarters, with further distinctions between upper and lower echelons. All people receiving restricted materials were to return them once a month to be checked and destroyed by a security officer. There also were briefings by high government and party officials at which strict instructions were given regarding what items should be used and how they should be treated. Finally, there were censors who had to stamp approval on each page before it could be printed or broadcast.

A State of the Union address by the president of the United States could serve as an example. Its complete text probably would be restricted. A critical reference to the Czechoslovak government or one of its officials would not be reported at all, and might not even be included in the material provided to chief editors, reaching only those in higher party offices. Broadcasters, therefore, might have to transmit or comment on a talk by the American president without ever seeing its entire text.[19]

One observer who compared Radio Prague's domestic output in February 1963 with that of the corresponding month of 1967 noted that even though Czech programs in 1963 were the most interesting in Eastern Europe, they were even better in 1967. By then, old-fashioned popular music and propagandistic songs had been replaced by contemporary, popular, and serious music; extended reports of party activities had given way to abbreviated newscast coverage; and the propaganda aspects of news had been minimized. For several years before 1968, in fact,

Czechoslovakia had more freedom of publication than any other country in Eastern Europe.

Large editions of Western books were circulated, and two well-known Western newspapers—*The Times* of London and *Le Monde* of Paris— were readily available.[20] Although it has been reported that these publications still are sold in Czechoslovakia, the newsstands at the hotels where I inquired in September 1972 had no Western newspapers at all, even for tourists. Nevertheless, a party official told an American reporter at about that time that they intended to sell some Western publications in major cities. "We know we must compete with these influences," he said. "We must demonstrate that our party is attractive. The Government and party must show that the standard of living is so good that people will feel the party is doing things for them."

In June 1967 the Fourth Congress of the Czechoslovak Writers' Union passed a resolution favoring the elimination of all prepublication censorship.[21] But this went too far, and the Ministry of Culture thereupon assumed control of the union's weekly magazine, saying that it had become "a platform for opposition political views." The Union of Journalists ultimately disassociated itself from the resolution too. After the replacement of Novotny by Dubček in January 1968, the opposition of newspaper editors made censorship so unworkable that it was largely suspended on March 5, and on June 25 the National Assembly voted overwhelmingly to abolish censorship.* However, some controls were retained: although the former list of 8,000 unpublishable military and political items was reduced to 5,000, it was not eliminated. The next day the official publication of the Writers' Union issued "2,000 Words: A Statement on Democratization," signed by seventy intellectual leaders, which so severely criticized certain political leaders as to unnerve some of the reformers.[22]

On May 5, 1968, a letter to the newspapers from the Association of Czechoslovak Composers urged the modernization of the broadcasting system, the money to come from the savings that would result if foreign broadcasts were no longer jammed. The next day the minister of culture urged at a press conference that there be more imports of foreign newspapers.[23] Thereupon the minister of the interior announced that the jamming of officially recognized radio stations would be stopped. But the

* *New York Times*, June 27, 1968, p. 3. Of the 298 deputies, only 30 voted to retain the press law, while 17 abstained.

jamming of Radio Free Europe would be continued because it was not "recognized" and because it used unauthorized frequencies. Interference with RFE also was necessary in order to "prevent American spies and agents in Czechoslovakia from getting in free information."*

In March 1968 television news films showed speakers at meetings being wildly applauded for criticizing the government and the police.[24] But the mid-1968 radio series called "Songs with the Telephone" must have been the most unrestrained broadcast of the decade in the socialist camp. During the programs, which often ran as long as two hours, listeners were invited to call in questions for party and government officials. On May 18 queries about the upcoming visit of Soviet Defense Minister Andrei Grechkov were directed to an official in the Czech Defense Ministry, who learned the conversation was being broadcast only after he was on the air.

Such things did not go unnoticed in the Soviet Union. On May 16, on domestic programs as well as in its foreign service to Czechoslovakia, Radio Moscow said: "Recently Czechoslovakia has become the subject of special attention from bourgeois propaganda. Press, radio, and television pursue a clear course: first, to encourage those forces in Czechoslovakia who are following their own aims alien to the people; and, second, to undermine the friendship and fruitful cooperation between the countries of the socialist community, and to sow distrust in the relations between fraternal peoples." The assertion that the USSR was exerting economic pressure on Czechoslovakia by canceling certain previously arranged deliveries was cited as "a clear example of dirty imperialist propaganda." At that time the number of USSR external broadcasts in Czech and Slovak was increased from two to five half-hour programs a day, and shortly thereafter to 168 hours a week. Supplementing this, Poland reinstated external broadcasting in Czech and Slovak after an eighteen-year interval—in September it was putting out 140 hours per week, while Hungary and mainland China both initiated broadcasts to Czechoslovakia.[25]

The role of Czechoslovak radio and television during the invasion period has frequently been told. Troops entered Czechoslovakia at 11:00 P.M., August 20, and arrived before the Prague radio headquar-

* *Variety*, March 20, 1968, pp. 1, 50. Czechoslovakia had been jamming Western broadcasts periodically since 1951, and jailing or fining people guilty of passing along reports heard on those stations.

ters at 7:30 the next morning. Nevertheless, the Czechoslovaks managed to continue radio and television programming until August 29, thanks to the ingenuity, skill, and dedication of their engineering and program staffs.[26] Evicted from their headquarters and from studios elsewhere in the country, the Czechoslovaks worked from auxiliary and improvised studios, using mobile transmitters supplied by the army or by plants manufacturing electronic equipment. Even more surprising, television kept going.[27] While the invasion was in progress, the Western world received prompt relays of programs originated by the free Czech television transmitters as a consequence of plans drawn up in advance by Austrian and Czech broadcasters, which made it possible for the Austrians to record off-the-air pictures from secret mobile Czech transmitters. In addition, some Czech film was smuggled across the border. During the first week of the invasion, Austrian television received and relayed to rest of the world almost ten hours of such programs.[28]

The programs encouraged passive resistance, and the public was instructed to tell the Russians to go home because they were uninvited and unwanted guests. But it was emphasized that "to oppose them by force would be stupid suicide. Our only weapon now is absolute, complete passive resistance."[29] Television managed to present filmed reports of street fighting as well as of the meeting of the National Assembly, despite the presence of Russian soldiers in the building. Public figures often appeared on the air to oppose the invasion, despite almost certain identification and punishment once conservative forces won control. People were warned against agents provocateurs, invited to call in news reports to broadcasting headquarters, and instructed to confuse the occupying forces by obliterating or changing street signs and highway markers, as the British had done during World War II in anticipation of a possible German invasion. One of the more interesting stories was about the delayed arrival of the Soviet train carrying electronic equipment to locate secret transmitters. Taking their cues from the radio, railroad employees managed to delay the train for several days by "losing" it on sidings and by putting its locomotive out of commission.[30] However, the Russians jammed the freedom stations and occupied most of them by August 29, one week after the invasion.

The USSR and other Warsaw Pact members charged that the free Czechoslovak broadcasts were no different from those of the Voice of America, the BBC, or Radio Free Europe. They claimed that some of the equipment had been supplied by West Germany; that certain programs were rebroadcast by West Germany army facilities or by the Deutsche Welle; and that "Radio Free South Moravia" operated out of Vienna. Radio Moscow said that the "forces of counter-revolution within Czechoslovakia and international imperialism placed great hopes on the underground radio stations, not only in Czechoslovakia, but also in Austria and West Germany." But in October 1968 a spokesman for the Czechoslovak Central Communications Authority denied that West Germany had supplied any radio transmitters to Czechoslovakia during the August events.

The invading forces also had mobile broadcasting units, augmented by facilities in neighboring countries. The USSR's Radio Vltava, using transmitters in East Germany, broadcast programs denouncing Dubček and the other liberal leaders, and exposing alleged "Zionist" and "Imperialist" plots, that were written in Dresden and East Berlin and then read—with characteristic accents—by former Sudeten and Carpathian Germans exiled from Czechoslovakia after World War II.[31] Polish television programs for Czechs in the border areas said that the events in Czechoslovakia resulted from the activities of "counter-revolutionaries and Zionists," proof being "the incitement by illegal radio stations."

With the return to "normalcy" at the end of August, progressively tighter controls were restored. On August 27 Dubček announced temporary restrictions on freedom of expression. Censorship was officially restored on September 13, 1968, when the National Assembly reimposed the prepublication controls that had been removed a few months before.[32] When Czechoslovak television resumed regular broadcasting on September 4, 1968, Reuters reported that "the pretty fair-haired announcer could hardly speak for emotion when she said the television staff wanted to thank everybody for the calm and discipline they had shown in their efforts to get on with the job." Television workers, she declared, were prepared to follow President Ludvik Svoboda and Party Secretary Alexander Dubček.

After the return of Dubček and his colleagues from their trip to Moscow on August 27, the Czech media assumed they would have self-censorship from within rather than control imposed from the outside.[33] But things did not work out that way. The Soviet news agency complained that antisocialist propaganda continued despite agreement to end it. The media, said TASS, remained in the hands of the people who had attacked the Czechoslovak Communist party and opposed friendship with the Soviet Union.[34]

By January 8, 1970, 118 former Czechoslovak radio workers had left for abroad, including "editors and workers known for their activities in 1968 and later." The next day television announced that its most important task was "the return to the basic principles of the internal party life, and further the completion of the departure of all those who were direct bearers and distributors of rightist opportunist views." An American journalist reported from Prague in May 1971 that while spring had returned it was not the Prague Spring of 1968. "Television," he wrote, "has lost its variety meanwhile and the only dramatic viewing now is heavily immersed in political and party ideology."[35] According to foreign observers in Prague, these personnel changes also resulted in a much lower standard of program and production quality.

Networks and Programs

Czechoslovakia plans much of its broadcasting with reference to its ethnic and language groups. It maintains nationwide radio services, extensive wired receiver installations, and external services for European and world audiences. One of its two television networks has nationwide and the other limited coverage.

Czechoslovak radio, which claims to be the oldest in Central Europe, began regular broadcasting on May 18, 1923. There now are five networks plus regional and local services.[36] Together they are carried by some thirty AM transmitters in the long-, medium-, and short-wave bands, plus thirty-five FM stations.

The nationwide network known as "Hvĕdzda" ("The Star"), reorganized in that form on January 2, 1971, provides "topical political news accompanied by broadcasts of an entertaining character" in both Czech and Slovak.[37] On the air twenty-four hours a day, it is planned particularly for young listeners, its programs from 1:00 to 6:00 p.m. being especially for youth.

In addition there are two networks in the Czech and two in the Slovak sections of the country. The first Czech program ("Praha"), on the air daily from 3:30 a.m. (Sundays from 5:00 a.m.) until 11:00 p.m., provides Czech speakers with a varied schedule of music and information. The second Czech program ("Vltava"), on the air from 7:00 or 8:00

a.m. until 10:00 p.m., approximates the BBC's Third Programme.[38] Influenced also by similar services in West Germany and France, it is "intended . . . for listeners with serious interest in definite fields of science and culture."

The first Slovak program ("Bratislava"), on the air daily from 3:00 a.m. (on Sundays from 5:00 a.m.) to 11:00 p.m., offers a general service in the Slovak language. A recent addition is the second Slovak program ("Devin"), on the air from 9:00 a.m. (weekends from 7:00 a.m.) until 10:00 p.m. Certain transmitters used for the national services also carry regional and local programs, some of them in Ukrainian, Polish, and German. There are regional studios in seven outlying cities.[39]

Since 1954 Czechoslovakia has distributed radio programs by wire.[40] In 1962 a spokesman for the ministry in charge of this development explained why wired broadcasting was encouraged. Installation was cheaper than for wave receivers, because no aerials were required; yearly maintenance costs were much lower; and electrification was not necessary, since like telephone exchanges, each system had its own power supply (this article was written before transistor radios were widespread). Wired radio also offered static-free reception plus wide frequency range. The Czechoslovak wired systems provide only one program, and there are no plans to increase this as in the Soviet Union, where there may be a choice of three programs (on the Soviet installations, see above, pp. 70–71). The wired systems relay broadcast programs and also have some originations of their own.

Czechoslovak broadcasting authorities in 1959 categorized approximately 60 per cent of their radio output as music and 40 per cent as spoken word, with around 20 per cent of the total as "political." A 1967 analysis classified it as follows: music, 63.1 per cent; news and current affairs, 16.1 per cent; literature and drama, 10.9 per cent; programs for children and youth, 5.6 per cent; educational broadcasts, 3.3 per cent; and miscellaneous (including advertisements), 1 per cent.

For a decade Czechoslovak radio programmers have recognized the need for adapting to changing times and media. In 1961 one of them observed that radio had to be aware of "the development and growing influence of television," the introduction of transistors (which could bring radio "to the fields [and] swimming pools"), higher living standards, and shorter working hours.[41] The deputy director of radio characterized a 1961 meeting as "historical" because its participants were aware of the new listening patterns resulting from the introduction of transistor sets and changes in the way of life.[42] The session, incidentally, led to a new program structure the following year emphasizing faster moving programs and more participation by announcers.

In 1964 the same broadcaster stressed the need for cooperation between radio and television.[43] It was necessary, he said, to divide the assignments, though not because television had replaced radio. Despite the popularity of sports on television, for example, many people took transistor receivers to the games in order to hear play-by-play accounts as they watched. Recognizing the same factors which led American stations to specialize in different types of programming, the author suggested that "radio must concentrate on specialized groups of listeners and hold their attention by affording experiences which cannot be gained elsewhere by broadcasting special news items, or by ensuring profound artistic representation."

The first television experiments in Czechoslovakia were conducted in the 1920s, although it was not until 1934 that a Czech inventor demonstrated transmissions with a 30-line definition.[44] By 1939, 242-line definition had been achieved with a screen diameter of approximately nine inches. Suspended during World War II, experiments were resumed in 1948, and by 1952 the first Czechoslovak receiving set, with a screen diameter of ten inches, was manufactured.

Regular test broadcasts began May 1, 1953, for several hundred receivers in the Prague area, and there has been regular programming since 1954. Originating facilities were added in Ostrava in 1955, Bratislava in 1956, Brno in 1961, and Kosiče in 1962.[45] There also are film centers, whose principal function is to prepare news inserts, in a number of regional towns. OIRT system D is used for the first service, which is entirely in black and white, and system K with SECAM color for the second.[46] Although television is available throughout the country except for a few places in the Tatra Mountains, Slovaks complain that they do not have as good coverage as do the Czech regions. In January 1968, they said, hardly 70 per cent of Slovakia could receive television. Furthermore, whereas the Czech area had one television set for every 1.7 households, the figure in Slovakia was one set for every 2.32 households.

The first service, which reaches approximately 90 per cent of the population, is broadcast by seventeen VHF transmitters, plus a large number of low-powered satellites.[47] In 1973 the first network was on the air approximately seventy hours each week. In addition to morning broadcasts for shift workers, and morning and afternoon programs for schools, the schedule was approximately as follows: Monday through Friday, 3:30 or 4:00 until 10:30 or 11:00 P.M.; Saturday, 8:30 to 11:00 A.M. and 3:30 to 11:00 P.M.; Sundays, 9:00 A.M. to noon and 3:00 to 11:30 P.M.

Each evening at 7:00 there is a twenty- or thirty-minute newscast. Otherwise, different material is featured on successive evenings: drama on Monday; entertainment on Tuesday; literature and drama on Wednesday; films on Thursday; light entertainment on Friday; and major entertainment features and films on Saturday.

The second television network went on the air in May 1970, seventeen years after the first one. Available to the metropolitan areas of the four largest cities—Prague, Ostrava, Brno, and Bratislava—it reaches about 10 per cent of those who can see the first program. However, it is planned to increase coverage so that 40 per cent of the country will be served by 1975. Because it is only on UHF, it is difficult to develop an audience for the second service, since older receivers cannot pick it up. There were no color receivers until the second quarter of 1971, when some sets were imported from the Soviet Union. Harking back to the early days of television in many other countries, two Prague cafés were provided with color receivers so that people might watch programs. By 1976 it is hoped to have twelve hours of color programs each week.

Initially the second program was on the air Sunday, Tuesday, and Thursday evenings, from 7:00 until 10:30, but since January 1, 1972, it has broadcast Friday evenings too. Whereas the first network offers the same service to the entire country, except when local transmitters substitute their own programs, the second network has separate programs for the Czech and Slovak areas. The second channel is resolving the conflict resulting from the concentration of all programs on a single service, leaving the public no choices. Certain types of serious and educational programs, which previously were delayed to the late evening hours, now are scheduled in midevening on the new channel.[48]

Those analyses available of Czechoslovak television content show an emphasis on serious and political programs. At the beginning of 1961 the figures were as follows: social and political, 24.1 per cent; sports, 16.7 per cent; entertainment, 9.5 per cent; feature films, 9 per cent; drama, 7.6 per cent; opera, 1.2 per cent; musical comedy, 1.1 per cent; ballet, 0.7 per cent; puppet theater, 0.6 per cent; and miscellaneous (including concerts, short films, quizzes, and unclassified), 29.5 per cent.[49]

By 1964 programs about news and political affairs took 44 per cent of television time; broadcasts for children and youth, 18.7 per cent: artistic, literary, dramatic, and entertainment programs, 18.1 per cent; films, 15.9 per cent; and miscellaneous, 3.3 per cent.[50] A few years later about 40 per cent of the time was devoted to news, journalistic features, and popular science programs; 31 per cent to literary, dramatic, and musical entertainment programs; 16 per cent to programs for youth; and 11 per cent to films. (Included in these various categories was a 12 per cent share of adult education programs.[51]) An unofficial report in January 1971 indicated that news, documentaries, and sports then made up approximately 45 per cent of the schedule; culture and amusement, 35 per cent; and children's and educational programs, 20 per cent.[52]

Periodically television has five- or ten-minute blocks of advertisements. After noting that the income received from these was slight, one broadcasting official remarked to me: "But it all comes from and goes to the State anyway." Each cluster is introduced by a cartoon character who also appears between commercials and at the end tips his hat as if to say thank you. The advertisements themselves are combinations of still photographs, films, animation, and cartoons. One or two off-screen voices often read the accompanying text. Items advertised include foodstuffs, soap (washing powder, water-closet deodorants), toys, and household appliances. The presentations are quite skillful.

A Czechoslovak broadcaster told me in the summer of 1965 that the basic purpose of broadcasting was "to promote the policies of the Communist Party of Czechoslovakia with all the means available." Except for the interlude of the Prague Spring in 1968, this would appear to be the consistent objective. A Czechoslovak publication pointed out that to commemorate the fifteenth anniversary of the "liberation by the Soviet army" in May 1960, there would be radio programs to report "what had been achieved under the leadership of the Communist Party of Czechoslovakia and the people's government in cooperation with the USSR and other socialist countries as well as the brilliant prospects of the Czechoslovak people under the socialist and communist regimes."*

The Press Law of 1966 stated that the basic purpose of all the media is "to advance the interest of socialist society. . . [and] to promote the people's socialist awareness of the policy of the Communist Party as the leading force in society and state."[53] In a talk to Czechoslovak journalists in July 1969, Gustáv Husák, first secretary of the party, stated that freedom and democracy must be interpreted from the class point of view.[54] A resolution adopted almost unanimously by the 500 journalists present outlined proper journalistic conduct, which was to include opposition to "rightist-opportunist forces in the mass communications media" and the support of Marxist-Leninist positions. The resolution also instructed journalists to follow the basic party documents and to "strengthen party organizations and editorial offices so that they may guarantee the implementation of party policies." Among other things the media were to recognize such upcoming events as the one-hundredth anniversary of Lenin's birth on April 22, 1970, and the twenty-fifth anniversary of the liberation of Czechoslovakia on May 9, 1970. In connection with these two occasions, a news release said: "Both anniversaries and their celebrations will not . . . constitute a once-and-for all political campaign . . . but will penetrate and inspire not only our publicistic but also our artistic and children's broadcasts throughout the whole of 1970."[55]

A Czech native, after a period of viewing in 1969, reported a swing from news and documentary content toward entertainment as a consequence of the post-Dubček policies. "Politics is out," she wrote. "It's back to entertainment, a familiar role for Czechoslovak TV."[56] According to this observer, Czech television then offered many adaptations of novels, short stories, and plays; live performances directly from theaters; and much music, ranging from the Prague Spring Music Festival to jazz and rock features. Light dramatic programs included crime shows, and there were sports like ice hockey and soccer, plus international competitions from Intervision and Eurovision. Absent, however, was the overemphasis on cooperative and industrial activities so typical of Soviet television, as well as the free discussion programs which flourished in Czechoslovakia during 1968. This writer concluded that the Czechoslo-

* "Czechoslovak Radio," *OIRT Review* 1961/6, p. 9. Official releases frequently use the expression "liberation of Czechoslovakia by the Soviet army."

vak output resembled neither Soviet nor American television, but rather that of Western Europe, "since most Czechoslovaks feel their closest cultural affinity is to the West."

In September 1972 I had extensive talks with key members of the Information Center for Foreign Journalists in Prague that left no doubt about the current role of the Czechoslovak media. Their main purpose is to present the socialist as opposed to the Western point of view, an assignment that has been intensified since 1968. An important aspect of this is competition with foreign broadcasts, particularly those from Radio Free Europe, which are heard by many Czechoslovaks. In keeping with this, a recent magazine article said that the third radio network "should operate on a basis corresponding with its very essence, *i.e., the Marxist-Leninist conception of culture, art and policy.*"*

News and Public Affairs

Although news broadcasting policies during the period of the Prague Spring approached those of the West, this clearly was an atypical interlude, since statements of policy before and after 1968 accord with those from other socialist countries. In 1960 a Czechoslovak writer emphasized the political aspects of radio news: "The sole aim of these newscasts is to serve the new social order, the government of the people, socialism. This, in any case, is the characteristic feature of the whole radio."[57] The following year an article contended that television should "aid in the political education of wide circles of population . . . [and] lead the working people to correct understanding of all tasks, connected with [the] building-up of a mature socialist society and their fulfillment."[58]

In August 1969 the newspaper *Rudé Právo* said: "After an extended silence political commentators have recently reappeared on the radio. . . . [They] deserve support . . . [in their assignment] to restore— following all those unfortunate excesses of the past months—the prestige of the commentator's words, based on profound Marxist knowledge, sincere conviction, and determination to support the conclusions of the recent Communist Party meetings. . . ."

In 1970, to mark the centennial of the birth of Lenin and the twenty-fifth anniversary of the "liberation of Czechoslovakia by the Soviet

---

* "Problems of Exacting Selected Programmes and the VHF Transmissions," *OIRT Review* 1972/1, p. 14. Emphasis in original.

army," television news and commentary set out to show "by picture and spoken word, the progress of the Soviet Army in 1945, the gradual liberation of the state territory of Czechoslovakia and the course of the celebrations organized in 1970. . . . By means of a detailed daily news service we intended to acquaint viewers with all important official events connected with the Lenin Jubilee, celebrations, exhibitions, the unveiling of monuments, etc., not only in Czechoslovakia, but also abroad."[59]

Apparently there were some objections to the increased emphasis on such items, since on May 15, 1970, Radio Prague replied to criticisms that it broadcast too much political news. A commentator said that "as a result of the intensive work of opportunists and anti-socialist forces, many false ideas and incorrect views were brought forth during the last few years." In consequence, the public acquired a distorted concept of "the problems, needs, and perspectives of our socialist society, and thus also with their own future and life." Therefore, "we will continue to broadcast politics, and do not doubt that honest and thoughtful people will agree with us."*

News is supplied by the official agency Československá Tisková Kancelář (ČTK), with offices in twelve Czechoslovak cities and foreign bureaus in the principal capitals of the world.[60] Broadcasting has its own correspondents throughout Czechoslovakia as well as in such cities as Moscow, Berlin, Peking, Delhi, Bonn, Paris, and New York. Through ČTK it obtains news from the major foreign agencies, East and West, including TASS, the Associated Press, Agence France Presse, and Deutsche Presse Agentur.

A former employee of the Czechoslovak news agency, who later broke with his country, has provided information about the operation of ČTK.[61] In the early years after World War II, ČTK, like some other Eastern European agencies, was largely dependent upon TASS for foreign news, but this was unsatisfactory, partly because the service was too slow and partly because of the extent to which it reflected Soviet political judgments. Accordingly, ČTK became increasingly independent after 1954 and by 1962 had bureaus or correspondents in twenty-eight cities, including Paris, London, and New York.

* When I showed this paragraph to a former director of Czechoslovak television news, he reacted: "This is in sharp contrast to public reactions in February-August 1968, when TV received thousands of letters demanding that still *more* time be devoted to political programs . . . Viewers even demanded that, if necessary, some sportscasts be cancelled."

Between 1963 and 1967 Czechoslovakia made increasing use of Eurovision.[62] In 1963 it provided no news items, while receiving 17, and in 1964 provided 1 and received 10. In 1965 it provided 11 and received 23 items; in 1966 it provided 12 and received 22; and in 1967, although it provided only 10, it received 251 items. Since 1967, the EBU has provided few figures on Czechoslovakian news exchanges with Eurovision. Intervision reports that in 1972 Czechoslovakia received 1,334 news items from Eurovision and originated 30.

Taken together, the national, local, and regional radio services of Czechoslovakia broadcast news programs, varying in length from five to fifteen minutes, almost every half hour all day long.[63] Radio Free Europe provided a comparative analysis of its newscasts for Czechoslovakia and the Czechoslovak domestic programs on January 30 and 31 and February 1, 1967, which revealed many similarities between the two services. Both reported funeral plans for the American astronauts who had just died in the Apollo tragedy; certain developments in mainland China; the visit of Soviet President Podgorny to Pope Paul in Italy; and a trip by United Kingdom's Prime Minister Wilson to Brussels to discuss entry into the Common Market.

The major differences between the services resulted from their different propaganda objectives. The Czechoslovak programs placed greater emphasis on such items as strikes in the Western countries, student unrest in Spain, protests against "neo-Nazi" trends in West Germany, and the suicide of a former concentration camp official. Treated on Radio Free Europe were certain items omitted entirely or given abbreviated coverage on the Czechoslovak programs: news that the Czechoslovak authorities had refused a travel permit to a man scheduled to produce an opera in Munich; and certain political stories involving West Germany, including visits from Romanian officials to West Germany and of a Bavarian bishop to Prague. Nevertheless, there was a surprising amount of duplication between the two services.*

The first television service has a twenty- or thirty-minute newscast at

---

* According to RFE, "although radios Prague and Bratislava have become increasingly competitive with RFE, they are still not able to provide their audiences with newscasts that are consistently interesting, accurate and fresh . . .Time and again, RFE was first and most thorough with the major stories of the day. The regime radios have problems with political considerations which undoubtedly delay or completely eliminate the coverage of some stories . . . Live newscasts in which the main stories are reworked from hour to hour are the pattern on RFE's Czechoslovak station. Listeners to Radios Prague and Bratislava hear frequent

7:00 P.M., plus a half-hour program later in the evening. The second network simulcasts the 7:00 P.M. program those evenings it is on the air (Tuesdays, Thursdays, Fridays, and Sundays) and concludes its broadcasts each day with a news summary.[64]

Coverage of the election for the National Assembly and other offices on June 14, 1964, illustrated how Czechoslovak television then perceived its role at election time.[65] On preceding days information was broadcast about the lives and records of the candidates. "The TV agitation centre was . . . in operation, fulfilling explanatory and propagandistic tasks during the preparation of the elections," including reports on developments in various cities since the last elections. Election day coverage began at 9:00 A.M., and in the course of the day some older people recalled election procedures in the period between the two world wars. In 1972 I saw a thirty-minute program introducing several candidates in an upcoming election. Film vignettes showed them in their family and work settings as the announcer read information about them. From the Czechoslovak point of view, this was an effective political promotion piece.

I saw a number of newscasts in September 1972. Most lead stories pertained to the Warsaw Pact maneuvers held that week in Czechoslovakia, which were covered mainly through silent film reports showing soldiers, weapons, tanks, and planes. A long statement by a general, however, rated sound film, while on another occasion a Czechoslovak party member explained that everything was going well and that the socialist countries were working together. From five to ten minutes of each thirty-minute newscast were devoted to these maneuvers.

Other typical subjects included the distribution of decorations to Party leaders; visiting delegations; the fair in Brno; and an exhibition of East German industrial machinery. There also were sport summaries (some quite good), weather forecasts, and a short feature showing pictures of criminals being sought by the police. There were frequent switches back and forth from Czech-speaking Prague to Slovak-speaking Bratislava, since people knowing either of these languages can understand the other one.

Czechoslovak television news is about the poorest of any of the social-

---

word-for-word repeats. While regime radios tend to repare 'set' stories expected to last over a period of time, RFE newscasts seek new developments and fresh angles with which to update their casts."

ist countries, the principal reason being the extensive staff changes after 1968, when competent but politically suspect employees were replaced by "reliable" neophytes. Most of the film was silent film; party leaders spoke too long; announcers—both men and women—read poorly; and programs lacked finesse.

Children and Youth

In 1960 a representative of Czechoslovak television wrote that in-school programs were designed not to replace teachers but rather to aid them in their work by supplementing school lessons. Among other things the programs were to provide motivation.[66] Six years later a radio spokesman said approximately the same thing: although radio was to implement school objectives and curriculums, it should not replace teachers but help them, as "in many other socialist as well as capitalist countries."[67]

In-school radio broadcasting began in 1929. Programs for nursery schools were started in 1946, often with the fairy-tale format still used twenty years later, when there were three such broadcasts each week.[68] For school scheduling reasons the Czechoslovaks decided against broadcasts for upper classes. First-grade programs are on Mondays, second-grade programs on Tuesdays, and so on.

By 1960 most schools had their own receiving equipment. Some even had public address systems with a control room in the headmaster's office, which, it was observed, not only permitted him to make announcements but also to interrupt schoolwork! By 1973 most schools had AM-FM transistor receivers, and many had tape recorders too. Some in-school programs are available on tape. There are books about program utilization, and all schools receive supplementary printed materials.

"Magazine for Reckoners," introduced in 1966, was an innovation since it used radio for direct instruction.[69] A typical program had several sections which, for example, after dealing with the history of mathematics and introducing algebra, might conclude with a student contest. The section on the history of mathematics in one September 1968 program was described as follows: "A witty scene describing how men learned to count. A conversation between two bear-hunters: father and son. The roots of mathematics in the primeval ages of mankind. The need of men to know and express the amount of food, the number of game and enemies, etc. The sequence has an instructive core, but is presented in the form of a dramatized anecdote."

In 1970 a four-part series for the fifth form, "The Liberation Struggle," included interviews with people who had taken part in World War II. "Thus our radio strives to provide young people with a comprehensive and concise idea of the greatness and importance of the events that transformed the lives of the Czech and Slovak peoples."[70]

In-school television began in 1953, the year television went on the air, although regular broadcasts did not start until 1958.[71] These included a half-hour program for nursery schools; broadcasts on biology and science for eighth and ninth grades; and programs on history, chemistry, biology, music, and natural science. Some were scheduled during school hours and others right after school, so that children could view them with their teachers without interrupting classes. Presentation techniques included puppets (in 1960 there were fifteen professional and over 2,000 amateur puppet ensembles in Czechoslovakia), storytellers, pictures, demonstrations, and clowns. At present programs are available for all ages from nursery school to mid-teens.

Both media have out-of-school programs for children. In 1962 a Czech writer observed that the two most popular radio programs were the evening news and the Sunday afternoon fairy tale, the latter being heard not only by children but by their elders too. This might be an implied criticism of the rest of the programming: "Maybe listeners like the fairy-tale because it brings them things that they do not find in many spoken programs: delightful speech, easy structure and a clear solution."[72] At any rate, Czechoslovak radio still offers fairy tales ("to educate children for the socialist society"), and since 1961 has had "Good Night Children" as an early evening fixture. At a meeting of youth broadcasters from Bulgaria, Czechoslovakia, Hungary, Mongolia, Poland, Romania, the Soviet Union, and Yugoslavia, it was concluded that television had not eliminated the appeal of radio for young people. One reason was that "transistor receivers (preferred by young people) and radio sets in public places, cars and means of public transport have made radio more omnipresent than before."

The chief editor of broadcasts for children and youth showed insight in noting certain differences between young people and adults.* "Today's youth," he wrote, "does not consider social reality to be something for

* Ferdinand Smrčka, "The Pedagogical Radio Propaganda," *OIRT Review* 1964/3, pp. 3–5. For comparable viewpoints from the Soviet Union, see pp. 135–136.

which it should be grateful to adults, but a simple, necessary and obvious reality whose shortcomings they criticize very sharply. They do not compare the actual situation with the past, but with the ideal which the community sets itself."

Radio programs for young people have included talks, interviews, readings from fiction, and dramatizations. Their director indicated awareness of the need for authenticity—along with a lack of concern for privacy—when he wrote: "Talks recorded by a hidden microphone in the consulting room of pediatrists or psychological consulting centres are very effective, but cannot be transmitted without a commentary." The "Hvězda" network, a nationwide service in both Czech and Slovak, allocates the time from 1:00 to 6:00 P.M. to programs for youth, with short news items (including local cut-ins) and rock-and-roll music.

In 1961 the head of young people's programs expressed certain concerns about children's television shared by observers in many countries.[73] "Articles by physicians, psychologists and pedagogues appearing in Western magazines often point out the ill effects of television on the development of children." Unfortunately, "by sitting in front of a TV set the child learns only to accept passively a ready-made programme which captures all its senses, causing it to discard books and more complicated toys without interest. . . ." To avoid this, the writer went on, Czechoslovak television encourages children to be active. Small children are asked to draw or to find mistakes in pictures shown on the program. Older children can reply to questions. At all times children should be led from the "active viewing of programmes, to creative work of their own after the programme is finished." The author also suggested that parents permit their children to watch only suitable programs and that in any case viewing be limited: small children should go to bed at 8 P.M., right after the news.

In 1964 television began "Stories of Life," which reviewed the accomplishments of the past in such fields as science, exploration, and sports.[74] A 1970 news release reported that children often said, "I won't go to bed if the TV has not said good night to me yet!" At that time "Good Night" programs were broadcast on Sundays, Tuesdays, and Thursdays but by 1973 there were programs every evening.[75] In 1972 I saw some of these productions. A combination of cartoon sequences and live actors, they were very well done, as usually is the case with such programs in the socialist world. One that impressed me particularly told a charming story with the moral that one should not needlessly kill wildlife.

Children often go on the air to act, sing, play, or be interviewed. For the fifteenth anniversary of the Czechoslovak Pioneer Organization, an entire day from 7:00 A.M. to 9:00 P.M. was devoted to broadcasts by, for, or about children—"and there was not a single protest."[76] In "Our Country," broadcast once a month on Sunday mornings, Czech and Slovak children compete to demonstrate their knowledge of the other part of the republic regarding its music, theater, technology, literature, nature, and history. The programs include references to those who "either remember or directly participated in the liberation struggles."[77]

Young people's programs underwent changes during the liberalization period. Some broadcasts even criticized the party structure as too rigid and condemned the regime's approach to the younger generation. A Czechoslovak sociologist wrote: "The young need more freedom of expression because they have ceased to think." A comparison of Radio Prague programs during the first weeks of February in 1963 and 1967 revealed that programs for youth underwent the greatest changes of all. For one thing, the state had taken the place of the party. Furthermore, current popular music, which so largely determines the character of radio, had been ingeniously worked into youth programs to make them more attractive.

But by 1970 the emphasis had changed back. In connection with the twenty-fifth anniversary of the end of World War II and the Lenin centenary, it was observed that programs for youth will "systematically follow both anniversaries, in particular . . . [addressing] adolescents who in the past years were influenced by great illusions and unrealistic ideas about the world. . . . The 25th anniversary of the liberation will thus afford an opportunity to remind our youth of the historic and decisive role played by the Soviet Union in the termination of the Second World War. The Leninist theme . . . will also be utilized to promote the education of our future generation, the rehabilitation in the eyes of young people of the ideas of communist society and the validity of the Marx-Leninist theory in the contemporary world divided into classes."[78]

Adult Education

Radio and television are used extensively in adult education. A government document published in 1963 emphasized the need to follow up school experiences, stating that "the main aim of all adult education for working people in Czechoslovakia is to raise their qualifications. . . . This means to acquaint without delay the broad masses of the working people with the latest developments of science and technology."[79] A television representative was included on the Central Commission for the Education of the Working People set up by the Ministry of Education and Culture in 1963, since television was regarded as "inseparably linked with the main educational endeavours of the whole of society. The role and function of television is understood to be an indivisible part of the instruments of our cultural policy."

In 1966 the chief of research and documentation in the National Institute of Adult Education in Bratislava wrote that "the high level of the country's industrialisation calls for an ever-greater number of qualified experts in various trades to enter industry and agriculture, and makes it necessary for the most able working people with the required practical experience to improve their general and specialised knowledge." The same year, during a UNESCO meeting in Prague, a Czech academician spoke of "the dangers of a new wave of illiteracy within a highly differentiated industrial society. Film, radio and television, however, are in a position to rapidly and effectively fight this situation, regardless of its extent and its conditions."[80]

The deputy program director of the second television network, which emphasizes education, wrote in 1972 that educational programs, "intended to provide instruction, competent information and up-to-date knowledge, constitute a component part of the programmes of perhaps all television organizations of the world with the exception of purely commercial capitalist channels."[81] In addition to presenting general information, he went on, "socialist television also considers it its task to *contribute to their education*, to spread the ideas of marxism, [and] to promote the viewer's world outlook. Thus, educational broadcasts are becoming a necessary and regular component of the programme of all television organizations in socialist countries."

Educational programs on Czechoslovak television benefit from long-term planning.[82] Typically, the staff member in charge of a project develops it cooperatively with related educational institutions and agencies, later involving media experts in a process which may take six months or longer for a major series. Although they are paid, most participants regard their telecasts as "an honour and social necessity" to serve "the common cause of socialism." Those taking part are carefully chosen and then given some broadcast training. Research has shown that the best time for adult education materials is 6:00 P.M. or 10:00 P.M., "although it must be assumed that at that [later] time the viewers' power of absorption is reduced."

Both radio and television have language courses.[83] Television began language instruction in 1960 with Russian, later adding English, German, Spanish, and French. (All schools teach both Russian and English.) The radio Spanish course in 1964 included a competition in which the ten finalists went to Prague for oral examinations consisting of conversations in Spanish and questions on Cuban history, with a member of the Cuban embassy in Prague as one of the judges. The winners received two-week trips to Cuba.

There are several graded series of Russian lessons on television, each consisting of thirty half-hour programs repeated twice at different hours, in separate Czech and Slovak versions, with native Russians reading the Russian texts. Visual aids include blackboards, films, and drawings. "From the beginning the viewers were led to understand, speak and think in the language of the course. The content of the lesson was summarized at the end, usually in the form of dialogue, and then homework was given."[84] Although most viewing is on an individual basis, there is group viewing in village cultural centers with teachers to assist. Registrants can take final examinations for credit. For a French course over 100,000 manuals were sold, while 130,000 brochures were distributed in connection with an English series.[85]

Television has courses at the secondary level to help working adults reinforce their school studies, much like those in the Soviet Union, Poland, and the German Democratic Republic, along with broadcasts for workers studying for school-leaving examinations.[86] Subjects include mathematics, physics, biology, chemistry, geometry, and geology, taught by university professors, along with courses in such practical subjects as dairying and the use of the slide rule. The programs, which vary in length from twenty to forty minutes, are broadcast alternate weeks, and each lesson is given twice, once in the morning and once in the evening. There are consultation centers in some cities to which students may come for advice and assistance. However, there are no examinations or certificates for these programs, since their purpose is to provide knowledge and skills to those who need them, rather than to contribute toward formal schooling requirements.

Although Czechoslovakia has had radio and television "universities" for some years, their programs are informal rather than credit oriented. Since 1949 the Radio University has dealt with such subjects as atomic energy, biochemistry, geophysics, music, sociology, and psychology.[87] The term "Television University" was introduced in 1955, although at times its programs have been canceled because of greater viewer interest in dramatic and entertainment broadcasts, films, and sports transmissions.[88] During late afternoon and early evening hours the Television University may present information on nutrition, science, parent education, and history. In 1960–1961 "Science and Technology on the Way to Man's Progress" reviewed discoveries of the late nineteenth and early twentieth centuries. During the first half of 1963 a five-part series, "Tomorrow Starts Today," discussed "the main ideas of building socialism in Czechoslovakia." In March 1968 an eight-part Television University cycle, "Man among People," dealt with the psychology of children, adolescents, and adults.[89] Various audiovisual devices are used to make such programs more than talks, and there are answers to viewers' questions.

Generational problems are universal. In 1962 a news release announcing a radio series about parent education referred to the problem of relating the older to the younger generation.[90] Many parents had learned that "their children are not as they imagined them to be and do not attain successes they could achieve if they were only a little more diligent." One woman listener wrote that her son "is rude and irresponsible in every respect." Another reported that although she and her seven siblings had pleased their parents by learning well, her own daughter had no interest in schooling. But some parents said that what they wanted were not discussions of abnormalities but "talks on daily problems with normal children."

In 1963 radio offered a series of talks by architects on house construction and the modernizing of old homes.[91] In 1964 Bratislava had a television cycle, "Man—the Creator of Beauty," consisting of twenty broadcasts dealing with successive periods in the history of the plastic arts.[92] In the same year, to mark the twentieth anniversary of the 1944 uprising in Slovakia, there were special programs on both radio and television. "Great attention was also devoted to depicting the transformations undergone by the formerly backward Slovakia during the twenty years of the people's rule."[93]

Television has used quiz programs to present information to general audiences.[94] "Ten Times Reply" consisted of ten telecasts during which ten people competed in ten areas of knowledge in which they were not professionally involved. Each contestant was asked one question per evening, the questions becoming progressively more difficult. Other contests have dealt with the history and development of different parts of the country, national historical figures, and great works of literature, music, and art. The project descriptions make it appear that Czechoslovak telecasters have tried ingeniously to employ entertainment techniques in general educational programs.

In 1972 I saw an interesting program about the art and architecture of an old castle. The program began with some paintings, filmed in their original baroque settings and accompanied by a background of appropriate music. Later there were excerpts from operas in settings similar to the artworks being discussed. Three art experts, in addition to constituting a discussion panel, took the audience on walking tours of the building. It was an effective production.

Programs of adult education, like all the rest, were affected by the Prague Spring. Between 1963 and 1967 Radio Prague dropped much of its direct propaganda emphasis and developed series like "Club of Engaged Thinking," to which people were invited to send questions for discussion by participants prepared even to criticize party-oriented thinking and to praise objectivity. In May 1968 Czechoslovak television introduced a weekly thirty-minute series, "Between Us," led in turn by four well-known journalists, on which there were some very frank discussions by prominent people. The programs were transmitted live, the questions not determined in advance, and the answers spontaneous.[95] *The Listener* reported that television was making "a major contribution in transforming a state, in liberating a people."[96]

But in due course the traditionalists returned to control, and an official release in 1970 explained their plans: "In their broadcasts our television publicists will try to analyze the key events of the past 25 years by means of specific television forms intended to help especially the young generation to find the correct approach as well as the correct evaluation of the enormous work done by the Party since 1945. . . . In the [Lenin] jubilee year the chief attention . . . will be centered on economic problems and the involved and effective promotion of the constructive Party efforts to lead our society out of its prolonged crisis."[97] Since 1970, "after the end of the political crisis," economics courses have been added for party leaders, workers, and peasants.[98]

Music

Beethoven is reported to have said that the Bohemians are the best musicians in Europe, while the head of Czechoslovak radio music recently wrote that the country's motto is "Every Czech a musician." However this may be, the musical traditions of Czechoslovakia are among the best.

In 1964 a member of the Radio Music Education Department reviewed the methods used to develop interest in serious music. It was important, he said, to broadcast from concert halls: "In comparison with a recording, a live relay has the undeniable advantage that it turns the listener into a direct participant in an artistic performance, affording him also the acoustic atmosphere of a concert hall which increases the sensation of listening to music."[99] Another person wrote that live relays were particularly attractive to "provincial listeners to whom they offer the possibility of being present."[100] Even in Czechoslovakia the audience for concert music needs to be built. The author went on: "Raising of the level of musical taste of the public is a question of a long-term educational process. No efforts should be spared because the character of the concert audiences and listeners depends also on the radio."

The director of music for Czechoslovak radio—whose name, incidentally, is Antonín Dvořák—told an OIRT music meeting in Moscow early in 1972 that the current trend in his country was to emphasize the "social-political orientation" of music, in order to deal with "the relations prevailing between music and society."[101]

Music education for adults is a continuing assignment of Czechoslovak radio, which has offered the "People's Conservatory," "Evening Talks on Music," "The Great Masters of Czech Music," "Chapters from the History of German Music," "Chapters from the History of Russian Music," and "Do Not Be Afraid of Modern Music"—a genre which a member of the Music Department staff said people would like if "presented in a suitable and interesting manner."[102] A radio staff member and OIRT official wrote that one way to win support for twentieth-century music was to have the composers themselves on the air.[103] In

1972 the director of radio music re-emphasized the importance of presenting serious music to the widest possible audience.[104]

The serious music repertoire is extensive. It includes relays of concerts by the broadcasting and other orchestras—and Czechoslovakia has a number of very fine symphony orchestras.[105] There have been live FM relays of concerts by the Czech Philharmonic Orchestra; broadcasts of Brahms instrumental works recorded by the Berlin Philharmonic Orchestra under Herbert von Karajan; complete cycles of the Mahler symphonies; the recorded repertoire of Arturo Toscanini; and presentations of Wagner performances from the Bayreuth Festival.

The observance of anniversaries is pressed to the point of monotony.[106] There were special programs for the 70th birthday of Bohuslav Martinů; the 5th anniversary of the death of Arthur Honegger; the 120th anniversary of the birth and the 60th anniversary of the death of Antonín Dvořák; the 50th birthday of the contemporary Polish composer Witold Lutoslawski; the 140th anniversary of the birth and the 80th and 85th anniversaries of the death of Bedřich Smetana; the 100th anniversary of the birth and the 40th anniversary of the death of Leoš Janáček; the 210th birthday of Mozart (who rated a Mozart Week); the 130th anniversary of the birth and the 75th anniversary of the death of Tchaikovsky; and an elaborate cycle in 1970 to mark the 200th anniversary of the birth of Beethoven, concluded with a broadcast from Leipzig of the Ninth Symphony performed by the Gewandhaus Orchestra.

Political occasions also are noted. In 1968 programs marked the 50th anniversary of the founding of the Czechoslovak Republic.[107] To observe the 50th anniversary of the Czechoslovak Communist party radio had "many portraits" of composers whose music could somehow be related to party policy.[108] In 1970, in connection with the 25th anniversary of liberation, radio had several cycles illustrating musical developments during the previous quarter century, plus "Combatant Music" by postwar Czech and Slovak composers.[109]

There are competitions too, such as the one for folk bands in 1961.[110] To observe its own 40th anniversary in 1963, Czechoslovak radio had a contest for the best "Song of Friendship" to "express the idea of friendship and peaceful co-existence among nations."[111] There were entries by 300 composers from twenty-three countries, including not only the socialist countries but also Belgium, Brazil, France, Greece, Ireland, Italy, Japan, Great Britain, New Zealand, and the United States. The first and second prizes, consisting of three-week visits to Czechoslovakia, were awarded to British and French contestants.[112] To commemorate the 40th anniversary of the founding of the broadcasting symphony orchestra, there was a competition for symphonic works.[113] In September 1970 a radio competition for young performers was held before a jury of musicians from Bulgaria, Czechoslovakia, Yugoslavia, and the USSR. The winners were from Czechoslovakia, Hungary, Japan, Poland, West Germany, and the USSR.[114] In 1971 Radio Bratislava had a competition for the best recordings of folk music, with entries from sixteen countries, including Bulgaria, Finland, Hungary, Poland, Romania, Yugoslavia, and the USSR.[115]

The various musical festivals of Czechoslovakia are another program source. There has been a Prague Spring Music Festival every year since 1945.[116] In 1961 Leopold Stokowski and Paul Hindemith were among guest conductors from the West, while in 1965 the Cleveland Orchestra took part under George Szell. Herbert von Karajan and Wolfgang Sawallisch also have appeared. Many of these programs are recorded for use by stations in other parts of the world, including the United States.[117] Czechoslovakia broadcasts recordings of festivals, particularly those held in foreign socialist countries, such as the Soviet "Russian Winter" and "White Nights," the Berlin Biennial of Contemporary Music, and the Hungarian "Liszt-Bartŏk" festival.[118]

Czechoslovakia also has many programs of entertainment music, and takes part in the annual OIRT International Festival of Light and Dance Music in Leipzig.[119] There was a five-day International Jazz Festival in Prague in 1965, much of which was broadcast and recorded for distribution abroad.[120] In 1967 a complete Louis Armstrong concert in Prague was televised and subsequently rebroadcast several times. But some popular music is ideologically unacceptable. A Reuters news dispatch from Prague in 1969 quoted the deputy director of Prague television as saying: "Energetically we will take steps to end these beat programmes where most of the songs are sung in English." In November of the same year the party newspaper *Rudé Právo* sharply criticized a program on the first radio network as too "Western" in approach, complained about introducing English words into Czech presentations, and objected to certain "questionable songs." One selection was described as "open propaganda of a religious and rather demagogical nature. I have nothing against those who believe in God, as long as they act like good citizens otherwise. . . . But that which belongs in church does not belong in the programs of a state communications medium. . . . The issue is not just this one song, which does not amount to much anyway. The issue is a fundamental one. It is a question as to whether there is someone who controls what is being broadcast and what is included in this 'Top 20' of ours." But as noted above, the Czechoslovaks are keenly aware of the competition between themselves and various foreign broadcasters, and hoping to attract and hold the youth audience, schedule much contemporary music, particularly between 1:00 and 6:00 P.M. on the "Hvĕzda" radio network.

Drama, Literature, Films, Documentaries, and Sports

Czechoslovak broadcasters always have stressed the ideological aspects of their programs, particularly since 1968. A spokesman for the department that produces radio programs about literature wrote in 1972 that socialist society should influence "the rational and emotional aspects of human perceptivity," so as to affect "human ideas on life and the world, to foster man's sensibility and taste."[121] Yet one reason for the many programs on literature and drama is the fact that their format permits points of view not in complete agreement with the regime to be expressed more readily than is possible on straightforward news or discussion broadcasts.

The chief editor of literary-dramatic broadcasts for Radio Bratislava believes that radio can "revive the category of artistic reading and recitation," and quoted a Czechoslovak writer to illustrate his point: "The poetic word becomes live on the radio. This invention has raised it from lyrical books and enabled it to resound again."[122] Reading cycles on radio are intended to "acquaint listeners with outstanding works of our literary heritage and to introduce the best contemporary works which have something important to say about the life of today, as well as some artistically significant books which are less known or somewhat neglected."[123]

There are programs each week on which both Czechoslovak and foreign authors are read, such as Gogol's *Taras Bulba*; Robert Louis Stevenson's *Dr. Jekyll and Mr. Hyde*; and Dickens's *Pickwick Papers*.[124] When a six-month cycle of "educational-esthetic" broadcasts was announced in 1963, it was explained that "The Small School of Poetry" was to introduce people to poetry, show them how to read it, and help them develop "fuller understanding of its intellectual and emotional wealth."[125] At the time of the fiftieth anniversary of the Czechoslovak state a cycle of nine half-hour broadcasts reviewed national trends in poetry during the previous half century.[126] Two years later, in connection with the twenty-fifth anniversary of the liberation of Czechoslovakia and the one hundredth anniversary of the birth of Lenin, the Department of Artistic Spoken Programmes prepared the cycles "Man at the End of War," "25 Years of Czech Prose," and "Portraits of the Worker in Czech Poetry."[127]

Under the title "Literary Instructive Broadcasts," radio has book reviews.[128] Very ambitious was the series in 1971 and 1972 called "We Wish for a New Life in the World!" subtitled "A Hundred Years of Workers' Destinies as Reflected in Literature," consisting of twelve thirty-minute programs "providing a true picture of the turning points in the development of our workers' movement while simultaneously evaluating our realistic fiction of the 19th and 20th centuries." Along with this went "Great Personalities of Soviet Literature" and "Scandals of World Literature," of which the latter devoted twenty-five programs to a study of "the close relations of truly great literature to social development and the share of literature in the mobilization of progressive ideas."

Television has a weekly Sunday "Minutes of Poetry," which in 1972 took up socialist poetry, including works by the USSR's Yevtushenko.[129] I was much impressed by one of these in September 1972. Against a rear-screen projected water scene and music from Debussy's "Girl with the Flaxen Hair," a professional actor read with great feeling.

An American observer surveying broadcasting in any European country immediately notices that the growth of television has not reduced the quantity or quality of radio drama. One reason for this is the lower value placed on audience ratings. European broadcasting organizations receive much or all of their income from license fees, and since radio's share has not been reduced by the increased popularity of television, funds still are available for extensive dramatic productions. Another reason is the emphasis on education and culture: radio drama is continued because it has artistic value.

Two articles illustrate the Czechoslovak point of view. In 1962, before television became a factor, someone wrote that "the radio play has a special artistic genre."[130] Without such "exterior wrappings" as scenery and visible action, words can "bring to life the listener's phantasy, correspond closely to the conceptions and images of the words preserved inside them, activizing and arousing them to life." In 1970 a theater

critic proudly stated that Slovak radio plays were "an important component of this country's national culture" and that they "concentrate on
man's internal world, on his existential problems."[131]

The radio dramatic repertoire is extensive, and ideology is often—
though not always—emphasized. One Czech play was a "satire on the
militarist and revanchist" policies of some Western countries.[132] In 1953
"The Kitchen," by the British author Arnold Wesker, was described as
"a play written in a capitalist society about the capitalist society, i.e.,
what becomes of people for whom earning money is the centre of their
lives."[133] Between 1967 and 1969 more than forty original plays were
presented by Slovak radio, and in one month in 1969 the First Festival
of Slovak Radio Plays included fourteen original productions.[134]

Domestic and international festivals are organized involving all the
Eastern and some Western European countries.[135] The International
Radio Play Review, begun in 1966, and now under joint OIRT and
EBU auspices, has participants from many countries. In 1968, when
there were ninety-seven entries, the winners were from Belgium, Denmark, Great Britain, Italy, Japan, New Zealand, Switzerland, West Germany, and Yugoslavia. In 1970, to "promote the development of creative
activity," the director of Czech Radio announced competitions for a
play and a musical work to deal with "the 25th anniversary of the liberation of Czechoslovakia by the Soviet army."[136] The announcement
stated: "The themes of the competition works are . . . to be based on
the progressive traditions . . of the Czech and Slovak nations, [are
to] deal with past and present social conflicts, and [should] present a
picture of the socialist development of Czechoslovak society or a many-
sided image of contemporary man."

There is both live and recorded television drama from studios—and
occasionally theaters—in Prague, Ostrava, Brno, Plzeň, and elsewhere.[137]
In 1961 an adaptation of František Kožik's book *The Law of Faithful
Guards* told the story of a young Prague boy who had an adjustment
problem when he transferred to a village school. The plot emphasized
the role of a teacher who provided leadership in helping students develop
the correct attitude toward life.[138] In 1964 there were dramatizations of
Sergeant Grischa's Justice, based on the novel by Arnold Zweig; *Corruption in the Palace of Justice*, by Hugo Betti, showing "the crooked morale
of law and justice in fascist Italy"; a live relay from a Brno theater of
The Green Fields by the American Marc Connelly; and a dramatization

of Robert Louis Stevenson's *The Strange Case of Dr. Jekyll and Mr. Hyde*.[139] There were series too, such as the original "Three Men in a Cottage," broadcast in eighteen monthly installments during the early 1960s, which depicted "problems of a contemporary cooperative village."[140]

A day devoted to Soviet television, on December 7, 1967, included a dramatization of Soviet intelligence activities during World War II.[141] Intelligence activities also were the basis for a thirteen-part series adapted from German Democratic Television which told about a German participant in the French resistance during World War II.[142] During the period of liberalization, there was a relaxation of controls which previously had been stricter for the broadcast media with their mass audiences than for the theaters with more limited clientele. But this was changed when the conservatives returned to power. For the Lenin jubilee in 1970 there were original dramatic works: Karvaš's trilogy, *The Bastion*, dealing with "the social and revolutionary struggle of the Slovak working people," and *Murder Gorge*, about "the heroism of honest people during the Second World War." There also were repeat performances of plays by Russian classical authors, along with contemporary Soviet productions based on episodes from the life of Lenin.[143]

High interest in film is shown by programs about it on radio. "Do You Know World Film Personalities?" broadcast in 1967, reviewed the contributions of producers like the American Orson Welles, the Italians Michelangelo M. Antonioni and Federico Fellini, the Swede Ingmar Bergman, and the Pole Andrzej Wajda. There also were references to actors Henry Fonda and Claudia Cardinale, as well as some Czechoslovak stars.[144]

Television broadcasts cinema films along with films produced especially for television. In 1962 "The Theater and Film" presented outstanding Soviet, British, and American films. There were Soviet adaptations of Gogol's *Dead Souls* and Shakespeare's *Romeo and Juliet* and *The Taming of the Shrew*; an American version of Rostand's *Cyrano de Bergerac*; and English versions of *The Importance of Being Earnest* and *Hamlet*. Normally, films are dubbed into Czech or Slovak, although a few are broadcast with the original sound track late in the evening for people wishing to learn languages. In September 1972 I saw portions of a Russian-made version of Tolstoy's *War and Peace* which had been dubbed into Czech.[145]

Television films are made by the broadcasting organization as well as by other film units in the country. Czechoslovak Television produced "Zoo Variety" in Brno about zoo animals.[146] Short portraits of native singers and instrumentalists, some in color in anticipation of color television, were recorded in 1971.[147] There also were films on sculpture, creative art ("Stone, Iron, and Concrete"), and music ("Music of Seven Countries," in eight parts). Short Film in Prague did programs for the second network on science (modern medical achievements, transportation) and light music.[148]

Ostrava television produced the documentary "The Dispatcher and a Girl from the Settlement" by the Czech writer Jaroslav Dietl, portraying the life of a miner's family, with musical accompaniment "provided by a miners' brass band."[149] A Network II series, "We Travel throughout the World," included films by Czech producers about Mongolia, Romania, the USSR, Ireland, Alaska, and Africa. When timber was floated down the Vltava River for the last time, television recorded the event.

On September 15, 1969, Prague television carried a seventy-five–minute Soviet documentary, "Czechoslovakia, A Year of Trials," dubbed into Czech. After flashbacks to 1918, the film showed the occupation of Czechoslovakia by Nazi Germany in 1938, its liberation by the Soviet army in 1945, and the victory of communism in 1948. The program explained that there had been much activity by a right-wing antisocialist group preceding the 1968 invasion. The announcer pointed out that by failing to oppose various opportunist and antisocialist forces, the leaders of the Czechoslovak Communist party had allowed these dissidents to gain control of the mass media. Therefore, the Warsaw Pact countries had to defend socialism by sending in troops. In conclusion the announcer said: "The Czechoslovak year of trials belongs to the past. However, problems and difficulties still exist, but socialism will dispose and finally erase all false demagogic slogans." Telefilms also are acquired from Italy, the BBC (*The Forsyte Saga*), and the United States, examples of the latter being *Bonanza, Flipper, Mr. Ed, Alfred Hitchcock Presents*, and some New York Philharmonic concerts with Leonard Bernstein.

In 1961 the Political Information Department of Czechoslovak Television was responsible for broadcasts pertaining to "the whole sphere of physical education, sports, and military education."[150] Czechoslovaks take an affirmative attitude toward the broadcasting of spectator sports. One writer stated in 1961 that "sports broadcasts should not only satisfy the interests of fans," but also should encourage active participation in sports events.[151] Accordingly, Czechoslovak radio organized the Youth Cup in Light Athletics in which 6,000 young people took part. By 1970 there were 13,000 entrants from 430 schools in the Czechoslovak Radio Cup Competition, whose purpose was to contribute "to the promotion of basic athletic disciplines among youth."[152]

A Czechoslovak television representative provided an interesting rationale for sports broadcasts.[153] Play-by-play accounts, he wrote, should do three things: they should inform; they should propagate and instruct; and they should entertain. The first function needed no explanation. As to the second, "every relay should be a mass instruction for thousands of sportsmen." Figure skating and handball were two sports whose popularity he ascribed to television. "It is also our wish that all our relays be not only a school of the rules of the game concerned, but also of fair play and correct conduct on the field and beyond the barriers. We wish to contribute considerably to the moral education of sportsmen." In regard to the third point, television wishes to entertain its viewers and "to provide them with thrilling and good entertainment after which they can return refreshed to their own work." Therefore, the article stated, a good sports commentator must have a "wide range of cultural-political knowledge"; know the sports he describes; be able to do so without "garrulousness"; avoid taking sides; speak fluently; be alert; and, have a "deep knowledge of the mother tongue and technique of speech."

An interesting sidelight on sports broadcasting was provided by an article in *Rudé Právo* on August 6, 1969, which accused certain television sportscasters of trying to "maliciously denigrate the prominent successes" of some East German athletes. The story said that the announcer, in broadcasting a track meet with European and American contestants, had credited the success of several GDR participants to drugs. After defending this practice as constituting "the introduction of scientific methods in sports," the article suggested sarcastically that the announcer should "find out where he can find some drugs permitting a serious evaluation of sports performances."

Czechoslovak radio and television cover domestic and international soccer, ice hockey, basketball, tennis, skiing, and skating contests, in addition to which sports items are reported on newscasts. Because of high interest, programming sometimes is planned around sports schedules, especially on Saturday and Sunday afternoons. Bilateral exchanges with other countries provide accounts of some international competitions, while Intervision and Eurovision bring others. In 1968 Czechoslovak television took 151 Eurovision programs, with a duration of 222 hours and 30 minutes, a major portion of which were Olympic Games transmissions from Grenoble, while in 1972 it relayed many contests from the Munich Olympic Games.

Sports coverage, in fact, is one of the brighter aspects of Czechoslovak television—probably because it has few, if any, political aspects. On several newscasts I noticed effective use of films of high jumping, relay races, soccer, basketball, and tennis. I was much impressed with the treatment given a motorcycle race. A diagram of the course was superimposed over a map of the country, and films showed various phases of the contest. Because a heavy rain had caused slippery roads and deep mud, the race was very exciting. In Moscow I saw an Intervision relay of an ice hockey game played in Prague by teams from Czechoslovakia and Canada. It was a lively contest with much crowd interest, since it took place only several days after Canada had won a close series from the Soviet Union. But the telecast had one incongruous touch: as was pointed out above, in addition to showing advertisements on the rinkside, television also carried shots of a timing device bearing the name of the Swiss manufacturer Longines.

Audience Research

In Czechoslovakia, as in all countries, letters from listeners provided the first basis for audience study. A research department was organized in 1946, but it was too small to do very much, although it did collect books on the mass media from other countries and circulate reports on them to the broadcasting staff.[154] In 1962 the emphasis still was on letters, and a short report on the television audience was headed "Viewers Write to the Czechoslovak Television."[155] But in the same year the deputy head of radio research wrote that the polling of listeners had begun, and explained how 900 volunteers were reporting the reactions of their groups.[156]

In 1966 the television research department called a selected panel each morning to learn what programs they had viewed the night before and how they reacted to them.[157] For a series on economics the panel might include a philosopher, several economists, and a producer-cameraman-soundman combination; and for a documentary a sociologist, a jurist, a judge, and an author, plus television producers and engineers. Each member would react in terms of his background, the findings being analyzed, and the results circulated within the broadcasting organization. Currently, television has a carefully chosen thousand-member group who keep diaries of their viewing. The results are analyzed by computer and made available eight days after the broadcasts take place.

Czechoslovakia is well supplied with radio and television receivers. In 1966 there were 3,179,143 radio and 2,375,105 television licenses, the rates per hundred of population being 26.78 and 16.61, respectively. Although by 1971 the number of radio licenses had dropped to 3,173,-653, the number of television licenses had increased to 3,091,243, the rates per hundred being 26.74 and 21.41, respectively (see Table 10). In 1966, 649,504 of the 3,179,143 radio licenses were for wired receivers, and by 1971 there were 687,290 wired receivers. Approximately 78 per cent of the television licenses were held by the 69 per cent of the population living in the Czech-speaking area of the country, and only 22 per cent by the 31 per cent in the Slovak portion. An American trade journal reported from Prague in July 1970 that Czechoslovakia was eighth among European nations in receiver distribution, since 99 per cent of its homes had radio sets and 83.8 per cent television sets.[158] This increase in television set ownership has taken place despite the fact that black-and-white receivers cost around 4,000 crowns and color sets 12,000 crowns, while the average monthly income is only 2,000 crowns. However, many families have more than one wage earner, which somewhat eases the burden.

A study made in the early 1960s indicated that in Bohemia people with access to television receivers averaged 5.37 hours of viewing per week, somewhat less than 1 hour a day, while in Slovakia the average viewer watched 16.58 hours per week or 2.4 hours a day.[159] The difference was explained on the grounds that in Slovakia television was newer and had greater appeal as a novelty, while in Bohemia there were more cultural centers, clubs, and other diverting activities. At a UNESCO mass media seminar in Prague in 1966, it was reported that the average Czechoslovak with a television set viewed it from 1½ to 3 hours a day, in addition to listening to the radio from 1½ to 2 hours a day.[160] Favorite viewing times were between 7:00 and 9:00 P.M.; but it should be noted that half the country's population then got up before 5:00 A.M., and only a minority after 6:00 A.M., so that a drop-off in viewing after 9:00 was to be expected.*

Research findings accord generally with those from other parts of the world. Between 1961 and 1963 a large sample reported their television program preferences as follows: films, 95.2 per cent; variety shows, 84.8 per cent; sports, 84.7 per cent; plays, 77.8 per cent; news and comment, 74 per cent; musical programs, 57 per cent; educational programs, 30.4 per cent; programs for farmers, 21.6 per cent; and opera and serious music, 15.5 per cent.[161]

Reflecting what may be a national inferiority complex about their country's cultural attainments, Americans are apt to believe that the average European is more prone to like serious music than is his American counterpart. But the figures do not support such conclusions. One reason only 15.5 per cent of the respondents reported preference for operatic and serious music was that 21.6 per cent of the sample seldom watched or listened to opera and 32.7 per cent never did. The greatest interest in such music, as one would expect, was among the upper socio-economic groups. Commenting on this low rating, the report observed: "This state of affairs is not in keeping with the rich national traditions of the Czech and Slovak people, nor does it correspond to the wide scope which exists in Czechoslovakia in this sphere."[162]

In 1966 the Czechoslovak program magazine invited its readers to report their reactions to the Saturday and Sunday evening television schedules.[163] The 14,000 respondents indicated preferences for various types of programs, and also recorded "extreme votes" for or against each program type. The results, though not highly scientific, provide some interesting data. A good majority of the respondents preferred entertainment programs to all others. Detective and adventure stories were first choice on Saturday evenings, receiving 70 points (including 43 extreme points for and only 0.3 extreme against). Other Saturday evening ratings included comedies, 31.5; humorous programs, 29; variety, 22.5; songs and music, 19; and old film comedies, 7. The most favored Sunday evening programs were feature films with 61 points (33 for and only 1.5 against). Other high preference categories were as follows: classical plays, 48; dramatic programs, 43; and operettas and musicals, 33. The

---

* The Robinson study found that in the middle 1960s the average person in Czechoslovakia did 65 minutes of primary and 71 minutes of secondary viewing, for a total of about 2¼ hours each day. See above, pp. 185–186.

category of "journalistic broadcasts" received a rating of −6.5; opera, −41 (2.1 for and 21 against); cultural life, −44; and poetry, −57.5 (0.6 for and 19.0 against).

Variety shows ranked high with viewers in villages, receiving lower ratings from respondents in larger cities and from the better educated. Younger viewers liked entertainment music, but respondents over fifty-nine years of age put it in eighth place. Old film comedies were very popular with viewers over sixty, although people between sixteen and twenty-four did not like them at all. Preferences for classical plays related to educational status. Although the vote was against opera 10 to 1, the report observed that those who liked it represented approximately 500,000 viewers, "an audience which would fill all European opera houses for an evening." Furthermore, while the vast majority preferred dance music, villagers and older people liked brass bands, and "the youngest viewers voted uncompromisingly for big beat." Taken together, these several sets of figures indicate that program preferences in Czecho-slovakia are much like those everywhere else.

Between May and December 1970 Radio Free Europe sponsored interviews by independent polling agencies on the domestic listening and viewing habits of 1,423 Czechoslovaks visiting Western countries.[164] It was found that the entire sample heard Czechoslovak radio programs, and that 54 per cent listened daily and 34 per cent several times each week. The favorite listening times were from 6:00 to 9:00 A.M., 11:00 A.M. to 1:00 P.M., and 3:00 to 11:00 P.M., with evening listening peaking between 7:00 and 8:00, when 54 per cent of the sample tuned in. Almost the entire sample, 97 per cent, viewed television—the largest percentage of the five countries covered by the survey (Czechoslovakia, Hungary, Poland, Rumania, and Bulgaria), with 31 per cent viewing daily and 43 per cent several times a week. Peak viewing came between 7:00 and 10:00 P.M., the highest rate of 90 per cent (again, the highest of the five countries covered) between 8:00 and 9:00 P.M.

Data from outside sources also show a fair amount of listening to programs from abroad. In 1971 the West German short-wave service reported that a survey of 16,000 Czechoslovaks found that 77 per cent preferred the Voice of America to all other foreign stations, although 52 per cent reported listening to Radio Free Europe.[165] An RFE publica-tion, on the other hand, indicated preference for its programs. RFE, which broadcasts over nineteen hours each day in Czech and Slovak, has periodically attempted to determine the size and nature of its audience by having independent research institutes in six Western European countries interview Czechoslovaks visiting temporarily in the West.[166] According to these reports, Czechoslovak listening to Western broadcasts increased greatly after the events of 1968. Whereas 37 per cent of the sample reported listening regularly to RFE before the invasion, 65 per cent did afterward, and there were increases for the other Western services too, including rises from 30 to 42 per cent for Radio Vienna, 26 to 35 per cent for the Voice of America, and 18 to 30 per cent for the BBC. Putting it another way, whereas before August 21, 1968, two out of three persons in Czechoslovakia heard at least one Western station regularly, after that date nine out of ten did so.

An RFE survey made shortly after the invasion provided additional data. Both before and after the occupation, newscasts were the most heard RFE programs, with commentaries a close second, interest in the latter increasing immediately after the arrival of the foreign troops. There was a strong preference for domestic over foreign items, especially following the invasion. Music was less attractive, while sports and religion trailed in preference. Beat and jazz music were preferred by young respondents and older popular hits by older persons, while opera and contemporary serious music received low ratings all around.

Another RFE study reported that 45 per cent of a sample of 1,214 Czechs and Slovaks interviewed between June 1971 and February 1972 listened regularly to Radio Free Europe, 26 per cent to Radio Luxembourg, 23 per cent to the BBC, 22 per cent to the Voice of America, and 18 per cent to Radio Vienna. Only 25 per cent of the sample did not listen regularly to any Western programs.[167] The average RFE listener spent thirty-four minutes a day listening to RFE programs.

Of the RFE listeners 81 per cent said they tuned to Radio Free Europe because it supplied "objectively, truthfully, and quickly" information suppressed by the domestic media. However, RFE listenership in Czechoslovakia underwent considerable variation between 1962 and 1971. Of the various samples interviewed, 33 per cent declared themselves regular listeners in 1962, and the number steadily increased up to a 1967 peak of 51 per cent. This dropped sharply to 37 per cent during the first part of 1968, at the time the domestic media were freest. Although it rose to 65 per cent immediately after the invasion, it declined to 45 per cent in 1971, coincidental with heavy jamming of Western programs, particularly those from Radio Free Europe.

External Broadcasting

Czechoslovak Radio indicated in 1967 that its external services were maintained "to inform foreign listeners about life in Czechoslovakia," about political, economic, and cultural developments, and "about the success and problems of socialist construction. The external broadcasts also present . . . the Czechoslovak point of view on world events. . . ."[168] Although discontinued during World War II, external broadcasting was resumed in May 1945, and by 1973 Czechoslovakia was broadcasting to Europe in Czech, Slovak, Arabic, English, French, German, Italian, and Spanish; to Africa in Czech, Slovak, Arabic, and English; to South Asia in Czech, Slovak, and English; to the Far East and Australia in Czech, Slovak, and English; to North America in Czech, Slovak, and English; and to Latin America in Czech, Slovak, Portuguese, and Spanish.[169] Programs for Europe were on the medium- and short-wave bands, and those for the rest of the world on short-wave.

The external, like the domestic services reacted to the Prague Spring interim, and delayed reverting to the pre-Dubček policies as long as possible. In January 1969 Radio Prague said it was trying to tell its listeners the truth about Czechoslovakia. English-language broadcasts to Africa and Asia stated that the only choices were support for the Svoboda-Dubček liberal line or "an open conflict which could have only tragic results." The Svoboda-Dubček team, said a program to Britain, "whatever reservations one may have about its policy," was vastly better than any conceivable alternative.

With its relatively small size and elongated shape, Czechoslovakia is well covered by radio and television signals from all its neighbors and by short-wave services from countries farther away. The man who was director general of Czechoslovak television from 1963 to 1968 reported that one way to get the hard currency necessary to purchase Eurovision coverage of important soccer matches was to point out that if the games were not carried at home the Czechoslovaks would tune them in from Austria.[170] North to south, Czechoslovakia's width varies from 180 to a mere 60 miles. Consequently, domestic broadcasts from Poland, West and East Germany, Austria, Hungary, and the USSR reach well into

Czechoslovak territory. Also available are the programs of Radio Free Europe, which broadcasts to Czechoslovakia on both the medium- and long-wave bands, as well as the short-wave services of the Voice of America and the BBC.

Periodically, Czechoslovakia jams the signals of stations it does not wish its citizens to hear. During a debate in the United Nations in 1959, a Czechoslovak spokesman joined a representative of the USSR in defending jamming as a means of opposing "an organized campaign of radio propaganda which constitutes a direct threat to peace, is based on misinterpretation, mixed information and distortion of facts, and is beamed daily for 11 full hours to my country" (see above, page 219). In 1968 the minister of the interior announced that Czechoslovakia had ceased jamming all officially recognized radio stations—although continuing to jam Radio Free Europe—but widespread jamming was resumed in 1969, and in 1972 in Prague I picked up jamming signals at various points on the dial.[171] In 1970 and 1971, when 2,821 Eastern Europeans visiting the West were asked why they did not listen to Radio Free Europe, 34 per cent of the nonlistening Czechoslovaks said that the jamming of RFE was a major factor.[172]

In December 1970 a twenty-eight-year-old American was arrested in Prague, accused of being a foreign agent, and sentenced to four years imprisonment on charges of subversion. The basis for his conviction was that he had once worked as a researcher for Radio Free Europe, the court ruling that since RFE was a foreign organization conducting subversive activities against Czechoslovakia, his work for them justified imprisonment.[173] But he was released after serving seven months of his sentence and returned to the United States.

Nevertheless, Czechoslovak broadcasting officials are quite aware that their people hear and view many foreign programs, and during conversations in September 1972 told me that for years one of their cardinal program objectives had been countering such impressions from abroad. Reinforcing this was the report of an American newspaperman who quoted a Communist party spokesman as saying: "We have nearly 2 million Czechs watching Austrian and West German television on our borders now. It is difficult to disrupt these programs from the technical point of view. If we disturb them, we disturb our own programs."[174]

Czechoslovakia exchanges programs and production teams with all the socialist and many other countries.[175] To mark the national holiday of

Romania in 1961, Czechoslovak radio had a Week of Romanian Music, with old and new folk, popular, and dance music.[176] The Week of Polish Culture, broadcast in 1964 to mark the twentieth anniversary of the People's Republic of Poland, presented a Polish play; readings from a Polish novel; musical compositions by such contemporary composers as Penderecki, Lutoslawski, and Szymanowski; and a youth-produced variety show broadcast by radio and television in both countries.[177] In connection with the national holiday of Hungary and to mark the twenty-fifth anniversary of that country's liberation by the Soviet army, Czechoslovak radio in 1970 broadcast thirty-nine programs about Hungarian life, music, literature, culture, and economics.[178] Tape recordings of Czechoslovak music and voice programs, including some of music festivals, are offered to foreign countries directly by the external broadcasting division, as well as through such agencies as the Broadcasting Foundation of America, which distributes them to many American—especially educational—stations.

In 1964 a Czechoslovak-Austrian agreement led to five radio quiz programs and a jointly produced entertainment telecast, the latter originating in a Czechoslovak castle.[179] But a news story from Vienna dated September 8, 1967, reported that Austrian broadcasting had canceled all Czechoslovak television programs until Czechoslovakia stopped "shooting refugees trying to flee the country" and returned the son of a refugee family to his parents in Austria. Until the dispute was resolved, said the Austrians, they would deal with Czechoslovakia only in news stories.

Relationships between Czechoslovakia and the Soviet Union have been predictably close. In 1965 the USSR broadcast "The Week of Czechoslovak Television" and Czechoslovakia scheduled "The Week of Soviet Television" as a part of the "Month of Czechoslovak-Soviet Friendship."[180] But in spite of such projects, high USSR officials often complained—even before 1968—that cooperation in the fields of television news and public affairs did not "properly" inform Czechoslovakia about Soviet life. In 1968 a protocol provided for a variety of exchanges, with special attention to the 150th birthday anniversary of Karl Marx and the 50th anniversary of the Soviet army.[181] Of somewhat different nature were the programs for Soviet soldiers in northern Bohemia broadcast by Czechoslovak radio during a fourteen-day period in December 1968. In the same month there was a television series, "Greetings to Friends," one program of which included three Czechoslovak army films in Russian plus some light entertainment. The USSR's Radio Volga, located in East Germany, regularly beams programs to Soviet troops stationed in Czechoslovakia.[182]

Plans for Czechoslovak-Soviet cooperation were renewed in an agreement signed in Prague March 2, 1970.[183] The leader of the Soviet delegation, who was the chairman of the USSR State Broadcasting Committee, said he was convinced the protocol would help "restore and strengthen those good and direct friendly relations which always existed between the mass information media of Czechoslovakia and the Soviet Union." He went on to point out that "unfortunately relations between our organizations were disturbed in August 1968 by the initiative of the rightists who work in the mass information media in Czechoslovakia."

Like most countries, Czechoslovakia sends musical groups on frequent trips abroad. Its Radio Symphony Orchestra visited West Germany, Switzerland, and France in 1961.[184] In 1965 its String Quartet went to the Scandinavian countries, Radio Jazz Orchestra to East Berlin, and Radio Symphony Orchestra, Radio Choir, and Ballet Corps to Italy.[185] The following year the Radio Symphony Orchestra toured West Germany playing music by Russian, French, Czech, Belgian, and Austrian composers.[186] In 1967, to mark the 1,000th anniversary of the founding of the Mont-Saint-Michel monastery in France, the Radio Symphony Orchestra and Choir gave a performance of Bach's B Minor Mass in the monastery, the performance being relayed live by Czechoslovak radio.[187] In 1970 the Symphony Orchestra gave concerts of Czech and Soviet music in Poland.[188]

For some years Czechoslovakia has had exchanges with Eurovision (see Tables 1 and 2). In 1960, though originating no programs, it received 73 broadcasts with a total duration of 68 hours. The next year it originated 11 programs (23 hr.) while receiving 41 programs (62 hr.). In 1967 13 programs were originated (28 hr.) and 53 programs received (77 hr., 45 min.). In 1968, an Olympic Games year, while only 4 programs (5 hr.) were originated, 151 programs (222 hr., 30 min.) were received. (During the invasion Intervision stations received a great deal of Western film about the Czech events, which they may have collected for use by their security agents in identifying demonstrators, rather than for broadcasting.) The number increased slightly the following year, since in 1969 Czechoslovakia originated 29 programs (47 hr.) while receiving 155 programs (222 hr., 45 min.). The 1972 figures, however, showed 36 programs originated (83 hr., 30 min.) and 142 programs received (277 hr., 15 min.). Intervision reported that in 1971 Czechoslovakia contributed 10 programs to Eurovision (25 hr., 29 min.), while receiving 69 programs (140 hr., 38 min.). The corresponding figures for 1972 were 42 programs contributed (94 hr., 52 min.) and 42 programs received (104 hr., 44 min.).

Despite close ties with the socialist countries, Czechoslovakia has actively promoted international festivals involving East and West, the outstanding example being the Prague Television Festival held annually since 1964. Described as an unofficial link between Eurovision and Intervision, it has entries from all over the world.[189] First-year winners included two quite dissimilar American productions, one featuring Jackie Gleason and the other Leonard Bernstein.[190] In the sixth festival in 1969, which had the motto, "the television screen at the service of better understanding among nations," forty-three films from thirty-three countries were entered, and awards were given to programs from Belgium, Bulgaria, Czechoslovakia, Denmark, France, the German Democratic Republic, the German Federal Republic, Italy, Japan, the United Kingdom, and the USSR.[191] However, the Club of Czech Television Critics announced at the opening press conference of the 1969 Festival that its members would not participate in judging that year, because situations might arise "to which motives other than purely professional may be attributed." Their statement probably was a reference to the entries from the Soviet Union.

IX

Hungarian People's Republic

Hungary regards itself as a Central rather than an Eastern European country, and substantiates this claim by citing both geography and history. Surely Budapest is more like Vienna or Munich than are most Eastern European capitals, and a visitor immediately becomes aware of these similarities—though not because of language, since Hungarian is a unique tongue. In any case, the 1956 Revolution was an important determinant of Hungary's role in the socialist bloc. It also involved broadcasting, since some programs beamed to Hungary by Radio Free Europe led to international concerns and investigations.

Facts about Hungary

The Hungarian People's Republic is bordered by Czechoslovakia on the north, Austria on the west, Yugoslavia on the south, Romania on the east, and the Soviet Union on the northeast. Its area of 35,919 square miles is about the size of the state of Indiana (36,291 square miles). The population in 1971 was 10,347,000, of whom 60 per cent lived in rural and 40 per cent in urban areas. Budapest, the capital, with approximately 2,000,000 residents, is the largest city.[1]

The major religious groups are the Roman Catholics (70 per cent), Calvinists (21 per cent), and Lutherans (4.3 per cent). Hungarians (Magyars) compose about 96 per cent of the population, with minority nationalities including Germans, Slovaks, Gypsies, Serbs, Croats, and Romanians. The Hungarian language, which uses the Latin alphabet and

361

has a historical relationship to Finnish, Lappish, and Estonian, is quite different from those used in the other countries of the socialist bloc. It is not mutually understandable with any other language.

Budapest is a very pleasant city. Its setting on the banks of the Danube gives it a head start for attractiveness, but the Hungarians have not left things to chance: buildings are in good repair, shop windows attractive, sales people accommodating, and streets clean. Its principal tourist hotels are well maintained, and have excellent food and service. Such conveniences as Western European newspapers are readily available. I was told that diplomatic personnel from other Eastern European countries look forward to being posted in Budapest.

The first Hungarian Republic was founded during the Revolution of 1848–1849, when independence was proclaimed from Austria, but the insurrection was put down by Habsburg and Russian troops. However, Hungary did receive a measure of self-government when the Compromise of 1867 created the Austro-Hungarian dual monarchy under which the emperor of Austria served also as king of Hungary, while Hungary maintained its own government and parliament. On the losing side in World War I, Hungary had to give up territory to several of its neighbors and emerged as a small country separated from Austria. A second Hungarian Republic was proclaimed on November 15, 1918, after which came the short-lived Socialist Federated Soviet Republic. From 1920 to 1944 Hungary was a "kingdom without a king," with Admiral Miklos Horthy as regent.

After its alliance with the Axis powers during World War II, Hungary was occupied by Soviet troops in 1944. This event—described officially as the "liberation"—is the occasion for many anniversary broadcasts. Following two years of relatively free parliamentary government with a Communist minority, the Communist party won control in 1947 and promulgated a Soviet-style constitution in 1949.

The most dramatic event in recent Hungarian history—comparable with developments in Poland the same year and in Czechoslovakia in 1968—was the uprising from October 23 to November 4, 1956. As with the Prague Spring, it was preceded by a period of liberalization.[2] Beginning in 1954 there had been pressures to free Hungary's cultural and intellectual life, and in 1955 and 1956 some journalists tried to develop a free press in the democratic style. But this ended when Soviet forces put down the Revolution—the same day Cardinal Mindszenty entered the

United States Legation in Budapest to spend fifteen years in silent protest against his country's policies, until he left for Rome in September 1971.

After several years of retaliation, a trend set in toward political, economic, and intellectual relaxation, and the Hungarian mass media have been freer and livelier in recent years than in any time during the decade before 1956. But 60,000 Soviet troops are quartered in the country. They are reported to be well disciplined. I saw a number of them in Budapest, and was impressed by their neat appearance and good behavior. (There also are Soviet troops in Poland, Czechoslovakia, and East Germany.)

There has been much debate over whether broadcasts from Radio Free Europe incited the Hungarian Revolution and thereafter intensified it by promising armed intervention. Leslie B. Bain, a Hungarian-speaking American who was in the Budapest embassy during most of the revolutionary days, wrote that although "no one said that military help would be forthcoming, . . . promises of all-out help were implicit in the broadcasts, and if the Hungarians understood that to mean military aid, the fault lies in the ambiguity of the broadcasts."[3] But a knowledgeable American observer, rejecting the suggestion that RFE made any promises, put it this way: "The Hungarians in their emotional state at that time would have read promises into stock-market quotations."

An American scholar, Robert T. Holt, after a careful study of the entire episode, concluded that RFE was blameless, although he stated that judgment was difficult in view of the large number of contradictory articles appearing in the American and European press in November and December of 1956.[4] Dr. Holt grouped the charges into three categories: (1) the RFE had incited the revolt; (2) although its broadcasts might have appeared otherwise to Americans, the effect on Hungarians living in a "charged situation was in fact inciting"; and (3) the very fact that RFE, along with VOA, had been on the air for six years implied that the United States would support any armed attempts to drive the USSR out of Hungary.

"The most serious indictment, namely, that RFE incited the revolution and, when it had burst into flame, added oil to the fire by promising western armed intervention, is simply not supported by a study of RFE's scripts," concluded Dr. Holt. Because of a furor in the German press over the entire episode, the German government formally investigated RFE's broadcasts during the Hungarian uprising, and decided that RFE had not encouraged the revolt by promising Western aid.

Dr. Holt argued that the second charge was hard either to prove or to disprove, but pointed out that the Hungarians may have heard what they wanted to hear rather than what RFE broadcast. As to the third charge, the problem was not that the United States maintained RFE (which in 1956 was claimed to be a private, nongovernment organization), but rather that American policy in regard to the Hungarian events was incompletely formulated and vaguely stated.

János Kádár, who succeeded Matyas Rakosi as party leader at the end of 1956, has followed a relatively liberal line. By conforming to Soviet foreign policy he has won the right to considerable independence in domestic affairs. At home he has tried to gain support by avoiding conservative extremes, and has been quoted in the press as saying that he conducts a "two-front" struggle against both the left and the right.[5] Kádár introduced far-reaching economic reforms in 1968, one aspect of which was the decentralization of economic decision-making and an emphasis on competition along with material incentives and profit-making. This approach, comparable in some ways with that of Yugoslavia, is known as the New Economic Mechanism.

Kádár has made a great effort to develop foreign trade, upon which Hungary is more dependent than any other country in the Eastern European bloc. About 40 per cent of Hungary's national income depends on foreign trade, two-thirds of which is with the Eastern countries, television equipment being among the exports.[6] In 1970, 40 per cent of the value of Hungarian foreign trade was with the Soviet Union, other principal trading partners including the German Democratic Republic with 12 per cent; Czechoslovakia, 9 per cent; the German Federal Republic, 7 per cent; and Poland, 5 per cent. Hungary has very little trade with the United States. Tourism also is important. In 1970 approximately 80 per cent of Hungary's 6,320,000 tourists were from the Eastern European countries and only 3,987 from the United States. There is much tourist activity in the area around Lake Balaton, the largest lake in Central Europe, which is sixty-six miles southwest of Budapest.

Full diplomatic relations with the United States were resumed after World War II in 1945. Following the rise to power of the Communists two years later, relations became increasingly strained, a situation exacerbated by the 1956 uprising. However, in recent years things have improved. A consular convention was signed in 1972 and an agreement on claims for war-damaged and nationalized American property in 1973.[7]

A continuing problem is American possession of the royal crown taken at the end of World War II, an object of sentimental value for Hungarians, since it was presented to King Stephen by Pope Sylvester II on Christmas Eve in the year 1000.

Hungary is a member of COMECON, the United Nations, UNESCO, and the Warsaw Pact. Although it supplied a token force of 12,000 troops for the occupation of Czechoslovakia in August 1968, it did so with little enthusiasm, and the action was not popular among Hungarians. But Kádár explained it by saying: "It is the fundamental principle of our foreign policy to cooperate with the Soviet Union."[8]

Legal Structure

The Hungarian Constitution, adopted August 20, 1949, follows the Soviet pattern. Its Preamble states: "The armed forces of the great Soviet Union liberated our country from the yoke of the German fascists, crushed the power of the great landowners and capitalists who were ever hostile to the people, and opened the road of democratic progress to our working people."[9] After several more laudatory references to the USSR, the Preamble concludes by stating that the Constitution, in addition to consolidating certain fundamental changes previously achieved, "also indicates the direction of our further advance."

The Hungarian People's Republic is "a state of workers and working peasants" in which "all power belongs to the working people."[10] The country's major resources and activities, including postal, telegraph, telephone, and "wireless" services, are declared to be "the property of the state and of public bodies as trustees for the whole people."[11] Legislative power is assigned to the single-chamber national assembly, whose members are elected for four-year terms.[12] The highest organ of state administration is the Council of Ministers, controlled by the Presidential Council, which is elected by parliament from its own members.[13] There is the usual close relationship between the government and the party, in this case the Hungarian Socialist Workers' party, whose first secretary is the country's dominant political figure. As of November 1970, party membership was 662,397 out of a total population of 10,347,000.[14]

Section VIII, "The Rights and Duties of Citizens," guarantees among other things the rights to work, relaxation, recreation, health, education, equality for women, liberty of conscience, and education in their native tongues of all the country's nationalities.[15] In return all citizens are expected to "defend the property of the people, consolidate social assets, increase the economic strength of the Hungarian People's Republic, raise the living standard and cultural level of the workers and strengthen the people's democratic system."

The government pledges itself to support "all scientific work serving the cause of the working people, as well as the arts which depict the life and struggle of the people, which describe reality, and proclaim the victory of the people. It gives every support to the emergence of the intellectual workers loyal to the people."[16] References to freedom of expression contain the limiting clause often found in Eastern European constitutions: "*In accordance with the interests of the workers* the Hungarian People's Republic insures for its citizens freedom of speech, freedom of the press and freedom of assembly."[17]

Broadcasting became a state monopoly in 1925, with responsibility later assigned to a company known as the Hungarian Central Office of Information, whose share of capital was divided among various political parties and trade unions.[18] This agency also was responsible for telegraph service and advertising. In the early 1930s a new corporation with private shareholders was granted monopoly control by the Ministry of Posts, Telegraph, and Telephone, and this evolved into the Office of Hungarian Radio in 1950.

The fact that the current Hungarian authority was established the year following the reorganization of Soviet broadcasting may account for certain similarities in pattern. The top policy group is an advisory council of seven members made up of the president of Magyar Rádió és Televízió (MRT), his administrative assistant, four vice-presidents (two each for radio and television), and the secretary of the Socialist Workers' (Communist) party. The president holds ministerial rank and participates in the government, and the main department heads are appointed by the Council of Ministers. Program administration in both media is divided into four areas: politics; music; literature and youth; and children's programs. Each division has its own advisory committee.

During visits to Budapest in 1970 and 1972, I talked at length with people in radio and television as well as with Americans well informed about Hungarian affairs. They agree that broadcasting is related both to the Council of Ministers and to the party. As one Hungarian put it: "Television is an agency of the government." In 1965 a broadcasting official told me: "The closest and friendliest relations exist between broadcasters and the Party."

There is no need for formal censorship. Policies are stated and implied by party and government, and since the key members of MRT and many program officials are party members, they follow the line. No one sits with his finger on a red button to cut off picture and sound if the wrong thing goes out on the air. As one official commented, broadcasting is a very public activity, and whatever goes out is immediately a matter of public knowledge.

No broadcast may advocate basic changes in the government system, and there must be no attacks on the role of the party or on the country's relationship with the Soviet Union. Criticism, however, is allowed, "if it will strengthen the basis of communism." When I asked how the freedom permitted Hungarian broadcasters compared with that in other socialist countries, I was told—as in most of the others too!—that they are among the freest. There is good reason to believe that they are.

One problem which Hungary shares with other small countries—especially those with unique languages—is that of financing television. The country's relatively small size and population limit national income and curtail the potential for the license fees which supply basic support for the broadcast media. In addition, the sharing of programs—and hence of costs—with other countries is made difficult by the absence of any large foreign groups speaking Hungarian.

Advertising was eliminated from Hungarian radio in 1949, only to be restored in 1958. Commercials are restricted to socialized products and services, and are presented in blocks rather than being interspersed throughout the schedule. The first radio network has five-minute clusters at 12:30 P.M. Monday through Friday, 3:55 P.M. on Saturday, and 11:00 A.M. Sunday, while the second network has five-minute commercial periods on several evenings. There is a daily ten-minute block on television in the late afternoon or early evening. Income is not a major factor, however, the main reason for advertising being to help cooperatives sell their products. Revenues from receiving licenses, therefore, are the main source of support. The annual fee per household for radio is 120 florints ($11.19) and for television 600 florints ($55.50).

Networks and Programs

Hungarians point with pride to the fact that wired broadcasting was originated by their countryman Tivadar Puskás (1845–1883), at one time an assistant to Thomas Edison.[19] Puskás also is credited with contributing to the development of the world's first telephone exchange and with inventing the "tele-phonograph" demonstrated at the Paris World Exhibition of 1881, which made it possible to distribute programs by wire from a central point to a number of listening stations. The tele-phonograph system was put into operation in Budapest the following year, and soon a "rich" service of news and live music was provided for "an extensive network of receivers."*(The studio used for these early wired transmissions was located in the same building in which Hungarian wireless broadcasting began December 1, 1925.)

The Hungarian People's Republic currently operates three nationwide radio networks, five regional services, an external broadcasting organization, and one nationwide plus an embryonic second television service.† Program I (Radio Kossuth) is carried by two AM stations, one with 300 and the other with 15 kilowatts power, and is available to the entire country. Program II (Radio Petöfi), also nationwide, is carried by eight AM transmitters with power ranging from 400 watts up to 135 kilowatts, seven of which also provide local coverage for programs from five regional studios. Regular FM broadcasting began in 1963, and five transmitters operating in the Eastern European FM band offer the equivalent of a Third Programme, although it is not available to the entire country.[20] Experimental stereo broadcasts of music and drama, inaugurated January 1, 1970, are on the air one hour each afternoon. There are plans to build a new radio center in Budapest in the near future.[21]

---

* Asa Briggs in *The Birth of Broadcasting* (p. 43) accepts 1881 as the date for the Puskás invention and goes on to report similar developments in Britain ten years later.

† *WRTH 1973*, pp. 77–78; *OIRT Information* 1970/2, pp. 10, 12. Programs I and II are named after two Hungarian patriots involved in the Revolution of 1848: Louis Kossuth (1802–1894) and Sandor Petöfi (1823–1849). There is a statue of Petöfi in front of the Duna Intercontinental, the newest and best of Budapest's hotels. On April 11, 1972, it was reported from Vienna that the first demonstrations to take place in Budapest since the 1956 Revolution had been centered in Hero's Square, adjacent to City Park, and in front of the Petöfi statue. Student demonstrators read some of Petöfi's poems, one of which included the phrase, "We have been slaves until now," a reference to the 1848 uprising put down by Russian troops (*New York Times*, April 12, 1972, p. 7C).

The basic national network, Radio I (Radio Kossuth), on the air daily from 4:25 A.M. (Sundays 6:00 A.M.) to 12:30 A.M., broadcasts "the most important" programs of presumed majority interest. Program II (Radio Petöfi), on the air daily from 4:25 A.M. (Sunday 7:00 A.M.) to midnight, is more experimental, and devotes considerable time to such entertainment features as light music. Taken together, 60 per cent of the output of the two services is music and 40 per cent spoken word.[22] It could further be classified as follows: light music, 36 per cent; serious music, 24 per cent; topical programs, 21 per cent; literary programs, 10 per cent; and programs for youth, 7 per cent. The FM service, which broadcasts weekday evenings, with longer periods on Saturdays and Sundays, is patterned after the BBC's Third Programme, and emphasizes serious music plus literary and scientific material.*

Like radio broadcasters everywhere, those in Hungary are much aware of television. One of them identified three stages in the developing relationship between the two media: (1) the early years, when television was feeling its way; (2) the years of struggle and competition; and (3) the present period of "coexistence."[23] After first imitating radio, television found itself and developed its own formats and identity, at the same time that radio learned that news, information, and music were its strongest points. As one Hungarian release put it: "Systematic development of programmes in recent years has aimed at making radio an even fresher, quicker, and more accurate source of information on national and international events, while maintaining the traditional character of the Hungarian Radio: its combined role of providing information and creative culture."† It now is agreed that the two media should supplement rather than compete with each other.

Although the Hungarians claim a television pioneer in Dénes Mihály, who introduced his Telehor apparatus at the end of the 1920s, experi-

---

* Until recently Radio Kossuth and Radio Petöfi often repeated or simulcast each other's programs (*OIRT Information* 1966/12, p.15). By 1969, however, the pattern had changed, and there were "distinct, individual profiles to the three parallel programmes" (Lévái, p. 3). For philosophical comments on radio as a medium, see Kálmán Kis, "Introduction to Some Problems of the Radio Art," *OIRT Review* 1965/1, pp. 3–7. For a discussion of the current pattern of Hungarian radio, see Béla Lévái, "La Radiodiffusion Hongroise en 1969," *OIRT Review* 1971/1, pp. 2–6.

† Lévái, p. 2. In several Eastern European countries I have been told that one fault of broadcasting in capitalist countries is that the two media become destructively competitive rather than complementarily cooperative.

mental telecasting did not begin until 1953 and regular transmissions until 1957.[24] Studios are housed in the vast old stock exchange building located across a public square from the American Embassy. Some studio and transmission equipment, and all the country's receivers, were made in Hungary. Programs from the first network are carried by a dozen VHF transmitters to approximately 95 per cent of the country's territory as well as to viewers in the border areas of Czechoslovakia and Austria.[25] For monochrome the standard Eastern European D system is used, while the few color programs use system K with SECAM color. Color television experiments began in 1964, although limited color programming—now available on both services—did not start until March 1, 1969.

Television hours have been greatly extended since regular broadcasting began in 1957, when there were only two short broadcast periods a week. Network I is now on the air an average of forty-two hours a week. Except on Monday, when it does not broadcast, there are programs on weekdays from 4:00 until about 10:30 P.M. The Sunday schedule is almost continuous from 8:00 A.M. to 10:30 P.M. In addition there are morning and afternoon programs for schools.

In November 1970 the director of foreign relations for MRT told me that the principal problem in preparing for the second television channel was not funds but studios. Countries with only one service have a hard time pleasing their viewers, and Hungarian broadcasters report that before the inauguration of the second service, they had fewer critics among people in border areas who could see programs from abroad than among residents in the central part of the country. For one thing, there were conflicts between viewers wanting culture and education and those seeking light entertainment. On August 19, 1971, the second channel began broadcasting. It can be received only in Budapest, but nearly 25 per cent of the population and 40 per cent of the television receivers are there.[26] Originally on the air only two days a week, it began a three-day schedule at the end of 1972, broadcasting Wednesday, Friday, and Sunday evenings from 8:00 to 10:30 P.M. Although it is not planned to make the second service primarily educational, it will be more intellectually demanding than the first one.

The vice-president in charge of television wrote that at the outset they had to decide whether they were dispensing televised cinema or radio with pictures. In any case, the first programs consisted of such ready-made materials as films, pickups from theaters, and transmissions of sporting events.[27] But, as was pointed out above, television now has found its identity. In Budapest, I saw some fast-moving and lively programs, and my impressions of Hungarian television were generally favorable. One American reporter said he considered Hungarian television the most advanced in Eastern Europe after that of the German Democratic Republic.[28] Certainly, production is better than in the Soviet Union.

The weekly program guide *Rádió és Televízío Újság* (*Radio and Television News*) has the largest circulation of any Hungarian magazine—just as *TV Guide* is the largest circulated periodical in the United States.[29] In 1965, when its circulation was 570,000, every fourth adult was a reader; and in 1971, when its circulation reached 900,000, it became the most widely circulated magazine in the country. *Radio and Television News* prints the weekly schedules for both national and regional services, along with some feature articles about broadcasting. The growth of circulation is not left to chance, however, since there periodically are broadcasts with the chief editor as master of ceremonies, on which some writers and contributors also appear.[30] MRT publishes an annual yearbook and some research reports too.

Although the Hungarians have published less about the role of broadcasting in advancing government and party than have some of their Eastern colleagues, there is no doubt that their policy in the main coincides with those followed in the other socialist countries. In 1964 the director of educational television observed that because it was "the most powerful ideological weapon of our time," television should "contribute to the building-up of socialism" by "showing and analyzing [the] conflicts and problems of daily life."[31] Four years later the vice-president for television wrote that the medium's principal assignment was "to reinforce the socialist system . . . and to provide a socialist education for the population."[32] In 1970 I read to several Hungarian television executives the statement I had composed in the Soviet Union in 1958 about the need for broadcasting to support government and party, and found that they too accepted it (see above, p. 44).

News and Public Affairs

Hungarian radio averages a newscast every thirty minutes. Most of these are on the first and second networks, although the FM service also has news.[33] Newscasts usually are from five to ten minutes in length, although some last fifteen and thirty minutes. There also are regional newscasts and weather reports, some in German, Czech, Polish, Russian, or Serbian for foreign-speaking residents and tourists.[34] Television news programs are scheduled on the first network from 7:30 to 8:00 P.M. and at 10:30 P.M., preceding sign-off. On those days it is on the air, the second network presents a midevening tape-recorded repeat of the first network's newscast.

MRT gets its news from the national news agency, its own reporters, and from exchanges with Intervision and Eurovision. Magyar Tavirati Iroda (MTI) has bureaus throughout Hungary as well as in many world capitals.[35] Drawing upon a stuff of 800, including 180 journalists, 340 photographers, and 280 other employees, MTI provides each day 80,000 words in Hungarian, 1,500 in Russian, 2,000 in English, and 1,200 in German. It also exchanges news with such foreign agencies as Reuters, Agence France Presse, Associated Press, and TASS.

Hungarian broadcasting has its own correspondents at home as well as in Berlin, Moscow, Paris, and New York, and it monitors short-wave programs from the USSR, the United States, and other foreign countries.[36] For example, it tunes in Voice of America broadcasts of the president's news conferences for information about the United States. It may send reporters to Moscow, Prague, Belgrade, Bucharest, and Vienna, among other cities, and once dispatched its Moscow correspondent to cover the work of a Soviet polar station.[37] Television secures materials from both Intervision and Eurovision, and identifies itself as "one of the founders of Intervision . . . [while maintaining] active and valuable contact in programme exchange with Eurovision."[38]

In 1963 Hungarian television received 17 and in 1964, 26 news items from Eurovision. In 1965 for the first time it provided 6 while receiving 162 items; in 1966 it provided 11 and received 457; and in 1967 provided 7 and received 529. Intervision reports that in 1972 Hungarian television took 1,587 news items from Eurovision and originated 15.

Hungarian broadcasters speak frankly of the political functions of news. One staff member wrote: "TV news is part of the political broadcasts of the propaganda department."[39] The starting point for television news, she continues, is "the policy of the Party and Government." Both domestic and foreign items should stimulate "viewers to the fulfillment of tasks set by the building-up of socialism." Nevertheless, in Hungary, as in the Soviet Union and other Eastern European countries, shortcomings in performance are criticized in broadcasts, newspaper editorials, and letters to the editor. Furthermore, ever since 1963, agencies receiving such complaints are obliged by law to investigate them.[40]

News commentaries and discussions have basically the same objectives as do straight newscasts. In 1962 radio had several daily five- and ten-minute commentaries. Subjects included the relative importance of living luxuriously or rearing a child; a book about American economists; and United Kingdom economic problems.[41] But sometimes events speak for themselves, as with the recordings made at a conference during which President Kennedy's Latin-American economic adviser allegedly declared "that it was worthwhile to invest American capital in Latin American countries only when this could result in the desired political effects."

MRT newscasters recognize the importance of making their programs interesting and attractive. In 1961 they were "happy and proud" to be the second country in Europe to broadcast news of the launching of Soviet cosmonaut Yuri Gagarin.[42] "Without sinking to sensationalism," wrote the head of radio news in 1967, "we must be interesting and therefore we attach great importance to the beginning of the news, the first sentence replacing the headline."[43] A spoken rather than written style should be used, and every item must be "comprehensible on the first hearing." The author points out that although they reported the assassination of President John F. Kennedy several times on November 22, 1963, some people who tuned in at 6:00 A.M. the next morning probably were unaware of it, so the opening news bulletin was phrased accordingly. Hungarian newscasters monitor foreign stations for ideas about presentation as well as for news substance, since the head of radio news observed that "they repeat most items as we do."

Government officials often go on the air, as in the series of fifteen- and twenty-minute programs broadcast alternate weeks in 1961 called "Minister at the Microphone," during which reporters asked ministers questions about their departments.[44] Political leaders made many microphone appearances preceding the national elections in 1963. One participant was János Kádár, the first secretary of the Hungarian Socialist Workers' (Communist) party. A Hungarian news release stated that "radio and television were used as the best media of direct contact between politicians and the masses."[45] In 1969 representatives of various ministries answered listeners' questions.

On the live television series "Forum," telephone callers select items for discussion by prominent Hungarians appearing on the programs.[46] An official brochure published in 1970 reported this to be the most popular television series on the air and further said that "questions from listeners are answered immediately, and from time to time national leaders and authorities are interviewed."[47] Government ministers and party leaders have appeared for as long as ninety minutes on programs of this type, and as many as a thousand questions may be received during a single broadcast. Statements made on these programs often are reported in the press, thus providing additional circulation. There are similar programs on radio.

In 1970 a precedent was set when a congress of the Hungarian Socialist Workers' party was transmitted live on both radio and television. Because of these broadcasts the whole country was "present" at the meetings and "participated in the Congress."[48] In October 1972 there was live television coverage of the opening autumn session of the Hungarian parliament, the highlights being recorded for reuse on news programs.

I was favorably impressed by several newscasts in November 1970 and October 1972. Thirty-minute news programs normally included ten minutes of domestic and ten minutes of foreign news, plus at least several minutes of commentary. A wide range of items was covered; announcers were skillful; production was professional; and there were occasional light touches, in contrast with the unrelieved seriousness of many socialist newscasts.

In 1972 the programs covered the peace negotiations then being conducted in Paris by Henry Kissinger with still pictures and films. Reports of a "trial" of American policy in Denmark included statements from English-speaking participants, which were faded under the Hungarian translation, but still were audible. Stories from Washington were read behind slides of the White House and of Secretary of Defense Melvin Laird, and there was coverage of the American presidential campaign with pictures of McGovern and Nixon. There also were films of a demonstration in Washington. Other items included a British political meeting in Blackpool, a border conflict in Tibet, floods in Romania (with map and film), the launching of a Cosmos satellite in the USSR, a West German political story, and—on the lighter side—a nostalgic report of a steam train outing in the United Kingdom.

There was a commendable de-emphasis of industrial and agricultural achievements, although there nevertheless were scenes in a spinning factory, events in a shipyard, and views of some new blocks of flats (with a map showing their location). Perhaps because of the limited time given to success stories, there was room for some cultural events, including films of an art show and of an exhibit of works by Marc Chagall. Each program included sports results plus a weather forecast, the latter combining diagrams, symbols, and clouds which moved across the screen as they "dripped" rain onto the map of Hungary.

An obvious improvement had taken place between 1970 and 1972. The news selection was better, news readers more skillful, and production smoother. Although the Soviet line is—of necessity—followed, American observers report that the Hungarian media do reasonably well in reporting news from the United States.

Broadcasts for Children and Youth

The head of the Editorial Board of Broadcasts for Children and Young People wrote in 1960 that Hungarian schools must impart sound progressive knowledge, relate education to life, and see that the people "acquire the bases of the Marxist point of view . . . [in order to] become people of Communist character."[49] The director of School Television wrote in 1970 that the first consideration was "educating youth for a socialist society."

Although regular in-school radio broadcasting did not begin until 1963, Hungary had broadcasts for children at home in 1947, when schools were closed because of inadequate heating, and in 1961 experimented with programs in French and Russian.[50] Since the introduction of regular in-school broadcasting, there have been programs to assist in the teaching of various languages, arithmetic, literature, history, the arts, music, and science.

In-school programs are planned cooperatively by teachers and educational administrators. Scripts are written by free-lance writers and edited by the radio staff. Programs are closely related to school curriculums and textbooks, except for language lessons, which teachers may utilize in accordance with pupils' knowledge and skills. Broadcasts vary from fifteen to thirty minutes in length, and are scheduled in blocks at 10:00 A.M. and 3:00 P.M. There are some evening presentations, such as classical dramas, for supplementary listening. Each week's program guide contains a box listing all the radio in-school programs. Presentations include talks, recitations, and dramatizations.[51] Tape recordings of many programs are available to teachers. Appraisal is made through questionnaires, visits to schools, and analysis of pupils' and teachers' letters.

In 1964, 100 schools viewed experimental television programs on subjects including Russian and physics, and thereafter programs on biology, English, geography, chemistry, physics, and Russian were broadcast.[52] When regular in-school television began in 1970, the head of the department observed that its late start gave Hungary the advantage of being able to benefit from experiences elsewhere.

In-school television programs are broadcast weekdays from approximately 8:00 A.M. until noon, and some afternoons between 1:00 and 3:30. There are supplementary programs on Sundays between 7:40 and 9:00 A.M. Taken together, these are designed to supplement rather than to replace teachers. Subjects include natural science, Hungarian language and literature, foreign languages (French, German, and Russian), mathematics, and physics. There also are telecasts for teachers. The producers are television experts with educational orientation who work in close cooperation with teachers and subject matter experts. In 1969 there was a conference on "the role of television in the modern schools," during which Hungarian pedagogues met with television experts from eleven other countries.

Although the Ministry of Public Instruction encourages in-class viewing, teachers are free to decide whether or not to use television. If they do, there are manuals to assist them in effective utilization. As long ago as 1961, 61.5 per cent of primary and 80 per cent of secondary schools had receivers. On April 4, 1970, the twenty-fifth anniversary of the country's liberation, the director of in-school television announced that every school in the country had at least one television set and that some had sets in every room. All this is the result of carefully staged campaigns. In 1969 youth brigades collected money to purchase sets for schools that were not equipped with television, and in 1971 there was a drive to provide portable electric generators for schools and small communities without electric service.* In the same year there was a competition to encourage effective program usage in small communities, with receivers for prizes.

Like broadcasters in all socialist countries, those in Hungary take very seriously out-of-school programs for children and young people. In 1960 the head of the editorial board in charge of such programs wrote that "the main task of radio consists in maintaining close contacts with life and assisting in forming and improving the socialist consciousness of the new generation."[53] Another writer said that the most important function of such programs is "to help young people to find the correct way in life as well as their place in society and to answer problems preoccupying young people." A broadcaster wrote in 1967 that one of "the most important tasks faced by the community is the education of the future generations."[54] The director of Television Programming noted in 1970 "that the younger generation is growing up with an avalanche of information transmitted by the mass media." The implication of his six-page "Mass Media and Youth" was that the broadcasters' responsibility is a heavy one.[55]

A department in charge of out-of-school radio broadcasts for young people was established in 1949.[56] In 1962 the Youth Radio Theater had a program about Abraham Lincoln "on the occasion of the 100th anniversary of the decisive turning point in the American civil war."[57] The next year marked the 100th broadcast of a science series, "Club of the Curious."[58] Originated before a young people's studio audience was "The Cat in the Sack," whose purpose was to present information about little-known writers and artists, who appeared in person to discuss their work.[59] A series introduced in 1966 was called "The Portable Radio Set" because it was estimated that most of the half million transistor sets were used by young people. Like other socialist countries, Hungary had an International Festival of Children's Plays, with scripts from Czechoslovakia, the German Democratic Republic, Hungary, Poland, Romania, the USSR, and Yugoslavia. In 1972 the Youth Department of Budapest Radio organized a "Review of Radio Plays for Youth," and in connection

* *OIRT Information* 1969/11, p. 11; *OIRT Information* 1971/8–9, p. 3; *OIRT Information* 1971/4–5, p. 14. There is a contradiction between the Hungarian source that reported 100 per cent distribution of television sets in schools as of 1970 and the one that described a national campaign to provide generators to schools without electric service so that they might have television receivers.

with a Communist Youth Congress scheduled a "Youth Week of Art."[60]

In March 1957, when Hungarian television was still in its early stages, a physics professor named Jozsef Öveges began broadcasting science programs, and he continued these through the years with such success that a survey of Hungarian television printed in four languages in 1970 included his picture and described him as among "the most popular lecturers."[61] Young people's television in 1963 had filmed cycles about Hungarian history, question-and-answer programs, and other instructional features. One author declared: "An instructive programme for youth must offer topical, scientific and materialistic knowledge in a form *comprehensible to everybody*. To attain this aim any form can be used from a simple lecture up to a documentary feature. However, all the so-called 'television effects' must be avoided as they only obscure the contents." There was a series in 1966 for children between the ages of ten and fourteen entitled "Write the Continuation Yourself." During each broadcast the first half of a story was presented and the viewers were invited to provide the conclusion.[62] Sex education was introduced to Hungarian television in April 1971, when programs were presented for parents, teachers, boys aged fourteen, and girls aged twelve to fourteen. An opinion poll was planned to analyze the results, and more than local interest was indicated by the fact that the findings were to be reported to UNESCO in Paris.[63]

Competitions are used to build interest. In 1961 there were 1,775 entries in a radio series to celebrate the anniversary of the country's liberation.[64] In 1963 television scheduled competitions in biology, history, geography, and physics, the results of which showed a high level of knowledge among youth at the same time that they revealed certain shortcomings in school curricula.[65] In the same year a radio literary competition brought 1,600 entries from 1,250 boys and girls. The next year the Ministry of Culture announced that young people with high scores in the television series "Who Knows Best This Subject?" could enroll directly in university courses in the fields covered without taking entrance examinations.[66] In 1966 television had "Who Knows What?" "What Have You Learned?" and "In What Field Are You Master?" in which young people competed in mathematics, history, science, and other areas.[67]

Programs in which children participate are popular with both young people and adults.[68] Teams compete to demonstrate their knowledge in geography, music, sports, and other fields. Children also take part in variety broadcasts. Radio reporters visit children in their homes and meetings; interview them about their work, leisure-time activities, and problems; and edit the tapes for broadcasting. Other broadcasts are based on children's letters. During 1966 between 800 and 1,200 letters were received every month, mainly from villages and small towns, addressed to broadcast character "Uncle Miska," who was asked for advice about youth problems. In the course of an average year over 1,000 literary contributions—stories, poems, and dramatizations—are received and used as the basis for three or four programs.

There also are joint broadcasts with what the socialist world calls "friendly countries." Young people from Budapest and Prague compared knowledge about the art, history, literature, and music of Hungary and Czechoslovakia; East German and Hungarian students had a mathematics contest; and young people from Hungary and Poland had other competitions. To mark the twentieth anniversary of Hungarian liberation, 1,200 children from six countries took part in the broadcasts of a children's choir festival in Budapest. Hungarian radio has its own children's choir, which broadcasts and presents public concerts at home and abroad.

Adult Education

Although Hungarian broadcasters put less emphasis on instructional programs for adults than do their colleagues in some socialist countries, they nevertheless have for many years offered educational material for older audiences. In 1961 the article "Hungarian Radio" devoted most of its space to adult education, documentaries, discussions, features for rural listeners, and literary broadcasts, also mentioning a program entitled "How Soviet and Hungarian Soldiers Drank to Their Friendship."[69] The same year a review of "Hungarian Television" was concerned mainly with adult education.

In one series a popular comedian served as talent for lectures on good manners.[70] Another time television took viewers to places normally marked "no admittance," such as the mint or the closed reconstruction area of an old castle. In 1964 Budapest radio initiated "The Alphabet of Marriage," in which writers, physicians, and psychologists discussed problems of married life. Designed mainly for newlywed women, these programs dealt with "the importance of mutual respect for each other's likes and dislikes, frankness between man and his wife, mutual confidence, problems of parents-in-law, jealousy, and many others."[71] A television program about plastic surgery showed the treatment of a severely burned girl, the repair of the deformed nose of a young man, and an operation on the injured hand of a guitar player.

Once a month television invites viewers to its studios to question staff members about program policies and procedures. I saw one such program which dealt with violence on the air, and particularly with the question of whether or not there were too many war films. Two men who had gone through World War II objected to such films, while several young people said they liked them. It is commendable for a broadcasting service to put itself on public trial for its policies and programs.

Surprisingly, in addition to programs on religious subjects, there are radio broadcasts of religious services early Sunday mornings.* In 1965 a television series reviewed the history of the four major religions: Christianity, Islam, Buddhism, and Judaism.[72] In 1971 "The World of the Bible," which used a historical approach, was described in an official release as "one of the most popular transmissions of the Hungarian Radio." With international aspects were programs broadcast jointly from London and Budapest in which Hungarian and British scholars discussed the sociology of art, and there were plans to develop a similar exchange with the United States.[73] In 1972 I saw a television program on current art exhibitions which, through the effective use of film, brought the galleries right into the living room.

"News from the Future" was the title of an animated cartoon series begun in 1970 involving television's Mézga "family."[74] Regular participants "include the parents, a teen-aged daughter, a son who is very interested in technology, a dog and a cat and a relative from the 30th century who is able to solve all problems with the help of technology." The production of the series took over a year and involved a half million cartoons.

In 1968 television used helicopters and automobiles to record the time taken by cars which did and did not observe traffic regulations in driving from Budapest to Lake Belaton, sixty-six miles away, in order to demonstrate that the few minutes saved by careless driving did not justify the

---

* The government provides Hungarian churches with annual subsidies totaling 80 million florins ($6,672,000 by the official rate, $2,262,000 by the tourist rate), of which half goes to the Roman Catholic Church (*Statesman's Year-Book 1971/ 72*, p. 1028).

risks involved.[75] In subsequent years there were both radio and television programs on traffic safety. In 1969 television had a series in which the public was invited to join the search for wanted criminals. During the first broadcast a telephone call led to the arrest of one person while the program was still on the air.[76] The same year several radio series analyzed the causes of accidents, fires, and crime, with the objective of reducing their frequency.

MRT programmers like quizzes and competitions. In 1965 a television cycle drew its themes from twelve great literary classics whose authors ranged from the Greek Euripides (480–406? B.C.) to the Russian Maxim Gorki (1869–1956), the winners receiving trips to the countries of the authors concerned.[77] On Bastille Day—July 14—in 1965, Hungarian radio had a quiz, "Who Knows More about France?" In the same year the winners of the BBC and Moscow Radio competitions "Who Knows More about Hungary?" visited Budapest. In 1966 winners in a television series testing knowledge in biology, chemistry, mathematics, and physics were allowed to enter universities without entrance examinations and also received trips abroad. The same year radio and the Ministry of Culture joined forces for ten programs in the series "Do You Know Your Region?" In 1971 in the radio quiz "Direct Hit" participants were asked questions about geography, history, music, language, and sports. As a reward for correct answers, contestants received "torpedoes" to shoot at the ships of their adversaries. For sinking a whole fleet contestants received money prizes.

Although agriculture is not as important to Hungary now as it was before World War II, it still accounts for a third of the labor force, and there accordingly are many broadcasts for agricultural workers. A writer in 1960 said that the primary objective of these programs was to popularize and explain the agrarian policies of the party.[78] A series of thirty-minute television programs, "Country People," presented information about the problems of an average man living in a new type of rural village.[79] In 1964 radio took some farmers and a reporter on a flight to better observe developments in Hungarian agriculture.[80] One television series for rural listeners was entitled "In the Light of Lamps," a reference to the long winter evenings during which the programs were broadcast. Actually, the title was something of an anomaly, since unless they used battery-powered receivers, which was very unlikely, the homes in which the programs were viewed must have had electricity! There now are agricultural programs several evenings each week and on Sunday afternoons which present practical advice about farming problems. The Sunday telecasts include folk music, as do similar programs in Romania.*

Only recently have there been organized instructional programs for adults, although there was a "Radio University" in 1961 dealing with such areas as industry, literature, and science.[81] A beginning was made with television lessons in Russian in 1961, and soon there was instruction in English on both media. Study guides and texts for language courses are sold in bookstores. In 1965 a news release told about four "friends" who were teaching on television: Grisha and Andrei, who taught Russian, and the BBC's Walter and Connie, who taught English. There also are German lessons produced in East Germany, French lessons produced in Paris, and Russian lessons produced—surprisingly—in Hungary. The first television credit course was "Higher Mathematics," designed for part-time students taking evening or correspondence courses, which was broadcast alternate Sunday mornings beginning September 10, 1967.[82] On these programs a university lecturer appeared jointly with a student who represented the viewers. In 1968–1969 a pilot series in geometry was organized along with the weekly television program "Teacher's Forum." At present, however, no credit courses are offered on television.

Music

An indication of music broadcasting objectives was provided by an article published in 1961 which claimed "modest success in the propagation of musical knowledge."[83] The author stated that "Music for Everybody" had succeeded because of "the fine style of the lecturer," his talent for clarity, and the accompanying musical illustrations. "We lay great emphasis on the development of musical knowledge in the rising generations." In 1964 radio had weekly lectures about "the composer of the week," whose works were featured on concert broadcasts.[84]

In 1969, 65 per cent of all radio programs consisted of music, of which 60 per cent was "entertaining music" and 40 per cent "heavy music," although the content of the FM service was 80 per cent serious music.[85] This ratio, it was claimed, reflected public taste. There of course is music on both radio and television, but a spokesman for MRT pointed out that

---

* Audience surveys in Poland have indicated a preference for folk music by small town and rural residents. See above, p. 307.

although music was the heart of radio, "with what passion has the young television in the whole world set to capture this territory! Television can conquer conductors, by which we mean that they might continually give concerts in TV studios, but television can never become the first source of musical art."[86] But television keeps trying. In Budapest in 1972, I saw a telecast recital of music for oboe and piano, well done in respect to both music and production, plus an Intervision relay of a symphony concert from Sofia, Bulgaria—neither of which made any concessions to popular taste. Scheduled for October 1972 was live transmission of a public concert featuring violinist Yehudi Menuhin.

It always is impressive to learn how many musical ensembles are maintained by broadcasting organizations in small countries like Hungary, which has a fine radio and television symphony orchestra, a mixed choir, a children's choir, a dance music group (called Studio 11), and other light music combinations.[87] MRT also has extensive recorded resources. In 1971, 3,408,000 minutes of musical and spoken word programs were available on magnetic tape or long-playing records, this number representing 56,000 hours, 2,366 days, or 6½ years of consecutive broadcasting.[88] Hungarian Radio also collects recordings of the voices of famous people, such as Gandhi, Nehru, de Gaulle, Castro, Nixon, Che Guevara, Ralph Abernathy, Chaplin, Cocteau, Picasso, and Matisse.[89]

The symphony orchestra broadcasts and gives public concerts regularly, sometimes under such international conductors as Charles Munch and Hans Schmidt-Isserstedt. When Munch conducted in 1966, one critic described the concert as among "the greatest musical events of the last 25 years."[90] In 1967 the Hungarian Broadcasting and BBC symphony orchestras had a joint presentation, originated alternately in Budapest and London, during which both orchestras played compositions by British and Hungarian composers.[91] In Hungary, as in the United States, owners of tape recorders like to record music off the air, for which reason radio has special FM broadcasts for them, repeating the programs the following day on the standard broadcast band for listeners without FM receivers.[92]

One author wrote of the search for new ways to develop the radio music theater.[93] In addition to standard operettas by composers like Jacques Offenbach, Johann Strauss, Franz von Suppé, Arthur S. Sullivan, and Franz Lehár, radio produces contemporary works by Oscar Hammerstein, Cole Porter, and Leonard Bernstein. A search is made for compositions by less established Hungarian composers. The article concluded: "The tone of musical radio plays should be democratic and modern but, at the same time, popular and intellectual." If possible there should be "humorous moments."

Opera is claimed to be the favorite type of serious music in Hungary. Hungarian Radio reported in 1952 that it recorded some operas in its studios for broadcasting, one of them being Haydn's *The Infidel Smitten*. This particular opera, for which the manuscript had only recently been discovered, had received only three performances—all private—during the composer's lifetime.[94] But there also are live transmissions from opera houses, which the public likes since they bring listeners closer to the real experience.[95] On the other hand, operas, musicals, and other stage works sometimes are presented in theaters after first being broadcast. Radio has scheduled cycles of operas by Verdi and Mozart, along with the rest of the standard operatic repertoire.[96] The first performance of the new Television Musical Theater took place in 1970 with an adaptation of an operetta by Franz Lehár. Later another operetta, *Old Summer* by Lajos Lajtaj, was prepared jointly with Swedish television.[97]

Encouragement is given to Hungarian music through broadcasting works by both established and new composers. In observance of the eightieth birthday of Béla Bartók (1881–1945), 1961 became "Bartók's Year," and another Bartók anniversary was celebrated ten years later. The 1961 festival included a documentary review of the composer's life.[98] To mark the eightieth birthday of Zoltán Kodály (1882–1967), a concert was broadcast which included variations on a theme from his first string quartet written by some of his pupils.[99] In 1969 there were plans to record sixty-eight new Hungarian compositions—twenty-five orchestral, twenty-eight chamber, and fifteen choral. In 1971 a "Month of New Hungarian Music" featured ninety-three radio broadcasts consisting of compositions of the preceding twenty-five years.[100] During the same year there were weeks of Hungarian folk songs and jazz. In January 1972 a three-week cycle, "New Hungarian Music on the Radio," presented fifty works by thirty-one composers, the best compositions receiving prizes.[101]

With music as with sports, Eastern European broadcasters use the media to encourage participation. In addition to broadcasting concerts by amateur orchestras, Hungarian radio for years has sponsored competitions: in 1966 and 1967 for pianists; in 1967 for cellists; in 1969 for violinists; and in 1971 for singers.[102] Very ambitious was the Beethoven bicentennial competition in 1970, entered by thirty-one young pianists, in the last round of which each contestant had to play a Beethoven piano concerto.[103] In 1971 television organized competitions for young musicians from Intervision countries which were held in a famous castle belonging to the Esterhazy family. The winners were rewarded with concert tours abroad.[104]

In 1966 there were 476 and in 1967, 1,378 entries in the "Festival of Variety Songs."[105] To mark the twenty-fifth anniversary of the country's liberation, television sponsored a competition to focus attention on little-known folk songs, with separate categories for participants between fourteen and thirty-five years of age and those older.[106] In the autumn of 1970, 27 secondary schools in Budapest and 115 in other parts of the country entered a national competition for performances of music by Béla Bartók. After hearing twenty-four hours of contest material, the jury awarded the winning schools money to promote music education, while individual winners received trips abroad.[107] A similar competition on Hungarian Liberation Day, April 4, 1971, again honored Bartók. The same year there were eight radio programs on which contestants were asked about such musicians as Liszt, Bartók, Kodály, Mozart, Verdi, Wagner, and Puccini. The winners received cash awards, and one did so well that he was offered a position on the music faculty of a Budapest university.

As was pointed out above, a large percentage of radio time is devoted to light music, of which dance and jazz music compose the major portion. Back in 1952 Hungarian Radio announced that by offering cash prizes it had "done a good deal to encourage the writing of dance music acceptable to the working people."[108] In 1966 a new studio was built with the artificial reverberation and other effects needed for such broadcasts.[109] In 1968 a Hungarian quartet won third place in a jazz festival in Montreux in competition with ensembles from thirteen countries, and in the same year Hungarian Radio and the Union of Communist Youth sponsored a light music festival for young people under thirty years of age.[110] On another occasion radio organized an international light music competition with entries from Belgium, Canada, Czechoslovakia, Finland, the German Democratic Republic, the German Federal Republic, Ireland, Monaco, New Zealand, Portugal, Spain, Sweden, Turkey, and the USSR.[111] First prize was a two-week holiday at Lake Balaton.

From 10:00 A.M. to noon daily one of the radio services offers "Music for Holiday Makers," designed especially for foreigners visiting the Lake Balaton area, which includes advice "for tourists and mountaineers," not only in Hungarian, but also in English, Russian, and German.[112] In 1971, when seven concerts by world-renowned Hungarian and foreign jazz musicians were broadcast live, an announcement mentioned "the further popularization of the Hungarian jazz art which already has a number of outstanding interpreters."

Literature and Drama

MRT presents programs about literature, readings of poetry and prose, and dramatic productions ranging from adaptations of prose and stage works to material written especially for the media. In the early 1960s "The Pleasures of Reading" included short talks and conversations designed to increase listeners' knowledge of literature. Such programs still are broadcast.[113] To observe the twentieth anniversary of liberation in 1965, there were readings of the best stories published during the previous twenty years, and there regularly are twenty-minute programs during which professional readers go through five or six novels a year.[114]

In the mid-sixties, in connection with an annual book week, television had programs on which authors answered questions from the audience.[115] In 1969, radio scheduled a week of poetry to tell the public about legends, ballads, and folk songs from the "inexhaustible treasure of Hungarian national folklore."[116] In 1971, 30 amateur readers were chosen from over 500 applicants to read the poetry of a recently deceased Hungarian writer. The same year radio had another Week of Hungarian Poetry.[117]

The relaying of programs from theaters and opera houses is much more prevalent in Europe than in the United States. The BBC relayed them for many years, while the Eastern European countries continue to do so on both radio and television. The reason is that less sophisticated audiences like to be "in" the theater, and are willing to overlook technical limitations in order to have this experience. A Hungarian writer observed in 1960: "A listener living far from a communal centre and with no possibilities to go to the theatre, is taken there via the radio. He hears not only a play, but an opera or a concert and thanks to the broadcast, the theatre can influence him."[118] A decade later another article stated that pickups from theaters "have directly and indirectly influenced the development of Hungarian television dramaturgy."[119]

In 1958 radio broadcast 158 major literary works in a series entitled "The Theatre at the Microphone," of which 42 were relayed from theaters and the remainder were studio originations.[120] These 158 presentations exceeded the total number of performances given by all the theaters in Budapest the previous year. The repertoire included plays by Corneille, Euripides, Goethe, Racine, Schiller, Sophocles, and Oscar Wilde. In more recent years authors have included Guy de Maupassant, Maxim Gorki, James Hilton, Victor Hugo, Ben Jonson, John Milton, Ferenc Molnar, Eugene O'Neill, Luigi Pirandello, Shakespeare, and Voltaire.[121] There also are adaptations of short stories and novels by such authors as Charles Dickens, Ernest Hemingway, and Sinclair Lewis.[122] Television too had adaptations of both prose works and stage plays by authors like Flaubert, Hawthorne, Hemingway, Tolstoy, and Turgenev.[123] Television averages 100 plays a year, some produced in its own studios and others, because of inadequate space, by Hungarian film companies.

Much encouragement is given to Hungarian authors. In 1969 "Forgotten Hungarian Plays" featured seldom performed works by twentieth-century writers.[124] In the same year Jozsef Gáti did a special radio version of Shakespeare's *Macbeth* about which the commentary said that "with the help of modern radio means he succeeded in creating a psychological play without false 'topicality.'" In 1971 there was a television revival of a play written twenty years before the French Revolution which expressed "the eternal idea that a hero fighting for the interests of the people is conquered if he fights for the people but not with it."[125]

There also are plays written for the media. In 1965, in connection with the twentieth anniversary of the liberation, there were broadcasts of the best radio plays of the previous twenty years. Five years later, to observe the twenty-fifth anniversary, a competition for new plays was scheduled, along with an international festival of radio plays for children.[126] The International Radio Play Festival was organized in 1966 "to provide a fresh notion of the state of the radio play" and to show how the radio play has distinguished itself completely from other kinds of art. Plays were chosen from Czechoslovakia, France, the German Democratic Republic, the German Federal Republic, Hungary, Ireland, Japan, Poland, and the USSR.[127] In 1968 one Hungarian writer—Géza Hegedüs—completed his one hundredth radio play.[128] But despite much encouragement, an official statement in 1972 declared that short radio plays constituted "deficit goods" on Hungarian radio, for which reason yet another competition was launched.[129]

To an American, the term "serial drama" suggests the "soap operas" which filled radio's daytime hours for so many years and which now have their successors on television. But to European broadcasters it means sequential presentations of all sorts of material ranging from adaptations of literary masterpieces to continued stories created especially for the media. To mark Dante's 700th birthday, Hungarian radio did a three-part dramatization of the *Divine Comedy*, which was characterized as "an outstanding cultural event."[130] In 1969 there was a serial presentation of Franz Werfel's novel *The Forty Days of Musa Dagh*, along with a six-episode version of Homer's *Iliad*.

Hungary's most famous serial—and most popular radio program—tells the story of the Szabó Family.[131] Discussing this series, which began in 1959 and still is on the air, a staff member pointed out that serial plays date from the Dionysus festival in Greece, and that Aeschylus's tetralogies and the passion plays were other examples of the format. Hungarian radio serials are in "harmony with the rhythm of life of contemporary man," and "every installment is short and attractive." Britain had "Mrs. Dale's Diary" and "The Archers," while Poland had broadcast the "Matysiak Family" since late 1956 (see above, p. 295). Hungary's Szabó Family attempts "to contribute to the formation of social opinion by . . . stimulating listeners to improve and change the present state of affairs."

The Szabó serial portrays the real-life problems of a typical worker's family. Uncle Szabó is a self-taught Communist, while Auntie Szabó is "religious and good-hearted, but also talkative and quarrelsome." The children include "a driver, greedy for money," "a cheeky and pampered university student," and "an educated diplomat, a leader from the working class who has many problems and sprang from the class which for centuries was taught opportunism and obedience." The family "is typical of our socialism-building society." The Szabó Family, like the characters in broadcast serials in other countries, is regarded as real by many listeners, and accordingly receives New Year's greetings and gifts from the audience.[132] In 1969 it was joined by a television Kóvacs Family.

Films and Documentaries

There are radio and television documentaries in Hungary, and television broadcasts both cinema and telefilms. A country with a unique language like Hungary cannot exchange programs with other countries as easily as can those with shared languages. When Hungary imports films it must broadcast them with subtitles or dub them into Hungarian—with no way of sharing the costs. There are similar barriers to the exporting of Hungarian productions.

In earlier years films were televised in their original languages with subtitles, but dubbing into Hungarian began in 1961.[133] At present subtitles are used on documentaries only. In the 1960s foreign films with stars like Sophia Loren, Fred Astaire, and Michael Redgrave often were seen on television before they appeared in Hungarian cinemas.[134] In 1962 a cycle was organized around outstanding comedians like Mack Sennett, Ben Turpin, and Laurel and Hardy. The next year a directors' series introduced such names as Ernst Lubitsch, Vittorio de Sica, Sergei Eisenstein, David Griffith, and Frederico Fellini.

An American trade journal reported in 1972 that cinema theater attendance in Hungary was suffering because of television. At that time Hungary was making 20 cinema films a year and importing about 150, of which 10 per cent were French, 10 per cent Italian and American, and more than 20 per cent Soviet. The remainder were from both Eastern and Western European countries.[135] In Budapest I noticed that a ninety-minute cinema film, dubbed into Hungarian, took up about a third of one evening's schedule.

Enthusiastic audience acceptance in the early 1960s of some British telefilms about Robin Hood and William Tell led to the domestic production of a twelve-part series set in a Hungarian castle.[136] In 1972, along with many other countries, television presented with great success the BBC's *The Forsyte Saga*, at which time a Hungarian publishing house issued a new edition of Galsworthy's novels.[137] In addition to telefilms from Eastern Europe, Hungarian schedules have included the American *Bonanza* (disapproved by some viewers because of the "land baron" status of several of its characters), *The Flintstones*, *Flipper*, *Daktari*, some old Zorro films (which Hungarians love), reruns of Hitchcock movies, and some Leonard Bernstein concerts.* The propagandistic type-

---

* *New York Times*, January 12, 1972, p. 70M. The *New York Times* reported a Western diplomat as saying that "*Bonanza* . . . seemed to bore many Hungarians

casting of the Polish series "Four Panzers and a Dog," with its contrast between healthy handsome Poles and comic character Americans, amused many Hungarian viewers.

Anniversaries, particularly of patriotic nature, often occasion documentaries. In 1965 radio marked the twentieth anniversary of liberation with twelve programs reviewing the life of a working family in a Budapest suburb from the beginning of the twentieth century up to the mid-1960s.* The same year radio observed its own fortieth anniversary with a program about the Hungarian inventor Tivadar Puskás, whose tele-phonograph of 1881 was mentioned above. Several years later five more broadcasts on the history of Hungarian radio drew upon archival recordings.

But there are light touches too. In Budapest I saw an amusing forty-five–minute "ironical documentary film," as it was described in the program guide, dealing with no less a subject than bird droppings. Several cameramen documented the nuisance caused when sparrows, pigeons, and other birds frequent public buildings and squares. I also saw a well-produced film version of three O. Henry short stories, though it was amusing to watch scenes in which European-style railroad carriages were pulled by an Old World engine chugging through a convincing replica of the American countryside.

There always are the political aspects. A Hungarian author wrote that a consistent effort is made to show how technology pertains to the working man. "The release of the millionth ton of cast iron at the end of a 30-minute broadcast was very exciting. The expectation created tension and viewers, together with workers, kept their fingers crossed for the success of the fusion."[138] In 1967 an ambitious film series, "Our Century," ranged over the first cinema films, the funeral of England's Queen Victoria in 1901, the Russo-Japanese War, the Russian Revolution of 1905, World War I, and World War II.[139] With the title "Three Youths in the Army," a six-part series recounted the adventures of three heroes, at the same time acquainting its viewers with the "important weapons and the technical equipment of the Hungarian People's Army."[140] In 1972 a Hungarian radio team went to the Soviet Union to collect material for a series "dealing with the original motherland of the Hungarian people."[141]

---

who can figure what is going to happen after seeing two or three episodes . . . but the Flintstones . . . is wildly popular."

* OIRT Information 1965/3, p. 10; OIRT Information 1963/11. p. 10; OIRT Information 1965/6, p. 17.

The United States comes in for its share of treatment too. Six months after the death of President John F. Kennedy a radio documentary reviewed the assassination, the subsequent investigation, and related political factors.[142] In 1971 a radio play, "The McNamara Dossier," based upon the Pentagon Papers published by the *New York Times* and the *Washington Post*, "aroused vivid interest."[143] In 1972 Angela Davis was the subject of a weekly series which not only showed "the hunt of the communist philosopher but also the daily world policy news."[144]

Like the other Eastern European countries, Hungary's current regime likes to point out the inadequacies of its predecessors, often with reference to Admiral Miklos Horthy, regent from 1920 to 1944. Since Horthy allied Hungary with Germany and Italy during World War II, the present People's Republic frequently refers to the earlier governments as Fascist. In 1961 radio had a cycle of programs about the history of fascism in Hungary, and in 1964 another series dealt with the secret archives of the old Ministry of Foreign Affairs and with Adolf Hitler.[145]

But Admiral Horthy is the real *bête noire*, and so in 1961 television produced a cycle to expose some of his collaborators "on the basis of little known documentary films, newspapers, books, photos."[146] In 1964 a three-part film, described at the time as "the most important production of the Hungarian television," showed how in October 1944 "the Horthy-ite Regime proved its weakness in its final historical test." These films were broadcast by some foreign television organizations too. A song popular in Hungary before World War II, "You Are Beautiful, Hungary, You Are Beautiful," provided the title for a 1964 documentary which in addition to reviewing news and hit songs from that period castigated Admiral Horthy.[147] In 1971 a radio program told "about the ill famed forgery of francs under Horthy's Regime."

Entertainment and Sports

Although a great deal of Hungary's broadcast time consists of light entertainment, MRT spokesmen minimize the nature and extent of such programs, emphasizing instead their educational and informational output. However, available reports indicate considerable ingenuity in developing entertainment formats. During the summer of 1963, in "It's Not My Scene" ("the most successful of the programmes of the Hungarian Radio of last summer"), singers, artists, and entertainers competed doing things outside their respective specialties.[148] In the mid-1960s the "Young Talents Show," one of television's most popular features, was supplemented by "The Old Talents Show" on radio, in which amateurs over thirty years of age competed.[149] In 1966 a prominent woman chess player offered a cycle of broadcasts for young chess enthusiasts, while in 1969 there were crossword puzzle telecasts for which the answers were hidden in a music series.[150]

Interest is high in sports, and sportscaster György Szepési became a national figure as a consequence of his play-by-play reports. In 1963 he received a prize from the National Journalists' Association, and in the same year went to the German Democratic Republic to voice some programs about the historical relationships of the two countries which were quite unrelated to sports.[151] In 1970 a Hungarian publication in English, German, French, and Russian, summarizing Hungarian broadcasting for foreign readers, included a picture of Mr. Szepési, who was identified as "the noted reporter."[152] The next year a news release referred to the death of another "famous sports commentator, István Pluhár, who was very popular in Hungary."[153] In October 1971 television transmitted "a whole women's football match."[154] During the winter of 1971–1972, when radio carried live some Italian football (soccer) games, almost a million people placed bets by purchasing "Toto" tickets.

In both 1964 and 1968 the number of television sets increased markedly in anticipation of broadcasts of the Olympics. In the latter year, television took 114 programs of 216 hours' duration from Eurovision, most of which were Olympic Games fed from Grenoble.[155] Preceding the 1972 Summer Olympics were many news reports, and most of the actual events were transmitted live from Munich in color. Some 250,000 copies of a book containing the broadcast schedule, together with tables of records and information about past games, were put on sale. In October Hungarian television relayed the Davis Cup tennis matches from Bucharest, in which Romania and the United States were the contestants. From time to time during the programs comments on the play were made from the Budapest studios.

Hungary often provides origination facilities for foreign organizations covering international contests. In 1963 broadcasts of the European figure skating championships were relayed from Budapest by seventeen countries, and in 1966 television organizations from thirty-four countries and radio stations from twenty-five carried reports of the European Athletic Championships.[156] The same year Hungarian television used seven cameras to cover an athletic contest, along with facilities for radio coverage. The total project involved 54 employees who turned out approximately 291 hours of programs, of which French television took the greatest amount—29 hours.[157] In 1971, when Hungarian radio had an early morning broadcast from Rio de Janeiro of a football match between Hungary and Brazil, there was an enthusiastic audience despite the hour.[158]

Countries like Hungary, with limited resources and budgets, often are glad to get entertainment programs—even if dated—from other countries. In Budapest I saw a program featuring Paul Anka which had been recorded several years earlier in the Olympia in London. Typically, he cavorted for his teenage fans as they squealed and shouted approval. Hungary also carries features like the Polish Sopoty Festival, the Intervision equivalent of the Eurovision Song Contest (see pp. 304–305).

Audience Research

In 1961 Hungarian television and the Department of Pedagogy of Budapest University sent questionnaires to several thousand viewers with children in order to study the effects of television on young viewers.[159] Two years later radio established a department "to elaborate wide and scientific method [s] of evaluation of listeners' opinions and gain a number of collaborators working on a voluntary basis."[160] Procedures were more sophisticated by 1969, when researchers over a four-day period questioned listeners and viewers in Budapest, 34 provincial towns, and 110 villages to obtain reactions to a new program structure.[161] In 1970 the MRT Communications Research Center polled a panel of 1,400 listeners and viewers every fifth week to secure information on such subjects as reactions to news broadcasts and the effects of the media on the world outlook of youth.[162] The results of these studies, however, are not available, although the MRT research department does issue Hungarian-language publications in addition to periodically reporting in English the results of some of the international conferences it organizes.

In 1966 the EBU reported 2,497,000 radio and 1,000,000 television licenses in Hungary, the rates per hundred being 24.56 and 9.84, respectively (see Table 10). Data from Hungarian sources indicate that in 1968 from 80 to 85 per cent of all families had radio sets, with the proportion in Budapest being about twice that in most rural areas. According to this report, in large Hungarian cities—as throughout the United States—the number of radios exceeded the number of people, indicating the increasing popularity of transistor sets.[163]

EBU figures show that by 1972 the number of radio licenses had increased to 2,542,213 (24.64 per hundred), and the television total to 2,100,000 (20.35 per hundred.) A Hungarian release reported that during 1971, 247,000 television and 579,000 radio receivers were sold, the number of portable transistors being six times that of table models.[164] In Hungary small transistor radios are priced from 120 to 550 florins; larger sets from 1,000 to 1,500 florins; and a black-and-white television set at around 7,500 florins. The average income of a Hungarian worker is between 2,000 and 2,500 florins per month.

There are concerted campaigns to increase the number of receivers. In 1963 favorable trade-in allowances were made on radio sets, and in 1971 and 1972, with the objective of having at least one receiver in every home, inexpensive sets were placed on sale with payments on an installment basis.[165] In addition, new owners were exempt from license fees for the first six months and received free copies of the program guide for a time.

The Robinson study reported in 1965 a daily average of forty-two minutes of television viewing as a primary and forty-five minutes as a secondary activity, for a total of about an hour and a half of television viewing per day (see Table 4). (It should be noted, however, that television schedules in Hungary were much shorter in 1965 than now.) As of that date, the amount of viewing in Hungary was somewhat greater than in Bulgaria, about the same as in the USSR and Yugoslavia, and considerably less than in East Germany, Poland, and Czechoslovakia.

The relative newness of television in Hungary permits certain types of studies to be made of the effects of set ownership on leisure-time activities. A national survey by the Mass Communications Research Center of Hungarian Radio and Television in 1968 compared people who did and did not own receivers with non–set owners who watched programs with friends.[166] A consistent finding was that owners and non–owner viewers were much more active and attended more public events than did nonowners and nonviewers: 27.8 per cent of owners compared with 13.7 per cent of nonowners attended the theater several times a year, and 14.6 per cent of owners compared with 4.8 per cent of nonowners went to operettas and revues. The same results were found in regard to cinema shows and sports events: 42.1 per cent of owners compared with 34.4 per cent of nonowners attended the cinema several times a year, and 24.0 per cent of owners as compared with 16.6 per cent of nonowners attended sports contests. Even more striking were the differences in regard to attendance at intellectually demanding events: 6 per cent of owners compared with 2.8 per cent of nonowners attended concerts of serious music several times a year, and 14.7 per cent of owners compared with 8.0 per cent of nonowners went to museums. But attendance rates for educational lectures and amateur performances were about the same for both groups.

The study concluded that television viewing itself was not the reason for these differences, but rather that television ownership tended to coincide with higher economic status, which was accompanied by more interests outside the home. Other data indicated that television had become the principal means of acquiring knowledge for the average adult. There was increased visiting by non–set owners in the homes of television-equipped friends. But whereas it was traditional in Hungarian villages to serve food to guests, when people came over to watch television it was not considered necessary to talk to them before or after the program or provide them with refreshments. The study concluded that Hungary had undergone the same changes in regard to cultural and leisure activities as a consequence of television as had the rest of the world.

Studies of radio and television audiences usually lead to similar conclusions no matter where conducted, one example being an analysis of listening and viewing in Hungary made in 1970.[167] The peak radio audiences were in the early morning hours, at noon, and in the evening, and there was less listening in the evening than in the morning or at noon. But the Monday evening radio audience was large, because there then was no television on Mondays. Viewing peaked between 8:00 and 10:00 P.M. and was highest on Saturdays and Sundays, when more viewers were available.

The most popular "literary" radio program was the Szabó Family (see above, p. 388). Close seconds were crime stories and comedy features, while poetry was among the least popular literary offerings. By all odds, dance and variety music were the favored musical programs, although folk music was liked by many. Serious music—including symphony, chamber music, choral music, and opera—rated low. Taken together, these figures confirmed again that people are fundamentally the same everywhere and that mass media preferences do not vary greatly from country to country.

Audience research reports from Radio Free Europe contain some interesting data about listening to both domestic and foreign broadcasts. Between May and December 1970, 1,525 Hungarians visiting in six Western countries were asked about their listening to domestic radio programs.[168] Almost all—99 per cent to be exact—reported listening to Hungarian programs, 66 per cent daily, and 29 per cent several times each week. The favorite hours were from 6:00 to 9:00 A.M., noon to 1:00 P.M., and 4:00 to 11:00 P.M., with the greatest amount of listening between 6:00 and 8:00 in the evening, when 50 per cent tuned in. Eighty-eight per cent watched television, 26 per cent viewing daily, and 35 per cent several times a week. The favorite viewing time was from 7:00 to 10:00 P.M., with the peak between 8:00 and 9:00 in the evening when 80 per cent viewed.

RFE also reported on its own Hungarian audience. Normally RFE broadcasts twenty hours a day to Hungary, and since 1964 there has been no jamming in that country. Between May and December of 1970 RFE engaged research institutes in five Western European countries to question 1,531 Hungarian nationals staying temporarily in the West about their major sources of information on world events.[169] Their replies were as follows: radio, 80 per cent; newspapers, 66 per cent; television, 23 per cent; and others, 4 per cent. Asked to name their preferred radio information sources on world events, 93 per cent said Radio Budapest, 45 per cent RFE, 16 per cent BBC, 10 per cent Voice of America, and 14 per cent others.

College-educated respondents were more likely to be BBC listeners, while the audiences for Radio Budapest and Radio Free Europe represented a wider educationl range. As to preferred sources of information for domestic news, 46 per cent said newspapers and 44 per cent radio. Among radio stations, Radio Budapest led with 81 per cent, RFE was second with 47 per cent, the BBC third with 16 per cent, and the Voice of America fourth with 8 per cent. Again the chances were that people with elementary or secondary education would prefer Radio Budapest, RFE, or VOA and that those with more formal schooling would choose the BBC.

Another survey of Hungarians visiting the West inquired into sources of information preceding and following the December 1970 demonstrations in Poland.[170] The first 1,525 interviews were conducted between May and early December of 1970 (before the demonstrations took place), and the second 204 interviews (all with respondents who had been in Hungary during the demonstration) between January and March 1971. Of the first sample, 73 per cent listened to broadcasts from the West during the six months preceding those events, and of the second sample 81 per cent listened immediately afterward, the greatest increases in listening being to Radio Free Europe (from 55 to 78 per cent) and the BBC (from 24 to 40 per cent). Some 50 per cent first learned about the events from RFE as compared with only 5 per cent from Radio Budapest. Asked, "How did RFE handle this subject," 88 per cent said, "Very well." But 54 per cent indicated "little confidence" and 38 per cent "no confidence" in the coverage of Radio Budapest.

A subsequent RFE survey found that 53 per cent of a sample of 1,265 Hungarians visiting in Western countries in 1971 listened regularly to RFE, 25 per cent to the BBC, and 18 per cent to the VOA, while only 35 per cent never listened to Western broadcasts.[171] The percentage of regular listeners among the Hungarian population rose from 49 in 1963 to 55 in 1968; dropped to 52 in 1969; went up again to 55 in 1970 (as a direct result of the Polish events); and dropped to 53 in 1971. From these several studies RFE concluded that its audience increases in times of crisis when Hungarian citizens feel the need to supplement domestic reports with news from outside sources.

A further report based on the same data indicated that when asked, "What role does RFE play in your life?" 73 per cent of 675 Hungarian RFE listeners replied that it supplied—to use the phrase in the report—"Needed (often suppressed) information objectively, truthfully, and quickly."[172] When asked why they did not listen to RFE, 9 per cent of 644 Hungarians in another survey gave jamming as the reason, an interesting answer since Hungary had not jammed foreign broadcasts for almost a decade. The RFE report ascribed this to a "residual belief" that jamming was going on.[173]

External Broadcasting

In 1972 Hungarian external broadcasting averaged 111 hours per week, which placed it second lowest to Yugoslavia among the Eastern countries.* Programs are beamed to Europe in English, German, Greek, Hungarian, Italian, and Spanish; to the Near East in Turkish; to North America in English and Hungarian; and to Latin America in Hungarian and Spanish. There also have been programs in Esperanto. Hungarian External Broadcasting publishes the magazine *Our Native Country* to tell foreign listeners about a program of the same name transmitted for Hungarians living abroad.

Agreements for program exchange have been signed with most of the socialist countries as well as with the Netherlands, Italy, and Austria, although exchanges are not limited to those countries.[174] The broadcasting organizations of Austria, Bulgaria, Czechoslovakia, France, West Germany, Sweden, and Switzerland have had Hungarian days, evenings, or weeks, with reciprocal arrangements in Hungary.[175] In 1971 Hungarian television transmitted a thirteen-part film made in Bulgaria dealing with Bulgarian heroes of the International Labor Movement. But international visits are not limited to program projects, since in 1972 a Hungarian delegation went to London to observe the BBC and the ITA.

Italian personnel came to Budapest to shoot film about Hungarian women, while a Finnish crew came to make a program about Zoltán Kodály.[176] The French did a program about Béla Bartók; the Austrians filmed a Hungarian horse farm; the East Germans reported on Hungary's agricultural and industrial development; and the British produced portions of a documentary about a trip from Paris to Istanbul on the Orient Express.[177] Hungarian crews went to the Soviet Union to make a film about a pipeline, and to Romania to make one on oil refineries.[178] To observe the fiftieth anniversary of the October Revolution, Hungarian producers shot footage in Leningrad for a ballet to be danced to Prokofiev's Seventh Symphony.[179] A cameraman-editor-reporter filmed scenes in Damascus and Cairo over a six-week period, and a crew traveled 37,250 miles to report on Antarctica.[180]

There have been live exchanges with Czechoslovakia, France, Switzerland, and Yugoslavia.[181] Hungary worked with Bulgaria, Czechoslovakia, Poland, Romania, the USSR, and Yugoslavia to arrange joint radio broadcasts for young people, while a light entertainment project involved fifteen-minute contributions from Belgrade, Berlin, Bratislava, Budapest, Bucharest, Moscow, Prague, Sofia, Warsaw, and Zagreb.[182]

---

* See Table 9. *WRTH 1973*, p. 78; *OIRT Information* 1966/5, p. 11; *OIRT Information* 1972/3, p. 8.

In 1960 Hungary received 43 Eurovision programs totaling 37 hours in length (see Tables 1 and 2). In 1961 it originated 3 programs (6 hr.), while receiving 19 programs (23 hr.). By 1966, 14 programs (37 hr.) were originated, and 69 (107 hr.) received. Although Hungary originated only 4 programs (7 hr.) in 1968, because of the Olympic Games it received 144 programs (216 hr.). In 1971, according to the EBU, only 5 programs (9½ hr.) were originated, although 94 programs (196 hr.) were received. But Intervision reported that during 1971 Hungary contributed 6 programs (8 hr., 47 min.), or 7.3 per cent of all Intervision feeds to Eurovision, while receiving 76 programs (154 hr., 23 min.). During 1972, again to cite Intervision figures, Hungary contributed 9 programs (14 hr., 34 min.), while receiving 43 programs (84 hr., 44 min.). Of these, 70 per cent were sports, 15 per cent culture, and 12 per cent entertainment.

An important aspect of external broadcasting is the placing of programs on foreign stations. In 1961 Hungarian concerts were carried by 27 broadcasting organizations, while 8 requested recordings of lectures on Hungarian composers.[183] In 1965, when broadcasts were exchanged with 115 countries, 60 stations devoted 208 broadcasts to 48 works by contemporary Hungarian composers. A number of American stations use Hungarian material. In 1965 an English-language report of a Hungarian puppet theater's presentation of Shakespeare's *A Midsummer Night's Dream* was carried by 60 stations.[184] In these exchanges Hungarian radio works closely with the Broadcasting Foundation of America. On one occasion the BFA provided 55 American stations with a 30-minute feature program about the city of Debreczen.

MRT musical organizations regularly play abroad. The Hungarian Radio and Television Symphony Orchestra has toured Australia, England, Italy, Romania, the Soviet Union, Switzerland, the United States, and Yugoslavia, and the Radio Jazz Orchestra has played in Italy and the Soviet Union, among other countries.[185] When the broadcasting symphony orchestra, which is probably Hungary's best, visited the United States in 1971, some aspects of the tour were filmed and subsequently televised at home. The Radio Children's Choir toured Japan twice, as well as Austria, Belgium, and West Germany.[186]

X

Socialist Republic of Romania

Romania is one of the more independent states of the Eastern European socialist bloc. It was the only Warsaw Pact country to oppose the Soviet invasion of Czechoslovakia in 1968. The following year President Nixon visited Bucharest, the first time an American president had visited a Communist country. Romania also has cultivated friendly relations with the People's Republic of China, despite Sino-Soviet tensions. Yet, in domestic affairs Romania applies Communist doctrine very strictly.

Facts about Romania

The Socialist Republic of Romania is bounded on the north and northeast by the Soviet Union, on the northwest by Hungary, on the southwest by Yugoslavia, and on the south by Bulgaria. Over 140 miles of its eastern border is on the Black Sea. With a total area of 91,699 square miles, Romania is slightly smaller than the state of Oregon, which occupies 96,981 square miles.

The population of Romania in July 1970 was 20,253,000, and its capital city, Bucharest, had 1,575,000 inhabitants.[1] Approximately 86 per cent of the population are Romanians, the principal minorities being Hungarians (1.5 million) and Germans (400,000), both concentrated in Transylvania along the Hungarian border. Other minorities include Yugoslavs, Ukrainians, Greeks, Gypsies, and Jews. The Romanian Orthodox Church, with 14 or 15 million followers, is the dominant faith, although the government is not sympathetic to religion, and there are no religious broadcasts. The Roman Catholic Church, with approximately 1,300,000 members (mostly Hungarians and Germans in Transylvania), is the second largest. Smaller religious groups include 700,000 Calvinists (mainly Hungarians), 180,000 Evangelicals (Germans), and some 110,000 Jews.

Historically Romania's economy has been agricultural, in spite of extensive petroleum deposits. But since 1950 official policy has encouraged industry, which now contributes over half the national income. Despite attempts to remain independent of Soviet economic control, the bulk of Romanian trade is with the USSR and other socialist states. In 1970, 30 per cent of the value of all foreign trade was with the USSR.[2] Then came the German Federal Republic with about 9 per cent, Czechoslovakia with 8 per cent, the German Democratic Republic and Italy with approximately 6 per cent each, and France with 5 per cent.

In the future an increasing amount of Romania's trade will be with the United States. In October 1970, as a result of the visit of President Nicolae Ceauşescu to Washington, an agreement was signed with the American Metal Climax Company to supply a $10,000,000 aluminum sheet rolling plant to Romania.[3] In December of the following year President Nixon authorized the Export-Import Bank to extend credits for the sale of American goods to Romania, thus ending a three-year ban on government-backed credits to socialist bloc nations.

Romanians are quick to tell visitors that they are not Slavs, and that their language, based on Latin, is a Romance language. (French, in fact, is the second language of the country.) The Romanians are descended from Roman settlers of the second century. Although in succeeding centuries Goths, Huns, Slavs, Magyars, and Turks overran the territory, the language remains predominantly Latin in vocabulary and uses Latin script. In recent years the government has officially changed the English spelling of the country's name form the Slavic Rumania to the Latinized Romania. Accompanying this cultural cleavage from the Slavic group is a pronounced tendency toward political independence.

In 1878 the Congress of Berlin recognized Prince Carol—the former German Prince Karl of Hohenzollern—as king of an independent Romania. In the course of his reign, which extended to 1914, parliamentary government was established, although Romania never developed democratic traditions like those of Czechoslovakia. During World War I Romania remained neutral until 1916, when it joined the Allies. In the postwar settlements it received some territorial gains. Early in World War II Romania was occupied by Germany, but following a coup d'état changed sides and fought against the Axis powers. After Soviet troops took over in 1944, a Communist government was established. Officially, however, the country remained a kingdom until the end of 1947, when the Romanian People's Republic was proclaimed. Romania is a member of the United Nations, UNESCO, the Warsaw Pact, and COMECON, although it takes the position that membership in COMECON should be open to nonsocialist states.

During its first Communist years Romania was very responsive to the Soviet Union, but recently has followed a courageously independent course.[4] Ceauşescu was the first Eastern European leader to establish diplomatic relations with West Germany in 1967, thereby provoking Soviet anger—although in 1973 the USSR did so too.[5] In June 1973 Ceauşescu visited West Germany for five days to seek trade arrangements, that being the first official trip to West Germany by an Eastern European head of state. Romania did not join the other bloc countries in severing relations with Israel during the Middle East War in 1967, and in August 1968, a few days before the occupation of Czechoslovakia, President Nicolae Ceauşescu visited Prague to show his support of Alexander Dubček.* When the USSR did invade, Romania alone among the Warsaw Pact nations not only failed to send troops, but publicly denounced the invasion. Despite rumors that the Soviet army might march into Romania too, it did not do so. Ceauşescu, contradicting the Brezhnev doctrine, insisted on the right of socialist nations to control their own domestic affairs, and described the invasion of Czechoslovakia as a "great mistake and a grave danger to peace in Europe, to the fate of socialism in the world" (on the Brezhnev doctrine, see above, page 315). The Romanians have rejected military as well as economic integration. There are no Russian troops in Romania, and there have been no Warsaw Pact maneuvers on Romanian territory since 1962, although early in 1973 the Warsaw Pact allies held a ten-day staff exercise—without troops—in Romania.[6]

When President Richard Nixon paid an official visit to Romania in August 1969, it was the first time an American president had visited a

* *New York Times*, August 22, 1968, p. 1. Yugoslavia likewise did not send troops, and Tito also condemned the Soviet action, but Yugoslavia was not a Warsaw Pact member.

Communist capital. The Romanians like to mention this during conversations with Americans. In October 1970 President Ceaușescu returned the visit, and while in the United States he also addressed the United Nations.[7] Two years later Secretary of State William P. Rogers visited Romania—the first time an American secretary of state had ever done so—and signed a consular convention, the first between the two countries since 1881.[8] In 1973 Mr. Ceaușescu concluded a six-day tour of Italy by visiting Pope Paul VI at the Vatican, with whom he discussed the status of Romania's million Roman Catholics.[9] (President Nikolai V. Podgorny of the USSR had visited the Pontiff in 1967, and President Tito of Yugoslavia in 1971.) In addition to gaining prestige both at home and abroad from such contacts, Ceaușescu probably feels that closer relations with the United States and other Western nations may deter the effects of the Soviet Union to increase its influence over his country.

After the invasion of Czechoslovakia it was not until March 1971 that a Romanian defense minister attended a meeting of the Warsaw Pact powers.[10] In the summer of 1971 President Ceaușescu visited Peking, and in August of that year Romania was the only bloc country not represented at a Moscow meeting which denounced Chinese deviation from the Soviet line.[11] At that time President Ceaușescu said that although "forms of cooperation may naturally be varied . . . this must not lead to the transgression of national sovereignty."[12] Again rejecting the Brezhnev doctrine, Ceaușescu declared later the same month: "The Communist movement can no longer be led by any center. No place in any part of the world needs a Communist center. It is necessary for each party to be self-dependent."[13]

On August 23, 1971, "Liberation Day," Romanian newspapers published side-by-side congratulatory telegrams from Party Chief Leonid Brezhnev and Chairman Mao Tse-tung.[14] More recently, the Soviet Union has tried to ease tensions with Bucharest in various ways, such as by providing an unusually cordial reception upon the arrival of a new Romanian ambassador in Moscow, but relations between the two countries have periodic ups and downs.[15]

These attempts to maintain Romanian independence in foreign affairs should not be taken, however, as indicating a departure from Communist orthodoxy at home. In fact, a Western reporter observed that whereas in 1968 Dubček had administered Czechoslovakia loosely, in 1971

Ceauşescu was holding "the tightest rein in Eastern Europe."[16] One reason for this undoubtedly is concern lest too much freedom provide an excuse for an invasion similar to that of Czechoslovakia. Yet this did not interfere with the opening of a United States library in Bucharest in 1971, the only American cultural facility in a Communist country (except Yugoslavia) located off American Embassy premises. Thousands of Romanians have participated in the center's activities and have used its library without apparent interference from Romanian authorities—which has not been the case in many of the socialist countries. (In the same year all Romanian citizens were required to report their contacts with foreigners to state security officials, although the enforcement of this rule subsequently was relaxed!)[17]

Legal Structure

The Romanian Constitution of 1965, which succeeded constitutions of 1948 and 1952, declared the country to be "a socialist republic" in which the "whole power . . . belongs to the people, free and masters of their destiny."[18] The concept of progression from socialism to communism is clearly set forth: "People's power is based on the worker-peasant alliance. In close union, the working class—the leading class of society—the peasantry, the intelligentsia and the other categories of working people, regardless of nationality, build the socialist system, creating the conditions for transition to communism."

The Constitution declares that "the leading political force of the whole of society is the Rumanian Communist Party" and that the country has "a socialist economy, based upon the socialist ownership of the means of production."[19] "Telecommunication" is classified as a natural resource, along with minerals, forests, and "state socio-cultural institutions," all of which "belong to the whole people and are state property."[20]

The purpose of "state activity" is "the development of the socialist system and the prosperity of the nation."[21] To this end the state "plans and conducts the national economy," defends socialist property, "guarantees the full exercise of citizen rights," "develops education at all levels," and "ensures the conditions for the development of science, the arts and culture."

The fundamental rights and duties of citizens are set forth as in the other socialist constitutions. All citizens have "equal rights" and are assured specifically the rights to work, leisure, and education.[22] All citizens eighteen years of age or older may vote. However, "the most advanced and conscious citizens . . . unite in the Rumanian Communist Party, the highest form of organization of the working class, its vanguard detachment." The party assumes "the role of leader in all the fields of socialist construction, and directs the activity of the mass and public organizations and of the state bodies."[23]

All citizens "are guaranteed freedom of speech, of the Press, of reunion, of meeting and demonstration."[24] But in Romania, as in other socialist states, these freedoms "cannot be used for aims hostile to the socialist system and to the interests of the working people. Any association of a fascist or anti-democratic character is prohibited. Participation in such associations and propaganda of a fascist or anti-democratic character are punished by the law."[25]

The "sole legislative body of the Socialist Republic of Rumania" is the National Assembly, elected by popular vote for a four-year term.[26] Subject to it is the State Council, "the supreme body of state power with a permanent activity," elected by the Assembly from its members, and composed of a president, four vice-presidents, and twenty-two other members.[27] The Council of Ministers, "the supreme body of state administration," also is elected by the National Assembly.[28] One member of this council is the minister of posts and telecommunications.

The single political party, the Romanian Communist party, created in 1921 and given its present name in 1965, has about 2,100,000 members.[29] The Socialist Unity Front, founded in 1968, relates various worker groups and professional organizations to the party. The general secretary of the Central Committee of the Romanian Communist party, Nicolae Ceauşescu, who also is a member of the Permanent Presidium, is the national president.

Broadcasting is the responsibility of the Radio and Television Committee of the Council of Ministers.[30] This committee, however, receives much policy guidance from the National Council on Radio and Television, created in March 1971. The council is headed by a member of the party's Central Committee, and includes prominent political and national leaders. Basic plans must have the prior approval of the Council of Ministers.

The president of the broadcasting committee also is vice-chairman of the National Council. In addition, the committee has four vice-presidents

who direct its major activities. They and the heads of the various program departments are expected to work closely with the government,
the party, and the trade unions.

The broadcasting organization itself is divided into three sections:
radio (domestic programs, external broadcasts, and engineering); television (programming, films, production, and engineering); and what are
described as "common departments" (ideological broadcasts, music,
education, foreign exchange, staff training, and research).

It was pointed out above that Romania's independent foreign policy
is accompanied by orthodox Communist domestic policies. In July 1971
President Ceauşescu stated: "It is necessary to strengthen the party
leadership and guidance of the whole cultural-artistic life of this country.
There must be a single concept [and] ideology—the revolutionary ideology and concept of the working class. The arts must serve a single
purpose—the socialist communist education."[31] He identified the press
as "an instrument of the party," which therefore must disseminate party
policy "in all domains of activity."

In October 1971 the Romanian government withdrew its display from
the International Book Fair in Frankfurt, West Germany, to protest the
"unfriendly act" of publication of a novel by former Romanian political
prisoner Paul Goma.[32] The following month five pages in the party newspaper were devoted to a speech in which President Ceauşescu announced
tighter controls over government, science, and art. The party, he said,
must have more control over such groups as the writers' and artists'
unions. Artists should "render in art the grand socialist transformations
of the country; the enthusiastic work of millions of people."

In view of such statements from the president, it is not surprising to
find broadcasters writing in the same vein. The chairman of the Radio
and Television Committee stated in 1961: "During the period of the
people's government . . . [radio and press] have become an important
means of mobilizing the creative energy of the working people for the
building-up of a new socialist life in the Rumanian People's Republic. . . . In evaluating the important role of radio and television, our
Party and Government have created suitable conditions so that these
'guides' of culture and progress might incessantly develop and fulfill
successfully the tasks which confront them."[33]

In 1963 another spokesman declared: "At present radio and television
represent an enormous force in the communist education of the people

and in political and cultural work among the masses. Together with the press, radio and television have become mass media of information. . . . [Accordingly] they reflect daily the numerous and variegated aspects of life in our country and speak about people working in factories, fields and laboratories, and the enthusiastic and devoted work of all those who are completing the building-up of socialism."[34]

I asked the head of television news—himself an active and obviously highly trusted member of the party—if my description of the relationship between the Communist party and broadcasting in the Soviet Union applied as well to Romania (see above, page 44). He replied that, generally speaking, it did. This accorded with the statement by President Ceauşescu in July 1971 about the importation of films from abroad: "We cannot admit radio and television programmes which by their content do not actively contribute to the communist, patriotic, revolutionary education of the youth, of the people."[35] Freedom of creation, he went on to say, must give way before the right of the government "to interfere in literature and in the fine arts, also in music, to admit only what it considered to harmonize with socialism."

A recent statement from the broadcasting organization declares that its programs "aim at contributing to the education of a wide range of listeners, to the creation of the advanced revolutionary characteristics of the new man, to the mobilization of the large masses in the achievement of the socialist society, and to keeping public opinion informed on domestic and international events. Romanian radio and television strive to develop the socialist conscience of the masses."

Although Romania permits its media more freedom than do some socialist countries, they nevertheless are well controlled. A spokesman for television assured me in 1972: "No one can dictate to radio and television." But he did not claim the right to examine basic beliefs, even though he insisted they could criticize operations, and that they enjoy considerable programming independence. There are, in fact, live programs on which ministers and other high government officials are questioned about the work of their departments. There is no censorship as such, however, since all key positions are held by people whom the government and the party can trust.*

* In 1964 Buzek (p. 11) wrote that the Romanian press, like those of Bulgaria, Albania, and East Germany, tried "to retain as long as possible the stalinest concept of strict party rule," while those in Poland, Yugoslavia, and Hungary "relaxed

Networks and Programs

Romanian Radio and Television (Radiodifuziunea si Televizinea Română) operates three nationwide radio networks, five regional programs, an external broadcasting organization, and two television services.

In 1972 Romania's three radio networks were on the air a total of fifty-one hours a day: Program I broadcast twenty-four hours, Program II nineteen hours, and Program III eight hours.[36] These networks complement rather than duplicate one another's offerings. Program I, brought to the entire country by one 1,200-kilowatt long-wave transmitter supplemented by several medium-wave and FM transmitters, is a general service with news, information, sports, drama, entertainment, and children's programs.

Program II, on the air daily from 4:00 A.M. to 11:00 A.M., carries the principal educational programs, material for in-school use, discussion broadcasts, serious drama, and some classical music. It is available to most of the country from a number of medium-wave transmitters (including one of 1,000 and another of 950 kilowatts power), as well as some FM transmitters. Program III, broadcast daily from 2:00 P.M. until 10:00 P.M. on FM only, is basically a music service.*

These nationwide networks are supplemented by five regional services, which present programs of local interest in Romanian, German, Hungarian, and Serbian. During the summer months since 1967, "Radio-Repos," at Mamaia on the Black Sea, has broadcast information and entertainment for vacationing Romanians and foreign tourists.[37] Leisure Radio, to use its English name, offers Romanian and foreign light music, a news service in five languages (Romanian, Russian, German, English, and French), weather forecasts, medical advice, recipes, and a course in colloquial Romanian.

Regular television programming began December 31, 1956.[38] Program I is on the air daily from 9:00 A.M. to 1:00 P.M. and from 4:00 to 10:30 or 11:00 P.M. The Sunday schedule is continuous from 6:15

. . . controls . . . [giving] more freedom for journalists to work within a broader party line." The following year Raymond B. Nixon, ranking Romania with 116 other countries on a 9-point scale for press freedom and control (1 indicating a free press, and 9 a completely controlled one), classified Romania as 8: "Controlled press system, but with less rigid controls [than 9] and/or some opportunity for debate within system" ("Freedom in the World's Press," pp. 6, 13).

* Romanian FM broadcasting, done in the Eastern European FM band, includes some stereophonic transmissions.

A.M. to 9:00 P.M. The first network uses seventeen VHF transmitters and approximately seventy low-power repeaters to cover 90 per cent of the population. Program II, which began in 1968, covers the greater Bucharest area from a single transmitter. Originally on the air only three nights a week, since 1969 it has broadcast daily from 6:00 to 9:00 P.M.*

In 1966, when there was only one service, the twenty-six hours a week of television broadcasts were categorized as follows: music, 19 per cent; news, 12 per cent; programs for children and youth, 18 per cent; films, 18 per cent; drama, 9 per cent; and sports, 8 per cent.[39] Program I is a general service, including news, films, sports, drama, music, educational features, and light entertainment. Program II is more intellectual and cultural, with full-length operas, plays, and educational features. It also repeats some first network programs.

There are advertisements for both Romanian and foreign products on the first two radio networks and on both television channels, although the income derived from them represents only 1 or 2 per cent of the total broadcasting budget. The first radio network schedules ten minutes of commercials at 4:50 P.M. Tuesday through Friday, while the second network has a fifteen-minute cluster at 3:45 P.M. on Sunday and twenty-minute clusters at 6:00 P.M. Tuesday through Saturday. The first television service has five-, ten-, and fifteen-minute blocks of commercials at various times during the day. I saw several of these, including advertisements for a soft drink which utilized some clever and ingenious cartoons, for the National Lottery, and for a space heater.

The lovely women television announcers of Europe deserve special mention. On almost all stations, both East and West, several carefully coiffured and neatly dressed young women, chosen for appearance, personality, voice quality, and diction, appear on screens at the beginning and end of transmissions and between programs to make announcements and, what is more important, to serve as hostesses and to provide continuity for the program schedule. In some cases their names appear on the screen—but no telephone numbers! The reason for including this paragraph in the section on Romania is that the Romanian *speakerines*— as they are called in French, *Ansagerinen* in German—were the prettiest I saw in all of Eastern Europe.

---

* The Eastern European System D is used, although color will employ the Western European PAL rather than the French and Eastern European SECAM system.

There are fine radio and television buildings in Bucharest. The radio center, completed in 1951, contains eight large studios for music and dramatic programs, plus a number of smaller ones for talks and interviews. The drama studios have floors of contrasting materials, reverberation chambers, and the other paraphernalia necessary for such productions. The most impressive feature of the building is its fine concert hall, completed in 1960, with seating for 1,000 people.[40] The stage, which will accommodate 120 instrumentalists and a choir of 125, is backed by an impressive pipe organ. As many as 12 microphones can be used, and there are reverberation chambers. There is sufficient lighting for television pickups.

The television center was begun in 1966, first used in 1968, and completed in 1972. My hosts reported with pride that the basic planning was done by Romanians and that all the equipment not manufactured in Romania was from Western Europe rather than the Soviet Union.[41] The total floor space of the four buildings in the center is approximately 645,000 square feet, the principal units being an office tower of thirteen stories and a studio section with seven studios and related facilities. There is another studio for sound recordings, and future plans include facilities for the production of television films. On my tour of the building in 1970 I saw much excellent equipment, but noted a complete absence of video tape recorders. The American prohibition against selling such recorders to the Communist countries because of their potential military value had up to that time prevented their acquisition in Bucharest, although the Romanians hoped to get some in the future. At present there are no television studios in other Romanian cities, although there are portable remote facilities.*

News and Public Affairs

The first and second radio networks together broadcast news at least once an hour, in addition to which there are newscasts on the third net-

* My very cordial tour guides, including both engineering and program personnel, seemed to hold nothing back in what they showed or said. However, I could not overlook the guards with submachine guns on each floor, indicating that in Bucharest as in all Communist countries, a high level of security is maintained in broadcasting installations. Admission normally is possible only upon the recommendation of responsible staff members, and may—although it did not in Bucharest—involve almost as much checking of identification papers as admission to the country itself. So, the guards in the Bucharest television center must be accepted as normal for that part of the world.

work, on the five local services, and on the Mamaia summer service in the Black Sea area. These programs range from brief headlines to thirty-minute reviews. Television offers a daily news program from 7:30 to 8:00 P.M., a shorter late evening summary, and some news-oriented features.

Basic to these broadcasts are the reports of the Romanian Press Agency (Agentia Romana de Presa, or Agerpres), which is legally part of the government.[42] Agerpres has branches in all major Romanian cities plus foreign bureaus in the socialist and many other countries, including Austria, France, Italy, Japan, Switzerland, and the United States. The 500-person staff, in addition to its basic Romanian output, turns out each day 14,300 words in English, 9,400 in French, 6,550 in Spanish, 13,250 in Russian, and 2,600 in German. Television also receives material from from UPI, IPN, and Visnews, as well as from daily Intervision and Eurovision exchanges.

But Eurovision records show limited use of its news service (see Tables 1 and 2). In 1963 Romania provided no items and received 16. After a year of no participation, in 1965 Romania provided 1 and received 1 item. In 1966 it provided 5 and received none, and in 1967 provided 4 and received 1. Intervision reports that in 1972 Romanian television received 1,532 news items from Eurovision and originated 10.

In 1960 a representative of Romanian radio wrote that because radio was the fastest way to disseminate information, it must be twenty-four hours ahead of the press.[43] But radio reporting should not "anticipate events on the basis of presumptions or unverified information. Informative material must be a document, and thus authentic and true and we must therefore edit it in this way." Newscasts, he went on, should supplement straight reading with on-the-spot reports and interviews, and should bring "real people" to the microphone. Seven years later a radio news editor stressed the importance of direct pickups of gala occasions, political congresses, sports contests, and events like the completion of a hydroelectric project.[44]

Radio has thirty news broadcasts every day. These include ten complete newscasts plus a number of shorter summaries.[45] Since 1971 there has been a two-hour program from 6:00 to 8:00 each evening ("lasting 7,200 seconds") which aims to transmit scientific, cultural, and sports events "almost at the moment" they occur, in order to achieve maximum impact from "simultaneity."

News accounts for about 25 per cent of the television output. On Program I there is a daily half-hour newscast at 7:30 P.M. plus a fifteen-minute late evening summary, while Program II offers a ten-minute late evening roundup. In May 1972 television launched a Saturday evening program, "The Week in Pictures," providing "a survey of the most important national and international events with film shots, telephotos and video recordings."[46] The news department also is responsible for documentary treatments of both domestic and international subjects, and frequently sends reporting and film teams abroad to collect material for such programs. When President Ceauşescu visited the United States in 1970, reporters and cameramen accompanied him and relayed reports home by film and satellite.

During a long and probing discussion, I exchanged ideas with the head of television news. He was editor in chief, he said, not because he belonged to the Communist party, but because he was professionally competent—which he obviously was. Not all his key staff members were party members: at one time membership was indispensable, but that was no longer the case. He himself had traveled extensively, spoke good English, had made several trips to the United States, and obviously was well informed about developments in all parts of the world. One of the several telephones on his desk, he said, was connected directly to Communist party headquarters—not to receive instructions "but to check the facts."

Newscasts emphasize industrial growth and expansion, he said, in order to encourage high work standards and to report on the expenditure of public funds. Living standards are steadily improving, but it still is necessary to assure the public that their sacrifices and taxes are bringing results. For example, a recent program had documented the reconstruction of a town destroyed in a flood the previous spring.*

We also discussed news broadcasting in other countries. The United States, he thought, overemphasized commentary and provided inadequate coverage of foreign developments. Comparing the Voice of America with the BBC and Radio Free Europe, all of which broadcast in Romanian, he ranked the BBC first as most objective, and said the

---

* This is consistent with the emphasis of some educational programs on good work habits as well as with the talk President Ceauşescu gave to agricultural and factory workers in March 1971 when he urged them to show more energy, imagination, and discipline (*New York Times*, March 18, 1971, p. 8C).

British output still benefited from its wartime record and its European orientation. Furthermore, it was more independent of government than the VOA, even though it still reflected national opinion. Least acceptable was Radio Free Europe.

Romanian television never speculates about the course of events. If there were doubt, for example, whether President Ceauşescu would attend the Nasser funeral (Nasser had died a few days before), they would not guess at his plans lest it weaken the party or the country abroad. But self-criticism was another thing. As a consequence of his visit to America, Ceauşescu was making surprise visits to supermarkets in Romania and comparing them—to their disadvantage—with their American counterparts. All this was well covered by television—though whether by coincidence or design I did not learn. In effect, however, the media were cooperating with the president to improve merchandising practices. Discussing such things, the director of television news remarked that whenever the Romanian media criticized the president, his ministers, or national developments, they did so to help rather than merely to complain.

Several telecasts in November 1970 reported the current visit to Romania of Premier Gomulka of Poland. Other items included the death of General Charles de Gaulle; progress on apartment construction; the completion of a hydroelectric plant; a kidnapping in Montreal; the trial in Italy of some Americans charged with hijacking an airplane; and several sporting events. There was great emphasis on President Ceauşescu and on the heads of state of other socialist countries. Generally speaking, the main international items broadcast by the English language services of the Voice of America and the BBC also were covered on Romanian Television. Romania, incidentally, was one of the two socialist countries to carry all or most of the American moon walks in November 1969. Many Romanians stayed up all night to watch, while some people in neighboring countries either tuned to Romanian stations or visited Romanian friends to see the broadcasts. There also was coverage of Eastern European events. I happened to visit the new television center just as they were relaying the annual November 7 parade from Moscow in 1970.

Programs in October 1972 were improvements over those of 1970, and represented enormous advancements over what I had seen in 1965. There, of course, were some typical socialist touches: the lead story usually was a report of industrial achievement or an item about the party or President Ceaușescu. But most of the items could have appeared on television screens anywhere. At the time of my visit in 1972, heavy rains had caused serious flooding, and so there were films of the damage and of soldiers helping with the harvest. Still pictures of Henry Kissinger were held on the screen while an announcer read reports about the peace negotiations in Paris. The fighting in Vietnam was illustrated with films and maps, and maps also accompanied stories about some current developments in Yemen.

There was film coverage of a political meeting in West Germany and of an exhibit of vintage airplanes. A photograph of Soviet Foreign Minister Andrei Gromyko filled the screen while a related news item was read. Needless to say, there were films and commentary about the upcoming Davis Cup matches between Romania and the United States. Almost half of a Sunday evening news summary pertained to sports, including highlights from the games of the day.

In 1970 I felt that Romanian television news was not as professional in content or production as the elaborateness of the studios had led me to expect. Often there was uninteresting reading with little if any visual material. But by 1972 presentation had improved, even though the emphasis was on silent rather than sound film. News readers clearly had gained in confidence and ability. The total impression was of a steadily improving service.

Americans in Bucharest report that Romanians tend to admire the United States, and that this is reflected in broadcast news coverage. At any rate, although they must follow the Soviet model in at least some respects, Romanian newscasts treat the United States quite well. As one person put it, although the recently completed tour of Angela Davis was "dutifully reported," the Romanian media were more objective in their treatment than were some other socialist bloc countries.

Children and Youth

Romanian radio and television have educational and instructional programs for all ages. It is not surprising that political education is an important objective for many of them. In 1962 a Romanian wrote that "the feature common to all [these programs] . . . is active contribution to communist education of the young generation of our country."[47]

Love of work is stressed, and some stories and dramatizations emphasize the importance of developing skills to contribute to "the building-up
of socialism and the transition to . . . communism."[48] There also are
references to internationalism and to "the fight of the working class of
other countries . . . and friendship with socialist countries." But there
is a nationalistic aspect too: an official concerned with children's programs, probably with an eye toward the Soviet Union, told me that it
is important to tell children about the sacrifices made by their forebears
so they will understand the importance of maintaining national independence. Programs for school-age children are intended "not to replace
the educational influence of the family and school, being rather to assist
those directly concerned with the education of children."[49]

For some years both radio and television have had programs to supplement schoolwork, but only recently have they developed programs
for in-school use. In 1966 the head of children's radio reported that the
three networks then offered twenty-seven broadcasts each week for pre-
school and school children, in addition to which there were originations
in regional studios and village wired broadcasting centers.[50] Currently
the Radio School presents material to supplement the teaching of biology,
natural science, philosophy, the philosophy of scientific socialism, and
Romanian language and literature. There also are programs to help
children prepare for school leaving and secondary school entrance examinations. Programs are broadcast six days a week at 10:30 A.M. and 3:00
or 3:30 P.M., and most programs are repeated one or more times. A
thirty-page guide, available on news stands throughout the country, contains supplementary material for both radio and television offerings.

In-school television was only recently introduced although it now is
being expanded. The Teleşcoală, broadcast daily at 9:00 A.M. and
4:00 P.M., has programs in biology, chemistry, economics, geography,
history, mathematics, philosophy, physics, and Romanian language and
literature. There also are programs in English, French, German, and
Russian, designed primarily for adult viewers, but broadcast not only
at 5:30 P.M. for them but also at 10:00 A.M. for the convenience of
classes wishing to use them.

The things written about Romanian out-of-school programs for children indicate a conscientious approach, and that also was my impression
after discussing the broadcasts with the people responsible for them. In
1962 a writer pointed out that dramatizations and interviews were used

rather than "dry and serious descriptions and lectures" in order to heighten student interest.[51] The political objectives mentioned above were evident in the series "Bright Pioneer Greeting," which related to "communist education." Pioneers were encouraged to do such helpful things as collecting scrap iron. "Materials describing the life and activity of pioneers in friendly countries and those reflecting the hard life of the children of working people in capitalist countries and colonies are included in this programme too."

Great explorers and scientists also are subjects for programs.[52] An article on scientific broadcasts for children concluded with the sentence: "The young dreamers of today are the bold builders of tomorrow."[53] Because science is an important area of knowledge, "scientific and technological problems occupy one of the most important places in the themes of broadcasts for children."

Many devices are used to sustain interest. "Captain Wind," a thirty-minute program broadcast twice a month in 1963, introduced viewers to scientific information.[54] According to the head of the Department of Scientific Broadcasts for Children, "such broadcasts not only stimulate children's fantasy, but also foster their love for science and technology."[55]

In 1963 "Children's Mail" answered letters from young viewers.[56] In 1967, on a weekly twenty-minute series, two children asked a well-informed "uncle" such questions as "Where does the sun hide at night?" "What is a submarine?" and "What is hail?" In 1971 a forty-five–minute monthly television series explored various trades and professions, as experts answered questions telephoned or written in by young people. For minority nationality children there are programs in Hungarian, German, and Serbian.[57] Currently radio has plays for children, "Radio Tom Thumb," "Always Forward" (for Pioneers and schoolchildren), "I Want to Know" (about science and technology), "100 Romanian Legends," and—inevitably—"Good Night Children," broadcast daily from 7:50 to 8:00 P.M.

Children often take part in programs, since producers believe that young listeners and viewers will then feel more involved.[58] Child readers, actors, announcers, performers, and singers are selected competitively, and some of them go on to professional careers. Climaxing all such projects is an annual competition organized cooperatively by the Minister of National Education and the Union of Working Youth in which 3 million children participate. Through a series of eliminations, the best readers, singers, instrumentalists, folk dance groups, and choirs are chosen, and the winners go on the air.

In Romania I saw some interesting programs for young people, ranging from calisthenics to hobby broadcasts. Each Sunday morning from 8:30 to 10:00 there is the ninety-minute "Red Ties" ("Cravatele Rosii," in Romanian), named for the red ties worn by Pioneers. This program, by and for children aged seven through fourteen, included an interview with a teen-ager who discussed and demonstrated some of his own electronic experiments plus a short NBC film about Flipper, the dolphin, broadcast in English with subtitles. (Amusingly, through an error, the transmission included the line, "Insert Commercial Here.") Television now is trying to bring *Sesame Street* to Romanian screens, the principal problem being that of language: should the programs be broadcast in English with subtitles, dubbed into Romanian, or what?

There also are children's programs during prime evening time, including "1001 de seri" (1001 Nights for Children"), broadcast daily from 7:20 to 7:30 P.M. One clever animated sequence involved an egg man, an egg cup, a rolling pin, and other kitchen appliances. In another a lamb was gamboling with three wolves. This series has been on the air for six years, and television personnel report that parents as well as children complain if it is delayed or omitted. One evening between 8:00 and 8:30 I saw some amusing skits by a well-known Romanian actor and a talented child performer, followed by children's cartoons, one with a moral about care with fire.

From 9:00 to 10:30 Monday evenings television has "The Romantic Club," a program by and for teen-agers, including light entertainment, together with discussions of political problems of interest to young viewers. The program I saw featured an attractive young woman professional singer who appeared both as performer and interviewee.

Adult Education

Romanian radio and television offer a variety of educational and instructional programs for adults, although these are not as highly structured as in some socialist countries. In 1964 an article described "Through the Towns and Regions of Our Country" as a fifteen-minute series broadcast twice a month "to show the great transformations which have occurred in the years of the people's rule."[59] Somewhat similar was "Industrial Geography," a monthly twenty-minute program reporting new developments in sections of the country that formerly were economically retarded.

The weekly ten-minute series "People and Their Work" emphasized "the moral traits of the new man," along with "the development of the socialist conscience of the working people which is reflected in the new attitude to work." In contrast with these was a program filmed in a machine shop which I saw one evening from 6:00 to 6:30. After an interview with an older person, some teen-agers were seen operating various types of shop equipment.

In addition to programs with incidental ideological references, there are others whose main purpose is political. In 1971 the radio series "Moments from the History of the Party and Their Reflection in Literature" observed the fiftieth anniversary of the Romanian Communist party.[60] An official release said: "Devoted to the path covered by our people, under the leadership of the Party, for the liquidation of exploitation and oppression, for the revolutionary transformation of society, for the building-up of socialism in Romania, this broadcast reflects the way in which the principal moments of the history of the Party have been recorded on pages with extraordinary artistic vigour." Titles in another series broadcast the same year included "Communists and the Fate of the Rumanian Nation," "Contemporary Profile of the Working Class," "Lasting Unity between the Party and the People," and "Socialist Education—A Complicated and Heterogeneous Process."[61] Paralleling this was "Contemporary Rumania," which told young listeners about their country.

Inevitably there are language lessons. As mentioned above, in 1973 television lessons in French, English, Russian, and German were broadcast several days each week from 10:00 to 10:30 A.M. and 5:30 to 6:00 P.M. These were designed both for supplementary school use and for adults at home. The several programs I saw were well done, fully equal if not superior to similar programs on American educational television. A Russian lesson, done on an elaborate set, utilized rear screen projection, visual devices, subtitles, photographs, film, and dramatic vignettes. The film inserts on these programs usually are made on location in countries using the language. A weekly publication available on newsstands includes the texts of the dramatized portions of the broadcasts.

A Radio Technical University was introduced in 1952, and a Television Technical University the following year.[62] Although such programs still are broadcast, they are not formally organized credit courses, and the term "university" is used only in a general sense. When technical courses were first introduced, it was explained that they constituted a "fundamental part of the building-up of socialism in the Rumanian People's Republic." A special editorial board of professors, engineers, and scientists selected themes for series about metallurgy, chemistry, power engineering, and industrial electronics. The Television Technical University was intended "to contribute to wide propagation of foremost progressive methods of work and thus show the viewers the latest achievements in the fields of technology both in our country and abroad." Current problems in economics and science are treated in radio programs with names like "The Radio Tribune," "Radio Symposium," "Economic Survey," and "Science, Techniques, and Phantasy." Similar programs on television are entitled "Economic Topics," "Life in the Village," "Economic Cabinet," and "Scientific Achievements of the Twentieth Century."

To serve the large part of the population engaged in agriculture, both radio and television dispense "agricultural propaganda," with programs related to decisions of the party and "directed in general to the numerous aspects of the socialist transformation of our villages."[63] Beginning in 1960 radio presented "Foremost Agricultural Workers Compete," in which bicycles, radio receivers, and watches were given as prizes to those contestants from various agricultural units who best answered the test questions.[64] The series was intended to disseminate information in an entertainment format, subjects including seed selection, fertilizers, tree planting, and cattle breeding. In Dobrogea, the first region of Romania to have its land entirely collectivized, almost all the farmers took part, and over 3,500 people watched four competitive rounds.

A Sunday series, "He Who Knows Writes to Us," asked questions of listeners about cereal growing, cattle breeding, and viticulture.[65] A hundred thousand letters came in, the best receiving prizes like radio sets and bicycles. A series for collective viewing was to "popularize the policy of our Party and Government in the socialist transformation of agriculture."[66]

Programs for rural audiences are telecast Sunday mornings from 10:00 to 11:15. I saw one that had been developed with great care. Films of workers in fields illustrating approved agricultural procedures were set off by prerecorded interludes of traditional folk music.* On other broadcasts three documentary films, "We Are Peasants and Workers," observing the tenth anniversary of the collectivization of Romanian agriculture, reviewed the changes that had taken place in the lives of Romanian peasants during that decade. Radio observed the occasion with programs like "The Process of Socialist Transformation of Agriculture as Reflected in the Life of Our Village."[67]

Literature and Drama

"Full exploitation of the national culture is the chief characteristic trait of our literary and art broadcasts," wrote a representative of Romanian radio in 1968.[68] Radio, he continued, is "a propagator of culture," since Romanian writers now reach larger audiences through broadcasting than ever before. In 1972 radio was presenting over sixty literary programs each week, and television also did such programming.

The range of literary broadcasts extends from short poetry readings to full-length dramas. For years there have been readings from and discussions of poetry and prose, on which the authors themselves often appear.[69] On "Masterpieces of World Literature," a fifteen-minute radio series broadcast alternate weeks in 1964, teachers, writers, critics, and historians discussed significant literary works, while a ten-minute weekly program, "Meridians," emphasized the "riches and beauty of progressive literature" all over the world, and discussed poets and writers who were "fighters for peace and friendship among nations."[70]

In 1964 outstanding actors and producers from Bucharest and other cities contributed to a weekly fifteen-minute series reporting theatrical news. On the monthly ten-minute program "Radio Anthology," native and foreign writers read excerpts from their works. In 1968 there were weekly radio series dealing with poetry, prose, choreography, architecture, and folklore, titles including "Writers at the Microphone" and "First Readings."[71] These were among the programs contributing to an archival collection of the voices of poets, writers, artists, actors, and other creative persons, some of which were drawn upon for the "Golden Library" series.

Poetry receives much attention. Ever since 1964 "Literary-Musical

---

* It was observed above that both Polish and Hungarian rural audiences are also fond of such music. See pp. 307 and 382.

Recitals," transmitted from the 1,000-seat concert hall of the radio studio building, has presented works of famous poets, often in combination with related musical compositions. Topics have included "The Reflection of the Fight for Peace in Poetry and Music" and "Springtime in the Works of Poets and Composers."[72] Commentary on this series in 1971 described it as "an excellent means for aesthetic and patriotic education" because of the variety of its subjects and the way they were presented.[73] The series is so popular that tickets are sold out weeks in advance.

Several times each week radio has five- and ten-minute poetry programs, scheduled at times like 8:25 A.M. and 9:25 or 10:30 P.M., on which as many as eighty readers may participate during a year.[74] The weekly program guide sometimes has a special box listing the works to be read. Television has late evening programs of readings by professional actors or the poets themselves. In the latter case, these may be recorded in the homes of the writers. The one I saw introduced the poet, after which actors read his poetry while some imaginative camera work showed related sculpture and forest scenes.

Romanian broadcasting authorities believe that radio drama should bring the "national and universal cultural values" to the mass audience. Each week there are several dramatic programs, including material for children, serial presentations of extended literary works, and full-length plays. These usually include one or more short plays of some thirty minutes' duration especially written for radio, which are regarded as very suitable for the rhythm of modern life.[75] When I asked about the effects of television on radio drama, I was told—as in other socialist countries— that radio and television are complementary rather than competitive media, so that radio drama has not been reduced in quantity or quality.

In 1969 Romanian Radio Theater looked back on forty years of activity.[76] Although the "Microphone Theater" began with one or two programs a week, by the beginning of 1966 it was offering five programs at different hours, divided among the three networks. Universality was the guideline for repertoire, which included *Antigone* by Sophocles, *Mother Courage* by Brecht, *Egmont* by Goethe, *Pygmalion* by Shaw, and *Romeo and Juliet* by Shakespeare, plus other classics by such writers as Dostoevsky, Gorky, Ionesco, Ibsen, Chekhov, and Strindberg. In cooperation with the OIRT, Romania broadcast translations of dramas by contemporary writers in Czechoslovakia, Finland, East Germany, Hungary, Poland, and the USSR, and had some of its works presented in return. Some Romanian radio dramas have received Prix Italia awards.

Several series observed the fiftieth anniversary of the Romanian Communist party in 1971. In connection with a Radio Theater competition, a distinguished jury chose 11 scripts out of 397 entries, with themes ranging from "the glorious fifty-year fight of our party [and] the achievements of the Romanian people in building up our socialist society . . . to the topical problems of our young generation."[77] In April and May of the same year a "Month of Rumanian Radiodramaturgy" sampled the original output of the previous twenty-five years. Of twenty-one broadcasts, nine were first performances.

During a typical year television broadcasts approximately fifty plays, including both originals and adaptations. Each week there is a sixty- or ninety-minute production plus at least one shorter work. A recent example was *Robespierre* by Rolland. Sometimes local theater productions are brought into the television studios. There also are serial treatments of classics like Dumas's *The Count of Monte Cristo* and *The Three Musketeers*. In developing dramatic and film programs Romania faces problems similar to those of Hungary and other small countries with unique languages. Since it must produce all its own material, there is no appreciable foreign market with which to share costs.

Music

Romanian radio and television broadcast much music. Radio alone presents approximately 220 hours each week, the three services emphasizing different types of music. Program I offers mainly entertainment music; Program II symphonic, chamber, and operatic music; and Program III— the FM service—extended serious compositions.[78] There also is music on television.

Music, like other types of program material, has its ideological potentials. In 1963 a writer linked music appreciation to "the upsurge of socialist culture directed by the Party and the constant raising of the cultural level of the working people, striving to become acquainted with the treasures of world art."[79] Music, along with the other arts, "is a form of social consciousness," whose roots "lie in the life and work of the people." It therefore "is a bearer of a progressive mission containing and expressing national aspirations." Whereas "under the former bourgeois-landlord system" the public was denied opportunities to acquire a knowledge of the fine arts, great efforts have been made in recent years to bring music to "the wide masses of working people." In July 1971 President Ceauşescu stated: The government "has the right to interfere in literature and in the fine arts, also in music to admit only what it considers to harmonize with socialism." Freedom to create must not interfere with these concepts: "We do not understand and cannot accept any kind of freedom for the productions inspired by concepts alien to the ideology of the working class."[80]

Programs about music, therefore, have ideological as well as artistic objectives. In 1962 a series about the famous Romanian composer Georges Enesco reported that he was inspired by his country's folklore and that he "spread its glory far beyond the borders."[81] Treatments of composers like Beethoven, Chopin, Glinka, and Liszt have emphasized "the humiliations and poverty which these genii of mankind had to suffer because of the rulers of their epochs and systems of government based on exploitation." Although "Literature and Music" reviewed literary works which had provided the inspiration for well-known compositions, a 1971 series was a discussion of music as a "source of ideological energy."[82]

The extensive resources available to carry out these assignments include a symphony orchestra of 120 players which broadcasts weekly over both radio and television from the 1,000-seat concert studio—a highly competent group which provided me with an enjoyable concert one evening in Bucharest. There also are an 80-piece chamber orchestra, a 40-piece light orchestra, 8 or 10 small ensembles ranging from chamber music to jazz, a children's choir of 80 members, and a mixed chorus of 100. Eight or ten conductors are permanently attached to the Romanian broadcasting studios.*

National pride in folk music is indicated by the time given to it on both media. A commentary in 1962 observed that whereas formerly folklore provided the people with a way of expressing "their feelings of hate for exploiters and confidence in a better future," the socialist era had "brought a stream of fresh air into folk art [and had] provided it with new forces, light, and joy of life."[83] Widespread interest in folk art

---

* An article by the "sound editor" of Romanian radio and television details the attention given to the theory and practice of music reproduction (Dutu Dumitru, "Sound Pick-up in Musical Recordings on the World Technical Level," *OIRT Review* 1967/4, pp. 26–27).

was demonstrated by the Sixth Competition of Amateur Artists held in 1962 in which 24,000 amateur groups participated, including 6,147 choirs, 9,126 dance ensembles, 6,439 "brigades of artistic propaganda," and 2,347 instrumental ensembles, the whole project involving 600,000 performers. Radio and television have made thousands of recordings of folk music and have encouraged the composition of music in that style, "inspired by the Party, our country, peace, great socialist constructions, new towns, metallurgical workers, blast furnaces, oil refinery workers, miners, weavers, etc."[84] Encouraged are songs about "collective farms," the struggle to achieve high crop yields, agricultural works, and "the building-up of villages."

Each week there are ten or fifteen folk music programs, varying from fifteen to thirty minutes in length. Radio has the daily "Folk Music and Your Favorite Singer," answering listener requests; "365 Songs," a ten-minute feature; and "Recordings of the Institute of Ethnography and Folklore," whose purpose is to preserve folk music in its authentic form. Television has two or three programs a week by both amateur and professional groups. The colorful costumes of the folk musicians make such telecasts good viewing as well as enjoyable listening.

Basically, Romanian concert broadcasts resemble those of all countries. The recorded repertoire has included cycles of Beethoven sonatas played by Wilhelm Kempf; symphonies by Mahler and Tchaikovsky; and "Outstanding Conductors."[85] During the Beethoven bicentennial in 1970 the symphony orchestra played a cycle of the composer's works, soloists including Polish-born (but Mexican resident) violinist Henryk Szeryng and Russian pianist Emil Gilels, along with Polish-born conductor Paul Klecki.[86] In 1970 a radio opera by the Romanian Pascal Bentoiu, *L'Iphigénie sacrifiée*, received a Prix Italia award.

Deriving much of his inspiration from folk music was the best-known of Romanian composers Georges Enesco (1881–1955), noted also as violinist, pianist, and conductor.[87] The many broadcasts of his music include some of his own recordings along with performances by other artists. Each August there are special broadcasts on his birthday.

Other current program titles are "Opera and Ballet Evenings" and "The History of Music in Masterpieces." A daily radio Program I series is based on selections chosen by prominent Romanians, who usually appear to explain the reasons for their choices. Cycles include a music appreciation series, "Let's Understand Music"; "Concerts of Baroque

Music"; and "The Romanian Opera." "Applause for Tomorrow" consists of recitals by music students.

There is music on television every day, ranging from fifteen-minute fillers to two-hour concerts. A current week might include staged excerpts from Gounod's *Faust*; a ballet presentation from a provincial theater; a two-hour concert of music by Romanian composers; and a short recital by young players, in a series with the incidental objective of training performers.

One Sunday morning I saw a recorded rehearsal from East Germany during which a very competent conductor—who spoke German throughout—led soloists, a choir, and an orchestra through a major choral work. There were Romanian subtitles for local viewers. One evening there was an old Leonard Bernstein concert consisting of overtures by Rossini, Beethoven, and other composers, again with subtitles. Early one evening I saw an interesting music education program on which a nonprofessional orchestra played Enesco's First Romanian Rhapsody, a youth group performed some ultramodern music, and a large amateur organization rehearsed the opening of Richard Strauss's *Don Juan*.

Although most of the things written by the Romanians about broadcast music concern the concert repertoire, the majority of the programs are in lighter vein. Radio, in addition to much traditional folk music, presents a great deal of light music by Romanian and foreign performers, and on most days there is at least one thirty-minute program listed simply as "jazz." A typical television week might include recorded programs by artists like Jerry Mulligan, Dave Brubeck, or Dale Evans, as well as studio-staged features with Romanian talent. Supplementing, and in contrast to the GDR choral rehearsal mentioned above, the same week's schedule included recordings of popular selections made in East Germany. Late one evening I saw a Romanian popular music group, using both conventional and electronic instruments, in a lively production involving singing, dancing, and other entertainment. Both camera and sound were good.

Entertainment and Sports

Entertainment is an important part of all broadcast schedules. In addition to the programs of light music mentioned above, the Romanians have contests, competitions, and even chess games. Marathon programs are a New Year's Eve feature.[88] On December 31, 1970, there were twelve consecutive hours of entertainment on television. A portion of this was described as "an entertaining film which is neither theatre, cinematograph, mere music or mere ballet," but rather a combination in which "all these fields of culture are represented by expressive means specific of television." In November 1970 I saw a portion of that program in rehearsal, with a talented popular singer performing on attractive sets. On another occasion the Department for Entertainment Broadcasts organized an open air show during which singers, instrumentalists, and dancers performed before an audience of 35,000 seated on the decks of ships in the Galatz dockyards on the Danube River.[89]

In the early 1960s radio had programs about films, one weekly series providing a "detailed picture of the work of film workers . . . in the field of feature and documentary films."[90] Radio now offers "The Seventh Art" about current developments in—mainly Romanian—cinematography. Television has presented such foreign features as *Nothing But the Truth*, with Irene Dunne and Cary Grant, and *Minstral Camerei No. 19*, with Dirk Bogart and Jean Simmons. Currently there are films from Czechoslovakia, the German Democratic Republic, the Soviet Union, Yugoslavia, and other Eastern European countries, along with some of Western origin, of which typical examples are *Union Station* (American, 1950), *Bend of the River* (American, 1952), *Hiroshima, mon amour* (French, 1959), *Fear Strikes Out* (American, 1957), and *Cone of Silence* (English, 1961). Although listed in the television guide with Romanian titles, these are broadcast with their original sound tracks and Romanian subtitles.

Television uses such foreign telefilms as *Bonanza, Danger Is My Business*, and a BBC film about the Wars of the Roses.[91] During my visits to Bucharest I have seen *Flipper, Mannix*, and *The Untouchables*—although the latter has been dropped as a consequence of political emphasis on home production. Other film programs have included a report of reconstruction in the Yugoslav city of Skopje leveled by an earthquake and documentaries from the Soviet Union and other socialist countries. I also saw a literary program incorporating a film of Robert Frost walking in the woods while his poetry was read in Romanian.

Important sports events, both domestic and international, are carried on radio and television. Radio has live transmissions of competitive sports in Romania and abroad, and gives scores on news programs. Tele-

vision broadcasts soccer matches from Romanian and foreign stadiums. As with other socialist countries, the number of Eurovision feeds
increased greatly in 1968, when Romania took 128 programs with a
duration of about 212 hours, many of which consisted of the winter
Olympic Games in Grenoble. One afternoon I saw an old film of a fight
by Cassius Clay (before he became Muhammad Ali) and noticed frequent references to the Davis Cup matches scheduled for the following
week. The matches themselves were carried live by Romanian television
and were sent to other socialist countries (such as Hungary; see above,
page 392).

Audience Research

Initially, audience research was based on letters from listeners and
viewers, and a Romanian writer reported with pride that in the first half
of 1960 some 62,500 letters were received from domestic and 18,500
letters from foreign listeners.[92] In 1963 the Department of Political
Broadcasts offered prizes to correspondents who sent in "materials of
good quality reflecting facts which are of special interest for the department." But analysis of letters was increasingly supplemented by audience
polls.

When the Office of Studies and Surveys was set up in 1967, it was the
first organization in the country to conduct scientific research in the
mass media.[93] After a research plan is drawn up and approved by the
broadcasting authorities, studies are made by teams of specialists in
sociology, statistics, and psychology, most of whom have had broadcasting experience. The department cooperates with a number of research
institutions, including the Central Board of Statistics, the Institute of
Philosophy of the Academy, and the Academy of Social and Political
Education under the Central Committee of the Romanian Communist
party.

At the end of 1972 Romania had 2,304,482 radio licenses (plus
807,833 for wired receivers), a rate of 14.96 licenses per hundred
inhabitants (see Table 10). There were 1,944,182 television licenses,
or 9.35 per hundred. According to the European Broadcasting Union
figures cited throughout this study, this was fewer radio or television
licenses per hundred of population than for any other socialist country reported (cf. Bulgaria, Czechoslovakia, East Germany, Hungary,

Poland, and Yugoslavia). The annual cost of a radio license is 120 lei ($21.74), an additional license being required for an automobile radio. A license for a wired receiving set costs 80 lei ($14.50). A television license costs 180 lei ($32.62). A medium-sized transistor radio costs 500 or 800 lei; an all-wave receiver, 1,300 lei; a small television set, 3,000 lei; a black-and-white 21-inch set, 3,500 lei; and a radio-phonograph combination, 2,400 lei. Salaries range from 1,800 to 2,000 lei per month, with a charwoman earning 1,000, a physician 2,500, and a professional man 4,000 lei.

The Office of Studies and Surveys has examined the effects of television viewing on radio listening and leisure-time activities; the differences in viewing between urban and rural areas; and the opinions of viewers who can receive both Hungarian and Romanian television. It also has done basic research on the role of communications in society. The results have not been widely published, although we do know that the most popular program is the 7:30—8:00 P.M. television newscast.

The director of research for Romanian broadcasting conducted an inquiry into the knowledge of rural and small town inhabitants about the serious theater. A sample of 7,700 persons was asked to list three or more favorite plays, and to indicate how they learned about them. Of the 4,500 who named one or more plays, television provided the main source of information, with the theater itself ranking second, reading third, and radio fourth.[94]

Radio Free Europe sponsored an inquiry into the domestic listening and viewing habits of Romanians by arranging interviews with 1,505 Romanians visiting in six Western European countries between May 1970 and March 1971.[95] It was found that 99 per cent of the sample listened to domestic radio programs, 53 per cent daily and 32 per cent several times a week. Preferred listening hours were between 6:00 and 9:00 A.M. and 5:00 P.M. and midnight, with over 40 per cent tuned in between 6:00 and 11:00 P.M. (In Romania alone of the five countries covered by the survey, there is no peak during the noon hour.) Ninety per cent of the sample watched television, 31 per cent daily or almost daily and 24 per cent several times a week. Favored hours were between 7:00 and 10:00 P.M.

Radio Free Europe broadcasts approximately twelve hours a day in Romanian. These and other foreign programs are readily available, since

Romania has not jammed Western broadcasts since 1963.* Between June 1971 and February 1972, RFE surveyed 1,099 Romanians visiting temporarily in the West to obtain data on its own audience.[96] Of this sample 57 per cent listened regularly to RFE, 22 per cent to the BBC, 18 per cent to the Voice of America, and 14 per cent to Radio Paris (French being the second language of Romania). On the basis of the statistic that 59 per cent of the Romanian RFE audience listened an average of thirty-two minutes a day, the report commented that Romanians appeared to be the most regular of all RFE listeners. Asked why they listened, 61 per cent said because they found RFE programs more objective and quicker with the news than the Romanian media. Comparing listenership trends from 1963 to 1971, 41 per cent of the samples polled were regular listeners in 1963, 63 per cent in 1969, 57 per cent in 1970, and 66 per cent in early 1971.

Another survey indicated that during the Polish crisis at the end of 1970, 75 per cent of all Romanians were listening to Western programs, and 88 per cent of these to Radio Free Europe.[97] Nine per cent of another group reported that jamming was one reason for not tuning to RFE, despite the fact that there had been no jamming in Romana for almost ten years.

External Broadcasting

Romania uses both medium- and long-wave transmitters (some of the former shared with its domestic services) to provide European listeners with programs in English, French, German, Greek, Italian, Portuguese, Romanian, Serbian, and Spanish.† In addition, it maintains short-wave services in Arabic, English, and French to Africa; in Arabic and Turkish to the Near East; in English and Persian to Asia; in English to listeners in the Pacific area; in English, Romanian, and Yiddish to North America; and in Portuguese and Spanish to Latin America. Its total output is small, however, since it ranks sixth among the nine countries of the Eastern European bloc: only Bulgaria, Yugoslavia, and Hungary do less external broadcasting than does Romania.

Cooperative program agreements have been signed with most of the

---

* When I asked a broadcasting official in 1965 why they formerly had jammed, he answered with a twinkle in his eye: "Because others jammed."

† *WRTH 1973*, p. 88. See Table 9 above.

socialist and some Western countries, and exchange projects developed with Argentina, Australia, Belgium, Czechoslovakia, Denmark, East Germany, Finland, France, Italy, Japan, Poland, Sweden, the United States, and Yugoslavia, among others.[98] Related to this is the circulation abroad of Romanian programs, mainly music. In 1963 Romania sent 800 reports on various aspects of Romanian life along with 166 hours of music.[99] In addition it sent recordings of music by contemporary Romanian composers to many Western European countries. The United States has been involved in many of these exchanges. On July 4, 1965, Romanian television broadcast a film about the music camp at Interlochen, Michigan, supplied by the United States government. For a decade the Broadcasting Foundation of America has distributed Romanian programs to American stations.

There are the usual exchanges of musical groups. Romanian ensembles have performed in Czechoslovakia, Hungary, and both Germanys, while conductors have been exchanged with Belgium, France, and Yugoslavia.[100] In April 1971 the Radio and Television Symphony Orchestra visited sixteen cities in West Germany playing music by Enesco, Dumitrescu, Tchaikovsky, Franck, Brahms, Respighi, Richard Strauss, and Dukas.

For one week in May 1971 the National Broadcasting Company's *Today* show consisted mainly of programs taped in Bucharest.[101] The invitation for the program to originate in Romania came from the Romanian ambassador in Washington with support from the National Tourist Office. It was accepted with the understanding that there would be no censorship. The programs included pickups from a church service, interviews with some Romanian writers, and a shopping expedition, all handled by key members of the *Today* cast, who were flown to Bucharest especially for the project. The broadcasts coincided with the opening in Bucharest of the new Inter-Continental Hotel.

According to the European Broadcasting Union, Romania first took programs from Eurovision in 1963, when it received 5 programs with a duration of 9 hours (see Tables 1 and 2). The next year it received 29 programs (32 hr.), and in 1966, 45 programs (84 hr., 45 min.). In 1968—the year of the Olympic Games—it took 128 programs (211 hr., 45 min.), and in 1972—another Olympic Game year—171 programs (321 hr., 45 min.). However, Romania made very few contributions, the first being in 1965 when it provided 1 program with a duration of 4 hours, 15 minutes. In 1968 it originated 7 programs (17 hr., 30 min.) and in 1970, 20 programs (32 hr., 30 min.). In 1972 this dropped to 12 programs (30 hr., 15 min.). (According to Intervision figures, however, in 1972 Romania contributed 23 programs (48 hr., 42 min.).)

XI

People's Republic of Bulgaria

Broadcasting, like most other things in Bulgaria, clearly shows the influence of the Soviet Union. No other Eastern European country has such close historical and cultural ties with the USSR. No other country has received so much economic aid, and none is so "dependable" an ally. It therefore is not surprising that the programs of Bulgaria, more than those of any other socialist bloc country, exalt the status, culture, and politics of the Soviet Union. Only Bulgaria relays Soviet television programs one full evening each week. Finally, it should be noted that even though the Soviet Union discontinued jamming foreign radio transmissions for a time in the 1960s, Bulgaria never stopped at all.

Facts about Bulgaria

The People's Republic of Bulgaria is bounded on the north by Romania, on the west by Yugoslavia, on the south by Greece and Turkey, and on the east by the Black Sea. With a total area of 42,729 square miles, it is approximately the same size as the state of Tennessee, which has 42,244 square miles.

The population of Bulgaria in 1969 was 8,515,000.[1] For the most part Bulgaria is a country of villages: in that year the capital city of Sofia contained only 886,000 people and the next largest city, Plovdiv, 252,000. Bulgarians compose about 85 per cent of the population. Minority groups include Turks (8.6 per cent), Gypsies (2.6 per cent), and Macedonians (2.5 per cent). Insofar as they are significant, figures show that about

432

86 per cent of the population belongs to the Bulgarian Orthodox Church; approximately 12 per cent are Moslems, and there are some Roman Catholics and Protestants. The Bulgarian language, like Serbian, Ukrainian, Russian, and some other Soviet languages, uses the Cyrillic alphabet.

For many years Bulgaria has had close ties with the Soviet Union. The Russians gave Bulgaria support against its Turkish rulers in the nineteenth century. Although this was done in the hope of gaining influence in the Balkan Peninsula and eventual control of Constantinople, Bulgaria nevertheless remained deeply grateful to Russia. Following the defeat of the Turks by the Russians in 1878, Bulgaria was made self-governing by the Treaty of San Stefano, although some of the territory then gained was lost a few months later at the Congress of Berlin. Bulgaria became a fully independent country under Czar Ferdinand of Saxe-Coburg-Gotha as a consequence of the Young Turk revolt in 1908.

In World War I Bulgaria supported the Central powers and as an aftermath of their defeat lost some territory. During World War II Bulgaria sided with the Axis until threatened by Soviet forces in September 1944. When a Communist-controlled coalition—The Fatherland Front— seized power, the monarchy was abolished and a people's republic proclaimed in 1946. The first premier of the republic was Georgi Dimitrov (1882–1949), whose mausoleum in Sofia is the counterpart of Lenin's mausoleum in Red Square.

Although its attitudes toward the USSR have varied, Bulgaria has been the most subservient of the Soviet Union's Eastern European allies. When there was unrest in other socialist countries, as in Poland and Hungary in 1956 and in Czechoslovakia in 1968, Bulgaria remained firmly loyal. One reason for this was that Todor Zhivkov, first secretary of the Bulgarian Communist party, needed Soviet support in order to stay in power and therefore willingly made Bulgaria a model satellite.[2] In recent years Bulgaria has received the equivalent of over $2 billion in Soviet subsidies for the development of industry and agriculture.[3] Watching Bulgarian television during a visit to Sofia in November 1970, I was surprised to find that one evening's programs each week consisted of direct relays from Soviet television.* Several days later, when I asked

* On that particular evening the program included a film about Soviet cosmonauts. We saw them in training; looked back with them at the earth through the windows of their capsule; and watched them talk to their wives and children at home as they flew around in space. Then came a charming documentary built

my guide to translate the large sign hanging in the entrance hall of the radio headquarters building, she replied: "We are with you all the way—USSR."

Bulgaria's fertile soil is the reason for its large agricultural output. Approximately 40 per cent of the population works on the land, and Bulgarian farm produce, which constitutes some 55 per cent of the country's exports, is sold in over 60 countries.[4] In developing this resource, Bulgaria is not content to follow the old ways; during the last few years 172 agro-industrial complexes, with an average size of 54,000 acres, and utilizing small computers, radios, and closed-circuit television, have been set up.[5] An American tourist visiting the Balkan countries will find his best food buys in Bulgaria. But industry is being expanded too, and the 1971–1975 Five-Year Plan is aiming for a 55 or 60 per cent increase in output. The country's first nuclear power station, constructed under the supervision of Soviet engineers, is scheduled for completion in 1975.

In 1970, 80 per cent of Bulgaria's foreign trade was with other COMECON countries, most of it with the Soviet Union. In value of imports and exports, 62 per cent was with the USSR, 10 per cent with the German Democratic Republic, 6 per cent with Czechoslovakia, 4 per cent with Poland, slightly less than 4 per cent with Italy, and 3 per cent with the German Federal Republic.[6] In the same year 573,000 (23 per cent) of Bulgaria's tourists came from Turkey, 484,000 (19 per cent) from Yugoslavia, and 393,000 (13 per cent) from Czechoslovakia. Only 18,000 came from the United States. However, it is likely that a large proportion of the Turkish and Yugoslav tourists either were in transit or were on very short visits, so these figures need qualification as indicators of Bulgaria's tourist industry.

Bulgaria is a member of the United Nations, UNESCO, the Warsaw Pact, and COMECON. In contrast with its Romanian neighbor to the north, it advocates closer trade relationships with the Soviet Union and

---

around the experiences of an old organ-grinder playing his instrument as he walked through Moscow. A Bulgarian release said that these relays constitute "a useful tradition bringing good results since they acquaint us ever more closely with the rich Soviet culture." They are "a large window to the Soviet Union, a school of the exchange of experience and television journalism" (*OIRT Information* 1972/2, p. 3). Early in 1973 it was announced that future Friday evening relays would draw upon all four Moscow television services, some of which would be translated into Bulgarian, "others only annotated." Most of those chosen would be in color (*OIRT Information* 1973/1, p. 3).

other Eastern countries, rather than seeking primary markets elsewhere. Although Bulgaria has exchanged diplomatic missions with France, Norway, Sweden, the United Kingdom, and other Western countries, its contacts with the United States have been sporadic. An American minister went to Bulgaria in 1945, and full relations were established two years later, only to be broken off in 1950 and resumed in 1960. During the last decade Bulgarian contacts with Western countries have increased. Premier Zhivkov went to Paris in 1966 on his first official visit to a Western country. Nevertheless, Bulgaria is closer to the Soviet Union than is any other bloc country, a relationship which will be evident as its broadcasting policies and procedures are reviewed below.

Legal Structure

Bulgaria was declared a republic in 1946, and a constitution on the Soviet model was adopted the following year. After being amended in 1961 and 1965, it was replaced by a new constitution in 1971. This document declares the Bulgarian People's Republic to be "a socialist state of the working people from town and country, headed by the working class."[7] The Constitution goes on to say: "All power in the People's Republic of Bulgaria stems from the people and belongs to the people," being exercised "through freely elected representative bodies—a National Assembly and people's councils—or directly."[8] Natural resources, along with "railway, water and air transport, posts, telegraphs, telephones, broadcasting and television are state (all-people's) ownership."[9]

The National Assembly, whose 400 members are elected for five-year terms by all citizens eighteen years of age or older and are subject to recall, is the "supreme body of state power," its functions including the election and dismissal of the State Council, the Council of Ministers, and certain key government officials.[10] The State Council, which is expected to provide continuing leadership in both domestic and foreign affairs, consists of a president, deputy-presidents, a secretary, and some other members.[11] However, the Council of Ministers is the "supreme executive and administrative body of state power." One of its members is the minister of information and communications.[12]

The section of the Constitution headed "Basic Rights and Obligations of the Citizens" fits the usual socialist pattern. There are guarantees of sexual equality, plus the rights to work, leisure, and education. Although national minorities have the right to be educated in their own languages and to develop their own culture, the study of Bulgarian is compulsory.[13] Citizens are assured "freedom of conscience and of creed" and are authorized both to "perform religious rites and conduct anti-religious propaganda."[14] But "the misuse of the church and religion for political purposes, as well as the setting up of political organizations on a religious basis, are prohibited."[15]

The Constitution guarantees freedom of speech and press, secrecy of correspondence, and the rights of association and assembly. But freedom of expression does not include permission to form organizations "directed against the socialist system . . . which propagate a fascist or other anti-democratic ideology."[16] Furthermore, "war incitement and propaganda are prohibited and are punishable by law as grave crimes against peace and mankind."[17] Clearly, Bulgaria does not have freedom of speech in the Western sense. As a young Bulgarian playwright put it, although there "is no official censorship," the party retains control by appointing editorial personnel who can be counted upon to carry out its policies.[18]

The party is all important. The Constitution states: "The guiding force in society and the state is the Bulgarian Communist Party."[19] The Sixth National Assembly, elected for a five-year term in 1971, has 400 members, of whom 267 belong to the Bulgarian Communist party, 100 to the related Agrarian Union, and 19 to the Dimitrov Young Communist League. Only 13 are nonparty members.[20]

Broadcasting is the responsibility of the Committee for Television and Radio, which is under the Council of Ministers. But the committee does not report directly to any one minister, even though the minister of information and communication is involved with broadcasting. The Postal authorities are responsible for transmitters and connecting links.

Annual licenses are required for the operation of receivers. Homes with tube or transistor sets must pay 5 leva ($4.66) per set, and an additional license is required for an automobile radio. A license for a loudspeaker fed by a wired system costs 3.20 leva ($2.98). A television license costs 12 leva ($11.17) per set.

Networks and Programs

The Committee for Television and Radio of the Bulgarian Council of Ministers operates three radio networks, several regional stations, an extensive wired distribution system, one television network, and an external service.

Bulgarian radio has undergone several reorganizations during the last decade. As recently as October 1965 the second network was on the air less than seven hours a day, and the FM service, then limited to the Sofia area, broadcast only ninety minutes a day.[21] Since January 4, 1971, the objective has been to operate "three completely new programmes which are clearly differentiated."[22] Program I, "Horizon" on the air from 5:00 A.M. to 1:30 A.M. and planned eventually as a twenty-four–hour service, is somewhat like the Soviet Union's Mayda, its basic components being music and information. "It strives to be the first to present information on all the most topical events at home and abroad."[23] "Horizon" is carried to almost the entire country by several medium-wave AM transmitters with up to 250 kilowatts power, five FM transmitters, and one short-wave transmitter.

Program II, "Khristo Botev," named after a Bulgarian poet-patriot who died in the war of liberation against the Turks in 1876, is on the air from 7:30 A.M. to 11:30 P.M. over several AM and five FM transmitters. It is more serious than Program I, emphasizing in-depth news, documentaries, talks, and concert music, plus educational programs for all ages. Program II relays material from Moscow Radio daily from 5:00 to 5:30 P.M.[24] Program III, "Orpheus," patterned after the original BBC Third Programme and entirely on FM, is available only in the Sofia area. On the air daily from 6:30 to 11:30 P.M., it emphasizes serious music, literature, and dramatic programs.*

Although the bulk of domestic radio broadcasting is in Bulgarian, there also are programs in Macedonian and Turkish. During the tourist season, some stations in the Black Sea area transmit news and weather information in Russian, Czech, Polish, French, and English.[25] Regional studios in several cities outside Sofia originate programs for their areas as well as contributing to the national service. All told, domestic Bulgarian radio programs consist of about 70 per cent music and 30 per cent talk.

Programs also are distributed by wire, and more than one-third of all radio licenses in 1972 were for wired receivers (see Table 10). These

---

* *OIRT Information* 1971/1, p. 4; *OIRT Information* 1971/4–5, p. 3. Bulgarian FM operates in the Eastern European FM spectrum. Stereo was introduced March 28, 1971, and there are several hours of recorded stereo music each week.

services are especially important in rural areas, although there also are some in industrial communities. The government has made many of these the equivalent of local radio stations.[26] In 1961, when there were 1,340 wired centers, their staffs included not only program and engineering personnel but even small musical groups, and one center had 150 part-time news correspondents.[27] Much of their output consists of agricultural programs.

Television experiments began in 1954, and regular programming on November 7, 1959, the forty-second anniversary of the Russian Revolution, which was the subject of the initial broadcast.[28] The service is available to approximately 90 per cent of the population from a half dozen transmitters operating in the VHF band supplemented by forty-nine low-powered repeaters. Black-and-white transmissions use the Eastern European D system, while color is in SECAM. The first color origination took place September 9, 1972, the anniversary of the socialist revolution in Bulgaria.[29] Credited for this "new large cultural achievement" were the "great efforts exerted by the Party and the people's power" and "the fraternal assistance granted by the Soviet Television and the GDR Television." By the end of 1973 Bulgarian television was transmitting ten hours of color programs each week, including the Friday evening feeds from the Soviet national network.

Although present radio and television studios are modest, there are ambitious plans for new facilities in Sofia, to be constructed in stages with completion in 1980.[30] Between them, the National Radio and Television Center and the new Radio House will accommodate television, film, and radio. For television there will be 4 studios with 7,500 square feet of floor space each and 2 with 8,770 square feet each, plus sound recording studios and related facilities. Radio will have 6 floors including 4 music studios, 2 drama studios, 13 talk studios, and a concert hall with 600 seats. In 1972 the first television studios outside Sofia were established in the city of Plovdiv. Additional broadcasting centers are planned for other cities.[31]

In 1971 the schedule averaged sixty-five hours a week.[32] Normally Bulgarian television is on the air daily from 4:00 until 11:00 P.M., plus morning periods. Sunday hours are from 8:00 A.M. to 11:00. P.M. One Bulgarian writer explained that there are no television programs after 11:00 P.M. because broadcasts at that hour would interfere with "the normal work rhythm in the country."[33] The television output has been categorized as follows: news and political programs, 27 per cent; films, 16 per cent; cultural programs, 16 per cent (further subdivided into literature, 3 per cent; music, 5 per cent; entertainment, 4.5 per cent; and drama, 3.5 per cent); broadcasts for children and young people, 15 per cent; educational programs, 12.5 per cent; sports, 6.5 per cent; Intervision, 6 per cent; and advertising, 1 per cent.[34]

There have been advertising periods on Bulgarian radio since 1965, grouped into short clusters with such titles as "The Morning Cultural Diary," "Music and News," "Musical Greetings," and "Concerts for Work Collectives."[35] There also are commercial periods on television, although no advertisements are broadcast on Sundays. I saw an effective ten-minute commercial for several products, during which cartoons were ingeniously combined with photographs of the articles being promoted. When I asked if a foreign airline like West Germany's Lufthansa could advertise, the answer was "perhaps." But in any case, the revenue from broadcast advertising is limited.

After several days of watching Bulgarian television, I concluded that it is fairly undeveloped, with many production flaws. There were some good programs, of course. I saw a fine puppet show for children, coupled with a UNESCO cartoon about animals, with multilingual titles. I was impressed by a program about high school athletics in which interviews of players by their coach could have been on American television, but for the language difference. A domestically produced film about a train was excellent. It showed the engineer in his cab, the track ahead, scenes within the train, railroad stations, and switchyards. There were various cinema films, plus a travelogue for Ethiopian Airlines, originally narrated by Les Tremayne but on the telecast narrated in Bulgarian.

Nevertheless, my basic impression was of an emerging service. Perhaps in recognition of this, a new television head was appointed in 1970, at the same time that an article by the chief secretary of the Union of Bulgarian Journalists, after identifying television as the "newspaper of our era," documented various inadequacies. Many programs were cumbersome, he said. Films were not properly coordinated with news and commentary, and some lectures were broadcast that might better be circulated in printed form. Television, he concluded, needed more creative personnel to devise innovative programs.

Like their opposite numbers all over the world, Bulgarian broadcasters are aware of changing relationships among the mass media, although when they write about them they also dwell upon ideological factors. In 1970 a key staff member analyzed the functions of radio, television, and the press "under the conditions of contemporary socialist society."[36] In spite of the rivalries among these several media, he pointed out, each has its distinctive role: radio informs, television shows, the press explains.

Nowhere are the mass media more consistently assigned propaganda objectives. "Bulgarian Radio is continuously fighting to realize the policy of the Bulgarian Communist Party and the People's Government to build-up socialism and communism in our country," wrote a radio staff member in 1960. "In its broadcasts it explains their measures, it mobilizes the working people to fulfil the set tasks and it carries our socialist truth to the remotest corners of the country."[37] Two years later a news release stated: "Popularization of the decisions of the 8th Congress of the Bulgarian Communist Party is . . . one of the most important tasks of the Bulgarian Television."[38]

The deputy chief of the Communist Education Department of Bulgarian Broadcasting spelled this out further in 1965 when he said: "The education of a new man is the chief task of the Bulgarian Radio."[39] Accordingly, radio maintains a constant fight against "bourgeois ideology," and broadcasts series with such names as "Education and Reality" and "Under Capitalist Oppression," in order to expose "bourgeois democracy." "The Atheists' Tribune" waged "a systematic, planned and effective educational campaign against religion as a world outlook and ideology of the reactionary classes and a detrimental remnant from the past."* Broadcasting, concluded this key staff member, "is a powerful weapon" for the party in its "fight for the formation of . . . the new man, the builder of socialism and communism. To master this tool and to handle it in a creative and clever way is our task and our duty. . . ."

A review of radio trends in 1971 also emphasized the ideological approach.[40] Looking forward to the Tenth Congress of the Bulgarian Communist party and the Twenty-fourth Congress of the Communist party of the Soviet Union, the article announced plans to reinforce news and information programs, and to prepare a series of programs on ideology, some to be developed domestically and others jointly with the Soviet Union.

---

* One Bulgarian program executive told me that there are no religious programs because most people are not religiously inclined and because research has shown that such programs are not wanted.

News

Radio Program I ("Horizon") presents news and information every thirty minutes, while Program II ("Khristo Botev") has a halfdozen newscasts each day.[41] Program III ("Orpheus") begins and ends its transmissions with a fifteen-minute "informative bulletin," so that a listener who has tuned in for music or literary material "has the possibility of obtaining—on the same programme—the necessary information of the events of the day."[42] There are four or five television newscasts, including one at the beginning and one at the end of each day's schedule.

The basic news source is the Bulgarian Telegraph Agency, which has reporters throughout Bulgaria and exchanges material with agencies in other socialist countries.[43] BTA provides subscribers in seventy-five countries with its basic Bulgarian service or with a more limited output in Arabic, Czech, English, French, German, Italian, and Russian. Bulgarian broadcasting also receives news from TASS, Visnews, UPI, Eurovision, and Intervision, as well as from its own correspondents in Moscow, Bonn, Paris, Tokyo, New York, and elsewhere. However, the European Broadcasting Union reports very few news exchanges with Bulgaria between 1960 and 1968, even though Bulgarian television did take other types of Eurovision programs during those years (see Tables 1 and 2). In 1972, according to Intervision data, Bulgaria originated nine news items for Eurovision while receiving thirty-one.

In 1966 radio inaugurated a two-hour program from 6:00 to 8:00 A.M., which, like early morning programs on many American stations, combined domestic, foreign, and weather news with light music.[44] In 1968 the "Radio Diary" was introduced to "enrich" the reporting of domestic and international affairs. Correspondents at home and abroad contributed to programs which supplemented the main 8:30 P.M. news bulletin with detailed and on-the-spot reports.

On November 11, 1971, I saw a television newscast scheduled from 8:00 to 8:30 P.M., but on the air from 8:05 to 8:45 P.M., consisting mainly of unedited Soviet films pertaining to the USSR unmanned moon walk which had taken place that day. This was followed by pictures of United States military action in Vietnam, a feature on Bulgarian industrial development, and a report of an industrial project, the completion of which had been delayed by operational problems.

Bulgarian ideas on news editing are in accord with those expressed generally in the socialist bloc. A professor of radio journalism at the University of Sofia wrote in 1972: "Our information service is not and cannot be aimless. It conforms with the objective laws and demands of socialist society and social development. . . . [Publishers always have had] the task of finding and stressing the social value and importance of presented facts."[45]

I received many of the same impressions during an extended discussion with the editor in chief of radio news and the deputy editor of television news. They frankly admitted the identification of their newscasts with the Bulgarian government, but insisted that the American networks merely projected the views of the United States Establishment. I argued unsuccessfully that, although American newscasts might reflect the country's basic values, they did not necessarily speak for the government, and pointed out that President Nixon often complained that the media opposed his policies.

My Bulgarian hosts explained that their newscasts emphasize industrial growth and expansion because such things are important to the nation's welfare. In a socialist country those are everyone's business and therefore are a proper subject for programs, whereas in the United States broadcast advertising merely advances the interests of wealthy private entrepreneurs. Bulgaria does have self-criticism—as one Bulgarian put it, "positive criticism"—and the media often complain about performance failures. But we had difficulty—partly owing to translation problems—in agreeing on how much independence the broadcasters actually have in deciding what and how to criticize. Apparently they do have some freedom, although they usually inform the authorities about their plans in advance. But in view of the close connection between broadcasting and government, it is unlikely that they depart very far from the official line.

In separate meetings I asked the news chiefs and the radio program head if they covered the story about Solzhenitsyn receiving the Nobel Prize, and got the same answer both times: they carried the item, but accompanied it with a commentary explaining that the prize had been awarded for political rather than literary reasons. Do they broadcast much news about the United States? Yes, in amount and emphasis it is exceeded only by news about Bulgaria and the USSR. Bulgarian television did not cover the television moon walks in November 1969, but did carry excerpts.*

* Although key programming personnel in socialist countries often are political

Children and Youth

It is not surprising to find the propaganda-oriented media of Bulgaria emphasizing dedication to party in their programs for children, to which they devote a good share of their radio and 15 per cent of their television time.[46] "All activities of our department," wrote a staff member responsible for children's programs in 1966, "try to ensure that children participate in the building-up of communism in our country."[47] Among "the great tasks we have to solve every day," she said, are those of educating for "a rich human character and strong emotions, intellectual audacity and, chiefly, the utmost faithfulness to communism. Our radio broadcasts are the organizers of large campaigns and they are of great advantage in the realization of the communist education of the young generation."

In 1971 the director of the Radio Department for Instruction and Education said many of the same things. "In the contemporary world characterized by a violent ideological struggle the problem of forming a scientific communist world outlook in the young generation is of great importance."[48] Such broadcasts "can play an important role in the formation of the communist world outlook in adolescents. In addition to the broad and varied scope of knowledge they provide, educational broadcasts enrich the cultural life of young listeners, promote the aesthetic, patriotic and international education of young people and contribute to the formation of a scientific, marx-leninist world outlook." An official announcement of some new radio programs in 1972 referred to them as fulfilling "the great goal: the communist education of youth."[49]

There are in-school broadcasts on both radio and television. These do not "repeat the lessons given by teachers," but rather "open new pages from textbooks and illustrate the taught material. These broadcasts must arouse the interest of children in knowledge and also educate them. With their help we must develop also the tendencies towards active experimental work with young people."[50]

Accordingly, there are programs "to support literature, music, geogra-

---

rather than professional in background, this was not the case with the radio program head in Bulgaria. In the course of a long and very pleasant conversation he told me that both he and his wife had been educated as lawyers; that he had had one year of journalism training in college; that he had been in radio for eighteen years; and that he had occupied his present position for some time. In the course of our conversation I had our translator take a picture of the two of us standing beneath a picture of Lenin.

phy, history, and mathematics curricula" for reception both at school and at home. These include dramatizations of literature; geography lessons (with a helicopter that "flies" over foreign countries); and programs on music, outer space, and science. The programs are made as interesting as possible, since there is concern lest talks and dry facts "kill a live interest in science and technology and the imagination of children." Dramatizations are used, the children themselves take part, and famous authors, composers, and artists appear in person. "Blue Fires," a monthly thirty-minute television cycle, brings stories, games, and music to small children.[51] "The Break" is a series of fifteen-minute programs for secondary schools. Broadcast from a simulated studio classroom with pupil participants, these include material selected to be of interest for pupil viewing in the breaks between classes "such as jokes, games, interesting facts, etc." Television now has in-school programs during midmorning hours on mathematics, Bulgarian literature, world history, and geography.

Eastern European broadcasters, like those everywhere else, are accused of inducing passivity among their audiences, for which reason the Bulgarians have tried to involve children directly, either by putting them on programs or by urging them to join in follow-up activities. "The Team of Curious Children," a series for secondary school pupils begun in 1960 and still on the air in 1963, consisted of "meetings" at which Professor Znai (Professor Know-all) and several "curious children," with the aid of films, drawings, photographs, and other visual aids, presented "interesting facts from the fields of scientific research, technology, natural science, etc."[52] In 1963 television introduced the "Evening of Five Wishes" to meet the demands of schoolchildren for information about art, literature, industry, science, and technology. The programs were preceded by polls to determine the "wishes" of the children concerned.[53] The radio series "A Frank Talk" invited young listeners to form groups to discuss moral and ethical problems.

Guidance for out-of-school programs was provided by the director of children's radio in 1961, who introduced an article about the department's work by quoting from Maxim Gorki: "It is necessary to write for children in the same way as for adults, only a little better."[54] He then went on: "We must not only find an interesting subject . . . [but we also must choose] suitable forms and expressions, taking into account the specific features of children's perception." However, we should not "speak and write for children in a childish way. Such broadcasts are listened to by children with disgust and by adults with mockery."

There always are fairy tales. Beginning in 1961 television presented a Bulgarian version of "Good Night Children," based on national folklore and introducing a new television personality, "Syncho," whose name was derived from the Bulgarian word for "dream."* The couple who originated the East German series "Flax and Krummel" came to Bulgaria to do a puppet show on Bulgarian television.

In 1963 radio scheduled a Day of Fairy Tales, which was so successful that it was decided to repeat the project each year on the first Sunday of December.[55] In 1964 the program was divided into three blocks totaling four hours in length. The several sections were tied together by two sprites, who, with a group of children, set off by magic carpet to visit a country of fairy tales. Stories included selections from Bulgarian and Russian literature, as well as Perrault's *Puss in Boots* and Hans Christian Andersen's *Ole Lukøje*.

Broadcasts for children of preschool age, said an article published in 1967, constitute a "serious and responsible task which is directly connected with the problems of the education of pre-school children. This period is one in which many substantial traits of children's psychology and character are formed."[56] First emphasis is given to moral education, although moralizing is never the apparent purpose of the programs. Nevertheless, the series "Grandfather's Pipe," broadcast once a month for fifteen minutes on Friday mornings, had a strong moral emphasis. Its three permanent characters—a grandfather, a bullfinch, and a hare—traveled throughout the country meeting children, good and bad, industrious and lazy. Three other cycles completed the Friday morning sequence. "Khop Top Is Drawing" invited children to send in drawings. At an exhibition in 1963, 170 of the 7,500 entries received that year were put on display.[57] The series was still going strong in 1967. Another preschool series, "The Merry Train," visited interesting places, while "The Miraculous Window" opened once a week on a new book which talked about itself, assisted by dialogues and dramatizations.

Programs for older children are many and varied. At the end of 1962 there were five installments in the teen-agers' cycle "How Man Explored

---

* *OIRT Information* 1962/12, p. 1; *OIRT Information* 1962/8, p. 1. For references to comparable Soviet and GDR series, see above, pp. 141, 241.

the Earth," which dealt with expeditions from the seventeenth century up to the time of the exploration of the Antarctic.[58] A thirty-minute monthly program, "Friendly Pioneers," which told of "the life of Bulgarian children in pioneer groups," was in its third year in 1963. An interesting approach was used for the television series "Meetings on the Planet of Earth," transmitted monthly for periods varying from thirty to sixty minutes. All children dream of becoming cosmonauts, said an accompanying news release, and of flying to Mars or Venus. Yet, they need to know more about the planet on which they live. Accordingly, with the assistance of a mobile unit, these programs took their viewers to places like a bakery, a paper mill, an electric power station, a dairy, a telephone exchange, an observatory, a construction site, and an airport.

With patriotic motive was "The Unforgettable One," a series of fifteen- or twenty-minute episodes telling about young heroes who had fought and died for their country.[59] To mark the fiftieth anniversary of the Russian Revolution in 1967, a "radio excursion" was organized cooperatively with Soviet radio to take young Bulgarian listeners to the birthplace of Lenin as well as to places where Soviet and Bulgarian soldiers had fought together during World War II.

There also are competitions, such as "Do You Know Your Country?" begun on television in the spring of 1963, in which young people matched knowledge in fields like history, geography, music, and sports.[60] A national amateur contest for readers, dancers, actors, singers, and musicians provided public exposure for talented young people. To observe the twentieth anniversary of Bulgarian Liberation Day on September 9, 1964, a six-month competition was organized under the title "Brother, Liberator and Big Ally." Young people from all over Bulgaria took part in programs "devoted to the immortal Lenin, the glorious Communist Party of the Soviet Union, the great Soviet art, the remarkable achievements of communism, etc." "Youth and Our Socialist Mother Country," a radio series developed cooperatively in 1971 with the Komsomol, consisted of discussions of ideological and political themes intended to stimulate further talks in youth groups. A 1972 release also reported close contacts with Moscow radio in developing some new programs for youth: "Almost every broadcast includes sketches, reportages and interviews with young Soviet scientists, public workers, poets, writers and Comsomol functionaries."

Adult Education

Bulgarian radio and television also have educational programs for adult audiences, although few if any of them are directly instructional. In 1960 the "People's University" offered radio talks by "outstanding scientist-popularizers," but there were no credit arrangements as there are with comparable projects in the German Democratic Republic, Poland, the Soviet Union, or the United Kingdom.[61] In the autumn of 1964 television launched a two-year series of thirty-minute broadcasts in elementary German. Several of these dealt with life in the German Democratic Republic. The next year a Russian course was presented on Fridays from 6:00 to 6:30 P.M., each lesson being repeated at another time on another day. These programs assumed some knowledge of Russian, since the course aimed "at the classification of this knowledge and the enrichment of viewers' vocabulary with new words and expressions." Currently there are Russian and German lessons in the late afternoon and early evening.

A glance through news releases reveals a wide range of educational features. In 1963 Sofia radio developed a competition for workers in canning factories as well as two broadcasts to improve the quality of ready-made clothing.[62] (Having visited Sofia's principal department store in 1970, I can testify that seven years later there still was a great need to improve clothing quality!) Television observed the 400th anniversary of Shakespeare's birth by picking up live from a public park the country's first performance of *Love Labour's Lost*.[63]

In 1963 a young woman journalist traveled around the country recording interviews with railway men, sailors, engineers, pilots, and other workers, which were edited into television programs about transportation.[64] A television course on practical electronics was begun in 1965. The ten thirty-minute programs dealt with the basic laws of electricity, the installation of electric mains, and the repair of such household appliances as stoves, irons, washing machines, refrigerators, vacuum cleaners, and radio and television receivers. In 1971 radio launched "The World in the Seventies" in order "to present to radio listeners a broad panorama of the development of mankind in the present decade and to show the growing progressive forces on our planet." Subjects included the socialist system, the increasing importance of international communism, and the intensification of the anti-imperialist struggle.

Since nearly 40 per cent of the population is employed on the land, there are many agricultural programs. "The primary tasks of the Rural Broadcast Department of the Sofia Radio," said a writer in 1960, "are determined by the main tasks set up by the Communist Party of Bulgaria and the needs of socialist building-up regarding agriculture in Bulgaria."[65] Supplementing broadcasts are programs from the wired services—approximately a third of all the sets in the country are wired receivers. For several years a national competition, "Wide Ways Open," encouraged agricultural output.[66] A contest in which listeners provided information about farming was called "Perfection through Knowledge." But the wired networks' schedules were not limited to vocational information, since local literary circles and folk singers also contributed. The first live television relay from a village took place on January 10, 1965, from a dairy farm near Sofia in a series whose purpose was "to show the experiences of the best farms."[67]

Like other socialist countries, Bulgaria has broadcasts of "economic propaganda," although the reference is not to "propaganda" in the Western sense but rather to informational programs about economics and labor.[68] Their objective is to "arouse lively interest" and to "mobilize the efforts of the working people" for the fulfillment of economic tasks. Radio and the Central Council of Trade Unions stage competitions to stimulate cooperatives to overfill their work pledges. Over 35,000 miners took part in one of these, and there have been similar projects for workers in the building and engineering trades. More than 1,200,000 people entered a competition in 1964 to mark the twentieth anniversary of the socialist revolution, and some 70,000 of these received Certificates of Working Glory and Anniversary Badges.[69] Such programs are the responsibility of the two subdivisions of the Department of Economic Broadcasts dealing respectively with industrial and agricultural progress.

All socialist countries use anniversaries as occasions for patriotic exhortations. As noted, for the twentieth anniversary of the revolution, radio had a competition to stimulate industrial and agricultural output.[70] The names of farmers, factory workers, construction workers, and others who met their pledges for increased output were announced, each winner receiving a Certificate of Working Glory. Over sixty correspondents were involved in the feature "One Day of the Five-Year Plan," which reported activities during "a normal day in our country," ranging from work in factories to a symphony orchestra rehearsal, and from the assignments of frontier guards "safeguarding freedom" to "a description of how leisure hours are spent in towns and villages."[71] It all added up to reporting "the 20th anniversary of achievement of freedom."

In 1966 a special radio day marked the Ninth Congress of the Bulgarian Communist party, and shortly afterward a radio evening observed the anniversary of the Russian Revolution of 1917.[72] In the same year there were competitions in connection with the ninetieth anniversary of the country's liberation from five centuries of Turkish rule and of the death of the Bulgarian revolutionary poet Khristo Botev.[73] In 1970 a series of five-minute programs dealt with the 1,300th anniversary of the country's founding.

In 1972 the monthly series "Soviet Parallels" told Bulgarian listeners about the Soviet Union. Prepared in cooperation with Soviet organizations, and scheduled to coincide with the fiftieth anniversary of the establishment of the USSR, the programs were designed "to promote the mutual knowledge and rapprochement of our friendly peoples," by discussing little-known places of interest, "the everyday life of common people living in the multinational Soviet family," and interesting facts about "the building-up of communism."[74]

In 1971 the series "Shield and Sword" dealt with the struggle "against the subversive activity of hostile, espionage and ideological centers. On the basis of documents and actual events the broadcast unmasks the strategic plans of the West for the destruction of socialist society and the provocation of 'critical situations' similar to the Czechoslovak situation in 1968."[75] Some of these programs analyzed the reasons for "the penetration of bourgeois influence among certain parts of our youth and intelligentsia." In another cycle "renowned journalists, writers and publicists talk with listeners and impart their impressions regarding the anti-Bulgarian and antisocialist activity of some western ideological centres and their individual co-workers, particularly of the 'Free Europe' and 'The Voice of America' radio stations." There also was "Economy and Espionage," a series "devoted to the struggle . . . against hostile economic secret services, to its attempts to recruit our specialists for the foul aims of our enemy."

Literature, Drama, and Film

For many years Bulgarian radio has broadcast poetry and prose readings. In 1961 a reference to the series "Fifteen Minutes of Poetry" emphasized the relationship between politics and literature. "At the time of the excited discussion of UNO on the question of abolition of colonialism the wrathful protest of African poets against imperialist oppression could be heard over our radio, while at the time of the threats of American imperialism to the Cuban people poetry of heroic Cuba was broadcast."[76] The cycle "Fires of the Five-Year Plan" demonstrated how everyday life is reflected in the work of Bulgarian writers. There also were readings from such great writers of the past as Schiller, Chekhov, Gorki, and Tolstoy, along with "Our Sonorous Language," which consisted of "recordings of talks by popular narrators . . . [and] by people from various parts of the country and various strata of the population."

Beginning in 1964, on "Literary Saturday," roving radio editors presented material recorded locally about the literary and cultural activities of various Bulgarian towns.[77] In 1968 plans were announced for a radio novel to be broadcast in thirty-minute installments Sundays at 1:00 P.M. which would describe "the great changes brought about in the mutual relations, life and environment of villagers due to the socialist revolution in Bulgaria."[78] In 1972 the Literature and Arts Department of Bulgarian Radio presented the series "Now the Twanging Harp, Now the Jangling Sword," the title being taken from a poem by a Bulgarian writer, which set out "to acquaint listeners with some moments of the historical development of the Bulgarian language, with its beauty and wisdom, picturesqueness and sonority as reflected in works by Bulgarian writers."[79]

In the early 1960s, a radio serial, "The Story of a Large Family," dealt with "moments from the life" of a typical large family in a new village.[80] In the absence of more information about Bulgarian radio drama one may refer to an article about sound effects in radio plays published in 1961 which reads very much like the textbooks on script writing used in some American college courses.[81]

Approximately 3.0 per cent of television time is devoted to literary programs and 3.5 per cent to drama.[82] When television transmitted a play by the Bulgarian writer Nikola Rusve in 1962, it was announced as "the first [Bulgarian] play to be written especially for television."[83] In the following year there were plans for adaptations of "the best performances of the theaters of Sofia and other Bulgarian towns," along with programs for young people featuring both puppets and live actors. National productions were supplemented with "the most successful broadcasts of brotherly countries."

In 1963, 35 per cent of all Bulgarian telecasts were on film.[84] About half of these had been produced especially for television in both "socialist and capitalist countries." The remainder were films secured through exchanges with socialist countries, mainly the USSR, the German Democratic Republic, and Czechoslovakia, as well as from the Bulgarian state film archives. In 1971, 16 per cent of Bulgarian television programs were on film.[85]

Many of these filmed programs have propaganda aspects. "The World of the Future," a Bulgarian production about a man who had just become the father of a baby girl, was described as follows: "A bright and happy future awaits those who are born in our time. This future is firmly based on the long-term plans outlined by our Party."[86] On the eighty-fifth anniversary of the liberation of Bulgaria from the Turks, in which the Russians played a major role, there was an exchange of films between Bulgaria and the Soviet Union, and on the anniversary day itself, Bulgarian television transmitted a Soviet film, "The Pillar of Slavonic Valour."[87] To mark the eightieth birthdate of its Communist hero Georgi Dimitrov, Bulgarian television transmitted a Soviet film. "The film was shot in 1935 and 1936 upon the proposal of German antifascists who had emigrated to the Soviet Union and represents a valuable document because it affects the political atmosphere in Germany of that period, using documentary shots from the historical Leipzig trial."

Bulgaria now is producing its own films for television.[88] In 1964 its first "feature film" was a fictional treatment of World War II. In the same year another Bulgarian production received two prizes in the Leipzig Festival of Documentary Films. A Western critic writing about Bulgarian cinema films in 1970 observed that two-thirds of the new productions were coming to grips with contemporary problems, and that a more forward look had replaced the previous emphasis on the periods of Nazi domination and postwar reconstruction.*

Music

Although figures have not been published on the percentage of Bulgarian radio time devoted to music, 5 per cent of the television output is music,

* *Variety*, January 6, 1971, p. 106; *Variety*, June 21, 1972. In 1970 only 15 and in 1971 only 16 feature cinema films were produced in the entire country. In the former year 139 films were imported, and in 1971, 138. All told, up to the end of 1971, Bulgaria had produced 3,397 films, including 171 feature films, 1,345 scientific films, 1,700 documentaries, and 173 cartoons. At various international festivals 151 of these won a total of 222 prizes. About half the productions scheduled for the third quarter of 1972 concerned contemporary problems.

and the 4.5 per cent classified as entertainment probably includes much light music too.[89]

Radio Network I presents "the most modern and interesting musical compositions including light, dance and classical music of a high artistic standard," along with folk music.[90] Network II has music of all types, instrumental and vocal, while the FM service concentrates on music of "serious genres," including complete operas, "large cantatas and oratorios, complicated works from the field of symphony and chamber music and jazz, i.e. compositions raising creative problems."

The Television and Radio Committee refers to itself as "one of the most important musical institutes in our country popularizing and stimulating the creation of new Bulgarian symphony, light, choral, and other types of music."[91] Although most Americans know very little about music performance standards in Bulgaria, my limited concert going in Sofia left favorable impressions. In November 1970 I saw a good production of Rossini's opera *Cinderella*, sung, of course, in Bulgarian, in the old, attractive opera house in the capital city. Two years later, in Budapest, I viewed on television a good performance by a Sofia symphonic group of a composition by Kodaly.

A continuing effort is made to raise the national level of music appreciation. In 1967 a writer observed that radio has a responsibility to make the serious music of the twentieth century better known and understood.[92] For listeners with limited backgrounds there was the series "Meetings with Music"; for those with greater sophistication, "Musical Knowledge for All," dealing with theory, interpretation, and form; and for advanced listeners, a series analyzing works by composers like Scriabin, Schumann, and Beethoven. In addition to encouraging people to listen with more understanding, Bulgarian broadcasters suggest that their audiences join music clubs.[93]

Representative music programs chosen at random include broadcasts from the Second International Competition of Opera Singers in Sofia in 1963, in which singers from twenty-seven countries took part.[94] In 1966 "Pictures of Our Musical Past" reported the formation of the first Bulgarian orchestra, the composition of the first Bulgarian opera, and other events which "laid the bases of musical culture in Bulgaria." In 1970 "Music in the Course of Centuries" reviewed music through the ages. Bulgarian radio has extensive collections of records and tapes containing performances by famous musicians of the past together with talks by such men as Lenin, Dimitrov, and Yuri Gagarin, which are available for the production of all kinds of documentary programs.

In 1967 one of Bulgarian radio's "most popular broadcasts" was the international song competition "Musical Clover," presented twice a month.[95] There was participation by radio organizations from over twenty countries, including Cuba, Czechoslovakia, Great Britain, Hungary, Italy, New Zealand, Poland, Romania, the USA, the USSR, and Yugoslavia. Awards were based on listeners' reactions, and during the first quarter of the year letters were received from over 30,000 people. Operettas by Bulgarian composers are broadcast, together with standards like Johann Strauss's *Die Fledermaus,* Offenbach's *La Belle Hélène,* and Lehár's *The Count of Luxembourg.* In 1970 "Songs, Singers, Gramophone Records, the Public" reported successes achieved abroad by Bulgarian performers "in the field of entertaining music," and also introduced young performers of such music.

Bulgaria also has its folk music. In 1960, 300 singers and musicians from 30 or 40 villages with a total population of only 10,000 took part in a festival organized cooperatively with the Bulgarian Academy of Sciences and the Union of Bulgarian Composers. During a 3-day competition 1,400 participants, of whom 50 received prizes, performed before 40,000 people.[96] In 1964 a variety song competition attracted 21 composers and 15 lyricists. In 1967 the "Black Sea Coast Song Competition" encouraged the writing of variety and dance songs. In 1968 a jazz series was introduced to "provide a comprehensive explanation" of such music "and to stimulate a permanent inclination towards good jazz music." In 1970 in a café, I enjoyed an evening of folk dancing and music, with native costumes, which was first rate.

Entertainment and Sports

Although serious-minded socialist programmers regard their assignment as more to instruct than to entertain, Bulgarian radio and television nevertheless have many entertainment programs. In the case of television, 16 per cent of all programs are on film, undoubtedly including much entertainment; 4.5 per cent are classified as variety; and 6.5 per cent as sports.[97]

Quiz shows have included the Sunday "Radio Riddles," which put "interesting questions and tasks" to listeners.[98] On December 31, 1964, a three-hour broadcast, which began at 11:00 A.M., "included greetings to those who finished the year 1964 with great working successes." Then came an afternoon session, "Jokes and Music"; a ninety-minute program, "Five Minutes to Midnight"; a review with the provocative title "The Good Corkscrew"; a two-hour program, "Your Health"; and finally, a broadcast of dance music from midnight to 5:00 A.M. on New Year's Day.

In 1969 the head of radio humor, satire, and entertainment reviewed his department's output.[99] Over 2,000 replies may be received during pseudo-educational quizzes, he said, with prizes awarded for "original and acute" answers. In response to the question, "What should be done to prevent divorces?" 700 people replied, "Abolish marriages." Another hundred listeners wrote: "If men were deaf and women blind there would never be any divorces." One person said: "If men were more prudent, then not only would divorces be abolished, but also marriages." When the question was asked, "What would be the greatest surprise for you?" first prize went to the person who answered: "If our streets were not dug up this year."

Once a month—strangely enough, at 10:30 A.M. Sundays—a radio variety program is broadcast live from a concert hall. Many letters have been received about such programs. In 1967 there were 38,000 responses, and in 1968, 52,000, the latter figure being half of all the letters received by Bulgarian radio that year. An official announcement in 1970 indicated that entertainment was recognized as having therapeutic value: not only did it provide pleasant interludes, but it also removed some of the "deficiencies of our social-political, economic and cultural life."[100]

Both radio and television cover sports events. In 1962 the sports editor of Sofia Radio discussed and analyzed such programs.[101] It is not sufficient, he wrote, to broadcast only competitive sports in which there is great interest, like football, hockey, and boxing, because "radio, being an institution taking part in the completion of the cultural revolution and socialist education of man, cannot be guided by almost commercial viewpoints, such as listeners' demands. The radio must purposefully popularise all sports because many decisions of the party and government have set forth clearly the aim of interesting the overwhelming part of the population in active, all-round sports." The editor went on to say that an announcer should be a specialist in the game being broadcast, rather than a generalist covering all sports. Furthermore, his qualifications should include "wide general culture, good language, clear diction, the art of narrating, political-social preparation, and moreover a thorough knowledge of all sports events, quick and original observations, interesting ideas, with knowledge of the psychology of spectators, etc." Finally, play-by-play accounts should be "strictly objective," with the sportscaster never revealing personal preferences for one or another contestant.

The Bulgarian media, like those in Romania and other socialist countries, encourage active participation in sports. In the winter of 1965 hundreds of groups entered contests arranged by the broadcasting organization.[102] But this is not to say that radio and television do not carry play-by-play accounts of major events. The number of Eurovision programs relayed by Bulgaria reached its high point—121 programs of 224 hours and 30 minutes duration—in 1972, the year of the Olympic Games in Munich (see Tables 1 and 2). The second highest was 1968, when the Olympic Games were held in Grenoble. The final contests and closing ceremonies of the 1972 Summer Olympics were among Bulgaria's first color telecasts.[103]

Audience Research

In 1963 the Scientific-Methodological Department of Bulgarian Radio and Television was the only agency in the country engaged in broadcast research. At that time the department published monthly and quarterly bulletins reporting audience studies in other countries, and reprinting articles from foreign journals about the theory and practice of broadcasting. By 1964, however, it had "become a tradition" to study the audience.[104] In one instance researchers spent two days probing the reactions of people in several mountain villages. Among other things, they learned that rural listeners wanted more radio programs about agriculture, more entertainment programs, and more news. Even though television reception was not good in the mountainous areas studied, the residents nevertheless said they wanted more theatrical and operatic telecasts. A 1967 release stated: "One of the most important conditions determining an effective radio programme is the constant endeavour of the Bulgarian Radio to establish creative links with listeners."[105] One way to do this is to collect "opinions, criticisms, and recommendations" in cities of different sizes for consideration by all "departments of the radio broadcasting service."[106]

Although the results of these studies are not available, there are some data about the distribution of receivers.* In 1966, with 1,468,930 wave and 675,152 wired receivers, Bulgaria had 25.88 sound licenses per hundred, ranking below East Germany and Czechoslovakia but above Hungary, Poland, and Yugoslavia. At that time, its 287,880 television licenses placed it at the bottom of the socialist group, with 3.47 licenses per hundred. In 1972, with 1,520,510 wave and 710,944 wired receivers, Bulgaria's 26.34 radio licenses per hundred put it at the top of the socialist countries reporting, though it should be noted that no Czechoslovak, East German, or Polish data were published that year. Bulgaria's 1,285,848 television licenses, at the rate of 15.18 per hundred of population, put it third lowest ahead of Romania and Yugoslavia.

The Robinson study reported that in 1965 the average Bulgarian with access to a television receiver devoted seventeen minutes a day to primary and seventeen minutes a day to secondary viewing, for a total daily exposure of slightly over half an hour.[107] This indicates less viewing in Bulgaria than in any of the other countries here studied, although at that time Bulgarian television was just beginning, and had very limited broadcast hours, so that comparisons would not be meaningful.

Between May 1970 and March 1971 interviews sponsored by Radio Free Europe probed the domestic radio listening and television viewing habits of 546 Bulgarians visiting six Western countries.[108] All of the sample listened to domestic radio, 48 per cent daily and 47 per cent several times a week. Favorite listening hours were between 6:00 and 9:00 A.M., noon and 2:00 P.M., and 5:00 to 11.00 P.M., with the peak of the day's listening between 7:00 and 8:00 P.M., when 73 per cent of the sample normally listened to the radio. Reflecting the relatively few receivers, only 65 per cent reported regular television viewing, with 6 per cent watching daily and 21 per cent several times a week. But those who did view did so at the same hours reported by respondents in the other socialist bloc countries, between 7:00 and 10:00 P.M., with 60 per cent watching between 8:00 and 9:00 P.M.

Since Radio Free Europe also is interested in the audience for the 7½ hours of programs broadcast to Bulgaria every day, it engaged some independent research organizations to question 546 Bulgarians temporarily visiting in the West between June 1971 and February 1972 about their

* See Table 10. The EBU figures are supplied by the various broadcasting organizations, so that those not replying to the annual questionnaire are omitted from the tabulations.

listening to programs from abroad.[109] It was found that 46 per cent of the respondents listened to RFE regularly, compared with 23 per cent who listened to the BBC, 22 per cent to the Voice of America, and 12 per cent to Radio Luxembourg. However, 41 per cent did not listen to Western broadcasts at all, a larger figure than was reported by respondents from Czechoslovakia, Hungary, Poland, or Romania, partly because Bulgaria was the only country in the group which consistently jammed outside programs. When 2,821 Eastern Europeans, including 291 Bulgarians, visiting the West were asked why they did not listen to Radio Free Europe, 27 per cent of the nonlistening Bulgarians said jamming was a major factor.*

On an average day 40 per cent of the people who tuned to RFE listened for approximately half an hour, and 81 per cent of these did so because the "station satisfied their need for objective, truthful, quick, and frequently suppressed information." Since 1965, RFE listening in Bulgaria has steadily risen: 39 per cent of the sample listened in 1965, 42 per cent in 1968, 45 per cent in 1970, and 50 per cent in early 1971. From the end of December to March 1971, during and immediately after the "Polish events," 75 per cent of a sample of 147 Bulgarians interviewed in Western Europe reported listening to Western radio stations generally and 88 per cent to Radio Free Europe.[110]

External Broadcasting

Bulgaria maintains the usual external services, ranging from broadcasts for foreign reception to program exchanges. There have been broadcasts to foreign countries ever since the revolution, and each day Radio Bulgaria transmits twenty hours of material for listeners abroad.[111] According to BBC figures, in 1972 Bulgaria broadcast an average of 175 hours of external programs each week, which would put it well down among Eastern European countries in this respect (see Table 9). One medium- and approximately fifteen short-wave frequencies are used for these serv-

---

* Radio Free Europe, *Reasons for Not Listening to Radio Free Europe*, pp. 1, 5. Although several key Bulgarian radio and television staff members told me in 1970 that the country no longer jammed foreign broadcasts, my own observations indicated otherwise. American observers in Sofia reported much jamming of foreign broadcasts, and even guessed where the jammers were located, while official VOA reports indicate consistent jamming by Bulgaria. In my hotel room I heard more and louder jamming than in any other country visited, indicating not only that there was jamming, but that the jammers were located in central Sofia.

ices. For Europe and the Near East there are transmissions in Arabic, Bulgarian, English, Esperanto, French, German, Greek, Italian, Serbo-Croatian, Spanish, and Turkish; for Africa in English and French; for North America in Bulgarian and English; and for South America in Bulgarian and Spanish.[112]

A spokesman for Bulgarian broadcasting stated that these programs project the socialist point of view as developed by the Bulgarian Communist party; point out the advantages of living under socialism; tell the world about the great successes achieved by the people of Bulgaria and other socialist countries; popularize the policies of peaceful coexistence; contribute to the efforts to unify the International Communist Workers' Movement; and counteract anti-Bulgarian propaganda disseminated by imperialist countries.[113] Beginning in 1968 a special service was organized for Bulgarians living abroad, featuring talks "about everything dear to Bulgarians, to our countrymen outside the borders of our country, everything that lives in their heart and minds, everything that connects them with their native valleys and mountains." But this was discontinued at the end of 1970 partly because of objections from Yugoslavia, which apparently felt that Yugoslavs with Bulgarian leanings might be the intended target.[114] My limited listening to English-language programs from Bulgaria has shown them to be of mediocre quality and of questionable value in the achievement of these objectives.

There are cooperative agreements with all the socialist and many Western countries.[115] Radio normally exchanges programs with 100 broadcasting organizations in over seventy countries, while television maintains relations with forty foreign groups. In 1971, thirty television programs were exchanged each month with Czechoslovakia, and in the same year a reciprocal agreement brought a "Week of the Romanian Socialist Republic" to Bulgarian television and vice versa. There also have been exchanges with Western countries. For eighteen years Soviet radio has carried a program from Bulgaria entitled "Sofia Calling," while the second Bulgarian network now relays a program from Radio Moscow daily between 5:00 and 5:30 P.M.[116] Reference was made above to television relaying seven hours of Soviet television programs on Friday evenings. Bulgaria exchanges musical groups, including choirs, folk dancers, and symphony orchestras, with Romania, Yugoslavia, Czechoslovakia, the USSR, Italy, France, East Germany, Japan, the United Kingdom, Hungary, France, West Germany, and others.[117] A 1973 news release told how "in the summer of 1972 the unaffected, childishly pure and sincere, warm and thrilling song of the Children's Radio Choir of the Bulgarian TV and Radio Committee aroused enthusiasm and storms of applause of the extraordinarily responsive Japanese public for the fourth time." All told, the Children's Radio Choir had given 132 concerts in 85 Japanese cities during its several trips there, plus other performances in the United States, United Kingdom, Switzerland, West Germany, Denmark, Poland, Romania, Yugoslavia, and other countries.

Although 6 per cent of the television output is from Intervision, Bulgaria has had limited participation in Eurovision.* In 1964 Bulgaria received 19 Eurovision programs totaling 26 hours. The following year it took 14 programs (34 hr. 45 min.), and in 1966, 31 programs (57 hr. 45 min.). In 1967 Bulgaria made its first contributions—4 programs (7 hr. 15 min.)—while receiving 17 programs (30 hr. 15 min.). In 1968 although it supplied only one program (2 hr.), it responded to the appeal of the Olympic Games by taking 115 programs (187 hr. 15 min.). In 1971, according to Eurovision, Bulgaria provided 7 programs (22 hr. 30 min.), and received 70 programs (125 hr. 15 min.). But Intervision reported that in the same year Bulgaria contributed 8 programs (18 hr. 38 min.) to Eurovision, receiving 56 programs (107 hr. 35 min.). According to Eurovision, in 1972 Bulgaria contributed 2 programs (2 hr. 15 min.) while receiving 221 programs (224 hr. 30 min.). But Intervision reported that in the same year Bulgaria provided 7 programs (8 hr. 59 min.), all sports events, and received only 33 programs (74 hr. 31 min.).

* *Internationales Handbuch 1971/72*, p. F16. See Tables 1 and 2 above.

XII

The Socialist Federal Republic
of Yugoslavia

The Socialist Federal Republic of Yugoslavia is a bridge between the Western democratic and the Eastern socialist countries. To an American making his first visit to a socialist land, Yugoslavia may mistakenly appear to be a "typical" Communist one-party state. To a Soviet citizen who never has been to the West it may seem like a capitalist bulwark. But people familiar with West and East will find in Yugoslavia some of the features of both.

Facts about Yugoslavia

Yugoslavia is "a state with six republics, five South Slav peoples, four languages, three religions, two alphabets, and one political party."* The largest European socialist country after the Soviet Union and Poland, it contains 98,740 square miles, and is about the size of Wyoming, which with 97,914 square miles is the ninth largest American state. It shares land boundaries on the west with Italy, on the north with Austria and Hungary, on the northeast with Romania, on the east with Bulgaria, and on the south with Greece and Albania. On the west it has a 450-mile Adriatic coastline.

* John C. Campbell, "Yugoslavia," in Adam Bromke and Teresa Rakowska-Harmstone, eds., *The Communist States in Disarray 1965–1971*, p. 189. Although the quotation, with its references to four languages, makes a neat phrase, Yugoslavia in fact has only three principal languages: Serbo-Croatian, Slovenian, and Macedonian. Serbo-Croatian, in effect, is one language, written in the Cyrillic alphabet by the Serbs and the Latin alphabet by the Croats.

460

In 1971 the population of Yugoslavia was 20,550,000.[1] Its six republics include Serbia with 34,107 square miles and 8,432,108 people; Croatia, 21,824 square miles, 4,346,376 people; Macedonia, 9,925 square miles, 1,616,069 people; Slovenia, 7,817 square miles, 1,697,499 people; Montenegro, 5,331 square miles, 531,213 people; and Bosnia-Herzegovina, 19,736 square miles, 3,716,786 people. The national capital, Belgrade, with 1,209,360 inhabitants, is the largest city, and Zagreb, the capital of Croatia, is the second largest with 602,205. Other chief towns, which are republic or regional capitals as well as broadcasting centers, include Skopje, Macedonia (388,962 people); Sarajevo, Bosnia-Herzegovina (292,263); Ljubljana, Slovenia (257,647); Titograd, Montenegro (98,796); Novi Sad, autonomous region of Vojovodina (213,861); and Priština, autonomous region of Kosovo (152,744).

As a result of heavy emphasis on industry following World War II, 45.7 per cent of employed persons in 1970 worked in industry and mining, 10.9 per cent in agriculture and forestry, 10.9 per cent in construction, 9.8 per cent in trade and catering, 5.4 per cent in arts and crafts, and 18.92 per cent in other occupations. A Yugoslav remarked to me that his country has competition without capitalism, another respect in which Yugoslavia draws from both Western and Eastern Europe. However, Yugoslavia has more private enterprise than any of the other countries covered in this study, even though most of it consists of small business. Currently there is much debate whether private enterprise should be encouraged or stifled. But in any case, virtually all the farms are privately owned and operated, although holdings are limited to twenty-five acres each.[2] Large industrial, financial, and trade enterprises are nationalized, but managers and workers share in basic decisions, and profit-sharing plans provide workers with strong incentives to increase output. One consequence of this is that customers receive more attention and better service than in most socialist countries, something which assists the constantly expanding tourist industry.

There is more foreign trade with West than East, although Yugoslavia continues to trade with the socialist countries too. It has been a member of GATT (General Agreement on Tariffs and Trade) since 1966, and in March 1970 was the first socialist state to conclude a trade agreement with the European Economic Community.[3] Early in 1973 Yugoslavia and the United States signed an agreement to provide insurance and financial aid to American investors in Yugoslavia through the Overseas

Private Investment Corporation, it being the first such accord with a Communist country.[4] This guarantee, intended to stimulate private investment in Yugoslavia, came shortly after the receipt by Yugoslavia of the equivalent of $540,000,000 in Soviet aid. During the preceding two decades, however, the United States had provided Yugoslavia with over $2 billion in economic assistance and loans.

In dinar values, 17 per cent of Yugoslavia's foreign trade in 1970 was with Italy, 14 per cent with the United Kingdom, 9 per cent with the Federal Republic of Germany, 6 per cent with the USSR, 5.5 per cent with the USA, 4.5 per cent with Austria, 4 per cent with Switzerland, and 4 per cent with France. Of its 4,748,000 tourists, 26 per cent came from the Federal Republic of Germany, 17 per cent from Italy, 12 per cent from Austria, 6 per cent from the United Kingdom, and 3 per cent from Czechoslovakia. The 206,000 American visitors made up a little over 4 per cent. All other visitors combined composed 26 per cent of the total.

Yugoslavia's six republics have divergent historical backgrounds. For centuries Slovenia was part of Austria while Croatia belonged to Hungary. Serbia, Montenegro, and Macedonia formerly were controlled by Turkey, while Bosnia was divided among several countries. However, Bosnia and Herzegovina came under Austro-Hungarian control in 1878 and were annexed by the Austro-Hungarian Empire in 1908. The idea of a state incorporating all the south Slavs emerged among the Croats in the 1830s, and during the revolution of 1848–1849 there were unsuccessful attempts to liberate Croatia from Hungary. Croatia finally received autonomous status within the Habsburg Empire in 1868. Subsequently, Serbia became the leader of the Pan-Slav movement, of which an extremist member assassinated Austrian Archduke Franz Ferdinand at Sarajevo in 1914, precipitating World War I.

In 1918, following the collapse of the Austro-Hungarian Empire, the Kingdom of the Serbs, Croats and Slovenes, whose territory approximated the present Yugoslavia, was set up under the king of Serbia, who became Peter I. The new government, dominated by the Serbs, had centralist tendencies and abolished the old provinces, thus exacerbating the perennial nationality conflicts. This led in 1929 to a dictatorship under Alexander I, Peter's successor, at which time the country's name was changed to Yugoslavia.

Although the Yugoslav government in March 1941 signed an agreement to enter World War II on the side of the Axis, this action led to its overthrow several days later by a bloodless coup, after which the new government signed a nonaggression pact with the USSR. Shortly thereafter, Germany, Italy, Hungary, and Bulgaria invaded and occupied the country. There ensued a bitter civil war between one resistance group led by Draža Mihailović, sympathetic to the Royal Yugoslav government-in-exile in London, and another led by Josip Broz Tito, supported by the USSR. The conflict was marked by bitter fighting between Serbs and Croats, and it was charged that during the Nazi occupation Croat extremists killed 100,000 Serbs. Eventually the Tito group gained the ascendancy, and in 1945 proclaimed the People's Republic of Yugoslavia.

Continuing conflicts among national groups are such a major problem for Yugoslavia that they are regarded as a "clear and present danger" justifying severe limitations on freedom of expression. These divisions, based on historical, geographical, ethnic, linguistic, religious, and economic differences, extend over several centuries, and often have been exploited by the various foreign powers that at one time or another have ruled portions of the country. There are 8.3 million Serbs (including those known as Montenegrins); about 4.3 million Croats; nearly 1.6 million Slovenes; over 1 million Macedonians; and nearly 1 million Bosnians. Minorities include Albanians, Hungarians, Turks, and Italians.

There are three major and several minor religious groups. The Serbian Orthodox Church has over 8,000,000 adherents, most living in Serbia, Montenegro, Bosnia-Herzegovina, and Croatia. Most of the 6,000,000 Roman Catholics are in Slovenia and Croatia, while the 1 million members of the Macedonian Orthodox Church live mainly in Macedonia.[5] The Albanian and Turkish minorities are mainly Moslems, and there also are other Catholic groups, Evangelicals, Lutherans, Methodists, Jehovah's Witnesses, and a small Jewish population. The major language is Serbo-Croatian, written in the Cyrillic alphabet by the Serbs and the Latin alphabet by the Croats. The second language, Slovenian, uses the Latin alphabet, and the third language, Macedonian, the Cyrillic alphabet.

There is a continuing conflict between Serbs and Croats, two groups that developed national consciousness following the Napoleonic Wars.[6] After World War II a separatist movement developed in Croatia, led by a group known as the Ustashi, an extremist group which controlled Croatia in World War II in collaboration with Germany and Italy, and which was charged with many atrocities against Serbians.[7] Some current Ustashi leaders live in West Germany and Australia.

An example of nationalist feeling was provided in September 1971 by a student strike in Zagreb, the Croatian capital, which culminated in four nights of violent demonstrations. During the disturbances nearly 1,000 people were arrested, and thereafter 740 Yugoslav party members were purged and 174 persons forced out of their jobs. It was claimed that Croatian terrorists incited these and other demonstrations, and that they subsequently took sanctuary in West Germany where they were harbored as "anti-Communists."[8] In January 1972, when a group of Ustashi blew up a Yugoslav airplane flying over Czechoslovakia, all people aboard, except one stewardess, were killed. In June of the same year, well-armed Croatian émigrés crossed into Yugoslavia from Austria. Several were killed in gun battles with Yugoslav police. Three of those captured were subsequently tried and thereafter shot by a firing squad, although full disclosure of their capture and execution was delayed until the following April. In September 1972 three Croatians hijacked a Scandinavian Airlines plane and subsequently forced Sweden to release six Croatians who had been imprisoned for an attack on Yugoslav diplomats.

President Tito has tried valiantly to control these nationalist outbreaks—and he himself is a Croatian. In April 1971 he condemned those who "poison the atmosphere" with excessive nationalism, and a year later, concluding a three-day party conference, said that the nation had enemies at home as well as abroad, the former including certain Croatian terrorists who, when arrested, would be charged with treason.[9] Tito harshly rebuked the Croation authorities for not keeping the September 1971 outbreaks under control and called for "sharp measures" against "counter-revolutionary groups." The question remains what will become of these conflicts when Tito passes from the scene, since with his great prestige, he is better able to control them than could any of his apparent successors.

Internationally, Yugoslavia follows an independent—and sometimes opportunist—policy. In the first years after World War II, Tito and his colleagues were firmly in the Soviet orbit, but following pronounced differences with the USSR, were expelled from the Cominform in 1948. At that time Stalin said: "I will shake my finger and there will be no more Tito."[10] Thereafter Tito talked of national communism and turned to the West for economic aid. In the years since then, Soviet-Yugoslav relations have pendulumed back and forth. They improved for a time following the death of Stalin in 1953, and reached a high point in 1955 when Khrushchev visited Belgrade to offer some concessions. But they were strained again when the USSR intervened in Hungary in 1956. Yugoslavia—not a member of the Warsaw Pact—severely criticized the Soviet occupation of Czechoslovakia in 1968, even while fearing for its own safety and mobilizing forces against the possibility of an invasion.

Toward the end of 1970 President Nixon and Marshal Tito exchanged visits, in 1971 Leonid Brezhnev came to Yugoslavia, and in 1972 Tito went to Moscow. On the latter occasion the Soviets gave Tito a very warm welcome and one of the highest Soviet awards, the Order of Lenin. One explanation for this hospitality was that the USSR wanted to mend relations with Yugoslavia during Tito's lifetime (he then was eighty years old) in the hope of being in a position to exert more influence on his successors.

In view of this maneuvering back and forth, it is interesting to note that in the summer of 1972 an opinion poll in Serbia found that 26 per cent of a sample of 900 people regarded the Soviet Union as Yugoslavia's best friend, while only 4 per cent felt that the United States was, dissatisfaction over the American role in the Vietnam War being a major reason for the different ratings. Nevertheless, in the long run Yugoslavia is expected to continue its Western orientation. Its status as an independent socialist state, therefore, poses a continuing challenge to Moscow, since it disturbs the Soviet pattern in Eastern Europe. Perhaps the USSR's real view of Yugoslavia was expressed in a book published in Moscow in 1971 by the head of the Department of Science and Education of the Soviet Communist party's Central Committee. After blaming Tito for disruptive activities in Hungary and Czechoslovakia, he referred to Yugoslavia as a "right-revisionist [country] established by world imperialism within the Socialist camp."[11]

Legal Structure

The legal structure for broadcasting in Yugoslavia is provided by the (1) National Constitution, (2) the Law of the Press and other Media of Information, (3) the Basic Law on Radio Communications, and (4) the Basic Law on Radiobroadcasting Institutions.

The 1963 Constitution, which replaced earlier documents of 1946 and 1953, begins as do some other socialist constitutions, by referring to the overthrow of "the former class society based on exploitation, political oppression and national inequality." It describes Yugoslavia as "a community in which human labor and man will be delivered from exploitation and arbitrariness," and in which "each of the peoples of Yugoslavia and all of them together will find conditions for free and comprehensive development."[12]

Chapter I ("Introductory Provisions") states that the Socialist Federal Republic of Yugoslavia comprises the republics of Bosnia and Herzegovina, Croatia, Macedonia, Montenegro, Serbia, and Slovenia, and that Yugoslavia is to be "a socialist democratic community based on the powers of the working people and on self-government."[13] In view of the separatist movement in Croatia, it is interesting to note the recognition of "the right of every people to self-determination, including the right to secession." At one point there is the phrase, "From each according to his abilities; to each according to his work."*

Articles 6–31 ("Social-Economic Organization") deal with the worker-management structure found in a number of public agencies, including broadcasting. It is declared to be "the right and duty of the working people" to manage such organizations, either directly "or through organs of management elected by themselves."[14]

Articles 32–70 define "The Freedoms, Rights and Duties of Man and Citizen." There is to be equality of "nationality, race, religion, sex, language, education [and] social position."[15] All citizens eighteen years of age or older may vote, have the right to work (the working week must not exceed forty-two hours), and are guaranteed a social security system.[16]

Freedom of expression is assured, although subsequent provisions permit important limitations and controls. The Constitution says: "Freedom of the press and other media of information, freedom of association, freedom of speech and public expression, freedom of meeting and other public assemblage shall be guaranteed."[17] Specifically, citizens are guaranteed "the right to express and publish their opinions through the media of information, . . . to publish newspapers and other publications and to disseminate information by other media of communication." There also are religious guarantees: "Religious confession shall not be restricted and shall be man's private affair. The religious communities shall be

* For other references to this phrase see above, 3n, 272, 316.

detached from the State and shall be free to perform religious affairs and religious rites," including setting up schools to train clergy.[18]

About the mass media the Constitution states: "The press, radio and television shall truthfully and objectively inform the public and publish and broadcast the opinions and information of organs, organizations, and citizens which are of interest to public information."[19] In addition to leaving open the question of what information is "truthful and objective," the Constitution goes on to offer some firm qualifications: "These freedoms and rights shall not be used by anyone to overthrow the foundations of the socialist democratic order determined by the Constitution, to endanger the peace, international cooperation on terms of equality, or the independence of the country, to disseminate national, racial, or religious hatred or intolerance, or to incite to crime, or in any manner that offends public decency." Application of these restrictions "shall be determined by federal law." (Article 118 of the Criminal Code forbids "maliciously and untruthfully representing the social and political situation in the country." The maximum sentence for violating this statute is twelve years of imprisonment.)

Articles 71–95 describe "The Social-Political System." Yugoslavia is a decentralized federation of six republics, each with its own government. The Federal Assembly, whose members are elected to four-year terms, is the supreme organ of government.[20] The assembly elects the president, who in the future will be limited to two four-year terms. However, in view of his great prestige, Josip Broz Tito is exempt from these limitations, so that, in effect, he is president for life.[21]

Although Yugoslavia is the most democratic and free of all the socialist countries, it still is a one-party state. The League of Communists of Yugoslavia, with a separate party in each of the six republics, has a total membership of slightly over 1 million.[22] The League is paralleled by the Socialist Alliance of the Working People of Yugoslavia, with 8.5 million members, which is responsible for building socialism and for nominating candidates for election to the Federal Assembly and other representative bodies.

Also related to broadcasting is the Law of the Press, parts of which repeat sections of the Constitution.[23] Article 1 states that "the freedom of the press and other forms of information shall be guaranteed" so that the democratic rights of citizens may be ensured, public opinion strengthened, and information freely disseminated. Accordingly, all Yugoslav citizens, "regardless of the differences in . . . nationality, race, language or religion, shall have the right to express and publish their opinions through the media of information."[24] However, in agreement with Articles 40 and 41 of the Constitution, it is stipulated that these rights "shall not be misused for the purpose of undermining the foundations of the socialist democratic government established by the Constitution, for the purpose of jeopardizing peace, . . . for the purpose of stirring international, racial, or religious hate or intolerance, or for the purpose of initiating criminal actions; nor shall they be misused to the detriment of public morals." (This limiting clause was not in the 1960 version of the law, having been added in the 1965 revision.)

Nevertheless, there is to be "no censorship of the press and other forms of information, except in event of a state of mobilization or war; . . . [and] institutions and organizations devoted to the publication and dissemination of information shall be independent" in performing their functions.[25] The exchange of information between Yugoslavia and other countries is to be "free," although it could be restricted to protect the country's independence. Likewise, the publication of information "prejudicial to the honour, reputation and the rights of the citizens or to the interests of the social community shall constitute an abuse of the freedom of information and involve the liability established by law." These limitations are summed up by an interesting sentence: "Publication and dissemination of information may be limited only in order to prevent abuse of the freedom of information, to wit, in the cases expressly established by law."

Persons or organizations have the right to reply to broadcasts "injurious to their honour, rights or interests."[26] If a broadcasting institution denies the validity of a complaint and refuses air time, the aggrieved party may appeal to the courts. But once the right of reply is conceded, the reply must be aired within two days, usually at the same time and during a program of the same type as that in which the material originally as transmitted. In the case of television, the reply may be by radio only.

The Basic Law on Radio Communications, which took effect in 1965, is the Yugoslav equivalent of America's Communications Act of 1934.[27] Broadcasting stations may be established to transmit "messages of general interest in the field of information, education and culture; . . . for the requirements of national defence, internal affairs, road safety; and for other instances in which radio communication is needed for the performance of actions." Stations may be established by "state organs, working and other organizations and by citizens."[28]

Legal framework for the broadcasting system itself is provided by the Basic Law on Radiobroadcasting Institutions, which came into effect in 1965 as a revision of the original 1955 statute.[29] In recognition of the diverse legal, cultural, and linguistic composition of Yugoslavia's six republics and two autonomous regions, radio and television are decentralized, each of these eight subdivisions having its own broadcasting organization. One hundred and eighty local stations supplement the main broadcasting institutions.

At the outset the Basic Law defines the purposes of broadcasting: "Radiobroadcasting institutions inform the public . . . concerning all spheres of life in Yugoslavia and abroad, initiate discussions on matters of public interest and broadcast opinions of citizens, organizations and public organs on such matters."[30] They also "broadcast cultural, artistic, educational, entertainment and other programmes" to satisfy the "cultural requirements and other interests of citizens." The law stipulates that programs "are not subject to censorship."

The heart of the law is its provision for organizing stations as collectives: "Radiobroadcasting institutions may be established by the sociopolitical community and the working and other self-governing organizations under the conditions provided by law."[31] In effect, these are of two types: the 8 main institutions serving entire republics or provinces, and the 180 local institutions.

Organs of management for broadcasting institutions must include at least an advisory council, a board of management, and a director, although each organization may create additional management divisions.[32] A broad base of participation is assured by stipulating that advisory councils shall consist of members chosen by the workers in the institution along with representatives from the social community.

Typical main broadcasting institutions have councils of from 15 to 47 prestigious people drawn from such fields as education, politics, creative arts, and engineering.[33] The board of management is elected by this council from among its members and from the community. Radio Television Belgrade has 9 self-management bodies with a total membership of 191. The same pattern is followed elsewhere, although smaller organizations have simpler structures.

The director of a broadcasting institution and some other staff members are chosen in open competition. The senior members of a broadcasting institution include the director and several assistant directors; the heads of radio and television and their key staff members; the heads of music and perhaps some other program areas; and the chief engineer.[34]

Coordination and leadership for all of Yugoslav broadcasting are provided by Jugoslovenska Radiotelevizija (JRT), which, however, does not have supervisory authority over the various units. JRT was founded in 1952 by the main broadcasting institutions. Under the provisions of the 1955 law, membership was obligatory, but in 1965 it became voluntary.[35] But all eight main broadcasting institutions belong, including the radio and television organizations of Belgrade, Zagreb, Ljubljana, Sarajevo, Skpoje, Titograd, Radio Novi Sad, and Radio Priština.

JRT is charged with promoting and expediting the work of Yugoslav broadcasting.[36] Its projects include the development and operation of nationwide radio and television networks and the representation of Yugoslav broadcasting abroad.[37] JRT is supported by contributions from its members, and is operated by a board of management and a secretary general elected by its members.[38] Much of its work is done by committees, made up of specialists from within the organization, dealing with such things as programming, engineering, finance, and foreign relations.[39]

Yugoslav broadcasting is supported 74 per cent by license fees, 19 per cent by advertising revenue, and 7 per cent by funds from "other sources."[40] The law allows the six republics to set their own license fees, which accordingly vary from one republic to another. The rate for radio receivers in private homes—it is higher for those in public places—averaged 180 dinars per year ($11.16 in 1973), and charges for television receivers are 480 dinars ($29.76) per year.[41] In some republics combined radio and television licenses are available at 660 dinars ($40.92) per year. Broadcasting institutions are free to engage in such supplementary income producing activities as producing and selling films, recordings, and publications, and giving public concerts.

How much freedom of expression is there in Yugoslavia? Clearly, less than in West Germany, the United Kingdom, or the United States— although these countries too have a "clear and present danger" point beyond which it is curtailed. Yugoslavia, of course, imposes fewer controls than do any of the other socialist countries. Western newspapers and magazines are on sale, not only in tourist hotels but also in kiosks all over the country, and Yugoslavs may and do purchase and read them. Sometimes the authorities confiscate a particular issue or book which they may regard as offensive, but there is no precensorship, and the courts occasionally rule against the government when a publisher or importer stands his ground. Bookstores stock books that are not sympathetic to the regime or to communism generally, such as translations of the works of Aleksandr Solzhenitsyn or George F. Kennan's *Memoirs.*

This freedom is accompanied by more sex and pornography than is found in any of the other socialist countries. I saw girlie magazines on public sale in Belgrade and Zagreb and noticed advertisements in hotel lobbies for striptease acts that left nothing to the imagination. In 1971 a performance of *Hair* had been running in Belgrade for three years, at which time *Oh Calcutta!* was opened—incidentally, with lukewarm reponse.[42]

Yugoslavia has never jammed foreign radio broadcasts, and normally maintains friendly relations with both the BBC and Voice of America staffs. Recognizing the openness of the country, and the availability of diversified information sources to its citizens, neither Radio Free Europe nor Radio Liberty broadcasts to Yugoslavia, although the Voice of America and BBC both do. Most visitors are impressed with the frankness of the Yugoslavs they meet, and I have found their public officials much more outspoken than those in the other socialist countries.

JRT, rather than concealing the facts of its operation, has published an excellent series of yearbooks annually since 1963, which tell as much or more about Yugoslav radio and television as do the BBC handbooks about British broadcasting. These are available not only in Serbo-Croatian but also in English. Attendance at USIA libraries is good, and there normally is no harassment of Yugoslavs visiting them, although in December 1966 there were demonstrations at the libraries in both Belgrade and Zagreb by students protesting American actions in Vietnam.[43] In 1970 I visited these two libraries, and found them well stocked with books and well attended, in contrast with those in Poland and the Soviet Union, for example, where few people, except newspapermen or others on official assignments, venture.

But some things cannot be said. The basic Communist system is not to be criticized; the animosities of Yugoslavia's nationalities must not be incited; foreign intervention is not to be invited by undue criticism of the Soviet Union; and President Tito personally is above criticism.

As was pointed out above, the Constitution specifies that freedom of expression cannot be used "to overthrow the foundations of the socialist democratic order, . . . to endanger the peace, . . . to disseminate national, racial, or religious hatred or intolerance, or to incite to crime, or in any manner that offends public decency."[44] The Law of the Press reiterates these limitations. During a May Day television broadcast in 1971 President Tito declared: "We have placed democracy on a very high level, on a strong foundation. But there cannot be democracy for the enemies of our socialist system who fight against everything we wish to achieve. Up until now we have tolerated too much. We have tolerated such enemies and their actions too much, and they are at work in many areas."[45]

In 1955 Milovan Djilas, a former member of the Central Committee of the Yugoslav Communist party and the party's chief ideologist, was given a three-year suspended sentence for publishing "hostile propaganda" in a *New York Times* interview, and the next year was jailed for criticizing the Soviet invasion of Hungary.[46] Djilas was jailed several times in the 1950s and 1960s for such publications as *The New Class*, which criticizes the Communist system. In 1969 the authorities banned the importation and sale of his book *The Unperfect Society*, which had been published in the United States and West Germany several months before. Nevertheless, throughout 1972 he continued to write for the *New York Times*, criticizing both the Soviet Union and his own country.[47] For this he was attacked in various Yugoslav publications, one of them even calling him a "traitor and enemy of his country."

In 1965 the Yugoslav writer Mihajlo Mihajlov received a suspended sentence for an article allegedly insulting the Soviet Union, and in 1967 was sentenced to 4½ years imprisonment for propaganda against the state. He was released in 1970, after serving 3½ years of his sentence. But in the same year he wrote a piece for the *New York Times*, "Art as Enemy," supporting Aleksandr Solzhenitsyn. Early in 1971, after the police had questioned him about this article, the same newspaper published a letter from him recounting his experiences. Thereafter he was sentenced to fifteen days for the article and fifteen days for the letter.[48] The judge who sentenced him said he was being imprisoned because the *New York Times* was available and was read in Yugoslavia. Two years later Mihajlov again wrote for the *New York Times*, despite instructions that he was not to do any publishing until March 1974.

Unable thereafter to secure employment, he appealed directly to President Tito for permission either to emigrate or to publish, after which Tito found him a position in the Institute of Literature in Belgrade.

In 1971 a Belgrade court banned distribution of an article by the Russian Nikolai Berdyaev, entitled "Realm of Spirit and Caesar," in the Yugoslav magazine *Kultura*, which originally had been published in 1943. (The author died in 1948 outside the Soviet Union, and his works have been banned in the USSR.)[49] Described to the court as "extremely anti-Marxist," and said to speak "offensively of the nature of the Soviet socialist state and socialism in general," it was forbidden, lest it interfere with "friendly relations" between Yugoslavia and the Soviet Union. While at times the Yugoslavs have been very critical of the Soviet Union—for example, during the invasion of Czechoslovakia in August 1968—incidents like this surface periodically.

In September 1972 a court banned one issue of the Serbian Philosophic Society's quarterly journal for "false and alarming statements" calculated to "disrupt the brotherhood and unity of the Yugoslav nationalities."[50] The court declared that the article contained "assertions that might alarm citizens and endanger law and order." In 1973 a book was banned for being too skeptical about the future outlook of the worker-managed enterprises which are such an integral part of the country's economic system.[51] In the same year, issues of two scholarly journals were banned for criticizing the conviction of an academic imprisoned for publicly opposing some constitutional amendments whose purpose was to transfer certain powers from the federal government to the independent republics, all this being related to the continuing Serbo-Croat controversy.

Commenting on such cases, President Tito remarked that certain philosophers either should "go on pension or find a new line of employment." While conceding that some professors had made great contributions, he complained that "in the faculties of philosophy they often are philosophizing in all possible ways. Our Marxist philosophy is not much used there." Shortly thereafter it was reported from Belgrade that after some years during which "liberal ideology has held sway, the League of Communists is sternly reasserting authority over all aspects of the society, and demanding doctrinal conformity."[52] The league (the Yugoslav Communist party) criticized certain liberal trends among professors at the University of Belgrade, singling out a "small group of instructors and extremist students" which had "imposed itself, in a liberalistic political climate, in an extremely aggressive way as an alien body . . . which must be removed. . . ."[53] There also were attacks on the United States. The Voice of America was charged with allowing Yugoslav émigrés to go on the air inviting demonstrations against Yugoslav diplomats abroad; a project to show some musical films to Yugoslavs was banned; and certain American newspapers, including the *New York Times* and the *Washington Post*, were accused of hostile propaganda. All of which adds up to the fact that even though Yugoslavia continues to be the most liberal country in the Eastern European bloc, it still should not be equated with typical Western democracies.

Again to quote President Tito: in the spring of 1973, in the course of complaints about "deformations" of Yugoslav-Marxist development as a result of two decades of "liberalism," he declared: "We Communists have the right to interfere in everything. I am chairman of the League of Communists and I have the right to interfere. We have the right to interfere to insure the correct implementation of the general policy of the party, the proper development of socialism, the proper development of social relations and brotherhood and unity, for which we shed a sea of blood."[54]

Networks and Programs

Yugoslavia is a decentralized country with a decentralized broadcasting system.* The structure of Yugoslav broadcasting reflects the intense patriotism and individuality of its six republics and two autonomous regions. In the words of the 1970 annual report, decentralization encourages "the full development of national cultures and the use of national languages, as well as a more thorough coverage of political, economic and cultural events in individual republics and autonomous provinces."[55]

Six of the eight main broadcasting institutions operate from one to three radio networks each, plus a single television service; the other two offer radio programs only. The 163 local broadcasting institutions are, in effect, local radio stations. All these activities are coordinated—but not controlled—by Jugoslovenska Radiotelevizija, which provides the frame-

* Switzerland and West Germany are two other countries with federal governments and decentralized broadcasting systems, and to some extent this also is true of the Soviet Union, where each of the fifteen republics has extensive regional and local services.

work for national network services and is responsible for all external broadcasting.

An official source stated that before World War II, because of the country's poor economic status, in everything "including the domain of radio, Yugoslavia was among the last countries in Europe."[56] First transmissions were from a radio telegraph station on the Adriatic Coast in 1904, and the first broadcasting station was established in Zagreb on May 15, 1926, the date observed as Yugoslav Radio Day since 1956.

Among them, the eight main broadcasting institutions provide twenty-two separate and independent radio services for domestic reception.[57] Radio Belgrade has three networks for the republic of Serbia and a local service for the immediate metropolitan area; Zagreb has four networks; Ljubljana and Novi Sad operate three networks apiece; Skopje and Sarajevo have two; Titograd and Priština one each. When there are two or more networks, they supplement rather than duplicate each other. If there are two, the first usually is planned to have universal appeal with "something for everyone." The second is lighter, featuring entertainment fare. When there is a third program, it is serious, on the order of the BBC's Third Programme. Although most radio programming is on a regional or local basis, there is some networking involving adjacent republics or, in some cases, the entire country.

Radio Belgrade, with three republic-wide networks, may be taken as an example of the main broadcasting institutions.[58] The first of these is on the air twenty hours on weekdays and twenty-four hours on Sundays; the second broadcasts eight hours weekdays and thirteen hours Sundays; and the third transmits four hours each evening. A local service, Belgrade 202, is on the air eighteen hours a day for listeners in the metropolitan area only.

There is considerable variation among these services.[59] In 1971 the first devoted 14.23 per cent of its time to serious music, the second 4.96 per cent, and the third 66.86 per cent, whereas the local service (Belgrade 202) has no serious music at all. On the other hand, the corresponding figures for light music are as follows: Belgrade 202, 52.71 per cent; the first program, 27.65 per cent; the second program, 40.24 per cent; and the third program, 1.24 per cent.

Serbia also has eighteen local broadcasting institutions, located in as many cities. For example, Radio Niš, founded in 1950, broadcasts 6½ hours a day on weekdays, 11¼ hours on Saturdays, and 9 hours on

Sundays.[60] In 1971 it originated 2,687 hours of its own and relayed 3,461 hours from Radio Belgrade. Among them the country's local stations do much programming of local information, news, and music.

During 1971 the combined radio output of the eight main broadcasting institutions—excluding the 163 local stations—consisted of 62 per cent music and 38 per cent spoken word material.[61] Programs were further analyzed as follows: light music, 32.04 per cent; serious music, 14.06 per cent; folk music, 15.50 per cent; news, 7.84 per cent; commericals, 5.63 per cent; special broadcasts, 3.96 per cent; arts and culture, 3.26 per cent; entertainment, 3.75 per cent; general education, 3.20 per cent; home affairs, 2.53 per cent; economy, 1.87 per cent; foreign affairs, 2.24 per cent; physical culture and chess, 1.55 per cent; agriculture, 0.82 per cent; and miscellaneous, 1.75 per cent.

As would be expected in a multilingual country, there are programs in local as well as national languages. Among them the eight main and 163 local broadcasting institutions use Albanian, Hungarian, Macedonian, Romanian, Ruthenian, Serbo-Croatian, Slovakian, Slovenian, and Turkish. During the summertime, for tourists, there also are programs in English, French, German, and Russian.

At the end of 1971 Yugoslavia had 237 medium-wave radio transmitters, with power varying from 1 watt to 1,000 kilowatts, and 111 FM transmitters.[62] Serbia alone had 57 medium-wave and 31 FM transmitters. The latter, which operate in the Western rather than the Eastern FM band, range in effective radiated power from 30 watts up to 50 kilowatts. In Yugoslavia as in some other countries—the United Kingdom, for example—medium-wave reception is poor at night, for which reason power is being increased to 300, 600, and even 1,000 kilowatts.[63] In the daytime the first Belgrade service covers 100 per cent and the second and third services 85 per cent of the Serbian population, but night coverage is never better than 90 per cent. In the other republics coverage ranges from 40 to 100 per cent of the population during the day, and from 28 to 100 at night.[64] There is some kind of FM service for 100 per cent of the population in Serbia, Slovenia, and Vojvodina, and from 71 to 90 per cent elsewhere in the country.

Television, like radio, is decentralized, and the main broadcasting institutions maintain independent services. There are originating studios in the six capitals, although most production is done in Belgrade, Zagreb, and Ljubljana, and Skopje.[65] Titograd, which does not have studios, contributes only through film. The total national daily output is about 25½ hours, and for the most part the six networks carry the same programs, although not always simultaneously. There also is some cooperative programming: thus, important holidays and other major events are observed in programs prepared jointly by two or more centers. Nevertheless, in the words of the 1970 annual report: "Regional programmes remain the basis of television's future development in Yugoslavia."[66]

Normally stations are on the air from about 9:00 A.M. until noon, and from 3:00 or 4:00 until 11:30 P.M. On Sundays there are programs from about 8:30 A.M. until 11:00 P.M.[67] Most morning and afternoon programs are for schools, and there is adult education in the early evening. Peak viewing hours are devoted to news and entertainment, and the schedule concludes with a news summary at 10:30 P.M. Serbia's second service is on the air for short periods six evenings a week. The combined national program has been categorized as follows: cultural, artistic, and popular, 32.90 per cent; information, talks, and current affairs, 32.30 per cent; educational, 11:50 per cent; sports, 9.40 per cent; commercials, 6.20 per cent; miscellaneous, 7.70 per cent.[68] At present television programs are produced in three Yugoslav languages—Serbo-Croatian, Slovenian, and Macedonian—and in 1968 Television Belgrade also began broadcasting in Hungarian and Albanian.

Serbian television is on the air an average of seventy-eight hours a week. Of these, forty-four hours are produced in Belgrade, the remainder being secured through exchange agreements from the other television organizations.[69] The situation in Croatia is similar, with eighty-four hours of programs, of which sixty-two hours are originated locally.

There are plans for second services. Yugoslavia, like other countries with a single service, is limited in the range of programs it can offer its viewers. Television is designed to "widen the horizon of its most numerous viewers and to help them in forming their tastes," but the task is "not a simple one, because there are very sharp distinctions in the degrees of education of the population."[70] Although a second channel was scheduled for Ljubljana in 1972, the first alternative service, Television Belgrade, turned up in Serbia at the end of 1971, with three high-power UHF and six low-power repeater stations. Once a comprehensive second service is established, it will specialize in educational and serious programs, as well as in repeating programs originally broadcast by the first service.[71]

Nationwide, at the end of 1971, Yugoslavia had 48 television transmitters operating in the VHF band, plus 260 low-power repeaters.[72] These transmitters are connected by microwave relays, and there also are links with Bulgaria, Romania, Hungary, Austria, and Italy. From 76 to 96 per cent of the population of the various republics is covered by these signals, the national average being 87.4 per cent. All the six republic centers have their own studios, and there are plans to build studios in Novi Sad and Priština, the capitals of the two autonomous provinces, which have their own radio origination facilities but depend on Serbia for television production.[73] The number of studios in the existing six centers varies from one in Sarajevo to seven in Belgrade, the national total being seventeen. Otherwise, equipment includes a fair number of image orthicon and other cameras, twenty-two permanently installed video tape recorders, nine portable tape recorders, a number of remote vans, and related equipment.[74]

Black-and-white television uses West European system B. (Yugoslavia and East Germany are the only socialist countries employing this system; all the others use the Eastern European OIRT system D.) Stations in Belgrade, Ljubljana, and Zagreb have experiemented with color, and regular programs were appearing in 1973.[75] First transmissions, incidentally, included rebroadcasts of programs from Austria by transmitters intended eventually for the Yugoslav second service. As would be expected, Yugoslavia uses PAL color—because of its general Western orientation, because the Eurovision network uses PAL, and because this gives its electronics industry better chances to sell sets in Western Europe.[76]

The total Yugoslav broadcasting staff is quite large.[77] In 1971 the Serbian staff alone consisted of 1,902 radio and 1,171 television employees, for a total of 3,073. The main broadcasting institutions combined had 6,852 radio and 3,566 television employees, for a total of 10,418. Since there were 1,126 employees in the local broadcasting institutions, the grand total for the country was 11,544.

Both the radio and television networks of the eight main broadcasting institutions carry advertising, although procedures vary from republic to republic. On weekdays Radio Belgrade's first radio service schedules commercials, either in short blocks or interspersed among other items, at 4:35, 5:05, 5:45, and 6:15 A.M., and at 2:30, 4:30, and 6:30 P.M. and one other period.[78] Procedures in the second program are similar, while Belgrade 202 inserts advertisements between musical numbers throughout the day. The other broadcasting institutions use basically the same approach.

A considerable range of products is advertised. In 1969, nationwide, the categories were as follows (in percentages): foodstuffs, 14.05; chemical products, 10.18; personal hygiene, 7.91; sweets, cakes, and chocolates, 5.03; textiles, 6.60; electrical products, 8.33; alcoholic beverages, 5.63; tobacco products, 3.64; medical products, 2.57; and miscellaneous, 37.73. However, there was considerable variation from republic to republic in the proportions of these categories.

In 1971 advertisements took up 6.2 per cent of television time. Typically, these are aired from two to four times a day, there being a fifteen-minute block at 5:00 P.M., a nine-minute block at 5:30 P.M., and a ten-minute block at 8:25 P.M.[79] The major articles advertised include chemical products and foodstuffs, although there also is advertising of alcoholic beverages, tobacco products, pharmaceuticals, clothing, and even—though to a limited extent—automobiles. The advertisers include foreign firms, some of which are trying to sell such consumer goods as motor cars. Although considerable income is received from these advertisements—about 15 or 20 per cent of all television revenue comes from commercials—and the 1970 yearbook reported that "the audience enjoys watching them," I found them boring because of varying standards of production and frequent repetition. Among the items I saw advertised were filter cigarettes, shoes, toothpaste, radios, cognac, washing machines, automobile tires, mineral water, perfumes, cheese, clothing, a beverage mix, deodorants, razor blades, soft drinks, shoes, and banking services.

News and Public Affairs

Although the mass media in Yugoslavia are much freer to report the news than are those in any other socialist country, there still are restrictions. As Tito said in 1958: "During our country's revolutionary period of transition, the Press cannot be considered as an independent and autonomous factor in our society, since all the actions of society as a whole must converge towards one aim: the construction of Socialism."[80] Nevertheless, the Yugoslav media enjoy a high degree of freedom and there is no precensorship, although editors are aware of the limits and the ground rules.

Comment on how the system works was provided by a paper presented by a Yugoslav journalist at an international symposium; he noted the "constant conflict of journalists . . . between their freedom of creativity and their social responsibility."[81] With great frankness he wrote: "The journalist cannot be only an apologist of opinions and decisions of forums; if he consented to this he would meet the wishes of bureaucrats who want to hold a monopoly over socialist thought, who are afraid of the struggle of thoughts, breaking such monopoly and getting rid of decreed authority."

In 1971 information, talks, and current affairs made up 43.89 per cent of the spoken word broadcasts of the eight radio services and 16.83 per cent of their total broadcast time.[82] This was categorized further: news, 6.44 per cent; foreign affairs, 1.76 per cent; home affairs, 2.23 per cent; and economy, 1.78 per cent. There are variations from network to network. The first Serbian service devoted 8.12 per cent of its time to news; the second, 3.91 per cent; the third—essentially a literary and good music service—no time at all; and Belgrade 202, 1.16 per cent. The first service of Ljubljana devoted 14.86 per cent of its time to news, and the first Novi Sad service 11.56 per cent. In 1971, 32.30 per cent of the nation's television consisted of "information, talks and current affairs," including news.

Basic material, particularly about foreign affairs, is received from the national news agency, Janjug, which supplements its own resources through exchanges with several foreign agencies, including Reuters, Agence France Presse, and UPI.[83] In addition, radio draws upon 100 full-time and several hundred part-time reporters for domestic stories, which are distributed by teleprinter to all stations. Most of the 163 local stations have facilities for gathering news in their own areas. JRT and the eight main broadcasting institutions maintain full-time reporters in Beirut, Bonn, Cairo, Klagenfurt, London, Moscow, New York, Paris, Prague, Rome, Trieste, Vienna, and the United Nations.

Television stations supplement closed circuit exchanges of news among themselves, begun in 1967, with filmed items from VISNEWS and UPITN and with participation in Eurovision and Intervision.[84] Yugoslavia uses more Eurovision material than does any other socialist country, which is not surprising in view of its open information policy, its

Western orientation, and its EBU membership—it being the only EBU member among the Eastern European socialist countries. In 1963 it provided 35 and received 10 Eurovision items; in 1972 it originated 50 and received 2,675 items (see Table 1). Although not a member of the OIRT or of Intervision, Yugoslavia participated in 23 news exchanges with Intervision in 1971, in the course of which it received 35 items.[85]

Radio Belgrade illustrates how the Yugoslav services handle news and public affairs. In 1969 between its first and second networks, Radio Belgrade had approximately thirty newscasts each day, varying between five and fifteen minutes in length, plus newsflashes transmitted "the moment they are received" on Belgrade 202.[86] Other information features included "Good Morning to Early Birds," "Cup of Coffee," "The Whole Town with You," and "Here and There around Town." There also was "Welcome to Yugoslavia" (for tourists), "Our Agronomist," "From the Activities of the UN," and weather forecasts ingeniously titled "Overcoat, Scarf or Umbrella?" Audiences all over the country depend on the 163 local stations for local news, which is presented not only in the main languages but also in such minority tongues as Albanian, Hungarian, Romanian, Ruthenian, Turkish and Slovakian.[87]

Television now has regional newscasts at 5:30 on week days, while "TV Journal," the main news program, is broadcast from 8:00 to 8.25 P.M. Originally, this was always produced in Belgrade with contributions from other stations, but in 1968 some regions began originating their own programs at least several days a week.[88] Other information-oriented telecasts include "Time Machine" from Belgrade, reviewing past events, and "Lens 350" from Zagreb, devoted to "topical problems of social, economic and cultural life." Prominent public officials appear on these and other programs to answer questions from the public.

The "keynote" for information programs in 1969, said the 1970 *JRT Yearbook*, "was given by the Ninth Congress of the League of Communists of Yugoslavia."[89] Yugoslav radio and television do not emphasize political ideology to the extent found in the other socialist countries. Nevertheless, the *Yearbook* did say that economic developments, the growth of industry, increases in labor productivity, the expansion of agriculture, the tourist boom, and close ties with the European Common Market "were all spotlighted in the [radio] information programmes."

It was also reported: "Special attention was given to the April elections for representative bodies, with an organized, systematic and exhaustive coverage of pre-election activities, so that for several months most of the information broadcast[s] were taken up with election topics." The radio services try "to give more than just a factual report of events in various sectors of society; indeed they tried to present an active socialist forum of self-managers. This principle entails an endeavour for the radio listener to be an active participant rather than a passive consumer."

When visiting Belgrade in 1970, I discussed news output with a number of Americans, and watched some local and network newscasts. The programs were much closer to the Western norm than those in most socialist countries. Newscasts were generally fair to the United States, although they did repeat some of the socialist clichés, emphasized the party, and made too much of politically oriented ceremonials. But the proselytizing is not too obvious, and the emphasis on industrial and economic achievements is held within bounds. Performance failures are criticized and documented. The Yugoslav programs, incidentally, are more apt to report natural disasters and human interest stories than those in most socialist countries.

There is room for improvement, however, in production and presentation. Although some effective rear screen projection is employed, there is too much silent film, and too many items are read with only a slide on the screen, the total effect being that of a program that moves slowly, with too much talk. But there are some good announcers, both men and women. One Yugoslav television news summary impressed me as the best newscast I saw during seven weeks of viewing in seven Eastern European socialist countries in the fall of 1970.

Education

Radio and television have educational and instructional programs for all ages. There are broadcasts for reception in schools, programs for young people at home, and various features for adults. Nationwide, 3.26 per cent of all radio programs are classified as "Arts and Culture" and 3.20 per cent as "General Education." Of the television output, 11.50 per cent is "Education."[90]

Radio Ljubljana began experimental programs for schools in 1940.[91] After a wartime interruption these were resumed in 1945, and all six republics now have in-school radio, introduced in some cases along with changes and reforms in curricula and teaching methods. Yugoslavs have written perceptively about such programs: they substitute for teachers; they introduce new material; and they reinforce and repeat old material.[92] They are especially helpful "in those branches of learning where . . . the spoken word is the basic means of learning." Teachers are free to decide whether or not to use radio, but if they do, it is suggested that reception be regarded as a four-stage project: teacher preparation, pupil preparation, the broadcast itself, and follow-up.[93] Tape recordings often are available, and brochures provide information about schedules and utilization.[94]

In 1968 Radio Ljubljana had programs dealing with science, language, physics, and chemistry for elementary and secondary schools. Two series, "The Workers' Movement and History" and "Biology," were described as "particularly noteworthy": the first of these reviewed "the workers' movement from the beginning of the industrial revolution in the 19th century to contemporary workers' movements"; the second tried to explain "the change in nature from static systems to dynamic conceptions in modern natural sciences."

In 1969 Radio Belgrade presented in-school programs five times a week, totaling some 2½ hours of broadcast time; subjects included music, painting, science, geography, Russian, English, and French.[95] Zagreb has about fifteen in-school series, including "The Cars Are Starting to Move," about traffic education; "Interesting Grammar," which encourages students to "learn grammar through direct usage"; and "Current Topics," a current events program.[96]

Special attention is given to language study.[97] In 1969 Radio Novi Sad had five in-school series on Serbo-Croatian and fourteen on Hungarian language and literature. Radio Priština, serving an area with many Albanian-speaking residents, in addition to teaching French and English, had a number of programs on Albanian language and literature.

In-school television began in 1960, with some programs supplementing the school curriculum and others teaching directly subjects for which there was a shortage of qualified instructors.[98] Currently, most school television comes from Zagreb, which specializes in that field. In fact, 21.50 per cent of the Television Zagreb output in 1971 consisted of in-school broadcasts. These programs are intended to open a window on the world by telling the children about life beyond their immediate environments.[99] Furthermore, they are expected to communicate both information and concepts; develop children's understanding; encourage them to do their own research; and stimulate them to better understanding of basic academic subjects. Television, incidentally, is not allowed to duplicate radio in-school services. Printed material for teachers lists schedules along with suggestions for effective utilization. There also are supplementary slides and films.[100]

There are telecasts for all grades in the natural and social sciences, history, geography, literature, and foreign languages. Total in-school program time averages four hours a day, and programs are on the air midmornings Monday through Friday with afternoon and Saturday morning repeats for out-of-school viewing. Evaluation is achieved through periodic school visits by representatives of the broadcasting services, discussions with teachers and students, and questionnaire studies. Some schools are designed as experimental centers, with regular meetings of advisory committees and school personnel.[101] It was learned in 1969 that 86 per cent of the pupils and 82 per cent of the teachers in Croatia watched in-school television, although not always regularly. The official yearbook declared that "television is playing a role of growing importance in modernization and this is highly appreciated in the system of schooling."*

Broadcasts for young people at home are regarded as very important. The head of educational broadcasting in Zagreb ascribed to Tito the concept that "he who possesses youth possesses the future and is in a position to develop historically."[102] Therefore, Zagreb programs have "initiated and harmonized the process of the dynamico-dialectical individualization of young people." They give "much attention to the problem of the creative integration of young people in the modern world, especially as this world, like those before it, is not a painless straight-line prolongation of the preceding ones, but has been produced in the uneven course of history, through wars, conflicts and revolutions." Surprisingly though, in the course of this article the author made almost no direct references to Communist ideology.

---

* *JRT Yearbook 1971/72*, pp. 387, 325. An American television educator, after a brief on-site inspection of Yugoslav schools, summarized some of his reactions as follows: there is inadequate liaison between television and the schools; educational television objectives are unclear; despite some excellent productions, too many are "rather dull and lacking in impact"; many schools do not have television receivers; teachers have not been taught effective utilization; and some of the republics do not have the financial resources to prepare good programs (John A. Montgomery, "ITV Problems, Yugoslavian and American Similarities," *Educational Broadcasting*, November 1971, p. 26).

Radio Belgrade clearly attaches great significance to the programs for out-of-school listening on both its first and second networks. The 1970 yearbook stated that the first network "went beyond its initial conception as a popular music broadcast to become a kind of forum where thousands of young people throughout the country could talk about various problems of immediate concern to them," while the second network was "predominantly tailored for young audiences."[103]

Program titles included: "With Music and about Music," "Musical Forum of the Young," "Date at 9:05," "The Knowledge Game" (quiz), "A Thousand Occupations," and "Non-Stop Dance Hall." As a result of the series "The Most Beautiful Verses," 3,000 books of poetry were sold, and an art exhibit in the Belgrade Youth Center accompanied "The Most Beautiful Pictures." "When, Where and How" brought together a specialist, teacher, and journalist to answer children's questions and make suggestions about entertainment, sports, and amusements. Following the series "We Are Looking for the Best Friend," a work brigade named "The Best Friends" was formed, and subsequently won the pennant "Fifty Years of the Communist Youth Union."

Radio Ljubljana opened the day with the three-minute feature "Good Morning Children," consisting of songs, stories, and sketches.[104] There also were fairy tales and stories; travelogues; "Pioneers' Weekly," a half-hour program by and for young Pioneers; a weekly poetry program; and "Good Night Children," a ten-minute serial to send the "youngest listeners off to bed." For older children, Ljubljana has the weekly fifty-five–minute series "Youth for Themselves and for You," to which young people make extemporaneous contributions. On the competitive series "Let's Get to Know the World and Our Homeland," sixteen towns competed on programs of seventy-five minutes' duration.

The director of educational programming in Zagreb told of creative writing programs intended to stimulate young authors "to mature more quickly and to become individuals."[105] Other programs brought together young people with talent for music and journalism. "Pioneers' Journal" attempted to accustom its listeners to "democratic forms of communication, to discussions as a form of thinking and not just the exchange of thoughts, a way of reconciling different viewpoints and, most important, of reaching the independent agreement of direct producers in conflict situations."

"Do We Understand One Another?" dealt with conflicts between adolescents and adults, in order to educate them "for a healthy society of democratic self-management which Yugoslavia is trying to create." "The Intimate World of the Young" presented discussions by young people, doctors, psychologists, teachers, and artists "to prepare young people for a healthy, human and poetic relationship with the opposite sex, to combat the coarse reduction of love to a sexual instinct, and hence to make people speak a little more of heart-stirrings, poetry, love rather than of sexual techniques in the manner of *Ars Amatoria.*"

Currently Radio Belgrade is conducting an interesting experiment in broadcasting to the hard of hearing.[106] Proceeding on the assumption that deafness affects different frequencies with different persons, a twenty-seven-channel "frequency corrector" has been devised which can be adapted to each listener's problems. Programs, of both words and music, have been broadcast on FM over Belgrade's first network Friday and Saturday noons from 11:30 to 12:00 since November 1971. First reports were encouraging, and the head of the project writes that he would like to exchange "all information" with other workers conducting comparable experiments. The Yugoslavs must be among the first if not the only ones devising such programs.

Television devotes 5.7 per cent of its time to children and youth.[107] "Many of these programmes," explained the 1970 yearbook, "have become the children's main entertainment and their inseparable childhood companions." Therefore, they are prepared "by children's writers and journalists, who handle various themes in a light and less conventional manner than is the case at schools, so as to bring the little viewers as close to television as possible." For older children there are historical dramas and literary classics. Theatrical presentations have included Prokofiev's *Peter and the Wolf,* Saint-Saëns's *Carnival of the Animals,* and performances utilizing children. Programs from the literature of many nations have included Monroe Leaf's story of *Ferdinand,* Hans Christian Andersen's *The Snow Queen,* and L. Frank Baum's *The Wizard of Oz.*

Zagreb Television had "The Curiosity Shop," in which puppets and people shared adventures; "The Steadfast Tin Soldier," in which a box of tin soldiers came to life and danced; and "The Family Album," based on the diary of a ten-year-old girl. In 1969 World's Children Day was observed by telecasting a children's festival in which over 500 young people from various countries took part, the final performance being transmitted by both Eurovision and Intervision.

In Belgrade in November 1970 I saw an interesting program involving deaf children who used sign language and normal children who spoke. In the summer of 1972 Yugoslavia joined Poland in a three-month test of the popular American series *Sesame Street*, using the original English version with voice-over translations.

Adult education, too, occupies considerable air time. In 1971 the main broadcasting institutions devoted 3.20 per cent of their radio time to "General Educaiton," 2.24 per cent to "Foreign Affairs," 2.53 per cent to "Home Affairs," and 1.87 per cent to "Economy."[108] Radio Belgrade had "News from Science and Technology," "Do You Know Yugoslavia?" "Radio Answers Your Questions," and "Our Radio Doctor."[109] While the first network emphasized programs formally organized into series, the second used "the technique of integrating educational material in the overall programmes," and the third maintained "a general educational character designed for its own audience." Radio Zagreb's "It Happened on This Day" was "a radio encyclopaedia featuring outstanding people and events . . . designed for adults, young people, and children alike."

Among its cultural and artistic programs, Radio Ljubljana scheduled "We Invite You to Reading Class," a series to acquaint listeners "in a systematic fashion with avant-garde drama."[110] Ljubljana also has programs about native writers; reports on cultural life; readings from classical and modern prose; late evening poetry readings; a "Literary Riddle," in which listeners receive prizes for providing the right answers; and "Echoes from the Mountain," about environmental problems.

Although "Radio Universities" are offered by Belgrade, Ljubljana, Priština, Skopje, and Zagreb, there are no courses for credit on television or radio.[111] On the Zagreb Radio University, broadcast twice a week, eminent "Yugoslav and foreign scientists acquaint listeners with the achievements of modern science and technology." The third programs in Belgrade, Zagreb, Ljubljana, and Novi Sad all emphasize cultural, literary, and educational materials.

Belgrade Television began educational programming for adults in March 1964 with courses in French and biology.[112] These programs try "to create the viewer as an active collaborator, to arouse his curiosity and imagination, thus introducing him into the world of intellectual and emotional experiences." Programs include "Operation Thirty Letters," for illiterates (the Serbo-Croatian alphabets, both Cyrillic and Latin, have thirty letters); "Army without Barracks," on national defense; and "Encyclopaedia of Self-Management," dealing with "socioeconomic relations." In 1969 Television Skopje, recognizing the need for "information about basic social phenomena, changes and laws," scheduled "Man and His Social Reality."[113] Among them the various republics offer lessons in English, French, German, and Russian, as well as in their own minority languages, which is to be expected in a country which so freely permits its citizens to travel abroad and encourages foreign visitors.[114] On Belgrade Television I saw "Walter and Connie," a BBC English-language series, and several services now carry its successor, "English by Television."

A special project, "Literary Action by Television," begun in October 1968, is scheduled to run until 1975. Developed cooperatively by Belgrade Television and several educational groups, its purpose is to present educational materials to illiterate adults.[115] "ABC by Television" teaches reading to illiterates; "Mathematics" treats elementary arithmetic; and there also are programs on history. Illiteracy is a major problem in Yugoslavia. With 19.7 per cent of its population unable to read according to the latest published statistics, it is second lowest to Albania among Eastern European socialist countries in this respect.[116] Accordingly, great effort is made to provide meaningful experiences for the intended audiences. "ABC by Television," for example, presents in dramatized form the story of an illiterate country woman who meets the challenge of living in a city by learning to read and write. Audience research shows that half a million people follow this series regularly, more in fact than view some entertainment programs. "Mathematics" has 200,000 viewers.

Literature, Drama, and Film

All Yugoslav broadcasting organizations have literary programs. Belgrade and Zagreb may serve as examples. "Creators and Their Works" dealt with the National Theater, the National Museum, and the National Library.[117] "Before Midnight," on the air five times a week for fifteen minutes, was "increasingly successful in its presentation of poetry." Other "cultural and artistic programmes" included "Literary Club," "Highlights in the History of Mankind," "Little Anthology," and "Radio Novel." The Belgrade third program devotes a third of its schedule to spoken word presentations of cultural, artistic, literary, and dramatic material. In 1969 the first and third programs of Radio Zagreb broadcast essays on "Five Centuries of Croatian Literature," plus programs on American beatnik, Yugoslavian, Hungarian, and Eskimo poetry. Titograd and Novi Sad also have programs for lovers of poetry and literature.

All the main broadcasting institutions do radio drama. In 1971 Belgrade, Ljubljana, Novi Sad, Skopje, and Sarajevo together broadcast 783 plays, of which 358 were produced by Radio Belgrade. Prizes were awarded for the best new scripts.[118] An average of nine plays is broadcast by the three Serbian networks each week, scheduled to provide at least one performance every day. On Network I, "From the Stage" presents the best works from large and small theaters in all parts of the country. A special drama series honoring the fiftieth anniversary of the League of Communists was described as "one of Radio Belgrade's most outstanding contributions to the celebration of this important date in Yugoslav history." The second network's "Radio Novel" dramatized works like Gogol's *Dead Souls* and Flaubert's *Madame Bovary*. The third network presented 109 plays, of which 53 were premieres.

The television drama repertoire ranges from classical to modern, and includes pickups from theaters along with studio productions.[119] Whereas writers formerly concentrated on World War II and the recent past, they now are "turning toward contemporary life. There is a prevalence of psychological, love and social themes, but without very deep involvement. . . . Television takes the stand that the original TV dramas should have a permanent place in literature, but it has not yet succeeded in this."

There are originations in all studio centers. In 1970 Belgrade transmitted approximately sixty-seven productions, including works by Pushkin, Shakespeare, and contemporary Yugoslav authors. Many performances were taped in theaters in various parts of the country. The BBC's version of Shakespeare's *Twelfth Night* also was telecast. Attractive brochures advertising Zagreb programs for sale abroad list adaptations of the story by Nobel Prize winner Ivo Andrić, *The Neighbors*, as well as of Chekhov's *Ward Number Six*.

Live and taped presentations of radio and television drama are supplemented by the television film output. Radio, too, deals with film, as with Radio Ljubljana's essays entitled "Radio Film Library" and with "Film Merry-Go-Round," a forty-minute weekly program of news about the film world.[120] Films, including features, documentaries, programs for children, and cartoons, compose 18.1 per cent of the television output. Major programs are networked simultaneously to the entire country, according to a schedule set up by the six television centers: feature films, Tuesday, Saturday, and Sunday evenings; documentaries, Sunday evenings; serials, Thursday and Friday evenings; children's serials, Sunday noons; cartoons, late Wednesday afternoons; and popular science films, dinner hour on Wednesdays.

Most feature films are foreign made, and the majority are American.[121] However, Yugoslav television is trying to use more German, Swedish, and Canadian material. Foreign films are dubbed into Yugoslav languages. In Yugoslavia, as everywhere else, television producers and filmmakers are competitive. When cinema attendance dropped, presumably because of television, the film studios unsuccessfully asked television for subsidies. Thereafter, confronted with increased charges, television was forced to limit itself to only the oldest films "whose career in the commercial circuit is usually quite finished," although on important holidays the stations pool their resources to purchase more recent releases.

The list of a year's feature film presentations takes almost ten pages in the annual yearbook.[122] Sources include Britain, Canada, Czechoslovakia, France, Hungary, Ireland, Italy, Poland, Sweden, the United States, the USSR, and West Germany. Although there are many films from socialist countries, there are very few from the Soviet Union. In 1969 American films included *Destry Rides Again, Romanoff and Juliet, Bonjour Tristesse, Cat Ballou, Requiem for a Heavyweight, Anatomy of a Murder, Gunfight at Dodge City,* and a number of Charlie Chaplin shorts.

Because domestic output is "underdeveloped," many telefilms must be imported. Those used in 1969 included the BBC productions of *Jane Eyre, David Copperfield, Pride and Prejudice, Vanity Fair,* and—inevitably—*The Forsyte Saga,* which had a double run, one with Serbo-Croatian and one with Slovenian titles. In Yugoslavia, as in the United States, the series increased the circulation of the novels, available in Serbian, Croatian, Slovenian, and Macedonian versions as well as English.

Although the American telefilms used did not bring great distinction to the service, they received more air time than did those from the United Kingdom: "Casper" cartoons, *The Flintstones, Huckleberry Hound, The*

Jerry Lewis Show, The Pink Panther, Huck Finn, and *Peyton Place*. But quality was not entirely missing, since the schedule also included some New York Philharmonic Young People's Concerts with Leonard Bernstein.

At the end of 1972 it was announced that *Peyton Place* would be terminated after a two-year run because it fostered "petit-bourgeois values" among its viewers.[123] Whatever its effect, the series clearly was popular, since during its broadcast time early Sunday evenings, automobile traffic noticeably lightened. The decision to discontinue the series was only one aspect of a campaign against foreign influences in general, since there also were complaints about *Mod Squad*, and United States army-style insignia, popular with teen agers, were removed from sale. All this accords with comments by President Tito and others that too many Yugoslav officials have taken study tours to the United States.

By scheduling broadcasts of domestically produced documentaries and shorts, Yugoslav television has tried to assist filmmakers to "popularise the national short documentary film," since these have little box office appeal despite "their qualities and successes abroad."[124] In the meanwhile, on its own, television produces films on a wide range of subjects. Zagreb, for example, has "With Tito in Asia"; "Byroad to Money," about a new road along the Dalmation coast which threatened the life style of some villagers; "The Dark Paths of Life," a report on a women's prison, including interviews with inmates; and "In Ten Years' Time," during which children in a mountain village described how they imagined their village would be in ten years. Other subjects included a factory making railroad carriages, old village festivals, pop art, architecture, tapestries, and old buildings from castles to fortresses.

Music

The eight radio broadcasting institutions devoted about 63.52 per cent of their total time in 1971 to music, of which 52.46 per cent was light music, 23.11 per cent serious music, and 24.43 per cent folk music.[125] Yugoslav compositions and performances were emphasized: among the domestic radio services the proportion of Yugoslav music ranged from 2.13 to 100 per cent, while the extent of Yugoslav performances ranged from 2.57 to 100 per cent.

Music is provided by performers on the staffs of the broadcasting institutions as well as by outside organizations. Among them, the broadcasting institutions have forty-four musical groups ranging from chamber ensembles and choirs to jazz and symphony orchestras.[126] At the end of 1971 they owned over 120,000 phonograph records and twice that many tape recordings.

When a republic has two or more radio networks, they provide contrasting musical offerings. The first program of Radio Ljubljana offers "all types of music to appeal to a broad audience"; the second is "designed for listeners seeking relaxation and entertainment"; while the third "broadcasts exclusively serious music in the form of specialized music programmes."[127]

Radio Belgrade emphasizes "on the spot coverage of important events in public music[al] life"; each year broadcasts over fifty live public concerts; participates in festivals ranging from chamber music to jazz; and sends its own ensembles abroad. Its serious repertoire is suggested by such titles as "Sunday Concert," "From Operas You Love," "Yugoslav Artists at the Microphone," and "Concerts in the Studio."[128] Light music includes "Forum of the Young," "Community Singing," "Old Favorites," "Jazz Panorama," and "With Pop Music Soloists and Groups." The Belgrade third program, which concentrates on serious music, presents "Classics of This Century," "Baroque Masters," "Music in Stereo," "Chamber Music," and "Musical Festivals."

The Yugoslavs celebrate anniversaries, and in a typical year the main broadcasting institutions have observed those of Francis Poulenc, Hector Berlioz, Edward Elgar, Joseph Haydn, and Frédéric Chopin.[129] Hard work is clearly deemed deserving of musical accolades, since "Musical Youth" observed "15 years of work," while a number of Yugoslav citizens were feted by Radio Ljubljana for "25 years of work." There also is locally oriented music on the 163 local stations, all of which have some studio facilities plus turntables and tape recorders. Radio Novi Sad, serving a region with many minorities, provides music for listeners with Serbian, Hungarian, Romanian, Ruthenian, and Slovak backgrounds.[130]

Special attempts are made to preserve the folk-music heritage. Although a Yugoslav writing about "Folklore and Radio" conceded that folk music was "an art of former centuries, at a time when man is preparing to land on the moon and seeks his distraction in beat and electronic music," he nevertheless maintained that it should be presented "to the men and women of today as the splendid thing it is. Folklore is

not an art to be preserved in a museum, for its truly human values support our modern outlook."[131] Although the author regretted that many
people—especially youth—did not like folk music, Radio Sarajevo
reported that folk music had the largest audiences of all its musical programs. But in any case, Yugoslav broadcasters have set out to popularize folk music. Sometimes they record it on location and then put it
on the air. A more elaborate approach was the series "From Traditional
Tunes to Symphonic Music," in which "we start out with an original
folk melody and move on through the arrangement and the modern
popular tune to the symphonic dance or some other composition within
the field of serious music."

In 1969 television devoted 7.7 per cent of its time to "music and entertainment," although this category apparently included more entertainment programs than music.[132] Serious music was relayed from concert
halls and festivals or produced in studios, and there were recitals by
native and foreign artists. There also were music appreciation programs
"intended to arouse interest for this kind of TV music among the broader
sections of the population."

But for the most part television offered entertainment music, with such
titles as "TV Magazine," "You Are Entertained by . . .," "Concert
for the Crazy Young World," "Paris Sings," "A Festival of Popular
Songs," "Hits '69," and "Vienna through Song and Dance." I saw a
light music telecast by a group including singers and a few instrumentalists, which was well performed and effectively produced.

Entertainment and Sports

If one were to believe the statistics, there is very little entertainment on
Yugoslav radio and television. In 1969 the main broadcasting institutions
classified only 3.38 per cent of their radio output as entertainment
(apart from music), and the official analysis of television listed no
entertainment at all, such programs being included in other categories.[133]
Yet after hearing and viewing Yugoslav programs, I got the impression
that Yugoslav broadcasters are much more partial to entertainment than
are their colleagues in the other socialist countries, and that their output
is superior.

Radio Belgrade's schedule includes such programs as "Gay Evening,"
"Saturday Night," "Merry Village," "Melody Quiz," "Radio Comedy,"

"Sixty Carefree Minutes," "Non-Stop Dance Hall," and "Entertainment Album."[134] Radio Zagreb's first and second networks present variety programs most evenings, with titles like "Date at Studio Eight," "Humorous Inspection," "Saturday Night," "Taxi to Babylon," and "Bright Evening."[135] In 1969 Radio Sarajevo devoted 10.32 per cent of its time to entertainment, although some of these programs must have had an educational flavor, since one, "For Nature and Music Lovers," was reported to provide in "a journalistic and entertaining way" information "on the natural beauties of Yugoslavia, travel possibilities, and important cultural monuments which are not generally known."[136]

Music and entertainment together, which made up 7.7 per cent of all television in 1969, provide "a wide variety of pleasant viewing."[137] Belgrade and Zagreb originated most of these programs. One was called "You Are Entertained by Sammy Davis"; another had the intriguing title "Welcome, the Middle Ages and Renaissance." Ljubljana had a jazz series plus concerts by its own dance orchestra. Belgrade and Zagreb joined forces for some quizzes called "I Know—You Know" and "Who Knows." These were scheduled during the summer so that part of the year would not be a "dead television season." Subjects included folk and popular music, love songs, sports, politics, hobbies, and professions, the winners receiving "valuable prizes." But there were problems: "Despite efforts to make a good selection of contestants, the level of knowledge shown was not always very high, whereas the value of the prizes was often a subject of discussion in the press and among the viewers." But the programs had large audiences.

In November 1970 I saw some interesting and ingenious light entertainment on Yugoslav television. On the quiet side was a chess program during which a commentator moved men about a large magnetized chessboard as he analyzed the plays. Several light music programs, with vocalists and orchestras, were well done. I was much intrigued by a zany musical comedy produced in Zagreb about a young man visiting his aunt in a haunted castle. Visual and sound effects were ingeniously used to turn out one of the cleverest entertainment shows I saw on socialist television.

Sports now take up 9.4 per cent of television time, subtotals for the various republics ranging from 8 to 16 per cent.[138] The radio program analysis does not have a separate category for sports, although there certainly are such broadcasts. Very popular on television are live broadcasts of football, water polo, basketball, boxing, and skiing. With its several languages Yugoslavia has a problem in covering competitive events: local programs are done in local languages, but for nationwide coverage there has to be commentary in Serbo-Croatian, Slovenian, and Macedonian. I saw a telecast of a basketball game late one Sunday afternoon which was similar to sports broadcasts in the United States.

There also are Eurovision and Intervision relays of events from abroad, including the European Skating Championship from Sweden, the European Boxing Championship from Romania, the European Athletic Championship from Greece, and the European Basketball Championship from Italy. In 1971 Yugoslavia took 121 sports programs of 228 hours' duration from Eurovision, and 23 programs of 41½ hours' duration from Intervision.[139]

Because Yugoslavia encourages competitive profit-making, even though it is a socialist state, there are intense conflicts between the television and football organizations.[140] The latter objects to the telecasting of football matches while championship games are being played, and has refused to allow certain of its games to be broadcast, thus bringing about confrontations reminiscent of those between stations and sports promoters in the United States. One dispute was ended by a court verdict in favor of television. There also are discussions about what should be paid for broadcasting rights and about the location of advertising billboards on football fields, from which—in the words of the broadcasters—the sports organizations receive income "thanks to the phenomenon of television, yet without wanting to grant a certain bonus to television in the price for TV rights."

Audience Research

In view of its democratic orientation it is not surprising that for some years Yugoslavia has regarded research as "more and more indispensable in the work of broadcasting stations."[141] Like broadcasting itself, research is decentralized, most of the main broadcasting institutions maintaining their own study departments. Belgrade, for example, reviewed the radio drama repertoire, analyzed news bulletins, and studied the audience for the new Belgrade 202 station. On the television side, it analyzed reactions to spoken word programs, reviewed mail responses, collected the views of intellectuals on entertainment broadcasts, studied quiz shows, and did special research on a sex education series.

In Zagreb 5,000 people over the age of fourteen were asked forty-eight questions about "the position, role, effect, effectiveness and contents of both radio and television."[142] The replies provided information about public exposure to mass communications, the use of leisure time, music preferences, the extent of listening to foreign programs, and reactions to commercials. Ljubljana surveyed the reactions of Yugoslavs who had viewed television newscasts from Italy and Austria, while Sarajevo studied in-school programs. Unfortunately, detailed reports of most of these studies are not available.

In 1972 Yugoslavia had 3,627,106 radio and 2,359,357 television receivers, the rate being 17.37 per hundred for radio and 11.30 for television. Among the socialist countries, only Romania had fewer sets per hundred—14.96 for radio and 9.35 for television.* Why should there be relatively few radio and television receivers in a fairly prosperous country where freedom in programming should encourage a high rate of set ownership? One Yugoslav scholar wrote of the "unsatisfactory situation of the diffusion of mass communications [in Yugoslavia] which does not correspond to the degree of socioeconomic development."[143] He went on to point out that according to BBC data, the rate of set distribution in Yugoslavia was below that in any European socialist country except Albania; lower than in any country in Western Europe; behind the United States, Canada, and Japan; but above the rate in some countries in Latin America, the Near East, and parts of Africa and China. But the author did not explain why things were that way.

The young lady who directs research for Radiotelevision Zagreb told me they do not use telephone surveys because there are so few telephones in rural areas, but instead have teams of sociology and psychology students conducting up to 400 interviews a day. She said there are

---

* See Table 10. There are detailed statistics on the number of radio and television receivers in the *JRT Yearbook* 1971/72, pp. 110–121, although they are not as recent as the EBU figures cited here. A JRT spokesman pointed out to me that if unregistered sets also were counted, the total number of radio receivers would be 5,621,179 and television receivers 2,711,834. Registration was avoided, he said, because fees were high and because there was "a rather widespread inherited predisposition to avoid paying any taxes in those parts of Yugoslavia which had been for a long time under Turkish rule." However, the same generalization probably could be made for most of the other countries studied, so that the EBU figures given in Table 10 are used throughout.

few differences in the research findings of the various republics. Among other things it has been learned that television tends to stimulate people in backward areas to work harder; some broadcast advertisements sell and some do not; and there are few complaints about commercials.

Generally speaking, Yugoslav findings accord with those in other countries. In Belgrade in February 1969, it was found that the most popular radio program was an entertainment feature, other high ratings going to certain news and information broadcasts.[144] The preferred television program was the evening news, viewed by 44.2 per cent of the public, with entertainment programs only slightly behind. Well received was a "Frank Sinatra Show," seen by 36.1 per cent of the sample. Sarajevo found that half the children in its area heard in-school radio programs, but that the programs did not achieve their full potential because of poor school equipment, lack of space, and discrepancies between school curriculums and broadcast materials.[145]

A study conducted in Slovenia for Radiotelevision Ljubljana showed that 93.4 per cent of adults listened regularly to the radio, 58 per cent watched television at least once a week, and 36.1 per cent viewed every day. Radio remained the main source of information for workers and pensioners, although people of higher education preferred television. The study also found that 83.9 per cent of the sample depended on local radio stations for information about local events and problems.[146]

Yugoslavia is the only socialist country to publish reports about the reception of foreign programs by its nationals, although I have been told in several other Eastern European countries that they too have made such studies.* In Slovenia, in northwestern Yugoslavia adjacent to Italy and Austria, 40.6 per cent of a sample said they tuned in foreign television or radio newscasts; 53.1 per cent said they did not; and 6.3 per cent said they neither listened to the radio nor watched television.[147] There was considerable preference for radio programs from Italy, with the Voice of America second and Austria a close third. In the television part of the survey, 40.3 per cent said they watched only domestic pro-

---

* Since Yugoslavia is the only bloc country (excepting Albania) to which neither Radio Free Europe nor Radio Liberty broadcast (although the BBC and the Voice of America both do), neither of these stations has made studies of the Yugoslav audience.

grams, 32.5 per cent said they did not watch television at all, while 11.0 per cent watched foreign newscasts.

External Broadcasting

Although its external output is limited, Yugoslavia's international role in broadcasting is extensive. It cooperates with both the West's European Broadcasting Union and the East's International Radio and Television Organization, thus reflecting its overall international status, described to me by one of its broadcasting leaders in the phrase: Yugoslavia is the only truly nonaligned country in Europe.

Yugoslav programs for reception abroad are intended to give "a comprehensive picture of the Socialist Federal Republic of Yugoslavia as an open community of peoples and nationalities."[148] They also present information about "the internal development of the country, its life, activity and development." In the foreign field there is emphasis on Yugoslavia's "non-alignment, active coexistence and international cooperation." The broadcasts also indicate "the support which Yugoslavia offers to the United Nations in its efforts to ensure peace." Because of their international objectives, these programs are financed directly by the federal budget rather than from receiver license receipts. The external services are operated in Belgrade by Radio Television Belgrade, under an agreement between that organization and the Yugoslav government. Although it has been proposed that the external services become a separate independent institution, such changes have not yet been made.

Yugoslavia transmits approximately eighty-six hours per week of external programs, less than any other country in the socialist group (see Table 9). In 1973 there were services in Albanian, Arabic, Bulgarian, English, French, German, Greek, Russian, and Spanish, plus some domestic programs relayed for countrymen living abroad.[149] There were also broadcasts in their own languages for all of Yugoslavia's immediate neighbors. For these services Yugoslavia employs five transmitters working on nine frequencies in the short-wave band, with power varying from 10 to 100 kilowatts, in addition to several medium-wave transmitters.[150] In 1971 the external services devoted 37.89 per cent of their time to news, 12.61 per cent to foreign affairs, 9.06 per cent to home affairs, and 3.83 per cent to "economy."[151] Only 3.95 per cent of the output was classified as entertainment. The music figures were 15.31 per cent folk music, 5.41 per cent light music, and 1.12 per cent serious music.

In conformity with the national pattern, Yugoslavia cooperates more with foreign broadcasting organizations than does any other socialist country. JRT is a very active member of the European Broadcasting Union, of which its secretary general was a vice-president in 1973, and also works with such Western-oriented groups as the Fourth International Jazz Festival in Montreux.[152] Although it does not belong to the OIRT, Yugoslavia sends observers to some of its meetings.

Yugoslavia unquestionably is the principal socialist user of Eurovision programs, although it also takes feeds from Intervision (see Table 1). In 1961 Yugoslavia contributed 20 programs to Eurovision with a duration of 22 hours, while receiving 4 programs lasting 6 hours. Its participation increased steadily, and in 1971 Yugoslavia contributed 17 programs (37 hr.), receiving 191 programs (326 hr.). Although in 1972 the number of programs contributed did not greatly change (to 14 programs, with a duration of 26 hr.), the number of programs received increased enormously (266 programs, 472 hr. 15 min.) owing to the Munich Olympic Games. In 1971, JRT received 391 hours of programs from Eurovision and Intervision combined, of which about 84 per cent were from Eurovision and 16 per cent from Intervision.[153] Most of these pertained to sports, of which 207 hours were received from Eurovision and 38 hours from Intervision. News came next, with 51 hours from Eurovision and 4 hours from Intervision.

In 1969 about 100 foreign broadcasting organizations, both West and East, cooperated in one way or another with JRT.[154] People from all over the world, both West and East, visited Yugoslav broadcasting, while 800 members of its staff traveled abroad. There also were many program exchanges. For example, 82 foreign organizations received music from JRT and supplied JRT with much music in return. A review of the Yugoslav press produced by JRT was distributed to American stations, including many educational outlets, by the Broadcasting Foundation of America. Television films were sent to 50 countries, and over 800 films, serials, shorts, and documentaries were imported for use at home.

To stimulate the sale of their productions abroad, some Yugoslav television organizations have produced attractively illustrated brochures. An announcement from Television Zagreb lists a concert by I Solisti di

Zagreb; an opera about ninth-century Croatia by a contemporary Yugo-slav composer; ballets with music by Yugoslav composers; and a pro-gram called "Music Laboratory," in which classical compositions are performed in jazz arrangements. Also available is "TV Magazine," a light entertainment music and dance series, and "Videophone," a series of short concerts featuring a beat group and a popular singer.

XIII

People's Republic of Albania

Albanian broadcasting is interesting mainly for its external services. In 1970 this little country was second only to the Soviet Union among Eastern European nations in the amount of its programming for listeners abroad (see Table 9). But its policy line is Chinese rather than Soviet, since even a casual sampling of its output indicates that Albania is a European outpost for the Chinese People's Republic.

Albania is one of Europe's smallest countries. With 11,111 square miles of territory, it is about the size of Maryland, whose 10,577 square miles make it the forty-second American state in area. In 1969 Albania's population was 2,108,000, and Tirana, its capital and largest city, had about 180,000 people.[1] Of the population 97 per cent is Albanian, the few minority residents being Greeks, Bulgarians, and Serbs. Half as many Albanians live in adjacent Yugoslavia as in Albania itself. Albania's neighbors include Yugoslavia on the north and east, and Greece on the south. Its 225-mile coastline is strategically attractive to countries seeking influence in the Adriatic area, such as the Soviet Union and the People's Republic of China, and there have been reports that the USSR formerly and China more recently have had submarine bases there.*

For centuries Albania fought to achieve and maintain independence. Although it broke away from Turkey in 1912, it was overrun by the

* It is difficult to obtain authentic information about Albania. But for whatever it is worth, in December 1972 Agence France Presse quoted the Chinese news agency to the effect that in 1959, the first secretary of the Albanian Communist party, Enver Hoxha, reported that two years before the Soviet break with Albania Nikita Khrushchev had considered setting up missile and submarine bases in Albania. The story did not say, however, that this was ever done (*New York Times*, December 4, 1972, p. 17C).

501

armies of several nations during World War I. Following short periods as republic and monarchy, Albania was forcibly annexed by Italy shortly before World War II. When Italy surrendered to the Allies in 1943, German troops took over, after which Communist partisans gained control. Enver Hoxha, who led the liberation army that made Albania a people's republic in 1946, has been the dominant personality ever since.

During the first years after World War II, Albania was a Yugoslav satellite, but when Tito broke with the USSR in 1960, Albania feared that it might be absorbed by Yugoslavia, and so developed close relations with China. Since then, China has provided its small Adriatic ally with experts and advisers, along with millions of dollars worth of machinery, raw materials, and military supplies. Consistent with its shift of orientation from the USSR to China, Albania dropped out of COMECON and the Warsaw Pact.[2]

The yardstick of Albania's attitudes toward other Eastern European countries has been the nature of their relationships with the Soviet Union. In 1968, after Bucharest established contacts with mainland China and opposed the Soviet invasion of Czechoslovakia, the Albanians drew closer to Romania. But the following year Albania criticized Romania for receiving President Nixon, maintaining that his visit set back the continuing struggle against imperialism.

In recent years Albania has been the spokesman for mainland China in the United Nations, and in 1971 introduced the motion that led to the admission of the People's Republic of China and the exclusion of Taiwan.[3] Characteristically, in the speech proposing this, the Albanian foreign minister complained that the United States Sixth Fleet and certain units of the Soviet Navy were behaving in the Mediterranean "as arrogantly as if they were in their own territorial waters." Neither the United States nor the Soviet Union maintains diplomatic relations with Albania.

In 1944 Albania was almost semifeudal, and it still is a very backward country. However, a series of five-year plans initiated in 1951 led to great improvements, and during the most recent of these (1966–1970) industrial output rose by 3 per cent, agricultural production by 28 per cent, and national income by 55 per cent.[4] Financial support has come principally from China. In 1970, 70 per cent of Albania's foreign trade was with China, 24 per cent with other Communist countries, and 6 per cent with Western Europe. There was no trade at all with the Soviet Union.[5] Nevertheless, Albania is trading with some forty countries and is trying to develop more Western contacts, one aspect of this being the attempts to encourage tourism which began in the late 1960s.

The People's Republic of Albania is governed under a constitution adopted in 1946 and amended in 1970 which follows the basic socialist pattern.[6] Enver Hoxha is first secretary of the Central Committee of the Albanian Party of Labor, the name adopted in 1948 for the Albanian Communist party, which at the end of 1971 had approximately 87,000 members. Although Albanian Marxism has firmly rejected the political philosophies of the Soviet Union in favor of those expounded by China, it nevertheless remains Albanian in style, reflecting the nationalism which has been basic to the country's survival for many decades.

Only limited information is available about Albania's domestic broadcasting. The government-run radio and television, begun in 1944, offers two radio services for eighteen hours a day over several medium- and short-wave stations, plus wired broadcasting for industrial installations and clubs in various parts of the country.[7] Experimental television began in May 1968, and the single station in Tirana is on the air three evenings a week from 6:00 to 9:00 P.M.*

There are extensive international services. Albania's weekly output of 490 hours puts it second only to the Soviet Union among Eastern European socialist countries (see Table 9). According to BBC figures, the world leader in 1972 was the USA with 2,001 program hours per week (the total of the VOA, RFE, and Radio Liberty). Second was the USSR with 1,884 hours. Then came the Chinese People's Republic (1,292 hr.), the German Federal Republic (806 hr.), the United Kingdom (746 hr.), and Egypt (601 hr.). Next was little Albania with 490 hours, which was not much less than RFE's 574 or RL's 498 hours.

It is reasonable to assume that both equipment and funds for this extensive external output are provided by China. Surely Albania has neither the money nor the manufacturing capacity to set up such a large operation; the countries of the Soviet bloc would hardly subsidize it; and China has contributed generously toward other aspects of Albanian economic development. Also supporting this thesis is the fact that since

---

* The figures available about the number of receivers are conflicting. The *World Radio TV Handbook* reports 3,000 television sets; the *Europa Year Book* says there were 50,000 television receivers in 1971 and 420,000 radio receivers in 1970; and the EBU table cited frequently during this study provides no information at all, indicating that Albania did not answer requests for information. But in any case the number of sets cannot be great.

1968 Albania has rebroadcast, on both medium- and short-wave transmitters, various Chinese programs intended for audiences in Europe, Africa, and the Americas.[8] Currently, an Albanian station on 1,457 kilohertz relays various Peking programs in Czech, Polish, Italian, Serbo-Croatian, and Turkish daily from 4:00 to 7:00 A.M., 11:00 A.M. to 1:00 P.M., 2:00 to 3:00 P.M., 5:30 to 6:00 P.M., and 10:00 P.M. to midnight. Furthermore, Chinese viewpoints are consistently expressed on Albanian programs. These conclusions are shared by other researchers with whom I have discussed Albanian broadcasting, although no one has firm documentation to support them.

Albania transmits external programs in seventeen languages, maintaining a twenty-four-hour schedule on five medium- and eight short-wave transmitters, the latter operating in the usual international bands with power ranging from 50 to 500 kilowatts.[9] There are seventeen hours a day of broadcasts in English and fifteen in Russian. From six to nine hours are devoted to transmissions in each of fifteen other languages: Albanian, Arabic, Bulgarian, Czech, French, German, Greek, Hungarian, Indonesian, Italian, Polish, Portuguese, Romanian, Serbo-Croatian and Spanish. The entire world is covered by these signals. I have heard Albanian programs on short-wave in various parts of the United States and on medium- and short-wave in Europe.

The output of Radio Albania is unique in that it condemns with equal severity both the Soviet Union and the United States, as also does mainland China. An example was provided by a broadcast of August 2, 1972, which commented on an international conference held in Paris several days previously.[10] The English-language program from Tirana described the meeting as "a farce held in Paris but arranged in Moscow," although "suffocated" by the "rumbling of the American bombs in Vietnam." The broadcast went on to group together "the Soviet modern revisionists, these effective and close allies of the imperialist U.S. aggressors," later referring to "the framework of the Soviet-U.S. alliance."

It is hard to believe that these programs can have much effect. The scripts are poorly written, and the English-language material is read in a labored and stilted manner. Perhaps programs in other languages are better done, although a small country like Albania, offering limited financial returns and few amenities for foreign-language broadcasters, probably finds it difficult to employ expert personnel for program planning, production, and presentation.

XIV

Comments

How well do these broadcasting organizations serve their countries? How "good" are their programs?*

Broadcasting grows out of, serves, and helps mold its environment. Socialist—like all other—broadcasting reflects its political, cultural, and economic backgrounds. The USSR, for example, never had anything like freedom of expression under its former imperial regime, and hence lacked a liberal heritage upon which to build its post-1917 socialist system. On the other hand, the rich literary and musical traditions of all these countries underlie some of their most successful broadcasting.

Program policies all over the world reinforce national values, although few people are sufficiently objective to be aware of that in their own country. Very important throughout Eastern Europe is the Communist concept of using all the media to support party and government. But one cannot explain everything on the basis of communism, since it is a relatively new development in all these countries.

Distinctive program formats were slow to emerge in Eastern Europe, as in Europe generally, although the Western countries are much ahead in this respect. One reason may be the general slowness of Eastern European bureaucracies. Another is the fact of monopoly: when a number of services compete for audiences, a high premium is placed on attractive—and this often means unique—program formats. In recent years there has been marked improvement, but there still is a long way to go.

* For additional summary material, see Chapter II.

505

Presentation and production have improved a great deal over the dozen years that I have been visiting these countries. In 1958, 1965, 1966, 1968, 1970, and 1972, I heard radio and watched television in that part of the world, and have noted conspicuous improvements, especially since 1965. Planning is better, presentations smoother, the distinctive features of the media better realized, and there is more response to audience needs.

As to national rankings, East Germany goes to the top, because of the German tradition of excellence and in response to competition from West Germany. Czechoslovakia is at the bottom, largely because the 1968 upheaval replaced experienced personnel with staff members who may have been politically dependable but were neophyte broadcasters. Otherwise, the Soviet Union, Yugoslavia, and Hungary go in the upper tier, followed by Poland, Romania, and Bulgaria. Major determinants are economic conditions and natural resources. Other things being equal, those countries with less government control tend to produce better programs. But these are only generalizations, and each country has both excellent and poor programs.

Among program types, sports and education rank high. There is tremendous public pressure for good sports coverage, and at the same time it is difficult to dilute such programs with propaganda. Frequent international exchanges are a factor too, since they ensure regular comparisons with foreign norms. Education benefits from the general emphasis on study and training, although there is excessive ideology. Proselytizing aside, there is much good work in drama, documentary, and film. Music is well handled, light entertainment less so.

The socialist programmers would do well to make their propaganda less obvious. It clearly is national policy everywhere to surround the public with approved points of view in all the media from childhood to retirement. But the audience data cited above, together with my observations and those of other outsiders, indicate that this is overdone to the point of being counterproductive. In fact, even some Eastern European broadcast executives will admit this off the record. If newscasts were less consistent in praising government and party, if there were reduced emphasis on industrial achievement, and if self-criticism could go beyond complaints about operations, the good—and true—things said would gain credibility. There is, I feel, a gap between party ideologists and mass media practitioners, with the latter recognizing the limitations of the procedures they are required to follow, but lacking the power to change them.

What will be the total effect of the electronic media—especially of television—on these controlled societies? Will they breach the information barrier? The effects of the media, of course, cannot be judged without reference to other developments now bringing Eastern Europe closer to the rest of the world. Steadily increasing numbers of socialist nationals are traveling abroad, while tourism is bringing in more people from outside. Expanding diplomatic relations, more participation in international organizations, and increased foreign trade all are influential. But the broadcast media must be the most effective of all factors in surmounting these barriers.

Even the domestic media disseminate much information not previously available. A television newscast may show a striking General Motors worker carrying a placard, the intended message being that he is exploited by his capitalist bosses. But at the same time the Soviet viewer may see thousands of cars on parking lots adjacent to the factory. The American housewife who appears to complain about supermarket prices may tell her socialist viewers even more by the good clothes she is wearing. The telefilms that stress the seamy side of American life also may refute many inaccuracies taught in Eastern European schools. Often I have heard people say, "I saw it on television," referring to events in Paris, London, and New York.

Then there are the programs beamed in from outside. The fact that they frequently are jammed, and that the domestic media are instructed to counter their message, documents their effectiveness. The Eastern countries broadcast certain types of popular music to keep their young people from tuning to foreign stations. Gromyko's proposal for an international convention limiting direct television broadcasts by satellite further demonstrates these concerns. All this indicates that the electronic media do breach the information barriers with which these governments try to surround their people. In the long run they should have far-reaching effects on information, education, and life in Eastern Europe.

Broadcasting systems can be put into two categories: those in which broadcasting and government are closely related, and those in which they are not. In the former case, since the government usually provides the funding and often controls the output, broadcasting is apt to become a government mouthpiece. From the democratic point of view, this is undesirable, for which reason those Western countries with close government-broadcaster relationships make great efforts to ensure the freedom of the media. The United Kingdom has been outstandingly successful in this respect. The United States, facing this problem for the first time in funding public broadcasting, is having great difficulty working out a satisfactory solution. In the socialist countries, of course, closeness of media and government is considered an advantage.

When government and media are separated, operation usually is by private entrepreneurs, and support is by advertising. In such cases the operators often refer to broadcasting as an "industry"; stations—together with their frequencies or channels—are bought and sold like all kinds of private property; and program policies are greatly influenced—if not controlled—by the drive for economic gain. There clearly are unsolved problems about such services too. Although some superb programs are produced, others seem to develop without regard for the social responsibilities inherent in all the mass media.

When American broadcasting operates as it should, it provides the world with examples of how a free system can serve society. From their side, the media in the socialist countries can remind us of the role of broadcasting as a public service rather than as an industry—even though we reject many of their basic concepts. We can hope that someday they may accept certain of our ideas about freedom from government control. Meanwhile, our challenge is to determine program policies on the basis of social objectives rather than investment returns. Our goal must be to secure responsible performances from our mass media within the framework of our democratic system.

Appendix: Technical Information

The paragraphs below provide information about certain technical aspects of radio and television referred to periodically in the preceding pages.*

Radio

Radio waves are mainly of three types: ground waves, which travel along the surface of the earth; sky waves, which travel up to the ionized layers in the upper atmosphere and then are reflected back to earth; and direct waves, which travel on line of sight. The long-wave frequencies between 150 and 525 kilohertz, with excellent ground-wave propagation, provide good coverage over wide areas and are highly prized in Europe, where most countries wish to cover large areas with strong signals.[1] But they are not used for broadcasting in the United States, instead being assigned to maritime, aeronautical, and other point-to-point services.

The medium-wave or standard broadcast band, extending from 525 to 1,605 kilohertz, is the part of the spectrum to which are assigned most domestic broadcasting stations in Europe and the Americas. This band, with both ground-wave and sky-wave propagation, can provide good reception over a radius from fifty to several hundred miles during the daytime, and up to thousands of miles at night, depending upon the frequency and power used. In some cases, directional antennas are em-

---

* In preparing this description I had the assistance of Oscar Reed, Jr., director of the Telecommunications Consulting Department of the Atlantic Research Corporation, who read much of the section and made some helpful suggestions for its improvement, and of William Fuller Brown, Jr., professor of electrical engineering at the University of Minnesota, who provided a number of carefully written paragraphs about color television which are quoted here almost verbatim.

ployed to reduce coverage in order to avoid interference between stations.

The high-frequency or short-wave bands, because of their predominately sky-wave propagation, are especially good for long-distance communication and hence are used to reach listeners hundreds or thousands of miles away. Such overseas services as Radio Moscow, the Voice of America, and the BBC make extensive use of these bands.

In amplitude modulation or AM broadcasting, the most widely used method of radio broadcasting, the amplitude or strength of the transmission is varied by the volume of the sound. In frequency modulation or FM, it is the frequency of the radio carrier rather than the amplitude of the transmission carrier that is modulated.* AM broadcasting has the advantage of potentially greater coverage on low-frequency clear channels, while FM is limited mainly to reception within line-of-sight distance from the transmitter. But FM transmissions are almost static-free; they have a wider audio frequency range; and mutual interference is less troublesome, since an FM receiver tends to receive only the strongest signal on the frequency to which it is tuned. An FM transmitter also can transmit two or more signals simultaneously on the same carrier, thus facilitating stereophonic and multiplex broadcasting.

Both Europe and North America use the same bands for FM radio, though with variations: Western Europe 87.5 to 100 megahertz; Eastern Europe originally only 66 to 73 megahertz, but now also some spectrum space above 87.5 megahertz; and the United States 88.1 to 107.9 megahertz. The Soviet Union began experimenting with stereophonic FM in 1955. Two Russian authors have described the differences between Soviet and American procedures.[2] "The two systems are very similar, the difference lying only in the degree of suppression of the subcarrier frequency signal: in the American system the signal is suppressed in full and instead of it a pilot-tone is transmitted at a frequency equal to one-half of the subcarrier frequency." The Soviet engineers claim their system to be superior because it has less distortion, and because it also can be used for stereophonic sound in television, since "the subcarrier at 31.25 kHz coincides with the second harmonic of the line frequency of the television system."

Television

The determination of technical standards is a prerequisite to the establishment of any television service. If a television picture is to be satisfactorily broadcast and reproduced, transmitting and receiving apparatus must be matched in a dozen respects.[3] One of the most important of these

---

* Europe uses the terms "VHF" ("Very High Frequency") and "UKW" ("Ultra Short Wave"), referring to the frequencies employed as well as the American "FM," which refers to the type of modulation.

variables is the number of lines composing the picture, which is among the factors affecting the sharpness of image. In transmission, a television picture is divided into a number of horizontal lines, each of which is scanned from left to right by the camera pickup tube, much as the eye traverses printed lines in reading a page; but whereas each printed line is read as a series of words, the camera (in black-and-white television) "reads" successive light or dark spots. Other things being equal, the sharpness or resolution increases as more lines are scanned (provided that corresponding increases are made in the video picture bandwidth). For this reason, within limits, a premium is placed upon a greater number of lines per picture.

In noninterlaced "sequential" scanning each line is scanned in turn, just as a page is read, whereas with "interlaced" scanning all the odd-numbered lines (1, 3, 5, 7, etc.) are scanned first, after which the camera scans the even-numbered ones (2, 4, 6, etc.) to the bottom of the picture. Since the latter procedure reduces picture flicker, interlaced scanning is now universally used. Another important factor is the number of complete pictures transmitted per second, flicker diminishing as the frequency is increased. At present the United States uses a 525-line interlaced standard with 30 pictures per second, and most of the rest of the world, including all of Eastern Europe, uses a 625-line standard with 25 pictures per second.

In none of these cases, however, is the picture proper divided for transmission purposes into the full number of lines mentioned. In the American 525-line system, for example, only 498 lines are devoted to the picture itself, the remainder being used to transmit synchronizing impulses. Generally, the number of lines given for each system must be reduced by about 5 per cent to allow for vertical retrace time. Thus, in the American system there are 525 minus 27, or 498 active lines. Of the European 625 lines, 594 are active in actual picture transmission.

When the British went on the air in 1936 with the world's first regular television service, their 405 lines represented very high definition. But the American standard was set at 525 lines in 1941, and the French, striving for extremely fine picture detail, chose 819 lines in 1949 (after having previously operated on 441 lines, which was the standard originally proposed by some American manufacturers). The CCIR had discussed a 625-line standard as early as 1950, and this was adopted by most Western European countries. (The Western European standard often is identified as the "CCIR Standard," although the CCIR never officially endorsed any standard.) All European countries now are moving toward 625 lines. The second BBC and French networks, on the air since April 1964, both use 625-line systems in the UHF band. (CCIR—after its French name, Comité Consultatif International Technique des Communications Radioélectriques—or International Radio Consultative

Committee is one of the organs of the International Telecommunication Union in Geneva.)

Europe telecasts in both the VHF and UHF bands. In most cases the first stations in any country operate in the VHF band—equivalent to America's channels 2 through 13—but as more stations are added there is expansion to the UHF band—America's channels 14 through 82. At present most Eastern European stations are on VHF, although some of the emerging second services are on UHF, as are many of the low-powered repeater stations.

The Eastern European or OIRT 625-line standard, adopted officially in 1957, differs mainly from the Western 625-line standard in bandwidth details.[4] OIRT spokesmen claim that their standard provides better picture definition and also facilitates the development of high-quality color television. The OIRT system is used by all the Eastern countries except Yugoslavia and East Germany, which use the Western standard.

This lack of standardization leads to many complications. Because receivers designated to operate on one standard usually will not work on another, elaborate conversion systems must be used when programs are to be exchanged by countries using different standards. There also are the problems of receiving programs from transmitters in neighboring countries with different standards. Because the OIRT and Western 625-line systems are much alike, it is possible for receivers operating on one standard to be modified to receive programs broadcast on the other, although usually with a loss of picture quality. However, there is no problem in exchanging programs by cable, microwave relay, or satellite, since the same basic scanning methods are used by both systems.

For color television, it fortunately is not necessary to transmit all the colors of the rainbow.[5] It is sufficient to transmit only three signals, representing roughly the red (R), green (G), and blue (B) content of the picture. If these are properly combined on the receiver screen, the eye of the viewer will experience essentially the same color impressions as if he were observing the original scene.

To produce the three signals R, G, and B, the television camera is equipped with three optical filters that transmit respectively the red, green, and blue parts of the spectrum. The result is three voltages that change, each in its own way, as the camera scans the original scene. To reproduce the picture, voltages similar to these in the receiver must react on the picture tube.

The obvious way to transmit the picture would be to transmit each of the three signals, R, G, and B in the same way a black-and-white picture is transmitted; but this would require three separate frequency bands instead of one, and therefore a total bandwidth three times that necessary for black-and-white television. However, this is not the method used, primarily because a black-and-white receiving set then would have to select just one of the three signals. It therefore would produce blacks, grays, and whites determined by the red or green or blue content of the picture, rather than by the proper combination of all three. The intensities would be seriously distorted, and important parts of the picture would not be seen at all. It therefore is required that color transmissions be "compatible" with black-and-white transmissions—that is, they must produce a satisfactory black-and-white picture on the screen of a monochrome receiver.

This is accomplished by transmitting not the three signals R, G, and B, but three combinations of them, obtained by electronically adding and subtracting definite fractions of the corresponding voltages. One such combination, Y, is a combination which, in a black-and-white receiver, will produce a satisfactory black-and-white picture. Only this combination affects a black-and-white receiver. A color receiver, however, will accept all three combinations and will, again by electronic addition and subtraction, put them together to reproduce the original signals R, G, and B, which then can act on the picture tube just as if they had never been subjected to all this electronic algebra. The combination already mentioned, Y, represents roughly the intensity of the light; it is called the "luminance" signal. The other two combinations, approximately the differences $R - Y$ and $B - Y$, are called "chrominance" signals.

A further advantage of this method of transmission is that it does not require three times the bandwidth required for black-and-white transmission, but only the same bandwidth. The reason is basically that black-and-white television transmission is very inefficient in its use of a frequency band; color transmission, by using the three signals mentioned (Y, $R - Y$, and $B - Y$), is able to make more efficient use of the band already available without requiring expansion of the band. It does so by exploiting two facts. First, the eye is less sensitive to color detail than to intensity detail. The $R - Y$ and $B - Y$ signals therefore can be squeezed into a narrower frequency band than is required for the Y signal. Second, because of the line-scanning action, the energy in the main (Y) signal is bunched around certain frequencies. The other signals can therefore be put into the spaces between these frequencies.

The several color systems that have been developed differ primarily with respect to the method of transmitting the two color or "chrominace" signals ($R - Y$ and $B - Y$). In the NTSC (National Television System Committee) system, these are combined into a single signal, somewhat in the way that the signals from two microphones are combined into a single groove in a stereophonic disc recording. The method requires accurate maintenance of a "subcarrier" frequency at the transmitter, and accurate synchronization with it of the same frequency generated in the receiver. The method of accomplishing the synchronization is to radiate a short "burst" of a few cycles of this frequency in an appropriate part of the television waveform.

In the SECAM ("Sequential and Memory") system, one of the two color signals is delayed with respect to the other, so that they can be transmitted successively (during alternate line periods) rather than simultaneously. This method eliminates the need for accurate synchronization of a locally generated subcarrier frequency and makes recording of the signal on magnetic tape easier; but it increases the difficulty of achieving satisfactory black-and-white reception. The PAL ("Phase Alternating Line") system resembles the NTSC but reverses the phase of one of the two color signals between alternate lines. The purpose is to average out errors in color that result from unequal transmission of the two color signals.

Once the signals have been received, amplified, and recombined to the original R, G, and B, these three signals then control separate electron guns in the picture tube. Each of the three electron beams impinges, during scanning, on its own set of color-fluorescing dots on the screen of the picture tube. Each set of dots produces its own color, so that there are really three separate pictures on the screen; but because they are close together, the eye does not perceive them separately but combines them into the correct color image.

Despite the disadvantages involved, European television now uses two incompatible color standards. Originally three systems were under consideration: the American NTSC, the French SECAM, and the German PAL. In most respects these systems are similar; in fact, 95 per cent of their components are the same. Nevertheless, a set designed to work on one will not necessarily reproduce signals broadcast by another. Throughout all the discussions the proponents of each strongly urged its adoption, although average viewers could see little difference among them. Whichever is best, its superiority is slight as opposed to the tremendous advantage of Continent-wide standardization.*

Unfortunately, at a CCIR meeting about color television standards held in Vienna from March 25 to April 7, 1965, there was a three-way disagreement: Twenty-two nations voted for the French SECAM system

* The director of the technical center of the European Broadcasting Union believed that the NTSC system had the advantage of a ten-year test in the United States as well as of lower receiver cost. Furthermore, NTSC black-and-white reception would be better than PAL or SECAM. But the PAL and SECAM systems would be less sensitive to differential-phase distortion and would facilitate program exchange, while long-distance transmissions would be easier by either PAL or SECAM (Georges Hansen, "Colour-Television Standards for Europe," *WRTH 1965*, p. 28). Britain's *Financial Times* (April 8, 1965) wrote: "The foremost television experts stated here time and time again that on objective technical grounds there was no doubt that NTSC was the best system although PAL was perhaps better suited to Europe. No one here doubts that SECAM is the worst of the three systems."

(including all socialist countries except Yugoslavia); eleven for the German PAL; and six for the American NTSC. Politics, economics, and prestige, rather than electronic theory, brought about this impasse. Just before the Vienna meeting, France and the Soviet Union agreed privately to support SECAM, a decision widely interpreted as a consequence of the current political rapprochement between De Gaulle and the USSR.[6] In some cases national positions resulted from ambitions to control foreign transmitter and receiver markets for one or another color system. The USSR opposed the NTSC system partly because of its American origin; West Germany, as would be expected, pressed the case for its own PAL; while only the British, with assistance from the Netherlands, favored NTSC. In view of the similarity of the American NTSC and German PAL systems, it was hoped for a time that they could be merged for adoption by most Western European countries, the system to be called QUAM for "Quadrature Amplitude Modulation." But this did not happen.*

The matter was discussed again by the 650 delegates from 69 countries that attended the Eleventh Plenary Assembly of the CCIR in Oslo from June 22 to July 22, 1966.[7] Serious consideration was given to two developments of SECAM—SECAM III and SECAM IV—as well as to PAL. The NTSC system was out of the running because those countries previously in favor of it had switched their support to the West German PAL. In the end, PAL was supported by all the Western European countries except France, while SECAM III was favored by France, the Soviet Union, and all the other Eastern countries except Romania and Yugoslavia.

Although they were not prepared to recede from their position, Eastern as well as Western spokesmen regretted the breakdown. Following the failure to reach agreement in Vienna in 1965, the *OIRT Review* commented that "the failure to select a single colour television system will considerably complicate further international exchange of colour television programmes."[8] As things finally came out, all the Eastern European socialist countries except Romania and Yugoslavia use SECAM color, those two employing PAL.

* *New York Times*, April 9, 1965, p. 3. There was a long and bitter controversy in the United States before agreement was reached on the present NTSC standard. In 1946 the Columbia Broadcasting System asked the Federal Communications Commission to authorize commercial operation with its system. The FCC first refused but then accepted the CBS standard in 1950. Because CBS color could not be received on black-and-white sets, this decision was widely criticized. After a series of legal actions brought by RCA, which among other things had the objective of delaying the final decision, and after the suspension of television receiver manufacturing because of the Korean War in 1952–1953, the present compatible NTSC system was adopted by the FCC in December 1953. Accordingly, the United States, along with the rest of the North American continent, has a single color standard.

NOTES

Notes

III. Union of Soviet Socialist Republics:
Structure and Organization

1. United Nations, *Demographic Yearbook 1971*, pp. 114–115, 118.

2. *Ibid.*, pp. 118, 357–358, 364, 371, 373–375.

3. *Encyclopaedia Britannica*, 1965 ed., Vol. 19, p. 683; *Soviet Life*, December 1971, p. 28

4. *New York Times*, April 19, 1970, p. 3; "Nationalities," *McGraw-Hill Encyclopedia of Russia and the Soviet Union*, p. 379; "Ethnic Composition," in Robert Maxwell, ed., *Information U.S.S.R.*, pp. 95–100.

5. For tables based on the 1959 Soviet census showing the fifteen major USSR nationalities by place of residence, see Rosemarie Sträussnigg Rogers, *The Soviet Audience: How It Uses the Mass Media*, pp. 310–311.

6. "Languages of the Peoples of the USSR," in Maxwell, ed., *Information U.S.S.R.*, pp. 101–104. These data were published in the early 1960s.

7. *New York Times*, January 27, 1972, p. 5C; *New York Times*, February 26, 1973. p. 2C.

8. *New York Times*, December 27, 1972, p. 70M; *New York Times*, January 14, 1973, p. 56F.

9. *Europa Year Book 1972*, Vol. 1, p. 1240; *New York Times,* January 12, 1972, pp. 1, 58; *New York Times*, March 11, 1973, p. 22.

10. *Europa Year Book 1972*, Vol. 1, p. 1272; *Statesman's Year-Book 1972–1973*, pp. 579, 580, 1412.

11. *United Nations Statistical Yearbook 1971*, pp. 442, 448.

12. *McGraw-Hill Encyclopedia of Russia and the Soviet Union*, p. 152.

13. *Editor and Publisher International Year Book 1973*, p. 427; *UNESCO Statistical Yearbook 1970*, p. 697; *United Nations Statistical Yearbook 1971*, pp. 788, 805.

14. *Statesman's Year-Book 1971–1972*, pp. 1420–1421.

15. *Europa Year Book 1972*, Vol. 1, p. 1233; *Statesman's Year-Book 1972–1973*, p. 1395.

16. *Europa Year Book 1972*, Vol. 1, pp. 1252–1253.

17. *Ibid.*, p. 1257.

18. Charles Süsskind, "Popov and the Beginnings of Radiotelegraphy," *Proceedings of the IRE,* 50:10 (October 1962), pp. 2036–2037, hereafter cited as Süsskind.

19. Orrin E. Dunlap, Jr., *Marconi: The Man and His Wireless,* p. 13, hereafter cited as Dunlap.

20. R. N. Vyvyan, *Wireless over Thirty Years,* p. 12.

21. W. Rupert Maclaurin, *Invention and Innovation in the Radio Industry,* pp. 18–20.

22. G. Marconi, "Wireless Telegraphy," *Journal of the Institution of Electrical Engineers,* Vol. 28 (1899), p. 278.

23. Süsskind, p. 2039.

24. "1917–1957," *Radio Engineering and Electronics,* 2:11 (1957), pp. 1–2, hereafter cited as *REE.*

25. Süsskind, pp. 2039–2040, 2042–2043, 2046; *REE,* pp. 1–2.

26. Süsskind, p. 2046.

27. *Ibid.,* p. 2047.

28. *REE,* p. 3.

29. Erik Barnouw, *A Tower in Babel: A History of Broadcasting in the United States,* Vol. 1 (to 1933), pp. 4, 61–74, 79; hereafter cited as Barnouw.

30. This résumé of early British developments draws upon Burton Paulu, *British Broadcasting: Radio and Television in the United Kingdom,* pp. 8–12; Asa Briggs, *The Birth of Broadcasting,* pp. 46–50.

31. Kaftanov, pp. 218–219.

32. *Ibid.,* p. 220; *REE,* p. 5.

33. Kaftanov, p. 221.

34. *Ibid.*

35. *Ibid.,* p. 8.

36. *Ibid.,* pp. 10, 12, 225.

37. *Ibid.,* p. 12.

38. *Ibid.,* pp. 221–222.

39. *REE,* p. 17.

40. A. Y. Yurovskiy and R. A. Boretskiy, *Osnovy televizionnoy zhurnalistiki (The Fundamentals of Television Journalism),* pp. 39, 41, hereafter cited as Yurovskiy and Boretskiy.

41. Kaftanov, pp. 230–231.

42. Yurovskiy and Boretskiy, pp. 42–43. The British claim that the Scot John Logie Baird first demonstrated the transmission of moving silhouettes by wire in 1925, and the following year showed an assemblage of scientists and reporters that he could transmit through the air not only shadows, but "the details of movement, in such things as the play of expressions on the face" (*London Times,* January 28, 1926, p. 9).

43. Kaftanov, p. 231; *REE,* p. 18.

44. *REE,* p. 18.

45. Yurovskiy and Boretskiy, p. 45.

46. Kaftanov, p. 234.

47. *REE,* p. 18.

48. Kaftanov, p. 237.

49. Data supplied by State Committee for Radio and Television.

50. The early history of the Russian press is summarized in James W. Markham, *Voices of the Red Giants,* pp. 25–65, hereafter cited as Markham.

51. Excellent reviews are available in such sources as Antony Buzek, *How the Communist Press Works,* hereafter cited as Buzek; Wilbur Schramm, "The Soviet Communist Theory of the Press," *Four Theories of the Press,* pp. 105–146; Alex Inkeles, *Public Opinion in Soviet Russia: A Study in Mass Persuasion,* hereafter cited as Inkeles; Markham; Mark W. Hopkins, *Mass Media in the Soviet Union,*

hereafter cited as Hopkins; and Serge L. Levitsky, "Soviet Law and the Press," *Journalism Quarterly*, 34:1 (Winter 1957), pp. 51–57.

52. V. I. Lenin, *Collected Works*, Vol. 10, p. 47.

53. *Ibid.*, Vol. 25, p. 375.

54. *Ibid.*, Vol. 26, pp. 66–67.

55. Andrei Y. Vyshinsky, *The Law of the Soviet State*, p. 615, hereafter cited as Vyshinsky.

56. Lenin, *Collected Works*, Vol. 27, p. 205.

57. *Ibid.*, Vol. 28, pp. 460–461.

58. Quoted by Frank Luther Mott, "Newspapers," *Encyclopaedia Britannica*, 1958 ed., Vol. 16, p. 356.

59. Letter to G. Myasnikov, August 5, 1921, in Lenin, *Collected Works*, Vol. 32, p. 505. Emphasis in original.

60. Lenin, *Collected Works*, Vol. 5, pp. 20–22.

61. J. V. Stalin, *Works*, Vol. 5, p. 206.

62. D. Kuzmichev, quoted in International Press Institute, *The Press in Authoritarian Countries*, p. 23, hereafter cited as IPI Survey.

63. Translated in *The Current Digest of the Soviet Press*, 9:35 (October 9, 1957), p. 8, hereafter cited as CDSP.

64. Vladimir Gvoski, *Soviet Civil Law*, pp. 1, 63–64; "Constitution of the Union of Soviet Socialist Republics," Art. 118–133, in Amos J. Peaslee, *Constitutions of Nations*, Vol. 3, pp. 1004–1006, hereafter cited as *USSR Constitution*.

65. *USSR Constitution*, Art. 126.

66. *Ibid.*, Art. 127–129.

67. *Ibid.*, Art. 130–133.

68. Stalin, *Problems of Leninism*, pp. 692–693.

69. Vyshinsky, p. 610.

70. *Ibid.*, pp. 612–613.

71. *Ibid.*, p. 614.

72. *Ibid.*, pp. 614–615.

73. *Ibid.*, p. 615.

74. *Ibid.*, p. 616.

75. *Ibid.*, p. 617.

76. For the background of this practice see Inkeles, pp. 194–222. See also Alex Inkeles and H. Kent Geiger, "Typical Letters to the Soviet Press," in Alex Inkeles, *Social Change in Soviet Russia*, pp. 291–326.

77. Stalin, *Works*, Vol. 11, pp. 135–136.

78. Harold J. Berman, *Soviet Criminal Law and Procedure*, pp. 153–154.

79. Material on Glavlit may be consulted in Hopkins, pp. 78–79, 123–129; Inkeles, pp. 184–193; Markham, pp. 130–133; Maurice Friedberg, "Keeping Up with the Censor," *Problems of Communism*, 13:6 (November–December 1964), pp. 22–31; Buzek, pp. 140–144; Merle Fainsod, *Smolensk Under Soviet Rule*, pp. 364–377.

80. "Decree on the Press," published in *Pravda*, November 10, 1917; reprinted in *Lenin about the Press*, p. 205.

81. Friedberg, p. 23; John N. Hazard, Isaac Shapiro, and Peter Maggs, *The Soviet Legal System*, p. 88.

82. Fainsod, *Smolensk under Soviet Rule*, pp. 3, 364–377.

83. Friedberg, p. 23.

84. Fainsod, *Smolensk under Soviet Rule*, pp. 364–366.

85. Buzek, pp. 140–141; Hopkins, pp. 125–126.

86. *New York Times*, June 11, 1972, p. 23.

87. *New York Times*, January 20, 1973, p. 10C.

88. *New York Times*, May 28, 1973, p. 6C; *New York Times*, March 10, 1973,

p. 29M; *New York Times*, March 28, 1973, p. 15C; *Variety*, March 14, 1973, pp. 1, 70.

89. Hazard, Shapiro, and Maggs, *The Soviet Legal System*, p. 87.

90. *Effect of Underground Radio Stations in the USSR*, pp. 2, 4.

91. *Ibid.*, pp. 6–7.

92. Gabriel Lorince, "Inside Russia: Moscow's Radio Pirates," *New Statesman*, 74:1902 (August 25, 1967), p. 227. *Los Angeles Times*, December 3, 1973, pp. 1, 12.

93. *Effect of Underground Radio Stations in the USSR*, p. 3.

94. AP Radio Wire, June 13, 1972; F. Gayle Durham, *Amateur Radio Operation in the Soviet Union*, pp. 1–3.

95. Hopkins, p. 77; Inkeles, pp. 30–37; Buzek, pp. 35–37; *IPI Survey*, pp. 32–35.

96. Buzek, p. 36.

97. Hopkins, p. 91.

98. Fainsod, *Smolensk under Soviet Rule*, p. 367.

99. *IPI Survey*, p. 32.

100. Kaftanov, p. 218.

101. *REE*, p. 3.

102. Kaftanov, pp. 221, 223.

103. *Ibid.*, pp. 12, 225.

104. *Ibid.*, pp. 13–14.

105. *Ibid.*, p. 14.

106. *Ibid.*, p. 230.

107. *Ibid.*, p. 231.

108. *Ibid.*, pp. 14–15.

109. Quoted from *Izvestia*, November 27, 1933, in Inkeles, p. 227.

110. Kaftanov, p. 15.

111. Rose Ziglin, "Radio Broadcasting in the Soviet Union," *The Annals of the American Academy of Political and Social Science*, Vol. 177 (1935), pp. 70–71. hereafter cited as Ziglin; Inkeles, pp. 226–233.

112. Kaftanov, pp. 15, 237.

113. *Ibid.*, p. 239.

114. *Ibid.*, pp. 15, 239.

115. *Pravda*, April 19, 1962, translated in CDSP, 14:16 (May 16, 1962), p. 28.

116. *Europa Year Book 1972*, Vol. 1, pp. 1252–1253.

117. This description is based upon information provided by the State Committee in 1965, supplemented by Albert Namurois, *Structure and Organization of Broadcasting in the Framework of Radiocommunications*, pp. 107–108, hereafter cited as Namurois.

118. *Partiinaya zhizn*, No. 4 (February 1960), pp. 26–34, translated in CDSP, 12:10 (April 6, 1960), pp. 18–21.

119. Translated in *The Soviet Press in Translation*, 4:5 (January 1964).

120. U.S. Foreign Broadcast Information Service, "The 23rd Congress of the Soviet Communist Party. Proceedings and Related Materials," *Daily Report: Supplement, USSR and East Europe*, 10:20 (April 8, 1966); *New York Times*, April 9, 1966, p. 2.

121. "Gift to 10,000,000. Registration of and Subscription Fee for Use of Radios and Television Sets Abolished," *Izvestia*, August 27, 1961, translated in CDSP, 13:34 (September 20, 1961), p. 29.

122. B. Prokofyev, "Letter from the Editors: The State and He," *Izvestia*, September 20, 1961, p. 4, translated in CDSP, 13:38 (October 18, 1961), p. 27.

123. "Replies, Rejoinders and Proposals," *Izvestia*, September 30, 1961, p. 3, cited in CDSP, 13:39 (October 25, 1961), p. 32. For examples of techniques used

in locating unlicensed sets in some other countries, see Paulu, *Radio and Television Broadcasting on the European Continent*, p. 93.

124. Hopkins, p. 63.

125. Inkeles, p. 270.

126. There are general discussions of Soviet advertising in Markham, pp. 187–193, and Inkeles, pp. 270–271.

127. *New York Times*, March 26, 1971, p. 63C.

128. *Variety*, April 16, 1969, p. 39.

129. Kendall Bailes, *Soviet Television Comes of Age*, pp. 4–5.

130. Information received from International Radio and Television Organization. Printed sources include: Kaftanov, pp. 191–192; *Internationales Handbuch für Rundfunk und Fernsehen 1971/72*, pp. E24–E25, E43–E44, hereafter cited as *Internationales Handbuch 1971/72*; George A. Codding, Jr., *Broadcasting without Barriers*, p. 47; Kenneth Harwood, "The International Radio and Television Organization," *Journal of Broadcasting*, 5:1 (Winter 1960–1961), pp. 61–72; *WRTH 1973*, pp. 14–16; Namurois, p. 68.

131. Rolf Weissbach, "The O.I.R.T. Radio Programme Commission—Its Present State and Perspective," *Radio Television: Review of the International Radio and Television Organization*, 1970/3, pp. 5–7, hereafter cited as *OIRT Review*.

132. "Creation of the Intervision," *OIRT Review*, 1960/2, pp. 70–74; "Intervision," *OIRT Review*, 1962/2, pp. 3–5; "Experience in the Technical Operation of the Intervision Network," *OIRT Review*, 1963/2, pp. 26–49. For a review of some legal problems involved in the international circulation of radio and television programs, see Namurois, pp. 60–65.

133. Rubina and Ramsin, *Communications in the USSR*, p. 15; UNESCO, *World Communications: Press Radio Television Film*, p. 368.

134. Nikolai Skatchko, "Five Years," *OIRT Review*, 1965/2, p. 3.

135. *New York Times*, May 8, 1956, p. 35.

136. "On Improving Soviet Radio Broadcasting and on Further Developing Television," *Partiinaya zhizn*, No. 4 (February 1960), pp. 26–34, translated in CDSP, 12:10 (April 6, 1960), p. 18.

137. N. Psurtsev, "USSR Speaks and Transmits Pictures," *Izvestia*, May 7, 1960, p. 12, translated in CDSP, 12:19 (June 8, 1960), pp. 36–37. "To Millions of Viewers and Listeners," *Pravda*, March 17, 1971, p. 6, translated in CDSP, 23:11 (April 13, 1971), p. 31; Editorial, *Pravda* (December 15, 1971), p. 1, translated in CDSP, 23:50 (January 1, 1972), p. 11.

138. *Internationales Handbuch 1971/72*, pp. F196–F202.

139. "To Millions of Viewers and Listeners," *Pravda*, March 17, 1971, translated in CDSP, 23:11 (April 13, 1971), p. 31. Throughout Europe such transmissions are called "VHF" (Very High Frequency) and "USF" (Ultra Short Wave), referring respectively to the frequencies and the wave lengths employed, as well as the American term "FM," which refers to the method of modulation.

140. V. D. Sher and I. M. Kononovitch, "Stereophonic Broadcasting in the USSR," *OIRT Review*, 1968/6, p. 28.

141. *WRTH 1974*, pp. 106–107.

142. I. A. Chamchine, "Le Système de la radiodistribution à trois chaînes," *OIRT Review*, 1972/3, pp. 23–24.

143. "Multiprogramme Wired Broadcasting in the USSR," *OIRT Review*, 1962/6, pp. 27–31; "U.S.S.R. Speaks and Transmits Pictures," *Izvestia*, May 7, 1960, p. 12, translated in CDSP, 12:19 (June 8, 1960), p. 37.

144. UNESCO, *World Communications: Press Radio Television Film*, p. 367. There is an explanation of the technical aspects of three-channel systems, in I. A.

Chamchine, "Le Système de la radiodistribution à trois chaînes," *OIRT Review.* 1972/3, pp. 23–29.

145. "Wired Broadcasting Networks Automatization," *OIRT Review,* 1960/4, pp. 162–172.

146. Paulu, *British Broadcasting,* pp. 26–29.

147. UNESCO, *Statistics on Radio and Television 1950–1960,* p. 60.

148. Soviet data from Table 3; other data from Table 10 and *EBU Review,* 102: 35 (March 1967).

149. *EBU Review,* 126:34 (March 1971).

150. *BBC Handbook 1971,* p. 110.

151. Inkeles, p. 244.

152. *REE,* p. 18.

153. "Creative Forces for the Fulfillment of the Party's Decisions," *Pravda,* May 7, 1972, p. 2, translated in CDSP, 24:18 (May 31, 1972), p. 21. Considerable information about Soviet television facilities is given in *WRTH 1973,* pp. 281–282, and *Internationales Handbuch 1971/72,* pp. F209–F211.

154. "To Millions of Viewers and Listeners," *Pravda,* March 17, 1971, p. 6, translated in CDSP, 23:11 (April 13, 1961), p. 31; *Europa Year Book 1972,* Vol. 1, p. 1268. On January 1, 1972, the United States had 905 television transmitters on the air (*Broadcasting Yearbook 1972,* p. A–112).

155. *WRTH 1973,* p. 281.

156. *Soviet Life,* July 1, 1971, p. 29; Irina Bogatko, "Television in the USSR" (manuscript supplied by Novosti); *Europa Year Book 1972,* Vol. 1, p. 1268; *OIRT Information,* 1972/1, p. 12; *OIRT Information,* 1972/4–5, p. 10.

157. O. Rupsky, "The Country from Midnight to Noon: Interesting Experiment," *Izvestia,* January 1, 1963, p. 4, translated in CDSP, 15:1 (January 30, 1963), p. 42; I. M. Kononovitch, "A System of Bilingual Television Sound Accompaniment," *OIRT Review,* 1965/3, pp. 21–25.

158. I. I. Govollo et al., *Leading Television Center of the USSR;* I. I. Govallo and Y. B. Gruzdev, "Basic Concepts of the Design of the All-Union Television Center in Moscow," *OIRT Review,* 1968/1, pp. 27–33; V. C. Sher and V. S. Nemanov, "New Audio Equipment of a Multi-Programme Television Centre," *OIRT Review,* 1972/1, pp. 33–42; I. G. Galakhova, L. M. Vovsi, and N. V. Vyatkina, "Central Apparatus Unit at the '50th Anniversary of the October Revolution' Television Centre," *OIRT Review,* 1972/3, p. 39. There are some photographs in *OIRT Review,* 1971/3, pp. 27–33.

159. V. M. Doganovskai, "Eclairage special des studios de télévision du nouveau telecentre de Moscou," *OIRT Review,* 1968/3, pp. 28–38.

160. V. I. Parkhomenko and A. G. Spirin, "Experience Gained with Practical Operation of KADR Video Tape Recorders at the Soviet Central Television," *OIRT Review,* 1964/2, pp. 28–32; *OIRT Information,* 1964/2, p. 15; V. Parchomenko, "Nouveaux videoscopes soviétiques pour l'enregistrement de signaux de télévision en couleurs et en noir et blanc," *OIRT Review,* 1970/6, pp. 33–36.

161. Govallo and Gruzdev, "Basic Concepts of the Design of the All-Union Television Center in Moscow," *OIRT Review,* 1968/1, p. 29; *London Times,* December 1, 1965; N. I. Tchistaikov, "Evolution of Satellites and Orbits," *Communication in the Space Age: The Use of Satellites by the Mass Media,* pp. 138–146; *Sputnik,* July 19, 1972, pp. 114–115; *Soviet Life,* July 1971, p. 29; *Soviet Life,* October 1972, p. 31; *New York Times,* May 21, 1972, p. 38.

162. *New York Times,* December 13, 1972, p. 6C; *New York Times,* July 12, 1973, p. 4C.

163. *New York Times,* August 21, 1971, p. 40M; I. Petrov, " 'Intersputnik' International Space Communications System and Organization," *Telecommunication Journal,* 39:11 (November 1972), pp. 679–684. This article contains much

technical data along with maps showing the areas of visibility of Molniya satellites in their present elliptical orbits as well as of the projected stationary satellites to be located over the Equator.

164. Kenneth A. Polcyn, "The Joint United States–India Educational Broadcast Satellite Experiment," *Educational Technology*, 12:6 (June 1972), pp. 14–17; Kenneth A. Polcyn, "The Proposed Brazilian Educational Satellite Experiment," *Educational Technology*, 12:7 (July 1972), pp. 2–25; *New York Times*, January 5, 1973, p. 1M; *New York Times*, April 1, 1973, p. 12.

165. *New York Times*, October 16, 1972, p. 7C; AP Radio Wire Dispatch, November 13, 1972; *Variety*, May 2, 1973, p. 50.

166. *New York Times*, August 11, 1972, pp. 1, 4; *New York Times*, October 30, 1972, p. 7C. For the Soviet point of view on the legal aspects of direct broadcasts from satellites, see Yu. M. Kolosov, "Mass Information and International Law," *Sovetskoye gosudarstvo i pravo*, November 1972, pp. 89–95, translated in CDSP, 25:11 (April 11, 1973), pp. 11–12.

167. "Three Important Unsolved Problems," *Ekonomicheskaya Gazeta* (March 8, 1961), p. 3; translated in CDSP, 13:11 (April 12, 1961), pp. 31–32.

168. "From the Baltic to Sakhalin and from Murmansk to Asakabad," *Pravda*, December 2, 1963, p. 6, translated in CDSP, 14:49 (January 2, 1963), p. 22.

169. V. Kalmykov, "The Broad Front of Radioelectronics," *Izvestia*, May 7, 1963, p. 5, translated in CDSP, 15:18 (May 29, 1963), p. 25.

170. V. Kalmykov, "May 7 is Radio Day: Present-day Radioelectronics," *Izvestia*, May 7, 1966, p. 3, translated in CDSP, 18:18 (May 25, 1966), p. 38.

171. See F. Gayle Durham, *Radio and Television in the Soviet Union*, pp. 21–46, for a description of Soviet radio and television receivers as of its publication date of 1966.

172. UNESCO, *World Communications: Press Radio Television Film*, p. 367.

173. *WRTH 1972*, pp. 95–96; *Internationales Handbuch 1971/72*, pp. F205–F206.

174. *Internationales Handbuch 1971/72*, pp. F206–F207.

175. Yu. Gakov, "Herald of the Truth of Communism," *Sovetskaya kultura*, May 6, 1961, p. 1, translated in CDSP, 13:18 (May 31, 1961), p. 26.

176. These figures were supplied by the program director of Soviet television on October 6, 1972.

177. There is an analysis of the published schedules of the two Moscow channels between January 1 and June 30, 1960, in Richard Tuber, "A Survey of Programming on the Central Studios of Television, Moscow, USSR, January—June 1960," *Journal of Broadcasting*, 4:4 (Fall 1960), pp. 315, 323.

178. "On Improving Soviet Radio Broadcasting and on Further Developing Television," *Partiinaya zhizn*, No. 4 (February 1960), pp. 26–34, translated in CDSP, 12:10 (April 4, 1960), p. 18.

179. R. Boretsky, "When There Are Many Channels," *Sovetskaya kultura*, September 11, 1965, pp. 2–3, translated in CDSP, 17:39 (October 20, 1965), pp. 12–14.

180. Georgi Fere, "TV Viewing and Viewers," *Zhurnalist*, No. 4 (April 1967), pp. 38–39, translated in *The Soviet Press in Translation*, 6:1 (Fall 1967), p. 4.

181. "On Improving Soviet Radio Broadcasting and on Further Developing Television," *Partiinaya zhizn*, No. 4 (February 1960), pp. 26–34, translated in CDSP, 12:10 (April 6, 1960), pp. 18–19.

182. *OIRT Information*, 1961/7, p. 11.

183. *OIRT Information*, 1962/6, pp. 12–13.

184. A. Yakovlev, "Television: Problems and Prospects," *Kommunist*, No. 13 (September 1965), pp. 67–81, translated in CDSP, 17:39 (October 20, 1965), pp. 14, 17.

185. "Screen of Millions," *Pravda*, November 21, 1969, p. 1, translated in CDSP, 22:47 (December 22, 1970), p. 31.

186. A. Yurovsky, "On TV Screen, the Journalist Speaks," *Pravda*, December 19, 1969, p. 3, translated in CDSP, 21:51 (January 20, 1970), p. 36.

187. *OIRT Information*, 1963/11, pp. 16–17.

188. N. I. Chistyakov, "The Training of Telecommunication Engineers in the USSR," *Telecommunication Journal*, 37:7 (July 1970), pp. 515–517.

IV. Union of Soviet Socialist Republics: Programs

1. Kaftanov, pp. 225–226.

2. *Ibid.*, pp. 231, 234.

3. Ziglin, p. 71.

4. Kaftanov, p. 236.

5. Yurovskiy and Boretskiy, p. 54.

6. Kaftanov, p. 30.

7. "On Improving Soviet Radio Broadcasting and on Further Developing Television," *Partiinaya zhizn*, No. 4, (February 1960), pp. 26–34, translated in CDSP. 12:10 (April 6, 1960), pp. 18–19.

8. Kaftanov, p. 2.

9. "Mighty Weapon of Our Ideology," *Pravda*, May 7, 1963, p. 2, translated in CDSP, 15:18 (May 29, 1963), p. 23.

10. "Creative Forces for the Fulfillment of the Party's Decisions," *Pravda*, May 7, 1972, p. 2, translated in CDSP, 24:18 (May 31, 1972), p. 21.

11. N. Sakontikov, "The Experience of the Central Television of the USSR in the Field of Political Broadcasts," *OIRT Review*, 1962/6, p. 3.

12. Kaftanov, pp. 3–4.

13. *Ibid.*, p. 52.

14. *Ibid.*, p. 4.

15. "Ukrainian Radio," *OIRT Review*, 1961/5, p. 25.

16. Kaftanov, p. 32.

17. A. Yurovsky, "The Place in the General System: Specific Features of Television Broadcasting," *OIRT Review*, 1964/4, p. 15.

18. M. I. Tsarev, "A Powerful Means of Education," in Kaftanov, p. 28.

19. V. Nesterovitch, "The Way to Human Hearts," *OIRT Review*, 1961/3, p. 100.

20. *The Soviet Press in Translation*, 4:5 (January 1964), p. 2.

21. "Clearer and More Trenchant!" *Pravda*, December 23, 1965, p. 2, translated in CDSP, 17:51 (January 12, 1966), p. 35.

22. "On Improving Soviet Radio Braodcasting and on Further Developing Television," *Partiinaya zhizn*, No. 4 (February 1960), pp. 26–34, translated in CDSP, 12:10 (April 6, 1969), p. 19.

23. Kaftanov, p. 54.

24. *Ibid.*, pp. 48–49.

25. V. Nesterovitch, "The Way to Human Hearts," *OIRT Review*, 1961/3, p. 99.

26. "Music on Television," *OIRT Review*, 1960/1, p. 1.

27. "On Improving Soviet Radio Broadcasting and on Further Developing Television," *Partiinaya zhizn*, No. 4 (February 1960), pp. 26–34, translated in CDSP, (April 6, 1960), p. 18.

28. T. Bohlovskii and Z. L'vov, *Posledniye Izvestia po radio* (*The "Latest News" on Radio*), published by the Scientific-Methodological Department of the State Committee on Radio and Television, USSR, p. 6, translated in F. Gayle Durham, *News Broadcasting on Soviet Radio and Television*, pp. 3–4. Approximately the same thing was said by N. G. Palgunov, the former general-director of the Soviet

news agency TASS, in a lecture at Moscow University in 1954 (*Osnovy informatsii v gazetakh; TASS i yevo rol* (*Principles of Information in the Newspapers; TASS and Its Role*), translated in Buzek, p. 171).

29. Yuri Letunov, "Radio Information," *OIRT Review*, 1968/3, p. 11, hereafter cited as Letunov.

30. "On Improving Soviet Radio Broadcasting and on Further Developing Television," *Partiinaya zhizn*, No. 4 (February 1960), pp. 26–34, translated in CDSP, 12:10 (April 6, 1960), p. 19.

31. Bohlovskii and L'vov, *Posledniye Izvestia po radio* (The "Latest News" on Radio), p. 5, translated in Durham, *News Broadcasting on Soviet Radio and Television*, p. 5.

32. Yurovskiy and Boretskiy, pp. 57–58.

33. "Soviet Television," *Pravda*, August 19, 1965, p. 1, translated in CDSP, 17:33 (September 8, 1965), p. 28.

34. A. Yakovlev, "Television: Problems and Prospects," *Kommunist*, No. 13 (September 1965), translated in CDSP, 17:39 (October 20, 1965), p. 15.

35. A. Yakovlev, I. Chuprynin, and Yu. Orlov, "What Television Lacks: Mighty Means of Propaganda," *Sovetskaya pechat*, No. 6 (1965), translated in *The Soviet Press*, 5:1 (Spring 1966), p. 19.

36. *OIRT Information*, 1962/6, p. 12.

37. Yakovlev, "Television: Problems and Prospects," *Kommunist*, No. 13 (September 1965), translated in CDSP, 17:39 (October 20, 1965), p. 15.

38. S. Golyakov, *Komsomolskaya Pravda*, March 17 and 18, 1966, translated in CDSP, 18:14 (April 27, 1966, p. 34). See also "Slanders on the Airwaves," *Izvestia*, April 14, 1966, p. 2, translated in CDSP, 18:14 (April 27, 1966), pp. 36, 42.

39. Durham, *News Broadcasting on Soviet Radio and Television*, pp. 8–9.

40. "The Publicism of High Ideas," *Sovetskaya pechat*, No. 7 (July 1964), pp. 1–17, translated in CDSP, 16:42 (November 11, 1965), p. 13.

41. UNESCO, *World Communications: Press Radio Television Film*, pp. 365–367; International Organization of Journalists, *Handbook of News Agencies*.

42. Letunov, pp. 1213; Durham, *News Broadcasting on Soviet Radio and Television*, pp. 22–26; A. Cibotaru, "Les Sources d'information de la télévision moldave," *OIRT Review*, 1970/2, pp. 19–20.

43. Much information about television news was received from the "Vremya" producer in October 1970.

44. Waclaw Wygledowski, "IVN—Daily News Exchange on the Intervision Network," *OIRT Review*, 1971/1, pp. 9–10.

45. *EBU Review*, 123A (December 1970), p. 288.

46. "From the Diary of Soviet Radio and Television," in Kaftanov, pp. 217–243, lists a number of landmark news broadcasts between 1917 and 1959.

47. Kaftanov, p. 240; Letunov, pp. 11–12. There are charts and tables listing the news programs between 1963 and 1965 in Moscow, Leningrad, and Kiev in Durham, *News Broadcasting on Soviet Radio and Television*, pp. 11–13, 15–16, and in Gayle Durham Hollander (same author), "Recent Developments in Soviet Radio and Television News Reporting," *Public Opinion Quarterly*, 31:8 (Fall 1967), pp. 363–364.

48. Durham, *News Broadcasting on Soviet Radio and Television*, pp. 32–38; Hollander, "Recent Developments in Soviet Radio and Television News Reporting," *Public Opinion Quarterly*, 31:8 (Fall 1967), pp. 361–364.

49. Kaftanov, pp. 40–41.

50. Letunov, p. 14.

51. For a review of United States reporting by the Soviet printed news media, see

Nancy C. Jones, "U.S. News in the Soviet Press," *Journalism Quarterly*, 43:1 (Spring 1966), pp. 687–696.

52. Translated in FBIS *Daily Report*, No. 6 (January 11, 1971), p. IIIA2.

53. FBIS *Daily Report* (May 14, 1971), pp. Cl ff; FBIS *Daily Report* (June 15, 1971), pp. C1 ff; FBIS *Daily Report* (June 16, 1971), pp. C3 ff; FBIS *Daily Report* (June 17, 1971), pp. C1 ff; FBIS *Daily Report* (June 18, 1971), pp. C1 ff.

54. *New York Times*, June 27, 1971, p. 27.

55. *New York Times*, April 17, 1972.

56. *New York Times*, June 6, 1972, p. 21C.

57. *New York Times*, May 14, 1972, p. 10; *New York Times*, May 17, 1972, p. 15L; AP Radio Wire Report, May 27, 1972; *New York Times*, May 29, 1972, pp. 1, 3. All live pickups of President Nixon's visit relayed to America, incidentally, had to be made by Soviet technicians using Soviet equipment (*Broadcasting*, June 5, 1972, p. 48).

58. *New York Times*, October 29, 1972, p. 51.

59. *New York Times*, September 3, 1972, p. 11; *New York Times*, January 6, 1973, p. 1C; *New York Times*, May 4, 1973, p. 9C; *New York Times*, May 18, 1973, p. 20C; *New York Times*, June 11, 1973, p. 9C; *New York Times*, June 21, 1973, p. 17C; *New York Times*, July 9, 1973, p. 14C.

60. *New York Times*, June 3, 1973, p. 3.

61. *London Times*, September 1, 1962, p. 5; Buzek, pp. 135–137.

62. "Soviet Radio," *OIRT Review*, 1961/5, p. 21.

63. *New York Times*, April 24, 1971, pp. 1, 58.

64. *New York Times*, May 10, 1971, p. 10.

65. FBIS *Daily Report*, No. 111, June 9, 1971, p. 11.

66. *New York Times*, June 30, 1971, pp. 1, 8; *New York Times*, July 1, 1971, pp. 1, 30.

67. *New York Times*, September 12, 1971, p. 1.

68. *London Times*, April 4, 1970, p. 9.

69. *New York Times*, June 4, 1973, p. 18C.

70. *New York Times*, January 10, 1971, p. 21.

71. Markham, p. 197. For a discussion of letters to the press, see Inkeles, *Social Change in Soviet Russia*, pp. 291–296.

72. "Support Principled Criticism in the Press in Every Possible Way," Leningrad *Pravda*, July 16, 1962, p. 2, translated in CDSP, 14:28 (August 8, 1962), p. 28.

73. Lev Lukyanov and George Fere, "Radio Reporter's Seven Sides," *OIRT Review*, 1962/6, p. 15.

74. *The Soviet Press in Translation*, 5:1 (Spring 1966), p. 19.

75. Kendall E. Bailes, *Soviet Television Comes of Age*, p. 2.

76. Alexei Kalinin, "The Politics of Local Television," *Rasprostaneniye pechati*, No. 2 (February 1969), pp. 34–38, translated in *The Soviet Press in Translation*, 7:2 (Spring 1969), p. 24.

77. *New York Times*, October 29, 1972, p. 26.

78. *New York Times*, October 25, 1972, p. 5C.

79. *New York Times*, February 25, 1972, p. 4C.

80. Pavel Gurevich, "Soviet TV and Radio: Foreign News and Audience Reaction," *Zhurnalist* No. 8 (August 1968), pp. 61–62, translated in *The Soviet Press, in Translation*, 7:1 (Fall 1968), pp. 12, 13, 18, 19.

81. "The Publicism of High Ideas," *Sovetskaya pechat*, No. 7 (July 1964), pp. 1–17, translated in CDSP, 16:42 (November 11, 1965), p. 12. The phrases quoted are from the official report of the conference.

82. "Soviet Television," *Pravda*, August 19, 1965, p. 1, translated in CDSP, 17:33 (September 8, 1965), p. 28.

83. A. Yakovlev, "Television: Problems and Prospects," *Kommunist,* No. 13 (September 1965), pp. 67–81, translated in CDSP, 17:39 (October 20, 1965), p. 15.

84. A. Yurovsky, "On TV Screens: The Journalist Speaks," *Pravda,* December 19, 1969, p. 3, translated in CDSP, 21:51 (January 20, 1970), p. 36.

85. N. Ivankovich, "The Leninina of the Television Screen," *OIRT Information,* 1969/4, pp. 12, 13, 14.

86. A. A. Rapokhine, "Le 50e Anniversaire d'Octobre," *OIRT Review,* 1967/5, pp. 3–6; "On Your Television Screens," *Izvestia,* January 19, 1967, p. 6, translated in CDSP, 19:3 (February 8, 1967), pp. 32–33.

87. *OIRT Information,* 1961/8, p. 17.

88. *OIRT Information,* 1962/1, pp. 10–11.

89. Vaido Pant, "25 Years Ago Today," *OIRT Review,* 1969/5, pp. 3–5.

90. *New York Times,* February 1, 1972, p. 2C.

91. M. Kharlamov, "Mighty Weapon of Our Ideology," *Pravda,* May 7, 1963, p. 2, translated in CDSP, 15:18 (May 29, 1963), p. 23.

92. "On Improving Soviet Radio Broadcasting and on Further Developing Television," *Partiinaya zhizn,* No. 4 (February 1960), pp. 26–34, translated in CDSP, 12:10 (April 6, 1960), pp. 18–19.

93. "Clearer and More Trenchant!" *Pravda,* December 23, 1965, p. 2; translated in CDSP, 17:51 (January 12, 1966), p. 35.

94. N. A. Sakontikov, "The Need for Today: To Seek," *OIRT Information,* 1961/12, pp. 9–11.

95. N. Sakontikov, "The Experience of the Central Television of the USSR in the Field of Political Broadcasts," *OIRT Review,* 1962/6, p. 3.

96. Kaftanov, pp. 48–51.

97. *Ibid.,* pp. 127–129.

98. *OIRT Information,* 1962/3, p. 18.

99. N. A. Sakontikov, "The Need of Today: To Seek," *OIRT Information,* 1961/12, p. 3.

100. *OIRT Information,* 1971/8–9, p. 15; *OIRT Information,* 1972/6, p. 9.

101. Yurovskiy and Boretskiy, p. 68.

102. "The Publicism of High Ideas," *Sovetskaya pechat,* No. 7 (July 1964), p. 17; translated in CDSP, 16:42 (November 11, 1964), p. 13.

103. Bailes, *Soviet Television Comes of Age,* p. 4.

104. Alexei Kalinin, "The Politics of Local Television," *Rasprostraneniye pechati,* No. 2 (February 1969), pp. 34–38, translated in *The Soviet Press in Translation,* 7:2 (Spring 1969), p. 25.

105. *New York Times,* February 25, 1972, p. 4C. See above, p. 117.

106. Kaftanov, p. 53.

107. *OIRT Information,* 1961/12, p. 11.

108. E. Mezhov, "Television Criticism in the Soviet Union," *The Listener,* April 16, 1964, p. 631.

109. N. Sakontikov, "The Experience of Central Television of the USSR in the Field of Political Broadcasts," *OIRT Review,* 1962/6, p. 4.

110. Igor Llyinsky, "A Good Comrade," *Izvestia,* February 12, 1960, p. 3, translated in CDSP, 12:6 (March 9, 1960), p. 3.

111. *OIRT Information,* 1961/5, pp. 12–14.

112. *Ibid.*

113. *OIRT Information,* 1962/8, p. 16.

114. *OIRT Information,* 1969/9, p. 14.

115. Z. Erbsteinate, "Problèmes économiques à la télévision," *OIRT Review,* 1972/3, pp. 8–10.

116. *OIRT Information,* 1963/12, pp. 13–14.

117. *OIRT Information*, 1962/1, pp. 12–13.

118. A. Yakovlev, "Television Problems and Prospects," *Kommunist*, No. 13 (September 1965), pp. 67–81, translated in CDSP, 17:39 (October 20, 1965), p. 16.

119. "Educational Broadcasting (Sound and Television) in the Soviet Union," *Telecommunication Journal*, 37:7 (1970), p. 520.

120. John Tebbel, "Inside Soviet Television," *Saturday Review*, January 8, 1972, p. 48.

121. Kaftanov, p. 58.

122. *OIRT Information*, 1961/12, pp. 14–15.

123. Kaftanov, pp. 57–58.

124. *OIRT Information*, 1961/4, p. 21

125. *OIRT Information*, 1971/8–9, p. 15.

126. N. Sakontikov, "The Experience of the Central Television of the USSR in the Field of Political Broadcasts," *OIRT Review*, 1962/6, p. 3.

127. *OIRT Information*, 1961/3, pp. 12–13.

128. Yu. Vasilyev Fyodorov, "Listening to the Radio Gazette," *Pravda*, April 7, 1970, p. 3, translated in CDSP, 22:14 (May 5, 1970), pp. 19–23.

129. *New York Times*, May 27, 1970, p. 2.

130. Kaftanov, p. 71.

131. "On Improving Soviet Radio Broadcasting and on Further Developing Television," *Partiinaya zhizn*, No. 4 (February 1960), pp. 26–34, translated in CDSP, 12:10 (April 6, 1960), p. 20.

132. "Clearer and More Trenchant!" *Pravda*, December 23, 1965, p. 2, translated in CDSP, 17:51 (January 12, 1966), p. 36.

133. A. Menjshikova, "The Radio Broadcasting in the Out-of-School Education of Children," *OIRT Review*, 1965/5, pp. 15–16, hereafter cited as Menjshikova, *OIRT Review*, 1965/5.

134. "Horizon Tells and Shows," *Pravda*, September 14, 1965, p. 4, translated in CDSP, 17:37 (October 6, 1965), p. 42.

135. A. Yakovlev, "Television: Problems and Prospects," *Kommunist*, No. 13 (September 1965), pp. 67–81, translated in CDSP, 17:39 (October 20, 1965), p. 15.

136. I. V. Doubrovitski, "L'Education du jeune citoyen," *OIRT Review*, 1967/2, p. 18.

137. Menjshikova, *OIRT Review*, 1965/5, pp. 16, 18. There is an insightful review of the generation gap in Egypt, Latin America, Turkey, Czechoslovakia, China, Poland, Yugoslavia, Romania, and ancient Greece by C. S. Sulzberger in the *New York Times*, January 5, 1973, p. 29M.

138. Ziglin, p. 68.

139. Menjshikova, *OIRT Review*, 1965/3, p. 16. See also A. Menjshikova, "Travel into the World of Knowledge," *OIRT Review*, 1965/1, p. 14, hereafter cited as Menjshikova, *OIRT Review*, 1965/1; Marina Kartasevs, "La Radiodiffusion au service de la pédagogie," *OIRT Review*, 1969/3, pp. 19–22.

140. Menjshikova, *OIRT Review*, 1965/1, pp. 13–14; "Educational Broadcasting (Sound and Television) in the Soviet Union," Telecommunication Journal, 37:7 (1970), pp. 518–519.

141. Kaftanov, p. 93.

142. Menjshikova, *OIRT Review*, 1965/1, p. 14.

143. "Educational Broadcasting (Sound and Television) in the Soviet Union," *Telecommunication Journal*, 37:7 (1970), p. 519.

144. V. Klyucanski, "School on the Blue Screen," *Pravda*, November 25, 1967, p. 4, translated in CDSP, 19:47 (December 13, 1967), p. 27; conferences with educational television staff in Moscow in October 1972.

145. Aleksiej Gubin, "Television as a Means of Extramural Instruction in the

Ukraine," in UNESCO, *Television and Further Education of Employed*, p. 186, hereafter cited as Gubin.

146. *OIRT Information*, 1961/3, pp. 13–14.

147. Kaftanov, pp. 73–74.

148. Menjshikova, *OIRT Review*, 1965/5, p. 15.

149. Paulu, *British Broadcasting*, pp. 212, 307.

150. *OIRT Information*, 1961/8, p. 18.

151. *OIRT Information*, 1962/9, pp. 13–14.

152. *OIRT Information*, 1962/9, p. 13.

153. Menjshikova, *OIRT Review*, 1965/5, pp. 16–18.

154. *OIRT Information*, 1962/11, p. 12; Kaftanov, p. 95.

155. Menjshikova, *OIRT Review*, 1965/5, p. 17.

156. Kaftanov, pp. 74–75.

157. *OIRT Information*, 1963/5, p. 16.

158. "The Creative Activity of the Directors and Editors of the Programme of the IInd International Festival of Children's Radio Plays," *OIRT Review*, 1970/6, pp. 3–7.

159. Taysa Zhumar, "Radio Plays as a Means of Enabling Children to Learn to Know the Surrounding World," *OIRT Review*, 1971/3, pp. 3–6.

160. *OIRT Information*, 1962/3, pp. 18–19.

161. *OIRT Information*, 1962/8, p. 17.

162. *OIRT Information*, 1963/4, p. 17.

163. Kaftanov, pp. 94–95.

164. "A New Important Theme of the Ukrainian Radio Broadcasts," *OIRT Review*, 1960/1, pp. 9–10; Kaftanov, pp. 71–73.

165. Boris Vovk, "The Club of Sunday Meetings," *OIRT Review*, 1964/5, pp. 7–9.

166. *OIRT Information*, 1963/10, pp. 12–13.

167. *OIRT Information*, 1961/11, p. 17.

168. "Certaines Émissions pour la jeunesse de la télévision soviétique," *OIRT Review*, 1972/4, pp. 14–15.

169. "Educational Broadcasting (Sound and Television) in the Soviet Union," *Telecommunication Journal*, 37:7 (1970), pp. 518–519.

170. L. Leibzon, "Educational Role of Soviet Radio and Television," *Telecommunication Journal*, 37:7 (1970), pp. 521–524.

171. Ziglin, p. 70.

172. Kaftanov, pp. 55–77 *passim*.

173. J. Hansen, "Some Problems of the Presentation of Information on Radio," *OIRT Review*, 1971/2, pp. 17–19.

174. Kaftanov, p. 131.

175. N. Kartsov, "New Aspects in the Artistic Broadcasts of the Soviet Radio," *OIRT Review*, 1960/5, p. 193.

176. "Radio Cultural University," *OIRT Review*, 1962/1, pp. 5–7.

177. "Dissemination of Scientific Knowledge by Television," *OIRT Review*, 1961/2, pp. 71–73.

178. "Educational Broadcasting (Sound and Television) in the Soviet Union," *Telecommunication Journal*, 37:7 (1970), p. 520.

179. *OIRT Information*, 1962/11, p. 15.

180. Material for this section was taken in part from V. Klyuchansky, "School on the Blue Screen," *Pravda*, November 25, 1967, p. 3, translated in CDSP, 19:47 (December 13, 1967), p. 27, hereafter cited as Klyuchansky, "School on the Blue Screen." Reference also was made to both published and unpublished documents prepared by Soviet broadcasting authorities for the European Meeting of Experts on the Use of Television Broadcasting for Further Education of the Employed, Par-

ticularly at the University Level, held in Warsaw, September 9–16, 1968. These include three papers published in the UNESCO volume *Television and Further Education of Employed*: Vladimir Y. Kluchansky, "Television as a Teaching Aid," pp. 88–99, hereafter cited as Kluchansky, "Television as a Teaching Aid"; Gubin, pp. 186–190; and Borys Markov, "Television as a Means of Extramural Tuition," pp. 191–194, hereafter cited as Markov. ("V. Klyuchansky" and "Vladimir Y. Kluchansky" are the same person, although his name is transliterated differently in the references cited above.)

181. Gubin, pp. 187–188.

182. Markov, p. 191.

183. Kluchansky, "Television as a Teaching Aid," p. 94.

184. *Ibid.*, p. 98; Klyuchansky, "School on the Blue Screen," p. 27.

185. "Educational Broadcasting (Sound Television) in the Soviet Union," *Telecommunication Journal*, 37:7 (1970), p. 519.

186. Kluchansky, "Television as a Teaching Aid," p. 90.

187. Klyuchansky, "School on the Blue Screen," p. 27.

188. Markov, p. 192.

189. Kluchansky, "Television as a Teaching Aid," p. 93.

190. Markov, p. 192.

191. *Ibid.*, p. 193.

192. Klyuchansky, "School on the Blue Screen," p. 27.

193. Kluchansky, "Television as a Teaching Aid," pp. 96–97.

194. Markov, p. 193.

195. Kluchansky, "Television as a Teaching Aid," p. 98.

196. Markov, pp. 192–193.

197. Kluchansky, "Television as a Teaching Aid," pp. 92, 97.

198. Markov, p. 194.

199. "Music on Television (Experience of the Moscow Television Studio)," *OIRT Review*, 1960/1, pp. 1–2.

200. *OIRT Information*, 1963/1, p. 10.

201. A. Yakovlev, "Television: Problems and Prospects," *Kommunist*, No. 13 (September 1965), pp. 67–81, translated in CDSP, 17:39 (October 20, 1965), p. 16.

202. L. Leibzon, "Educational Role of Soviet Radio and Television," *Telecommunication Journal*, 37:7 (July 1970), p. 521.

203. Kaftanov, pp. 84–85.

204. *Ibid.*, pp. 36–37.

205. "The Education of Musical Tastes of Radio Listeners (from the Experience of the Soviet Radio)," *OIRT Review*, 1961/1, p. 11; I. Nestyev, "Music on the Radio," *Izvestia*, August 5, 1962, p. 2, translated in CDSP, 14:32 (September 5, 1962), p. 30; A. Zvorykin, *Cultural Policy in the Union of Soviet Socialist Republics*, p. 42.

206. "False Note," *Izvestia*, January 20, 1965, p. 4, translated in CDSP, 17:29 (August 11, 1965), p. 38.

207. Material supplied by broadcasting authorities, 1965.

208. I. Nestyev, "Music on the Radio," *Izvestia*, August 5, 1962, p. 2, translated in CDSP, 14:32 (September 5, 1962), p. 30.

209. *OIRT Information*, 1963/1, p. 13.

210. "Music on Television (Experience of the Moscow Television Studio)," *OIRT Review*, 1960/1, p. 1.

211. Examples are given in Kaftanov, pp. 84–91 *passim*.

212. Kaftanov, p. 88

213. V. A. Ratchkovskaia, "Le Travail de la rédaction musicale de la radio soviétique," *OIRT Review*, 1969/6, p. 16.

214. *OIRT Information*, 1962/1, p. 15–16.

215. Kaftanov, p. 132.
216. *Ibid.*, p. 85.
217. *OIRT Information*, 1961/8, p. 16.
218. *OIRT Information*, 1961/12, p. 15.
219. V. A. Ratchkovskaia, "Le Travail de la rédaction musicale de la radio soviétique," *OIRT Review*, 1969/6, p. 15.
220. V. S. Ostrovsky and I. D. Simonov, "Development of New Electromusical Instruments in the USSR," *OIRT Review*, 1963/6, pp. 29–33.
221. A. A. Zvorykin, *Cultural Policy in the Union of Soviet Socialist Republics*, p. 43, hereafter cited as Zvorykin.
222. "The Education of Musical Tastes of Radio Listeners (from the Experience of the Soviet Radio)," *OIRT Review*, 1961/1, pp. 11–13; "A propos des émissions musicales éducatives du point de vue de la propagande de la grande musique à la radio," *OIRT Review*, 1967/6, pp. 15–18.
223. "A propos des émissions musicales éducatives du point de vue de la propagande de la grande musique à la radio," *OIRT Review*, 1967/6, p. 17.
224. Kaftanov, p. 132.
225. *OIRT Information*, 1963/1, p. 10.
226. *OIRT Information*, 1962/2, p. 14.
227. *OIRT Information*, 1970/8, p. 10.
228. "Music on Television (Experience of the Moscow TV Studio)," *OIRT Review*, 1960/1, p. 4.
229. Kaftanov, pp. 86–87.
230. *OIRT Information*, 1963/1, p. 10.
231. *OIRT Information*, 1961/6, p. 21.
232. *OIRT Information*, 1962/1, p. 15.
233. Kazia Pouras, "Le Folklore sur les ondes," *OIRT Review*, 1971/6, pp. 3–7.
234. Kaftanov, p. 91.
235. Zvorykin, p. 42.
236. *OIRT Information*, 1969/9, pp. 17–18; *OIRT Information*, 1970/8, p. 10; *OIRT Information*, 1972/1, p. 10.
237. *The Soviet Press in Translation*, 4:5 (January 1964), p. 2.
238. V. Merkulov, "Some Ideas Regarding Intervision Musical Broadcasts," *OIRT Review*, 1964/2, pp. 21–22.
239. Kaftanov, p. 88.
240. V. Merkulov, "Some Ideas Regarding Intervision Musical Broadcasts," *OIRT Review*, 1964/2, p. 21.
241. *OIRT Information*, 1963/4, p. 16.
242. *OIRT Information*, 1963/10, pp. 7–8.
243. *Ibid.*, p. 8.
244. Kaftanov, p. 91.
245. "The Education of Musical Tastes of Radio Listeners (from the Experience of the Soviet Radio)," *OIRT Review*, 1961/1, p. 12.
246. Y. Gakov, "Tomorrow is Radio Day: Herald of the Truth of Communism," *Sovetskaya kultura*, May 6, 1961, translated in CDSP, 13:18 (May 31, 1961), p. 26.
247. "For Debate, Against Attacks," *Izvestia*, March 18, 1965, p. 4, translated in CDSP, 17:11 (April 17, 1965), p. 37.
248. "False Note," *Izvestia*, July 20, 1965, p. 4; translated in CDSP, 17:29 (August 11, 1965), p. 38.
249. Innokenty Popov, "Spots on the Musical Sun," *Ogonyok*, No. 40 (September 1968), pp. 25–27, translated in *Current Abstracts of the Soviet Press*, 1:7 (December 1968), p. 15.
250. *Ibid.*, p. 28; translated, p. 18.
251. Kaftanov, p. 35.

252. UNESCO, *World Communications: Press Radio Television Film*, pp. 367–368.

253. Richard Tuber, "A Survey of Programming on the Central Studios of Television, Moscow, USSR, January–June 1960," *Journal of Broadcasting*, 4:4 (Fall 1960), p. 323.

254. Victor Slavkin, "Television: 7% Fun," *Sovetskaya kultura*, September 9, 1965, translated in CDSP, 17:39 (October 20, 1965), p. 11.

255. Data from Soviet broadcasting authorities.

256. Ziglin, p. 67.

257. Kaftanov, pp. 77–78.

258. *Ibid.*, pp. 80–81.

259. *Ibid.*, pp. 78–79.

260. *OIRT Information*, 1971/10, pp. 9–10.

261. Irina Bogatko, "Television in the USSR," p. 5, hereafter cited as Bogatko.

262. Kaftanov, p. 78.

263. A. Zolevsky, "La Poésie sur les ondes de la radio bielorusse," *OIRT Review*, 1969/4, p. 21.

264. *OIRT Information*, 1961/5, p. 14.

265. Ziglin, p. 67; Kaftanov, p. 82.

266. Janina Babiliute, "Le Développement du théâtre radiophonique à la radio lithuanienne," *OIRT Review*, 1970/3, p. 9.

267. *OIRT Information*, 1972/1, p. 10. For a discussion of the importance of maintaining radio drama as an independent medium, see "Qu'est-ce que l'art radiophonique?" *OIRT Review*, 1971/1, pp. 6–10

268. Yurovskiy and Boretskiy, pp. 44–48.

269. *Ibid.*, pp. 62–63.

270. Radoslav Alexandrovich, "Problems of Television Plays," *OIRT Review*, 1969/5, pp. 10–13.

271. L. Tarasov, "Light and Shadow," *OIRT Review* 1963/4, pp. 12–14.

272. Yurovskiy and Boretskiy, pp. 46, 63; Serge Kuznetsov, "Films in the Moscow Television," *OIRT Review* 1964/3, p. 7–8; Bogakto, p. 4.

273. Yurovskiy and Boretskiy, p. 63; Kuznetsov, "Films in the Moscow Television," p. 7.

274. Yurovskiy and Boretskiy, p. 67; A. Yakovlev, "Television: Problems and Prospects," *Kommunist*, No. 13 (September 1965), pp. 67–81, translated in *CDSP*, 17:39 (October 20, 1965), p. 16.

275. *OIRT Information*, 1972/1, p. 12.

276. *OIRT Information*, 1972/1, p. 11.

277. *Variety*, April 8, 1970, p. 94.

278. *Variety*, June 3, 1970, p. 27.

279. AP Radio Wire Dispatch, June 11, 1972.

280. Bogatko, p. 9.

281. *Variety*, April 8, 1970, p. 94.

282. Bogatko, p. 9; *Variety*, July 1, 1970, p. 27; *New York Times*, July 9, 1971, p. 51M.

283. *Variety*, February 18, 1970, p. 34; *New York Times*, June 25, 1973; p. 18M; *Broadcasting*, April 26, 1971, p. 7.

284. "Music on Television (Experience of the Moscow Television Studio)," *OIRT Review*, 1960/1, p. 3.

285. Yurovskiy and Boretskiy, pp. 58–59.

286. Kaftanov, p. 70.

287. Victor Slavkin, *Sovetskaya kultura*, September 9, 1965, p. 3, translated in CDSP, 17:39 (October 20, 1965), pp. 11–12.

288. *New York Times*, May 31, 1972, p. 71M.

289. This description paraphrases and quotes from a feature article by Frank Crepeau in an AP radio dispatch of March 11, 1972.
290. *Nagel's USSR Travel Guide*, p. 187; Maxwell, ed., *Information U.S.S.R.*, p. 404.
291. Kaftanov, p. 47.
292. Yurovskiy and Boretskiy, p. 47; *OIRT Information*, 1963/5, p. 17; Bogatko, p. 6.
293. N. A. Skatchko, "Five Years," *OIRT Review*, 1965/2, p. 4.

V. Union of Soviet Socialist Republics: Other Services

1. Hopkins, p. 326.
2. *United Nations Statistical Yearbook 1971.*
3. Milan Cesky, "Central Antenna Arrays," *OIRT Review*, 1962/5, pp. 39–40.
4. "Letters from Radio Listeners," in Kaftanov, pp. 105–108.
5. Kaftanov, pp. 105, 107; *OIRT Information*, 1965/12; Soviet broadcasting authorities.
6. I. L. Ivanova, "L'Utilisation des lettres d'auditeurs dans les programmes de la rédaction principale des émissions musicales de Radio Moscow," *OIRT Review*, 1972/4, pp. 2–22.
7. Hopkins, p. 262.
8. *Ibid.*, p. 326. For a report on the USSR radio audience in the 1940s, see Inkeles, pp. 274–286. Durham, *Radio and Television in the Soviet Union*, pp. 74–86, provides some data on audiences in the early 1960s.
9. Zvorykin, p. 41.
10. Bailes, *Soviet Television Comes of Age*, p. 3.
11. Boris Firsov, *There Is No "Average" Viewer*. Translated from *Zhurnalist*, No. 12, December 1967. For a summary of USSR audience studies covering some of the sources cited here and others, see Gayle Durham Hollander, *Soviet Political Indoctrination: Developments in Mass Media and Propaganda since Stalin*, pp. 108–125.
12. A. Baskina, "Learn How to Spend Leisure Time," *Izvestia*, May 26, 1973, p. 5, translated in CDSP, 25:21 (June 20, 1973), p. 23.
13. George Fere, "TV Viewing and Viewers," *Zhurnalist*, No. 4 (April 1967), pp. 38–39, translated in *The Soviet Press*, 6:1 (Fall 1967), pp. 1–7.
14. G. Kuznetsov, "Television, My Friend, My Enemy," *Trud*, November 14, 1971, p. 3, translated in CDSP, 23:49 (January 4, 1972), p. 30.
15. Pavel Gurevich, "Soviet TV and Radio: Foreign News and Audience Reaction," *Zhurnalist*, No. 7 (July 1967), pp. 47–48, translated in *The Soviet Press*, 7:1 (Fall 1968), pp. 11–19.
16. Yuri Letunov, "Radio Information," *OIRT Review*, 1968/3, p. 13.
17. Igor Ilyinsky, "Attention! Listen, Radio Workers! A Good Comrade," *Izvestia*, February 12, 1960, p. 3, translated in CDSP, 12:6 (March 9, 1960), pp. 33–34.
18. "Workers! Tuning In from 7 to 10 P.M. Helps Us to Relax," *Izvestia*, February 12, 1960, p. 3, translated in CDSP, 12:6 (March 9, 1960), p. 34.
19. "On Improving Soviet Radio Braodcasting and on Further Developing Television," *Partiinaya zhizn*, No. 4 (February 1960), pp. 27–34, translated in CDSP, 12:10 (April 6, 1960), pp. 18–21.
20. "On Measures for the Further Improvement of the Work of Radio Broadcasting and Television," translated in *The Soviet Press in Translation*, 4:5 (January 1964); "The Publicism of High Ideas," *Sovetskaya pechat*, No. 7 (July 1964), translated in CDSP, 16:42 (November 11, 1964), pp. 11–16.

21. R. Boretsky, *Sovetskaya kultura*, September 11, 1965, translated in CDSP, 17:39 (October 20, 1965), pp. 12–16.

22. Article in *Molodaia Gvardiia*, cited in Bailes, *Soviet Television Comes of Age*, p. 1.

23. "The Voice of Local Radio," *Pravda*, October 28, 1970, p. 1, translated in CDSP, 22:43 (November 24, 1970), pp. 24, 32.

24. "What Has Been Done Since *Pravda* Spoke?" *Pravda*, January 15, 1971, p. 3, translated in CDSP 23:2 (February 9, 1971, p. 28.

25. Theodore E. Kruglak, in *The Two Faces of TASS*, argues that TASS combines the roles of journalist, propagandist, and spy. Frederick C. Barghoorn, *Soviet Foreign Propaganda*; L. John Martin, *International Propaganda: Its Legal and Diplomatic Control*, pp. 46–54, hereafter cited as Martin. For a good overview of international broadcasting today, see Francis S. Ronalds, Jr., "The Future of International Broadcasting," *The Annals of the American Academy of Political and Social Science*, November 1971, pp. 71–80. For a discussion of some of these issues see Don R. Browne, "The Limits of the Limitless Medium—International Broadcasting," *Journalism Quarterly*, 42:1 (Winter 1965), pp. 82–86, 164.

26. "The Publicism of High Ideas," *Sovetskaya pechat*, No. 7 (July 1964), pp. 1–17, translated in CDSP, 16:42 (November 11, 1964), p. 13.

27. Hopkins, p. 294.

28. Martin, p. 48; *Soviet Life*, October 1971, p. 53.

29. Charles A. Siepmann, "Propaganda and Information in International Affairs," *Yale Law Journal*, 55:5 (August 1946), p. 1266.

30. A. Yakovlev, "Television: Problems and Prospects," *Kommunist*, No. 13 (September 1965), pp. 67–81, translated in CDSP, 17:39 (October 20, 1965), p. 17.

31. *London Times*, January 30, 1969, p. 4. For another statement of the Soviet view, see Yu. M. Kolosov, "Mass Information and International Law," *Sovetskoye gosudarstvo i pravo*, November 1972, pp. 89–95, translated in CDSP, 25:11 (April 11, 1973), pp. 9–12.

32. John B. Whitton and John H. Herz, "Radio in International Politics," in Harwood L. Childs and John B. Whitton, eds., *Propaganda by Short-Wave*, pp. 3–4; Will Irwin, *Propaganda and the News, or What Makes You Think So?* pp. 129–132. Radio telegraphy, rather than voice broadcasting, was used in these early transmissions.

33. Kaftanov, pp. 217–220.

34. Victor Kuprianov, "Supplement from Moscow," *Journal of Broadcasting*, 4:4 (Fall 1960), pp. 336–338; Kaftanov, p. 100.

35. Arno Huth, *Radio Today: The Present State of Broadcasting in the World*, p. 200.

36. Paulu, *British Broadcasting*, pp. 383–389; Asa Briggs, *The War of Words*, pp. 81–82, 176–187.

37. Paulu, *Factors in the Attempts to Establish a Permanent Instrumentality for the Administration of the International Broadcasting Services of the United States*, pp. 13–22.

38. Martin, pp. 10–12.

39. *United States Code Annotated: Title 22, Foreign Relations and Intercourse, Sections 1432–End*, p. 393, Ch. 18.

40. United States Information Agency, *34th Semiannual Report to Congress*, January–June 1970, p. 13.

41. Kaftanov, p. 101.

42. *The Soviet Press in Translation*, 4:5 (January 1964), pp. 2, 4, 6–7.

43. *BBC Handbook 1970*, pp. 98–99.

44. *WRTH 1971*, pp. 98–100.

45. Kaftanov, p. 100; Zvorykin, p. 42.

46. *BBC Handbook 1973*, p. 103; "Creative Forces for the Fulfilment of the Party's Decision," *Pravda*, May 7, 1972, p. 2, translated in CDSP, 24:18 (May 31, 1972), p. 21.

47. *BBC Handbook 1973*, p. 105; United States Information Agency, *34th Semiannual Report to the Congress*, January–June 1970, p. 13.

48. *WRTH 1973*, pp. 103–104; James Kritchlow, "Broadcasting in the Uzbek SSR," *Central Asian Review*, 15:3 (Winter 1967), p. 261.

49. *WRTH 1971*, pp. 100–102; *WRTH 1973*, p. 64.

50. *WRTH 1973*, pp. 104–105; Hopkins, p. 262.

51. *London Times*, August 5, 1967, p. 4.

52. Material supplied by Soviet broadcasting authorities.

53. Information secured in conferences during several visits to the USSR, as well as from William S. Howell, "The North American Service of Radio Moscow," *Quarterly Journal of Speech*, 46:3 (Winter 1960), pp. 262–269; William S. Howell, "Program Production at Radio Moscow," *Journal of Broadcasting*, 4:4 (Fall 1960), pp. 336–338.

54. Comments on North American Service announcers in 1958 can be found in William S. Howell and E. W. Ziebarth, "The Soviet Airwaves," in Robert T. Holt and John E. Turner, eds., *Soviet Union: Paradox and Change*, pp. 198–200; William S. Howell, "Program Production at Radio Moscow," *Journal of Broadcasting*, 4:4 (Fall 1960), pp. 331–333.

55. Kaftanov, pp. 187–193; material provided by Soviet broadcasting authorities.

56. *New York Times*, June 1, 1973, p. 62M.

57. OIRT, *Catalogue of Transmissions Suitable for Exchange*, 1967/3, pp. 16–20; 1967/4, pp. 19–22.

58. *BBC Handbook 1973*, p. 122.

59. Information supplied by Radio Liberty.

60. April 27, 1966, pp. 1, 28.

61. *New York Times*, January 24, 1971, pp. 1, 18.

62. *New York Times*, July 12, 1971, p. 3C.

63. S. Golyakov, "An Alliance of Dirty Hands," *Komsomolskaya pravda*, March 17 and 18, 1966, p. 3, translated in CDSP, 18:14 (April 27, 1966), pp. 34–36.

64. *Variety*, July 1, 1970, p. 1.

65. *New York Times*, May 4, 1968, p. 8; *New York Times*, July 14, 1968, p. 11.

66. AP radio wire report, January 5, 1973.

67. "Measuring 'Imperialist Propaganda': Three Soviet Views," *USIA Communicator*, January 1973, pp. 14–16.

68. Alex Inkeles, "The Soviet Attack on the Voice of America: A Case Study in Propaganda Warfare," *American Slavic and East European Review,* Vol. 12 (1953), pp. 319–320. This article also is available in Inkeles, *Social Change in Soviet Russia*, pp. 356–379.

69. Radio Liberty Committee, *Annual Report 1972*, p. 16.

70. Codding, *Broadcasting without Barriers*, p. 74.

71. United States Information Agency, *33rd Semiannual Report to the Congress*, July–December 1969, p. 3.

72. Information supplied by Radio Free Europe.

73. Letter to the Editor by Kenneth R. Giddens, director, Voice of America, *Variety*, January 27, 1971, p. 38.

74. *London Times*, November 24, 1970, p. 8.

75. Martin, p. 85; *New York Times*, September 13, 1973, p. 16C.

76. United Nations General Assembly, *Official Records: Fifth Session*, 325 Plenary Meeting, December 14, 1950, pp. 666–667.

77. Delbert D. Smith, *International Telecommunication Control*, p. 9.

78. League of Nations, *Treaty Series*, 4301–4327, 186:303–317 (1938); United Nations, General Assembly Resolution 841 (IX), December 17, 1954.

79. M. Kharlamov, "Mighty Weapon of Our Ideology," *Pravda*, May 7, 1963, translated in CDSP, 15:18 (May 29, 1963), p. 24.

80. *The Soviet Press in Translation*, 4:5 (January 1964), p. 1.

81. *BBC Handbook 1971*, p. 103.

82. Don D. Smith, "Radio Moscow's North American Broadcasts: An Exploratory Study," *Journalism Quarterly*, 42:4 (Fall 1965), pp. 643–645.

VI. German Democratic Republic

1. *Europa Year Book 1972*, Vol. 1, pp. 730, 785.

2. *Europa Year Book 1972*, Vol. 1, pp. 783–784, 788, 790.

3. Melvin Croan, "East Germany," in Adam Bromke and Teresa Rakowska-Harmstone, eds., *The Communist States in Disarray 1965–1971*, pp. 73–94.

4. *New York Times*, November 19, 1972.

5. *Europa Year Book 1972*, Vol. 1, pp. 790–791.

6. *Ibid.*, p. 792; *Constitution of the German Democratic Republic*, p. 10, hereafter cited as *GDR Constitution*.

7. *GDR Constitution*, Art. 1.

8. Office of the U.S. High Commissioner for Germany, *Soviet Zone Constitution and Electoral Law*, p. 9.

9. *Europa Year Book 1972*, Vol. 1, pp. 794, 796.

10. *Internationales Handbuch 1971/72*, pp. C18–19, 143, 148. An earlier organization is described in Hans Brach, *German Radio and Television: Organization and Economic Basis*, pp. 28–29.

11. *New York Times*, December 2, 1971, p. 21C; *New York Times*, May 1, 1972, p. 6C; *New York Times*, August 3, 1972, p. 20C; *Variety*, September 27, 1972, p. 50.

12. Erich Richter, "The History of the German Democratic Radio," *OIRT Review*, 1965/5, pp. 24–25. There is a review from the Western viewpoint of the development of East German radio from 1945 until 1961 in Gerhard Walther, *Der Rundfunk in der sowjetischen Besatzungszone Deutschlands*.

13. *London Times*, March 22, 1968, p. 12; *New York Times*, March 22, 1968, p. 47.

14. Wolfgang Kleinert, "Organizational Role of Broadcasting," *OIRT Information*, 1960/4, p. 148.

15. Interview with Hermann Ley, chairman of the German Democratic State Radio Committee, *OIRT Information*, 1960/6, p. 253.

16. *OIRT Information*, 1969/9, p. 8.

17. *WRTH 1973*, p. 62.

18. G. Steinke, "Experience with Stereo Recording and Experimental Public Transmissions of Broadcast Programmes in the German Democratic Republic," *OIRT Review*, 1965/5, p. 26; *OIRT Information*, 1965/3, pp. 2–3; *Internationales Handbuch 1971/72*, p. 176E.

19. *OIRT Information*, 1970/8, pp. 8–9.

20. *OIRT Information*, 1964/8, p. 10; Manfred Klein, "The Role of the Second Programme of the German Democratic Republic Radio," *OIRT Review*, 1964/4, p. 18.

21. Ursula Meining, "The Dresden VHF Transmitter—A Regional Programme of the GDR Radio," *OIRT Review*, 1967/4, p. 19.

22. Deutscher Demokratischer Rundfunk, *Informationen*, p. 7, hereafter cited as Rundfunk, *Informationen*; *WRTH 1973*, p. 62.

23. *Internationales Handbuch 1971/72*, pp. C151–152.

24. Helmut Gralow, "Désirés par l'auditeur, offerts par la radio: les Services sur les ondes," *OIRT Review*, 1971/3, pp. 19–23.

25. Deutscher Fernsehfunk, *Information on Television in the GDR* (n.p.), cited hereafter as Fernsehfunk, *Information*; *WRTH 1973*, p. 276; *Internationales Handbuch 1971/72*, pp. C148–151; Klaus Roscher, "Television and VHF-FM Broadcasting Tower of the German Post in Berlin, Capital of the German Democratic Republic," *OIRT Review*, 1976/2, pp. 29–35.

26. German Democratic Republic, *Statistisches Jahrbuch 1971*, p. 391.

27. Dieter Schmotz, "Some Experience Concerning the Development of Colour Television in the German Democratic Republic," *OIRT Review*, 1970/5, pp. 3–7.

28. Erich Richter, "The History of the German Democratic Radio," *OIRT Review*, 1965/5, p. 25.

29. Willy Walther, "Ways to Radio Journalism," *OIRT Review*, 1967/5, p. 28.

30. Wolfgang Grosse, "Zur Montage von Rundfunknachrichten (II/Schluss)," *Rundfunkjournalistik in Theorie and Praxis*, 1969/6, pp. 14, 15, 18.

31. *OIRT Information*, 1970/8, pp. 8–9.

32. Siegbert Gedlich, "Repetition of Radio News," *OIRT Review*, 1969/1, pp. 16–17.

33. Wolfgang Grosse, "Zur Montage von Rundfunknachrichten (I)," *Rundfunkjournalistik in Theorie and Praxis*, 1969/5, pp. 13, 15.

34. International Organization of Journalists, *Hand Book of News Agencies*; UNESCO, *World Communications: Press Radio Television Film*, pp. 290–291.

35. *OIRT Information*, 1966/5, p. 7. For the translated text of a von Schnitzler commentary, see FBIS *Daily Report*, December 20, 1971, No. 244, pp. E1–E2.

36. *New York Times*, December 2, 1971, p. 21C.

37. FBIS *Daily Report*, August 14, 1972, No. 158, pp. E1–E2.

38. *OIRT Information*, 1964/5, p. 10; Manfred Klein, "The Broadcast Called 'Frankly,' " *OIRT Review*, 1965/1, pp. 8–9.

39. *OIRT Information*, 1972/4–5, p. 3.

40. *OIRT Information*, 1966/5, p. 2; *OIRT Information*, 1963/4, p. 7; *OIRT Information*, 1963/5, p. 8.

41. *Europa Year Book 1972*, Vol. 1, p. 784.

42. Inge Kalisch, "The Television Screen—Our Educational Medium (Pedagogical Tasks of Television for Children)," *OIRT Review*, 1960/1, pp. 12–14.

43. Ernst Heinze, "Methods of Pre-School Education in Radio GDR (German Democratic Republic)," *OIRT Review*, 1966/2, p. 7.

44. Johny Marhold, "Topical Questions of Broadcasts for Young People and the DT-64 Youth Studio," *OIRT Review*, 1967/6, p. 6.

45. S. Böhme, "Socialistic Programmes for Children on DR Television," *OIRT Review*, 1960/2, pp. 50–51.

46. *OIRT Information*, 1967/7, p. 10.

47. *OIRT Information*, 1968/11, p. 3; *OIRT Information*, 1968/12, p. 3.

48. *OIRT Information*, 1969/9, pp. 5–6.

49. Günther Hoppe, "La 'Radiovision'—un pas vers la radiodiffusion éducative," *OIRT Review*, 1971/5, pp. 9–11.

50. Ernst Heinze, "Methods of Pre-School Education in Radio GDR (German Democratic Republic)," *OIRT Review*, 1966/2, pp. 8–9.

51. Fernsehfunk, *Information*; Inge Kalisch, "The Television Screen—Our Educational Medium (Pedagogical Tasks of Television for Children)," *OIRT Review*, 1960/1, pp. 12–14. Much the same thing is said in S. Böhme, "Socialistic Programmes for Children on German DR Television," *OIRT Review*, 1960/2, pp. 50–56.

52. *OIRT Information*, 1966/2, p. 9.

53. Inge Kalisch, "The Television Screen—Our Educational Medium (Pedagogical Tasks of Television for Children)," *OIRT Review*, 1960/1, pp. 13–14.

54. "The New Structure of the Television Programmes for Children and Youth," *OIRT Information*, 1969/8, pp. 3–4.

55. *OIRT Information*, 1963/8, p. 5.

56. Brigitte Deckwerth, "Broadcasts for Children of the Berlin Radio," *OIRT Review*, 1966/1, pp. 5–6.

57. S. Böhme, "Socialistic Programmes for Children on German GDR Television," *OIRT Review*, 1960/2, p. 53.

58. *OIRT Information*, 1963/5, p. 12; *OIRT Information*, 1966/4, pp. 8–9; *OIRT Information*, 1968/2, p. 5; *OIRT Information*, 1970/6, pp. 7–8.

59. Johny Marhold, "Topical Questions of Broadcasts for Young People and the DT-64 U Studio," *OIRT Review*, 1967/6, pp. 6–7.

60. *OIRT Information*, 1965/8, pp. 6–7.

61. *OIRT Information*, 1961/3, pp. 6–7.

62. "Information about the Educational Broadcasts Provided Especially for Instructional Purposes of Further Education of Adults," *Television and Further Education of Employed*, pp. 168–170, hereafter cited as *Television and Further Education*.

63. *Television and Further Education*, pp. 170–172; *OIRT Information* 1963/3, p. 307.

64. *OIRT Information*, 1966/12, p. 11; *OIRT Information*, 1968/2, pp. 9–10.

65. *Television and Further Education*, pp. 172–173; Jürgen Heinecke, Cours de langues—quelques expériences acquises par la télévision en RDA," *OIRT Review*, 1971/5, pp. 3–8.

66. *OIRT Information*, 1963/4, pp. 6–8; *OIRT Information*, 1966/5, p. 9.

67. *OIRT Information*, 1963/6, pp. 13–14.

68. *OIRT Information*, 1965/4, p. 14; *OIRT Information*, 1967/11, p. 8; *OIRT Information*, 1966/6, p. 11.

69. Rolf Schmidt, "The Work of the Department of Economic Broadcasts of the German Democratic Radio," *OIRT Review*, 1964/3, pp. 16–17; *OIRT Information*, 1966/4, p. 7; *OIRT Information*, 1967/7, p. 10.

70. *OIRT Information*, 1962/3, p. 10.

71. *OIRT Information*, 1962/10, pp. 5–6; *OIRT Information*, 1963/3, p. 4.

72. "Educational Programmes of the Television of the German Democratic Republic," *OIRT Review*, 1968/2, pp. 23–24; *OIRT Information*, 1963/5, p. 10.

73. *OIRT Information*, 1966/7, p. 8; "Educational Programs of the Television of the German Democratic Republic, *OIRT Review*, 1968/2, p. 21; Willy Walther, "The 'Hour of Pedagogic Consultation' in the GDR Radio," *OIRT Review*, 1972/6, pp. 10–12.

74. *OIRT Information*, 1966/2, p. 8; *OIRT Information*, 1964/10, p. 2; *OIRT Information*, 1966/11, p. 9; *OIRT Information*, 1967/7, pp. 10–11.

75. *Hochschule für Film and Fernsehen der DDR, Informationsblatt: Film- und Fernsehausbildung*; *OIRT Information*, 1970/1, pp. 6–7; *OIRT Information*, 1970/9, p. 13.

76. *OIRT Information*, 1966/4, pp. 5–6.

77. *OIRT Information*, 1970/8, p. 9; *OIRT Information*, 1968/2, p. 10.

78. Horst Angermüller, "The Radio Play in the German Democratic Republic," *OIRT Review*, 1965/4, pp. 12–15.

79. Manfred Engelhardt, "1969 and the German Democratic Radio Plays," *OIRT Review*, 1970/4, pp. 4–5.

80. *OIRT Information*, 1971/3, pp. 7–8.

81. Werner Fehlig, "Development of Dramatic Art in the Television of the German Democratic Republic," *OIRT Review*, 1962/2, pp. 17–19.

82. Rundfunk, *Informationen,* p. 20. East German playwrights featured on GD Radio programs include Günter Rüchker, W. K. Schweickert, Rolf Schneider, Gerhard Rentzsch, Peter Hacks, Bernhard Seeger, Heiner Müller, and Manfred Bieler. There are frequent references to dramatic presentations in the *OIRT Information* brochures: 1966/4, p. 8; 1966/5, p. 3; 1966/9, p. 15; 1967/7, p. 12; 1968/7, p. 4; 1969/11, pp. 1–2.

83. *OIRT Information,* 1971/4–5, p. 10.

84. Gerhard Puls, "Feature in the German Democratic Radio," *OIRT Review,* 1969/4, p. 4; Gerhard Puls, "Feature in the German Democratic Radio: The Possibilities and Necessities of the Genre," *OIRT Review,* 1970/1, pp. 9–10.

85. *OIRT Information,* 1968/2, p. 10.

86. *OIRT Information,* 1969/7, pp. 7–8.

87. *OIRT Information,* 1963/7, p. 9.

88. Manfred Egelhardt, "1969 and the German Democratic Radio Play," *OIRT Review,* 1970/4, p. 5; *OIRT Information,* 1970/6, p. 6.

89. *OIRT Information,* 1961/2, p. 18; *OIRT Information,* 1963/11, pp. 4–5; *OIRT Information,* 1963/6, pp. 16–17.

90. *OIRT Information,* 1971/4–5, p. 10.

91. *Internationales Handbuch 1971/72,* p. C144.

92. *OIRT Information,* 1966/4, pp. 13–14; *OIRT Information,* 1966/5, pp. 3–4; *OIRT Information,* 1967/11, pp. 4–6.

93. *OIRT Information,* 1961/1, p. 13; *OIRT Information,* 1962/6, pp. 8–9.

94. *OIRT Information,* 1966/4, p. 14; *OIRT Information,* 1966/11, p. 5.

95. *OIRT Information,* 1971/4–5, pp. 12–13; *OIRT Information,* 1966/11, pp. 6–7.

96. *OIRT Information,* 1970/2, p. 9.

97. G. Steinke, "On the Way to a New Sound Art?" *OIRT Review,* 1965/6, pp. 19–21; *OIRT Information,* 1966/4, p. 11.

98. *New York Times,* April 17, 1966, p. 64L.

99. *OIRT Information,* 1965/7, p. 6.

100. *OIRT Information,* 1965/6, pp. 4–5; *OIRT Information,* 1966/5, p. 6.

101. *OIRT Information,* 1964/10, p. 1; *OIRT Information,* 1964/10, p. 4; *OIRT Information,* 1966/2, pp. 12–13; *OIRT Information,* 1965/6, p. 11; *OIRT Information,* 1966/11, pp. 7–8; *OIRT Information,* 1968/12, pp. 4–5; *OIRT Information,* 1966/4, p. 20; *OIRT Information,* 1968/4, pp. 2–3.

102. *OIRT Information,* 1965/5, pp. 6–7.

103. Fernsehfunk, *Information.*

104. *Introducing the GDR,* p. 221.

105. *OIRT Information,* 1964/4, p. 4; *OIRT Information,* 1961/6, p. 10.

106. Deutscher Fernsehfunk, *Fernsehdienst: Sonderausgabe.*

107. *FF Dabei,* No. 45 (1972), p. 6; *OIRT Information,* 1973/2, p. 4.

108. *OIRT Information,* 1961/6, p. 6; *OIRT Information,* 1961/11, p. 8; *OIRT Information,* 1962/1, p. 2.

109. *OIRT Information,* 1966/5, p. 8.

110. *OIRT Information,* 1966/7, p. 3; *OIRT Information,* 1966/12, p. 14; *OIRT Information,* 1968/4, p. 4.

111. *OIRT Information,* 1969/8, p. 1.

112. Deutscher Fernsehfunk, *Der Präsident im Exil: Information und Kommentare;* *OIRT Information,* 1969/9, p. 10.

113. *OIRT Information,* 1962/4, pp. 7–8.

114. *OIRT Information,* 1968/4, p. 5.

115. *OIRT Information,* 1969/8, p. 1.

116. *FF Dabei,* No. 46 (1972), pp. 19, 23.

117. Werner Cassbaum, "Full Use of Productional Possibilities of Television in Sports Transmissions," *OIRT Review*, 1963/2, pp. 12–13.

118. *OIRT Information*, 1964/6, pp. 5–6.

119. *OIRT Information*, 1969/7, pp. 9–10; *OIRT Information*, 1970/9, pp. 11–12.

120. *OIRT Information*, 1962/9, p. 3.

121. *OIRT Information*, 1962/11, p. 10.

122. Kurt Schulz, "Radio Information from the Cybernetic Point of View," *OIRT Review*, 1965/6, pp. 22–24.

123. Otto Stoll, "Die Hörenpost—Informationsquelle für den Rundfunkjournalisten," *Rundfunkjournalistik in Theorie and Praxis*, 1970/203, pp. 45–51; *OIRT Information*, 1970/8, p. 9; *OIRT Information*, 1961/6, pp. 7–8; *OIRT Information*, 1964/4, p. 3; *OIRT Information*, 1966/5, p. 1; *OIRT Information*, 1966/7, p. 4; Ursula Meining, "The Dresden VHF Transmitter—a Regional Programme of the GDR Radio," *OIRT Review*, 1967/4, p. 19.

124. Christa Oehme, "Television of the German Democratic Republic Department of Audience Research," in Tomas Szecsko, ed., *Public Opinion and Mass Communication*, pp. 181–193; Christa Oehme, "Le Sondage de l'auditoire et la programmation," *OIRT Review*, 1972/5, pp. 9–11.

125. W. Maltusch, "Sociological Research Section of the National Radio Committee of the German Democratic Republic," in Szecske, ed., *Public Opinion and Mass Communication*, pp. 195–196.

126. Günther Hansel, "A Whole Town in the Capacity of a Programme Council," *OIRT Review*, 1965/3, pp. 17–18.

127. *OIRT Information*, 1966/5, p. 1.

128. *OIRT Information*, 1966/7, p. 4.

129. M. Kurt Schulz, "Systèmes et résultats d'un sondage des auditeurs," *OIRT Review*, 1967/3, pp. 14–19.

130. *OIRT Information*, 1966/5, p. 10.

131. "Interview with Herman Ley, Chairman of the German Democratic Republic State Radio Committee," *OIRT Review*, 1960/6, pp. 253–254.

132. Richard Krause, "Experience of the Television of the German DR in the Instructive Broadcasts from the Field of Natural Sciences," *OIRT Review*, 1963/1, p. 11.

133. Fernsehfunk, *Information*.

134. *EBU Review*, 133A (June 1972), p. 142.

135. *WRTH 1973*, p. 62.

136. Rundfunk, *Informationen*, p. 8.

137. *OIRT Information*, 1965/7, pp. 5–6; *OIRT Information*, 1966/2, p. 13; *OIRT Information*, 1966/4, p. 9.

138. *OIRT Information*, 1965/6, pp. 9–10.

139. *OIRT Information*, 1966/6, p. 12.

140. *OIRT Information*, 1966/2, p. 14; *OIRT Information*, 1966/10, pp. 8–9; *OIRT Information*, 1969/11, p. 6.

141. *OIRT Information*, 1966/2, pp. 13, 15–17; *OIRT Information*, 1966/6, pp. 12–13.

142. *WRTH 1973*, pp. 62, 64.

143. Julius Waldschmidt, "Radio Broadcasts for Africa," *OIRT Review*, 1966/4, p. 23.

144. *OIRT Information*, 1972/7–8, p. 6.

145. "Television Wooing of West Germans," London *Times*, July 29, 1957, p. 6; "Germany's Radio War," *Economist*, January 20, 1962, pp. 234–235; Timothy Green, *The Universal Eye: The World of Television*, pp. 178–183, hereafter cited as Green.

146. Rundfunk, *Informationen*, p. 18.
147. *OIRT Information*, 1966/7, p. 11.
148. Gerhart Eisler, "Twenty Years of the German Democratic Radio," *OIRT Review*, 1965/2, p. 6.
149. *OIRT Information*, 1961/2, pp. 16–18.
150. *OIRT Information*, 1969/11, p. 1.
151. *OIRT Information*, 1969, p. 3; *OIRT Information*, 1971/11–12, p. 6.
152. *OIRT Information*, 1967/7, p. 12.
153. *OIRT Information*, 1966/2, pp. 16–18; *OIRT Information*, 1966/5, p. 10; *OIRT Information*, 1970/9, p. 9; *OIRT Information*, 1972/1, p. 9.
154. *Variety*, January 12, 1972, p. 54.
155. Any issue of the *OIRT Catalogue of Radio Broadcasts Suitable for Exchange* lists the current offerings.
156. *OIRT Information*, 1965/6, p. 7; *OIRT Information*, 1971/2, p. 10.
157. Rundfunk, *Informationen*, p. 19.
158. *Ibid.*; *OIRT Information*. 1965/10, p. 5.

VII. The Polish People's Republic

1. *Europa Year Book 1972*, Vol. 1, p. 1039.
2. "Constitution of the Polish People's Republic," in Peaslee, *Constitutions of Nations*, Vol. 3, pp. 709–724.
3. Information supplied by Polish broadcasting authorities. For further details see *Internationales Handbuch 1971/72*, pp. F158–159.
4. Buzek, pp. 144–145.
5. *Trybuna ludu*, December 5, 1971, translated in FBIS *Daily Report,* December 13, 1971, No. 239, Supp. 63, p. 44.
6. FBIS *Daily Report*, December 6, 1971, No. 242, Supp. 64, p. 30.
7. "Polish Radio," *OIRT Review*, 1971/2, p. 5.
8. John C. Merrill, Carter R. Bryan, and Marvin Alisky, *The Foreign Press: A Survey of the World's Journalism*, p. 170.
9. Buzek, p. 180.
10. *New York Times*, April 26, 1972, p. 54C; *New York Times*, February 15, 1973, p. 5C; *New York Times*, June 11, 1973, p. 11C. Raymond B. Nixon, ranking Poland and 116 other countries on a 9-point scale for freedom and control, with 1 indicating a free press, and 9 a completely controlled one, in 1965 classified Poland as 7: "Controlled press system, but with even less rigid controls and/or more opportunity for debate within the system than 8" ("Freedom in the World's Press: A Fresh Appraisal With New Data," *Journalism Quarterly*, 42:1 (Winter 1965), pp. 6, 13).
11. *OIRT Information*, 1966/3, p. 13; Stanislaw Miszczak, "Polish Radio in the Early Days after Liberation," *Polish Radio and Television Bulletin*, 1970/3, pp. 1–8, hereafter cited as *Polish Bulletin*; Stanislaw Miszczak, "Broadcasting in People's Poland," *Polish Bulletin*, 1969/7, pp. 1–4; Stanislaw Miszczak, *Historia radiofonii i telewizji w Polsce*, pp. 555–557.
12. Information supplied by Polish broadcasting authorities. Much of this material also is available in "Polish Radio," *OIRT Review*, 1971/2, p. 5; *WRTH 1973*, pp. 84–85.
13. Jan Mietkowski, "Le Troisième Programme de la Radio Polonaise: Le Répertoire et les formes d'émissions récréatives," *OIRT Review*, 1971/2, pp. 13–16.
14. Jacek Kunicki, "Permanent Education and Radio Broadcasting: Several Preliminary Comments," *OIRT Review*, 1972/5, p. 6.
15. UNESCO, *World Communications: Press Radio Television Film*, p. 316.
16. *OIRT Information*, 1966/3, p. 9.

17. Wydawnictwa Radio i Telewizji, *Z Anteny PR i Ekranu TV (Broadcasting Yearbook for Polish Radio and Television)*, p. 281. Local and regional services averaged 56.3 per cent spoken word and 40.9 per cent music, with 2.8 per cent miscellaneous.

18. Jósef Godlowski, "Les Stations Radiophoniques Regionales," *OIRT Review*, 1968/5, p. 305; Borys Mokryszewski, "This Is the Polish Radio Wroclaw," *Polish Bulletin*, 1970/4–5, pp. 1–6; L. Janowicz, "This Is Warsaw Calling," *Polish Bulletin*, 1970/1, pp. 6–8.

19. *OIRT Information*, 1970/3, p. 10; *OIRT Information*, 1972/1, p. 15.

20. Aleksander Landau, "Organization and Finances in the Polish Radio and Television," *OIRT Review*, 1962/5, p. 6.

21. Zbigniew Lipinski, "An Outlook for the Progress of Broadcasting," *Polish Bulletin*, 1971/1–2, pp. 4–5.

22. Information received from Polish television authorities. *OIRT Information*, 1972/1, p. 13.

23. Wlodzimierz Lozinski, "The Nearest Future of Polish Television," *Polish Bulletin*, 1971/1–2, pp. 10–11.

24. *OIRT Information*, 1969/10, p. 12.

25. *OIRT Information*, 1969/8, pp. 10–11; *OIRT Information*, 1970/5, p. 9; *OIRT Information*, 1971/6–7, p. 14.

26. Green, pp. 171–172.

27. "TV Centre in Gdansk," *Polish Bulletin*, 1969/9–10, pp. 1–3; "Television Centre in Szczecin," *Polish Bulletin*, 1969/6, p. 2.

28. *OIRT Information*, 1966/10, p. 11; *OIRT Information*, 1967/8, p. 4; *Polish Bulletin*, 1969/1, p. 7.

29. *Polish Bulletin*, 1970/2, p. 8.

30. Zbygniew Lipinski, "Radio Commentary," *OIRT Review*, 1960/4, p. 150.

31. Georges H. Mond, *L'Information et la "guerre psychologique" dans un pays socialiste: le cas de la Pologne*, p. 33.

32. UNESCO, *World Communications: Press Radio Television Film*, p. 316; Zdislaw Stankewicz, "Polish Radio," *OIRT Review*, 1967/5, pp. 13–16; International Organization of Journalists, *Handbook of News Agencies*.

33. Michal Skalenajdo, "Le Développement des formes des dernières nouvelles," *OIRT Review*, 1971/1, p. 11.

34. *Polish Bulletin*, 1970/3, p. 10.

35. Ryszard Wojcik, "A Thousand Angry People," *OIRT Review*, 1966/5, pp. 10–12.

36. *New York Times*, June 11, 1973, p. 11C.

37. FBIS *Daily Report*, No. 24, Supp. 64, December 16, 1971.

38. Green, p. 177.

39. *Ibid.*, p. 172.

40. Zofia Latalowa, "Radio and School," *OIRT Review*, 1965/6, p. 3.

41. *OIRT Information*, 1971/4–5, p. 17.

42. "Polish Television," *OIRT Review*, 1961/6, p. 18.

43. *Polish Bulletin*, 1970/7–8, p. 6.

44. *OIRT Information*, 1961/10, p. 13; *OIRT Information*, 1964/3, pp. 15–16; Zofia Latalowa, "Radio and School," *OIRT Review*, 1965/6, pp. 4–5; *OIRT Information*, 1969/12, p. 4.

45. Maria Wisniewska, "School Television Programmes in Poland," *OIRT Review*, 1965/1, p. 10.

46. *OIRT Information*, 1966/9, pp. 9–10; Miroslaw Dabrowski, "Musical Education on the Polish Radio," *OIRT Review*, 1972/4, p. 4.

47. *Polish Bulletin*, 1970/2, p. 1.

48. Miroslaw Dabrowski, "Musical Education on the Polish Radio," *OIRT*

Review, 1972/4, p. 4; OIRT Information, 1969/12, p. 4; Polish Bulletin, 1969/9–10, p. 4.

49. Information supplied by Polish broadcasting authorities.

50. OIRT Information, 1967/11, p. 5.

51. Maria Wisniewska, "School Television Programmes in Poland," OIRT Review, 1965/1, p. 12; OIRT Information, 1964/4, p. 14; OIRT Information, 1969/12, p. 4.

52. Irene Windholz, "Programmes for Youth of the Polish Radio and Young Listeners' Letters," OIRT Review, 1964/3, pp. 18–19.

53. Halina Hermelin, "Radio Broadcasts for Children of Pre-school Age," OIRT Review, 1966/5, pp. 17–22.

54. OIRT Information, 1969/8, p. 10; Polish Bulletin, 1969/2, p. 11.

55. "Popular Science Programs for Children Heard on the Polish Radio," Polish Bulletin, 1970/7–8, p. 3; OIRT Information, 1969/10, p. 14.

56. "Popular Science Programs for Children Heard on the Polish Radio," Polish Bulletin, 1970/7–8, p. 3.

57. OIRT Information, 1967/12, p. 4.

58. Communicator, 1:3, (April 1973), p. 16.

59. Tardeausz Kornecki, "Broadcasts of the Radio University in the Programme of the Polish Radio," OIRT Review, 1962/6, p. 7; Jerzy Kubin, "Coordination of the Work of Radio with the Work of Public and State Organizations in the Field of Popularization of Science," OIRT Review, 1963/4, pp. 6–11.

60. Jacek Kunicki, "Program and Problems of Education for Adults," Polish Bulletin, 1971/6, pp. 4–11.

61. Eugenia Gadzinska, "The International Radio University on the Polish Program," Polish Bulletin, 1971/6, pp. 25–27.

62. Jacek Kunicki, "Permanent Education and Radio Broadcasting: Several Preliminary Comments," OIRT Review, 1971/5, p. 4; Centre for Public Opinion and Broadcasting Research, Research Abstracts, No. 3.

63. M. Wisznewska, "Popular-Scientific and Educational Broadcasts of the Polish Television," OIRT Review, 1964/4, pp. 10–11.

64. Polish Bulletin, 1970/1, p. 12.

65. Alojzy Sroga, "Economic and Agricultural Broadcasts of the Polish Radio," OIRT Review, 1964/2, p. 17.

66. Polish Bulletin, 1970/2, p. 7.

67. Polish Bulletin, 1969/7, p. 6.

68. OIRT Information, 1966/3, p. 15; OIRT Information, 1969/12, pp. 6–7; Polish Bulletin, 1970/1, p. 11.

69. Polish Bulletin, 1969/6, p. 5; OIRT Information, 1962/12, pp. 13–14.

70. Material about the Television Technical College is drawn from the following sources: Henry R. Cassirer, "Television Extends Higher Education: A Pilot Project in Poland," UNESCO Chronicle, 12:9 (1966), pp. 346–356; "Polish University of the Air," Times Educational Supplement (November 24, 1967), pp. 1228–1229; UNESCO, Television and Further Education of Employed; UNESCO, Television for Higher Technical Education of the Employed: A First Report on a Pilot Project in Poland; and UNESCO, Television for Higher Technical Education of Workers: Final Report on a Pilot Project in Poland.

71. UNESCO, Television for Higher Technical Education of the Employed, pp. 7–10; Rocznik Statystyczny 1971 (Statistical Year Book 1971), p. 488; Janusz Tymowski, "Politechnika Telewizyjna," Multi-Media Systems in Adult Education: Twelve Project Descriptions in Nine Countries, p. 152, hereafter cited as Tymowski.

72. "Polish University of the Air," Times Educational Supplement (September 9, 1965), p. 496.

73. Tymowski, pp. 159–162.

74. UNESCO, *Television for Higher Technical Education of Workers*, pp. 11–15.

75. *Ibid.*, pp. 17, 18, 30, 34, 36, 37.

76. *Ibid.*, p. 20.

77. *"L'Université à Domicile" Symposium*, pp. 45–46.

78. UNESCO, *Television for Higher Technical Education of Workers*, pp. 68, 71, 73.

79. Witold Billip, "Polish Radio Dramaturgy," *OIRT Review*, 1970/4, pp. 9–10, hereafter cited as Billip.

80. *Polish Bulletin*, 1971/3–4, p. 6.

81. *OIRT Information*, 1971/1, p. 11; *Polish Bulletin*, 1971/3–4, pp. 6, 9; Billip, p. 12.

82. Billip, p. 10; *OIRT Information*, 1964/6, p. 12; *OIRT Information*, 1966/8, pp. 14–15; *Polish Bulletin*, 1971/3–4, p. 7.

83. *Polish Bulletin*, 1971/3–4, p. 8; *Polish Bulletin*, 1970/3–4, p. 10.

84. *OIRT Information*, 1965/7, pp. 17–18; *OIRT Information*, 1966/7, pp. 14–15; *OIRT Information*, 1965/1, p. 13; *OIRT Information*, 1969/10, p. 13.

85. *OIRT Information*, 1970/2, p. 14; *OIRT Information*, 1970/8, pp. 14–15; *OIRT Information*, 1971/1, p. 12.

86. Billip, p. 11.

87. Wladyslaw Zeslawski, "The Radio Novel," *OIRT Review*, 1965/2, pp. 13, 15.

88. *OIRT Information*, 1966/3, pp. 13–14; Anna Major, "A Report on the 'Szabó Family' and Serial Broadcasts in General," *OIRT Review*, 1965/6, pp. 15–18; *OIRT Information*, 1964/4, pp. 12–13. For a study of American serial listeners, see Herta Herzog, "On Borrowed Experience: An Analysis of Listening to Daytime Sketches," *Studies in Philosophy and Social Science*, 9:1 (1941), p. 85.

89. *Polish Bulletin*, 1970/4–5, p. 16; *OIRT Information*, 1972/1, p. 15.

90. *OIRT Information*, 1961/8, pp. 11–13.

91. *OIRT Information*, 1966/10, pp. 10–11.

92. *OIRT Information*, 1970/6, p. 10.

93. Irena Boltuc, "Polish Television Drama," *Polish Bulletin*, 1969/2, pp. 1–2.

94. *Polish Bulletin*, 1971/3–4, pp. 16–19.

95. Jozef Kadzielski, "On the Influence of Television Theatrical Culture in Poland," *Polish Bulletin*, 1970/1, p. 3; Irena Boltuc, "Polish Television Drama," *Polish Bulletin*, 1969/2, pp. 3–5.

96. Irena Boltuc, "Polish Television Drama," *Polish Bulletin*, 1969/2, p. 4; Jan Klowsowicz, "The Television Theater," *OIRT Information*, 1965/1, pp. 17–18.

97. *Polish Bulletin*, 1969/7, p. 7.

98. *OIRT Information*, 1971/8–9, p. 9.

99. Irena Boltuc, "Polish Television Drama," *Polish Bulletin*, 1969/2, p. 5.

100. *OIRT Information*, 1970/12, p. 9; *OIRT Information*, 1970/9, p. 15.

101. Mariusz Kwiatowski, "Les Emissions les plus populaires," *OIRT Review*, 1972/2, pp. 13–15.

102. *OIRT Information*, 1965/1, p. 14; *OIRT Information*, 1964/13, p. 14.

103. *OIRT Information*, 1966/1, p. 20; *OIRT Information*, 1970/8, p. 18.

104. *Variety*, June 24, 1962, p. 27.

105. *OIRT Information*, 1971/6–7, p. 14.

106. *OIRT Information*, 1970/1, p. 9; *FF Dabei*, No. 46 (1972), p. 33.

107. *OIRT Information*, 1966/4, p. 21; *OIRT Information*, 1967/0, pp. 2–3.

108. *OIRT Information*, 1964/2, p. 11; *OIRT Information*, 1965/9, p. 13; *Polish Bulletin*, 1969/5, pp. 8–9.

109. *Polish Bulletin*, 1969/3, pp. 4–5.

110. *OIRT Information*, 1970/12, p. 8; *OIRT Information*, 1970/9, p. 14; *Polish Bulletin*, 1970/2, p. 9.

111. *Polish Bulletin*, 1970/4–5, p. 20.
112. Green, p. 166.
113. *BBC Handbook 1972*, p. 103.
114. Miroslaw Dabrowski, "Le Rôle de la radiodiffusion dans la propagation massive de la culture musicale," *OIRT Review*, 1969/1, p. 3.
115. *OIRT Information*, 1964/6, p. 14; *Polish Bulletin*, 1970/2, p. 8.
116. Miroslaw Dabrowski, "Le Rôle de la radiodiffusion dans la propagation massive de la culture musicale," *OIRT Review*, 1969/1, p. 4; *Polish Bulletin*, 1969/1, p. 8.
117. *Polish Bulletin*, 1969/3, pp. 1–2; *OIRT Information*, 1963/8, p. 8.
118. *OIRT Information*, 1964/5, p. 11; *OIRT Information*, 1966/3, p. 10; Jozef Tatkowdik and Anna Skrzynska, "Le 15e Anniversaire du Studio Experimental de la Radio Polonaise," *OIRT Review*, 1972/3, pp. 3–7.
119. *OIRT Information*, 1961/2, p. 21; Miroslaw Dabrowski, "Le Rôle de la radiodiffusion dans la propagation massive de la culture musicale," *OIRT Review*, 1969/1, pp. 4–5; Miroslaw Dabrowski, "The Role of the Polish Radio in the Musical Life of Poland," *OIRT Review*, 1966/4, pp. 4–5.
120. "Some Problems of the Polish Television Musical Programmes Department," *OIRT Review*, 1960/1, pp. 6–7.
121. Ryszard Lindenberg, "Music on Channel II of Polish Television," *Polish Bulletin*, 1971/1–2, pp. 23–26.
122. *OIRT Information*, 1972/2, p. 7.
123. "Some Problems of the Polish Television Musical Programme Department," *OIRT Review*, 1960/1, p. 7.
124. *Polish Bulletin*, 1969/5, pp. 1–3.
125. Miroslaw Dabrowski, "The Role of the Polish Radio in the Musical Life of Poland," *OIRT Review*, 1966/4, pp. 4–5.
126. Miroslaw Dabrowski, "Musical Education on the Polish Radio," *OIRT Review*, 1972/4, p. 4.
127. Gendrik Svolken, "For the Active Participation of Radio-Listeners in Musical-Spoken Broadcasts," *OIRT Review*, 1968/6, pp. 3–5.
128. *Polish Bulletin*, 1970/7–8, pp. 1–2.
129. Miroslaw Dabrowski, "Musical Education on the Polish Radio," *OIRT Review*, 1972/4, pp. 3–6.
130. Gendrik Svolken, "For the Active Participation of Radio-Listeners in Musical-Spoken Broadcasts," *OIRT Review*, 1968/6, p. 3; *Polish Bulletin*, 1969/1, p. 4.
131. Miroslaw Dabrowski, "The Role of the Polish Radio in the Musical Life of Poland," *OIRT Review*, 1966/4, p. 4.
132. *OIRT Information*, 1963/10, p. 5; *OIRT Information*, 1969/10, p. 12; *Polish Bulletin*, 1970/7–8, pp. 9–10; *OIRT Information*, 1971/8–9, p. 7.
133. Józef Kadzielski, "Application of Results of Research on Program Activities of Radio and Television," *Polish Bulletin*, 1971/1–2, p. 13.
134. Andrzej Sicinski, "Public Polls in Radio and Television Broadcasting," *OIRT Review*, 1965/4, p. 3.
135. Józef Kadzielski, "Application of Results of Research in Program Activities of Radio and Television," *Polish Bulletin*, 1971/1–2, pp. 14, 16–17; material supplied by the Centre for Public Opinion and Broadcasting Research.
136. There is a list of these and other Centre publications in *Polish Bulletin*, 1970/2, pp. 1–6.
137. Radio Free Europe, *Some Aspects of Exposure to the Press and Radio as Measured inside Poland and by APOE-RFE*, p. 1.
138. *WRTH 1973*, p. 280.
139. *OIRT Information*, 1963/5, pp. 14–15.

140. *OIRT Information*, 1965/10, p. 11.

141. Józef Kadzielski, "The Interest of Audiences in Theater Programs of the Polish Radio and Television," *Polish Bulletin*, 1971/3–4, pp. 35–36.

142. Centre for Public Opinion and Broadcasting Research, *Research Abstracts*, No. 1.

143. Radio Free Europe, *Domestic Poll Results on Listening to Radio Warsaw*, pp. 1–3.

144. Józef Kadzielski, "The Interest of Audiences in Theater Programs of the Polish Radio and Television," *Polish Bulletin*, 1971/3–4, p. 38.

145. Radio Free Europe, *The Exposure to the Domestic Radio and Television in Eastern Europe*.

146. Radio Free Europe, *The Major Information Sources of Polish Respondents on Important Foreign and Domestic Issues*, pp. 1, 5, 11, 15, 20.

147. Radio Free Europe, *Listening to Western Radio in Poland before and after the "December Events,"* pp. 9–10.

148. Radio Free Europe, *Listening to Western Broadcasts in Eastern Europe*, pp. 2–3, 8.

149. *Ibid.*, table following p. 14.

150. *OIRT Information*, 1970/4, p. 8.

151. Zbigniew Lipinski, "An Outlook for the Progress of Broadcasting," *Polish Bulletin*, 1971/1–2, p. 4.

152. Radio Free Europe, *Reasons for Not Listening to Radio Free Europe*, p. 5.

153. Sergiusz Mikulicz, "The Essence and Principles of Collaboration with Foreign Countries," *Polish Bulletin*, 1971/1–2, p. 19.

154. *OIRT Information*, 1964/3, pp. 14–15.

155. *OIRT Information*, 1966/8, p. 13.

156. *OIRT Information*, 1967/8, pp. 4–5.

157. *OIRT Information*, 1968/10, pp. 1–2.

158. *OIRT Information*, 1964/5, p. 14; *OIRT Information*, 1964/7, p. 14; *OIRT Information*, 1965/1, p. 14.

159. *OIRT Information*, 1970/12, p. 7.

160. Sergiusz Mikulicz, "The Essence and Principles of Collaboration with Foreign Countries," *Polish Bulletin*, 1971/1–2, pp. 19–22.

VIII. The Czechoslovak Socialist Republic

1. *Europa Year Book 1972* Vol. 1, p. 608.

2. *Ibid.*, p. 611.

3. *New York Times*, November 16, 1972, p. 11C.

4. For a review of the events leading up to the invasion, see Avraham G. Mezerik, *The Invasion and Occupation of Czechoslovakia and the U.N.*, pp. 75–80. Later political developments in Czechoslovakia are discussed in H. Gordon Skilling, "Czechoslovakia," in Bromke and Rakowska-Harmstone, eds., *The Communist States in Disarray 1965–1971*, pp. 43–72.

5. *New York Times*, August 21, 1968, p. 1.

6. *New York Times*, May 7, 1970, p. 3.

7. *New York Times*, October 17, 1968, pp. 1, 2.

8. *London Times*, May 26, 1972, p. 5; *New York Times*, May 30, 1971, p. 8.

9. *New York Times*, July 28, 1972, p. 7C; *New York Times*, July 21, 1972, p. 14C.

10. *New York Times*, February 23, 1973, p. 2C; *New York Times*, July 2, 1973, p. 6C.

11. "Constitution of Czechoslovakia," in Peaslee, *Constitutions of Nations*, Vol.

3, p. 226, hereafter cited as *Czechoslovak Constitution.* The Constitution currently in effect, adopted July 11, 1960, replaced an earlier one of May 9, 1948.

12. *Europa Year Book 1972,* Vol. 1, p. 613.

13. *Statesman's Year-Book 1972–1973,* p. 854.

14. *Czechoslovak Constitution,* Art. 20–24.

15. Namurois, p. 108.

16. *EBU Review,* 138B (July 1971), p. 58.

17. Buzek, pp. 148–149, 174–175. Corresponding delays in reporting a flood in 1956 are cited on p. 181. Raymond B. Nixon, ranking Czechoslovakia and 116 other countries in 1965 on a 9-point scale for press freedom, with 1 indicating a free press and 9 a completely controlled one, classified Czechoslovakia as 8: "Controlled press system, but with less rigid controls [than in category 9] and/or some opportuntiy for debate within systems" ("Freedom in the World's Press: A Fresh Appraisal with New Data," *Journalism Quarterly,* 42:1 (Winter 1965), pp. 6, 13).

18. Kamil Winter, former editor, News and Current Affairs Programs, Czechoslovak Television, and former foreign editor, *Rudé Právo,* in a talk in Minneapolis, Minnesota, February 6, 1970.

19. A description of directives applied to newspapers in the early 1960s is given in Buzek, pp. 119–124.

20. *Europa Year Book 1971,* Vol. 1, p. 611; *Europa Yearbook 1972,* Vol. 1, p. 618; *New York Times,* November 16, 1972, p. 11C.

21. *Europa Year Book 1971,* Vol. 1, p. 611.

22. The text is given in A. G. Mezerik, *Invasion and Occupation of Czechoslovakia and the U.N.,* pp. 116–121.

23. *London Times,* May 7, 1968, p. 6.

24. John Morgan, "A Revolutionary Role for Czech Television," *The Listener,* April 11, 1968, p. 459.

25. *BBC Handbook 1970,* pp. 98–99.

26. Sláva Volny, "The Saga of Czechoslovak Broadcasting," *East Europe,* 17:12 (December 1968), pp. 13–15.

27. For a description of broadcasting during the occupation, see Joseph Wechsberg, "A Reporter at Large: The Air Alive with Words," *The New Yorker,* 44:36 (October 26, 1968), pp. 64–136, hereafter cited as Wechsberg. Throughout this chapter extensive use is made of off-the-air and other reports supplied by Radio Free Europe.

28. Green, p. 184.

29. Wechsberg, p. 72.

30. *Ibid.,* p. 94.

31. *London Times,* March 4, 1969, p. 10.

32. *Europa Year Book 1972,* Vol. 1, p. 618.

33. Adam Roberts, "The Face of Censorship," *The Listener,* October 24, 1968, pp. 523–524.

34. *London Times,* September 25, 1968, pp. 1, 4.

35. *New York Times,* May 17, 1971, p. 5C.

36. *WRTH 1974,* p. 55.

37. *OIRT Information,* 1970/9, pp. 5–6.

38. "Problems of Exacting Selected Programmes and VHF Transmissions," *OIRT Review,* 1971/1, pp. 11–13.

39. František Šmolík, "Le Centre de radiodiffusion de Prague," *OIRT Review,* 1966/5, pp. 13–16.

40. Jiří Komárek, "Eight Years of Wired Broadcasting in the Czechoslovak SR," *OIRT Information,* 1962/4, pp. 3–7.

41. "Czechoslovak Radio," *OIRT Review,* 1961/6, p. 10.

42. Rostislav Běhal, "Programme Blocks: New Type of Broadcast or a New Character of the Radio Programme?" *OIRT Review*, 1963/3, p. 5.

43. Rostislav Běhal, "The Role of Radio Broadcasting in Modern Life, The Prospects of Development of Radio, Cooperation between Radio and Television," *OIRT Review*, 1964/1, pp. 7, 9.

44. Information supplied by Czechoslovak Television.

45. Ctibor Tahy, "Czechoslovakia," in *Adult Education and Television*, p. 57, hereafter cited as Tahy.

46. For a discussion of the problems involved in transcoding PAL into SECAM color in Czechoslovakia, see Milam Ptáček, "Les Propriétés des méthodes de trancodage des systèmes de télévision en couleurs PAL-SECAM," *OIRT Review*, 1971/1, pp. 26–32.

47. *WRTH 1973*, p. 273.

48. Miroslav Marek, Milan Hromádka, and Josef Chroust, *Cultural Policy in Czechoslovakia*, p. 57.

49. "Czechoslovak Television," *OIRT Review*, 1961/5, p. 35.

50. UNESCO, *World Communications: Press Radio Television Film*, p. 274.

51. Tahy, p. 59.

52. *Variety*, January 6, 1971, p. 84.

53. *Europa Year Book 1972*, Vol. 1, p. 618.

54. *East Europe*, 18:8–9 (August–September 1969), pp. 50–51.

55. *OIRT Information*, 1970/2, p. 2.

56. B. Jicinska, "Watching Czechoslovakia's Television Screen," *East Europe*, 18:10 (October 1969), pp. 17–19.

57. Alois Šrubǎr, "The Czechoslovak Radio Newsreel," *OIRT Review*, 1960/5, p. 197.

58. "Political Information on the Czechoslovak Television," *OIRT Review*, 1961/3, p. 108.

59. *OIRT Information*, 1970/2, pp. 1–2.

60. International Organization of Journalists, *Handbook of News Agencies*; UNESCO, *World Communications: Press Radio Television Film*, p. 273.

61. Buzek, pp. 189–190, 193–194, and 198–205.

62. See above, pp. 62–64.

63. *WRTH 1973*, p. 47.

64. Zdeněk Michalec, "The Initial Experience of the 2nd Programme of the Czechoslovak Television," *OIRT Review*, 1971/4, pp. 4–5.

65. *OIRT Information*, 1964/7, p. 1.

66. Vladimír Kovařík, "Television Goes into Schools," *OIRT Review*, 1960/3, p. 93.

67. Milan Maralík, "Radio and School—Some Czechoslovak Experiences," *OIRT Review*, 1966/1, pp. 23–26.

68. *OIRT Information*, 1966/3, p. 2.

69. Bohumil Kolář, "Magazine for Reckoners," *OIRT Review*, 1968/6, pp. 23–25.

70. *OIRT Information*, 1970/3, p. 1.

71. Vladimír Kovařík, "Television Goes into Schools," *OIRT Review*, 1960/3, p. 91; Zdeněk Michalec, "Czechoslovak Television Programmes for School," *OIRT Review*, 1960/4, pp. 151–153; Valter Feldstein, "Programme Experience of the Czechoslovak Television," *OIRT Review*, 1960/6, p. 260.

72. Ferdinand Smrčka, "The Fairy Tale in Radio Programmes," *OIRT Review*, 1962/1, pp. 3–4; Ferdinand Smrčka, "Radio and Children," *OIRT Review*, 1966/1, p. 4.

73. Zdeněk Michalec, "Television and Children's Activity," *OIRT Review*, 1961/4, pp. 6–7.

74. *OIRT Information*, 1964/4, p. 2.

75. *OIRT Information*, 1970/4, pp. 2–3.

76. Olga Spalová, "Participation of Children in Radio Broadcasting," *OIRT Review*, 1965/4, p. 21; Július Farkaś, "Participation of Children in the Slovak National Radio Network," *OIRT Review*, 1966/1, pp. 27–29.

77. *OIRT Information*, 1970/3, p. 1.

78. *OIRT Information*, 1970/2, p. 3.

79. Tahy, pp. 55–56.

80. UNESCO, *Mass Media in Adult Education*, p. 37.

81. Zdeněk Michalec, "Educational Broadcasts on the Screen," *OIRT Review*, 1972/4, p. 9.

82. Tahy, pp. 76–82.

83. "Mass Media Man: Escapist, Non-Selective Sponge or Knowledge Seeker?" *Czechoslovak Life*, February 1967, p. 3; hereafter cited as "Mass Media Man"; Tahy, pp. 60–61; *OIRT Information*, 1964/8, p. 5.

84. Tahy, p. 61.

85. "Mass Media Man," p. 3; Tahy, pp. 62–63.

86. Zdeněk Michalec, "Educational Broadcasts on the Screen," *OIRT Review*, 1972/4, p. 13.

87. "Mass Media Man," p. 5; Tahy, pp. 65–66.

88. Zdeněk Michalec, "Educational Broadcasts on the Screen," *OIRT*, 1972/4, p. 9.

89. *OIRT Information*, 1968/4, p. 1.

90. *OIRT Information*, 1962/10, p. 4.

91. *OIRT Information*, 1963/4, p. 2.

92. *OIRT Information*, 1964/4, p. 2.

93. *OIRT Information*, 1964/8, p. 4.

94. Tahy, p. 67.

95. *OIRT Information*, 1968/5, p. 5.

96. John Morgan, "A Revolutionary Role for Czech Television," *The Listener*, April 11, 1961, p. 459.

97. *OIRT Information*, 1970/2, p. 2.

98. Zdeněk Michalec, "Educational Broadcasts on the Screen," *OIRT Review*, 1972/4, p. 13.

99. Miloslav Nedbal, "Musical Education and Popularization of Music on the Czechoslovak Radio," *OIRT Review*, 1964/5, p. 6.

100. Jiří Štilec, "Some Questions of the Popularization of Serious Music, Chiefly of the 20th Century, on the Radio," *OIRT Review*, 1967/6, p. 14.

101. Antonín Dvořak, "Some Problems of Musico-Publicistic Activity on the Czech Radio (with Regard to Serious Music)," *OIRT Review*, 1972/4, p. 27, hereafter cited as Dvořák.

102. Miloslav Nedbal, "Musical Education and Popularization of Music on the Czechoslovak Radio," *OIRT Review*, 1964/5, p. 6.

103. Jiří Štilec, "Some Questions of the Popularization of Serious Music, Chiefly of the 20th Century, on the Radio," *OIRT Review*, 1967/6, p. 13.

104. Dvořák, pp. 27–29.

105. *OIRT Information*, 1965/1, p. 7; *OIRT Information*, 1965/3, p. 4.

106. *OIRT Information*, 1961/1, pp. 5–6; *OIRT Information*, 1961/2, pp. 5–6; *OIRT Information*, 1961/9, pp. 1–2; *OIRT Information*, 1964/4, p. 1; *OIRT Information*, 1963/2, p. 5; *OIRT Information*, 1964/4, pp. 1–2; *OIRT Information*, 1969/6, p. 1; *OIRT Information*, 1968/11, p. 12; *OIRT Information*, 1966/2, p. 1; *OIRT Information*, 1968/12, p. 8; *OIRT Information*, 1970/8, p. 3; *OIRT Information*, 1970/8, p. 5.

107. *OIRT Information*, 1968/11, p. 2.

108. Dvořák, p. 28.
109. *OIRT Information*, 1970/5, p. 1.
110. *OIRT Information*, 1961/11, p. 7.
111. *OIRT Information*, 1963/4, pp. 2–3.
112. *OIRT Information*, 1964/2, pp. 4–5.
113. *OIRT Information*, 1965/1, pp. 7–8.
114. *OIRT Information*, 1970/6, p. 6.
115. *OIRT Information*, 1972/1, pp. 5–7.
116. For a comment on the Spring Festival of 1971, see the *New York Times*, May 18, 1971, p. 47C.
117. *OIRT Informaiton*, 1961/6, pp. 2–4; *OIRT Information*, 1965/6, p. 3.
118. Dvořák, p. 29.
119. *OIRT Information*, 1962/3, pp. 3–6.
120. *OIRT Information*, 1965/2, pp. 4–6.
121. Josef Štefánek, "Literary Instructive Series of Radio Broadcasts," *OIRT Review*, 1972/4, p. 7.
122. Leopold Slovák, "Literature on the Radio," *OIRT Review*, 1968/3, pp. 15–16.
123. *OIRT Information*, 1961/2, pp. 9–10.
124. *Ibid.*, p. 11.
125. *OIRT Information*, 1963/2, pp. 4–5.
126. *OIRT Information*, 1968/6, pp. 1–2.
127. *OIRT Information*, 1970/1, p. 2.
128. Josef Štefánek, "Literary Instructive Series of Radio Broadcasts," *OIRT Review*, 1972/4, pp. 7–8.
129. *OIRT Information*, 1972/4–5, p. 2.
130. Ivan Teren, "Radio Play—the Art of Our Century," *OIRT Review*, 1962/5, pp. 23–24.
131. Marián Mikola, "Ideological and Artistic Trends in Slovak Radio Plays," *OIRT Review*, 1970/4, p. 13.
132. *OIRT Information*, 1961/10, pp. 1–2.
133. *OIRT Information*, 1963/8, pp. 3–4.
134. Marián Mikola, "Ideological and Artistic Trends in Slovak Radio Plays," *OIRT Review*, 1970/4, pp. 13–14.
135. *OIRT Information*, 1964/5, p. 6; *OIRT Information*, 1966/1, p. 7; *OIRT Information*, 1966/8, p. 8; *OIRT Information*, 1968/2, p. 3.
136. *OIRT Information*, 1970/1, p. 1.
137. *OIRT Information*, 1971/6–7, pp. 2–3; *OIRT Information*, 1971/4–5, pp. 6–7.
138. *OIRT Information*, 1961/12, pp. 2–4.
139. *OIRT Information*, 1964/6, p. 6.
140. *OIRT Information*, 1961/11, pp. 7–8; *OIRT Information*, 1963/5, p. 7.
141. *OIRT Information*, 1968/1, p. 1.
142. *OIRT Information*, 1971/6–7, p. 3.
143. *OIRT Information*, 1970/2, p. 3.
144. *OIRT Information*, 1967/9, p. 1.
145. *OIRT Information*, 1962/3, p. 6. For an extended discussion of theory and practice in dubbing film for television, see Oldřich Kautský, "Television Dubbing," *OIRT Review*, 1969/6, pp. 18–24; *OIRT Review*, 1970/1, pp. 18–22.
146. *ORIT Information*, 1968/3, p. 2.
147. *OIRT Information*, 1971/4–5, p. 7.
148. *OIRT Information*, 1971/10, p. 2.
149. *OIRT Information*, 1971/6–7, p. 2.

150. "Political Information on the Czechoslovak Television," *OIRT Review*, 1961/3, p. 109.

151. "Czechoslovak Radio," *OIRT Review*, 1961/6, p. 10.

152. *OIRT Information*, 1970/11–12, p. 2.

153. Karel Mikyska, "Relays of Sports Events in Television," *OIRT Review*, 1963/5, pp. 8–9, 11–12.

154. Jiří Lederer, "Research of Listeners to the Czechoslovak Radio," *OIRT Review*, 1963/5, pp. 3–5.

155. *OIRT Information*, 1962/5, pp. 2–3.

156. Zdeňka Kadlecová, "The Czechoslovak Radio and Its Listeners," *OIRT Review*, 1962/1, pp. 21–23.

157. "Mass Media Man," pp. 3–4; Ludvik Baran, "Team Work Analyzed in Czechoslovakia TV Broadcasts," *OIRT Information*, 1966/10, pp. 1–3.

158. *Variety*, January 6, 1971, p. 84.

159. Tahy, p. 70.

160. "Mass Media Man," pp. 2, 4.

161. Tahy, p. 70.

162. *Ibid.*, p. 73. For a comparison of British and American radio program preferences which showed very similar tastes in those two countries, see Paulu, *British Broadcasting*, pp. 361–367.

163. *OIRT Information*, 1966/12, pp. 1–7. Since this survey covered only Saturday and Sunday programs, no votes were recorded for certain types of broadcasts, such as sports, which surely would have received high ratings had they been on the schedules.

164. Radio Free Europe, *The Exposure to the Domestic Radio and Television in Eastern Europe*.

165. *New York Times*, October 5, 1971, p. 23M.

166. Radio Free Europe, *Listening to Western Broadcasts in Czechoslovakia before and after the Invasion*, pp. 1–4; Radio Free Europe, *Listening to RFE in Czechoslovakia before and after August 21*, pp. 6, 7, 11, 12, 13–14.

167. Radio Free Europe, *Listening to Western Broadcasts in Eastern Europe*, pp. 2–5, table following p. 14.

168. Information supplied by Czechoslovak broadcasting authorities. For a review of Radio Prague broadcasts to North America, see William S. Howell and John Franklin White, "The North American Broadcast Service of Radio Prague," *Quarterly Journal of Speech*, 55:3 (October 1969), pp. 247–255.

169. *WRTH 1973*, p. 48.

170. Green, pp. 186–187.

171. *London Times*, May 7, 1968, p. 6.

172. Radio Free Europe, *Reasons for Not Listening to Radio Free Europe*, p. 5.

173. *London Times*, December 19, 1970, p. 4; *New York Times*, February 25, 1971, p. 10C.

174. *New York Times*, November 16, 1972, p. 11C.

175. *OIRT Information*, 1965/5, p. 1; *OIRT Information*, 1965/8, p. 3; *OIRT Information*, 1966/1, p. 7; *OIRT Information*, 1968/4, p. 1; *OIRT Information*, 1970/3, p. 2; *OIRT Information*, 1970/6, pp. 1–2.

176. *OIRT Information*, 1962/9, p. 1.

177. *OIRT Information*, 1964/8, p. 4.

178. *OIRT Information*, 1970/5, pp. 1–2.

179. *OIRT Information*, 1964/4, p. 1; *OIRT Information*, 1964/8, p. 5.

180. *OIRT Information*, 1965/7, p. 1.

181. *OIRT Information*, 1968/3, p. 1.

182. *Internationales Handbuch 1971/72*, pp. C151–152.

183. *OIRT Information*, 1970/4, p. 1.

184. *OIRT Information*, 1961/8, pp. 6–9; *OIRT Information*, 1965/6, p. 3.
185. *OIRT Information*, 1965/6, p. 3; *OIRT Information*, 1965/9, pp. 3–5.
186. *OIRT Information*, 1966/3, p. 2.
187. *OIRT Information*, 1966/8, p. 7.
188. *OIRT Information*, 1970/11–12, pp. 1–2.
189. *OIRT Information*, 1966/9, p. 12.
190. "The First International Television Festival, Prague, 1964," *OIRT Review*, 1964/5, pp. 15–16.
191. *OIRT Information*, 1969/7, pp. 3–4.

IX. The Hungarian People's Republic

1. *Europa Year Book 1972*, Vol. 1, p. 840.
2. Buzek, pp. 96–99.
3. "How We Failed in Hungary," *The Reporter*, 16:2 (January 24, 1957), p. 28.
4. Robert T. Holt, *Radio Free Europe*, pp. 196–199.
5. Ferenc A. Vali, "Hungary," in Bromke and Rakowska-Harmstone, eds., *The Communist States in Disarray 1965–1971*, p. 124.
6. *Europa Year Book 1972*, Vol. 1, p. 843.
7. *New York Times*, July 8, 1972, p. 3C; *New York Times*, March 7, 1973, p. 14.
8. Quoted from *Nepszabadsag*, October 26, 1968, in Ferenc A. Vali, "Hungary," in Bromke and Rakowska-Harmstone, eds., *The Communist States in Disarray 1965–1971*, p. 129.
9. "Constitution of Hungary," in Peaslee, *Constitutions of Nations*, Vol. 3, p. 432; hereafter cited as *Hungarian Constitution*.
10. *Ibid.*, Art. 2.
11. *Ibid.*, Art. 6.
12. *Ibid.*, Sec. III.
13. *Ibid.*, Arts. 19, 22, 23.
14. *Europa Year Book 1972*, Vol. 1, pp. 840, 848.
15. *Hungarian Constitution*, Arts. 59, 60, 61.
16. *Ibid.*, Art. 53.
17. *Ibid.*, Art. 55. Raymond B. Nixon, ranking Hungary and 116 other countries in 1965 on a nine-point scale for press freedom, with 1 indicating a free press and 9 a completely controlled one, classified Hungary as 7: "Controlled press system but with . . . less rigid controls and/or more opportunity for debate within the system than 8" ("Freedom in the World Press: A Fresh Appraisal with New Data," *Journalism Quarterly*, 42:1 (Winter 1965), pp. 6, 13).
18. Ferand Terrou and Lucien Solal, *Legislation for Press, Film and Radio*, pp. 199–200; François Pigé, *La Télévision dans le monde*, pp. 53–54, Walter B. Emery, *National and International Systems of Broadcasting*, pp. 396–397.
19. Béla Lévái, *Hungarian Radio and Television 1970*, p. 1, hereafter cited as Lévái. References are to the unnumbered pages of the English-language portion.
20. *OIRT Information*, 1963/2, p. 9; Lévái, pp. 23; *WRTH 1973*, p. 77.
21. *OIRT Information*, 1972/3, p. 9.
22. Lévái, p. 2.
23. Andor Szücs, "The Mutual Influence of Radio and Television in Hungary," *OIRT Review*, 1971/6, p. 10.
24. Lévái, p. 5.
25. *WRTH 1973*, p. 278.
26. Lévái, p. 5; *OIRT Information*, 1971/8–9, p. 5.
27. Ferenc Kulcsár, "Notre politique et certains traits de la programmation de la

Télévision Hongroise au cours des dix dernières années," *OIRT Review*, 1968/1, pp. 4–5.

28. *New York Times*, January 12, 1972, p. 70M.

29. *OIRT Information*, 1965/10, p. 8; *OIRT Information*, 1971/6–7, p. 11; Lévái, pp. 6–7.

30. *OIRT Information*, 1969/6, p. 2.

31. György Sándor, "The Experience of the Hungarian Television," *OIRT Review*, 1964/4, pp. 6–7.

32. Ferenc Kulcsár, "Notre politique et certains traits de la programmation de la Télévision Hongroise au cours des dix dernières années," *OIRT Review*, 1968/1, p. 9.

33. *OIRT Information*, 1971/11–12, p. 9; Lévái, pp. 2–3.

34. *OIRT Information*, 1966/8, p. 11.

35. International Organization of Journalists, *Handbook of News Agencies*; UNESCO, *World Communications: Press Radio Television Film*, p. 297.

36. Iván Földi, "Hungarian Radio," *OIRT Review*, 1967/5, pp. 10–11.

37. *OIRT Information*, 1970/10, p. 9; *OIRT Information*, 1971/8–9, p. 3.

38. Lévái, p. 5.

39. Rose Matuz, "TV News in the Framework of Television Political Programmes," *OIRT Review*, 1963/2, p. 3.

40. *Europa Year Book 1972*, Vol. 1, p. 849.

41. Ferenc Vajda, "Commentary on the Hungarian Radio," *OIRT Review*, 1962/4, pp. 7–8.

42. *OIRT Information*, 1961/6, p. 16.

43. Iván Földi, "Hungarian Radio," *OIRT Review*, 1967/5, p. 11.

44. *OIRT Information*, 1961/11, p. 11.

45. *OIRT Information*, 1963/3, pp. 12–13; Lévái, p. 3.

46. *OIRT Information*, 1969/10, p. 10.

47. Lévái, p. 6.

48. *OIRT Information*, 1971/1, p. 6.

49. Ferenc Takacs, "Aiding Polytechnical Education of Young People," *OIRT Review*, 1960/4, pp. 157–159; Endre Keleman, "La Télévision dans les écoles hongroises," *OIRT Review*, 1971/1, p. 17.

50. UNESCO, *Broadcasting to Schools*, p. 173; *OIRT Information*, 1961/12, p. 7; *OIRT Information*, 1964/12, p. 7; *OIRT Information*, 1965/7, pp. 15–17.

51. "Education of Young Citizens," *OIRT Review*, 1967/3, pp. 8–9.

52. *OIRT Information*, 1964/4, p. 7; *OIRT Information*, 1964/10, p. 6; Endre Kelemen, "La Télévision dans les écoles hongroises," *OIRT Review*, 1971/1, p. 17–21.

53. Ferenc Takacs, "Aiding Polytechnical Education of Young People," *OIRT Review*, 1960/4, p. 157.

54. József Békés, "Broadcasts for Youth of the Hungarian Television," *OIRT Review*, 1966/3, pp. 19–22; "Education of Young Citizens," *OIRT Review*, 1967/3, pp. 8–9.

55. György Sándor, "Les Moyens de communication de masse et la jeunesse," *OIRT Review*, 1970/3, p. 13.

56. *OIRT Information*, 1969/11, p. 11.

57. *OIRT Information*, 1962/10, p. 9.

58. *OIRT Information*, 1963/11, p. 8.

59. *OIRT Information*, 1964/7, p. 7.

60. *OIRT Information*, 1972/3, p. 7.

61. Pál Rockenbauer, "Instructive Television Programmes for Young People," *OIRT Review*, 1963/1, pp. 3–5; Lévái, p. 7.

62. *OIRT Information*, 1966/3, p. 6.

63. *Variety*, March 3, 1971, p. 47.
64. *OIRT Information*, 1961/6, p. 15.
65. *OIRT Information*, 1963/9, pp. 12–13.
66. *OIRT Information*, 1964/10, p. 5.
67. József Békés, "Broadcasts for Youth of the Hungarian Television," *OIRT Review*, 1966/3, pp. 19–22.
68. Gézané Földes, "Participation of Children in the Creation of Broadcasts for Children," *OIRT Review*, 1966/1, pp. 16–18.
69. "Hungarian Radio," *OIRT Review*, 1961/5, pp. 11–12; "Hungarian Television," *OIRT Review*, 1961/6, pp. 16–17.
70. *OIRT Information*, 1962/4, p. 16; *OIRT Information*, 1963/11, p. 8.
71. *OIRT Information*, 1964/1, p. 8; *OIRT Information*, 1964/7, p. 8.
72. *OIRT Information*, 1965/3, p. 13; *OIRT Information*, 1971/8–9, p. 4.
73. *OIRT Information*, 1969/10, p. 11.
74. *OIRT Information*, 1970/4, p. 4.
75. *OIRT Information*, 1968/9, pp. 9–10.
76. *OIRT Information*, 1969/8, p. 9; *OIRT Information*, 1961/10, p. 9.
77. *OIRT Information*, 1965/3, p. 9; *OIRT Information*, 1965/10, p. 9; *OIRT Information*, 1966/5, p. 11; *OIRT Information*, 1966/5, p. 13; *OIRT Information*, 1971/6–7, p. 8.
78. Mihály Kovács, "The Hungarian Radio," *OIRT Review*, 1960/5, p. 204.
79. "Hungarian Television," *OIRT Review*, 1961/6, p. 17.
80. *OIRT Information*, 1964/10, p. 6.
81. *OIRT Information*, 1961/12, p. 8; *OIRT Information*, 1961/10, p. 11; *OIRT Information*, 1964/12, p. 7; *OIRT Information*, 1965/3, p. 9; *OIRT Information*, 1972/7–8, p. 8.
82. Barbara Kovács, "The Role of Hungarian Radio and Television in Adult Education," UNESCO, *Television and Further Education*, p. 180.
83. "Hungarian Television," *OIRT Review*, 1961/6, pp. 16–17.
84. *OIRT Information*, 1964/12, p. 7.
85. András Sebestyén, "Contemporary Music and the Hungarian Radio Transmissions," *OIRT Review*, 1969/2, pp. 6–7.
86. Andor Szücs, "The Mutual Influence of Radio and Television in Hungary," *OIRT Review*, 1971/6, p. 15.
87. Lévái, p. 7.
88. *OIRT Information*, 1971/8–9, p. 5.
89. *OIRT Information*, 1972/11, p. 9.
90. *OIRT Information*, 1965/9, p. 5; *OIRT Information*, 1966/8, p. 10.
91. *OIRT Information*, 1967/10, p. 7.
92. *OIRT Information*, 1964/4, p. 8.
93. András Sebestyén, "The Search for New Ways of the Development of Musical Radio Theatre," *OIRT Review*, 1961/6, pp. 10–12.
94. *European Broadcasting Union Documentation and Information Bulletin*, 3:16 (November 15, 1952), p. 636.
95. András Sebestyén, "Contemporary Music and the Hungarian Radio Transmissions," *OIRT Review*, 1969/2, pp. 6–7.
96. *OIRT Information*, 1961/3, p. 9; *OIRT Information*, 1962/4, p. 17; *OIRT Information*, 1963/3, p. 13.
97. *OIRT Information*, 1970/10, p. 9.
98. *OIRT Information*, 1961/6, p. 14; *OIRT Information*, 1971/1, p. 5.
99. *OIRT Information*, 1963/2, p. 8.
100. András Sebestyén, "Contemporary Music and the Hungarian Radio Transmissions," *OIRT Review*, 1969/2, pp. 6–7; *OIRT Information*, 1971/6–7, p. 11; *OIRT Information*, 1971/1, p. 7.

101. *OIRT Information*, 1972/3, p. 9.
102. *OIRT Information*, 1971/1, p. 9.
103. *OIRT Informtaion*, 1970/4, p. 4.
104. *OIRT Information*, 1971/8–9, p. 3.
105. *OIRT Information*, 1967/10, p. 7.
106. *OIRT Information*, 1969/10, p. 11.
107. *OIRT Information*, 1971/1, p. 9; *OIRT Information*, 1971/6–7, p. 9; *OIRT Information*, 1971/1, pp. 8–9.
108. *European Broadcasting Union Documentation and Information Bulletin*, 3:16 (November 15, 1952), p. 626.
109. *OIRT Information*, 1966/11, p. 10.
110. *OIRT Information*, 1968/9, p. 10; *OIRT Information*, 1968/11, p. 11.
111. *OIRT Information*, 1970/4, p. 6.
112. *OIRT Information*, 1965/9, p. 8; *OIRT Information*, 1971/6–7, p. 11; *OIRT Information*, 1971/4–5, p. 14.
113. "Hungarian Radio," *OIRT Review*, 1961/5, p. 12.
114. *OIRT Information*, 1965/3, p. 10.
115. *OIRT Information*, 1964/7, p. 6.
116. *OIRT Information*, 1969/11, p. 8.
117. *OIRT Information*, 1971/1, p. 7; *OIRT Information*, 1971/6–7, p. 9.
118. Lájos Lorand, "The Theatre at the Microphone and Cultural-Educational Work," *OIRT Review*, 1960/1, p. 11.
119. Andor Szücs, "The Mutual Influence of Radio and Television in Hungary," *OIRT Review*, 1971/6, p. 11.
120. Lájos Lorand, "The Theatre at the Microphone and Cultural-Educational Work," *OIRT Review*, 1960/1, pp. 10–11.
121. *OIRT Information*, 1963/3, p. 11; *OIRT Review*, 1963/9, p. 4; *OIRT Information*, 1971/1, p. 7; *OIRT Information*, 1971/8–9, p. 3.
122. *OIRT Information*, 1961/12, p. 6; *OIRT Information*, 1968/2, p. 7; *OIRT Information*, 1964/12, p. 7.
123. *OIRT Information*, 1964/4, p. 10.
124. *OIRT Information*, 1969/10, p. 8.
125. *OIRT Information*, 1971/8–9, p. 4.
126. *OIRT Information*, 1965/3, p. 10; Lévái, p. 3.
127. *OIRT Information*, 1966/5, p. 14.
128. *OIRT Information*, 1968/11, p. 6.
129. *OIRT Information*, 1972/11, p. 7.
130. *OIRT Information*, 1965/9, p. 6; *OIRT Information*, 1969/10, pp. 7, 9.
131. Anna Major, "A Report on the 'Szabó Family' and Serial Broadcasts in General," *OIRT Review*, 1965/6, pp. 15–18.
132. *OIRT Information*, 1961/3, p. 8; *OIRT Information*, 1969/11, p. 10.
133. *OIRT Information*, 1961/12, p. 6.
134. *OIRT Information*, 1962/8, p. 11; *OIRT Information*, 1963/9, p. 12; *OIRT Information*, 1964/4, p. 9.
135. *Variety*, February 23, 1972, p. 28.
136. *OIRT Information*, 1963/11, p. 10.
137. *OIRT Information*, 1971/4–5, p. 14.
138. Károly Megyeri, "A Television Reportage Is Life Itself," *OIRT Review*, 1964/1, p. 12.
139. Peter Bokor, "L'Histoire et la télévision," *OIRT Review*, 1967/2, p. 3.
140. *OIRT Information*, 1971/11–12, p. 7.
141. *OIRT Information*, 1972/11, p. 6.
142. *OIRT Information*, 1964/7, p. 8.
143. *OIRT Information*, 1971/8–9, p. 3.

144. *OIRT Information*, 1972/7–8, p. 11.
145. *OIRT Information*, 1961/6, p. 16; *OIRT Information*, 1964/1, p. 8.
146. *OIRT Information*, 1961/12, p. 6; *OIRT Information*, 1964/1, pp. 7–8.
147. *OIRT Information*, 1964/7, p. 6; *OIRT Information*, 1971/6–7, p. 11.
148. *OIRT Information*, 1963/11, p. 7.
149. *OIRT Information*, 1965/3, p. 10.
150. *OIRT Information*, 1965/5, p. 11; *OIRT Information*, 1969/10, p. 10.
151. *OIRT Information*, 1963/2, p. 9; *OIRT Information*, 1963/3, p. 11.
152. Lévái, p. 3.
153. *OIRT Information*, 1971/1, p. 7.
154. *OIRT Information*, 1971/11–12, p. 9; *OIRT Information*, 1972/3, p. 8.
155. *OIRT Information*, 1964/12, p. 8; *OIRT Information*, 1968/11, p. 6; *OIRT Information*, 1972/7–8, p. 8; *OIRT Information*, 1972/11, p. 9.
156. *OIRT Information*, 1963/3, p. 12; *OIRT Information*, 1966/11, p. 15.
157. *OIRT Information*, 1966/12, p. 16.
158. *OIRT Information*, 1971/8–9, p. 4.
159. *OIRT Information*, 1961/7, p. 10.
160. *OIRT Information*, 1963/3, p. 12.
161. *OIRT Information*, 1969/10, p. 7.
162. *OIRT Information*, 1970/4, p. 5.
163. György Sándor, "Les Moyens de communications de masse et la jeunesse," *OIRT Review*, 1970/3, p. 12.
164. *OIRT Information*, 1972/3, p. 10.
165. *OIRT Information*, 1963/11, p. 9; *OIRT Information*, 1971/6–7, p. 8; *OIRT Information*, 1972/7–8, p. 11.
166. Miklos Gardos, ed., *Hungary 70*, pp. 88–93.
167. Erika Bácskai and György László, *A rádió és a televizió müsorainak fogadtatásáról*.
168. Radio Free Europe, *The Exposure to the Domestic Radio and Television in Eastern Europe*.
169. Radio Free Europe, *The Major Information Sources of Hungarian Respondents on Important Foreign and Domestic Issues*, pp. 1, 6, 7, 9, 12–13, 15. Since respondents could give more than one answer, totals exceeded 100.
170. Radio Free Europe, *Listening to Western Radio in Hungary before and after the "Polish Events,"* pp. 1, 2, 4, 9, 11, 13, 14.
171. Radio Free Europe, *Listening to Western Broadcasts in Eastern Europe*, p. 6; table following p. 14.
172. Radio Free Europe, *RFE's Role as Seen by Polish, Czechoslovak, and Hungarian Listeners*, pp. 1, 2, 5.
173. Radio Free Europe, *Reasons for Not Listening to Radio Free Europe*, pp. 1, 5.
174. *OIRT Information*, 1963/9, p. 11; *OIRT Information*, 1964/12, p. 9; *OIRT Information*, 1965/6, p. 17; *OIRT Information*, 1966/12, p. 15; *OIRT Information*, 1968/9, p. 8; *OIRT Information*, 1969/6, p. 3; *OIRT Information*, 1969/10, p. 7; *OIRT Information*, 1970/4, p. 5; *OIRT Information*, 1971/4–5, p. 16.
175. *OIRT Information*, 1964/4, p. 10; *OIRT Information*, 1964/12, p. 9; *OIRT Information*, 1968/11, p. 9; *OIRT Information*, 1969/10, p. 7; *OIRT Information*, 1971/6–7, p. 10; *OIRT Information*, 1971/8–9, p. 3; *OIRT Information*, 1971/11–12, p. 7; *OIRT Information* 1972/3, p. 7.
176. *OIRT Information*, 1963/9, p. 14; *OIRT Information*, 1968/11, p. 10.
177. *OIRT Information*, 1970/10, p. 10.
178. *OIRT Information*, 1966/12, p. 17.
179. *OIRT Information*, 1967/10, pp. 4–5.

180. *OIRT Information*, 1968/11, p. 10; *OIRT Information*, 1969/8, p. 8.
181. *OIRT Information*, 1963/11, p. 11; *OIRT Information*, 1966/3, p. 6; *OIRT Information*, 1966/8, pp. 11–12.
182. *OIRT Information*, 1966/3, p. 6; *OIRT Information*, 1970/4, p. 6.
183. *OIRT Information*, 1961/12, pp. 5–6; *OIRT Information*, 1965/6, p. 15.
184. *OIRT Information*, 1965/3, p. 11; *OIRT Information*, 1961/3, p. 10.
185. *OIRT Information*, 1961/3, p. 9; *OIRT Information*, 1961/9, p. 9; *OIRT Information*, 1970/10, p. 9; *OIRT Information*, 1971/1, p. 5; *OIRT Information*, 1961/9, p. 15; *OIRT Information*, 1971/1, p. 5; *OIRT Information*, 1972/3, p. 8.
186. *OIRT Information*, 1965/10, p. 10; *OIRT Information*, 1968/9, p. 7; *OIRT Information*, 1968/11, p. 8.

X. The Socialist Republic of Romania

1. *Europa Year Book 1972*, Vol. 1, pp. 1085, 1101.
2. *Europa Year Book 1972*, Vol. 1, p. 1089.
3. *New York Times*, October 27, 1970, p. 9; *New York Times*, December 1, 1971, pp. 1, 8.
4. For a survey of recent Romanian domestic and international politics, see Gabriel Fischer, "Rumania," in Bromke and Rakowska-Harmstone, eds., *The Communist States in Disarray 1965–1971*, pp. 158–179.
5. *New York Times*, June 27, 1973, p. 3C.
6. *New York Times*, February 23, 1973, p. 2C.
7. *New York Times*, October 27, 1970, p. 1; *New York Times*, October 20, 1970, p. 21.
8. *New York Times*, July 7, 1972, p. 2C.
9. *New York Times*, May 27, 1973, p. 7.
10. *London Times*, March 4, 1971, p. 7.
11. *New York Times*, August 3, 1971, p. 1; *London Times*, June 3, 1971, p. 15.
12. *London Times*, August 5, 1971, p. 12.
13. *New York Times*, August 21, 1971, p. 3C.
14. *London Times*, August 25, 1971, p. 5.
15. *New York Times*, March 2, 1972, p. 3C.
16. *New York Times*, September 13, 1971, p. 2C; *New York Times*, December 23, 1972, p. 3.
17. *New York Times*, June 13, 1973, p. 20C.
18. "Constitution of the Socialist Republic of Romania," Arts. 1 and 2, in Peaslee, *Constitutions of Nations*, Vol. 3, p. 767.
19. *Ibid.*, Arts. 3, 5.
20. *Ibid.*, Art. 7.
21. *Ibid.*, Art. 13.
22. *Ibid.*, Arts. 17, 18, 19, and 21.
23. *Ibid.*, Arts. 25, 26.
24. *Ibid.*, Art. 28.
25. *Ibid.*, Art. 29.
26. *Ibid.*, Arts. 42, 45.
27. *Ibid.*, Arts. 62, 65, 66.
28. *Ibid.*, Arts. 70, 71.
29. *Europa Year Book 1972*, Vol. 1, pp. 1098, 1100.
30. Information supplied by Romanian Radio and Television.
31. *London Times*, July 14, 1971, p. 5.
32. *New York Times*, October 17, 1971, p. 14; *New York Times*, November 5, 1971, p. 4C.
33. Ion Pas, "Rumanian Radio and Television," *OIRT Review*, 1961/1, p. 3.

34. "Rumanian Radio & Television and Its Audience," *OIRT Review*, 1963/5, p. 16.

35. *London Times*, July 14, 1971, p. 5.

36. Information supplied by Romanian broadcasting authorities; *WRTH 1973*, pp. 87–88; "La Radiodiffusion Roumaine," *OIRT Review*, 1971/2, pp. 9–10.

37. Léon Serecianu, "Radio-Repos," *OIRT Review*, 1971/6, pp. 8–9.

38. Information supplied by Romanian broadcasting authorities; *WRTH 1973*, p. 280.

39. "Television in Eastern Europe," *East Europe*, 15:4 (April 1966), p. 14.

40. "Concert Hall of the Rumanian Radio," *OIRT Review*, 1962/4, pp. 26–32.

41. N. Stanciu, "Le Nouveau Centre de Télévision de Bucarest," *OIRT Review*, 1971/4, pp. 29–31. Uzinexport, the State Foreign Trade Company, has published an attractive brochure advertising architectural and engineering services through Romanian radio and television, for the planning and installation of radio, motion picture, and television facilities.

42. International Organization of Journalists, *Handbook of News Agencies.*

43. "A Few Facts on Radio Information," *OIRT Review*, 1960/2, pp. 59–60.

44. M. Teodore Brates, "Reportage en direct," *OIRT Review*, 1967/3, pp. 22–24.

45. "La Radiodiffusion Roumaine," *OIRT Review*, 1971/2, pp. 9–10; *OIRT Information*, 1971/1, p. 13.

46. *OIRT Information*, 1972/6, p. 7.

47. "Educational Broadcasts of the Rumanian Radio for Children and Youth," *OIRT Review*, 1962/4, p. 20.

48. Victor Popa, "Broadcasts for Children of the Rumanian Radio and Television," *OIRT Review*, 1966/1, pp. 13–14.

49. "Educational Broadcasts of the Rumanian Radio for Children and Youth," *OIRT Review*, 1962/4, p. 20.

50. Victor Popa, "Broadcasts for Children of the Rumanian Radio and Television," *OIRT Review*, 1966/1, p. 11; information received from the Romanian broadcasting authorities.

51. "Educational Broadcasts of the Rumanian Radio for Children and Youth," *OIRT Review*, 1962/4, pp. 20–21.

52. "Educational Broadcasts of the Rumanian Radio for Children and Youth," *OIRT Review*, 1962/4, p. 21.

53. E. Jurist, "Science and Technology in Broadcasts for Children," *OIRT Review*, 1967/3, pp. 20–21.

54. *OIRT Information*, 1963/7, p. 15; Victor Popa, "Broadcasts for Children of the Rumanian Radio and Television," *OIRT Review*, 1966/1, pp. 11–15. I had an interview with Mr. Popa which covered much of the same material as his article.

55. E. Jurist, "Science and Technology in Broadcasts for Children," *OIRT Review*, 1967/3, p. 21.

56. "Children at the Small Screen," *OIRT Review*, 1963/2, pp. 10–11; E. Jurist, "Science and Technology in Broadcasts for Children," *OIRT Review*, 1967/3, pp. 20–21; *OIRT Information*, 1971/1, p. 17.

57. Victor Popa, "Broadcasts for Children of the Rumanian Radio and Television," *OIRT Review*, 1966/1, p. 11.

58. Alexandra Teodoriu, "The Participation of Children in Broadcasts Intended for Children," *OIRT Review*, 1967/4, pp. 16–17.

59. "New Broadcasts of the Rumanian Radio and Television," *OIRT Review*, 1964/2, p. 14.

60. *OIRT Information*, 1971/1, pp. 13–14.

61. *OIRT Information*, 1971/3, p. 12.

62. *OIRT Information*, 1963/7, p. 13; "New Broadcasts of the Department of

Political Broadcasts of the Rumanian Radio & Television," *OIRT Review*, 1963/4, pp. 15–16.

63. "New Broadcasts of the Department of Political Broadcasts of the Rumanian Radio & Television," *OIRT Review*, 1963/4, p. 16.

64. "Foremost Agricultural Workers Compete: Broadcasts of the Rumanian Radio," *OIRT Review*, 1962/4, pp. 24–25.

65. "Rumanian Radio and Television: New Interesting Type of Broadcasts," *OIRT Review*, 1961/3, p. 116.

66. "Rumanian Television," *OIRT Review*, 1961/5, p. 36.

67. *OIRT Information*, 1972/6, p. 7.

68. Julius Tundrea, "Literary and Art Broadcasts of Rumanian Radio Stations," *OIRT Review*, 1968/1, p. 19.

69. "Literary Artistic Reportage on the Rumanian Radio," *OIRT Review*, 1962/4, p. 23.

70. "New Broadcasts of the Rumanian Radio and Television," *OIRT Review*, 1964/2, pp. 14–15.

71. Julius Tundrea, "Literary and Art Broadcasts of Romanian Radio Stations," *OIRT Review*, 1968/1, pp. 17–20.

72. "New Broadcasts of the Rumanian Radio & Television," *OIRT Review*, 1964/2, p. 15.

73. "La Radiodiffusion Roumaine, *OIRT Review*, 1971/2, p. 11.

74. Constantin Sabareanu, "Studio de la poésie de la Radiodiffusion Roumaine," *OIRT Review*, 1969/4, pp. 10–11.

75. Pavel Cîmpeanu, "Le Petit Théâtre," *OIRT Review*, 1967/3, pp. 6–7.

76. Virgil Stonesco, "Le Théâtre au microphone roumain," *OIRT Review*, 1969/4, pp. 19–20.

77. *OIRT Information*, 1971/8–9, pp. 11–12.

78. Petre Brântuşi, "La Radiodiffusion et la dissémination de la culture musicale," *OIRT Review*, 1969/2, pp. 8–9.

79. "Musical-Educational Broadcasts," *OIRT Review*, 1963/2, p. 7.

80. *London Times*, July 14, 1971, p. 5.

81. "Educational Broadcasts of the Rumanian Radio for Children and Youth," *OIRT Review*, 1962/4, pp. 20–22.

82. *OIRT Information*, 1963/7, p. 14; *OIRT Information*, 1971/3, p. 13.

83. *OIRT Information*, 1962/5, pp. 14–15.

84. Ovidiu Varga, "The Role of Radio in the Research, Evaluation and Propagation of Folklore," *OIRT Review*, 1963/3, p. 4.

85. *OIRT Information*, 1963/7, p. 15.

86. *OIRT Information*, 1971/1, pp. 15–16; Radu Gheciu, "L'Iphigénie sacrifiée de Pascal Bentoiu," *OIRT Review*, 1970/1, pp. 7–8.

87. "Broadcasts Devoted to the Life and Work of Georges Enescu," *OIRT Review*, 1963/1, pp. 6–7.

88. *OIRT Information*, 1971/1, p. 16.

89. *OIRT Information*, 1971/8–9, p. 14. For pictures of the new Bucharest television building and of rehearsals of several programs, including a New Year's Eve broadcast, see *OIRT Review*, 1971/2, pp. 20–22.

90. "New Broadcasts of the Rumanian Radio & Television," *OIRT Review*, 1964/2, p. 15; "Literary Artistic Reportage on the Rumanian Radio," *OIRT Review*, 1962/4, p. 23.

91. Green, pp. 166–167.

92. Ion Pas, "Rumanian Radio and Television," *OIRT Review*, 1961/1, p. 5; "The Use of Listeners' Letters in the Department of Political Broadcasts," *OIRT Review*, 1963/4, p. 22; "Romanian Radio & Television and Its Audience," *OIRT Review*, 1963/5, pp. 16–18.

93. Pavel Câmpeanu, "The Office of Studies and Surveys of the Radio and Television," *The Romanian Journal of Sociology*, Vol. 6, pp. 143–147.

94. Pavel Câmpeanu, "La Télévision et les connaissances en matière de théâtre du public rurale," unpublished report released in June 1971.

95. Radio Free Europe, *The Exposure to the Domestic Radio and Television in Eastern Europe.*

96. Radio Free Europe, *Listening to Western Broadcasts in Eastern Europe*, pp. 2–3, 10–11, tables following p. 14.

97. Radio Free Europe, *Critical Developments and Listening Behavior in East Europe*, p. 5; Radio Free Europe, *Reasons for Not Listening to Radio Free Europe*, p. 5.

98. *OIRT Information*, 1962/5, pp. 12–14; *OIRT Information*, 1963/7, pp. 11–12; *OIRT Information*, 1966/2, pp. 18–19.

99. *OIRT Information*, 1964/3, pp. 16–18. Most issues of the *Catalogue of Transmissions Suitable for Exchange* published by the OIRT list Romanian dramatic and musical programs.

100. *OIRT Information*, 1966/2, p. 19; *OIRT Information*, 1971/8–9, p. 13.

101. *Variety*, June 23, 1971, p. 2.

XI. The People's Republic of Bulgaria

1. *Europa Year Book 1972*, Vol. 1, p. 572.

2. Michael Costello, "Bulgaria," in Bromke and Rakowska-Harmstone, eds., *The Communist States in Disarray 1965–1971*, p. 136.

3. *New York Times*, November 6, 1972, p. 2C.

4. *Europa Year Book 1972*, Vol. 1, p. 570.

5. *New York Times*, November 8, 1972, p. 69.

6. *Europa Year Book 1972*, Vol. 1, p. 575.

7. *Constitution of the People's Republic of Bulgaria*. Art. 1; hereafter cited as *Bulgarian Constitution*.

8. *Ibid.*, Art. 2.

9. *Ibid.*, Art. 16, Sec. 1.

10. *Ibid.*, Arts. 66, 68, 78.

11. *Ibid.*, Art. 92.

12. *Ibid.*, Art. 98.

13. *Ibid.*, Arts. 35, 36, 40, 42, 45.

14. *Ibid.*, Art. 53, Sec. 1.

15. *Ibid.*, Sec. 4.

16. *Ibid.*, Art. 52.

17. *Ibid.*, Art. 63.

18. Velko Verin, "Getting into Print in Bulgaria," *East Europe*, 18:1 (January 1969), p. 22. Raymond B. Nixon, ranking Bulgaria with 116 other countries on a 9-point scale for press freedom and control, with 1 indicating a free press and 9 a completely controlled one, classified Bulgaria as 8: "controlled press system but with less rigid controls and/or some opportunity for debate within system" ("Freedom in the World Press: A Fresh Appraisal with New Data," *Journalism Quarterly*, 42:1 (Winter 1965), pp. 6, 13).

19. *Bulgarian Constitution*, Art. 1.

20. *Europa Year Book 1972*, Vol. 1, p. 581.

21. *OIRT Information*, 1966/1, p. 4.

22. *OIRT Information*, 1971/1, pp. 2–4; *WRTH 1973*, p. 46. For additional comments on the current distinctions among the three radio services see "Nouvelles tendances dans le développement des programmes radiodiffusés: La Radiodiffusion Bulgare," *OIRT Review*, 1971/2, pp. 3–4.

23. *OIRT Information*, 1972/1, pp. 1–2.
24. *Internationales Handbuch 1971/72*, p. F16.
25. *OIRT Information*, 1966/8, pp. 1–2.
26. *OIRT Information*, 1961/1, pp. 3–4; *OIRT Information*, 1961/3, pp. 1–2; *OIRT Information*, 1961/7, pp. 1–2.
27. *OIRT Information*, 1962/6, pp. 3–5.
28. UNESCO, *World Communications: Press Radio Television Film*, p. 270; *WRTH 1973*, p. 273.
29. *OIRT Information*, 1972/10–11, pp. 1–2; *WRTH 1974*, p. 281.
30. *OIRT Information*, 1972/2, pp. 1–3.
31. *OIRT Information*, 1972/6, p. 1; *OIRT Information*, 1972/10–11, p. 2.
32. *OIRT Information*, 1971/4–5, p. 2.
33. Pavel Pisarev, "Current Questions of Bulgarian Television," *Bulgarski Zhurnalist*, July 1969.
34. *Internationales Handbuch 1971/72*, p. F16.
35. *OIRT Information*, 1967/7, p. 2.
36. Mikhaïl Minkov, "Certains problèmes de la radio et l'interaction de la radio, de la presse et de la télévision dans les conditions de la société socialiste," *OIRT Review*, 1970/2, p. 25.
37. "Rubrics of Sofia Radio," *OIRT Review*, 1960/2, p. 56.
38. *OIRT Information*, 1963/6, p. 1.
39. Penyu Ivanov, "The Bulgarian Radio in the Fight for the Formation of a New Man," *OIRT Review*, 1965/2, pp. 22–25.
40. "Nouvelles tendances dans le développement des programmes radiodiffusés: La Radiodiffusion Bulgare," *OIRT Review*, 1971/2, pp. 3–4.
41. *WRTH 1973*, p. 46. For a theoretical discussion of radio journalism, see the article by Mikhail Minkov, "The Problems of Genres in Radio Journalism," *OIRT Review*, 1972/2, pp. 3–8.
42. *OIRT Information*, 1971/1, p. 4. Information received from radio and television news staffs.
43. International Organization of Journalists, *Handbook of News Agencies*.
44. Vesséline Dimitrov, "De six à huit," *OIRT Review*, 1969/5, pp. 6–9; *OIRT Information*, 1968/5, p. 1.
45. Mikhail Minkov, "The Problems of Genres in Radio Journalism," *OIRT Review*, 1972/2, p. 3.
46. *Internationales Handbuch 1971/72*, p. 16F.
47. Snezhina Kraleva, "Broadcasts for Children of the Bulgarian Radio," *OIRT Review*, 1966/1, pp. 19–20.
48. Shelyaska Kupenova, "Instructional and Educational Broadcasts and the Formation of a World Outlook in Youth," *OIRT Review*, 1971/5, pp. 21–24.
49. *OIRT Information*, 1972/6, p. 2.
50. Snezhina Kraleva, "Broadcasts for Children of the Bulgarian Radio," *OIRT Review*, 1966/1, pp. 20–21.
51. *OIRT Information*, 1966/1, pp. 2–3.
52. *OIRT Information*, 1963/9, p. 1.
53. *OIRT Information*, 1964/1, pp. 4–5; *OIRT Information*, 1964/2, p. 1.
54. Dimitr Tochev, "Broadcasts of Bulgarian Radio for Children," *OIRT Review*, 1961/2, pp. 65–66.
55. *OIRT Information*, 1964/1, p. 2.
56. Rosen Vasilev, "Broadcasts for Children of Pre-School Age," *OIRT Review*, 1967/1, pp. 19–21.
57. *OIRT Information*, 1963/7, p. 3.
58. *OIRT Information*, 1963/2, p. 1; *OIRT Information*, 1963/8, p. 2; *OIRT Information*, 1965/1, pp. 4–5.

59. *OIRT Information*, 1965/1, p. 5; *OIRT Information*, 1967/11, p. 1.

60. *OIRT Information*, 1964/1, p. 3; *OIRT Information*, 1964/5, p. 3; *OIRT Information*, 1965/1, pp. 1–2; *OIRT Information*, 1971/3, p. 2; *OIRT Information*, 1972/6, p. 2.

61. Maria Gheorghieva, "Popularization of Scientific and Technical Knowledge on the Air," *OIRT Review*, 1960/6, p. 270; *OIRT Information*, 1965/1, pp. 2–3; *OIRT Information*, 1965/4, p. 1.

62. *OIRT Information*, 1963/10, p. 3; *OIRT Information*, 1964/1, p. 4.

63. *OIRT Information*, 1963/9, p. 2.

64. *OIRT Information*, 1963/6, p. 2; *OIRT Information*, 1965/1, p. 4; *OIRT Information*, 1971/2, p. 2.

65. "The Bulgarian Radio," *OIRT Review*, 1960/5, pp. 202–203.

66. *OIRT Information*, 1961/12, pp. 16–17; *OIRT Information*, 1961/7, pp. 2–5.

67. *OIRT Information*, 1965/4, p. 2.

68. "Our Experience in the Field of Economic Radio Propaganda," *OIRT Review*, 1963/6, pp. 8–9.

69. Vlado Marianov, "Economic Broadcasts of Sofia Radio," *OIRT Review*, 1967/1, pp. 12, 14.

70. *OIRT Information*, 1964/5, p. 2.

71. *OIRT Information*, 1964/8, pp. 1–4.

72. *OIRT Information*, 1966/12, pp. 1–2.

73. *OIRT Information*, 1966/8, pp. 3–4; *OIRT Information*, 1971/2, p. 2.

74. *OIRT Information*, 1972/6, p. 2.

75. *OIRT Information*, 1971/2, pp. 2–3; *OIRT Information*, 1971/3, pp. 1–2.

76. Veselin Nikolov, "New Literary Broadcasts of the Sofia Radio," *OIRT Review*, 1961/4, pp. 9–10.

77. *OIRT Information*, 1965/2, p. 1; *OIRT Information*, 1966/8, p. 3.

78. *OIRT Information*, 1968/9, pp. 1–2.

79. *OIRT Information*, 1972/3, p. 1.

80. *OIRT Information*, 1963/7, p. 2.

81. Khristo Kovachev, "Sound in Radio Plays," *OIRT Review*, 1961/1, pp. 10–11.

82. *Internationales Handbuch 1971/72*, p. F16.

83. *OIRT Information*, 1962/3, p. 1; *OIRT Information*, 1963/6, p. 1.

84. *OIRT Information*, 1963/11, p. 2.

85. *Internationales Handbuch 1971/72*, p. F16.

86. *OIRT Information*, 1963/6, p. 3.

87. *OIRT Information*, 1963/4, p. 1; *OIRT Information*, 1963/11, p. 3.

88. *OIRT Information*, 1965/1, p. 3.

89. *Internationales Handbuch 1971/72*, p. F16.

90. *OIRT Information*, 1971/1, pp. 3–4.

91. *OIRT Information*, 1967/7, p. 2.

92. Stoïan Anghélov, "The Role of Radio Broadcasting in the Enrichment of the Listeners' Musical Culture," *OIRT Review*, 1967/2, pp. 23–25; Stoïan Anghélov, "Musique contemporaine dans les programmes radiodiffusés," *OIRT Review*, 1969/2, pp. 3–5.

93. *OIRT Information*, 1969/7, p. 2.

94. *OIRT Information*, 1963/10, p. 2; *OIRT Information*, 1966/8, pp. 2–3; *OIRT Information*, 1970/9, p. 3; *OIRT Information*, 1971/4–5, p. 3.

95. *OIRT Information*, 1967/7, p. 1; Emil Karamanov, "Le Genre musico-dramatique radiophonique et la Radiodiffusion Bulgare," *OIRT Review*, 1969/6, pp. 13–14; *OIRT Information*, 1970/7–8, p. 2.

96. Georghi Boyadjiyev, "Competitions of Amateurs," *OIRT Review*, 1961/4,

p. 11; *OIRT Information*, 1964/5, p. 3; *OIRT Information*, 1967/7, p. 2; *OIRT Information*, 1968/9, p. 2.
    97. *Internationales Handbuch 1971/72*, p. F16.
    98. *OIRT Information*, 1963/7, p. 2; *OIRT Information*, 1965/2, p. 3.
    99. Marko Stoychev, "Entertaining Broadcasts of the Bulgarian Radio," *OIRT Review*, 1969/4, pp. 16–18.
    100. *OIRT Information*, 1971/3, p. 3.
    101. *OIRT Information*, 1962/6, pp. 1–2.
    102. *OIRT Information*, 1965/2, pp. 3–4.
    103. *OIRT Information*, 1972/10–11, p. 2.
    104. *OIRT Information*, 1964/5, p. 1.
    105. *OIRT Information*, 1967/7, p. 3.
    106. *OIRT Information*, 1968/5, p. 3.
    107. See above, pp. 185–186.
    108. Radio Free Europe, *The Exposure to the Domestic Radio and Television in Eastern Europe*.
    109. Radio Free Europe, *Listening to Western Broadcasts in Eastern Europe*, pp. 2, 12, 13; chart following p. 14.
    110. Radio Free Europe, *Critical Developments and Listening Behavior in East Europe*, pp. 1, 5.
    111. Alexej Chichov, "Une Fenêtre toujours ouverte sur la Bulgarie," *OIRT Review*, 1970/6, pp. 11–16.
    112. *WRTH 1973*, p. 46.
    113. Alexej Chichov, "Une Fenêtre toujours ouverte sur la Bulgarie," *OIRT Review*, 1970/6, p. 12.
    114. *OIRT Information*, 1968/5, p. 3.
    115. *OIRT Information*, 1971/4–5, pp. 1–3.
    116. *OIRT Information*, 1972/6, p. 2; *Internationales Handbuch 1971/72*, p. 16F.
    117. *OIRT Information*, 1963/10, p. 2; *OIRT Information*, 1964/2, p. 3; *OIRT Information*, 1964/12, p. 2; *OIRT Information*, 1965/9, p. 2; *OIRT Information*, 1970/9, p. 3; *OIRT Information*, 1971/4–5, p. 3; *OIRT Information*, 1973/1, p. 3.

XII. The Socialist Federal Republic of Yugoslavia

    1. *Europa Year Book 1973*, Vol. 1, p. 1510.
    2. *New York Times*, October 29, 1972, p. 5F.
    3. *Europa Year Book 1972*, Vol. 1, pp. 1421, 1427–1428.
    4. *New York Times*, January 19, 1973, p. 47C.
    5. *Europa Year Book 1972*, Vol. 1, pp. 1435–1436.
    6. *New York Times*, January 25, 1972, p. 3C; *New York Times*, December 17, 1971, p. 8C. Anatole Shub, "After Tito—Who Can Keep Together the Serbs, Croats, Slovenes, Macedonians, Bosnian Moslems, Albanians, Hungarians and Montenegrins?" *New York Times Magazine*, January 16, 1972, p. 14–15, 38, 44, 50.
    7. *New York Times*, April 28, 1971, p. 5C.
    8. *New York Times*, December 3, 1971, p. 8C; December 20, 1971, p. 8C; December 17, 1971, p. 8C; January 1, 1972, p. 2C; January 23, 1972, p. 15; January 28, 1972, p. 3C; February 17, 1972, p. 2; September 16, 1972, p. 2; October 1, 1972, p. 15; April 13, 1973, p. 6C.
    9. *New York Times*, January 28, 1972, p. 3C; *London Times*, April 7, 1971, p. 7; *New York Times*, December 3, 1971, p. 8C.
    10. *New York Times*, September 23, 1971, p. 10C; *New York Times*, June 6,

1972, pp. 1, 11; *New York Times*, June 11, 1972, p. 25; *New York Times*, October 8, 1972, p. 6.

11. *New York Times*, September 23, 1971, p. 10C.

12. "Constitution of Yugoslavia," in Peaslee, *Constitutions of Nations*, Vol. 3, p. 1236; hereafter cited as *Yugoslav Constitution*.

13. *Ibid.*, Arts. 1, 2.

14. *Ibid.*, Art. 9.

15. *Ibid.*, Art. 33.

16. *Ibid.*, Arts. 35–38.

17. *Ibid.*, Art. 40.

18. *Ibid.*, Art. 46.

19. *Ibid.*, Art. 40.

20. *Ibid.*, Arts. 78, 81.

21. *Ibid.*, Arts. 220–221.

22. *Europa Year Book 1972*, Vol. 1, p. 1434.

23. *Law of the Press and Other Forms of Information*, hereafter cited as *Law of the Press*. There is an interesting discussion of Yugoslav press law in Mate Oreč, "Application of International Principles on Freedom of Information in Yugoslavia," *Mass Media and International Understanding*, pp. 384–391.

24. *Law of the Press*, Art. 2.

25. *Ibid.*, Arts. 3, 5, 6, 7.

26. *Ibid.*, Arts. 34–39, 82–83.

27. "Basic Law on Radio Communication," in *Jugoslovenska Radiotelevizija Yearbook 1971/72*, pp. 479–480, hereafter cited as *JRT Yearbook*.

28. *Ibid.*, Arts. 2, 3.

29. "Basic Law on Radiobroadcasting Institutions," in *JRT Yearbook 1971/72*, pp. 467–475.

30. *Ibid.*, Arts. 2, 5.

31. *Ibid.*, Art. 11.

32. *Ibid.*, Art. 24; *JRT Yearbook 1971/72*, p. 10.

33. *JRT Yearbook 1971/72*, pp. 10, 425–431.

34. Further details about the organization of Yugoslav broadcasting are given in *JRT Yearbook 1971/72*, pp. 408–419.

35. *JRT Yearbook 1971/72*, pp. 13–17, 72.

36. "Statute of the Community of Broadcasting Institutions of the Federal Socialist Republic of Yugoslavia—Jugoslovenska Radiotelevizija," *JRT Yearbook 1971/72*, pp. 489–500, Art. 1, hereafter cited as "JRT Statute." There is an outline of the work of JRT in the *JRT Yearbook 1971/72*, pp. 72–77.

37. "JRT Statute," Art. 12.

38. *Ibid.*, Arts. 14, 21.

39. *Ibid.*, Art. 33.

40. *JRT Yearbook 1971/72*, pp. 449, 483–488.

41. Information supplied by Yugoslav broadcasting.

42. *New York Times*, May 21, 1971, p. 23C.

43. *New York Times*, December 28, 1966, p. 3.

44. *Yugoslav Constitution*, Art. 40; *Law of the Press*, Arts. 6, 7.

45. *New York Times*, May 2, 1971, p. 3.

46. C. S. Sulzberger, "A Conversation with Yugoslavia's Djilas: 'We Are Going toward the Death of All Isms,'" *New York Times Magazine*, June 9, 1968, pp. 30–31, 110–120; *London Times*, October 24, 1969, p. 7.

47. *New York Times*, January 7, 1971, p. 35; July 31, 1972, p. 27C; August 1, 1972, p. 33M; August 2, 1972, p. 35M; June 21, 1973, p. 7C.

48. *New York Times*, February 10, 1972, p. 11C; *New York Times*, December 21, 1972, p. 35C; *New York Times*, January 29, 1973, p. 7C.

49. *London Times*, August 24, 1971, p. 4.
50. *New York Times*, September 17, 1972, p. 11.
51. *New York Times*, January 18, 1973, p. 4C; *New York Times*, March 18, 1973, p. 6: *New York Times*, April 22, 1973, p. 12.
52. *New York Times*, January 2, 1973, p. 37C.
53. *New York Times*, April 1, 1973, p. 18.
54. *New York Times*, April 8, 1973, p. 14.
55. *JRT Yearbook 1971/72*, p. 10.
56. *JRT Yearbook 1971/72*, pp. 122–123, 129, 397.
57. *JRT Yearbook 1971/72*, pp. 10, 153.
58. *JRT Yearbook 1971/72*, p. 13.
59. *JRT Yearbook 1971/72*, chart following p. 160.
60. *JRT Yearbook 1971/72*, p. 23. The *Yearbook* (pp. 20–72) lists all 163 local stations and provides information about their equipment, hours on the air, and programs.
61. *JRT Yearbook 1971/72*, p. 158, chart following p. 160.
62. *JRT Yearbook 1971/72*, pp. 78–86, 86–87.
63. *JRT Yearbook 1971/72*, p. 12.
64. *JRT Yearbook 1971/72*, pp. 89–91.
65. *JRT Yearbook 1971/72*, pp. 9–10, 284–285, 293, 339.
66. *JRT Yearbook 1970*, p. 240.
67. A typical week's schedule is given in *JRT Yearbook 1971/72*, pp. 296–300.
68. *JRT Yearbook 1971/72*, pp. 293, 339.
69. *JRT Yearbook 1971/72*, pp. 13–14.
70. *JRT Yearbook 1971/72*, pp. 11–12, 294–295, 305.
71. *JRT Yearbook 1971/72*, pp. 11–12, 294–295; *WRTH 1973*, p. 282.
72. *JRT Yearbook 1971/72*, pp. 78, 103–109.
73. *JRT Yearbook 1971/72*, pp. 284, 292–293.
74. *JRT Yearbook 1971/72*, p. 110.
75. *EBU Review*, 124B (November 1970), p. 81; *EBU Review*, 126A (April 1971), p. 77; *JRT Yearbook 1971/72*, p. 294.
76. *JRT Yearbook 1971/72*, p. 295.
77. *JRT Yearbook 1971/72*, p. 422.
78. *JRT Yearbook 1971/72*, pp. 275–280.
79. *JRT Yearbook 1970*, pp. 287–288; *JRT Yearbook 1971/72*, pp. 327–329.
80. *Europa Year Book 1972*, Vol. 1, p. 1436.
81. Milan Pogačnik, "Independence and Responsibility of Yugoslav Journalists," *Mass Media and International Understanding*, pp. 325–326.
82. *JRT Yearbook 1971/72*, pp. 162, 300, chart following p. 160.
83. *JRT Yearbook 1971/72*, pp. 162, 303, 369.
84. *JRT Yearbook 1971/72*, pp. 284, 303.
85. *JRT Yearbook 1971/72*, p. 373.
86. *JRT Yearbook 1971/72*, pp. 165–167.
87. *JRT Yearbook 1971/72*, pp. 176–177.
88. *JRT Yearbook 1971/72*, pp. 300–302.
89. *JRT Yearbook 1970*, pp. 142–143.
90. *JRT Yearbook 1971/72*, p. 324, chart following p. 160.
91. Hrvoje Juračić, "Broadcasting and the Schools," *EBU Review*, 72B (March 1962), pp. 6–7.
92. *JRT Yearbook 1970*, pp. 160, 166.
93. Hrvoje Juračić, "Teaching Children Their Mother Tongue through Literature Broadcasts," *EBU Review*, 79B (May 1963), pp. 16–17.
94. *JRT Yearbook 1970*, pp. 167, 172–173.
95. *JRT Yearbook 1970*, pp. 159–160.

96. *JRT Yearbook 1970*, pp. 166–167.
97. *JRT Yearbook 1970*, pp. 183, 186.
98. *JRT Yearbook 1971/72*, p. 324.
99. Hrvoje Juračić, "The First Year of School Television," *EBU Review*, 69B (September 1961), p. 33.
100. *JRT Yearbook 1970*, pp. 284–285.
101. Golina Jankovic, "Educational Sound Programmes in Yugoslavia," *Proceedings of the International Conference of Broadcasting Organizations on Sound and Television School Broadcasting*, pp. 74–78.
102. Nedjeljko Kujundžić, "The Individualization of Young People: What Is the Influence of Radiotelevizija Zagreb in This Sphere?" *EBU Review*, 130B (November 1971), pp. 41–42.
103. *JRT Yearbook 1970*, pp. 160–161.
104. *JRT Yearbook 1970*, pp. 173–174.
105. Nedjeljko Kujundžić, "The Individualization of Young People: What Is the Influence of Radiotelevizija Zagreb in This Sphere?" *EBU Review*, 130B (November 1971), pp. 41–42.
106. Branko Petrovic, "An Experimental Programme for the Hard of Hearing," *EBU Review*, 24:2 (March 1973), pp. 29–32; *JRT Yearbook 1971/72*, p. 180.
107. *JRT Yearbook 1971/72*, pp. 314–315.
108. *JRT Yearbook 1971/72*, chart following p. 160.
109. *JRT Yearbook 1970*, pp. 159, 167.
110. *JRT Yearbook 1970*, pp. 171–172.
111. *JRT Yearbook 1971/72*, pp. 178, 180, 184–185, 194–195, 199.
112. *JRT Yearbook 1970*, pp. 285–286.
113. *JRT Yearbook 1970*, p. 245.
114. *JRT Yearbook 1971/72*, pp. 191, 296–300, 324–325.
115. John Maddison, *Radio and Television in Literacy: A Survey of the Use of the Broadcasting Media in Combating Illiteracy among Adults*, p. 14.
116. United Nations, *Demographic Yearbook 1970*, pp. 589–590.
117. *JRT Yearbook 1970*, pp. 157, 165, 181–182.
118. *JRT Yearbook 1971/72*, pp. 183–184, 189, 194, 197.
119. *JRT Yearbook 1971/72*, pp. 305–311.
120. *JRT Yearbook 1971/72*, pp. 184, 316.
121. *JRT Yearbook 1971/72*, pp. 293, 316–318.
122. *JRT Yearbook 1970*, pp. 274–284.
123. *New York Times*, December 5, 1972, p. 8C.
124. *JRT Yearbook 1971/72*, pp. 316–317.
125. *JRT Yearbook 1971/72*, charts following pp. 160 and 240.
126. *JRT Yearbook 1971/72*, pp. 269–274, 391–392.
127. *JRT Yearbook 1970*, p. 192. Detailed information about radio music is given on pp. 187–232.
128. *JRT Yearbook 1970*, pp. 188–190.
129. *JRT Yearbook 1970*, pp. 199–200.
130. *JRT Yearbook 1970*, p. 197. Local station programs are described on pp. 17–57.
131. Djordje Karaklajić, "Folklore and Radio," *EBU Review*, 103B (May 1967), pp. 58–59; *JRT Yearbook 1970*, p. 194.
132. *JRT Yearbook 1970*, pp. 267–270.
133. *JRT Yearbook 1971/72*, chart following p. 160; p. 241.
134. *JRT Yearbook 1970*, p. 158.
135. *JRT Yearbook 1970*, p. 165.
136. *JRT Yearbook 1970*, pp. 174–176.
137. *JRT Yearbook 1970*, pp. 267–269.

138. *JRT Yearbook 1971/72*, pp. 303–304, 339.
139. *JRT Yearbook 1971/72*, pp. 333–334.
140. *JRT Yearbook 1971/72*, p. 304.
141. *JRT Yearbook 1965*, p. 7.
142. *JRT Yearbook 1970*, pp. 315–319.
143. Igor Leandrov, "Mass Communications in Yugoslavia," *Mass Media and International Understanding*, p. 319. The study covers newspapers and theaters as well as broadcasting.
144. *JRT Yearbook 1970*, p. 314.
145. *JRT Yearbook 1970*, p. 319.
146. *JRT Yearbook 1970*, pp. 317, 318, 320.
147. *JRT Yearbook 1970*, p. 317.
148. *JRT Yearbook 1970*, pp. 302, 305.
149. *WRTH 1973*, p. 109.
150. *JRT Yearbook 1971/72*, p. 86.
151. *JRT Yearbook 1971/72*, chart following p. 160.
152. *JRT Yearbook 1971/72*, pp. 367–368, 370–371.
153. *JRT Yearbook 1971/72*, p. 333.
154. *JRT Yearbook 1970*, pp. 307, 310–312.

XIII. The People's Republic of Albania

1. *Europa Year Book 1972*, Vol. 1, p. 510.
2. For information on the political status of Albania, see William E. Griffith, *Albania and the Sino-Soviet Rift*; Anton Logoreci, "Albania and China: The Incongruous Alliance," *Current History*, 52:308 (1967), pp. 227–231, 245; and Peter R. Prifti, "Albania," in Bromke and Rakowska-Harmstone, eds., *The Communist States in Disarray 1965–1971*, pp. 198–220.
3. *New York Times*, October 6, 1971, p. 12C.
4. *Europa Year Book 1972*, Vol. 1, pp. 508, 513.
5. *Statesman's Year-Book 1971–1972*, p. 734.
6. *Europa Year Book 1972*, Vol. 1, pp. 514, 516.
7. *WRTH 1973*, pp. 41, 273; *Internationales Handbuch 1971/72*, p. F4; *OIRT Information*, 1961/5, pp. 1–3.
8. *BBC Handbook 1973*, p. 103; *WRTH 1973*, p. 41.
9. *Internationales Handbuch 1971/72*, p. F4.
10. FBIS *Daily Report*, No. 151, Vol. 2 (August 3, 1972), pp. B1–B2.

Appendix. Technical Information

1. George A. Codding, *Broadcasting without Barriers*, pp. 77–78.
2. V. D. Sher and L. M. Kononovitch, "Stereophonic Broadcasting in the USSR," *OIRT Review*, 1968/6, p. 37.
3. Tables providing detailed information about the world's television systems are printed in each edition of the *World Radio TV Handbook*—for example, *WRTH 1973*, p. 272. They are reproduced in Paulu, *Radio and Television Broadcasting on the European Continent*, pp. 249–252.
4. Details of the OIRT system are outlined in S. V. Novakovskij and D. I. Ermakov, "Consideration of Fundamental Characteristics of the OIRT Monochrome Television Standard," *OIRT Review*, 1960/3, pp. 111–123.
5. In preparing this description of color television process, Professor Brown drew upon John Patrick Hawker, *Radio and Television*, Ch. 20.
6. *New York Times*, March 23, 1965, p. 1.

7. *London Times*, July 19, 1966, p. 1; *London Times*, July 23, 1966, p. 1; "Colour Television in Europe," *EBU Review*, 98A (August 1966), pp. 138–141; Georges Hansen, "Colour-Television Standards for Europe," *WRTH 1965*, pp. 28–30. The assembly also was concerned with other matters pertaining to television as well as with FM radio and magnetic tape recording, although television standards were the most important item discussed.

8. "Meeting of CCIR Study Groups and XI in Vienna," *OIRT Review*, 1965/4, p. 41.

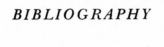

BIBLIOGRAPHY

Bibliography

There are no comprehensive studies of radio and television broadcasting in the socialist countries of Eastern Europe. As mass media courses are introduced in the universities, and research departments established by broadcasting organizations, some publications are emerging; but there are very few of them and they are of uneven quality. There also is little documentation of the sort turned out so extensively by Western parliamentary bodies and government agencies. Except for Yugoslavia none of these countries has a yearbook like those published by a number of broadcasting organizations in Western Europe. Because there are no large collections of material, the scholar must collect information as best he can, item by item, rather than working in well-equipped libraries containing much of what he needs.

Among the more useful books are those listed below by Gayle Durham Hollander, Mark W. Hopkins, and Walter B. Emery. But even these deal with single aspects of the subject, are concerned mainly with the print media, or devote limited space to the Eastern European countries.

The publications cited in the footnotes of this book, together with some others containing important information, are grouped below in two categories: books and pamphlets, and newspapers and periodicals. When citation is by an abbreviation not readily apparent from the full title, the short form is given following the entry.

Books and Pamphlets

Bácskai, Erika, and György László. *A rádió és a televizió müsorainak fogadtatásáról.* (Tomegkommunikacios kutatokozpont III 1.) Budapest, 1971.

Bailes, Kendall. *Soviet Television Comes of Age: A Review of Its Accomplishments and a Discussion of the Task Facing It.* New York: Radio Liberty Committee, 1968. Radio Liberty Research Paper, No. 24.

Barghoorn, Frederick C. *Soviet Foreign Propaganda.* Princeton: Princeton University Press, 1964.

Barnouw, Erik. *A Tower in Babel (A History of Broadcasting in the United States,* Vol. 1, to 1933). New York: Oxford University Press, 1966.

Bartlett's Familiar Quotations: A Collection of Passages, Phrases and Proverbs Traced to Their Sources in Ancient and Modern Literature. 14th ed. Emily Morison Beck, ed. Boston: Little, Brown, 1968.

BBC Handbook 1970. London: British Broadcasting Corporation, 1970.

BBC Handbook 1971. London: British Broadcasting Corporation, 1971.
BBC Handbook 1972. London: British Broadcasting Corporation, 1972.
BBC Handbook 1973. London: British Broadcasting Corporation, 1972.
Berman, Harold J., and James W. Spindler, trans. *Soviet Criminal Law and Procedure; the RSFSR Codes.* 2nd ed. Cambridge, Mass.: Harvard University Press, 1972. Russian Research Center Studies, No. 50.
Brack, Hans. *German Radio and Television: Organization and Economic Basis.* Geneva: European Broadcasting Union, 1968. Legal and Administrative Series, Monograph No. 6.
Briggs, Asa. *The Birth of Broadcasting (The History of Broadcasting in the United Kingdom,* Vol. 1). London: Oxford University Press, 1961.
————. *The War of Words (The History of Broadcasting in the United Kingdom,* Vol. 3). London: Oxford University Press, 1970.
Broadcasting Yearbook 1972. Washington: Broadcaasting Publications, 1972.
Bromke, Adam, and Teresa Rakowska-Harmstone, eds. *The Communist States in Disarray 1965–1971.* Minneapolis: University of Minnesota Press, 1972. The Carleton Series in Soviet and East European Studies.
Bulgaria. *Constitution of the People's Republic of Bulgaria,* adopted by a national referendum on May 16, 1971. Sofia: Sofia Press, 1971.
Buzek, Antony. *How the Communist Press Works.* New York: Frederick A. Praeger, 1964. Praeger Publications in Russian History and World Communism, No. 147.
Câmpeanu, Pavel. "La Télévision et les connaissances en matière de théâtre du public rurale." Unpublished report released in June 1971.
Childs, Harwood L., and John B. Whitton, eds. *Propaganda by Short Wave.* Princeton: Princeton University Press; London: H. Milford, Oxford University Press, 1942.
Codding, George A., Jr. *Broadcasting without Barriers.* Paris: UNESCO, 1959.
Communication in the Space Age: The Use of Satellites by the Mass Media. Paris: UNESCO, 1968.
Czechoslovak Government Information Office. *The Constitution of the Czechoslovak Republic.* A reprint of the English rendition published in Prague in 1920. New York, 1944.
Deutscher Demokratischer Rundfunk. *Informationen.* 1968. Cited as Rundfunk, *Informationen.*
Deutscher Fernsehfunk. *Fernsehdienst: Sonderausgabe.* 1969.
————. *Information on Television in the GDR.* 1967.
————. *Der Präsident im Exil: Information und Kommentare.* 1969.
Dunlap, Orrin E., Jr. *Marconi, the Man and His Wireless.* Rev. ed. New York: Macmillan, 1938.
Durham, F. Gayle. *Amateur Radio Operation in the Soviet Union.* Cambridge, Mass.: Center for International Studies, Massachusetts Institute of Technology, 1965. Research Program on Problems of Communication and International Security.
————. *News Broadcasting on Soviet Radio and Television.* Cambridge, Mass.: Center for International Studies, Massachusetts Institute of Technology, 1965. Research Program on Problems of Communication and International Security.
————. *Radio and Television in the Soviet Union.* Cambridge, Mass.: Center for International Studies, Massachusetts Institute of Technology, 1965. Research Program on Problems of International Communication and Security.
Editor and Publisher International Year Book 1973. New York: Editor and Publisher Co., 1973.
Effect of Underground Radio Stations in the USSR. Washington: Joint Publications Research Service, 1968.

Emery, Walter B. *National and International Systems of Broadcasting: Their History, Operation, and Control.* East Lansing: Michigan State University Press, 1969.

Encyclopaedia Britannica. Chicago: Encyclopaedia Britannia, 1958; 1965.

The Europa Year Book 1965. A World Survey. 2 vols. London: Europa Publications, 1965.

The Europa Year Book 1971. A World Survey. 2 vols. London: Europa Publications, 1971.

The Europa Year Book 1972. A World Survey. 2 vols. London: Europa Publications, 1972.

The Europa Year Book 1973. A World Survey. 2 vols. London: Europa Publications, 1973.

Fainsod, Merle. *Smolensk under Soviet Rule.* New York: Vintage Books, 1963. Vintage Russian Library.

Firsov, Boris. *There Is No "Average" Viewer: A Soviet TV Survey.* Translated from *Zhurnalist*, No. 12 (December 1967). New York: Radio Liberty Committee, 1967.

German Democratic Republic. *Charter of Freedom and Humanity.* Draft Constitution of the Socialist State of the German Nation, presented to the Seventh Session of the GDR People's Chamber by the chairman of the State Council [1968].

_____. Hochschule für Film und Fernsehen. *Informationsblatt: Film- und Fernsehausbildung.* Berlin.

_____. Staatliche Zentralverwaltung für Statistik. *Statistisches Jahrbuch 1971 der Deutschen Demokratischen Republik.* Berlin: Staatsverlag der Deutschen Demokratischen Republik, 1971.

_____. *Ulbrichts Grundgesetz: Die sozialistische Verfassung der DDR*, mit einem einleitenden Kommentar von Dietrich Müller-Römer. Cologne: Verlag Wissenschaft und Politik, 1968.

Gordos, Miklos, ed. *Hungary 70.* Budapest: Pannonia Press, 1970.

Govallo, I. I., and Y. B. Gruzdev. *Leading Television Center of the USSR.* Washington: Joint Publications Research Service, 1968.

Green, Timothy. *The Universal Eye: The World of Television.* New York: Stein and Day, 1972.

Griffith, William E. *Albania and the Sino-Soviet Rift.* Cambridge, Mass.: MIT. Press, 1963. Massachusetts Institute of Technology, Center for International Studies, Studies in International Communism.

Gsovski, Vladimir. *Soviet Civil Law: Private Rights and Their Background under the Soviet Regime.* Comparative Survey and Translation of the Civil Code, Code of Domestic Relations, Judiciary Act, Code of Civil Procedure, Laws on Nationality, Corporations, Patents, Copyright, Collective Farms, Labor, and Other Related Laws. 2 vols. Ann Arbor: University of Michigan Law School, 1948–1949. Michigan Legal Studies.

Hawker, J. P. *Radio and Television: Principles and Applications.* New York: Hart, 1968.

Hazard, John N., Isaac Shapiro, and Peter B. Maggs. *The Soviet Legal System: Contemporary Documentation and Historical Commentary.* Rev. ed. Dobbs Ferry, N.Y.: Oceana Publications, 1969. Parker School Studies in Foreign and Comparative Law.

Hollander, Gayle Durham. *Soviet Political Indoctrination: Developments in Mass Media and Propaganda since Stalin.* New York: Praeger, 1972. Praeger Special Studies in International Politics and Public Affairs.

Holt, Robert T. *Radio Free Europe.* Minneapolis: University of Minnesota Press. 1958.

————, and John E. Turner, eds. *Soviet Union: Paradox and Change*. New York: Holt, Rinehart, and Winston, 1963.

Hopkins, Mark W. *Mass Media in the Soviet Union*. New York: Pegasus, 1970.

How to Listen to the World 1971. Hvidovre, Denmark: World Radio-TV Handbook, 1971.

Huth, Arno, *Radio Today: The Present State of Broadcasting in the World*. Geneva: Geneva Research Centre, 1942. Geneva Studies, Vol. 12, No. 6.

Inkeles, Alex. *Public Opinion in Soviet Russia: A Study in Mass Persuasion*. Cambridge, Mass.: Harvard University Press, 1958. Russian Research Center Studies, No. 1. Cited as Inkeles.

————. *Social Change in Soviet Russia*. Cambridge, Mass.: Harvard University Press, 1968. Russian Research Center Studies, No. 57.

International Organization of Journalists. *Handbook of News Agencies*. Prague, 1969.

International Press Institute. *The Press in Authoritarian Countries*. Zurich, 1959. IPI Survey, No. 5. Cited as IPI Survey.

Internationales Handbuch für Rundfunk und Fernsehen 1971/72. Hamburg: Verlag Hans-Bredow-Institut, 1972.

Irwin, Will. *Propaganda and the News, or, What Makes You Think So?* London: Whittlesey House; New York: McGraw-Hill, 1936.

Jugoslovenska Radiotelevizija Yearbook 1965. Belgrade: 1965. Cited as *JRT Yearbook 1965*.

Jugoslovenska Radiotelevizija Yearbook 1970. Belgrade: 1970. Cited as *JRT Yearbook 1970*.

Jugoslovenska Radiotelevizija Yearbook 1971/72. Belgrade: 1972. Cited as *JRT Yearbook 1971/72*.

Kaftanov, S. V., et al., eds. *Radio and Television in the USSR*. Washington: U.S. Joint Publications Research Service, 1961.

Kruglak, Theodore E. *The Two Faces of TASS*. Minneapolis: University of Minnesota Press, 1962.

League of Nations. Treaty Series, 4301–4327. 186: 303–317 (1938).

Le Compte, Andrew C. "Soviet Broadcasting Today." M.A. thesis, Ohio State University, 1971.

Lenin, V. I. *Collected Works*. 44 vols. Moscow: Progress Publishers, 1960–1970.

Lenin about the Press. Prague: International Organisation of Journalists, 1972. Journalist Library, Vol. 1.

Lévái, Bela. *Hungarian Radio and Television 1970* Budapest: Hungarian Radio and Television, 1970.

Maclaurin, W. Rupert. *Invention and Innovation in the Radio Industry*. New York: Macmillan, 1949. Massachusetts Institute of Technology. Studies of Innovation.

Maddison, John. *Radio and Television in Literacy: A Survey of the Use of the Broadcasting Media in Combating Illiteracy among Adults*. Paris: UNESCO, 1971. Reports and Papers on Mass Communication, No. 62.

Marek, Miroslav, Milan Hromádka, and Josef Chroust. *Cultural Policy in Czechoslovakia*. Paris: UNESCO, 1970.

Markham, James W. *Voices of the Red Giants: Communications in Russia and China*. Ames: Iowa State University Press, 1967.

Martin, L. John. *International Propaganda: Its Legal and Diplomatic Control*. Minneapolis: University of Minnesota Press, 1958.

Marx, Karl, and Frederick Engels. *Selected Works in One Volume*. New York: International Publishers, 1968.

Mass Media and International Understanding. Symposium. Ljubljana, 1968.

Maxwell, Robert, ed. *Information U.S.S.R.: An Authoritative Encyclopaedia about*

the Union of Soviet Socialist Republics. Oxford: Pergamon Press, 1962. Countries of the World, Information Series, Vol. 1.
McGraw-Hill Encyclopedia of Russia and the Soviet Union. New York: McGraw-Hill, 1961.
Merrill, John C., Carter R. Bryan, and Marvin Alisky. *The Foreign Press: A Survey of the World's Journalism.* Baton Rouge: Louisiana State University Press, 1970.
Mezerik, Avraham G. *The Invasion and Occupation of Czechoslovakia and the U.N.* New York: International Review Service, 1968.
Miszczak, Stanislaw. *Historia radiofonii i televizji w Polsce.* Warsaw: Wydawnictiwa Komunikacji i Lącznósci, 1972.
Mond, Georges H. *L'Information et la "guerre psychologique" dans un pays socialiste: Le Cas de la Pologne.* 7th General Assembly of the Association Internationale des Etudes et Recherches sur l'Information, Constance, 1970. Unpublished.
Multi-Media Systems in Adult Education: Twelve Project Descriptions in Nine Countries. Munich: Internationales Zentralinstitut für das Jugend- und Bildungsfernsehen, 1971.
Nagel's U.S.S.R. Travel Guide. New York: McGraw-Hill, 1965. The Nagel Travel Guide Series.
Namurois, Albert. *Structures and Organization of Broadcasting in the Framework of Radiocommunications.* Geneva: European Broadcasting Union, 1972. EBU Legal Monograph, No. 9.
Paulu, Burton. *British Broadcasting: Radio and Television in the United Kingdom.* Minneapolis: University of Minnesota Press, 1956.
————. "Factors in the Attempts to Establish a Permanent Instrumentality for the Administration of the International Broadcasting Services of the United States." Ph.D. thesis, New York University, 1949.
————. *Radio and Television Broadcasting on the European Continent.* Minneapolis: University of Minnesota Press, 1967.
Peaslee, Amos J. *Constitutions of Nations.* Rev. 3rd ed. 4 vols. The Hague: Martinus Nijhoff, 1965–1970.
Pigé, François. *La Télévision dans le monde: Organisation administrative et financière.* Paris: Ministère de l'Education Nationale, 1962.
Poland. Glówny urząd statystyczny. *Rocznik statystyczny 1971.* Warsaw, 1971.
R.A.I. *Proceedings of the International Conference of Broadcasting Organizations on Sound and Television School Broadcasting.* Rome: Edizioni Radio Italiana, 1961.
Radio Free Europe. *Critical Developments and Listening Behavior in East Europe.* Munich, 1972.
————. *Domestic Poll Results on Listening to Radio Warsaw.* Munich, 1972.
————. *The Exposure to the Domestic Radio and Television in Eastern Europe.* Munich, 1971.
————. *Listening to Western Broadcasts in Czechoslovakia before and after the Invasion.* Munich, 1969.
————. *Listening to Western Broadcasts in Eastern Europe.* Munich, 1972.
————. *Listening to Western Radio in Hungary before and after the "Polish Events."* Munich, 1971.
————. *Listening to Western Radio in Poland before and after the "December Events."* Munich, 1971.
————. *The Major Information Sources of Hungarian Respondents on Important Foreign and Domestic Issues.* Munich, 1971.
————. *The Major Sources of Polish Respondents on Important Foreign and Domestic Issues.* Munich, 1971.

_____. *RFE's Role as Seen by Polish, Czechoslovak, and Hungarian Listeners.* Munich, 1972.

_____. *Reasons for Not Listening to Radio Free Europe.* Munich, 1972.

_____. *Some Aspects of Exposure to the Press and Radio as Measured inside Poland and by APOE-RFE.* Munich, 1972.

Radio Liberty Committee. *Annual Report 1972.* New York and Munich, 1972.

Reith, J. C. W. *Into the Wind.* London: Hodder and Stoughton, 1949.

Rogers, Rosemarie Sträussnigg. "The Soviet Audience: How It Uses the Mass Media." Ph.D. thesis, Massachusetts Institute of Technology, 1967.

Roper Organization. *What People Think of Television and Other Mass Media 1959–1972.* New York: Television Information Office, 1973.

Rubina, P., and F. Ramsin. *Communications in the USSR.* Moscow: Novosti Press Agency Publishing House, n.d.

Siebert, Fred S., Theodore Peterson, and Wilbur Schramm. *Four Theories of the Press: The Authoritarian, Libertarian, Social Responsibility and Soviet Communist Concepts of What the Press Should Be and Do.* Urbana: University of Illinois Press, 1956.

Smith, Delbert D. *International Telecommunication Control: International Law and the Ordering of Satellite and Other Forms of International Broadcasting.* Leyden: A. W. Sijthoff. 1969.

Stalin, J. *Problems of Leninism.* Moscow: Foreign Languages Publishing House, 1953.

Stalin, J. V. *Works.* 13 vols. Moscow: Foreign Languages Publishing House, 1952–1955.

Statesman's Year-Book. Statistical and Historical Annual of the States of the World for the Year 1971–1972. John Paxton, ed. London: Macmillan, 1971.

Statesman's Year-Book. Statistical and Historical Annual of the States of the World for the Year 1972–1973. John Paxton, ed. London: Macmillan, 1972.

Szecskö, Tomas, ed. *Public Opinion and Mass Communication.* Budapest: Mass Communications Research Center, Hungarian Radio and Television, 1972.

Television Factbook 1969–1970. Washington: Television Digest, 1969.

Terrou, Fernand, and Lucien Solal. *Legislation for Press, Film and Radio; Comparative Study of the Main Types of Regulations Governing the Information Media.* Paris: UNESCO, 1951. Press, Film and Radio in the World Today.

USSR Central Statistical Board. *Narodnoye khozyaystvo SSSR v 1958 g.* Moscow, 1959.

_____. *Narodnoye khozyaystvo SSSR v 1962 g.* Moscow, 1963.

_____. *Narodnoye khozyaystvo SSSR v 1965 g.* Moscow, 1966.

_____. *Narodnoye khozyaystvo SSSR v 1968 g.* Moscow, 1969.

_____. *Narodnoye khozyaystvo SSSR v 1970 g.* Moscow, 1971.

_____. *Narodnoye khozyaystvo SSSR 1922–1972 gg. Yubileynyy statisticheskiy yezhegodnik.* Moscow; statistika, 1972.

_____. *Soviet Union 50 Years. Statistical Returns.* Moscow: Progress Publishers, 1969.

_____. *The U.S.S.R. Economy. A Statistical Abstract.* London: Lawrence and Wishart, 1957.

UNESCO. *Adult Education and Television: A Comparative Study in Three Countries.* London: National Institute of Adult Education, 1966.

_____. *Broadcasting to Schools: Reports on the Organization of School Broadcasting Services in Various Countries.* Paris: UNESCO, 1949.

_____. *Mass Media in Adult Education.* 1967. Publications of the International Central Institute for Youth and Educational Television, No. 2.

_____. *Statistics on Radio and Television 1950–1960.* Paris: UNESCO, 1963.

_____. *Television and Further Education of Employed.* Warsaw, 1969.

_____. *Television for Higher Education of the Employed: A First Report on a Pilot Project in Poland.* Paris, 1969. Reports and Papers on Mass Communications, No. 55.

_____. *Television for Higher Technical Education of Workers: Final Report on a Pilot Project in Poland.* Paris: UNESCO, 1973. Reports and Papers on Mass Communications, No. 67.

_____. *World Communications: Press Radio Television Film.* 4th rev. ed. Paris: UNESCO, 1964.

United Nations. *Demographic Yearbook 1970.* New York, 1971.

_____. *Demographic Yearbook 1971.* New York, 1972.

_____. *Statistical Yearbook 1971.* New York, 1972.

United Nations General Assembly. *Official Records: Fifth Session,* 325 Plenary Meeting, December 14, 1950.

United Nations. General Assembly Resolution 841 (IX), December 17, 1954.

U.S. Bureau of the Census. *U.S. Census of Population: 1970. Number of Inhabitants.* Final Report PC(1)-Al United States Summary.

United States Code Annotated: Title 22, Foreign Relations and Intercourse, Sections 1432–end.

U.S. High Commissioner for Germany. *Soviet Zone Constitution and Electoral Law.* 1951.

United States Information Agency. 33rd Semiannual Report to the Congress, July–December 1969.

_____. 34th Semiannual Report to the Congress, January–June 1970.

L'Université à Domicile Symposium. Montreal, 1972.

Vyshinsky, Andrei Y. *The Law of the Soviet State.* Hugh W. Babb, trans. New York: Macmillan, 1948.

Vyvyan, R. N. *Wireless over Thirty Years.* London: G. Routledge and Sons, 1933.

Walther, Gerald. *Der Rundfunk in der sowjetischen Besatzungszone Deutschlands.* Bonn: Deutscher Bundesverlag, 1961. Bonner Berichte aus Mittel- und Ostdeutschland.

The World Almanac, 1972. ed. New York: Newspaper Enterprise Association, 1971.

World Radio TV Handbook 1971. Hvidovre, Denmark, 1971. Cited as *WRTH 1971.*

World Radio TV Handbook 1972. Hvidovre, Denmark, 1972.

World Radio TV Handbook 1973. Hvidovre, Denmark, 1973.

Wydawnictwa Radio i Televizji. *Z anteny PR i ekranu TV. Rocznik 1971.* Warsaw, 1971.

Yezhegodnik bol'shoy sovyetskoy entsiklopediy 1964. Vypusk vos'moy. Izdatel'stvo "Sovyetskaya entsiklopediya," 1964.

Yugoslavia. *Law of the Press and Other Forms of Information.* Belgrade: Union of Jurists' Association of Yugoslavia, 1960. Collected Yugoslav Laws, 2nd Ser., II, No. 3.

Yurovskiy, A. Y., and R. A. Boretskiy. *Osnovy televizionnoy zhurnalistiki.* Moscow: Izdatel'stvo Moskovskogo Universiteta, 1966. Cited as Yurovskiy and Boretskiy.

Zvorykin, A. A., with the assistance of N. I. Golubtsova and E. I. Rabinovich. *Cultural Policy in the Union of Soviet Socialist Republics.* Paris: UNESCO, 1970. Studies and Documents on Cultural Policies, No. 8.

Newspapers and Periodicals

American Slavic and East European Review. Menasha, Wisconsin.

The Annals of the American Academy of Political and Social Science. Philadelphia.

Broadcasting. Washington.
Bulgarski zhurnalist. Sofia.
Business Week. New York.
Central Asian Review. London.
Centre for Public Opinion and Broadcasting Research. *Research Abstracts.* Warsaw.
Current Abstracts of the Soviet Press. Columbus, Ohio.
Current Digest of the Soviet Press. Washington. Cited as CDSP.
Current History. New York.
Czechoslovak Life. Prague.
East Europe. New York.
EBU Review. Geneva.
Economist. London.
Educational Technology. Englewood Cliffs, New Jersey.
European Broadcasting Union Documentation and Information Bulletin. Geneva.
FF Dabei. Berlin.
Financial Times. London.
Foreign Broadcast Information Service. *Daily Report.* Washington.
Journal of Broadcasting. Philadelphia.
Journal of the Institution of Electrical Engineers. London.
Journalism Quarterly. Urbana, Illinois.
Life. Chicago.
The Listener. London.
Los Angeles Times. Los Angeles.
Minneapolis Tribune. Minneapolis, Minnesota.
New Statesman. London.
New York Times. (Almost all *New York Times* references are to the (early) City Edition, so that date and page citations may differ from those in the Final Edition stocked by most libraries.)
The New York Times Magazine. New York.
The New Yorker. New York.
OIRT. *Catalogue of Transmissions Suitable for Exchange.* Prague.
OIRT Information. Prague.
Polish Radio and Television Bulletin. Warsaw. Cited as *Polish Bulletin.*
Problems of Communism. Washington.
Proceedings of the IRE. New York.
Public Opinion Quarterly. Princeton, New Jersey.
Quarterly Journal of Speech. Chicago.
Quarterly of Film, Radio and Television. Berkeley, California.
Radio Engineering and Electronics. New York.
Radio Television. Review of the International Radio and Television Organization. Prague. Cited as *OIRT Review.*
The Reporter. New York.
The Romanian Journal of Sociology. Bucharest.
Rundfunk und Fernsehen. Hamburg.
Rundfunkjournalistik in Theorie und Praxis. Berlin.
Saturday Review. New York.
Soviet Life. Washington.
The Soviet Press in Translation. Madison, Wisconsin.
Sputnik. Moscow.
Studies in Philosophy and Social Science. New York.
Telecommunication Journal. Geneva.
Times. London.
Times Educational Supplement. London.
Trybuna ludu. Warsaw.

UNESCO Chronicle. New York.
USIA Communicator. Washington.
Variety. New York.
Windsor Star. Windsor, Ontario.
Winnipeg Free Press. Winnipeg, Manitoba.
Yale Law Journal. New Haven, Connecticut.

INDEX

Index